Footprint

Colombia

The travel guide

Handbook

Peter Pollard

*Many stories have been heard
that the sun will go out,
the world will come to an end.
But if we all act well, and think well, it will
not end.
That is why we are still looking after
the sun and the moon and the land.*

Mama Valencia (Kogi Indian) from The Heart
of the World by Alan Ereira

Colombia Handbook
Second edition
© Footprint Handbooks Ltd 2000

Published by Footprint Handbooks
6 Riverside Court
Lower Bristol Road
Bath BA2 3DZ. England
T +44 (0)1225 469141
F +44 (0)1225 469461
Email discover@footprintbooks.com
Web www.footprintbooks.com

ISBN 1 900949 71 7
CIP DATA: A catalogue record for this
book is available from the British Library

In USA, published by
NTC/Contemporary Publishing Group
4255 West Touhy Avenue, Lincolnwood
(Chicago), Illinois 60712-1975, USA
T 847 679 5500 F 847 679 2494
Email NTCPUB2@AOL.COM

ISBN 0-658-00660-6
Library of Congress Catalog Card
Number 00-136131

Credits

Series editors
Patrick Dawson and Rachel Fielding

Editorial
Editor: Alan Murphy
Maps: Sarah Sorensen

Production
Typesetting: Richard Ponsford, Leona
Bailey and Angus Dawson
Maps: Robert Lunn and Claire Benison
Colour maps: Kevin Feeney

Cover: Camilla Ford

Design
Mytton Williams

Photography
Front cover: Impact Photo Library
Back cover: Impact Photo Library
Inside colour section: Eye Ubiquitous,
Impact Photo Library, getty one Stone,
Jamie Marshall, Robert Harding Picture
Library, South American Pictures

Print
Manufactured in Italy by LEGOPRINT

Colombia

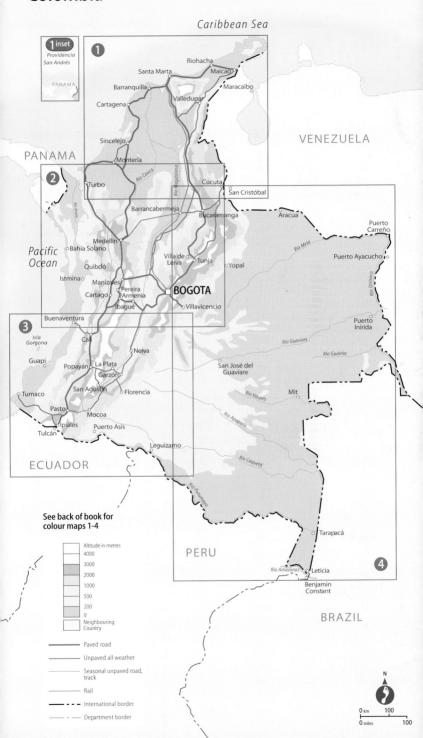

Caribbean Sea

PANAMA

VENEZUELA

1 inset
Providencia
San Andrés

PANAMA

Riohacha
Santa Marta
Maicao
Barranquilla
Valledupar
Maracaibo
Cartagena
Sincelejo
Montería
Rio Cauca
Rio Magdalena
Turbo
Cúcuta
San Cristóbal
Barrancabermeja
Bucaramanga
Arauca
Puerto Carreño
Medellín
Bahía Solano
Villa de Leiva
Tunja
Yopal
Rio Meta
Puerto Ayacucho
Quibdó
Rio Orinoco
Istmina
Manizales
Pereira
Cartago Armenia
BOGOTA
Ibagué
Villavicencio
Puerto Inírida
Buenaventura
Rio Guaviare
Cali
Isla Gorgona
Neiva
Rio Guainía
Guapi
Popayán
La Plata
Garzón
San José del Guaviare
San Agustín
Florencia
Mit
Tumaco
Rio Vaupés
Pasto
Ipiales
Mocoa
Rio Apaporis
Tulcán
Puerto Asís
Leguizamo
Rio Caquetá

Pacific Ocean

ECUADOR

PERU

Rio Putumayo

Tarapacá

See back of book for colour maps 1-4

Rio Amazonas
Leticia
Benjamin Constant

BRAZIL

Altitude in metres
4000
3000
2000
1000
500
200
0
Neighbouring Country

Paved road
Unpaved all weather
Seasonal unpaved road, track
Rail
International border
Department border

N

0 km   100
0 miles   100

2

Contents

A foot in the door

Right: Stony-faced. The amazing collection of
precolumbian statues around San Agustín are
a wonderful sight to behold and their exact
purpose continues to defy explanation.
Below: Cartagena by night. This most
beautiful of colonial cities has a vibrant
nightlife which makes it an equally appealing
prospect after dark.
Previous page: Rhapsody in blue. An angel
looks down from above in the stunning
Zipaquirá cathedral which is made entirely
of salt.

Above: Beach scene at Morgan Cove on San
Andrés island, one of Colombia's top resorts.
Right: In the heart of throbbing Bogotá lies La
Candelaria, the best-preserved colonial district
in any Latin Anmerican capital.

Highlights

If ever a country has a serious image problem, then it's Colombia. Despite the fact that it's perhaps the most beautiful country in Latin America, with mountains, Caribbean and Pacific beaches, precolumbian ruins and a vast swathe of the Amazon, most people associate it with drugs, guerrilla violence and kidnapping. Yet, ask any self-respecting lover of all things South American what is their favourite country and nine out of ten will immediately answer "Colombia". That may just be the *aguardiente* talking, but there's one thing for sure: this most notorious of places maintains a powerful hold on those who know it.

Worth its salt

Colombia's capital, Bogotá, is as manic and exciting as any other Latin city. It's a vast, sprawling urban nightmare of choking traffic, emerald sellers on street corners and legions of homeless kids living in the sewers. However, it also happens to be the cultural and intellectual hub of the country. The old colonial district of La Candelaria, in the heart of the city, must be the best-preserved historical centre of any major city on the continent. Here, you'll find irascible old intellectuals in furious debate with writers and artists in cafés and in the narrow, cobbled streets theatres and universities jostle for space with elegant colonial mansions and churches. The city's most valuable tourist asset, though, is the fabulous gold museum, which no one should miss, and only an hour or so away by bus is the remarkable Zipaquirá salt cathedral, a tasty prospect for even the most seasoned of travellers.

Paradise found

Those not arriving in Bogotá will touch down in Cartagena, the finest colonial city in the Americas. Cartagena is also one of Colombia's top Caribbean resorts, so if all that colonial architecture gets too much, you can head off to the beach and soak up some rays. To the east is Santa Marta, another historic Spanish port with wonderful beaches. Only 50 km away are the highest mountains in the country, the Sierra Nevada de Santa Marta, which rise straight out of the Caribbean to over 5,000 m. Santa Marta is the starting point for one of South America's greatest experiences, the trek through beautiful rainforest up to *Ciudad Perdida*, the Lost City, centre of the ancient Tayrona culture who lived here a thousand years before Columbus was even a twinkle in his father's eye. After the strenuous trek you can chill out in a hammock on the delicious beaches of Tayrona National Park, the ultimate Caribbean paradise.

Sights for sore eyes

Southwest of Bogotá, in lush sub-tropical valleys, lie the country's most impressive precolumbian sites, around the little town of San Agustín. Here, in the Valley of the Statues, are hundreds of huge stone figures of men, animals and gods, some over 5,000 years old. Nearby is Tierradentro, a spectacularly beautiful area riddled with ancient burial tombs, where you can wander in the hills for weeks and not see another tourist. The main city in the south is Cali, probably best known for its drug cartel which vied with Medellín's for control of the country's trade. Uninformed visitors are in for a shock, however. This is a vibrant, sexy city, with the friendliest, most fun-loving people you could ever hope to meet. A night spent drinking rum and dancing salsa in Cali is not forgotten quickly – or the following day's hangover!

Living la vida loca

Colombia certainly has more than its fair share of stunning scenery and classic sights, but that's only half the story. Its single greatest attraction is surely its people. Not for nothing is Colombia also known as 'Locombia' – mad country. Its people are so terminally-optimistic, insanely exuberant and hopelessly romantic. it's impossible not to fall in love with them. For in common with all countries blighted by violence and civil war, Colombians are just happy to see anyone visit their country.

A thousand years of attitude

A thousand years ago, the indigenous peoples of Colombia were developing all manner of crafts, practical and ornamental, using the wide variety of materials available in this abundant country. Earthenware pots of many styles have been found in many ancient sites. In centres such as Ráquira, you can see items being made that are virtually unchanged from those made by the Muiscas and, on the Pacific coast, the Chocó Indians still weave their traditional baskets, of exceptional quality, from palm fibres. Wooden mask making is another craft widely established with its roots in the Indian culture.

Gold bringer Before the arrival of the Spaniards, gold had become very important to the Indians. Among the treasures of Colombia today are the collections of gold artifacts in the museums around the country, the best of all the fantastic Gold Museum in Bogotá. With the Spaniards came horses and cattle which introduced leatherwork in practical form and fine tooled ornamental work. Pasto, in the south of the country, is famous for leather furniture. Examples of items made from all manner of fibres, bamboo, nuts, metals and stone can be found in various centres around the country, such as the gold filigree work done in Mompós on the lower Magdalena.

Preservation order The Spaniards had a major impact on Colombia for several centuries and many of the major towns still bear a strong reminder of their colonial heritage. The grid pattern of the streets, the plazas, churches and elegant houses, often still filled with furniture and art of the period, are their legacy. Even more satisfying are the smaller towns, some well outside the stream of modern development, where little has changed.

Kicking the habit Unfortunately, Colombia's recent past has been dominated by violence mostly connected to the drugs trade. A few spectacular villains in the narcotics business created an easy target for international criticism. Although they were eliminated (one way or another) the best part of a decade ago, the image given to Colombia will be around for a long time. Guerrilla groups control a few remote areas, well away from places of interest, but if you keep away from these sensitive no-go areas, you'd be hard pushed to tell there was a problem. There is very little urban violence now and the cities of Medellín and Cali, formerly synonymous with the warring drugs cartels, are now great places to visit in their own right.

Rythym & muse Colombia's best known exports may be coffee and cocaine, but a third 'C' should be added to that list – culture. In literature, Colombia has one of the world's greatest contemporary writers in Gabriel García Márquez, who created a new literary genre now called Magic Realism. In the visual arts, there have been many indigenous artists whose work can be seen in the museums, churches and public places up and down the land. Colombia has some outstanding sculptors, led by Rodrigo Arenas Betancur and Fernando Botero whose work inspires the visitor and is the pride of the Colombians. And music? Well, where do you start? Colombia could rightly claim to be the music capital of South America, with a variety of styles unmatched anywhere on the continent. They also know how to strut their stuff. From vallenato to cumbía, via the ever-popular salsa, dancing in Colombia is practically the national sport.

Left: Indigenous culture is alive and well in Colombia and this lady shows that they even managed to keep some of their own gold!
Below: These sinister-looking chaps are Makuna Indians taking part in their Peach Palm festival.

Above: Fruits of their labour. A woman pauses for a few moments' reflection on Boca Chica beach, Cartagena.
Left: Mind the gap! A lonely canoe negotiates the near-impenetrable jungles of the Darién.
Next page: Marlboro country. Colombia's vast plains – Los Llanos – are home to only a few remote indigenous tribes and the hardy llaneros, famous for their exuberant hospitality and sentimental ballads.

Essentials

2

Essentials

Planning your trip

Where to go

A country so large and varied as Colombia has a bewildering list of places worth visiting. A comprehensive look at the country will require a good deal of time and planning. If you have limited time and want to see as much as possible, you should consider using the extensive internal airline network for which you can buy reduced cost 'air passes' with your international ticket. If you have more time, there are good Pullman and minibuses, but remember that distance and variable road quality will take time.

You will almost certainly arrive in the country via Bogotá or Cartagena, and a look at those two cities makes a good start.

Bogotá

Like most capital cities, at least in Latin America, **Bogotá** is crowded, noisy, polluted and disorganized. Yet it is a proud, cosmopolitan city with impressive modern buildings and services. The historical centre, La Candelaria, has a wealth of fine colonial churches and buildings. For a great view of the city, take the cable car to the top of Monserrate. A visit to the Gold Museum, a dazzling collection of the art of the pre-Columbian cultures, is a mind-boggling experience. There is excellent accommodation in all categories that can be used as a base for trips to surrounding areas. Bogotá is the best place for information on the whole country with quality bus services and the comprehensive air network based here. For local travel, taxis can be hired for the day and car hire (though rather expensive) can be arranged at the airport or in town. Places to visit nearby include Guatavita, Zipaquirá, the many towns down to the west towards the Río Magdalena eg Guaduas, and the Parks of Chicaque, Chingaza and Sumapaz (check for security). You may, quite rightly, decide to overnight away from Bogotá, and there are plenty of places to stay, particularly good value midweek.

Cartagena

Cartagena is more relaxed than Bogotá, though not without some of the problems of a big modern city. It is Colonial Spain's finest legacy in the Americas, impressive in every respect, and the most visited city by tourists and the many who come to the national and international conventions. A visit to Cartagena must be for several days since there is so much to see. It is also the best centre for the Caribbean coast and the islands. Check out the beaches and the water sports available. For the straightforward Caribbean holiday, all the facilities are here in the wonderfully historic setting. Beaches along the coast and on the offshore islands can be visited from Cartagena and the strange mud volcanoes nearby. To the northeast, Barranquilla has its attractions including the last bridge over the Río Magdalena and its spectacular carnival, perhaps the finest in Latin America after Rio de Janeiro. Mompós, a superb colonial town also on the river can be visited from Barranquilla or Cartagena but you will have to stay overnight. Cartagena is the gateway to San Andrés, a popular island resort, attractive to Colombians as a major holiday destination, and to neighbouring island of Providencia, a charming place and still relatively unspoilt.

Medellín

Medellín is, perhaps, the biggest surprise. With a recent legacy of over-industrialisation and violent drug cartels, you are now confronted by a modern, vibrant city with many fine new buildings, complementing the old, restored architecture. There is plenty of modern art, a friendly, outgoing people and many fascinating places to visit in the surrounding Department of Antioquia. The *Paisas* (as the locals are known) leave in droves at the weekends for the countryside and there are many places geared up to receive them which are also, of course, available to the tourist. Santa Fé de Antioquia, a remarkable, preserved colonial town, is an easy day's trip, but you are more than likely to be seduced to stay the night. Rionegro is not only interesting in itself but to get there you pass through some beautiful countryside. To the north, El Peñol, the towering black rock overlooking Guatapé and its huge lake, should not be missed, and there are many other delightful places with lakes and waterfalls in this region and further north around Don Matías. Equally, to the southwest of Medellín, you should visit Jericó and particularly, Jardín, truly a garden village. Medellín is also the jumping off point for Quibdó, the Chocó and the northern part of Colombia's Pacific coast.

Cali   The 'capital' of the south of the country is **Cali**, about the same size as Medellín with a similar recent unhappy past. It is now reinvigorated with an attractive, lively atmosphere springing from an interesting mixture of people, who have combined to make this the finest popular music centre of the continent, well illustrated by their passion for *salsa*. Remember, when in Cali, this is the second city of Colombia, whatever the statistics may or may not say about Medellín! After a while you will want to explore outside the city. The Farallones de Cali National Park is only a few kilometers to the west and with good facilities near the entrance at Pance. To the north, Darién with its Calima museum and lake is a recommended trip. Buenaventura is accessible from Cali, together with the central section of the Pacific coast and the island of Gorgona.

Around the rest   A quarter of the population live in these four cities, but we must look for the heart of
of the country   Colombia elsewhere. One thing you will quickly realise is that the country is strongly regionalised. This comes from the rugged terrain and the early history when many different Indian groups lived separately here. The Spaniards colonised the territory from three directions – the Caribbean coast, from Venezuela (as it is today) and from the south. All roads do not lead to Bogotá; hence the importance today of the *Departamentos* and their capitals. In the 19th century some, eg Antioquia, were independent countries for a short time. These were often Spanish settlements and the fierce pride of the later inhabitants ensured the preservation of their heritage. Virtually all are worth a visit, but of particular interest are **Popayán, Tunja, Pereira, Ibagué** and **Bucamaranga.**

Smaller places that express even better the feel of colonial Colombia are spread around the western part of the country. They include **Villa de Leiva, Santa Fé de Antioquia, Mompós, Monguí,** and **Barichara.** There are many others detailed in the text. If you are looking for fine scenery, it is all here: from dry semi-desert **(Guajira)** to the wettest area of the Americas **(Chocó)**, from one of the hottest places in South America **(Norte de Santander)** to the snows of the **Nevados**. Beaches and coral reefs line the Caribbean coast with **Providencia** a most attractive tropical island. There are deep river gorges **(Chicamocha** and **Upper Magdalena)** and high rocky mountain chains **(Cocuy** and **Sierra de Santa Marta)**, and many areas of fine high *páramo* for walking and trekking. Equally there are large areas of attractive undulating countryside comfortably near the larger cities where every type of country pursuit can be enjoyed. Also, Colombia has its own stretch of the Amazon, and **Leticia** is recommended as a good, well organized place to experience the jungle environment.

For those passionate about birds, butterflies, orchids, ecology and wildlife in general, there are many opportunities. The diversity of climate and the land has endowed the country with one of the widest collections of all these things in the world. On top of this, there are 46 National Pakrs spread virtually all over the country, each with its specialities.

Finally, there are some particularly outstanding attractions that it would be a pity to miss. The archaeological sites of **Ciudad Perdida, San Agustín** and **Tierradentro,** the wax palms above **Salento**, the flamingos near **Riohacha**, the mud volcanoes near **Arboletes** and **Galerazamba** and the wonderful rich green countryside of the **Zona Cafetera.** Four specific objectives that the visitor to Colombia really should not miss are: The **Gold Museum** in Bogotá, **El Peñol** rock, 50 km east of Medellín, **Las Lajas** sanctuary, near Ipiales in the extreme south of the country and the **Zipaquirá** Salt Cathedral two hours north of Bogotá by bus, car or even weekend train.

When to go

The best time for a visit is December to February, on average the driest months. However, many Colombians are then on holiday so prices can be somewhat higher in the most popular places, and transport including internal airlines, can be busy. In this period, a number of major annual fiestas are held, for example in the south (Popayán and Pasto) in January and, at the opposite end of the country, Carnival in Barranquilla in February. These events bring out the locals in force and it is a fun time to visit. Equally, Easter is a local holiday time. Accommodation prices tend to rise also in July/August because of holiday times in the northern hemisphere, but then local facilities are at a higher level for tourists.

The climate does not vary much during the year, and apart from the Chocó (North **Climate** West Colombia) where it rains almost every day, you will see plenty of sun. If you venture into the eastern departments, rains can make travelling very difficult in the plains between March and September. There is occasional heavy rain in many places in April/May and October/November though intermittent downpours can fall at any time almost anywhere.

Temperature is almost entirely a matter of altitude: there are no seasons to speak of, though some periods are wetter than others. When travelling, note the altitudes in the text, and ensure you have the right clothing available. By and large, over 2,000 m you will notice that the sun can be hot in the middle of the day, but it can be distinctly cool at night. Quite a number of important towns are over 2,500 m and are distinctly cold at night. Sleeping bags for camping are not a luxury in the high country. If you are intending to go into the peaks or the volcanoes of the *cordilleras,* read the section on high altitude in the main **Health** section, on page 52. One exception to the general rule is that travellers frequently report that in the eastern jungles and on the coasts, a light blanket at night is welcome, even on the Equator at a few metres above sea level.

Tours and tour operators

Austral Tours, 120 Wilton Road, London SW1V 1JZ, T020-72335384, F020-72335385. **In the UK** *Destination South America,* 51 Castle St, Cirencester, Gloucs, T01285-885333, **& Ireland** F01285-885888, www.destinationsouthamerica.co.uk Wide range of tours throughout the continent. *Dragoman/Peregrine,* Camp Green, Debenham, Suffolk, IP14 6LA, T01728-861133, F01728-861127, info@dragoman.co.uk, www.dragoman.co.uk; camping and hotel trips, with choice of comfort/difficulty level, length of trip and countries visited; several of the South American segments include Colombia. *Ecolatina*, PO Box 395, Richmond, Surrey, TW10 7FE, T020-85499430, F020-84081080, ecolatino@btinternet.com; concentrate on Colombia with wide-ranging tours from 7 days upwards. *Encounter,* 267, Old Brompton Road, London SW5 9JA, T020-73706845, F020-72449737, adventure@encounter.co.uk; multicountry tours including Colombia. *Exodus Travels,* 9 Weir Road, London SW12 0LT, T020-86755550, F020-86730779, www.exodus.co.uk; Cartagena and Bogotá added to other country tours. *Explore Worldwide,* 1 Frederick St, Aldershot, Hants, GU11 1LQ T01252-319448, F01252-343170. *Guerba Expeditions,* Wessex House, 40 Station Rd, Westbury, Wilts BA13 3JN, T01373-826611, F01373-858351, info@guerba.co.uk, www.guerba.co.uk; some South American tours include Colombia. *Journey Latin America,* 12-13 Heathfield Terrace, Chiswick, London W4 4JE, T020-87473108 (flights), 020-87478315 (tours), F020-87421312, www.journeylatinamerica.co.uk; also at 51-63 Deansgate, Manchester

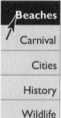

M3 2BH, T0161-8321441, F0161-8325151; long established (20 years) company running escorted tours throughout the region as well as offering a wide range of flight options. *Scott Dunn Latin America* (formerly *Passage to South America)*, Fovant Mews, 12 Noyna Road, London SW17 7PH, T020-87678989, F020-87672026, latin@ scottdunn.com, wwwscottdunn,com; interesting tours to Colombia, tailor made arrangements. *South American Experience*, 47 Causton St, Pimlico, London SW1P 4AT T020-79765511, F020-79766908, sax@mcmail.com; www.sax.mcmail.com; flights, accommodation and tailor-made trips. *Trailfinders,* 194 Kensington High Street, London W8 7RG, T020-79383939. Trips Worldwide, 9 Byron Place, Clifton, Bristol, BS8 1JT, T0117-9872626, F0117-9872627, www.tripsworldwide.co.uk Tailor-made holidays in Latin America and the Caribbean.

Ladatco Tours, 2020 Coral Way, Miami, Fla 33145, USA, T305-8548422 or 1-800-3276162, F305-2850504. Run themed explorer tours.

In North America

Finding out more

National tourism is handled by the **Dirección de Turismo**, **(DITUR)** a part of the Ministry of Economic Development, Calle 28, No 13A-59 18th floor, Bogotá, T3522120, F2841001. This is the umbrella organization and the controlling authority for hotels (**COTELCO** – Hotel Association of Colombia), travel agencies (*ANATO* – Association of Travel Agencies) and government funds allocated to the industry (*Fondo Mixto de Promoción Turistico* – Tourist Promotion Fund). Some information is available from these entities but only of a general nature.

Websites:
COTELCO www.hotelesc olombia.org;
ANATO www.elexpreso. com;
Tourist Promotion Fund www.turismocolo mbia.com

    Detailed information on each Department in the country will be found in the Department capitals (including Bogotá), names of the entities involved are in the travelling text.

Essentials

Essentials

 Colombian Embassies & Consulates

Australia *2ⁿᵈ floor, 101 Northbourn Ave, Canberra, PO Box 2892. ACT 2601, T2572027, F2571448. Consulate: Sydney.*

Austria *Stadiongasse 6-8A, 3005 1010 Vienna, T4054249, F4088303.*

Belgium *Av Franklin Roosevelt 96A, 1050 Brussels, T6495679, F6494329.*

Brazil *Ses Av Das Nacoes, Lote 10 70444, Brasilia DF, T2268902, F2244732. Consulates: Manaus, Rio de Janeiro, São Paulo Tabatinga.*

Canada *360 Albert Street, Suite 1130, Ottawa, Ontario, K1R 7X7, T(613)230-3760, F(613)230-4416. Consulates: Montreal, Toronto, Vancouver.*

Chile *Ave Presidente Errazuriz 3943, Las Condes, Santiago, T2061999, F2080712.*

Costa Rica *Barrio Dent de Taco Bell, San Pedro 150m Oeste, T2836871, F2836818.*

Denmark *Kastelsvej 15, st tv 2100, Copenhagen, T263026, F262297.*

Ecuador Av Colón, No 11-33, Edif Arista, 7 piso, Quito, T222486, F567766. Consulates: Cuanca, Esmeraldas, Guayaquil, Nueva Loja, Santo Domingo de los Colorados, Tulcán.

France *22 rue de L'Elysée, 75008, Paris, T42654608, F42661860.*

Germany *Kurfürstenstr 84 50G 10787, Berlin, T26396110, F26396125. Consulates: Bonn, Frankfurt, Hamburg and Munich.*

Greece *Vrassida 3, Athens, T7236848, F7246270.*

Guatemala *12 Calle, 1-25, Zona 10, Edif Geminis, Guatemala City, T3352906, F3353603.*

Holland *Groot Hertoginnelaan 14, 2517 EG The Hague, T3614545, F3614636. Consulate: Amsterdam.*

Israel *52 Pinkas St, Apt 26, floor 6, 62261 Tel Aviv, T5461434, F5461404.*

Italy *Via Giuseppe Pisanelli 4, 00196 Rome, T3612131, F3225798. Consulate: Milan.*

Japan *310-53 Kami-Osaki, Shinagawa-ku, Tokyo 141, T34406451, F34406724.*

Mexico *Paseo de la Reforma 1620, Colonia Lomas de Chapultepec, Mexico City, T52027299, F55209669. Consulate: Monterrey.*

New Zealand *10 Brandon Street, Wool House, level 11, Wellington, T4721080, F4721087.*

Panama *Calle Manuel María Icasa, Edif Grobman p6, Panama City, T2649266, F2231134. Consulates: Colón, Puerto Obaldía.*

Peru *Av Jorge Basadre 1580, San Isidro, Lima, T4429653, F4419806. Consulate: Iquitos.*

Portugal *Av Conde Valbo 30-9, 1050 Lisbon, T3557096, F3528665.*

Spain *Gen Martínez Campos 48, 28010 Madrid, T7004770, F3102869. Consulates: Barcelona, Bilboa, Pamplona, Seville.*

Sweden *Ostermalmsgatan 46, Stockholm, T218489, F216205.*

Switzerland *Dufourstrasse 47, 3005 Bern, T3511700, F3527072.*

UK *3 Hans Crescent, London SW1X OLR, T020-75899177, F020-75811829. Consulate: 15-19 Great Titchfield Street, London W1P 7FB, T020-76379893, F020-76375604.*

USA *2118 Leroy Place, NW Washington, DC 20008, T(202)3878338, F(202)2328643. Consulates: Atlanta, Boston, Chicago, Houston, Los Angeles, Miami, New Orleans, New York, San Francisco.*

Venezuela *2A Av de Campo Alegre/Av Francisco Miranda, Torre Credival, Caracas 1060, T2616592, F2638974. Consulates: Barquisimeto, El Amparo de Apure, Maracaibo, Mérida, Puerto Ayacucho, Puerto La Cruz, San Antonio del Táchira, San Cristóbal, Valencia.*

However, the specialist travel agencies (and hotels eg *Platypus)* in Bogotá are very well informed and willing to help you to make the most of your stay.

Outside the country, you will find the Embassies Consulates and offices of the national airline, Avianca, helpful.

An excellent source of information is **South American Explorers** (SAE), formerly the South American Explorers Club. This is a non-profit educational organization functioning primarily as an information network for South America. It is useful for travellers to Colombia and can be contacted in the USA at 126 Indian Creek Rd, Ithaca, NY 14850, T607-2770488, F607-2776122, www.samexplo.org

Another sueful source is **The Latin American Travel Advisor.** This is a complete travel information service providing up-to-date, detailed and reliable information concerning travel conditions in Colombia and 17 other South and Central American countries. Comprehensive country profiles, detailed "how to" advice, a large selection of maps and a directory of local services are all available online. Public safety, health, weather and natural phenomena, travel costs, economics and politics are highlighted for each country. F1-888-215-9511 (toll free), www .amerispan.com/lata/

Essentials

Language

The official language is Spanish. There are several Indian languages and many dialects in use in the remoter parts of Colombia but, unlike Peru or Guatemala, you are unlikely to hear them unless you go well off the beaten track. English is understood to a limited extent in hotels, airports, travel organisations, stores and restaurants; French, German and Italian can be used here and there. Some Spanish is essential outside the main towns. Colombia has arguably the best spoken (and written) Spanish in Latin America, clearly enunciated and not too desperately fast. Spanish, even a little, can be very helpful in the smaller places. Furthermore, local people appreciate your efforts to tackle their language, and it will enhance the enjoyment of your visit. A Basic Spanish for travellers will be found at the end of the book but we urge you to take a good phrase book and dictionary with you.

Before you travel

Entry requirements

A passport is always necessary. An onward ticket is officially required, but is not always asked for at land borders or airports. Visitors are sometimes asked to prove that they have US$20 for each day of their stay (US$10 for students).

Passport & visas

   You are normally given 90 days permission to stay on entry, though this is not automatic. If you intend to stay more than 30 days, make sure you ask for longer. If not granted at the frontier, extension (*salvoconducto*) for 15-day periods can be applied for at the DAS (security police) office in any major city up to a maximum of six months. There may be delays, so apply in good time. Better, apply at the DAS office, Calle 100, No 11B-27, Bogotá (see under Bogotá, Useful Addresses) who are empowered to grant longer stays immediately. Alternatively, if you have good reason to stay longer (eg for medical treatment), apply at the embassy in your home country before leaving. Note also that if you are going to take a Spanish course, you must have a student visa. You may not study on a tourist visa. Leaving the country and re-entering to get a new permit is not always allowed.

To visit Colombia as a tourist, nationals of Afghanistan, Angola, Algeria, Benin, Botswana, Burkina Faso, Burundi, Cape Verde, Cameroon, Central African Republic, Chad, China, Comoros, Congo, Cuba, Czech Republic, Djibouti, Dominican Republic, Egypt, Equatorial Guinea, Eritrea, Ethiopia, Gabon, Ghana, Guinea, Guinea Bissau, Haiti, Hong Kong, India, Iran, Iraq, Ivory Coast, Jordan, Kenya, Lebanon, Lesotho, Liberia, Libya, Madagascar, Malawi, Mali, Mauritius, Mauritania, Morocco, Mozambique, Namibia, Nicaragua, Niger, Nigeria, North Korea, Pakistan, Palestine, Rwanda, São Tomé and Principe, Senegal, Seychelles, Sierra Leone, Somalia, South Africa, Sri Lanka, Sudan, Syria,

These requirements change frequently – check with the appropriate consulate in good time before your trip

Swaziland, Taiwan, Tanzania, Togo, Vietnam, Yemen, Zaire, Zambia, and Zimbabwe need a visa (this information was correct according to the Colombian consulate in London, April 2000). Visas are issued only by Colombian consulates. A list of Colombia's overseas representations is shown in the box above. Note that there are consuls in many provincial cities abroad, check details locally. When a visa is required you must be prepared to show three photographs, police clearance and medical certificates, an application form (£16 or equivalent), as well as a passport (at least 48 hours is necessary if the applicant is resident of the country where the application is made; 14 days otherwise).

Special visas Various business and temporary visas are needed for foreigners who have to reside in Colombia for a length of time. Fees range from £54 (or equivalent) for a student visa, £112 for a business visa, to £131 for a working visa. You may find that your onward ticket, which you must show before you can obtain a visa, is stamped 'non-refundable'.

To leave Colombia you must get an exit stamp from the DAS. They often do not have offices at the small frontier towns, so try to get your stamp in a main city near to your exit point.

NB It is highly recommended that you have your passport and entry stamp photocopied, (for added insurance, witnessed by a notary). This is a valid substitute for normal identification purposes, and your passport can then be put into safe-keeping. Also generally acceptable in Colombia for identification purposes (eg to enter Government buildings) is a driving licence (or similar identification document) provided it is of plastic, credit card size and has your photograph. Also, keep separately photocopies of your TCs, flight ticket and any other essential documents. For more information, check with your consulate. However, for drawing money across the counter in banks and other official purposes, you will need original documents.

Customs Irregular customs checks take place at airports and frontiers for both arriving and leaving travellers. Do not be caught with drugs or firearms of any kind, and take care that no-one tampers with your baggage.

Duty free allowance Duty-free admission is granted for portable typewriters, radios, binoculars, personal and ciné cameras, but all must show use; 200 cigarettes or 50 cigars or up to 500 g of manufactured tobacco in any form, 2 bottles of liquor or wine per person.

What to take

A good principle is to take half the clothes, and twice the money, that you think you will need

Everybody has their own list. Obviously what you take depends on your individual travel style, your budget and what you plan to do. Listed below are a few things which are particularly useful for travelling in Colombia. There are a million-and-one other travel accessories and gadgets on the market, all of which may well prove useful under the appropriate circumstances. At the same time however, you should try to think light and compact. The less weight you have to carry around and the fewer your belongings which might be lost or stolen, the more carefree and enjoyable will be your travels. All but the most specialized products are available in the major cities, while many basic commodities are readily purchased throughout the country.

The essentials A **moneybelt or pouch** is absolutely indispensable for everyone Be sure to bring an adequate supply of any **medications** you take on a regular basis, plus two weeks spare, as these may not be available. **Sturdy comfortable footwear** is a must for travels anywhere, and Colombia's uneven sidewalks, dirt roads and muddy country trails are no exception. **Sun protection** is very important in all regions of the country and for visitors of all complexions. This should include a **sun hat, high quality sun glasses and sun** screen for both skin and lips. Take **insect repellent** if you plan to visit the coast or jungle. Also recommended are **rubber sandals or thongs** for use on the beach, at hot springs and in hotel showers, where they protect against both athlete's foot and electric shock when instant-heating shower heads are used. If you use contact lenses, be sure to also bring a pair of **eye glasses**. A **small lightweight towel** is an asset, as is a short length of **travel clothesline**, which can be purchased or made of braided elastic, eliminating the need for pegs. A **compact torch (flashlight)**, **alarm watch** and **pocket knife** may all be useful. Always carry some **toilet paper**, as this is seldom found in public washrooms unless it is sold at the entrance.

Have a check up with your doctor if necessary and arrange your immunizations well in advance. Try ringing a specialist travel clinic if your doctor is unfamiliar with health in Colombia. You should be protected by immunization against polio (10 years), tetanus (also 10 years), and typhoid fever. There is a moderate risk in Colombia of yellow fever, hepatitis B (through sex contact, contaminated blood, needles and syringes) and a lower risk of contracting cholera and hepatitis A. Children should be protected against tuberculosis. Risks are higher in rural and jungle areas especially where standards of hygiene are lower. Malaria is present in Colombia but normally only below 800 m in the eastern *llanos*, Amazonia, the Pacific coast and the lower river valleys of the Magdalena, Cauca and Atrato rivers, inland from the coast. Whilst at time of writing no health certificates are required to enter Colombia, if you are going elsewhere in Latin America, you may not be allowed to cross the border (or board a plane) without valid health protection, eg Brazil requires yellow fever inoculations at least 10 days before you arrive. Before you travel, make sure that you have adequate medical insurance.

Vaccinations
See the Health section on page 52

See the Health section on page 52

Money

The monetary unit is the peso, divided into 100 centavos. There are coins of 50, 100, 200, 500 and 1000 pesos; there are notes of 1,000, 2,000, 5,000, 10,000 and 20,000 pesos. A 50,000 peso note is expected in 2000-01. Large notes of over 5,000 pesos are often impossible to spend on small purchases as change is in short supply, especially in small towns, and in the morning.

Currency

There is a limit of US$25,000 on the import of foreign exchange, with export limited to the equivalent of the amount brought in.

Cash and travellers' cheques can in theory be exchanged in any bank, except the *Banco de la República.* Banks generally open about 0900 and close about 1600 though bank hours are generally getting longer. They may close for the lunch break. On the last day of the month they close at 1200 or even all day. Go early to banks in the smaller places to change cash or travellers' cheques: some close the service as early as 1000. In most sizeable towns there are some *casas de cambio*, more limited in the services they offer but which are quicker to use than banks, and may be open when banks are closed. Always check which rate of exchange (including any 'commissions') is being offered and shop around if you have the time. Hotels may give very poor rates of exchange, especially if you are paying in dollars, but practice varies. It is generally dangerous to change money on the streets, and you are likely to be given counterfeit pesos. Also in circulation are counterfeit US dollar bills. Do not accept torn or damaged notes, no one, not even banks, will take them off you. If you do not present your passport when changing money (a photocopy is not always acceptable), you may be liable for a 10% tax charged to residents on foreign exchange. Try to get the pesos you need in Bogotá or the departmental capitals, elsewhere it can be difficult or impossible. In the past couple of years, however, the situation has been getting progressively better.

Exchange

Travellers' Cheques When changing travellers' cheques, a photocopy of your passport may be taken, best to take a supply of photocopies with you. Owing to the quantity of counterfeit American Express travellers' cheques in circulation, you may experience difficulty in cashing these cheques so it is a good idea to take another brand with you. For changing American Express cheques, use Bancolombia. You must always provide proof of purchase. The procedure is always slow, maybe involving finger printing and photographs. Obtaining reimbursement for lost American Express travellers' cheques can be straightforward if you have the numbers recorded (preferably proof of purchase), a police certificate (*diligencia de queja*) covering the circumstances of loss, and apply to their office at Calle 85, No 20-32, T5311919, open 0900-1730 or *Tierra Mar Aire*, Bogotá (see Bogotá, Exchange) may be able to help. Take dollar travellers' cheques in small denominations, but, better still, take a credit card or two (see below). Thomas Cook/Mastercard refund assistance point in Bogotá is Aviatur, Avenida 19, No 4-62, T2865555, Bogotá. Non US dollar travellers' cheques are practically impossible to change in Colombia.

Credit/Debit Cards For obtaining pesos, credit and debit cards are the most satisfactory method, and better take two or three from different systems for maximum flexibility. Banks will advance cash against cards at the counter against signature and identification (normally passport) if you have the right symbols on the card.

Mastercard and Visa are widely accepted for payment in shops, restaurants etc; Diner's Club is also accepted, while American Express is only accepted in high-priced establishments in Bogotá. Less hassle are Automatic Teller Machines (ATMs), which are often open 24 hours, usually have no queues and normally operate in Spanish and English. Many banks' machines will accept Visa (Visaplus and ATH logos): *Bancafe, Banco Ganadero, Banco Agrario* and *Banco Popular*. Similarly, for Mastercard/Cirrus, (Maestro and Multicolor logos) go to *Bancolombia, Banco del Occidente, Conavi* and many of the Savings and Loan associations. American Express credit cards are rarely accepted for cash advances. At present cash advances against credit/debit cards give the best rates of exchange though the amount you will be charged is not predictable as the voucher indicates only the amount in pesos (not dollars) and the rate of exchange is determined at the time the charge is posted to your account. However, you must have patience: machines may advertise 'all cards accepted' – they don't. They may be out of cash, or just out of order. Try another machine. Look for the machines that return your card immediately it has been 'read'. It is a comfort when it decides not to cooperate.

In addition to counterfeit US$ notes, Colombia has been flooded with large quantities of legitimate US$ cash which have come into the country through the drugs trade. Thus cash dollars are difficult to exchange and rates for cash are lower than for credit cards and travellers' cheques. The latter can be exchanged in the main branches of banks in Bogotá, Medellín, and Cali and some of the other major centres. Difficulties and very poor rates of exchange can be expected in smaller towns and tourist resorts. Many banks are reluctant to exchange money for anyone but account holders. Because of the great difference between the rates of exchange available (official, cash, travellers' cheques and credit cards), travellers may find variations of between 10 and 20% for prices of services and those quoted in the text.

NB Most banks are closed on the last working afternoon of the month or for the whole of that day (hopefully for balancing the books!). This can be especially annoying if that is a Friday, so beware.

Money Transfers Money can be transferred between banks. Before leaving, find out which Colombian bank is correspondent of your home bank and ask them the best way to arrange transfers when you are there. This will normally entail an email, telex or fax message from you, and a wait of 48 hours or so for the nominated bank in Colombia to pay you against identification. AmEx MoneyGram agents are *Bancolombia*. Alternatively, use Western Union to send or receive money. Addresses of their offices are in the text.

The Colombian peso has been slowly depreciating against other currencies at about 20% per annum for the last few years paralleled by local inflation. Generally, prices are lower than Europe or North America for services and locally produced items, especially food, but more expensive for imported and luxury products. In 1999/2000 inflation has remained about 20% but the currency has deteriorated at a faster rate and an economic slowdown in the country has held down price increases. The net result is very favourable for the visitor and prices are among the cheapest in South America.

In Bogotá, Cartagena and special areas eg the northwest Pacific coast, reasonable, modest accommodation will cost about US$8 per person per night, but elsewhere, in normal circumstances, US$6 should be sufficient. Out of 'high' season you will find plenty of room in hotels and *residencias* and asking for discounts is always worth a try. There is fierce competition in road transport, and there are often special air fare promotions worth seeking out. If you are travelling widely, and remember, Colombia is a big country, transport costs can be an important part of the visitor's budget. Food is generally inexpensive everywhere compared with other countries. Meals in cheaper restaurants (*comida corriente*): soup and main dish US$1.50-$2, breakfast: eggs, bread, beverage US$1-$1.75. At the upper end too, good restaurants and hotels will give you good value for money.

Cost of living /travelling

Essentials

Getting there

Air

International flights arrive principally at Bogotá and Cartagena, but there are also direct flights to Medellín, Cali, Pereira, Barranquilla and San Andrés. Fares are significantly lower in the low season, the 'high' season being July, August and December (the 'high' being the North American and European holiday period rather than the best time to visit the country). There was talk in 2000 that Easter may be designated 'high season' in future.

From **London,** British Airways has a three times weekly service to Bogotá, via Caracas, and Avianca three a week direct. From **Madrid,** five direct flights a week each by Iberia and Avianca. From **Paris,** three flights each a week by Air France and Avianca. From **Frankfurt**, three a week each Lufthansa and Avianca. There are good connections from other main European cities.

From UK, Ireland & Europe

From **New York** to Bogotá, two daily direct services by Avianca and one daily Continental, also Servivensa via Caracas; American originates some flights from New

From North America

Essentials

 Discount flight agents in the UK and Ireland

Council Travel, 28a Poland St, London, W1V 3DB, T020-74377767, www.destinations-group.com
STA Travel, 86 Old Brompton Rd, London, SW7 3LH, T020-74376262, www.statravel.co.uk They have other branches in London, as well as in Brighton, Bristol, Cambridge, Leeds, Manchester, Newcastle-Upon-Tyne and Oxford and on many university campuses. Specialists in low-cost student/youth flights and tours,

also good for student IDs and insurance.
Trailfinders, 194 Kensington High Street, London, W8 7RG, T020-79383939.
Usit Campus, 52 Grosvenor Gardens, London, SW1 0AG, T0870 240 1010, www.usitcampus.co.uk Student/youth travel specialists with branches also in Belfast, Brighton, Bristol, Cambridge, Manchester and Oxford. The main Ireland branch is at 19 Aston Quay, Dublin 2, T01-602 1777.

York calling at Miami. From **Miami,** several daily flights by American, and Avianca; Lan Chile stops three times a week en route to Chile. From Los Angeles Avianca four times a week.

There are direct services also from Miami to Barranquilla, Cartagena, and Medellín. At certain times of the year, there may be scheduled flights direct to Cali and Pereira. Enquire when you book if there are special offers for internal flights.

From neighbouring countries There are direct flights to Bogotá from Aruba, Bonaire, Buenos Aires (Avianca and Aerolineas, both daily), Caracas (five a day), Curaçao, Guayaquil, Havana, Lima, Mexico, Panama, Quito, Rio de Janeiro/Sao Paolo and Santiago; to Medellín from Aruba, Barquisimeto, Bonaire, Caracas, Curaçao, Panama and San Antonio(Venezuela); to Cartagena from Panama and Miami (both daily) and Caracas; to San Andrés from San José (Lacsa) daily. Connections from Central America are principally through Panama City.

For taking a car by air to Colombia, see under Darién in the text.

The cheapest way to fly from Quito to Colombia is to fly to Tulcán, cross the border by road to Ipiales where you have the option of going on to Cali or Bogotá by air.

Baggage Allowance Airlines will only allow a certain weight of luggage without a surcharge; this is normally 30 kg for first class and 20 kg for business and economy classes, but these limits are often not strictly enforced when it is known that the plane is not going to be full. On some flights from the UK special outbound concessions are offered (by Iberia, Air France, Avianca) of a two-piece allowance up to 32 kg, but you may need to request this. Passengers seeking a larger baggage allowance can route via USA, but with certain exceptions, the fares are slightly higher using this route. On the other hand, weight limits for internal flights are often lower; it's best to enquire beforehand.

Prices & Discounts
For special deals for travelling by air within Colombia, see page 34
It is generally cheaper to fly from London rather than a point in Europe to Latin American destinations. Fares vary from airline to airline, destination to destination and according to time of year. Check with an agency for the best deal for when you wish to travel.

Most airlines offer discounted fares of one sort or another on scheduled flights. These are not offered by the airlines direct to the public, but through agencies who specialize in this type of fare (see Discount Flight Agent boxes). There are similar arrangements in provincial cities in the UK, European, North American and Far Eastern centres and elsewhere.

The very busy seasons are 7 December – 15 January and 10 July – 10 September. If you intend travelling during those times, book as far ahead as possible. Between February-May and September-November special offers may be available.

● ●

Discount flight agents in Australia and New Zealand

Flight Centres, *82 Elizabeth St, Sydney,*
T13-1600; 205 Queen St, Auckland, T09-309
6171. Also branches in other towns and
cities.
STA Travel, *T1300-360960,*
www.statravelaus.com.au; 702 Harris St,

Ultimo, Sydney, and 256 Flinders St,
Melbourne. In NZ: 10 High St, Auckland,
T09-366 6673. Also in major towns and
university campuses.
Travel.com.au, *80 Clarence St, Sydney,*
T02-929 01500, www.travel.com.au

● ●

Essentials

Other fares fall into three groups, and are all on scheduled services:

Excursion (return) fares (A) with restricted validity eg 5-90 days. Carriers are introducing flexibility into these tickets, permitting a change of dates on payment of a fee.

Yearly fares (B) these may be bought on a one-way or return basis. Some airlines require a specified return date, changeable upon payment of a fee. To leave the return completely open is possible for an extra fee. You must fix the route (some of the cheapest flexible fares now have 6 months validity).

Student (or Under 26) fares some airlines are flexible on the age limit, others strict. One way and returns available, or 'Open Jaws' (see below). Do not assume that student tickets are the cheapest; though they are often very flexible, they are usually more expensive than A or B above. On the other hand, there is a wider range of cheap one-way student fares originating in Latin America than can be bought outside the continent. NB If you foresee returning home at a busy time (eg Christmas-beginning of January, August), a booking is advisable on any type of open-return ticket.

For people intending to travel a linear route and return from a different point from that which they entered, there are 'Open Jaws' fares, which are available on student, yearly, or excursion fares.

Road

There are three official vehicle border crossings to neighbouring countries, one to Ecuador (Ipiales-Tulcán) and two to Venezuela (Cúcuta-San Antonio and Maicao-Sinamaica for Maracaibo). There are various other places where roads cross to Venezuela (usually over river bridges) for local traffic only.

There are buses which run across the frontiers from Ecuador and Venezuela. There is one line (Ormeño) which runs from Lima(Peru) to Caracas (Venezuela), but this is expensive and unreliable. Better is to take buses to the border and take the much more frequent national services. **International Buses**

Proof of ownership of the vehicle, valid driving licence and insurance (local insurance can usually be purchased at the border or obtained in the nearest town) will be requested at the border. A *carnet de passage* is not obligatory but will help. To obtain a *carnet* apply to a motoring organization in your own country. **Driving**

Sea

There are many ways of getting to Colombia by short sea crossing to the Caribbean coast and some via the Pacific, none of them are easy. A full description of the alternatives and how to transport a vehicle will be found in the Darién section. The sea link with Ecuador is given in the text under Tumaco.

Discount flight agents in North America

Air Brokers International, 323 Geary St, Suite 411, San Francisco, CA94102, T01-800-883 3273, www.airbrokers.com Consolidator and specialist on RTW and Circle Pacific tickets.

Council Travel, 205 E 42nd St, New York, NY 10017, T1-888-COUNCIL, www.counciltravel.com Student/budget agency with branches in many other US cities.

Discount Airfares Worldwide On-Line, www.etn.nl/discount.htm A hub of consolidator and discount agent links.

International Travel Network/Airlines of the Web, www.itn.net/airlines Online air travel information and reservations.

STA Travel, 5900 Wilshire Blvd, Suite 2110, Los Angeles, CA 90036, T1-800-777 0112, www.sta-travel.com Also branches in New York, San Francisco, Boston, Miami, Chicago, Seattle and Washington DC.

Travel CUTS, 187 College St, Toronto, ON, M5T 1P7, T1-800-667 2887, www.travelcuts.com Specialist in student discount fares, Ids and other travel services. Branches in other Canadian cities.

Travelocity, www.travelocity.com Online consolidator.

Possibilities for long distance sea voyages and cruises from Europe and North America to Colombia are available. Enquiries regarding passages should be made through agencies in your own country, or through John Alton of Strand Cruise and Travel Centre, Charing Cross Shopping Concourse, The Strand, London WC2N 4HZ, T 0171-836 6363, F 0171-497 0078. Strand Cruise and Travel are booking agents for all shipping companies, except Fyffes, whose booking agent is Cargo Ship Voyages Ltd, Hemley, Woodbridge, Suffolk, IP12 4QF, T/F 01473-736265 (who can also advise on the other sailings). In Europe, contact Wagner Frachtschiffreisen, Stadlerstrasse 48, CH-8404, Winterthur, Switzerland, T (052) 242-1442, F 242-1487. In the USA, contact Freighter World Cruises, 180 South Lake Avenue, Pasadena, CA 91101, T (818) 449-3106, or Travltips Cruise and Freighter Travel Association, 163-07 Depot Road, PO Box 188, Flushing, NY 11358, T (800) 872-8584.

For short trans-Caribbean cruise travel, there are frequent trips that include Cartagena and/or Santa Marta on their itinerary. Most originate in Miami, any good travel agent will be able to tell you what is on offer.

Other crossings

If travelling independently on foot, there are many more places for entering or leaving Colombia, all difficult to access and requiring time and care to ensure your documents are in order and the routes are safe. These include to Ecuador via Puerto Asís (not advised in 2000), and to Venezuela across the Río Orinoco, details in the text. It is also possible to enter Colombia from Peru and Brazil through Leticia.

Touching Down

Airport information

For details of services at your arrival airport and ground transport alternatives available, see under the relevant destination.

You should always reconfirm your onward flights 24-48 hours before departure time and leave a contact phone number. Arrive for check-in two hours before departure for international flights and one hour before domestic flights (unless told otherwise). At main airports, there are several security checks which can take extra time. Do not arrive late: planes are often overbooked and you don't want to be the one left behind.

Airport Departure Information

There is an airport tax (*tasa aeroportuario*) of US$24 (in cash, dollars or pesos), that every passenger leaving the country has to pay. In addition, there is an exit tax (*impuesto salida*) of US$18 for stays of over 60 days. Make sure you are going to fly before you pay the tax. If for any reason you have to change airlines, you may have to pay again. When you arrive, ensure that all necessary documentation bears a stamp for your date of arrival; without it you will have to pay the exit tax on leaving. If your stay was less than 60 days, you should obtain the tax exemption certificate (for the *impuesto salida*) from the '*Exención de impuestos*' desk. Travellers changing planes in Colombia and leaving the same day are exempt from both taxes.

Airport Departure Tax

There is a 17% tax on all international air tickets bought in Colombia for flights out of the country (7½% on international return flights). It is not possible to avoid the purchase tax by buying tickets outside the country, as the charge is included automatically. Do not buy tickets outside Colombia for domestic flights (other than the official airpasses see below); they are much more expensive. There is also an airport tax of US$3.25 on internal air tickets, not normally included in price quotations.

Tourist information

Details of the national tourist agencies is given on page 15. For offices at airports and bus stations, see under the relevant destination in the travelling text. Other tourist agencies, mainly Departmental and City ones, now have offices responsible for providing visitors with information. See text for local details. These offices should be visited as early as possible not only for information on accommodation and transport, but also for details on areas which are dangerous to visit. Enquire at Colombian embassies and consulates abroad for information on the country and at your own embassy in Colombia.

Maps of Colombia and route maps are obtainable at the Instituto Geográfico Militar, Agustín Codazzi, Cra 30 y Calle 45, open 0800-1530, Bogotá, or from their offices in other large cities. Drivers' route maps are also included in the *Auto Guia* by Publicación Legis, reviewed annually, price (2000) US$7. See also under Bogotá, Maps.

Special interest groups

Provision for the disabled is limited in Colombia. Wheelchairs and assistance are available at major airports but inconsistent. Modern and public buildings are being provided with ramps and relevant lifts, and some streets have sidewalk breaks mainly for vendor trollies and cycles, but usually adequate for wheelchairs. As yet, serious concern for the disabled is not evident in the country.

Disabled travellers

But, of course, only a minority of disabled people are wheelchair-bound and it is now widely acknowledged that disabilities do not stop you from enjoying a great holiday.

Essentials

Touching down information

Business Hours Monday to Friday, commercial firms work 0800 to 1200 and 1400 to 1730 or 1800. Certain firms in the warmer towns such as Cali start at 0700 and finish earlier. Government offices follow the same hours on the whole as the commercial firms, but some prefer to do business with the public in the afternoon only. Embassy hours for the public are very variable but 0900 to 1200 is the most common. For banks, see above under **Exchange**. Standard shopping hours are 0900 to 1230 and 1430 to 1830, including Saturdays.

Voltage 120 volts AC, is general for Colombia. A transformer must be 110-150 volt AC, with flat-prong plugs (all of same size).

Official Time Colombia is 5 hours behind GMT.

Direct Dialling Code +57

Weights and measures Weights and measures are metric, and weights should always be quoted in kilograms. Litres are used for liquid measures but US gallons are standard for the petroleum industry. Linear measures are usually metric, but the inch is quite commonly used by engineers and the yard on golf courses. For land measurement the hectare and cubic metre are officially employed but the traditional measures vara (80 cm) and fanegada (1,000 square varas) are still in common use. As in many other countries food etc is often sold in libras (pounds), which are equivalent to about ½ kg.

Some travel companies are beginning to specialize in exciting holidays, tailor-made for individuals depnding on their level of disability. A Global Access-Disabled Travel Network website is: www.geocities.com/Paris/1502 It is dedicated to providing travel information for "disabled adventurers" and also includes a number of reviews and tips from members of the public. You might also want to read *Nothing Ventured*, edited by Alison Walsh (Harper Collins), which gives personal accounts of worldwide journeys by disabled travellers, plus advice and listings.

Gay & lesbian travellers Major cities have facilities (bars, clubs etc) for homosexuals and lesbians, but, as in Latin America generally, there is no general public acceptance. Contact can be made through 'classified' newspaper advertisements, and information is available at some hotels.

Student travellers If you are in full time education, you will be entitled to an International Student Identity Card (ISIC), which you can obtain through student travel offices and many travel agencies in 77 countries. You will need this for special prices on transport (air, sea, road etc), and access to a variety of other concessions and discounts. The ISIC is recognized in Colombia and is useful for identity purposes. Make sure it has a photograph. We try to show in the travelling text where students are allowed a discount eg entry to National Parks, but it may depend on the official at the gate. It is always worth trying.

Travelling with children The Colombians often go on local holidays as families, and attractive localities within reach of large cities frequently have spacious hotels with pools and facilities for family stays. Many are busy at weekends but good bargains are available during the week.

Make sure you pack that favourite toy. Nothing beats a GameBoy, unless it's 2 GameBoys & a link cable

Bus travel People contemplating overland travel in South America with children should remember that a lot of time can be spent waiting for transport, especially for aeroplanes. On bus journeys, if the children are good at amusing themselves, or can readily sleep while travelling, the problems can be considerably lessened. If your child is of an early reading age, take reading material with you as it is difficult, and expensive to find.

On all long-distance buses you pay for each seat, and there are no half-fares if the children occupy a seat each. For shorter trips it is cheaper, if less comfortable, to seat small children on your knee. Often there are spare seats which children can occupy after tickets have been collected. In city and local excursion buses, small children generally do not pay a fare, but are not entitled to a seat when paying customers are standing. On sightseeing tours you should *always* bargain for a family rate – often children can go free. (In trains, reductions for children are general, but not universal.)

Food can be a problem if the children are not adaptable. It is easier to take biscuits, drinks, bread etc with you on longer trips than to rely on meal stops where the food may not be to taste. Avocados are safe, easy to eat and nutritious; they can be fed to babies as young as six months and most older children like them. A small immersion heater and jug for making hot drinks is invaluable, but remember that electric current varies. Try and get a dual-voltage one (110v and 220v). In restaurants, you can normally buy children's helpings, or divide one full-size helping between two children.

Hotels   Try to negotiate family rates. If charges are per person, always insist that two children will occupy one bed only, therefore counting as one tariff. You can almost always get a reduced rate at cheaper hotels. Occasionally when travelling with a child you will be refused a room in a hotel that is 'unsuitable'; ie intended for short-stay couples.

Travel with children can bring you into closer contact with Latin American families and, generally, presents no special problems – in fact the path is often smoother for family groups. Officials tend to be more amenable where children are concerned and they are pleased if your child knows a little Spanish.

Generally, women travellers should find visiting Colombia a relatively hassle-free experience. However, machismo is alive and well here and you should be prepared for this and try not to over-react. When you set out, err on the side of caution until your instincts have adjusted to the new culture.

Women travellers

It is easier for men to take the friendliness of locals at face value; women may be subject to much unwanted attention. Minimize this by not wearing suggestive clothing and do not flirt. By wearing a wedding ring, or carrying a photograph of your "husband" and "children", you may dissuade an aspiring suitor. If politeness fails, do not feel bad about showing offence and departing. When accepting a social invitation, make sure that someone knows where you went and when you left. Ask if you can bring a friend (even if you do not intend to do so).

If, as a single woman, you can befriend a Colombian woman, you will learn much more about the country as well as finding how best to deal with the barrage of suggestive comments, whistles and hisses that might come your way. However, don't be too flattered either. Your average *latino* would whistle at his own grandmother if she walked past wearing a potato sack for a dress. Travelling with another *gringa* may not exempt you from this attention, but at least should give you moral support.

Rules, customs and etiquette

Never give money or sweets to children. Their parents often spend the whole day working for less than the kiddies earn begging. This only encourages more begging, and a generation of kids with no education and no way of making a living. Also a generation of those who believe gringos are nothing more than a dollar piggy bank to be dipped into at will. It's a better idea to give books, pens, toothbrushes, soap etc to the schools and orphanages, or play a game with the kids instead.

Begging

Essentials

Clothing   Colombians, if they can afford it, devote great care to their clothes and appearance. It is appreciated if visitors do likewise. **How you dress is mostly how people will judge you.** Bogotá, in particular, is conservative in a business and social context, with dark suits and formal dresses worn on appropriate occasions. That said, on informal occasions there are few restrictions, particularly on beaches and in the hot lowland areas. Elsewhere, locals do not normally wear shorts and men do not go bare-chested. There are good quality clothes at reasonable prices available in the main towns which will help you to look less like a tourist, and well worth bringing home.

Conduct   Remember that politeness – even a little ceremoniousness – is much appreciated. In this connection professional or business cards are useful. Men should always remove any headgear and say 'con permiso' when entering offices, and be prepared to shake hands; always say 'Buenos días' (until midday) or 'Buenas tardes' and wait for a reply before proceeding further. Always remember that the traveller from abroad has enjoyed greater advantages in life than most Colombian minor officials, and should be friendly and courteous in consequence. Never be impatient and do not criticize situations in public: the officials may know more English than you think and they can certainly interpret gestures and facial expressions. Politeness can be a liability, however, in some situations. Most Colombians are disorderly queuers. In commercial transactions (buying a meal, goods in a shop etc) politeness should be accompanied by firmness, and always ask the price first.

Politeness should also be extended to street traders; saying 'No, gracias' with a smile is better than an arrogant dismissal.

Prohibitions   It is very important to realize that no matter how simple it seems, it is not worth your time to try to take anything illegal out of the country – this includes drugs. The security personnel and customs officials are much smarter than you and are experts at their job. It's best to understand that this is a foolhardy idea and save yourself the wasted time, money and energy of 10 years in jail. Never carry firearms. Their possession could land you in serious trouble.

Time-keeping   Colombians, as with most Latin Americans, have a fairly 'relaxed' attitude towards time. They will think nothing of arriving an hour or so late on social occasions. If you expect to meet someone more or less at an exact time, you can tell them that you want to meet 'en punto'.

Tipping   Upmarket restaurants, up to 10%. However, many such restaurants include a 'voluntary' service charge on the bill. Normally this is accepted by the customer and no further tip expected. If the service has not been up to standard, it is perfectly acceptable to delete it and pay only the base amount. In cheaper restaurants, no tipping is expected though if you do not pay the exact amount, they may infer the 'small change' is a tip. Taxi-drivers are not normally tipped but many are friendly and helpful with baggage etc and a tip is always appreciated.

Responsible tourism

Travel to the furthest corners of the globe is now commonplace and the mass movement of people for leisure and business is a major source of foreign exchange and economic development in many parts of South America. In some regions (eg the Galápagos Islands and Machu Picchu) it is probably the most significant economic activity.

The benefits of international travel are self-evident for both hosts and travellers – employment, increased understanding of different cultures, business and leisure opportunities. At the same time there is clearly a downside to the industry. Where

Preserving the environment

'Bueno, uno exagera un poco. Si no lo hiciéramos asi, las exageraciones se extinguirían y sería otra especie más que desaparecería del planeta.'

Translation *Yes, one exaggerates a little. If we did not, exaggerations would disappear and that would be another species lost to the planet.*
Andrés Hurtado García

Essentials

visitor pressure is high and/or poorly regulated, adverse impacts to society and the natural environment may be apparent. Paradoxically, this is as true in undeveloped and pristine areas (where culture and the natural environment are less 'prepared' for even small numbers of visitors) as in major resort destinations.

The travel industry is growing rapidly and increasingly the impacts of this supposedly 'smokeless' industry are becoming apparent. These impacts can seem remote and unrelated to an individual trip or holiday (eg air travel is clearly implicated in global warming and damage to the Ozone layer, resort location and construction can destroy natural habitats and restrict traditional rights and activities) but, individual choice and awareness can make a difference in many instances (see box), and collectively, travellers are having a significant effect in shaping a more responsible and sustainable industry.

In an attemot to promote awareness of and credibility for responsible tourism, organizations such as Green Globe (T+44 020-79308333, greenglobe@compuserve.com) and the Center for Environmentally Sustainable Tourism (CERT, T+44 01268-795772) now offer advice on destinations and sites that ave achieved certain commitments to conservation and sustainable development. Generally these are larger mainstream destinations and resorts but they are still a useful guide and increasingly aim to provide information on smaller operations.

Of course travel can have beneficial impacts and this is something to which every traveller can contribute – many National Parks are part funded by receipts from visitors. Similarly, travellers can promote patronage and protection of important archaeological sites and heritage through their interest and contributions via entrance and performance fees. They can also support small-scale enterprises by staying in locally run hotels and hostels, eating in local restaurants and by purchasing local goods, supplies and arts and crafts.

In fact, during the past decade there has been a phenomenal growth in tourism that promotes and supports the conservation of natural environments and is also fair and equitable to local communities. This 'ecotourism' segment is probably the fastes growing sector of the travel industry and provides a vast and growing range of destinations and activities in Colombia. For example, in Chocó Province, the Utria Ensenada range of ecotourism experiences (see page 285) and the Serranía de la Macarena area offers ecological and archaeological experiences.

While the authenticity of some eco-tourism operators claims need to be interpreted with care, there is clearly both a huge demand for this type of activity and also significant opportunities to support worthwhile conservation and social development initiatives.

Organizations in the USA such as Conservation International (T+1 202 4295660, www.ecotour.org), the Eco-Tourism society (T+1 802 4472121, www.ecotourism.org), Planeta (www2.planeta.com/mader) and, in the UK, Tourism Concern (T+44 020 77533330, www.gn.apc.org/tourismconcern) have begun to develop and/or promote eco-tourism projects and destinations and their web sites are an excellent source if information and details for sites and initiatives throughout South America. Additionally, organisations such as, Earthwatch (T+44 01865 311601, www.earthwatch,org) and Discovery International (T+44 020 72299881, www.discoveryinitiatives.com) offer opportunites to participate directly in scientific research and development projects throughout this region.

Colombia offers unique and unforgettable experiences – often based on the natural environment, cultural heritage and local society. These are the reasons many of us choose to travel and why many more will want to do so in the future. Shouldn't we provide an opportunity for future travellers and hosts to enjoy the quality of experience and interaction that we take for granted.

Safety

Most travellers confirm that the vast majority of Colombians are honest and very hospitable. However, the following local conditions should be noted.

Con tricks Remember the city (or beach) con artist is always looking for the unwary. The best advice is: be suspicious of anyone who approaches you. If you are told there are marks on your clothing, they probably put them there. A simple request for information may be designed to get you to stop. A plainclothes policeman (possibly one of a team) may be nothing of the kind. If in doubt, make sure you are taken to an official police station before showing any identification or money to them. Try walking away politely but determinedly and see what happens. Similarly, after drawing cash from a bank or cash machine, move quickly out of range of anyone who could have been watching you.

In the text, we try to tell you where this kind of trouble is likely. In the vast majority of places you will visit, there will be none of these problems. However, this is a 'third world' country and people will be less well off than you are. If you inadvertently leave something behind, and it is returned to you, please offer an appropriate reward to the finder.

Drugs As is all too well known, Colombia is part of a major drug-producing and smuggling route. Police and customs activities have greatly intensified and smugglers increasingly try to use innocent carriers. Do not carry packages for other people without checking the contents (indeed taking suspicious packages or gift-wrapped presents of your own through customs could give problems). Be very polite if approached by policemen or if your hotel room is raided by police looking for drugs. Colombians who offer you drugs may well be setting you up for the police, who are very active on the north coast and San Andrés island, and other tourist resorts. There are established penalties which include prison, fines and deportation of any foreigner caught using any drug.

Guerrilla There is sporadic guerrilla activity in Colombia. At present it is mostly confined to rural **activity** areas down the eastern part of the country (the Llanos and Amazonia), near the frontier with Panama and in some parts of the lower Río Magdalena. It can be related to oil production and pipeline areas and to the current destruction of drug crops by the authorities, causing local hardship and resentment. For the most part, tourists are not targeted, though they may be involved with everyone else if they stray into areas of known difficulty. Detailed local enquiry is essential before entering any potentially hazardous area.

In 2000, there were several events which closed certain main roads in Antioquia, Santander and in the south. These were to do with the efforts of the main guerrilla groups to obtain control of country areas (*despejadas*) for bargaining purposes with the Government. One of these was established in the southeast of the country in November 1998. Another, along the west bank of the Río Magdalena near Barrancabermeja was under discussion in 2000. There are also groups of 'bandits' taking advantage of current instabilities to rob groups of passers by.

Local informed authorities agree that you should not travel between cities and towns anywhere by night at present, and therefore make sure you time your arrival at your destination well before 1800. Smaller vehicles are less likely to be stopped than larger. In towns, keep away from 'no-go' zones detailed in the text. Read the safety section carefully for each town you visit which has been compiled from the best information available in mid-2000.

Violent robbery tends to be localised in areas that favour the criminal. These places are **Robbery** known and many are detailed in the travelling text. If you are caught, cooperation almost always saves you from getting harmed. Opportunistic thieves operate in busy streets, markets and the like: don't tempt them by wearing or carrying items of value and leave what you don't immediately need in a safe place. Most hotels will have safety box arrangements, use them. Vulnerable places include airports and, in particular, some bus stations and on the buses themselves. The warning against accepting cigarettes, chewing gum, sweets or any other type of food or drink, even water from fellow bus passengers, applies mainly in the southern part of Colombia. The purpose may be to disable you and steal your baggage.

The standard suggestions to avoid theft apply. Keep all documents secure; hide what cash, travellers cheques and credit cards you are carrying in different places under your clothes: extra pockets sewn inside shirts and trousers using zips or safety pins, money belts preferably out of sight, neck or leg pouches, a thin chain attached to the body to stop a purse or bag being snatched. If you have a shoulder bag, wear it in front of you, a back pack should be lockable at its base.

Where to stay

There is a very wide range of accommodation available in Colombia. At the top end, the best will stand comparison with anywhere in the world, and surprising for the quality of service and the reasonable prices. Part of the reason for this is that there has been a great deal of investment in new hotels in Bogotá and the main cities in anticipation of continuing economic prosperity and increased tourism which has proved, so far, to be over-optimistic. The result is a good choice and, usually, it is worth asking for a lower price than the standard quoted. We give a selection of these hotels, all of which have been visited by ourselves or recommended to us by our readers. This applies to the middle and lower ranges also where there can be even more difficulty for the visitor to make a choice. Within the hotel listings there are a few outstanding places to stay, some at the upper end where you can be assured of a memorable experience or we advise you to have a look around anyway, and at the lower cost level, a number of places in the main cities we have used the phrase 'excellent travellers guest house'. This indicates that not only will the younger traveller find value for money and plenty of information on where to go and what to do, but the management is dedicated to the interests of the guests and to giving any help required.

You will notice that 'recommended' appears in the text sparingly. We recommend only those hotels (and restaurants etc) where we have consistently good references from all sources

In Colombia there are a number of quite exceptional hotels, not necessarily very expensive, usually in colonial towns, that are well worth seeking out. You will spot them in the text. There is a small network of Youth Hostels, though of varying quality, used extensively by Colombian groups, but international members welcomed.

There are many names in Colombia for hotels including *posada, pensión, residencía,* **Advice &** *hostal, hostería, hospedaje, hospedería, mesón* and *hotelito*. Ignore them all and simply **suggestions** look at the price range for what to expect.

In the past, the more expensive hotels and restaurants added on 16% IVA (value added tax) to bills, but this was suspended (temporarily?) in late 1999. Some hotels add a small insurance charge.

Hotel Classifications

Classifications given in accommodation listings are for a standard double room for two people sharing including any taxes charged. If breakfast is included, it will say so in the text - this will be continental style though often a more substantial menu will be available for a supplementary charge. Single rooms are not common in Colombian hotels so travellers on their own will normally pay around 75% of the charge quoted (more in busy periods) for a room to themselves. The alternative is to share. Cheaper hotels charge per person, as quoted in the text. The following is a general description of what to expect in each of the category bands. However, you will get less for your money in Bogotá, Cartagena and the special tourist areas such as the north west Pacific coast than in the rest of the country.

LL to L (US$100 up) luxury hotels with full range of services, often part of international chains, restaurants, pool, sauna etc, email services and a predictable atmosphere.

AL to A (US$46-99) comfortable hotels, often the best in an important provincial town, or an older hotel in a big city, family facilities, restaurant and bar, shower/toilet standard in all rooms, cable TV, possibly a pool, they may have their own transport service and will most likely accept credit cards.

B to D (US$12-45) a wide range of quality from good comfortable but "faded" hotels to very pleasant smaller establishments. Cost may depend on location. You should expect your own shower/toilet, hot water, TV, restaurant in hotel or at least next door, air conditioning (if appropriate), reasonably sized rooms and comfortable beds. In towns, shared bathrooms and fan rather than air conditioning may be normal at this price range.

E and F (US$4-11) the best in these categories will be clean, have some degree of comfort, at least some rooms with shower/toilet, soap and towel, possible breakfast included, luggage store, cycle/motorcycle parking arrangements. However, some may be included because they are the only place to stay in the area and are not up to the normal standard. The travelling text gives specific details and will help you to find the best bargains.

G (up to US$3) almost always the price is per person, and you will get little more than a cubicle and a bed. In most you will find communal facilities and will need your own towel, soap, toilet paper etc. In colder climates, a sleeping bag may be handy, and the closeness to the bus station may make sleeping after 5 am problematical. We try to include only those that have a reputation for cleanliness, safety and helpful management.

Between 15 December and 30 April, 15 June and 31 August, some hotels in main holiday centres may increase prices by 20-30%. In some hotels outside the main cities you can only stay (very cheaply) at *en pension* rates but no allowance is made for missing a meal.

The Colombian hotel federation (COTELCO) has lists of authorized prices for all member hotels which can be consulted at tourist offices. In theory, new laws require all hotels to be registered, but to date this is incomplete particularly with regard to cheaper hotels. Most hotels in Colombia charge US$1 to US$6 for extra beds for children, up to a maximum (usually) of 4 beds/room. Prices are normally displayed at reception, but in quiet periods it is always worth negotiating and ask to see the room before committing.

When booking a hotel from an airport or bus station, try to speak to the hotel yourself, most will understand at least simple English and possibly French, German or Italian. If you use an official tourist agent, you will probably pay a little more as a booking fee. If you accept help from anyone else, you could be putting yourself at risk.

Essentials

In cheaper hotels, beware of electric shower heaters which can be dangerous through faulty wiring. Hotels are sometimes checked by the police for drugs. Make sure they do not remove any of your belongings. You do not need to show them any money. Cooperate but be firm about your rights.

Toilets may suffer from inadequate water supplies. In all cases, however, do not flush paper down the pan but use the receptacle provided. Carry toilet paper with you as cheaper establishments as well as restaurants, bars etc may not provide it. If you are concerned about the higiene of the facility, put paper on the seat.

Cockroaches are ubiquitous and unpleasant. They can also be surprisingly large. However they are not dangerous and if you are staying in cheaper hotels, take insecticide; Baygon (Bayer) has been recommended. Stuffing toilet paper in any holes in the walls can also keep them at bay.

Camping

Sites are given in the text. The local tourist authorities have lists of official sites, but they are seldom signposted on main roads, so can be hard to find. Permission to camp with tent, camper van or car may be granted by landowners in less populated areas. Many *haciendas* have armed guards protecting their property: this can add to your safety. Do not camp on private land without permission. Those in camper vans may camp by the roadside, but it is neither particularly safe, nor easy to find a secluded spot. Vehicles may camp at truck drivers' restaurants or ask if you may overnight beside police or army posts. Check locally very carefully before deciding to camp: you may be exposing yourself to significant danger.

Colombia is one of the few countries which sells 'white gas' for camping stoves etc, so stock up here. Also available is Coleman fuel imported from the US sold at 19 Avenida/Calle 123, Bogotá; Calle 3, No 42-135, Cali; and Avenida 30 de Agosto, No 37-23, Pereira.

Youth hostels

The Colombian Youth Hostel network (*La Federación Colombiana de Albergues Juveniles*) is affiliated to the International Youth Hostel Federation (IYHF) and has 11 hostels around the country centered on Bogotá, where there are 105 beds at Carrera 7, No 6-10, in Candelaria, T2803041, F2803460, in the old centre of the city. The other hostels are in Cartagena, Leticia, Medellín, Neiva, Paipa, Pasto, Santa Marta (2), Villa de Leiva and Villavicencio. Hostels are often full at holiday periods, December-January and June to mid-July, best to telephone beforehand at these times. Otherwise, there is usually room. Details are in the travelling text. Membership can be taken out in Colombia: Hostelling International Cards are recognised and qualify for discounts.

Homestays

You will find local families who offer rooms to let in many places (at the end of the sleeping sections). If you are interested in informally learning Spanish in a family

Essentials

environment, see also in the text or check with the tourist offices. However, if you take formal classes, you should have a student visa. See also the Staying on coffee farms section in La Zona Cafetera chapter.

Getting around

Air

Internal air services are flown principally by Avianca/ SAM, Aces, Aires, AeroRepublica and Satena. They serve the whole country, the larger towns and cities receiving flights usually daily, the smaller places perhaps only once or twice a week. There are other feeder lines including Aerotaca (towns to the northeast of Bogotá), and West Caribbean Airways (San Andrés and Providencia).

Airpasses Avianca offers a five coupon Air Pass for travel within the country valid for 21 days on Avianca, Aires or SAM, which must be bought outside Colombia in conjunction with an international air ticket. Children up to 12 pay 67%, infants 10%. The Air Pass is non-refundable unless the whole has been unused. You cannot pass through a city more than once (except for transfers), and a proposed itinerary (not firm) must be submitted when buying the ticket (Leticia and San Andrés may be included at the higher charge marked * below). Prices are determined by high season (June-August and December), or low season (rest of year). Air Pass 1 is open to all nationalities including Colombians legally resident abroad. Passengers must fly Avianca into Colombia.

Air Pass 1 costs US$200 ($290*) high season; US$180 ($260*) low season, for five coupons, with the option to add three extra coupons at US$40 each. With Air Pass 2 (which is not available to Colombians), any other carrier may be used. This costs US$419 ($539*) high; US$399 ($509*) low for five stops, plus US$40 each for up to three extra coupons. These prices and conditions change from time to time, enquire at any Avianca office.

Another Air Pass is offered by Aces. It is valid for 30 days, must be bought outside Colombia, children 2-11 pay 75%, infants free. Refunds permitted if unused and proportionately if used in part. High season is 15 December-15 January, low season is the rest of the year except one week before/after Easter when the Air Pass is not available. Air Pass A is open to those who travel from international points on Aces (Miami, Panama City and Dominican Republic) or from anywhere else on any airline: three coupons US$150 (high) $130 (low) which do not include San Andrés and Capurganá (on the border with Panama); additional coupons which do include these destinations, US$60 (high) $50 (low). Air Pass B is open to those who travel on competing airlines from the international points named above: three coupons US$150 (high) $155 (low) with additional coupons US$65 (high) $55 (low).

There is yet another air-pass arrangement offered by AeroRepública, for purchase within Colombia, which allows seven trips on that airline between Bogotá, Cali, Medellín, Bucamaranga, Cúcuta and Montería for US$440, or six trips anywhere on the network for US$565, which adds, amongst others, Leticia, San Andrés, and the *llanos* destinations of Puerto Carreño and Puerto Inírida. Both passes are valid for one year.

For those who wish to make Bogotá their base and travel to other cities and return to Bogotá, the Avianca air-pass is good value. If you wish to do a round trip in Colombia, Aces is probably the best. Check the networks before deciding. Note also that these air-pass arrangements are subject to change at any time.

For single flights, the army airline Satena tends to be cheaper than Avianca. Satena flies to 34 destinations in Colombia. Since many of these are remote locations, their timekeeping is not good but they fly modern, comfortable aircraft and you can see a lot more of Colombia from the air. Avianca's domestic shuttle flights go from Bogotá to Medellín, Cali, and other destinations but book a ticket as for an ordinary flight: just turning up will involve a long wait. Ask about discount fares which may be available on certain days of the week. There are good bargains directed to Colombian travellers advertised in the press, usually on Thursdays, eg weekends Bogotá to San Andrés or Cartagena; these can work out cheaper than an air-pass.

Domestic airports are good, though the tourist facilities tend to close early on weekdays, and all day Sunday. Most airports levy a US$3.25 tax, payable before issue of a boarding pass. In-flight service is generally good but airline services on the ground tend to be patchy. Security checks are thorough everywhere; watch your luggage particularly before and while checking in and hand items before passing into the departure lounges.

Bus

Public transport is standard Latin American, noisy, mostly uncomfortable, unpredictable and usually too fast.

The bus network is very comprehensive and for most journeys you have a choice of quality, type and operator. Travel in Colombia is far from dull. The scenery is generally worth seeing so travel by day if possible: this is also strongly recommended for safety reasons and you can keep a better eye on your valuables. On main routes you usually have choice of operator and of type of bus. The cheapest (*corriente*) are basically local buses, stopping frequently, uncomfortable and slow but offering plenty of local colour. Try to keep your luggage with you, if asked to leave the bus en route for any reason, take all your luggage with you. *Pullman* (each company will have a different name for the service) are long distance buses usually with air conditioning, toilets, hostess service, videos (almost always violent films, Spanish/Mexican or dubbed English) and limited stop. Be prepared for lack of air conditioning and locked windows. Sit near the back with your walkman to avoid the video and the need to keep the blinds down but best not at the back, especially if the roads are likely to be in poor condition. Luggage is normally carried in a locked compartment against receipt. *Colectivos*, also known as *vans* or *busetas*, run by Velotax, Taxis Verdes, etc are usually 12-20 seat vehicles, maybe with air conditioning, rather cramped but fast, saving several hours on long journeys, though the driving can be hair-raising! You can keep your eye on luggage in the back of the van.

Fares shown in the text are middle of the range where there is a choice but are no more than a guide. The cost of bus travel rose steeply for several years in the 1990s, particularly for the more comfortable services, but recently have gone down a little in dollar terms due to strong inflation. The companies with the best reputations include Expreso Bolivariano, Copetran and Los Libertadores. If you have time and a tight budget, shop around for your appropriate service. Note that meal stops can be few and far between, and short; bring your own food and water. Be prepared for climatic changes on longer routes. If you entrust your luggage to the bus companies' luggage rooms, remember to load it on to the bus yourself; it will not be done automatically. There are few interdepartmental bus services on holidays. If you are joining a bus at popular or holiday times, not at the starting point, you may be left behind even though you have a ticket and reservation. Always take your passport (or photocopy) with you: identity checks on buses can happen at any time.

Car

The road network has been improved during the past few years, with a new road in the Magdalena valley connecting Bogotá with the north coast significantly shortening journey times. A connecting highway from Medellín is now in course of major roadworks, and elsewhere reconstruction and improvements are under way. For information, a useful website of the National Road Institute is: www.invias.gov.co If you are driving, beware of unexpected bad patches: especially in the mountains, rockfalls, landslips and heavy rains frequently cause damage.

East of the Andes, good roads lead to Yopal, Villavicencio and Florencia in the foothills and peter out shortly afterwards. Tracks lead on towards the Orinoco river but, in the *llanos*, you are left to make your own way in the dry season. In the wet, these quickly become impassable. Further south, in Amazonia, there is virtually no land transport.

The best road connections are given in the text. Before taking a long journey, ask at your hotel and elsewhere for information on the state of the road including for personal safety. Roads are not always signposted. If driving yourself, avoid night journeys. The roads may not be in good condition, lorry and bus drivers tend to be reckless, and stray animals are often encountered. If you find yourself on a stretch of road normally busy and there is no oncoming traffic for a period, stop and wait: there may be a guerrilla road block ahead. Police checks can be frequent in troubled areas, keep your documents handy. There are toll stations (*peajes*) every 60-100 km or so on major roads: tolls vary but are around US$1.80. Motorcycles and bicycles don't normally have to pay. In town, try to leave your car in an attended car park (*parqueadero*), especially at night. If you are planning to sleep in your car, it is better to stop in a *parqueadero*; you will be charged a little extra. Alternatively, find a police station and ask to sleep in your car nearby. You can also stay overnight in *balnearios campestres*, which normally have armed guards.

National driving licences may be used by foreigners in Colombia, but should be accompanied by an official translation if in a language other than Spanish. International drivers licences are also accepted. Motor fuel: 'premium' 95 octane, about US$1.80/US gallon; 'corriente' 84 octane, US$1.25/US gallon. Diesel US$1.20. Carry driving documents with you at all times.

Spare parts are plentiful for Renault, Mazda and Chevrolet cars, which are assembled in Colombia. VW is also well represented.

The machine What kind of motoring you do will depend on what kind of car you set out with. While a normal car will reach most places of interest, high ground clearance is useful for badly surfaced or unsurfaced roads and for fording rivers. Four-wheel drive vehicles are recommended for greater flexibility in mountain and jungle territory, although you may not get far in Amazonas, where roads are frequently impassable. Wherever you travel you should expect from time to time to find roads that are badly maintained, damaged or closed during the wet season, and delays because of floods, landslides and huge potholes. There is also the possibility of hold-ups from major roadworks. Do not plan your schedules too tightly.

Preparation Preparing your own car for the journey is largely a matter of common sense: obviously any part that is not in first class condition should be replaced. It's well worth installing extra heavy-duty shock-absorbers (such as Spax or Koni) before starting out, because a long trip on rough roads in a heavily laden car will give heavy wear. Fit tubes on 'tubeless' tyres, since air plugs for tubeless tyres are hard to find, and if you bend the rim on a pothole, the tyre will not hold air.

Take spare tubes, and an extra spare tyre. Also take spare plugs, fan-belts, radiator hoses and headlamp bulbs; even though local equivalents can easily be found in cities, it is wise to take spares for those occasions late at night or in remote areas when you might need them. You can also change the fanbelt after a stretch of long, hot driving to prevent wear (eg after 15,000 km/10,000 miles). If your vehicle has more than one fanbelt, always replace them all at the same time (make sure you have the necessary tools if doing it yourself).

Find out about your car's electrics and filters and what spares may be required. Similarly, know how to handle problems arising from dirty fuel. It is wise to carry a spade, jump leads, tow rope and an air pump. Fit tow hooks to both sides of the vehicle frame. A 12 volt neon light for camping and repairs will be invaluable. Spare fuel containers should be steel and not plastic, and a siphon pipe is essential for those places where fuel is sold out of the drum. Take a 10 litre water container for self and vehicle. Note that in some areas gas stations are few and far between. Fill up when you see one: the next one may be out of fuel.

Security Spare no ingenuity in making your car secure. Your model should be the Brink's armoured van: anything less secure can be broken into by the determined and skilled thief. Use heavy chain and padlocks to chain doors shut, fit security catches on windows, remove interior window winders (so that a hand reaching in from a forced vent cannot open the window). All these will help, but none is foolproof. Anything on the outside – wing mirrors, spot lamps, motifs etc – is likely to be stolen too. So are wheels if not secured by locking nuts.

Try never to leave the car unattended except in a locked garage or guarded parking space. Remove all belongings and leave the empty glove compartment open when the car is unattended. Also lock the clutch or accelerator to the steering wheel with a heavy, obvious chain or lock. Adult minders or street children will generally protect your car fiercely in exchange for a tip. Be sure to note down key numbers and carry spares of the most important ones (but don't keep all spares inside the vehicle).

Documents
See page 23, for required documents

Be very careful to keep all the papers you are given when you enter, to produce when you leave. Bringing a car in by sea or air is much more complicated and expensive: generally you will have to hire an agent to clear it through customs, expensive and slow.

Insurance for the vehicle against accident, damage or theft is best arranged in the country of origin, but it is getting increasingly difficult to find agencies who offer this service. In Latin American countries it is very expensive to insure against accident and theft, especially as you should take into account the value of the car increased by duties calculated in real (ie non devaluing) terms. If the car is stolen or written off you will be required to pay very high import duty on its value. Get the legally required minimum cover for third party insurance, not expensive, as soon as you can, because if you should be involved in an accident and are uninsured, your car could be confiscated. If anyone is hurt, do not pick them up (you may become liable). Seek assistance from the nearest police station or hospital if you are able to do so.

Car hire The main international car rental companies are represented at principal airports but may be closed Saturday afternoons and Sundays. There are also local firms in most of the departmental cities. In addition to passport and driver's licence, a credit card may be asked for as additional proof of identity (Visa, Mastercard, American Express), and to secure a returnable deposit to cover any liability not covered by the insurance. Check the insurance carefully; it may not cover you beyond a certain figure, nor 'natural' damage such as flooding. Ask if extra cover is available. A charge may be put through on your card after the hire charge passes a certain figure; enquire when you take the vehicle. You should be given a diagram showing any scratches and other damage on the car before you hired it.

Car hire, though relatively expensive especially if you are going to the remoter areas and need four-wheel drive or specialist vehicles, is convenient for touring, and the better hotels all have safe parking.

Taxi Whenever possible, take a taxi with a meter, and ensure that it is switched on. Some cities do not have metered taxis, in which case bargain and fix a price. All taxis are obliged to display the normal legal tariffs including any higher rates that may be

Essentials

charged in the evenings, on Sundays and fiestas. Try not to take a taxi which is old; look for 'Servicio Público' on the side. There is a small surcharge for Radio Taxis, but they normally offer reliable service. The dispatcher will give you the cab's number which should be noted in case of irregularities. You should always take a radio taxi at night in the main cities. If the taxi 'breaks down', take your luggage out if you are asked to push, or let the driver push; it may be a trick to separate you from your luggage - but you will probably not be in an official taxi if this happens.

Motorcycling

Before taking a motorbike to South America, we strongly advise that you consult the technical details including the type of machine, the general state of the roads, altitude, quality of fuel available etc with competent specialists in your home country.

People are generally very amicable to motorcyclists and you can make many friends by returning friendship to those who show an interest in you.

The machine   It should be off road capable, eg the BMW R80/100/GS for its rugged and simple design and reliable shaft drive, but a Kawasaki KLR 650s, Honda Transalp, XR600, or XR250, or the ubiquitous Yamaha XT600 Tenere would also be suitable. A road bike can go most places an off-road bike can go at the cost of greater effort.

Preparations   Many roads are rough. Fit heavy duty front fork springs and the best quality rebuildable shock absorber you can afford (Ohlins, White Power). Fit lockable luggage such as Krausers (reinforce luggage frames) or make some detachable aluminium panniers. Fit a tank bag and tank panniers for better weight distribution. A large capacity fuel tank (Acerbis), +300 mile/480 km range is essential if going off the beaten track. A washable air filter is a good idea (K&N), also fuel filters and fueltap rubber seals. A good set of trails-type tyres, as well as a high mudguard, are useful. Get to know the bike before you go, ask the dealers in your country what goes wrong with it and arrange a link whereby you can get parts flown out to you. If using a fully enclosed chaincase on a chain driven bike, an automatic chain oiler, to stop it getting it, is a good idea. The Scott-Oiler (106 Clober Road, Milngavie, Glasgow G62 7SS, Scotland) has been recommended. Fill it with Sae 90 oil. A hefty bash plate/sump guard is invaluable.

Spares   Reduce service intervals by half if driving in severe conditions. A spare rear tyre is useful but you can buy modern tyres in most capital cities. Take oil filters, fork and shock seals, tubes, a good manual, spare cables (taped into position), a plug cap and spare plug lead. A spare electronic ignition is a good idea, try and buy a second-hand one and make arrangements to have parts sent out to you. A first-class tool kit is a must and if riding a bike with a chain then a spare set of sprockets and an 'o' ring chain should be carried. Spare brake and clutch levers should also be taken as these break easily in a fall. Parts are few and far between, but mechanics are skilled at making do and can usually repair things.

Take a puncture repair kit and tyre levers. Find out about any weak spots on the bike and improve them. Get the book for international dealer coverage from your manufacturer, but don't rely on it. They frequently have few or no parts for modern, large machinery.

Clothes &   A tough waterproof jacket, comfortable strong boots, gloves and a helmet with which
equipment   you can use glass goggles (Halycon) which will not scratch and wear out like a plastic visor. The best quality tent and camping gear that you can afford and a petrol stove which runs on bike fuel is helpful.

This is not a problem in most parts of the country. Try not to leave a fully laden bike on its own. An Abus D or chain will keep the bike secure. A cheap alarm gives you peace of mind if you leave the bike outside a hotel at night. Most hotels will allow you to bring the bike inside. Look for hotels that have a courtyard or more secure parking and never leave luggage on the bike overnight or whilst unattended. **Security**

Passport, International Driving Licence, bike registration document are necessary. Temporary import papers are given on entry, to be surrendered on leaving the country. **Documents**

You must drain the fuel, oil and battery acid, or remove the battery, but it is easier to disconnect and seal the overflow tube. Tape cardboard over fragile bits and insist on loading the bike yourself. **Shipping**

Bringing a bike in by land from Venezuela or Ecuador only takes a few minutes. For bringing a bike by sea or air from North America or Panama, see under Shipping a vehicle in the Darién section. Parking at night can be a problem, but some hotels listed have patios or their own lock up garages nearby. Otherwise use *parqueadores* (see Motoring above). Local insurance costs around US$30 for a bike over 200 cc. You may find that wearing helmets is inadvisable in trouble spots. Check also for special rules for motorcyclists in Colombia. In early 2000, for instance, all motorcyclists in Bogotá were required to wear a high visibility vest with the number plate of the vehicle clearly shown on it.

Spare parts, tyres, etc readily available in Colombia for Yamaha and Honda (although supplies are less good for models over 500 cc), so Colombia is a suitable country for rebuilding a bike on a long trip. Medellín is the best place for spare parts. Other recommended places:

Bogotá BMW, Triumph spares sold by Germán Villegas Arango, Calle 1 B, No 11A-43, T2894399. Pereira *Racing Lines Ltda*, Avenida 30 de Agosto, No 40-51, T3361970. Two other motorbike shops nearby. Cali *Motoservicio Asturias*, Cra 5, No 24-35, T8893616. *Marcus Germayer*, Avenida 7 AN, No 56-196, T/F6643958. English and German spoken.

Cycling

Cycling is popular in Colombia; there are many bicycles about at weekends including racing and mountain-bikes, so much so that special arrangements are made for them eg: *ciclovía* in Bogotá on Sundays. Although distances are great and the Andes formidable barriers to east-west travel, cyclists are well received by local people. It is often possible to find routes which keep you off the lethal main roads. Cyclists have many advantages over travellers using other forms of transport, since they can travel at their own pace, explore more remote regions and often meet people who are not normally in contact with tourists. For longer trips, contact local cycling groups and you may be able to join them for journeys.

Unless you are planning a journey almost exclusively on paved roads – when a high quality touring bike such as a Dawes Super Galaxy would probably suffice – a mountain bike is strongly recommended. The good quality ones (and the cast iron rule is never to skimp on quality) are incredibly tough and rugged, with low gear ratios for difficult terrain, wide tyres with plenty of tread for good road-holding, cantilever brakes, and a low centre of gravity for improved stability. Although touring bikes – and to a lesser extent mountain bikes – and spares are available in the larger cities, remember that most locally manufactured goods are shoddy and rarely last. Buy everything you possibly can before you leave home. **Choosing a bicycle**

A small but comprehensive tool kit (to include chain rivet and crank removers, a spoke key and possibly a block remover), a spare tyre and inner tubes, a puncture repair kit **Bicycle equipment**

Essentials

Essentials

with plenty of extra patches and glue, a set of brake blocks, brake and gear cables and all types of nuts and bolts, at least 12 spokes (best taped to the chain stay), a light oil for the chain (eg Finish-Line Teflon Dry-Lube), tube of waterproof grease, a pump secured by a pump lock, a Blackburn parking block (a most invaluable accessory, cheap and virtually weightless), a cyclometer, a loud bell, and a secure lock and chain. *Richard's Bicycle Book* makes useful reading for even the most mechanically minded.

Luggage and equipment Strong and waterproof front and back panniers are a must. When packed these are likely to be heavy and should be carried on the strongest racks available. Poor quality racks have ruined many a journey for they take incredible strain on unpaved roads. A top bag cum rucksack (eg Carradice) makes a good addition for use on and off the bike. A Cannondale front bag is good for maps, camera, compass etc. (Other recommended panniers are Ortlieb – front and back – which is waterpoof and almost 'sandproof', Mac-Pac, Madden and Karimoor.) 'Gaffa' tape is excellent for protecting vulnerable parts of panniers and for carrying out all manner of repairs.

All equipment and clothes should be packed in plastic bags to give extra protection against dust and rain. (Also protect all documents etc, carried close to the body, from sweat.) Always take the minimum clothing. It's better to buy extra items *en route* when you find you need them. Naturally the choice will depend on the terrain you are planning to cover, and whether rain is to be expected.

Useful tips Wind, not hills, is the enemy of the cyclist. Try to make the best use of the times of day when there is little; mornings tend to be best but there is no steadfast rule. Take care to avoid dehydration, by drinking regularly. In hot, dry areas with limited supplies of water, be sure to carry an ample supply. For food, carry the staples (sugar, salt, dried milk, tea, coffee, porridge oats, raisins, dried soups etc) and supplement these with whatever local foods can be found in the markets. Give your bicycle a thorough daily check for loose nuts or bolts or bearings. See that all parts run smoothly. A good chain should last 3,200 km or more but be sure to keep it as clean as possible – an old toothbrush is good for this – and to oil it lightly from time to time. Remember that thieves are attracted to towns and cities, so when sight-seeing, try to leave your bicycle with someone such as a café owner or a priest. Country people tend to be more honest and are usually friendly and very inquisitive. However, don't take unnecessary risks; always see that your bicycle is secure (most hotels will allow bikes to be kept in rooms). In more remote regions dogs can be vicious; carry a stick or some small stones to frighten them off. Traffic on main roads can be a nightmare; it is usually far more rewarding to keep to the smaller roads or to paths if they exist. Most cyclists agree that the main danger comes from other traffic. A rearview mirror has been frequently recommended to forewarn you of vehicles which are too close behind. You also need to watch out for oncoming, overtaking vehicles, unstable loads on trucks, protruding loads etc. Make yourself conspicuous by wearing bright clothing and a helmet. Most towns have a bicycle shop of some description, but it is best to do your own repairs and adjustments whenever possible. In an emergency it is amazing how one can improvise with wire, string, dental floss, nuts and bolts, odd pieces of tin or electrical 'Gaffa' tape!

The Expedition Advisory Centre, administered by the Royal Geographical Society, 1, Kensington Gore, London, SW7 2AR, has published a useful monograph entitled *Bicycle Expeditions*, by Paul Vickers. Published in March 1990, it is available direct from the Centre, price £6.50 (postage extra if outside the UK). (In the UK there is also the Cyclist's Touring Club, CTC, Cotterell House, 69 Meadrow, Godalming, Surrey, GU7 3HS, T01483-417217, cycling@ctc.org.uk, for touring and technical information.)

There are good shops for spares in all big cities, though the standard 622/700 size touring wheel size is not very common.

Recommended for spares and service are: Bogotá *Almacen Mountain Bike Shop*, Calle 96, No 10-65, T2560915, F6361665, Enrique Arango or Jerónimo Echeverrí; *Bike*

House, Calle 93B, No 15-34, Of 208, T2573107/2364691, open Mon-Sat 1000-1300, 1400-1900. Other bicycle shops around Calle 13/Cra 15. Medellín *Bicicletas de Montaña*, Calle 23, No 43A-104, T2627249. Manizales *Todo Terreno Bike Shop*, Cra 23, No 55-37, T8856845, F 8848861. Pereira *Almacen Kamikase*, Avenida Circunvalar No 9-29, T3330971, Santiago Robledo. Cali *Almacen BTT*, Avenida 8N, No 16N-51, T6615831, Jorge Bueno or Maritza. Tuluá *Ciclo Raleigh*, T 240468/244654, Luis Alberto Tejada. Popayán *Ciclovia Popayán*, Cra 11, No 6-40, T8210070, Otto Arras. Pasto *Almacen Bicos*, Cra 23, No 17-31, T235029, Eduardo Valencia.

Hitchhiking

Hitchhiking (*autostop*) has become more difficult in 2000 as road communications have been under threat. However, it is not impossible but you must make very careful enquiries before attempting longer journeys. Try to enlist the co-operation of the highway police checkpoints outside each town and toll booths. Truck-drivers are often very friendly, but be careful of private cars with more than one person inside, especially if you are travelling on your own (but lone females should not try to hitchhike in Colombia). The best number is probably two, any more in the party together may have to wait a long time for a lift. If there is no mention of payment before the end of your ride, ask 'Le debo algo?' (Do I owe you anything?). You may not have to pay, but it leaves a favourable impression.

Rail

The only passenger train services currently operating are weekend tourist trains from Bogotá and Medellín, and a daily service from Medellín to Barrancabermeja. See under those cities for details.

There has been much talk about reviving sections of the national rail system, but apart from isolated freight lines in various parts of the country, little has been achieved.

River

The days of paddle-steamer journeys have long since gone but river transport is still surprisingly important in some parts of Colombia. It is possible to travel in *lanchas* up long stretches of the Río Magdalena and sections of the western rivers Atrato, San Juan and Cauca. In the Orinoco and Amazon regions, fast boats (*voladores*) are the only normal way for visitors to get around. They are efficient, and seasoned travellers say are better timekeepers than buses or planes elsewhere. They can, however, be expensive, partly because fuel costs are high in the remoter regions. Remember to take water with you, sun protection and an inflatable cushion to make a long journey more comfortable. The better boats will have life-jackets, and if any sea transport is involved, they are indispensible.

Keeping in touch

Details of organizations which can help sort out problems or give advice can be found in the travelling text under Embassies & consulates and Cultural centres

Points of contact

The internet is expanding rapidly in Colombia and has replaced postal and telephone services for the vast majority of travellers. Cyber cafés are found in all cities and many towns, and many hotels also offer email facilities. If you are looking for the most economical price, you will have to shop around. Look for information under the relevant Directory or Sleeping sections of the various towns and cities.

Internet

Post There are two parallel postal systems; Avianca operated by the national airline, and Correos de Colombia, the post office proper. Both have offices in all major cities, but only Correos can be found in small towns and rural areas. Both will accept mail for all destinations. Adpostal, part of Correos, will take parcels for overseas: correspondents report 10 day delivery to the UK. Prices are usually but not always identical for overseas airmail (which is carried by Avianca in any event), but Correos/Adpostal is much more economical, and can be more efficient, for internal services. Anything of importance should be registered. Avianca controls all airmail services and has offices in provincial cities. It costs from US$0.65 to $0.80 to send a letter or postcard to the US, US$0.90 to $1.60 to Europe or elsewhere; a 1 kg package to the US costs US$16, to Europe, US$18 by air.

Many international courier services operate in Colombia. One recommended is DHL, for which *Aviatur* act as agents. See under Tour companies and travel agents for their local addresses.

Telephone Local calls from public telephones cost a minimum of US$0.05. Inter-city and international calls are best made from Telecom offices unless you have access to a private phone. Long-distance pay phones are located outside most Telecom offices, also at bus stations and airports. They take 100 peso and larger coins, or you can obtain operator assisted calls at the counter. A deposit may be required before the call is made; for person-to-person and reverse-charges calls, enquire of the operator. The best value is to purchase a phone card, valid for local and international calls, and dial direct yourself.

Three separate telephone services are at present available though there is only Telecom's equipment and lines. For local calls, dial the number given. However, for inter-city calls, you have the choice of ORBITEL (code 05), ETB (07) or TELECOM (09), followed in each case by the area code (*indicativo*) and the local number. For international calls, the codes are ORBITEL (005), ETB (007) and TELECOM (009), followed by country code and the number you are calling. International phone charges are high: around US$7 for three minutes to USA, US$8 to Europe, US$12 to Australia but these can be substantially reduced at off peak times, weekends and holidays. At these times, the three systems compete for your business. Watch the press for special offers or ring the information services (ORBITEL 150 or 158, ETB 170 or 177 and TELECOM 190 or 198) to see what prices are available. Mobiles (*celulares* or '*cel*') begin with 033 from normal phones - omit the 033 if calling from another mobile.

Fax to the US costs about US$2.20/page and to Europe US$4/page, but it can be almost double this from hotels.

Media

Newspapers **Bogotá:** *El Tiempo,* www.eltiempo.com.co, *El Espectador,* www.elespectador.com.co, *La República.* **Medellín:** *El Mundo, El Colombiano.* **Cali:** *El País, Occidente, El Pueblo.* **Cartagena**: *El Heraldo.* All major cities have daily papers. *Latin American Post*, owned by Miami Herald, is available weekly in English in Bogotá and major cities.

Magazines Magazines are partisan, best are probably *Semana,* www.semana.com and *Cambio,* www.cambio.com.co, which is owned by a group of journalists and Gabriel García Márquez. US and European papers can be bought at *Librería Oma*, Carrera 15, No 82-58, or at Mario's stand outside *Tacos de la 19* near the corner of Carrera 7/Calle 19 in the centre of Bogotá, average price, US$2.50. Worth bargaining for a better price. Good selection also at *Papeles de la Candelaria*, Calle 11, No 3-89, Bogotá.

On Thursdays, *El Tiempo* publishes a good weekly guide to Bogotá called ESKAPE which lists many local and national events including hikes and day trips, inside and outside the capital. Also on Thursdays they produce a special travel supplement

(VIAJAR) useful for short trips to San Andrés etc. *El Espectador* has similar Thursday supplements called *Buen Viaje*. Elsewhere in the country there are similar arrangements.

South America has more local and community radio stations than practically anywhere else in the world; a shortwave (world band) radio offers a practical means to brush up on the language, sample popular culture and absorb some of the richly varied regional music. International broadcasters such as the BBC World Service, the Voice of America, Boston (Mass)-based Monitor Radio International (operated by Christian Science Monitor) and the Quito-based Evangelical station, HCJB, keep the traveller abreast of news and events, in both English and Spanish.

World band radio

Compact or miniature portables are recommended, with digital tuning and a full range of shortwave bands, as well as FM, long and medium wave. Detailed advice on radio models ($150 for a decent one) and wavelengths can be found in the annual publication, *Passport to World Band Radio* (Box 300, Penn's Park, PA 18943, USA). Details of local stations is listed in *World TV and Radio Handbook* (WTRH), PO Box 9027, 1006 AA Amsterdam, The Netherlands, US$19.95. Both of these, free wavelength guides and selected radio sets are available from the BBC World Service Bookshop, Bush House Arcade, Bush House, Strand, London WC2B 4PH, UK, T0171 257 2576.

In some areas of Colombia, including Bogotá, there is often poor reception for BBC World Service and some of the other international stations. News is retransmitted by Radio Universidad Nacional on 98.5 FM: Voice of America 0430-0500 followed by news in english from Radio Netherlands, 0500-0600 daily. On the same wavelength, news in French is relayed from RFI at 2030-2130.

The two principal television channels are RCN (state owned) and Caracol (private). Main daily news on both services is at 2130. Caracol is good for sport, especially football. Colombian TV is well known for its 'soaps' *(telenovelas)* which are exported to Spanish speaking countries. Regional TV stations are in the main towns all over Colombia. City TV was launched by *El Tiempo* newspaper in 1999 in Bogotá, good for city news.

Television

Food and drink

In the main cities (Bogotá, Cartagena, Medellín and Cali) you will find a limitless choice of menu and price. The other departmental capitals have a good range of specialist restaurants and all the usual fast food outlets. Only in the smaller towns and villages, not catering for tourists, will you find a modest selection of places to eat. Watch out for times of opening in the evenings, some city areas may tend to close around 1800 (eg La Candelaria in Bogotá), and times may be different at weekends. On Sundays it can be particluarly difficult to eat in a restaurant and even hotel restaurants may be closed. On the other hand, some national chains eg *Punto Rojo,* have a 24-hour service. These cafeterias are useful if you are confused about the local dishes – you can see what you are ordering and the price you will pay. If stuck, you will probably find something to eat near the bus station.

Eating out

The basic Colombian meal of the day is at lunchtime, the *almuerzo* or *comida corriente*, with soup, main course and drink of fruit juice, or soft drink *(gaseosa)*. If you are economising, ask for the *plato del dia, bandeja* or *plato corriente* (just the main dish). This can be found everywhere, many restaurants will display the menu and cost in the window.

The cheapest food available is in markets (when they are functioning) and from street stalls in most downtown areas and transport terminals. The problem is whether it is safe and also if it will agree with you. The general rules apply – keep away from uncooked food and salads, and eat fruit you have peeled yourself. Watch what the locals are eating

Markets

as a guide to the best choice. Wash it down with something out of a sealed bottle. Having said that, take it easy with dishes that are unfamiliar especially if you have arrived from a different climate or altitude. On the other hand, you will find that fresh fruit drinks, wherever prepared, are irresistable and you will have to take your chance!

Restaurants Restaurants are more difficult to evaluate than hotels because, as everywhere, they come, change and go. We try to give you a tested choice at all available price levels. Food is generally good, occasionally very good. Note that more expensive restaurants may add 15% IVA tax to the bill.

Vegetarians Most of the bigger cities have specific vegetarian restaurants and you will find them listed in the text. The *Govinda* chain is widely represented. Be warned that they are normally open only for lunch. In towns and villages you will have to ask for special food to be prepared.

Cuisine However, you will surely wish to try some of the local specialities, which may depend on where you are. Colombia's food used to be very regional. Now, however you will find regional restaurants in all the major cities, though local variations creep in.

Some of the standard items on the menu are: *Sancocho,* a meat stock (may be fish on the coast) with potato, corn (on the cob), yucca, sweet potato and plantain. You can have *sancocho* for breakfast in some places. *Arroz con pollo* (chicken and rice) the standard Latin American dish, is excellent in Colombia. *Carne asada* (grilled beefsteak), usually an inexpensive cut, is served with *papas fritas* (chips) or rice and you can ask for a vegetable of the day. *Sobrebarriga* (belly of beef) is served with varieties of potato in a tomato and onion sauce. *Huevos pericos,* eggs scrambled with onions and tomatoes, are a popular, cheap and nourishing snack available almost anywhere, especially favoured for breakfast. *Tamales* are meat pies made by folding a maize dough round chopped pork mixed with potato, rice, peas, onions and eggs wrapped in banana leaves (which you don't eat) and steamed. Other ingredients may be added such as olives garlic, cloves and paprika. Colombians eat *tamales* for breakfast with hot chocolate. *Empanadas* are another popular snack; these are made with chicken or various other meats, or vegetarian filling etc inside a maize dough and cooked in a light oil. *Patacones* are cakes of mashed and baked *platano* (large green banana). *Arepas* are standard throughout Colombia – these are flat maize griddle cakes often served instead of bread or as an alternative. *Pandebonos* is cheese flavoured bread. *Almojábanas,* a kind of sour milk/cheese bread roll, great for breakfast when freshly made. *Buñuelos* are 4-6 cm balls of wheat flour and eggs mixed and deep-fried, also best when still warm. *Arequipe* is a sugar based brown syrup used with desserts and in confectionary, universally savoured by Colombians. *Brevas* (figs) with *arequipe* are one of the most popular items to take home with you.

Some regional specialities that may be found elsewhere but are best tried in the original region: **In Bogotá and Cundinamarca** *Ajiaco de pollo (ajiaco santafereño)* is a delicious chicken stew with maize, manioc (*yuca*), three types of potato, herbs (including *guascas*) and sometimes other vegetables, served with cream and capers, and pieces of avocado. It is a Bogotá speciality. *Chunchullo* (tripe), *longanisa* (long pork sausage) and *morcilla* (blood sausage) are popular dishes. *Cuajada con melado* is a dessert of fresh cheese served with cane syrup, or *natas* (based on the skin of boiled milk.

In Boyacá *Mazamorra* is a meat and vegetable soup with broad and black beans, peas, varieties of potato and corn flour. *Care* – or *mazamorro* in Antioquia and elsewhere – is a milk and maize drink, which, to confuse matters further is known as *peto* in Cundinamarca. *Puchero* is a stew based on chicken with potatoes, *yuca*, cabbage, turnips, corn (on the cob) and herbs. *Cuchuco,* another soup with pork and sweet potato. *Masato* is a slightly fermented rice beverage.

In Santander and Santander del Norte *Mute* is a traditional soup of various cereals including corn. Goat and pidgeon appear in several local dishes. *Hormigas culonas* is the most famous culinary delight of this area is (large bottomed black ants) served toasted, and particularly popular in Bucamaranga at Easter time. Locals claim they have aphrodisiacal powers. *Bocadillo veleño* is similar to quince jelly but made from *guava*. It takes its name from Veléz, but can be found elsewhere in Colombia. *Rampuchada* is a North Santander stew based of the fish of the Zulia river which flows into Venezuela. *Hallacas* are cornmeal turnovers with different meats and whatever else is to hand inside typical of neighbouring Venezuela, like an oversized *tamal*. Dishes featuring chick-peas and goats milk are popular in this part of Colombia.

On the Caribbean coast, fish is naturally a speciality. *Arroz con coco,* rice here is often prepared with coconut. *Cazuela de mariscos* is a soup/stew of shellfish and white fish, maybe including octopus and squid, is especially good. *Sancocho de pescado* is a fish stew with vegetables, usually simpler and cheaper the *cazuela. Chipichipi,* a small clam found along the coast in Barranquilla and Santa Marta, is a standard local dish served with rice. *Empanada* (or *arepa) de huevo,* which is deep fried with eggs in the middle and is a good light meal. *Canastas de coco* is a good local sweet: pastry containing coconut custard flavoured with wine and surmounted by meringue.

In Tolima *Lechona* suckling pig with herbs is a speciality of Ibagué. *Viudo de pescado* is a dish based on small shellfish from the Opía (a local)river. *Achiras* a kind of hot biscuit.

In Antioquia *Bandeja antioqueña* or *paisa* consists of various types of grilled meat, *chorizo* (sausage) pork crackling, sometimes an egg, served with rice, beans, potato, manioc and a green salad; this has now been adopted in other parts of the country. *Natilla,* a sponge cake made from cornflour and *salpicón,* a tropical fruit salad.

In Cali and South Colombia, in contrast to most of Colombia, menus tend not to include potato (in its many forms). Instead, emphasis is on corn, plantain, rice and avocado with the usual pork and chicken dishes. *Manjar blanco,* made from milk and sugar or molasses, served with biscuit is a favorite dessert. *Cuy, curí* or *conejillo de Indias,* guinea pig, is typical of the southern Department of Nariño. *Mazorcas,* baked corn-on-the-cob, typical of road side stalls in southern Colombia.

Fruits are exceptional in Colombia – another aspect of the wide range of altitude and climate. Fruits familiar in northern and mediterranean climates are here, though with some differences:

Fruit & juices

Apples – *manzanas;* bananas *bananos;* grapes – *uvas;* limes – *limones* (lemons, the larger yellow variety are rarely seen); mangoes – *mangos;* melons – *melones;* oranges – *naranjas* (usually green or yellow in Colombia); peaches – *duraznos;* pears – *peras.* Then there are the local fruits: *chirimoyas* (a green fruit, white inside with pips), *curuba* (banana passion fruit) *feijoa,* a green fruit with white flesh, high in vitamin C, *guayaba* (guava), *guanábana* (soursop), *lulo* (a small orange fruit), *maracuyá* (passion fruit), *mora* (literally blackberry but dark red more like a loganberry) and *papayas,* and the delicious *pitahaya,* taken either as an appetizer or dessert, *sandía* (watermelon), *tomate de arbol* (tree tomato, several varieties normally used as a fruit) and many more.

All of these fruits are served as juices (either with milk, hopefully fresh or water, hopefully bottled or sterilised). Most hotels and restaurants are careful about this and you can watch the drinks being prepared on street stalls). You will be surprised how delicious these drinks are and the adventurous will experiment to find their favourite. Fruit yoghurts are nourishing and cheap – *Alpina* brand is good; *crema* style is best. Also, *Kumis* is a type of liquid yoghurt. Another drink you must try is *champús,* a corn base, with fruit and lemon.

Hot drinks
Colombian coffee is always mild. *Tinto*, the national small cup of black coffee, is taken at all hours. If you want it strong, ask for *café cargado;* a *tinto doble* is a large cup of black coffee. Coffee with milk is called *café perico; café con leche* is a mug of milk with coffee added. If you want a coffee with a little milk, order a *tinto y leche aparte* and they will bring the milk separately.

Tea is popular but herbal rather than Indian or Chinese: ask for *(bebida) aromática*, flavours include *limonaria, orquídea* and *manzanilla*. If you want Indian tea, *té Lipton en agua* should do the trick. Mint tea (*té de menta*) is another of many varieties available but you may have to go to an upmarket café or *casa de té* which can be found in all of the bigger cities. Chocolate is also drunk, *chocolate Santafereño* often taken during the afternoon in Bogotá with snacks and cheese. *Agua de panela* is a common beverage (hot water with unrefined sugar), also made with limes, milk, or cheese.

Cold drinks
Soft bottled drinks are universal and standard, commonly called *gaseosas*. If you want non-carbonated, ask for *sin gas*. Again you will find that many of the special fruits are used for bottled drinks. Water comes in bottles, cartons and small plastic packets: all safer than out of the tap.

Beer & spirits
Many acceptable brands of beer are produced, until recently almost all produced by the Bavaria group. However, in January 1995, a new brand, Leona, appeared, brewed by a rival drinks group, appropriately accompanied on the same day by an earthquake that shook Bogotá. It has quickly become popular. There are also many imported beers, which are more expensive, and Mexican beers are popular.

A traditional drink in Colombia is *chicha*. It is corn (maize) based but sugar and/or *panela* are added and it is boiled. It is served as a non-alchoholic beverage, but if allowed to ferment over several days, and especially if kept in the refrigerator for a while, it becomes very potent.

The local rum is good and cheap; ask for *ron*, not *aguardiente*. One of the best rums is *Ron Viejo de Caldas*, another (dark) is *Ron Medellín*. Try *canelazo* cold or hot rum with water, sugar, lime and cinnamon. As common as rum is *aguardiente* – literally fire water – a white spirit distilled from sugar cane. There are two types, with *anis* (aniseed) or without. Local table wines include *Isabella;* none is very good. Wine is very expensive, as much as US$15 in restaurants for an acceptable bottle of Chilean or Argentine wine, more for European and other wines.

Warning Care should be exercised when buying imported spirits in some bars and small shops. It has been reported that bottles bearing well-known labels have been 'recycled' and contain a cheap and poor imitation of the original contents and can be dangerous. You are probably safe purchasing in supermarkets. Also note that ice may not be made from potable water.

Shopping

Bargaining
Bargaining is standard in markets, stallholders will expect it, so don't disappoint them. Watch others before wading in. A rule of thumb is to offer about half, or a bit less, of the asking price. The art, fascinating to watch, is to negotiate rather than haggle, arrive at a good price then ask for a better item (the one you really want) for a little more, the shrug of the shoulders, the walk away when you know you will be called back, and a host of other techniques. All done in the very best of humour, and for the right length of time. There may be others waiting to be served. Also, it does no harm to think of what the same item would cost in your home country. You cannot bargain everywhere, there are fixed prices in supermarkets, department stores etc, but if in doubt, it does no harm to try.

Colombian emeralds are world famous and can be bought cheaply in Bogotá, and even cheaper in Muzo, but if you want the best quality, buy from authorized dealers and ask for a certificate. Handworked silver and gold are generally excellent and Indian pottery and textiles are of fine quality. *Artesanías de Colombia* (see under Bogotá) have a comprehensive selection of craft work. In Antioquia buy the handbag/sachel *carriel antioqueño* traditionally made from otter skin, but nowadays from calf skin, attractive and practical. Clothing and shoes are cheap in Medellín. The Colombian *ruana* (poncho) is attractive and warm in any cool climate, and comes in a wide variety of colours. Leatherwork is generally good and not expensive especially in southern Colombia. See the Arts and Crafts section in the Background chapter for local specialities. Usually the best place to buy and the largest selection is where these articles are made..

What to buy
For information try: www.ecomerz.rds.org.co a combined site of handicraft cooperatives around the country

Essentials

Holidays and festivals

National public holidays are on the following days:

1 January: **Circumcision of our Lord**; 6 January: **Epiphany***; 19 March: **St Joseph***; Maundy Thursday; Good Friday; 1 May: **Labour Day**; Ascension Day*; Corpus Christi*; Sacred Heart*; 29 June: **SS Peter and Paul***; 20 July: **Independence Day**; 7 August: **Battle of Boyacá;** 15 August: **Assumption***; 12 October: **Columbus' arrival in America***; 1 November: **All Saints' day***; 11 November: **Independence of Cartagena***; 8 December: **Immaculate Conception**; 25 December: **Christmas Day**.

When those marked with an asterisk do not fall on a Monday, the public holiday will be on the following Monday.

Sport and special interest travel

Adventure tourism

Colombia has more to offer than most of its Latin American neighbours in terms of tropical oceans, snowy mountains, major rivers, remote, unspoilt countryside and wild dramatic places. Adventure tourism development is at an early stage but there are groups of adventure travel enthusiasts who are dedicated to exploring many of the exciting places that the country has to offer.

For those sports that will take you into the remoter parts of the country, it is important that you check on safety factors before going. Seek advice from adventure tour operators in the main cities, and the National Parks Authority referred to as **MA** (for *Medio Ambiente* ie Environment) in the text, as some of the parks have been used as hideouts by the guerrillas, and drug-traffickers *(narcotraficantes)*. If you understand Spanish it is a good idea to read the local press and ask local people.

There are no regulatory bodies at present to control or organise adventure tourism as in Chile or Ecuador. This introduction gives just a brief selection of what is on offer.

There are interesting caves to explore in several parts of the country. Near **San Gil**, caving *(espeleología)* centres on limestone near **Curití** and **Páramo**, enquire in San Gil. Near the Magdalena river are the caves of the **Río Claro** and the **Río Nus**. The **Cueva de Los Guácharos** is a National Park in the south of the country near Pitalito with many caves.

Caving

Colombia has nearly 3000 km of coastline on the Caribbean and Pacific with a near perfect year-round climate. As the infrastructure grows, it is becoming interesting as

Diving

Essentials

an international diving centre. Hiring equipment is easy at the main diving centres: **Cartagena,** the **Caribbean Islands, Santa Marta (Rodadero and Taganga)** on the Caribbean, and **Bahía Solano** on the Pacific.

The clear waters off the coast of Cartagena and the abundance of coral reefs off **San Andrés and Providencia** add to the pleasure of doing a course at these sites. The **Islas de San Bernardo** and **Isla Fuerte** off the coasts of Sucre and Córdoba respectively are two of the newer destinations. Trips can be organised from **Tolú**, and Cartagena, from Bogotá and Medellín or locally. **Capurganá**, near the border with Panama, is also becoming very popular as a diving destination with its secluded coves and warm waters. The cost of doing a PADI or NAUI certificate course averages US$140 for a five day course but you may be able to bargain in quiet periods. For information on the possibilities, contact Pedro Roa, T6138038, Bogotá, aquasub_dive@uole.com who can put you in touch with the *Asociación Colombiana de Instructores de Buceo (ACIB)* to which diving instructors belong.

The more adventurous may wish to dive at **Malpelo**, a rocky outcrop 300 km out in the Pacific, but getting there is a day's journey and expensive. Awaiting you, however, is cold water diving in a rich marine environment among Hammerhead and Whale sharks. One week trips to Malpelo can be arranged departing from Buenaventura, costing about US$800, food and board on the boat included. Contact Gonzalo Concha, an experienced diver, T3396858, (Cali) for further information. Pacific diving is also possible around **Gorgona**, enquire in Cali and Buenaventura. Currents in this part of the ocean can be very strong and dangerous which makes these dive sites for professionals only.

Maurice Thorin is another highly experienced diver, who can be contacted at mobile (*celular*) T033-7238807, colmoredive@hotmail.com or through *Bienvenidos Turismo Ltda*, Carrera 62, No 127-72, Bogotá, T/F2714517, T2531754, biencol@cable.net.co

Mountain Biking
There are many local cycling clubs and this is one of the sports in which Colombia excels. Mountain biking in difficult terrain is organised through clubs and bike shops, see in the text. It is not advisable to make independent plans without consulting on safety issues with local groups, hotels and specialised travel agents such as Eco-Guías in Bogotá (see address in text) for details. Elsewhere, ask in the main towns and cities for advice eg in Ibagué, Fernando and Janet Reyes, who run a tour agency in Ibagué, Carrera 11 No 1-21, T2639027, can arrange trips to Los Nevados National Park.

Mountaineering
The best possibilities in Colombia for climbers are in the National Parks of **Los Nevados, Huila** and **Sierra Nevada del Cocuy.** The scenery is breathtaking, particularly in Cocuy and it is easy to climb a number of peaks there in a 10 day to two week period. Colombia's mountains are easily accessible and technically not too difficult. In the northern part of Los Nevados Park, **Nevado del Ruiz** is a popular climb while **Nevado del Tolima** at the southern end presents more of a challenge, the last section is a very steep ice slope. There is good climbing also on **Nevado del Huila** volcano, Colombia's second highest mountain.

Some of the best climbing in Colombia is in the **Sierra Nevada de Santa Marta** but access to the mountains has been restricted in recent years. This is because the indigenous people who live in the Sierra, the Kogi and Arhuaco – two of the last remaining traditional high Andean civilisations – have become increasingly disturbed by groups of trekkers walking through their territory. Climbing and trekking in the Sierra was officially prohibited in 1996.

There has been renewed local interest in mountaineering with two recent Colombian expeditions to Cho Oyu in the Himalaya, the seventh highest of the world's peaks. Members of the team regularly guide groups in the Colombian Andes.

For up to date information on Santa Marta and the other mountain areas, contact the National Parks office (see under **Bogotá**). Guides are available for all areas. In some eg Los Nevados, there are official associations of guides, detailed in the text. If you have a guide or are invited on a mountain tour, make certain that all arrangements, costs/charges etc are clear before you start.

The best source of information on mountaineering generally is Mauricio Afanador who can be located at his restaurant Café y Crepes, Diagonal 108, No 9-11, T2145312 (see **Bogotá – Eating** listing) There are slide shows here from time to time. The Mountaineering Club at the *Universidad Nacional* meets on Thursday nights at 1800 and they welcome new members. Also the *Jorge Tadeo Lozano University*, Cra 4/Calle 22, T3341777, Ext 1263 has a *Club de Montañismo*, whichclimbs at weekends and in holidays. Good for information with website www.yavida.freeservers.com

Maps can be obtained from the IGAC, (see under **Bogotá - Maps**), but they are rather out of date.

Equipment is expensive in Colombia as it is nearly all imported. It is almost impossible to hire gear. There are a few shops that sell equipment and generally know the latest details about climbing in the different areas: *Almacén Aventura*, Carrera 13, No 67-26, Bogotá, T3133219, F2482639, (ask for Gonzalo Ospino), who are also at Avenida 7, No 116-28, T2132415; *Camping Vive*, Calle 57, No 9-29, local 301, Bogotá, T2118141/2357265; *Sierra Nevada*, Carrera 7, No 55-32, Bogotá, T2171512/2123411, open Monday-Saturday 1000-1900 and *Deportivos del Campo*, Calle 64, No 18-15, T5479405 also Bogotá. Light equipment, rucksacs etc of reasonable quality can be bought in markets.

Rock and Ice Climbing   A popular area for rock climbing, conveniently 50 km north of Bogotá, is at **Suesca** near Nemocón, which has some of the best rock climbing in the country. There is plenty of challenge for climbers of all grades. It is busy at weekends and holidays but also attended during the week. The *Gravedad Escuela de Montaña* is based in Suesca, ask for Fernando González-Rubio, Director, T8563290 (Bogotá) or cellular T033 3443729.

The eastern flank of the **Sierra Nevada del Cocuy** also has some spectacular rock climbs. All technical equipment should be brought from home though some items may be available in Suesca.

There is some technical ice climbing in **the Nevados, Cocuy** and on **Nevado de Huila**. The climbing clubs at the Jorge Tadeo Lozano University and at the National University, in Bogotá, are the best sources of information. For further details, see the travelling text.

Parapenting   This is available in various locations with contrasting conditions. In the warmer areas such as **Melgar** (near Bogotá), **Armenia** and the area around the **Mesón de los Santos** and the **Cañon de Chicamocha** south of Bucamaranga, are ideal locations and allow spectacular views of the countryside. There is parapenting also at **Embalse de Neusa**, near Zipaquirá at weekends. Some parapenting is now available in the high Cordillera, near **Bogotá** and in **Los Nevados.**

There are several local clubs, two in Bogotá – *Escuela de Parapente*, T2956988 and *Escuela Aerea Colombiana*, T6256432 – who can put you in touch with clubs elsewhere in Colombia including *Club Los Cóndores* T6604804, Cali; *Centro de Vuelo Libre*, T6610032, Cali; *Free Gliders* T4123886, Medellín. Also, contact Stefano Cagnucci, T6314501, Bucamaramga. All clubs are affiliated to the *Fédération Aéronautique International (FAI)*, France. Colombians participate in international parapenting events associated with the Paragliding World Cup. A qualifying course for FAI membership can be completed in Colombia, normally eight full-day classes, US$260. Tandem flights, approximately one hour, US$25.

It is not yet possible to buy equipment in Colombia, so you will have to bring your own.

Rafting   In a country with over a thousand rivers it is surprising that this is not yet a major adventure sport. At the moment, the best opportunities are in Santander on two rivers near San Gil: the **Río Fonce** and on the **Río Chicamocha.** The centre for this and other local adventure activities is beside the entrance to the Parque Gallineral in San Gil, T7240000/7247679. The trips do not include Grade V experiences, but many runs from beginners up to that level. Recently, a new area has opened up, about 100 km west of Bogotá on the **Río Negro**, centred on La Vega, Tobia and Villeta. For further information, call Kumandai, T2557518/2127478.

Trekking   Colombians enjoy trekking and it is popular with foreign travellers in many parts of the country. The best trodden path is the trek to the archaeological site of **Ciudad Perdida** in the Sierra Nevada de Santa Marta. This can be organised through any of the hotels in Santa Marta, see text for details. It is also possible to organise the trek through several tour operators around the country.

   Another major trekking adventure is the **Darién Gap** between Colombia and Panama. You will find full details in the text. Unfortunately, there have been serious security difficulties in the last few years in Panama and the Katíos National Park where the trail enters Colombia. Hopefully, this trek will become available again soon. There are many trails in other National Parks promoted for tourism, eg **Amacayacú, Los Nevados** and **Puracé**.

   The departments of Santander and Boyacá are becoming popular as weekend destinations and there are many old pathways, or *caminos reales*, dating from the Colonial times. The former tourist corporation, CNT, disbanded in 1997, published a series of guidebooks on trekking in these departments. They are out of print but look around for copies. The walks range from easy day excursions to 3-4 day strenuous treks.

There are many local walking groups, several are Bogotá based. Highly recommended is *Sal Si Puedes*, founded in 1988 with a big selection of walks graded for all levels of fitness, contact Carrera 7, No 17-01, office 640 and 641, T2833765. Details of this and other groups will be found under Bogotá and other cities that have organised walking and trekking associations (see under **Sports** sections).

   For specific area details, see under Sierra Nevada del Cocuy, Valledupar, Ibagué, Manizales and Pereira. For rock climbing, see Suesca. If you intend to climb, bring all your own equipment. It may be impossible to find easily in Colombia, eg compass. Some equipment available at *Almacén Aventura*, Carrera 13, No 67-26, Bogotá, T 248-1679, F 201-9543, rope, boots etc; *Deportivos del Campo*, Calle 64, No 18-15, Bogotá, T 248-1855, F 217-4756, tents, mattresses etc, mostly imported; *Sierra Nevada* shops: Carrera 24, No 72-75, T 225-0827, Bogotá; Avenida 37, No 41-53, T 648029, Ibagué; Carrera 39, No 8-03, T 268-4296, Medellín. Also at *Eco-Guias*, T 284-8991, Bogotá. Light equipment, rucksacks etc of reasonable quality, can be bought in markets.

Windsurfing   Many of the hotels in Bocagrande (Cartagena) can organise windsurfing and the hire of equipment. Prices are much in line with resort areas around the world.

   For windsurfing on local lakes, contact Erhard Martin, T/F 2493002/3480705 (Bogotá) or at **Embalse de Sisga** (Cundinamarca), T(91)8562174. He offers instruction and is very informative.

Archaeology

There are three major sites of interest to those looking for pre-conquest settlements, two in the south – **San Agustín** and **Tierradentro** – and **Ciudad Perdida** in the north. All over the highlands there are smaller sites which have been preserved, and plenty of places in the lowlands that have been explored and documented. The latter are less dramatic, however, since the higher temperatures and water damage have eroded away much of the past.

Earlier history can be explored near **Villa de Leiva** where several dinosaurs have been found, and further north near **Guane** (Santander), there are many fossils from the Cretaceous Era.

Birdwatching

The extravagantly wide range of bird life in Colombia, with over 1800 species of birds recorded, is of particular interest to birdwatchers. Many of the National Parks have interesting bird populations, with many unique endemic species and a comparatively low level of visitors to many of the remoter Parks has allowed them to thrive undisturbed.

Around Bogotá in the Eastern Cordillera Parks and north of the city in the marshland of **Humedal La Conejera,** there is good bird territory. In the Cordillera Central, particularly rich in upland birdlife are **Los Nevados, Ucumarí** and **Puracé** Parks. Near the Río Magdalena, there are parrots, woodpeckers and oilbirds to be seen in the **Río Claro** Reserve. The Cordillera Occidental near Cali has a fine collection of hummingbirds. The private reserve of **La Planada**, near Pasto in the south of the country is specially recommended: for details, see the travelling text. From the UK, birding trips to Colombia are run from time to time by *Birdquest*, Two Jays, Kemble End, Birdy Brow, Stonyhurst, Lancs, BB7 9QY, T01254-826317, F01254-82670, birders@birdquest,co,uk Locally in Bogotá, the tour operators *Eco-Guías* have very good information.

Ecotourism

The Colombians are well aware of the dangers to the environment of unrestricted development for tourism in sensitive areas of the country. The Ministry of the Environment (*Medio Ambiente*) has the responsibility for the extensive National Park system. One or two of the Parks, notably Tayrona on the north coast, have suffered and have been closed from time to time to assess what needs to be done. So far, however, the low level of contemporary visitor density has had little impact, and high entry fees together with limited numbers of visitors allowed at any one time, is helping to preserve this valuable national resource. Unhappily, this service is under-funded and there is a continual danger that local people are driven by economic necessity to move into 'protected' areas.

An interesting ecological lesson was learned when a major improvements to the Caribbean coast road from Barranquilla to Ciénaga were made resulting in the gradual destruction of over half the natural vegetation of the area, covering many hundreds of square kilometers. Between 1992 and 1999, much has been done to repair the damage, leading to the return of flora and wildlife (see under **Ciénaga de Santa Marta**).

If you are particularly interested in biodiversity and environmental issues, contact *Eco-Fondo*, T6913452/63/74. This is an umbrella group for all the Non-Governmental Organizations working in this field in Colombia.

Fishing

There are regular deep sea fishing competitions, especially on the Pacific coast, Bahía Tebada is particularly good. Fishing is particularly good at Girardot, Santa Marta, and off Barranquilla marlin is fished. There is good trout fishing, in season, in the lakes in the Bogotá area, and in Boyacá, particularly at Lago Tota, in the mountains.

Many of the upmarket travel agencies in Bogotá and Medellín can arrange trips. Fresh water fishing is common throughout the highland regions; ask at local travel agencies and hotels.

Sailing

Sailing is becoming more popular with Colombians, both offshore and on inland lakes. The Caribbean coast from Cartagena to the Guajira and beyond to Venezuela and the islands in the Caribbean are also frequented by European and North American sailors every year. Information is available at the *Club Nautico* (Yacht Club) in Cartagena. For the ocean hitch-hiker, it is possible to get a passage along the coast or further afield to Central America or the Caribbean, but be patient! The notice board at the club is a good place to look for a passage. The Yacht club has information on charters and sailing off the Caribbean coast.

For sailing on inland lakes, one of the biggest clubs is the *Club Nautico El Portillo* in Tominé, north of Bogotá. Courses can be arranged, a full 32-hour course taken over four weekends in J-12 class boats, US$150. Call Maritza or Roberto Vargas, T(91)8577218, www.elportillo.com.co, english and german spoken. The *Federación Colombiana de Vela*, Bogotá, T2459232/2877963 organises competitions at national and international levels in various classes. Locally, these are held on **Represa de Tominé** and other nearby lakes. There is also sailing at **Embalsa Calima** near Cali and on lakes near Medellín.

Spectator sports

Association football is the most popular game and is of high quality, especially in Cali and Medellín. American baseball is played at Cartagena and Barranquilla. There are bullrings at Bogotá, Cali, Manizales, Medellín, Sincelejo, Cerrito and a number of smaller places. Polo is played at Medellín and Bogotá. Most of the larger towns have stadia. Cockfights, cycling, boxing and basketball are also popular.

The game of *tejo* is played in Cundinamarca, Boyacá, Tolima, Valle, Caldas and elsewhere. A stone is thrown from a set distance at a mudbank in which an explosive device is embedded. Hopefully, the winner survives! Another similar game is played in Pasto and Popayán under the name of *sapo* (toad). This is the Spanish *juego de la rana*, in which a small quoit has to be thrown from an improbable distance into a metal frog's mouth.

Health

For anyone travelling overseas health is a key consideration. With the following advice and routine sensible precautions the visitor to Colombia should remain as healthy as at home. Most visitors return home having experienced no problems at all apart from some travellers' diarrhoea.

The health risks, especially in the lowland tropical areas, are different from those encountered in Europe or North America. It also depends on where and how you travel. There are clear differences in risks for the business traveller, who stays in international class hotels in large cities and the backpacker trekking in remote areas, and there is huge variation in climate, vegetation and wildlife. There are no hard and fast rules to follow; you will often have to make your own judgement on the healthiness or otherwise of your surroundings.

There are English (or other foreign language) speaking doctors in major cities who have particular experience in dealing with locally-occurring diseases, but don't expect facilities to international standards away from the major centres. Your Embassy representative will often be able to give you the name of local reputable doctors and most of the better hotels have a doctor on standby. If you do fall ill and cannot find a recommended doctor, try the Outpatient Department of a hospital – private hospitals or *clínicas* are usually less crowded and may offer a more acceptable standard of care to foreigners.

Before travelling

Take out medical insurance. Make sure it covers all eventualities, especially evacuation to your home country by a medically equipped plane if necessary. You should have a dental check up, obtain a spare glasses prescription, a spare oral contraceptive prescription (or enough pills to last) and, if you suffer from a chronic illness (such as diabetes, high blood pressure, ear or sinus troubles, cardio-pulmonary disease or nervous disorder), arrange for a check up with your doctor, who can at the same time provide you with a letter explaining the details of your disability in English and if possible Spanish. Check the current recommendations for malaria prophylaxis (prevention). If you are on regular medication, make sure you have enough to cover the period of your travel plus two weeks spare.

Children

More preparation is probably necessary for babies and children than for an adult and perhaps a little more care should be taken when travelling to remote areas where health services are primitive. This is because children can be become more rapidly ill than adults (on the other hand they often recover more quickly). Diarrhoea and vomiting are the most common problems, so take the usual precautions, but more intensively.

Breastfeeding is best and most convenient for babies, but powdered milk and formulas are widely available in Colombia and so are baby foods in the larger cities. Papaya, bananas and avocados are all nutritious and can be cleanly prepared. The treatment of diarrhoea is the same as for adults, except that it should start earlier and be continued with more persistence. Children get dehydrated very quickly in hot countries and can become drowsy and uncooperative unless cajoled to drink water or juice plus salts.

Upper respiratory infections, such as colds, catarrh and middle ear infections, are also common and if your child suffers from these normally take some antibiotics against the possibility. Outer ear infections after swimming are also common and antibiotic eardrops will help. Wet wipes are always useful and sometimes difficult to find in Colombia. Disposable nappies (diapers) on the other hand, can be found throughout the country, all too often improperly disposed of; please be conscientious in this regard..

Medicines

There is very little control on the sale of drugs and medicines in Colombia. You can buy anything except drugs of addiction without a prescription. Be wary of this because pharmacists can be poorly trained and might sell you drugs that are unsuitable, dangerous or old. Many drugs and medicines are manufactured under licence from American or European companies, so the trade names may be familiar to you. This means you do not have to carry a whole chest of medicines with you, but remember that the shelf life of some items, especially vaccines and antibiotics, is markedly reduced in hot conditions.

Buy your supplies at the better outlets where there are refrigerators, even though they are more expensive, and always carefully check the expiry date of all preparations you buy. Immigration officials occasionally confiscate scheduled drugs (Lomotil is an example) if they are not accompanied by a doctor's prescription.

What to take

Self-medication may be forced on you by circumstances so the following text contains the names of drugs and medicines which you may find useful in an emergency or in out-of-the-way places. You may like to take some of the following items with you from home:

Vaccination & immunization Smallpox vaccination is no longer required anywhere in the world. Neither is cholera vaccination recognized as necessary for international travel by the World Health Organization – it is not very effective either. Nevertheless, some immigration officials may rarely request proof of vaccination against cholera.

Vaccination against the following diseases are recommended:

Yellow Fever This is a live vaccination not to be given to children under nine months of age, pregnant women or persons allergic to eggs. Immunity lasts for 10 years, an International Certificate of Yellow Fever Vaccination will be given and should be kept because it is sometimes asked for. Yellow fever is not very common in Colombia, but the vaccination is practically without side effects and almost totally protective. Yellow fever is a fatal disease and you should not visit the jungle without being vaccinated.

Typhoid A disease spread by the insanitary preparation of food. A number of new vaccines against this condition are now available; the older TAB and monovalent typhoid vaccines are being phased out. The newer, eg Typhim Vi, causes less side effects, but are more expensive. For those who do not like injections, there are now oral vaccines.

Poliomyelitis Despite its decline in the world this remains a serious disease if caught and is easy to protect against. There are live oral vaccines and in some countries injected vaccines. Whichever one you choose it is a good idea to a have booster every three to five years if visiting developing countries regularly.

Tetanus One dose should be given with a booster at six weeks and another at six months, and 10 yearly boosters thereafter are recommended. Children should already be properly protected against diphtheria, poliomyelitis and pertussis (whooping cough), measles and HIB, all of which can be more serious infections in Colombia than at home. Measles, mumps and rubella vaccine is also given to children throughout the world, but those teenage girls who have not had rubella (german measles) should be tested and vaccinated. Hepatitis B vaccination for babies is now routine in some countries. Consult your doctor for advice on tuberculosis inoculation: the disease is still widespread in some parts.

Infectious Hepatitis is less of a problem for travellers than it used to be because of the development of two extremely effective vaccines against the A and B form of the disease. It remains common, however, in Colombia. A combined hepatitis A & B vaccine is now available – one jab covers both diseases.

Other vaccinations might be considered in the case of epidemics. There is an effective vaccination against rabies which should be considered by all travellers, especially those going through remote areas or if there is a particular occupational risk, eg for zoologists or veterinarians.

Further information Further information on health risks abroad, vaccinations etc may be available from a local travel clinic. If you wish to take specific drugs with you such as antibiotics these are best prescribed by your own doctor. Beware, however, that not all doctors can be experts on the health problems of remote countries. More detailed or more up-to-date information than local doctors can provide are available from various sources.

In the UK there are hospital departments specializing in tropical diseases in London, Liverpool, Birmingham and Glasgow, and the Malaria Reference Laboratory at the London School of Hygiene and Tropical Medicine provides free advice about malaria, T(0891)600350. In the USA the local Public Health Services can give such information and information is available centrally from the Centre for Disease Control (CDC) in Atlanta, T(404)3324559, www.cdc.gov In Canada information is available from the McGill University Centre for Tropical Diseases, T(514)9348049, www.medcor. mcgill.ca/~tropmed/td/txt

There are additional computerized databases which can be assessed for destination-specific up-to-the-minute information. In the UK there is MASTA (Medical Advisory Service to Travellers Abroad). To obtain a health brief tailored to your journey call the MASTA Travellers Health Line, T0906-8224100 (calls charged at 60p per minute). For travel health products, call T0113-2387575, and for general health advice visit the website www.masta.org Other information on medical problems overseas can be obtained from the book by Dawood, Richard (Editor) (1992) *Travellers' Health: How to stay healthy abroad*, Oxford University Press 1992, £7.99. We strongly recommend this revised and updated edition, especially to the intrepid traveller heading for the more out of the way places. General advice is also available in the UK in *Health Information for Overseas Travel* published by the Department of Health and available from HMSO, and *International Travel and Health* published by WHO, Geneva.

Essentials

Staying healthy

The commonest affliction of visitors to Colombia is probably traveller's diarrhoea. Diarrhoea and vomiting is due, most of the time, to food poisoning, usually passed on by the insanitary habits of food handlers. As a general rule the cleaner your surroundings and restaurant, the less likely you are to suffer.

Intestinal upsets

Foods to avoid: uncooked, undercooked, partially cooked or reheated meat, fish, eggs, raw vegetables and salads, especially when they have been left out exposed to flies. Stick to fresh food that has been cooked from raw just before eating and make sure you peel fruit yourself. Avoid raw food, undercooked food (including eggs) and reheated food. Food that is cooked in front of you and offered hot all through is generally safe. Always wash and dry your hands before eating.

Shellfish are always a risk eaten raw (as in *ceviche*) and at certain times of the year some fish and shellfish concentrate toxins from their environment and cause various kinds of food poisoning. The local authorities notify the public not to eat these foods. Do not ignore the warning.

Heat treated milk (UHT), pasteurized or sterilized in Tetra-Brik or similar containers, is safe and available in all but the smallest villages as is pasteurized cheese. Standards very for ordinary pasteurization however and the milk sold refrigerated in plastic bags cannot always be trusted. If you can, boil it before drinking. On the whole matured or processed cheeses are safer than the fresh varieties and fresh unpasteurized milk from whatever animal can be a source of food poisoning germs, tuberculosis and brucellosis. This applies equally to ice-cream, yoghurt and cheese made from unpasteurized milk, so avoid these homemade products – the factory made ones are probably safer.

Tap water anywhere in Colombia is unsafe to drink. Filtered or bottled water (with or without gas) is universally available and safe. Ice for drinks should be made from boiled water, but rarely is, so stand your glass on the ice cubes, rather than putting them in the drink. The better hotels have water purifying systems. Stream and well water, if you are in the countryside, is often contaminated by communities or livestock living surprisingly high in the mountains.

This is usually caused by eating food which has been contaminated by food poisoning germs. Drinking water is rarely the culprit. Sea water or river water is more likely to be contaminated by sewage and so swimming in such dilute effluent can also be a cause.

Travellers' diarrhoea

Infection with various organisms can give rise to travellers' diarrhoea. They may be viruses, bacteria, eg Escherichia coli (probably the most common cause worldwide), protozoal (such as amoebas and giardia), salmonella and cholera. The diarrhoea may come on suddenly or rather slowly. It may or may not be accompanied by vomiting or by severe abdominal pain and the passage of blood or mucus, when it is called dysentery.

How do you know which type you have caught and how to treat it?

If you can time the onset of the diarrhoea to the minute ('acute') then it is probably due to a virus or a bacterium and/or the onset of dysentery. The treatment in addition to rehydration is Ciprofloxacin 500 mg every 12 hours; the drug is now widely available and there are many similar ones.

If the diarrhoea comes on slowly or intermittently ('sub-acute') then it is more likely to be protozoal, ie caused by an amoeba or giardia. Antibiotics such as Ciprofloxacin will have little effect. These cases are best treated by a doctor as is any outbreak of diarrhoea continuing for more than three days. Sometimes blood is passed in amoebic dysentery and for this you should certainly seek medical help. If this is not available then the best treatment is probably Tinidazole (Fasigyn), one tablet four times a day for three days. If there are severe stomach cramps, the following drugs may help but are not very useful in the management of acute diarrhoea: Loperamide (Imodium) and Diphenoxylate with Atropine (Lomotil). They should not be given to children.

Any kind of diarrhoea, whether or not accompanied by vomiting, responds well to the replacement of water and salts, taken as frequent small sips of some kind of rehydration solution. There are proprietary preparations consisting of sachets of powder which you dissolve in boiled water or you can make your own by adding half a teaspoonful of salt (3.5 g) and four tablespoonsfuls of sugar (40 g) to a litre of boiled water.

Thus the lynch pins of treatment for diarrhoea are rest, fluid and salt replacement, antibiotics such as Ciprofloxacin for the bacterial types and special diagnostic tests and medical treatment for the amoeba and giardia infections. Salmonella infections and cholera, although rare, can be devastating diseases and it would be wise to get to a hospital as soon as possible if these were suspected.

Fasting, peculiar diets and the consumption of large quantities of yoghurt have not been found useful in calming travellers' diarrhoea or in rehabilitating inflamed bowels. Oral rehydration has on the other hand, especially in children, been a life saving technique and should always be practised, whatever other treatment you use. As there is some evidence that alcohol and milk might prolong diarrhoea they should be avoided during and immediately after an attack.

Diarrhoea occurring day after day for long periods of time (chronic diarrhoea) is notoriously resistant to amateur attempts at treatment and again warrants proper diagnostic tests (most Ecuadorean towns have laboratories for stool samples). There are ways of preventing travellers' diarrhoea for short periods of time by taking antibiotics, but this is not a foolproof technique and should not be used other than in exceptional circumstances. Doxycycline is possibly the best drug. Some preventatives such as Enterovioform can have serious side effects if taken for long periods.

Paradoxically **constipation** is also common, probably induced by dietary change, inadequate fluid intake in hot places and long bus journeys. Simple laxatives are useful in the short-term and bulky foods such as maize, beans and plenty of fruit are also useful.

High altitude Spending time at high altitude in Colombia, is usually a pleasure – it is not so hot, there are fewer insects and the air is clear and spring like. Travelling to high altitudes, however, can cause medical problems, all of which can be prevented if care is taken.

On reaching heights above about 3,000 m, heart pounding and shortness of breath, especially on exertion, are a normal response to the lack of oxygen in the air. A condition called acute mountain sickness (*soroche*) can also affect visitors. It is more likely to affect those who ascend rapidly, eg by plane and those who over-exert themselves (teenagers for example). *Soroche* takes a few hours or days to come on and presents with a bad headache, extreme tiredness, sometimes dizziness, loss of appetite and frequently nausea and vomiting.

Insomnia is common and is often associated with a suffocating feeling when lying in bed. Keen observers may note their breathing tends to wax and wane at night and their face tends to be puffy in the mornings – this is all part of the syndrome. Anyone can get this condition and past experience is not always a good guide.

The treatment of acute mountain sickness is simple – rest, painkillers (preferably not aspirin based) for the headache and anti sickness pills for vomiting. Oxygen is actually not much help, except at very high altitude. Various local treatments, such as Coramina, glucosada, Effortil and Micoren are popular and *mate de coca* (an infusion of coca leaves widely avaiable and legal) will alleviate some of the symptoms.

To **prevent** the condition: on arrival at places over 3,000 m have a few hours rest in a chair and avoid alcohol, cigarettes and heavy food. If the symptoms are severe and prolonged, it is best to descend to a lower altitude and to reascend slowly or in stages. If this is impossible because of shortage of time or if you are going so high that acute mountain sickness is very likely, then the drug Acetazolamide (Diamox) can be used as a preventative and continued during the ascent. There is good evidence of the value of this drug in the prevention of *soroche*, but some people do experience peculiar side effects. The usual dose is 500 mg of the slow release preparation each night, starting the night before ascending above 3,000 m.

Watch out for **sunburn** at high altitude. The ultraviolet rays are extremely powerful. The air is also excessively dry at high altitude and you might find that your skin and lips dry out and the inside of your nose becomes crusted. Use a moisturiser for the skin and lips and some vaseline wiped into the nostrils. Some people find contact lenses irritate because of the dry air. It is unwise to ascend to high altitude if you are pregnant, especially in the first three months, or if you have a history of heart, lung or blood disease, including sickle cell.

A more unusual condition can affect mountaineers who ascend rapidly to high altitude – **acute pulmonary oedema**. Residents at altitude sometimes experience this when returning to the mountains from time spent at the coast. This condition is often preceded by acute mountain sickness and comes on quite rapidly with severe breathlessness, noisy breathing, coughing, blueness of the lips and frothing at the mouth. Anybody who develops this must be brought down as soon as possible, given oxygen and taken to hospital.

A rapid descent from high places will make sinus problems and middle ear infections worse and might make your teeth ache. Lastly, don't fly to altitude within 24 hours of Scuba diving. You might suffer from 'the bends'.

Full acclimatization to high temperatures takes about two weeks. During this period it is normal to feel a bit apathetic, especially if the relative humidity is high. Drink plenty of water (up to 15 litres a day are required when working physically hard in the tropics), use salt on your food and avoid extreme exertion. Tepid showers are more cooling than hot or cold ones. Large hats do not cool you down, but do prevent sunburn. Remember that, especially in the highlands, there can be a large and sudden drop in temperature between sun and shade and between night and day, so dress accordingly. Warm jackets or woollens are essential after dark at high altitude. Loose cotton is still the best material when the weather is hot.

These are mostly more of a nuisance than a serious hazard and if you try, you can prevent yourself entirely from being bitten. Some, such as mosquitoes, are, of course, carriers of potentially serious diseases, so it is sensible to avoid being bitten as much as possible.

Sleep off the ground and use a mosquito net or some kind of insecticide. Preparations containing Pyrethrum or synthetic pyrethroids are safe. They are available as aerosols or pumps and the best way to use these is to spray the room thoroughly in all areas (follow the instructions rather than the insects) and then shut the door for a while, re-entering when the smell has dispersed. Mosquito coils release insecticide as they burn slowly. They are widely available and useful out of doors. Tablets of insecticide which are placed on a heated mat plugged into a wall socket are probably the most effective. They fill the room with insecticidal fumes in the same way as aerosols or coils.

You can also use insect repellents, most of which are effective against a wide range of pests. The most common and effective is diethyl metatoluamide (DET). DET liquid is best for arms and face (care around eyes and with spectacles – DET dissolves plastic). Aerosol spray is good for clothes and ankles and liquid DET can be dissolved in water and used to impregnate cotton clothes and mosquito nets. Some repellents now contain DET and Permethrin, insecticide. Impregnated wrist and ankle bands can also be useful.

If you are bitten or stung, itching may be relieved by cool baths, antihistamine tablets (care with alcohol or driving) or mild corticosteroid creams, eg hydrocortisone (but take great care: never use if there's any hint of infection). Careful scratching of all your bites once a day can be surprisingly effective. Calamine lotion and cream have limited effectiveness and antihistamine creams are not recommended – they can cause allergies themselves.

Bites which become infected should be treated with a local antiseptic or antibiotic cream such as Cetrimide, as should any infected sores or scratches.

When living rough, skin infestations with body lice (*piojos*, crabs) and scabies (*rasca bonita*) are easy to pick up. They may be treated with topical Benzyl Benzoate (Benzoato de Bencilo) or Gamma-benzene Hexachloride (Davesol or Lindano), available in most pharmacies. Fleas (*pulgas*) are generally harmless but annoying and usually acquired in crowded busses or markets. Bedbugs (*chinches*) are occasionally a plague in very cheap hotels, and leave you incredibly itchy.

Crotamiton cream (Eurax) alleviates itching and also kills a number of skin parasites. Malathion lotion 5 (Prioderm) kills lice effectively, but avoid the use of the toxic agricultural preparation of Malathion, more often used to commit suicide.

They attach themselves usually to the lower parts of the body often after walking in areas where cattle have grazed. They take a while to attach themselves strongly, but swell up as they start to suck blood. The important thing is to remove them gently, so that they do not leave their head parts in your skin because this can cause a nasty allergic reaction some days later. Do not use petrol, vaseline, lighted cigarettes etc to remove the tick, but with a pair of tweezers remove the beast gently by gripping it at the attached (head) end and rock it out in very much the same way that a tooth is extracted.

Certain tropical flies which lay their eggs under the skin of sheep and cattle also occasionally do the same thing to humans, with the unpleasant result that a maggot grows under the skin and pops up as a boil or pimple. The best way to remove these is to cover the boil with oil, vaseline or nail varnish so as to stop the maggot breathing, then to squeeze it out gently the next day.

The burning power of the tropical sun, especially at high altitude, is phenomenal.

Always wear a wide brimmed hat and use some form of suncream lotion on untanned skin. Normal temperate zone suntan lotions (protection factor up to seven) are not much good; you need to use the types designed specifically for the tropics or for mountaineers or skiers with protection factors up to 15 or above. Glare from the sun can cause conjunctivitis, so wear sunglasses especially on tropical beaches, where high protection factor sunscreen should also be used.

This very common intensely itchy rash is avoided by frequent washing and by wearing loose clothing. It's cured by allowing skin to dry off through use of powder and spending two nights in an air-conditioned hotel!

This and other fungal skin infections are best treated with Tolnaftate or Clotrimazole.

Other risks and more serious diseases

Remember that rabies is endemic in Colombia, so avoid dogs that are behaving strangely and in the Llanos and Amazonia cover your toes at night from the vampire bats, which also carry the disease. If you are bitten by a domestic or wild animal, do not leave things to chance: scrub the wound with soap and water and/or disinfectant, try to have the animal captured (within limits) or at least determine its ownership, where possible, and seek medical assistance at once.

The course of treatment depends on whether you have already been satisfactorily vaccinated against rabies. If you have (this is worthwhile if you are spending lengths of time in developing countries) then some further doses of vaccine are all that is required. Human diploid vaccine is the best and is now available in many parts of the country; other, older kinds of vaccine, such as that derived from duck embryos, may be the only types available in some small towns. These are effective, much cheaper and interchangeable generally with the human derived types. If not already vaccinated then anti rabies serum (immunoglobulin) may be required in addition. It is important to finish the course of treatment whether the animal survives or not.

AIDS (*SIDA*) in Colombia is increasing and is not confined to the well known high risk sections of the population, ie homosexual men, intravenous drug abusers and children of infected mothers. Heterosexual transmission is now the dominant mode and so the main risk to travellers is from casual sex. The same precautions should be taken as with any sexually transmitted disease.

The Aids virus (HIV) can be passed by unsterilized needles which have been previously used to inject an HIV positive patient, but the risk of this is negligible. Sterile disposable syringes are routinely available throughout Colombia. The risk of receiving a blood transfusion with blood infected with the HIV virus is greater than from dirty needles because of the amount of fluid exchanged. Supplies of blood for transfusion should now be screened for HIV in all reputable hospitals, so again the risk is very small indeed.

Catching the AIDS virus does not always produce an illness in itself (although it may do). The only way to be sure if you feel you have been put at risk is to have a blood test for HIV antibodies on your return to a place where there are reliable laboratory facilities. The test does not become positive for some weeks.

Malaria is present in Colombia but only in the eastern *llanos*, Amazonia, the Pacific coast and the lower river valleys of the Magdalena, Cauca and Atrato rivers, inland from the coast. Mosquitos do not thrive above 2,500 m, so you are safe at altitude. There are different varieties of malaria, some resistant to the normal drugs. Make local enquiries if you intend to visit possibly infected zones and use a prophylactic regime.

Start taking the tablets a few days before exposure and continue to take them for six weeks after leaving the malarial zone. Remember to give the drugs to babies and children also. Opinion varies on the precise drugs and dosage to be used for protection. All the drugs may have some side effects and it is important to balance the risk of catching the disease against the albeit rare side effects. Until recently, only the

Essentials

older less efficacious drugs such as Chloroquine (Aralen) and Fansidar could be routinely purchased. This is currently changing and a variety of anti-malarial preparations including Mefloquine (Larium) and Proguanil (Paludrine) should soon be available, either at pharmacies or directly through physicians.

The increasing complexity of the subject is such that as the malarial parasite becomes immune to the new generation of drugs it has made concentration on the physical prevention from being bitten by mosquitos more important. This involves the use of long sleeved shirts or blouses and long trousers, repellants and nets. Clothes are now available impregnated with the insecticide Permethrin or Deltamethrin, or it is possible to impregnate the clothes yourself. Wide meshed nets impregnated with Permethrin are also available, are lighter to carry and less claustrophobic to sleep in.

If your itinerary takes you into a malarial area, seek expert advice before you go on a suitable prophylactic regime. This is especially true for pregnant women who are particularly prone to catch malaria. You can still catch the disease even when sticking to a proper regime, although it is unlikely. If you do develop symptoms (high fever, shivering, headache, sometimes diarrhoea), seek medical advice immediately. If this is not possible and there is a great likelihood of malaria, the treatment is:

Chloroquine, a single dose of four tablets (600 mg) followed by two tablets (300 mg) in six hours and 300 mg each day following.

Falciparum type of malaria or type in doubt: take local advice. Various combinations of drugs are being used such as Quinine, Tetracycline or Halofantrine. If falciparum type of malaria is definitely diagnosed, it is wise to get to a good hospital as treatment can be complex and the illness very serious.

The main symptoms are pains in the stomach, lack of appetite, lassitude and yellowness of the eyes and skin. Medically speaking there are two main types. The less serious, but more common is Hepatitis A for which the best protection is the careful preparation of food, the avoidance of contaminated drinking water and scrupulous attention to toilet hygiene. The other, more serious, version is Hepatitis B which is acquired usually as a sexually transmitted disease or by blood transfusions. It can less commonly be transmitted by injections with unclean needles and possibly by insect bites. The symptoms are the same as for Hepatitis A. The incubation period is much longer (up to six months compared with six weeks) and there are more likely to be complications.

A vaccination against Hepatitis A (Havrix) gives immunity lasting up to 10 years. After that boosters are required. Havrix monodose is now widely available as is Junior Havrix. The vaccination has negligible side effects and is extremely effective; it is available in Colombia.

Hepatitis B can be effectively prevented by a specific vaccine (Engerix) – three shots over six months before travelling. If you have had jaundice in the past it would be worthwhile having a blood test to see if you are immune to either of these two types, because this might avoid the necessity and costs of vaccination or gamma globulin. There are other kinds of viral hepatitis (C, E etc) which are fairly similar to A and B, but vaccines are not available as yet.

This can still occur and is carried by ticks. There is usually a reaction at the site of the bite and a fever. Seek medical advice.

These are common and the more serious ones such as hookworm can be contracted from walking barefoot on infested earth or beaches; try to wear sandals or thongs.

Various other tropical diseases can be caught in jungle areas, usually transmitted by biting insects. They are often related to African diseases and were probably introduced by the slave labour trade. Leishmaniasis (Espundia) is carried by sandflies and causes a sore that will not heal or a severe nasal infection. Wearing long trousers and a long sleeved shirt in infected areas protects against these flies. DET is also effective. Be careful about swimming in piranha or caribe infested rivers. It is a good idea not to swim naked: the Candiru fish can follow urine currents and become lodged in body orifices. Swimwear offers some protection.

Leptospirosis occurs in Colombia, transmitted by a bacterium which is excreted in rodent urine. Fresh water and moist soil harbour the organisms which enter the body through cuts and scratches. If you suffer from any form of prolonged fever consult a doctor.

This is a very rare event indeed for travellers. If you are unlucky (or careless) enough to be bitten by a venomous snake, spider, scorpion or sea creature, try to identify the creature, but do not put yourself in further danger. Snake bites in particular are very frightening, but in fact rarely poisonous – even venomous snakes bite without injecting venom.

What you might expect if bitten are: fright, swelling, pain and bruising around the bite and soreness of the regional lymph glands, perhaps nausea, vomiting and a fever. Signs of serious poisoning would be the following symptoms: numbness and tingling of the face, muscular spasms, convulsions, shortness of breath and bleeding. Victims should be got to a hospital or a doctor without delay.

Commercial snake bite and scorpion kits are available, but usually only useful for the specific type of snake or scorpion for which they are designed. Most serum has to be given intravenously so it is not much good equipping yourself with it unless you are used to making injections into veins. It is best to rely on local practice in these cases, because the particular creatures will be known about locally and appropriate treatment can be given.

Reassure and comfort the victim frequently. Immobilize the limb by a bandage or a splint or by getting the person to lie still. Do not slash the bite area and try to suck out the poison because this sort of heroism does more harm than good. If you know how to use a tourniquet in these circumstances, you will not need this advice. If you are not experienced do not apply a tourniquet.

Avoid walking in snake territory in bare feet or sandals – wear proper shoes or boots, preferably the knee-high rubber boots used by most Colombian *campesinos*. If you encounter a snake stay put until it slithers away, and do not investigate a wounded snake. Spiders and scorpions may be found in the more basic hotels. If stung, rest and take plenty of fluids and call a doctor. The best precaution is to keep beds away from the walls and look inside your shoes and under the toilet seat every morning.

Certain tropical sea fish when trodden upon inject venom into bathers' feet. This can be exceptionally painful. Wear plastic shoes when you go bathing if such creatures are reported. The pain can be relieved by immersing the foot in extremely hot water for as long as the pain persists.

This is increasing worldwide, including Colombia. It can be completely prevented by avoiding mosquito bites in the same way as malaria. No vaccine is available. Dengue is an unpleasant and painful disease. Symptoms are a high temperature and body pains, but at least visitors are spared the more serious forms (haemorrhagic types) which are more of a problem for local people who have been exposed to the disease more than once. There is no specific treatment for dengue – just pain killers and rest.

Essentials

This is a chronic disease, present in a few parts of the country. It is very rarely caught by travellers and difficult to treat. It is transmitted by the simultaneous biting and excreting of the Reduvid bug, locally known as the *chinchorro*. Somewhat resembling a small cockroach, this nocturnal bug lives in poor adobe houses with dirt floors often frequented by opossums. If you cannot avoid such accommodation, sleep off the floor with a candle lit, use a mosquito net, keep as much of your skin covered as possible, use DET repellent or a spray insecticide. If you are bitten overnight (the bites are painless) do not scratch them, but wash thoroughly with soap and water.

When you get home

Remember to take your antimalarial tablets for six weeks after leaving the malarial area. If you have had attacks of diarrhoea it is worth having a stool specimen tested in case you have picked up amoebas. If you have been living rough, blood tests may be worthwhile to detect worms and other parasites. Report any untowards symptoms to your doctor and tell the doctor exactly where you have been and, if you know, what the likelihood of disease is to which you were exposed.

See the literature section in Background for details of Colombian authors

The following list is only a a brief, introductory selection.

John Hemming, *The Search for Eldorado*; Alexander von Humboldt, *Travels*. For an account of the problems of the drugs trade, Charles Nicoll's *The Fruit Palace* is recommended. For a sensitive account of the Kogi Indians of the Sierra Nevada de Santa Marta, *The Heart of the World*, by Alan Ereira (1990); *Colombia – Inside the Labyrinth* by Jenny Pierce (1990); *Kingdom of the Sun God* by Ian Cameron (1990); *Whitewash – Pablo Escobar* by Simon Strong (1995); *Colombia* (and many other titles) by G Reichel Dolmatoff (1965); *Colombia in Focus* by Colin Harding (1996). *An introduction to climbing: mountaineering in the Andes* by Jill Neate (1994). For birdwatchers, *A guide to the Birds of Colombia*, by Steven Hilti and William Brown, is recommended, Princeton University Press (1986). Colombian literature: Jorge Isaacs, *María* (1867); José Eustacio Rivera, *La Vorágine* (*The Vortex*, 1924); and, of course, the novels and short stories of Gabriel García Márquez. *Colombian News Letter*, published monthly by the Colombian American Association Inc, 150 Nassau Street, New York, NY 10038.

As an introduction to Colombia, interesting early travel books on the country include: *Cartagena and the Banks of the Sinú*, R B Cunninghame Graham 1920; *Colombia Land of Miracles*, Blair Niles 1925.

Useful websites

www.conexcol.com Colombian search engine covering many topics. **www.uniandes.edu.co/Colombia/** History, geography, news, tourism, music, recipes etc in Spanish from the *Universidad de Los Andes*

www.colombia-travelnet.com Travel and practical information in Spanish.

www.ideam.gov.co Weather and climate information.

www.invias.gov.co *Instituto Nacional de Vias*, (National Road Institute). Current detail on the state of the roads with maps etc.

www.igac.gov.co *Instituto Geográfico Agustín Codazzi*. Details of official maps of the country.

www.ecomerz.rds.org.co Colombian handicrafts cooperatives site, connected with the Sustainable Development Network.

http://move.to/colombia Has information on travel, jobs, safety.

www.colostate.edu/Org/LASO/Colombia/colombia.html A site of Colorado State University and the Latin American Student Organisation with introductory material on history, geography society, the arts.

www.minambiente,gov.co Colombia Ministry of the Environment. Environmental legislation can be checked as well as general information.

www.humboldt.org.co Site of Institute Von Humboldt, probably the most important environment research organization in Colombia. Excellent site with descriptions of the different ecosystems in the country and projects with ethnic communities. For local offices, see under Villa de Leiva.

www.conservation.org Conservation International site. Click on Andean Programme for details about projects in Colombia. Their local offices are at Calle 72, No 9-55, of 1001, T2354046/2111582, Bogotá.

www.iucn.org International Union for the Conservation of Nature. One of the best sites for information on biodiversity protection worldwide with links to South America/Colombia including projects in protected areas and National Parks.

www.coama.org.co Details of conservation projects in Amazon and Orinoco regions.

www.natura.org.co *Fundación Natura* website, scientific information on several National Parks where they have projects.

www.survival-international.org Information on indigenous communities in Colombia.

Essentials

Bogotá

3

Bogotá

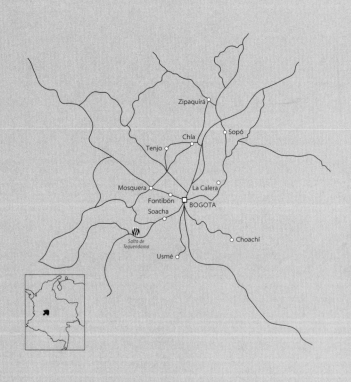

Colombia's capital is a vast, sprawling, disorganized city standing at over 2,500 m surrounded by the high ranges of the Cordillera Oriental immediately to the east and much lower ridges to the north, south and west. Like other Latin American capitals, Bogotá suffers from traffic gridlock, choking pollution and shocking extremes of wealth and poverty. The huge, depressing shanty towns which encircle it come as a rude awakening after the glitzy excess of the northern part of Bogotá. This is the commercial centre, and, in reality a new city, with all the swanky shopping centres, expensive restaurants and sumptuous, high-security homes you'd expect to see in Europe or North America.

The old centre is La Candelaria, a fascinating district to explore, with countless fine colonial buildings lining the narrow cobbled streets, theatres, universities and cafés buzzing with intellectual debate. Here also is Bogotá's most valuable attraction, the Gold Museum, a dazzling collection of precolumbian treasures.

If you tire of the traffic fumes and noise, there's attractive countryside and many places of interest in nearby towns for day and weekend excursions out of the city. Number one on everyone's list, and rightly so, is the extraordinary salt cathedral of Zipaquirá.

Highlights of Bogotá

★ *The ride up and the view from the monastery of Monserrate.*

★ *Walking the old cobbled streets round Plaza del Chorro de Quevedo.*

★ *Almojábanas for breakfast at Cafetería Salón Fontana.*

★ *Haggling for precious emeralds.*

★ *The flea market on Sunday.*

★ *The Jardín Botánico, Bogotá's miniature National Park.*

★ *And don't forget the Gold Museum!*

Ins and Outs

Getting there

Phone code: 91
Population: 6.4 mn;
Altitude 2,650 m;
Average temperature
14°C (58°F)

Air The International airport has 2 terminals, **El Dorado** and the **Puente Aéreo**, the latter 1 km before the main terminal. Both are on Av El Dorado. Most international flights arrive at El Dorado; however some Avianca flights from the USA come into Puente Aéreo. The arrival procedure is much the same at both terminals. If you are changing planes in Bogotá, there is complimentary transport between terminals.

The taxi fare from airport to city is a fixed charge, US$6, more at night and early morning. Make sure you get a registered taxi, normally yellow, found to your right as you leave the main terminal and ask the driver to quote the fare before you get in. You can also go left to the far end of the main terminal to domestic arrivals where you can get a ticket, from the booth just inside the building, which will fix the price of your journey. There is a separate taxi rank outside. You will be expected to tip if you are helped with any luggage. Unofficial taxis are not advisable. Use only uniformed porters. There are *colectivos* (US$1 plus luggage per person) to the centre. In the city centre take buses and black and red *colectivos* marked 'Aeropuerto' to the airport. Watch belongings inside and outside airport, especially at night. See below under **Getting around** and **Transport** for full details.

Bus The long-distance bus terminal, Terminal de Transportes, is near Av Boyacá at C 33B, No 69-59. There is also access from Cra 68. To get into town take buses marked 'Centro' or 'Germania'. The 'Germania' bus goes up through the centre and La Candelaria. To take a taxi, go to the appropriate exit and obtain a computer slip which shows the exact fare to your destination. Taxi fares from the terminal to the city are about US$3.50, depending on the destination, with a surcharge at night. Do not take unofficial taxis, which are normally touting for particular hotels.

Getting around Visitors should not be too active for the first 24 hrs. Some people get dizzy at Bogotá's altitude. Be careful with food and alcohol for a day or two. Walking in the downtown area and in Candelaria is recommended, as distances are short and the traffic is heavy. North Bogotá is more spacious and buses and taxis are more convenient. Between the two and elsewhere, transport is necessary.

Local bus Bus fares are from US$0.30 up, depending on length of route and time of day. Most buses have day/night tariff advertised in the window. *Busetas* charge a little more. There are some red and white *ejecutivo* routes with plush(!) seats, at US$0.40. Fares are a bit higher at night and on holidays. Urban buses are not good for sightseeing because you will most likely be standing.

Car rental Whilst not cheap, if you are in the city for several days this could be a good option, see details in the **Transport** section.

Taxis Taxis are the best way to get between sectors of the city, and at night are recommended for all journeys. All taxis have meters, insist that they are used. The starting charge is US$0.70 and an average fare from North Bogotá to the centre US$3.50. For more details, see under **Transport.**

Arriving by air at night

If your plane arrives late at night, particularly after midnight and you need a place to stay, phone a selected hotel to ensure they have space and ask about the best method of transport, normally by official taxi. The popular hotels in each area have full night service. There is, unfortunately, no hotel close to the airport. Most of the restaurants and commercial establishments close between 2100 and 2200, but the main seating areas are patrolled throughout the night. If uncertain, find somewhere comfortable and move on after dawn (around 0545).

Orientation

Bogotá

The Calles (abbreviated 'C', or 'Cll') run at right angles across the Carreras ('Cra' or 'K'). It is easy enough to find a place once the address system, which is used throughout Colombia, is understood. The address C 13, No 12-45 would be the building on C 13 between Cra 12 and 13 at 45 paces from Cra 12; however *transversales* (Tra) and *diagonales* (Diag) can complicate the system. The Avenidas (Av), broad and important streets, may be either Calles (like 26) or Carreras (like 14) or both (like 19 which is Calle in the Centre and Carrera in the North). Av Jiménez de Quesada, one of Bogotá's most well known streets, owes its lack of straightness to having been built over a river-bed (which, incidentally was opened up again in 2000). The Calles in the south of the city are marked 'Sur' or 'S'; this is an integral part of the address and must be quoted.

Ciclovía Every Sun and public holiday, Cra 7 from C 17 to C 116 and many other streets to the west are closed from 0700 to 1400 to motor traffic and dedicated to cyclists, joggers, roller skates etc. If you go to watch (or participate), beware of pickpockets. Traffic has become accustomed to this phenomenon and is little disrupted.

Traffic problems Bogotá has had serious transport difficulties (see below). Several palliatives have been tried, the latest is to restrict private cars to only 3 of the 5 working days of the week at rush hours (0700-0900, 1730-1930), controlled by the last digit of the licence plate. If you hire a car, find out if restrictions apply to you. In addition, many main city roads are in poor condition and a good deal of resurfacing and general road works are taking place. Leave plenty of time for your city journeys, at least until the TransMilenio has arrived.

TransMilenio After many years of indecision (and stung by the success of Medellín's Metro), Bogotá will have inaugurated a new public transport service by the end of 2000. Essentially it is an articulated bus system along dedicated tracks; the first line north-south along Autopista Norte and Av Caracas, with interchange points for future lines to the western suburbs at C 80 and 13 (Av Jiménez de Quesada). A good deal of chaos is predicted in the early stages but in the long term, the TransMilenio could massively improve the city's traffic problems. Check out the latest situation when you arrive.

Safety

As in any city of this size, take care not to tempt thieves by careless display of money or valuables. Also, anyone approaching you with questions, offers to sell something or making demands, may well be a thief or a con-artist. Beware, they may be well dressed and plausible, may pose as plain-clothes officials, and often work in pairs. Read the **Safety** section in **Essentials** carefully and the comments in the various paragraphs below. Especially recommended is to take taxis, preferably radio-taxis, if travelling in the city at night. Also, do not forget to watch where you are going, especially in the wet. Potholes in both roads and pavements can be very deep. La Candelaria district is relatively safe by day, and in the evening too there are many people about including hundreds of students attending classes until around 2000. You may be hassled by beggars, a problem aggravated by the economic downturn in

1998/2000. If returning to your hotel at night, take a taxi and keep the doors locked. Watch out for 'con' men in and near the Plaza de Bolívar. One well dressed group, speaking English and other languages, known as the 'Venezuelan tourists' may ask you questions as their opening gambit. Best to ignore anyone who approaches – a wave of the hand is sufficient.

If you do have problems, contact the police at a *Centro de Atención Inmediata (CAI)* for assistance. Downtown: Av Jiménez/Cra 6, T2860477; also Cra 1, No 18A-96, T3364725/2868972; Candelaria: Cra 7, No 4-12, T2467203. There are many offices throughout the city, the general number is T156. For the Tourist Police, T3374413.

Tourist information
A useful website for information on Bogotá is: www.laciudad.com

Municipal tourist office, *Instituto Distrital de Cultura y Turismo*, Cra 8, No 9-83, T3366511 turismo@idct.gov.co, www.idct.gov.co; they also have representation at the airport, Mon-Fri 0800-1900, Sat 0800-1700, and at the bus terminal, operated by the City of Bogotá. Good local guide books and maps available. *Corporación La Candelaria*, C 13, No 2-58, T3360888, helpful, sells posters, T-shirts, booklets etc. Tourist Police will also give information and guidance: Main office, International Center, Cra 13, No 26-62, T3374413. For information on 24-hr chemists (pharmacies), events, attractions, etc, T2820000 or T113. The National Parks Office, **(MA)** is at Cra 10 No 20-30. The Ecotourism office for information on the parks is on the 4th floor. Full details are given in the **Background** section, **National Parks**.

Climate
Bogotá has a pleasant temperate climate with the sun hot in the middle of the day but normally much cooler at night, when a light sweater is useful. Theoretically there is a wet season from Apr to Nov but there is not much rain in the middle of the year and nowadays there can be showers at any time.

Best time to visit
Bogotá is an all-year-round-city. Holiday times eg Easter, Christmas are quiet, but attractions are closed, as many are on Mon if they have been open over the weekend.

History

The city of Santa Fé de Bogotá (also written Santafé and with or without accent) was founded by Gonzalo Jiménez de Quesada on 6 August 1538 in territory inhabited by the Muisca Indians. The name of the king, Bacatá, was adopted for the new city. In 1575, Philip II of Spain confirmed the city's title as the 'very noble and very loyal city of Santafé de Bogotá', adopting the name of Jiménez de Quesada's birthplace of Santa Fé in Andalucia. It was the capital of the Viceroyalty of Nueva Granada in 1740. After independance in 1819, Bogotá became the capital of **Gran Colombia,** a confederation of what is today Venezuela, Ecuador, Panama and Colombia and remained capital of Colombia as the other republics separated.

For much of the 19th century, Bogotá suffered from isolation in economic terms mainly due to distance and lack of good transport. Population in 1850 was no more than 50,000. By 1900, however, a tram system unified the city and railways connected it to the Río Magdalena. Migrants from the Colombian countryside flocked to the city and by 1950, the population was 500,000, and the move to develop the north of the city accelerated. Since then it has reemphasised its position as the dominant city in Colombia.

The official name of the city is now simply Bogotá, the urban area of the metropolis is known as the Distrito Capital (D.C.), and it is also the capital of the surrounding Department of Cundinamarca.

Bogotá today

The central part of the city is full of character and contrast. **La Candelaria** is the historic centre, occupying the area of some 70 city blocks to the south of Avenida Jiménez de Quesada, north of Calle 6 and east of Carrera 10 (see map). There is some modern infill but many of the houses are well preserved in colonial style, of one or two storeys with tiled roofs, projecting eaves, wrought ironwork and carved balconies. Many are brightly painted. The churches, museums and palaces are concentrated around and above the Plaza de Bolívar. There are also many intriguing cobbled streets further out from this nucleus. Some hotels are found in this part, more along the margins, eg Avenida Jiménez de Quesada. The streets are relatively uncrowded and safe although care should be exercised after dark. West of Carrera 10 and south of Calle 6 is seedier and not recommended for pedestrians.

Downtown Bogotá, the old commercial centre with shops, offices and banks, runs in a band northwards from Av Jiménez de Quesada. It is very patchy, with a thorough mix of styles including modern towers and rundown colonial and later buildings, together with a few notable ones. This commercial hub narrows to a thin band of secondary shops extending between Carrera 7 and Avenida Caracas to around Calle 60. The streets are full of life; they are also paralyzed by traffic and choked with fumes much of the time. The pavements can be very congested too, particularly Carrera 7 and Avenida (Calle) 19. Many of the budget hotels and some of the better ones are found in this area, which is rated as low to moderate risk.

Beyond Calle 60, the main city continues north to a comparatively new area **North Bogotá**, where there has been great commercial expansion with the development of wealthy suburbs around. Most of the best hotels and restaurants are in this area which is regarded as relatively safe. Small towns, such as Chapinero, Chicó and Usaquén have been absorbed, and the city now extends north to around Calle 200. Many commercial and financial companies have moved here but most government offices and many businesses remain in the very busy downtown sector.

To the south and southwest of the city centre, are areas of industrial development and poor housing. There is little to attract the visitor and generally should be avoided. However, if visiting these zones or any outside the narrow north-south strip, it is helpful to know the name of the *barrio* you are visiting. Taxi drivers respond to these names (there are over a thousand of them) even though the grid system has all the logic.

Information on Bogotá is arranged with these three zones in mind.

Sights

Monserrate

First, no visitor will fail to notice the range of mountains to the east and several peaks which have antennae and buildings on the summits. The most important of these is Monserrate.

There is a very good view of the city from the top of Monserrate (3210 m), the lower of the two peaks rising sharply to the east. It is reached by a funicular railway (built in 1929) and a cable car (1955). A small hermitage was founded here in 1650 dedicated to Santa María de la Cruz de Monserrate. The new convent at the top is a popular shrine. Inside, the figure of Christ, which is the objective

The times of the funicular and cable car frequently change, so check before going, T2845700

of pilgrimage, is a sculpture by Pedro de Lugo y Albarracín, dating from 1656. At the summit, near the church, a platform gives a bird's-eye view of the city's tiled roofs and of the plains beyond stretching to the rim of the Sabana. Also at the top are several restaurants, including *Casa San Isidro*, T2819309, with a French menu and a spectacular view; open Monday-Saturday 1200-2400, Sundays 1200-1500. It is expensive but good. There are also snack bars (good *tamales*, US$1), and the Calle del Candelero, a reconstruction of a Bogotá street of 1887, with plenty of street stalls. Behind the church are popular picnic grounds. The fare up to Monserrate is US$4 adult return (US$2 child). The funicular normally works daily from 0800-0900 extended to 0530-1800 on Sundays and holidays; the cable car operates 0900-2400 daily, (expect to have to queue for an hour at weekends if you want to go up before about 1400, and for coming down).

Bogotá orientation

Related maps
A North Bogotá, page 90
B Bogotá Downtown, page 86
C Bogotá Candelaria, page 76

0 metres 500
0 yards 500

■ Sleeping
1 Casa Berlinesa
2 Casa Medina
3 Centro Internacional
4 Fiesta Avenida
5 Hospedaje Turístico
6 Hostal Linden
7 La Cabaña
8 La Casona del Patio Amarillo

To La Calera
To Carretera del Norte
To Autopista del Norte
To Medellín

A good time to walk up is Saturday or Sunday about 0500, before the crowds arrive. There are enough people then to make it quite safe and the view of Bogotá at sunrise is spectacular. The path is dressed stone and comfortably graded all the way up with refreshment stalls at weekends every few metres. It takes about 1¼ hours up (if you don't stop). Sunset is also spectacular from the top but on no account walk down in the dark and take a taxi from the bottom station into town. There are usually taxis waiting by the footbridge across the road. It is best not to go alone. On weekdays, it is not recommended to walk up and especially not down. You should also take a bus or taxi to the foot of the hill Monday-Friday. The walk up to Guadalupe, the higher peak to the right of Monserrate, with its huge statue of the Virgin on the summit, is more dangerous and not recommended at any time.

Bogotá

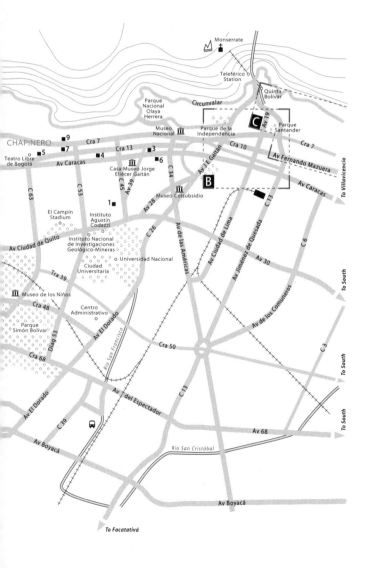

At the foot of Monserrate is the **Quinta de Bolívar**, Calle 20, No 2-91 Este, T2846819, (see the Candelaria map), a fine colonial mansion, with splendid gardens and lawns. There are several cannons captured at the battle of Boyacá. The house was once Bolívar's home, and he lived there off and on between 1820 and 1829. Some of the trees in the garden were planted by Bolívar himself. It is now an important museum showing some of his personal possessions, contemporary weapons, documents, uniforms and medals. Paintings depict events in his career. ■ *Open Tue-Sat 0900-1700, Sun 1000-1600, entry US$1, reductions for children and students, expected to fully reopen after renovations by the end of 2000.*

Candelaria

The Plaza de Bolívar, marked out by the city's founders (as Plaza Mayor), is at the heart of the city. Around the Plaza are the narrow streets and mansions of the **Barrio La Candelaria**, the historical and cultural heart of the city. Because the main commercial and residential focus of the city moved down the hill and to the north early on, much of the original colonial town remains. It is one of the best preserved major historical centres in Latin America, and as such has attracted artists, writers and academics to fill the sector with theatres, libraries and universities, for which Colombia has a very high reputation in the Spanish speaking world. The interested visitor will be delighted by what is available to see, especially the colonial houses with their barred windows, carved doorways, red-tiled roofs and sheltering eaves. The local authorities are helping to preserve and renovate properties and the cobbled streets, a feature of Candelaria. A new initiative in 1999 encouraged property owners to repaint their houses, providing the materials free. Many did so. Many of the best of Bogotá's churches and colonial buildings are in this district.

Traffic can be problem here, notably buses, using the Carreras to reach the suburbs to the south. Some sidewalks are narrow and uneven (to say the least!). Take care. Otherwise, 'walking' Candelaria will be one of the highlights of your visit to Colombia.

A walking tour of Candelaria You may find the following tour a convenient guide to the attractions. Note, however, that two or three days will be needed to do justice to the full tour.

The numbers below refer to the map of Candelaria. Note that most museums and tourist attraction are open Tuesday-Sunday from around 0900-1700, but may be closed for a period in the middle of the day. Times are frequently changed. Entry is often free but may be a modest US$1 or so. Very little is open on Mondays. The best time to visit the churches is before or after Mass (best not during!), around 0700, 1200 and 1800.

1 Casa de Poesía Silva, Calle 14, No 3-41, T2865710. The poet José Asunción Silva lived here until his death in 1895. This is a good introduction to the restored colonial house, with a peaceful garden patio. There is a museum, bookshop and a fine audio and book library with taped readings of almost every Spanish-speaking author. Tapes can be bought in the bookshop for about US$5. Also there are lectures and poetry readings. ■ *Open Mon-Fri 0900-1300, 1500-1800.*

Up from the Casa de Poesía to Calle 14/Cra 2, turn right up a delightful narrow way (Callejón del Embudo) to the:

2 Plaza del Chorro de Quevedo, which is believed to be the centre of the Muisca Indian village of Teusaquillo (or Tibsaquillo) and certainly was where Jiménez de Quesada took possession of the territory in the name of King Charles

24 hours in Bogotá

There's a lot to see in this city, so if you only have one day in passing, make the most of it!

First thing to do is to make for **Candelaria***; the Plaza de Bolívar is a good place to start. Choose some of the attractions detailed below, including the Cathedral, the Casa de Moneda and the new Botero display next door. A walk up to the Iglesia María del Carmen will give you a feel of the old city. Across the Av Jiménez de Quesada is the* **Gold Museum,** *on Plaza Santander – the one thing you must not miss. Set aside at least 1½ hours. For lunch, head for one of the many good*

restaurants in Candelaria: eg La Casa Vieja, where you can try ajiaco or pargo rojo (red snapper) and patacones.

After lunch you can indulge in a spot of retail therapy at any number of good craft shops, such as Artesanías de Colombia, Museo de Artes y Tradiciones Populares or Mi Viejo on Calle 11. Then take a walk (or taxi) along Av 7 (Septima) to the **National Museum,** *one of the best in South America, set in the busy commercial heart of Bogotá and with a new café for a well-earned coffee break. And before leaving, why not buy some Colombian coffee;. supermarkets sell Oma Linea Selecta at US$1.60 for 500g.*

Bogotá

of Spain to form the kingdom of New Granada on 6 August 1538. The centre of the city later moved down to flatter ground (around what is now the Parque Santander), but a commemorative chapel (now a cultural centre) was built on the corner of this plaza and many other houses were built around and below. The name dates from about 1800 when Father Francisco Quevedo provided a well (chorro) for the local people. From time to time during the day you will see many students here taking a break from their studies at the several universities nearby, adding to the activity (and the safety) of the area until around 2000 in the evening. (Note there are public toilets in a corner of the plaza).

3 Down Calle 13 is the first home of the **Teatro Libre de Bogotá**, Calle 13, No 2-44, T2814834. It still houses a professional acting school with occasional public performances. The main home of this company is now in Calle 62, Chapinero, (see under entertainment).

4 Also on this street is the **Corporación La Candelaria**, Calle 13, No 2-58, T 336-0888, part of the government of the Barrio and an information point. Look in at the attractive colonial patio, with its trees and lawns. At present, under the guidance of the Corporacíon, efforts are being made to reinstate the 'cobbled' streets with modern techniques but with very successful results. They have another office across the street which also has information and sells T-shirts etc.

5 At Cra 3 turn left (south) to Calle 12/Cra 3. Half way up Calle 12 is the **Teatro de La Candelaria**, Calle 12, No 2-59, T2814814, whose resident group has travelled widely in Latin America and Europe. Presentations normally Wednesday-Sunday at 1900.

6 Back to the corner of Cra 3, you will be intrigued by the neogothic building on the corner. This was originally a convent but later abandoned. After years of neglect, it was purchased by the national government and became the headquarters of the secret police for some twenty years. Again abandoned, it was purchased privately in the 1990s and converted into apartments. Now known as the **Conjunto Residencial Calle del Sol,** it is unfortunately closed to the public but worth a try to see the attractive gardens and the restored arches of the convent courtyard. The entrance is at Cra 3, No 11-55.

7 Continue along Cra 3, and down Calle 11. On the corner of Calle 11/Cra 4 is **Iglesia de La Candelaria**, part of an Augustinian friary originally established in 1560. This is an 18th century three-nave colonial church with some fine carving and a gilded reredos. The structure is in poor shape and desperate steps have been taken to buttress the southwest corner.

Bogotá Candelaria

Sleeping

1 Ambala	12 Youth Hostel	8 Biblioteca Luis Angel Arango
2 Avenida Jiménez	13 Zaragoza	9 Casa de La Moneda
3 Dann Colonial		10 Museo Militar
4 Hostería de la Candelaria	**Historical route**	11 Fundación Rafael Pombo
5 Internacional	1 Casa de Poesía Silva	12 Teatro Colón
6 La Opera	2 Plaza del Chorro de Quevedo	13 Palacio de San Carlos
7 Platypus	3 Teatro Libre de Bogotá	14 Museo de Arte Colonial
8 Residencia Aragón	4 Corporación La Candelaria	15 Iglesia de San Ignacio
9 Residencia Dorantes	5 Teatro de La Candelaria	16 Plazuela de Rufino Cuervo
10 San Sebastián	6 Conjunto Calle del Sol	17 Museo de Trajes Regionales
11 Santa Fé	7 Iglesia de La Candelaria	18 La Imprenta

8 On down Calle 11 and running the full block between Cra 4 and Cra 5 is the **Biblioteca Luis Angel Arango**, Calle 11, No 4-14, T2864610/3431212, a facility of the Banco de la República, and one of the best endowed libraries in Latin America. There are three reading rooms, research rooms and art galleries. The cafeteria on the 6th floor has a good view and reasonable food. They also have

19 Colegio de San Bartolomé	Populares	Señora del Rosario
20 Plaza de Bolívar	**29** Museo del Siglo XIX	**39** La Bordalita
21 Palacio Arzobispal	**30** Observatorio Astronómico	**40** Plazoleta del Rosario
22 Capilla del Sagrado	**31** Santa Clara	**41** Iglesia de San Francisco
23 Catedral	**32** Casa de los Comuneros	**42** Palacio de San Francisco
24 Museo Arqueológico	**33** Capitolio Nacional	**43** Iglesia de la Veracruz
25 Iglesia de Nuestra	**34** Alcaldía	**44** La Tercera Orden
Señora María del Carmen	**35** Palacio de Justicia	**45** Museo del Oro
26 Iglesia de San Agustín	**36** Museo 20 de Julio (Casa del Florero)	
27 Palacio de Nariño	**37** Palacio de Telecomunicaciones	
28 Museo de Artes y Tradiciones	**38** Colegio Mayor de Nuestra	---▶-- Historical route

premises on the other side of Calle 11. There is a splendid concert hall, where public concerts are usually cheap or free. Free internet service is available for 30 minutes but in great demand. The library is very popular with students, who will be found queueing an hour before it opens at 0800 to secure a study place in the reading room. The building separately houses the **Museo de Arte Religioso** which has as one of its functions to recover neglected religious art from around the country. Notable recent 'finds' are on display. Unfortunately, it was closed in 2000 for remodelling. The architecture of the whole complex is impressive. As you are going down past the library, note the good view of the cathedral towers and dome over the rooftops. ■ *Library open Mon-Sat 0800-2000, Sun 0800-1600, free. Exhibitions closed Mon.*

9 At Calle 11, No 4-93, T3431331, is the **Casa de Moneda** (The Mint). The mint was established on this site in 1620 and the present building dates from 1753, constructed with traditional materials including stone and adobe. Note the courtyard and thick walled arcades. The exhibition traces the history of currency from the earliest trading in gold, salt and tumbago to the present day. There is good commentary (much also in English) with interactive exhibits. The hoard of 1630 coins, known as the *Tesoro del Mesuno* which was found in 1936 on a small island in the Río Magdalena is displayed. There is a coin and banknote exhibition upstairs and occasional extra art shows. ■ *Open Tue-Sat 1000-1900, Sun and holidays 1000-1600, free.*

Next door, a permanent display of Fernando Botero's work was opened in 2000 as *Donación Botero*, with many of his works and his private collection of Picasso sketches. Well worth a visit. ■ *Open Wed-Mon 1000-2100, T3431212.*

10 The **Museo Militar** is at Calle 10 No 4-92, T2813131. The building was originally constructed to house part of the National University but is now a museum devoted to the Colombian armed forces and has a interesting collection of weapons. There is also a detailed presentation of the independence campaign of 1819. ■ *Open Tue-Sat 0900-1530, US$1.*

11 On the northwest corner of Calle 10/Cra 5 is the **Fundación Rafael Pombo**, Calle 10, No 5-22, T2814534, named after the writer of children's books, who lived here. The foundation is dedicated to services to children, including a library, workshops and a film studio.

12 The **Teatro Colón** is next door at Calle 10, No 5-32, T3410475. It opened in 1892 on the fourth anniversary of Columbus' discovery of America. It presents operas, ballets, plays and concerts and is the home of the Colombian Symphony Orchestra which performs there regularly. The auditorium is late 19th century, lavishly decorated and seats 1200. Guided tours can be arranged Mondays-Fridays 0900-1700 or ask if you can have a look around when the theatre is not in use.

13 Opposite is the **Palacio de San Carlos**, Calle 10, No 5-51, T2827811, where Bolívar lived for a time. He is said to have planted the now huge walnut tree in the courtyard. On 25 September 1828, there was an attempt on his life and his mistress, Manuela Sáenz, thrust him out of the window (a plaque facing Calle 10 marks the event) and he was able to hide for two hours under the stone arches of the bridge across the Río San Agustín, now Calle 7. Santander, suspected of complicity, was arrested and banished. Later, it was the home of the Presidents of Colombia at various times until 1980. At present it houses the Ministry of Foreign Affairs.

14 On the corner of Calle 10/Cra 6 is the **Museo de Arte Colonial,** Cra 6, No 9-77, T2841373/2866768, one of the finest colonial buildings in Colombia. It belonged originally to the Society of Jesus, and was once the seat of the oldest

Thomas Paine - Rights of Man

Thomas Paine was born in Norfolk, England on 29 January 1737, the son of a Quaker. After a modest upbringing and minimal education, he took up various jobs, at all of which he failed, including working as a custom's officer. Here he published a strong argument calling for an increase in officers' wages as a way of ending corruption in the service. He was dismissed.

By chance in 1774, he met Benjamin Franklin, who encouraged him to emigrate to America, where he found a post with the Pennsylvania Magazine. In 1775, he wrote an article proposing that the colonists should not only revolt against taxation, but should demand full independence. This piece, entitled 'Common Sense' sold more than 500,000 copies and was one of the key documents leading to the Declaration of Independence of 1776. He served in various governmental capacities but was constantly in trouble because of his outspoken criticism of politicians.

He returned to England in 1787 to find the French Revolution brewing and was soon in print on the subject. He was an admirer of Edmund Burke's views on the American Revolution, but when Burke's 'Reflection on the Revolution in France' appeared in 1791, which was critical of the new order, Paine countered with his 'Rights of Man', championing republicanism and calling for popular education, relief for the poor and unemployed, pensions for the elderly and progressive taxation. The English hierarchy were outraged and he was indicted for treason. He escaped to France where, in something of a volte-face, he pleaded for the life of King Louis XVI, leading to several years in jail there.

He eventually was released and returned to the new USA. His earlier contributions had been forgotten and in 1809 he died in obscurity in New York. It took 100 years for his contribution to history to be recognised, but Paine is now regarded as one of the foremost thinkers of his times.

Yet the impact of his writings in Spanish America was immediate. The incipient revolutions in the northern provinces were greatly encouraged by the American and French revolutions and within a few months of appearing, the 'Rights of Man' had been translated into Spanish by Antonio Nariño. He however fared no better than Paine and was sentenced by the Spaniards to 10 years imprisonment in exile. Nevertheless he later returned as a leader of the Independence movement in Colombia and a province was named for him. Nariño is commemorated particularly in Bogotá at the 'Imprenta' where his translation was printed, and in Villa de Leiva where his house is now a museum.

Bogotá

University in Colombia and of the National Library. It has a splendid collection of colonial art and paintings, including a whole room of works by Gregorio Vázquez de Arce y Ceballos, all kinds of silver, furniture, glassware and utensils of the time. Particularly impressive is the collection of portable writing cabinets with inlay marquetry in one of the upstairs rooms. There is a private chapel and two charming patios. ■ *Open Tue-Fri 0900-1700, Sat-Sun 1000-1600, US$0.50.*

15 The **Iglesia de San Ignacio,** further down Calle 10, No 6-35, was built by the Jesuits between 1605 and 1635 with plans from Rome. Over the choir and the galleries is a rich ceiling in Moorish style and emeralds from Muzo in Boyacá were used in the monstrance. Paintings by Gregorio Vázquez de Arce y Ceballos are in the nave.

16 Opposite is the **Plazuela de Rufino Cuervo**, one of the few original squares in Candelaria, a garden of trees and flowers with balconied buildings around and the dome of the Capilla del Sagrario visible above. The Palacio Arzobispal (Cardinal's Palace) is to the left. To the right of the square is:

17 The **Museo de Trajes Regionales,** Calle 10, No 6-36, T/F2811903, with a display of present and past regional dress, and a collection of hand woven textiles showing pre-Columbian techniques. This is the house where Manuela Sáenz, Bolívar's mistress, lived. ■ *Open Mon-Fri 0930-1630, Sat 1000-1300, US$1.*

18 At the back of the square is **La Imprenta**, where Antonio Nariño's translation of Thomas Paine's 'Rights of Man' was published in 1794, This had a profound influence on the growing demand for independence from Spain (see above). You can read an extract from the text in Spanish on the wall of the building.

19 At the bottom of Calle 10 is **Colegio de San Bartolomé**, Cra 7, No 9-96, T4442530, originally Bogotá's oldest university founded in 1573 and where many notable Colombians of the past were educated, including Antonio Nariño, Antonio Ricaurte and the future General Santander. The imposing early 20th century classical building, now an important secondary school, fits appropriately into the corner of:

20 Plaza de Bolívar, the central square of Bogotá, with a statue of the Liberator at its centre.

21 On the eastern side is the **Palacio Arzobispal**, Cra 7, No 10-20, with splendid bronze doors.

22 Next to it is the **Capilla del Sagrario**, Cra 7, No 10-40, T2436626, built at the end of the 17th century. There are two aisles with wooden balconies above and a fine red/gilt ceiling and screen. The inside of the dome was painted by Ricardo Acevedo Bernal. There are several paintings by Gregorio Vázquez de Arce y Ceballos. Mass is celebrated at 0800 and 1700 during the week.

23 The **Catedral,** T2439794 completes the block. This is the fourth building on the site. The first was completed in 1553 to replace a small chapel where Fray Domingo de las Casas said the first mass in Bogotá. The present building was constructed between 1807 and 1823. It has a fine, spacious interior, redecorated (1998) in cream and gold with high ceilings across three naves. There are lateral chapels in classical style, a notable choir loft of carved walnut, wrought silver on the altar of the Chapel of El Topo and elaborate candelabras. Treasures and relics include paintings attributed to Ribera and the banner brought by Jiménez de Quesada to Bogotá in the sacristy, which also houses portraits of past Archbishops. There are monuments to Jiménez and to Antonio Nariño inside the Cathedral. In one of the chapels near the altar is buried **Gregorio Vázquez de Arce y Ceballos** (1638-1711), the most notable painter in colonial Colombia. A number of his paintings can be seen in the Cathedral, which is open most days from 0900-1200.

24 Retrace your route along Cra 7 past the Colegio Bartolomé and up Calle 8 to Cra 6. To the right along Cra 6 is the **Museo Arqueológico**, Cra 6, No 7-43, T2820760, which is sponsored by the Banco Popular. This is the restored mansion of the Marqués de San Jorge, which is itself a beautiful example of 17th century Spanish colonial architecture. The museum is arranged in themes rather than periods and is not well annotated. However it is an impressive and comprehensive collection of anthropomorphically decorated ceramics from all the early cultures of Colombia. The restored murals of the original house are also interesting. ■ *Open Mon-Sat 0800-1200, 1300-1630, entry US$1.30.*

25 You will have noticed the eye-catching church further up Calle 8. This is the **Iglesia de Nuestra Señora María del Carmen**, Cra 5, No 8-36, T3420972, the most striking church in Bogotá. The architecture is bright and interesting with a graceful western tower and fine cupola over the transept, all in red and white, brick/stone construction. It has recently been repainted to brighten this

Catedral de Bogotá

Bogotá

corner of Candelaria. Inside the red/white motif continues with elegant arches and an impressive altar. The stained glass windows, unusually illustrating fruit and flowers, are slanted to give maximum light to the congregation and the windows in the apse are particularly fine. The overall impression of freshness and light is emphasised by the detail in the rose windows of the clerestory and the intricate ornamentation inside and outside the building. Time your visit to see inside; masses are normally at 0700, 1200 and 1800.

Next to the church along Cra 5 is the **Colegio Salesiano Leon XIII,** a boys college. Inside, a cobbled 'street' leads upwards with three courtyards and the buildings of the former Carmelite community on the left, all in the same style as the church, now serving the school. On the corner of Cra 5/Calle 9 is the former Carmelite chapel with its bell tower above and a rounded balcony on Calle 9 housing the altar of the chapel. This building, known as the **Camarín del Carmen** was faithfully restored as a colonial building in 1957 and is now used as a theatre. The entrance is Calle 9, No 4-77, T2831772.

26 Return down Calle 8, left along Cra 7 to the corner of Calle 7 and the **Iglesia de San Agustín,** built between 1637 and 1668, the tower being a later addition. It is strongly ornamented with an interesting coffered ceiling in the crypt. Note also the ceilings in the nave and the chandeliers. It was restored in 1988 and inside has a bright, cheerful appearance. There are several paintings by Gregorio Vázquez de Arce y Ceballos. The Image of Jesus was proclaimed 'Generalisimo' of the army in 1812.

27 Opposite on Calle 7 is the **Palacio** (or **Casa**) **de Nariño,** T5629300, the presidential palace. It has a spectacular interior with a fine collection of contemporary Colombian paintings. Enquire if there are guided tours, the position frequently varies. The ceremonial guard is normally changed daily at 1730.

28 Down past the front of the Palacio de Nariño to Calle 7/Cra 8, is the **Museo de Artes y Tradiciones Populares,** Cra 8, No 7-21, T3421266, in the old 16th century monastery of San Agustín, with an interesting collection of traditional arts and crafts, particularly ceramics, wood and textiles. It has a colourful shop, a reasonably priced bar and a good restaurant serving Colombian food accompanied by regional music. Some building reconstruction continues in 2000. ■ *Open Tue-Fri 0900-1700, Sat 0930-1300, 1400-1700, entry to museum US$1. The restaurant is also open Mon.*

29 North towards Plaza de Bolívar at Cra 8/Calle 8 is the **Museo del Siglo XIX**, Cra 8, No 7-93, T2817362, formerly a private house, renovated in the republican style around 1880. It was acquired by Bancafé in 1977 and now has a collection of 19th century paintings, clothes and furniture. The *Botica de los pobres* is a fascinating recreation of a 'poor man's chemist' shop of the period. Note the decoration of the rooms on the second floor and the staircase wood-work. A 19th century-style coffee shop was opened in 2000, good coffee to order, mini sandwiches and snacks, not cheap but very pleasant. Newspapers and books to read. ■ *Open Mon-Fri 0830-1300, 1400-1730, Sat 0900-1300, entry US$0.50.*

30 To the right you will see the **Observatorio Astronómico**, built in 1802, one of the first in Latin America.

31 A little further along Cra 8, is the museum of **Santa Clara**, Cra 8, No 8-91, T3376762, formerly the church of the convent of Clarissa nuns, built between 1619 and 1630 and preserved very much as it was in the 17th century. There is a comprehensive collection of religious art including paintings by Gregorio Vázquez de Arce y Ceballos, and some fine interior decoration with coffered ceilings and lattice screens and windows behind which the nuns attended Mass concealed from the public. Note the extensive remains of the original wall paintings. Though discreet signs on the walls tell you what to look for, a guide is a great help, ask at the entrance. Concerts are occasionally staged here. ■ *Open Tue-Fri 0900-1300, 1400-1700, Sat-Sun 1000-1600, entry US$1.*

32 A further block brings you back to the Plaza de Bolívar. On the corner of Cra 8/Calle 10 is the **Casa de Los Comuneros**, Cra 8 No 9-83, T3365803. The building dates from the 17th century when it housed commercial premises with living quarters above and typical wrought-iron balconies. There are also preserved examples of later modifications to the building from the 19th and 20th centuries. It now belongs to the *Instituto Distrital de Cultura y Turismo* and includes the main tourist office of the city. It can be visited during normal business hours.

33 On the south side of the Plaza de Bolívar is the **Capitolio Nacional**, T3500048, originally the site of the Viceroy's Palace. In 1846, Thomas Reed, born in Tenerife and educated in England, was commissioned to build the Capitolio, but it was fraught with difficulties from the start. Construction was suspended in 1851, to be recommenced in 1880 by Pietro Cantini, who finished the façade to the original design in 1911. The rest was finally 'finished' in 1927 by Alberto Manrique Martín. Many other architects and engineers were involved at various times. In fact it is still being restored, now by the Instituto Nacional de Vías (National Road Institute), which has a department that specialises in maintaining national monuments. The Capitolio houses several Ministries, the Supreme Court, Consejo de Estado and Congress.

34 The **Alcaldía**, Cra 8, No 10-65, T2832600, Bogotá's City Hall, is on the west side of the Plaza. It is known as the Lievano Building, and is in the French style of the early 20th century. Until 1960, the ground floor galleries were business premises.

35 On the north side of the Plaza you will see the **Palacio de Justicia.** The former building was badly damaged when the Army recaptured it from the M19 guerrillas who attacked and took it over in 1985. Eventually it was pulled down and a new one was completed in April 1999.

36 On the northeast corner of Calle 11/Cra 7 is the **Museo 20 de Julio**, Calle 11, No 6-94, T2826647, also known as the **Casa del Florero** in a colonial house which houses the famous flower vase that featured in the 1810 revolution. The owner of the vase, the Spaniard José González Llorente refused to lend the vase for the decoration of the main table at an event in honour of Antonio Villavicencio, a prominent 'Creole'. This snub was used as a pretext by the Creoles for the rebellion against the Spaniards which led to the independence 9 years later of Nueva Granada. A copy of the Declaration of Independence is on display. The museum has collections of the Independence War period, including documents and engravings and some fine portraits of Simón Bolívar. ■ *Open Tue-Sat, 0900-1615, Sun 1000-1515, entry US$1, reduction for ISIC cards.*

Two doors above the museum (Calle 11 No 6-42) is an attractive inner courtyard, now a restaurant, which is worth a look.

From here, Cra 7, which was the first important street of Bogotá, runs 4 blocks to Av Jiménez de Quesada, connecting the administrative centre of the city with Parque Santander, the first residential area and now the commercial hub of the capital. This street is locally known as the Calle Real del Comercio.

37 On the corner of Cra 7/Calle 12A is the **Palacio de Telecomunicaciones,** T2811460, the headquarters of the country's postal services on the site of the colonial church of Santo Domingo. In the building there is the **Museo Postal**, same address, T2838006, which is only of interest to philatelists.

Up Calle 13 and left at Cra 6 there are two universities: **La Gran Colombia,** and **38 Colegio Mayor de Nuestra Señora del Rosario** near the corner at Calle 14, No 6-25. The latter school is the second oldest in Bogotá, was founded by Father Cristóbal de Torres of the order of Santo Domingo in the 16th century and is a typical cloistered school of the period. **José Celestino Mutis**, the botanist, taught natural sciences and medicine here (see page 104). You can buy a good cheap lunch at the cafeteria and great crêpes.

39 Alongside is the chapel of the Order - **La Bordalita**. Inside is an embroidered Virgin made by Queen Isabel de Borbón for Fr Cristóbal on his appointment as Archbishop of Santa Fé de Bogotá. Note the coffered ceilings and the huge altar. The elegant façade has some fine stone carvings above the entrance.

40 Cross diagonally the **Plazoleta del Rosario** and over Av Jiménez de Quesada. Although not strictly in the Barrio de Candelaria, the cluster of interesting buildings around the **Parque Santander** are appropriately part of Old Bogotá, with three of the finest churches in Colombia. After crossing Jiménez de Quesada, the **41 Iglesia de San Francisco** is immediately to your left. It is an interesting mid-16th century church with paintings of famous Franciscans, choir stalls, a famous ornate gold high altar (1622), and a fine Lady Chapel with blue and gold ornamentation. The remarkable ceiling is in Spanish-Moorish (*mudéjar*) style. Try to see this church when fully illuminated.

Around Parque Santander

42 Behind it along Av Jiménez de Quesada is the **Palacio de San Francisco,** Av Jiménez No 7-50, built between 1918 and 1933 for the Gobernación de Cundinamarca, on the site of the Franciscan friary. Designed in the republican style, it has a fine façade and competed to some degree with the Capitolio Nacional. It is now part of the *Rosario* University.

43 Next to the San Francisco church and overlooking Parque Santander is the **Iglesia de la Veracruz**, first built eight years after the founding of Bogotá, rebuilt in 1731, and again in 1904. In 1910 it became the Panteón Nacional e Iglesia de la República. José de Caldas, the famous scientist, was buried under the church along with many other patriots - victims of the Spanish 'Reign of Terror' around 1815. It has a bright white and red interior and a fine decorated ceiling. Fashionable weddings are held here.

Bogotá

44 Across Calle 16 is the third major church **La Tercera Orden**, a colonial church famous for its carved woodwork along the nave and a high balcony, massive wooden altar reredos, and confessionals. It was built by the Third Franciscan Order in the 17th century, hence the name.

Museo de Oro **45** Finally, on the northeast corner of the Parque de Santander is the **Museo del Oro** (the Gold Museum), in the splendid premises of the Banco de la Republica at Cra 6, No 15-82, T3421111, F2847450. This collection is a 'must', and perhaps the finest museum in all of South America. There are more than 35,000 pieces of pre-columbian gold work in the total collection, most of which is held here. The rest is divided between other regional *Museos de Oro* (all of which are worth a visit) sponsored by the Banco de la Republica throughout Colombia. Many thousands of pieces are displayed, some are rotated from time to time.

On two upper floors, a full presentation is made of the dozen or so pre-Spanish Indian groups that have been identified in Colombian territory, and how they found and worked gold and other metals. It is a fascinating story, illustrated by many examples of their work. They used techniques, some might say, unsurpassed by goldsmiths of today.

The first display floor sets the scene, each culture set in its geographical and historical environment, explaining the characteristics of their art. There are illustrative models including one of Ciudad Perdida as it would have looked when inhabited. In each section there are helpful portable A4-sized boards with explanatory notes in English which paraphrase the Spanish notes on the display cabinets. The second floor has many more examples of the extraordinary goldwork of these pre-columbian peoples. The centrepiece of the exhibition is the Salón Dorado, a glittering display of 8000 pieces inside an inner vault – an unforgettable experience.

On the ground floor there is a souvenir/bookshop, and exhibition rooms. Audio guides can be hired at the ticket office (Spanish US$1.50, English/French US$2.50). On the first floor, 20-minute films are shown throughout the day, times and languages are displayed. ■ *The museum is open Tue-Sat 0900-1630; Sun and holidays, 1000-1630, entry US$1.50. NB closed Mon.*

Other colonial churches Although the Museo del Oro completes our suggested tour of the Old City, devotees of colonial architecture should also see the following churches on the fringes of Candelaria, marked on the map by name:

Iglesia de Santa Bárbara, Cra 7, No 5-26, T2463565, a mid 16th century church, and one of the most interesting. There are some paintings in the nave by Gregorio Vázquez de Arce y Caballos. Conservation work is being undertaken by the Instituto Nacional de Vías, who are also involved with the Capitolio Nacional.

Iglesia de La Concepción, Calle 10, No 9-50, T2486084, an attractive interior, on a busy market street.

Iglesia San Juan de Dios, Calle 12, No 9-93, T3349194, on the corner of one of the busiest streets of Bogotá, well patronised, worth a visit.

Also marked on the map is the large open air theatre known as **La Media Torta,** Calle 18/Carretera de Circunvalación, which has all kinds of presentations usually at 1100 Sundays and holidays, run by the city of Bogotá, often introducing visiting troupes. There is room for 1500 spectators.

Universities Anyone who has 'walked' Candelaria will have noticed the number of students, even out of normal term time, and observed some of the many schools of the area. The Universities are noteworthy. Two have been mentioned above, others include **Universidad Autónoma de Colombia,** Cra 5, No 11-43, T3424296; **Universidad Externado de Colombia,** Calle 12, No 1-17E, T2826066, and in particular the large **Universidad de la Salle,** Cra 2, No 10-70, T2830900, and **Universidad de los Andes,** Cra 1, No 18A-70, T3520466. The campus of the latter is well worth a visit. It is high on the hillside with good views of the city and has a fine reputation. Although a fraction of the size of the Universidad Nacional, it has produced more than its fair share of the political and business leaders of the country. There is a good restaurant if you can make it to the top of the complex. Nearby is **Quinta Bolívar** see under **Monserrate.**

Downtown Bogotá

Bogotá

The commercial centre of Bogotá has been weakened in recent years by the migration north of company headquarters and offices, yet the area seems busier than ever. For the visitor there are plenty of attractions. The immediate area of Parque de Santander has been covered under Candelaria. Other attractions marked on the 'Bogotá Downtown' map include:

Iglesia de San Diego, Cra 7, No 26-37, was built about 1606 by the Franciscans and a chapel to the Virgin was added in 1629. There is a fine statue of Our Lady in the chapel dedicated to the countryside (which surrounded it when it was built). The monastery was built about 1560, and the fine moorish ceiling can still be seen. Local craft items are sold in part of the old San Diego monastery adjacent to the church.

Iglesia de Nuestra Señora de las Aguas, Cra 3 No 18-66. This charming 17th century church has a wide façade with seven bells overlooking a small park and Avenida Jiménez de Quesada. The name refers to the San Francisco river which now flows under the avenida. It has a single nave and a baroque altar, with a wood carving of tropical fruits at its base. The convent next door has been inhabited by Dominicans for over a century. It has served as a hospital and a school since then, now it is occupied by *Artesanías de Colombia*, one of the best places to buy local crafts.

Museo Nacional, Cra 7, No 28-66, T3348366, F3347447. The museum was founded by Santander in 1823 and later moved to this building, a former prison built around 1900, designed by Thomas Reed (see Capitolio Nacional). It houses a very well displayed archaeological collection, one of the best in the country. If you are short of time, try to see this display. There is a collection of gold items in the vault. The top floor has a fine art section, comprising 20th century national paintings and sculptures. Expensive but good café and tasty cakes. Also salads and desserts named after exhibits. ■ *Open Tue-Sat 1000-1800, Sun 1000-1600, entry US$1 (pensioners free). Café open Mon-Sat 1100-1500.*

Museo de Arte Moderno, Calle 24, No 6-00, has an appropriately modern building, inaugurated in 1953. It has an interesting, well displayed collection of modern Colombian artists, with sculptures, the graphic arts etc represented. Good café and bookshop. If you want to photograph in the museum you must obtain permission from the office. ■ *Open Tue-Sat 1000-1900, Sun 1200-1800, entry US$0.80, half price for students.*

Museo de Ciencias Naturales, Calle 26/Cra 7, T3344571, has a comprehensive collection of the country's flora and fauna. In 2000 it is in the process of transferring to the new Maloka Science and Technology Centre in the west of the city (see below).

Planetarium, Calle 26/Cra 7, T3344548, offers lectures, courses, seminars etc as well as the public astronomical show. *Son et lumière* shows are presented from time to time. ■ *Open Tue-Sun 1100-1700.*

Parque de la Independencia, beside the Planetarium, is popular at weekends though not recommended for visits during the week. Beside the park is:

Plaza de Toros (Bull ring – details under **Sports), 9 Parque de los Mártires** (Park of the Martyrs), Cra 14 (Av Caracas)/Calle 10-11, with monument, on the site of the Plaza in which the Spanish shot many patriots during the struggle for independence.

Teatro Jorge Eliécer Gaitán, Cra 7, No 22-47, T3346800, built in art deco style around 1945 as a movie house, it is now one of the biggest theatres in the country, holding an audience of over 1500 for shows, concerts and theatre productions. It was totally refurbished in 1998. Tickets around US$7.

The centre of Bogotá comes to a natural end where Cras 7 to 13 come together beyond the Centro Internacional (marked on the Downtown map), a large complex that includes the *Tequendama Hotel.*

In the link between Central and North Bogotá, there are a number of places of interest:

Casa Museo Jorge Eliécer Gaitán, Calle 42, No 15-52, is the former residence of the populist leader whose assassination in April 1948 triggered the infamous 'Bogotazo', at the outset of La Violencia (see page 400). The museum is dedicated to this period of Colombia's history.

Bogotá downtown

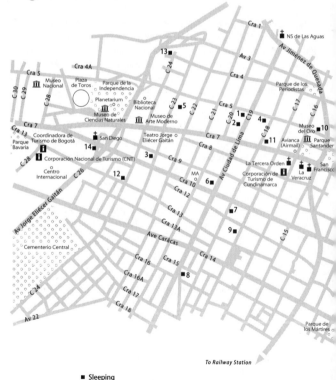

■ **Sleeping**

1 Bacatá	6 Los Cerros	11 Regis
2 Dann	7 Los Cristales	12 San Diego
3 Del Duc	8 Príncipe de Viena	13 Santa Mónica
4 El Virrey	9 Quiratama	14 Tequendama
5 La Sabana	10 Regina	

0 metres 100
0 yards 100

Instituto Nacional de Investigaciones Geológico-Mineras (INGEOMINAS) has a library and pleasant museum at Diagonal 53, No 34-53. It is in the corner of the Universidad National campus, close to other Earth Science institutions including the Instituto Geográfico Agustín Codazzi (see under **Maps**). ■ *Entry US$0.20.*

Museo de los Niños, Cra 48, No 63-97, T2257587. Natural sciences explained for children, created by Sra Ximena Rosas with funding from industry. ■ *Open Tue-Fri 0830-1600, Sat, Sun and holidays 0900-1600.*

Museo Colsubsidio, Calle 26, No 25-42, T3431899. Exhibitions of contemporary artists, and has other special events.

The **Universidad Nacional** is housed in the Ciudad Universitaria, and with about 13,000 students is much the largest in the country. Unlike the older centres of learning in Candelaria, it has plenty of space, and is still expanding.

Teatro Nacional, Calle 71, No 10-25, T2174577. Traditional presentations by national and international artists with important facilities for training young people. They have other premises in North Bogotá.

Teatro Libre de Bogotá, Calle 62, No 10-65, T2171988. Frequent presentations, formerly in Candelaria where they still have a base.

Jardín Botánico-José Celestino Mutis, Av 57, No 61-13, T4377060, www.jbb.gov.co These interesting and well organised botanical gardens have a collection of over 5,000 native orchids, plus roses, gladioli and trees from all over the country. If you can't get to the National Parks, you can at least see many of the local species here. It has a fine documentation centre with resident experts. For more on **José Celestino Mutis** see page 104.

Maloka Centro Interactivo de Ciencia y Tecnología, Cra 68D, No 40A-51, T4272707, F4272747. A complex of science exhibits and instructive entertainment for all ages. There are over 200 exhibits in 9 halls, a 135° large screen cinema, internet rooms, restaurants and other facilities. A full visit takes about three hours. ■ *Open Tue-Sun 0900-1800.*

North Bogotá

North of Calle 68 is an expanding band of wealthy suburbs, business centres, shopping malls and classy restaurants. The best hotels are scattered through this area, which is regarded as relatively safe.

North Bogotá is noted for its huge, lavish shopping malls, which have sprung up in the last few years. They are worth a visit even if the prices don't grab you. The **Hacienda Santa Bárbara** (No **3** on the map) has been constructed within a large country mansion, and parts of the colonial architecture, arches, and stone floors have been incorporated. Even some of the old gardens have been retained.

Museo Mercedes de Pérez, formerly the Hacienda de El Chicó, a fine example of colonial architecture, is at Cra 7, No 94-17. It contains a world-wide collection of mostly 18th century porcelain, furniture, paintings, etc. ■ *Open Tue-Sun, 0930-1230, 1430-1700.*

Usaquén was once one of the more important towns and is now absorbed by the growing metropolis of Bogotá. The small plaza in the centre has become an attractive shopping and restaurant area, popular in the evenings. The railway station can be used for the Tourist Train to Nemocón at weekends (see under **Transport - trains**).

World Trade Center, Calle 100, No 8A-49, T2183484, is a large convention and exhibition centre with all the usual services. The *Bogotá Royal Hotel* is alongside.

Essentials

Sleeping

Accommodation is plentiful in Bogotá. All three sections of the city have top class and middle range hotels but budget travellers will find more choice in the Downtown and Candelaria areas. If possible, book hotels in advance, even if only from the airport or bus terminal. IVA tax (of 16%) charged by middle and more expensive hotels was suspended in late 1999.

Note: Taxi drivers at the airport or bus station occasionally say that the hotel you have chosen is 'closed', 'not known' etc, especially the cheaper ones listed in Candelaria. Insist they take you to the address we quote.

La Candelaria to Av Jiménez de Quesada

AL *La Opera*, C 10, No 5-72, T3362066, F3374617 sales@hotelopera.com.co Next to Teatro Colón, with breakfast, conversion of two colonial houses, opened 1997, personal service, nice restaurant, recommended.

B *Dann Colonial*, C 14, No 4-21, T3411680, F3349992. With breakfast, laundry, TV, popular with groups, safe parking, friendly. **B San Sebastián,** Av Jiménez de Quesada 3-97, T5666889, F2829825. Spacious rooms, restaurant, TV, telephone.

C *La Hostería de la Candelaria* C 9, No 3-11, T2861479. Quiet and relaxed, charming patio, restaurant (Café Rosita), suite with good view of old Bogotá, good for longer stays.

D *Santa Fé,* C 14, No 4-48, T3420560, F3421879. Shower, good service, quiet, clean, friendly, safe, good restaurant, popular with locals. **D** *Zaragoza*, Av Jiménez de Quesada, No 4-56, T2845411. With bath, hot water, OK. **D** *Residencia Dorantes*, C 13, No 5-07, T3346640, F3415365. Very clean, (cheaper without bath), hot water, high ceilings, 1950s décor, most rooms with good view of Monserrate, reasonable, safe. Recommended. **D** *Ambala*, Cra 5, No 13-46, T2863751, F2863693. Cheap, clean, friendly and central. **D** *Avenida Jiménez,* Av Jiménez de Quesada, No 4-71, T2436685. Helpful, friendly, sauna, safe.

E *Internacional*, Cra 5, No 14-45, T3418731. With bath, cheaper without, friendly, hot water, excellent kitchen, good value, safe deposit, popular with Israelis (take care to specify the address, there are several other hotels with similar names). **E** *Platypus*, C 16, No 2-43, T/F3412874/3104, platypushotelyahoo.com Clean, pleasant, kitchen facilities, hot water, free coffee, friendly informative owner, very good book exchange, excellent travellers guest house. Highly recommended. **E** *Residencia Aragón,* Cra 3, No 14-13, T3425239/8325. Clean, safe, friendly, honest, usually hot water, will store luggage, parking facilities. Recommended.

In Downtown Bogotá (Av Jiménez de Quesada up to Calle 31)

LL *Tequendama*, Cra 10, No 26-21, T2861111, F2822860, bogha@interconti.com Restaurant serves excellent *ajiaco*, good for breakfast, important location, full service hotel.

AL *Bacatá*, C 19, No 5-20, T2838300/3364231, F2817249, hbacata@colomsat.net.co On busy street, cheaper at weekends, worth asking at other times, restaurant not recommended. **AL** *Dann*, C 19, No 5-72, T2840100, F2823108. Buffet breakfast, very helpful. **A** *Santa Mónica*, Cra 3, No 24-11, T3368080, F3363601. A/c, restaurant, cable TV, pleasant location, good.

B *Del Duc*, C 23, No 9-38, T3340080. Negotiate for longer stays, friendly, clean, restaurant. **B** *El Virrey*, C 18, No 5-56, T3341150. Modern, hot showers, TV, good value restaurant, friendly. Recommended. **B** *Los Cerros*, C 19, No 9-18**,** T3340711, pleasant, good restaurant. **B** *Quiratama*, C 17, No 12-44, T2824515, F3413246. Very nice rooms, TV, telephone, good service. **B** *San Diego*, Cra 13/C 24, T2842100. Friendly, clean, large rooms, good value.

C *Regina*, Cra 5, No 15-16, T3345137. With private bath, TV, phone, friendly, good. **C** *La Sabana,* C 23, No 5-23, T2844361, F2846552. Central, quiet, clean, English spoken, small restaurant, Visa accepted. **C** *Príncipe de Viena*, C 19, No 15-35, T3420090. Big old rooms, with bath, TV, friendly, laundry service, bar, restaurant.

D *Los Cristales*, C 18, No 10-65, T2848008. Clean, safe, cold water, TV. **D** *Regis*, C 18, No 6-09 (also known as *Residencias María*). With bath, cheaper without, hot water, old-fashioned, rundown but safe, clean, safe parking for car or motorcycle.

LL *Casa Medina*, Cra 7, 69A-22, T2170288, F3123769. In the French 'Relais et Châteaux' chain, nice interior, good restaurant, chic.

Between Calles 32 & 75

AL *Centro Internacional*, Cra 13A, No 38-97, T2885566, F2880850. Suites available, popular, good location.

A *Fiesta Avenida*, Av Caracas, No 47-28, T2853407. Clean, friendly, safe, restaurant, TV. Recommended. **A** *Las Terrazas*, C 54A, No 3-12, T2555777. Very clean, 'rustic charm', pleasant, nice view of city. **A** *Hostal Linden*, C 36, No 14-39, T2874239. Central, small, 2 rooms with kitchenette, credit cards accepted.

C *Casa Berlinesa*, C 45A, No 21-40, T2328504. German and English spoken, full breakfast available. **C** *La Casona del Patio Amarillo*, Cra 8, No 69-24, T2128805, F2123507. Various room sizes, some with bath, negotiate price, good for groups, pleasant area, friendly, helpful. Recommended.

D *La Cabaña*, C 58, No 9-55. Safe, good value. **D** *Hospedaje Turístico 61*, C 61, No 10-18, T2170383. Clean, friendly, discounts for stays over 3 days, those with less stamina can pay by the hour.

LL *Bogotá Royal*, Av 100, No 8A-01, T2189911, F2183261. Excellent. **LL** *Victoria Regia Sofitel*, Cra 13, No 85-80, T6212666, F6220692, PO Box 250-718. Superior rooms and suites, all services, pool, restaurant. **LL** *La Fontana*, Av 127, No 21-10, T6154400, F2160449. Distinctive, very good (*Los Arcos* restaurant in hotel, superb, elegant). **LL** *Los Urapanes*, Cra 13, No 83-19, T2181188, F2189242. Very pleasant, smart, smaller hotel. **LL** *Portón de La Cabrera*, C 84, No 7-65, T6166611, F6110960. Friendly, very good, excellent restaurant, business facilities. **LL** *Cosmos 100*, C 100, No 21A-41, T6217750, F2571035. Friendly staff, great view, good breakfasts. Recommended.

In North Bogotá, Calles 76 & upwards

L *La Bohème*, C 82, No 12-35, T6171177, F6180003. European style, well-equipped rooms, attractive, good location. **L** *Casa Dann Carlton*, C 94, No 19-71, T6338777, F6338810. New in 1998, good location, high standard. **L** *Morrison*, C 84, No 13-54, T6223111. With breakfast, comfortable modern hotel, gym, sauna. **L** *Richmond Suites,* C 93, No 18-81, T6167121. Convenient, quiet, excellent rooms. **L** *Windsor House*, C 95, No 9-97, T6168766, F6166445. Large suites, English style furnishings, very good.

AL *Rincón del Chicó*, C 101, No 13-32, T2147371. Hot water, clean, safe, family atmosphere, TV, helpful, good restaurant. **AL** *Apartamentos 82*, Cra 14, No 81-34, T 2566751. Self-catering flatlets, good service, pleasant, safe, recommended.

C *Hostal Moreno*, Transversal 33 No 95-28, T2579127. Meals available, house taxi driver, nearby frequent bus service to centre, very friendly, safe for left luggage, quiet, comfortable, hot water, good value. Highly recommended.

Furnished rooms are available for longer stay visitors. In Candelaria these include C 11, No 2-98, Bertha Herrera, T 284-7973, around US$160/month.

There are any number of small, unregistered hotels and *hostales* in other parts of the city, many of which are cheap, some of which are clean. However, such areas may be regarded from time to time as unsafe for tourists and are remote from places of interest.

Youth Hostels Colombian Youth Hostels are administered by the *Federación Colombiana de Albergues Juveniles (FCA)*, Cra 7, No 6-10, a block beyond the Palacio de Nariño (Presidential Palace), T2803041/2803202, F2803460. The FCA is affiliated to the International Youth Hostels Association. At this address there is a clean and well run hostel, safe area, with 90 beds, US$4.50 members, US$5.50 non-members per night, lunch available US$2, 1200-1500. Ask for full information about other hostels here.

Eating

Restaurants are spread throughout the city. The more exotic and fashionable places to eat are in North Bogotá but Candelaria has its bistros and good value, typical Colombian food. Take local advice if you want to eat really cheaply in markets or from street stalls. For the traveller on a budget, *bandeja* (the local *plato del día*) can cost US$1.30-2.00 for a 2-course meal at the right places.

Up market restaurants may cost from US$20/25 to US$40 a head and add a 'voluntary' 10-15% service charge.

In Candelaria *Casa Vieja*, Av Jiménez 3-73, T3348908. Traditional Bogotá food including *ajiajo*, live music, also in North Bogotá and 2 other branches. *Eduardo*, C 13, No 8-66, T2430118. Good business restaurant upstairs, more popular downstairs. *Cafetería Romana*, Av Jiménez, No 6-65. All meals, very clean, reasonable pasta, good food, excellent but expensive breakfast menu. *Sorrento*, C 14, No 6-64. Wide range of popular dishes. *Café L'Avenir,* C 11, No 2-98. French style, *crêpes* a speciality, pleasant atmosphere, friendly owners, useful notice-board, 1000-2200, recommended. *Andante ma non Troppo,* Cra 2, No 10-92. Good menu, good comida US$2.50, Mon-Sat 1200-1500. *Los Secretos del Mar,* Cra 5, No 13-20. Fish, run by Colombians from Chocó, good. *Mi Viejo,* C 11, No 5-37, T3415178. Argentine steakhouse, popular at lunchtime.

North Bogotá

■ **Sleeping**
1 Apartamentos 82
2 Bogotá Royal
3 Casa Dann Carlton
4 Cosmos 100
5 Hostal Moreno
6 La Bohème
7 La Fontana
8 Los Urapanes
9 Morrison
10 Portón de la Cabrera
11 Richmond Suites
12 Rincón del Chicó

Bogotá

Recommended. *El Café Rosita*, C 9, No 3-11, T2861479, good food, open till 2100 weekdays, good *ajiaco* on Sun. *S.E.A.P (Sociedad Económico de Amigos del País)*, C 11, No 6-42, T3365849. Up-market, delightful colonial setting, good, open lunchtimes. *Los Ultimos Virreyes*, C 10, No 3-16, T3426580. Good meals, popular at lunchtime. *La Puerta Falsa*, C 11, No 6-50. Good *tamales* and other local dishes, open 0700-2200. *Empanadas Don Camillo*, Cra 4, No 12-15. Excellent filled *arepas*, clean, friendly, warmly recommended. *Cafetería Salon Fontana*, C 14, No 5-98. Excellent busy breakfast place, try their fresh *almojabánas*. Recommended. *Lotus Azul*, C 15/Cra 6, good quality and good value vegetarian food.

In Downtown Bogotá (Av Jiménez de Quesada up to Calle 31)

La Fragata, Cra 13, No 27-98, T2432959. Very good fish, other locations in North Bogotá. *Refugio Alpino*, C 23, No 7-49, T2846515. French/Swiss, good value international restaurant. *Casa San Isidro*, on Monserrate (see under **Sights**). *Salerno*, Cra 7, No 19-43, popular menu, good value, closes at 2100. *Ramses*, Cra 7, No 18-64, T2438401. Excellent, inexpensive Arab food, open to 2200. *El Patio*, Cra 4A, No 27-86, T2826141, and *Il Caffe*, next door. Both under same management, good Italian and international. Recommended. *Urbano*, Cra 4A, No 27-03, T3341432. Weird décor, varied menu, good. *La Barra*, C 22, No 9-23, T2832302. Near bullring, Spanish, popular, busy before *corridas*. *San Lorenzo*, Cra 13, No 28A-31, T2888731, Mexican food, popular with business people. *El Boliche*, C 27, No 5-64, T2811549. Italian and good crêpes. *Empanadas La 19*, Av 19, No 8-56. Good, cheap meals and snacks. *Marandúa*, Av 19, No 4-37. Excellent sandwiches, imported meats. *Estrella de los Ríos*, C 26B, No 4-50, T3340502. Caribbean coast food, closed weekends. *La Tienda de Don Zoilo*, Cra 4, No 19-56. Student pub, good food, friendly atmosphere, recommended.

Vegetarian *La Berenjena*, C 19, No 3A-37 directly above Olímpica supermarket, good, lunch US$2.50. *El Champiñon*, Cra 8, No 16-36, 2 other branches, good vegetarian lunches, fish also served.

Cafeterias *Punta Roja*, Cra 7/ C 22. Good 3-course meal for US$2, open 24 hrs. *Punto Rápido*, Cra 7, No 22-60 and Cra 7, No 19-49. Self service, good meals, reasonable, friendly, 24 hrs service. Supermarkets also often have good value, fast food counters.

Cafés and tea rooms (Pastelerías) *Benalcázar*, near Plaza de las Nieves on Cra 8, No 20-25, excellent pastries. *La Suiza*, Calle 25, No 9-41. Excellent pastries. *Panadería Florida*, Cra 7, No 20-82. Also has good pastries and is the place to try *chocolate santafereño*.

Between Calles 32 & 75

Kalinka, Cra 9, No 70-34, T3429871. Russian food and décor, good. *Pizzería El Sol de Nápoles*, C 69, No 11-58, T3453207. Small, cosy, excellent antipasto. *Armadillo*, Cra 5, No 71A-05, T3459994. Good steaks, and service, nicely decorated, pricey, good selection of cocktails. *Le Poivre*, Cra 10A, No 69-38, T2496485. French, good. *Chalet Suizo*, Av 22, No

13 Victoria Regia
14 Windsor House

39A-48, T2456115. Delicious fondues and good steaks. *Samovares*, Cra 11, No 69-89 T2494549. Vegetarian, lunch only, fixed menu, nice atmosphere, also Cra 11, No 67-63, T2496515 and Av Caracas No 32-64 T2856095.

North Bogotá **Seafood** *La Bodega Marina*, Cra 11A, No 93A-46, Cra 9, No 81-49, and 2 other
(Calle 76 branches. Fine fish menu. *La Fragata*, C 100, No 8A-55, 12th floor of World Center,
& above) revolving; also in *Hotel Radisson*, C 114, No 9-65 and at Cra 13, No 27-98 and Diagonal 127A, No 30-26, L1. Expensive, excellent fish. *Pesquera Jaramillo*, Cra 11, No 93B-31. Good seafood, moderate prices, branches also at Cra 8, No 20-65 and C 125, No 29-23, T2145595. *El Buque*, Calle 101, No 18-18, T2561979. Interesting menu, maritime décor, good seafood, excellent but expensive.

Italian *Il Piccolo Caffe*, Cra 15, No 96-55. Pasta etc, very good quality. *Il Pomeriggio*, Cra 11 y C 82 in Centro Andino, Local 158. Light popular meals, good atmosphere, expensive. *Il Fogolar*, C 98, 10-08, T2577114. North Italian, good. *Luna*, C 83, No 12-20, T2572088. Popular, reservation advisable, very good. *Di Lucca*, Cra 13, No 85-32, T6115665. Freshly made pasta, excellent cooking, open daily 1200-2400. *Archie's Pizza*, C 82, No 13-07, T6109162. Very good pizzas, other branches in North Bogotá.

Spanish *La Casa de la Paella*, C 93 No 13A-46, T6104242. Very good, moderate prices. *Cuatro Estaciones*, Cra 8, 98-38, Good *paella*. *Las Tapas*, Av 19, No 114-13. Spanish bar-restaurant. *Pajares Salinas*, Cra 10, 96-08, T6161524. Very good classical Spanish. *Tacos*, Cra 15, No 83-21. Good, nice décor.

French/Swiss *Le Petit Bistrot*, C 76, No 10-28, T 249-4058. Excellent cuisine, popular. *Bilbouquet*, C 83, No 12-19, T6105210. Authentic French, good wine list, nice atmosphere. Recommended. *La Tour,* C 99, No 10-46, T 256-6485. Near World Trade Centre, very good cuisine. *Le Bistrot Suisse*, Cra 7, No 128-31, T6141198. Good fondues. *Mammas*, C 93A, 11A-47, T2362764. Elegant, good menu, Sun brunch.

Colombian *El Mondongo y Algo Más*, Cra 11, No 97A-38. Very good local menu. *El Atico los Olivos,* Transversal 22, No 122-13, T6123904. Rustic style, excellent cooking. *Fulanitos*, C 81, No 9-13. Good Valle Cauca food, friendly atmosphere. *Casa Vieja*, Cra 11, No 89-08. Good local food, other branches in the city.

Steaks *Casa Brava*, Km 4.5, Vía La Calera. Superb view, very good food. *Tienda de Café*, C 119, No 6-16, T2133118. Good steaks, full menu, children's menu includes small hamburger with potatoes and ice cream(!). *Vaquero Parilla*, Calle 101, No 18-50, T2561979. High quality steaks.

Asian *Welcome*, Cra 14, No 80-65, T2564790. Japanese, good cooking supervised by perfectionist owner. *Hatsuhana*, Cra 13, No 93A-27, T2363379. Japanese, excellent, very expensive. *Gran China*, C 77, No 11-77, T2495938. Chinese, chef from Beijing. *H Sasson*, C 83, No 12-49, T6102619. Very good Asian food, open 1200-0100. *Shushi Bar*, C 96, No 10-28. Authentic Japanese.

US *Fridays*, C 82, No 12-18. US$10-12, good value, recommended. *Tony Roma's*, C 86A, No 13A-10, T6127968. Good quality food, and excellent service, try their ribs. *TGI Fridays*, C 93A, No 11-27, T2570604. Usual overpriced burgers etc. *Houston's*, Cra 17, No 93-17, T2365417. Mexican and international, very popular, US style, crowded Sun. *San Angel,* Cra 11A, 93B-12, T2361019. Good American menu, open daily to 0100, Sun to 1900.

Others and international *Chicanos*, Cra 11, No 88-70, T2496212. Mexican, authentic, good. *La Taquería*, C 82, No 12-80. Mexican, large portions. *La Academia de Golf*, Cra 15, No 85-42, and Cra 15, No 102-20. International, very good. *Na Zdarovia*, Cra 14, No 80-71, T2185072. Russian, very good. *Viva Brasil*, Av 19, No 114A-27, T2137686. Good food, good steaks, lively atmosphere. *El Khalifa*, Cra 11, No 88-46, T2361374. Arab, excellent Sun brunch US$25, authentic atmosphere, expensive. *Estancia Chica*, C 93A, No 13B-50, T6115401. Full range, Argentine menu, good. *Afrikafe*, Cra 11A, No 93-93. African décor, general menu, bar, good, open Sun.

Bogotá

Cafés and Tea Rooms *Café Libro*, Cra 15, No 82-87. Bar with live music, also serves lunches, several others in the city. *Café Oma*, several locations, including Cra 15, No 82-58, Av 19, No 118-78, Cra 5, No 14-71, and airport Puente Aéreo local 2-33, all associated with bookshops. Good food and coffee, nice atmosphere but relatively expensive, most are open till 0100. *Café y Crêpes*, Diagonal 108, No 9-11, T2145312. Good food, good atmosphere, climbers meet here, run by Mauricio Afanador, open 1200-0100 every day; another branch at Cra 16, No 82-17, T2362688, open Mon-Sat 1100-0100. *La Espiga*, Cra 15/C 82, and other locations. Excellent bread and pastries.

Vegetarian *El Integral Natural*, Cra 11, No 95-10. Health food shop with a few tables at street level, restaurant downstairs, fixed menu US$2.

Fast food *Punta Rápido*, Cra 7, No 19-49, self-service, good meals, reasonable, 24 hrs.

Bars and nightclubs

Bars and clubs are concentrated in the Cra 11-13, C 80-86 region, known as the Zona Rosa – a lively, up-market area where there are many restaurants open late. Some of these have live entertainment. Also the downtown section, including Candelaria, has its share of late-night hangouts.

Café Libro, Calle 81, No 11-92, T2568018 and at Cra 15, No 82-87, good music including salsa. Many other bars in the neighbouring streets. Also many popular bars around Cra 4/C 15, which is a relatively safe area. *El Viejo Almacé*, Cra 4, No 13-14. Run by an aged Colombian lady who plays old tango records and sells reasonably priced beer and *aguardiente* (Thur-Sat only). *Escobar y Rosas*, Cra 4, No 15-01, T3417903. Converted pharmacy, popular spot, moderate prices, food available, Cuban rock. **Gay Bars** 3 bars on Cra 7 between Calle 17 y 18, all no cover, expensive drinks. *Boys Club*, Av Caracas 37-68. *Safari*, Av Caracas 73-26, T2178262. *Bianca*, C 72, No 16-48. **Bars**

Salome Pegano, Cra 14, No 82-16, T2184076. Cuban *son* and salsa. *Music Factory*, Cra 14. No 82-76, T6215630. Techno and house, cover charge US$5. *Johnnny Cay*, C 84, No 13-64. Caribbean music. *Café Bohemia*, Cra 15A, No 46, reggae and rock. *Goce Pegano*, Cra 13A/C 23. One of the best salsa spots, no cover but expensive drinks; also at Av Jiménez de Quesada No 6E, T2432549, on the Parque Germania, new, very popular. *Antifaz*, C 13, No 4-30. Young crowd, popular salsa disco. *Disco del Teatro de Candelaria*, C 15 between Cras 4 and 5, good atmosphere especially Fri and Sat. Other small salsa discos around Cra 30/C 50. **Nightclubs**

Entertainment

For general information about what's on in Bogotá, see *Agenda Cultural*, published monthly by Jorge Tadeo Lozano University, in newsagents and bookshops US$1.50, and also see www.utadeo.edu.co

There are commercial cinemas all over the city showing Spanish-language films and English language releases, some dubbed, most with sub-titles. Some new luxury cinemas, with airline-style seats, food and drink services and showing the latest films have recently opened in the main shopping areas eg: *Cinebar Lumière*, Cra 14, No 85-59, T2363957/6360485. *Cinebar Paraíso*, Cra 6, No 119B-56, T2155361,(Usaquén). Tickets at these cinemas cost about US$4.50, but midweek only US$2. Prices are much cheaper in the older cinemas. Check details in the press. **Cinema**
Consult El Espectador or El Tiempo for what is on; there are frequent programme changes. You can also dial 113 for cinema information. See also under Festivals

Foreign films old and new are shown on weekend mornings in some commercial cinemas and there are many small screening rooms which run the occasional feature. *Cineclub El Muro*, Cra 4, No 14-15. Foreign films daily, free coffee. *Cinemateca*

● ●

 Theatre Festival

The Bogotá **Festival Iberoamericano de Teatro** is an exciting bi-annual event and groups come from all over the world to perform. One of the most popular presentations in 1998 and 2000 was *Strange Fruit* from Australia. They gave spectacular outdoor circus-type performances with crowd participation, full of colourful, heart-stopping moments. They are illustrated on the cover of the Handbook. Hopefully they will be booked for 2002.

● ●

Distrital, Cra 7, No 22-79. Foreign films. The *Museo de Arte Moderno* shows different films every day.

Theatre
Details of theatres are also given in the Sights section

Teatro Colón, C 10, No 5-32, T3410475. Frequent major productions. *Teatro Libre de Bogotá*, C 62, No 10-65, T2171988. Specializes in modern theatre; also a studio theatre in Candelaria. *Teatro Nacional*, C 71, No 10-25, T2358069/2174577. *Teatro La Candelaria*, C 12, No 2-59, T2814814. *Teatro Popular de Bogotá*, Cra 5, No 14-71, T 342-1675. *Teatro al Aire Libre La Media Torta*, Av Circunvalar/C 18. Tickets for major productions usually around US$5, often cheaper with a student card. Much less for other shows.

Festivals

There are no city-wide festivals as such in Bogotá. Local communities have their celebrations notably on their Saint's days, and cultural activities are going on all the time. At national holiday times, eg Easter, Christmas/New Year, and when a Mon holiday extends the weekend break (called a *puente*), Bogotáños tend to leave the city so it is an easier time for visitors to get around. Activities that do specifically draw visitors include: **Temporada taurina** (bullfighting fair), in Jan, see under **Sports**.

Feria Internacional del Libro (International book fair) is held every year in Apr/May in *Corferias*, Cra 40, No 22C-67, T3810000, and is supported by publishers from all over the world.

Festival de Jazz, annually in Sep, in the Parque de Independencia, in theatres, universities and all over the city.

Feria Internacional de Bogotá, an industry and trade fair in Jul 2000 and every 2 years.

Festival Iberoamericano de Teatro, a wide-ranging international theatre event in Mar/Apr 2000 and every other year, celebrated in many places, indoors and outdoors. For information: www.festivaldeteatro.com.co

Expoartisanías, a crafts fair held in Dec attracting the best of Colombia's artisans from all over the country.

An **International Film Festival** is held in Sep/Oct and **European Film Festival**, in Apr/May.

Shopping

Bookshops
Books in Colombia are generally expensive

Oma,(also known as *Libros y Discos*) Cra 15, No 82-58 T2565621, good art and literature books, international newspapers, also sells this *Handbook* and other *Footprint* titles, open 1000-2000 every day, later to at least 2300 weekdays. Other branches are at Av 19, No 118-78, T2137083, open 1200-2000 every day; in the Centro Comercial Bulevar, Cra 52, No 125A-19, local 3-13, T2266911, same hours, and in the Puente Aéreo section of the Bogotá airport. *Librería Nacional*, Cra 7, No 17-51 (has small selection of English novels), other branches including airport. *Librería Francesa*, Cra 8, No 63-45, good selection of international magazines, also imports English books.

Bogotá

Librería Lerner, Av Jiménez, No 4-35 and C 92, No 15-23, T2360580, (specializes in 'libros colombianos'). *Librería Buchholz*, Cra 7, No 27-68, T2452023, also at Cra 13, No 52A-24, T2350552, most books in Spanish; useful advice in a number of languages. *Sociedad Colombiana de Arquitectos*, Cra 6, No 28-85, good bookstore on ground floor. *Librería Tercer Mundo*, Cra 7, No 16-91, knowledgeable. *Villegas Editores*, Av 82, No 11-50, Int 3, T6161788, great coffee table books on Colombia, prize winning editions. *Panamericana*, Cra 7, No 14-09, has some guidebooks and maps. *Biblos Librería*, Av 82, No 12A-21, T 2181831, some books in English, café upstairs. *Exopotamia*, C 70, No 4-47, T2493900, good selection of books and music, strong on Colombian music and Latin jazz, also branch by the entrance to *Biblioteca Luis Angel Arango* in Candelaria. *Librería Central*, C 94, No 143-92, foreign language books, interesting, informative owner.

Newspapers: US and European papers can be bought at Librería Oma, at *Tacos de la 19*, near the corner of Cra 7/C (Av) 19, or at Papeles La Candelaria, C 11, No 3-89, T3361228, F5620705, prices about US$1.50, open daily, also has Internet, fax and sells Latin American cultural magazines, US, European and other papers 2 days after publication.

Artesanías de Colombia, Claustro de Las Aguas, Cra 3A, No 18-60, T2861766, next to **Handicrafts** the Iglesia de las Aguas, has good, but expensive selection of folk art and crafts. *Almacén San Diego*, in the old San Diego church, Cra 10, No 26-50. A wide selection of handicrafts is available in Pasaje Rivas, C 10/Cra 10 with lots of stalls and small shops. The main downtown market here has been closed. There is a shop in the *Museo de Artes y Tradiciones Populares*, which is recommended. *Almacén Fascinación*, local J36-38, T2810239. *Mercado de Pulgas* (fleamarket) on Cra 7/C 24, in car park beside *Museo de Arte Moderno*, on Sun afternoons and holidays. Another, higher quality flea market, is held on Sun and holidays all over Usaquén in North Bogotá. *Galerías Cano*, Edif Bavaria, Cra 13, No 27-98 (Torre B, Int 1-19B), also at Unicentro Local 218, at Centro Andino and the Airport, sell textiles, pottery as well as gold and gold-plated replicas of some of the jewellery on display in the Gold Museum. *Galería Belarca*, C 69, No 10-81, T3217021, good selection of local artists, fair prices.

The pavements and cafés along Av Jiménez, below Cra 7, Parque de los Periodistas, **Jewellery** and C 16 and Cra 3, are used on weekdays by emerald dealers. Great expertise is needed in buying: bargains are to be had, but synthetics and forgeries abound. *La Casa de la Esmeralda*, C 30, No 16-18, wide range of stones. *Emerald Trade Centre*, Av Jiménez, 5-43, first floor, German/English spoken. *Joyas Verdes Ltda*, Cra 15, No 39-15 also. Other jewellery shops in the *Hotel Tequendama*. See *H Stern's* jewellery stores at the International Airport, and *Tequendama Hotel*. *Galería Minas de Colombia*, C 20, No 0-86, T2816523, at foot of Monserrate, good selection of gold and emerald jewellery at fair prices.

The best current maps of Bogotá are by IGAC, scale 1:30,000, published 2000, US$9, or **Maps** Cartur, scale 1:25,000, 1994, US$4 and of Colombia, Mapa Vial de Colombia by Rodríguez, scale 1:2,000,000, also 1994, about US$4.

You may have to try several bookshops. Hiking, topographical, town and general maps, also a good road atlas of the country (*Hojas de ruta)* from **Instituto Geográfico Agustín Codazzi**, Av Ciudad de Quito (Cra 30), No 48-51, T3683666, F3680998, www.igac.gov.co, who also have a relief map of the country: Mapa Vial y Turístico, 1:1,500,000, 1995, US$5.80. The topographical details of the walking maps are generally accurate, but trails and minor roads less so. The Institute is open 0900-1500, maps are mainly from US$2.50 to $6 and you pay at the bank next door. There is a library open to 1630 and refreshments available at lunchtime.

Esso and other road maps from some service stations, about US$2.

Photography *Poder Fotográfico,* Cra 5, No 20-70, T3424130, for good developing in 2-3 hrs, used by professionals, also camera repairs. Other photo shops nearby. *Foto Japón*, branches all over the city, gives free film, branch at Cra 7, No 50-10, develops slides in 1 hr. Film, including slide film, tends to be cheaper in Colombia than in Ecuador and Peru.

Shopping Malls *Unicentro,* a large shopping centre on Cra 15, No 123-30 (take 'Unicentro' bus from centre, going north on Cra 10 takes about 1 hr). *Centro Granahorrar,* Av Chile (Calle 72), No 10-34, is another good shopping centre; also *Metrópolis,* Av 68, No 75A-50 (with *Exito* supermarket opposite); *Hacienda Santa Bárbara,* Cra 7 y C 116; *Bulevar Niza,* Cra 52, No 125A-59; *Centro Comercial Andino,* Cra 12 between C 82/83; *Salitre Plaza,* Cra 68B No 40-39, next to *Maloka* science centre. *Exito, Pomona* and *Carulla* chains are probably the best supermarket groups in Bogotá. Some stores have pay by weight salad bars.

Miscellaneous Heavy duty plastic for covering rucksacks etc, is available at several shops around C 16 and Av Caracas; some have heat sealing machines to make bags to size. At the airport there are machines for sealing items of luggage.

Sports

Bullfighting There are *corridas* on Sat and Sun during the season (Jan and sometimes Feb), and occasionally for the rest of the year, at the municipally owned Plaza de Santamaría, near Parque Independencia. The brick bull ring was built in 1927 and has a capacity of 16,000. In season, the bulls weigh over 335 kg; out of season they are comparatively small. (Local bullfight museum at bullring, door No 6.) **Boxing matches** are held here, too.

Football Tickets for matches at El Campín stadium can be bought in advance at *Federación Colombiana de Fútbol,* Av 32, No 16-22. It is not normally necessary to book in advance, except for the local Santa Fe-Millonarios derby, and of course, internationals. Take a cushion; matches Sun at 1545, Wed at 2000.

Hiking *Sal Si Puedes* hiking group arranges walks every weekend and sometimes midweek on trails in Cundinamarca, and further afield at national holiday periods eg Semana Santa; very friendly, welcomes visitors. Hikes are graded for every ability, from 6 km to 4-day excursions of 70 km and more, camping overnight. The groups are often big (30-60), but after the preliminary warm-up exercises, and the Sal Si Puedes hymn, the regime relaxes and it is possible to stray from the main group. Reservations should be made and paid for a week or so in advance at Cra 7, No 17-01, offices 639 to 641, T2839086 or 3415854, F2815624, open 0800-1200 and 1400-1800. This is a very good way to see the National Park areas in the Cordillera Oriental near Bogotá, eg Chingaza and Sumapaz. They also occasionally go at holiday times to the major tourist attractions of Colombia eg Tayrona, San Agustín, Leticia and Gorgona. *Corporación Clorofila Urbana,* C 67, No 4A-80, T3102009/3100048, offers similar walking opportunities, costing around US$10 for the day, more if there is a significant transport cost. Another is *Confraternidad de Senderismo Ecológico El Respiro,* Transversal 48, No 96-48, T2530884/6178857. There are several other ecological/hiking groups that arrange outings at weekends and holidays. Good information on the weekend arrangements can be found in the *El Tiempo* newspaper on Thu in the *Eskape* section.

Horse riding This is another popular leisure activity. Try *Cabalgatas San Francisco,* Cra 5, No 129-38, T6158648, daily rides in the local mountains and *Sabana,* around US$15/hour; *Cabalgatas Carpasos,* Km 7 Via La Calera, T3687242, similar. **Horse racing** at Hipódromo los Andes, on Autopista Norte Km 21, races at 1400 (entrance US$1 and

US$0.35), and at the Hipódromo del Techo, in the southwest, on Sat, Sun and public holidays, but check before going that the meeting is taking place.

Sauna Los Andes, Cra 4, No 16-29, good service, open daily 1000-2200. *Sauna San Diego*, Cra 7 near C 25, massage, turkish bath and sauna recommended. Also available in the top hotels in North Bogotá.

Tour operators

Eco-Guías, Cra 3, No 18-56A, T3348042, F2848991, www.ecoguias.com, specialize in ecotourism, trekking, riding and tourism on coffee *fincas*. English and German spoken. Highly recommended. *Viajes y Turismo Los Alpes*, C 90, No 14-16, Of 110, T2183938, day trips around Bogotá. *Vitramar Ltda*, C 99, No 10-37, T6627075, F2360421, vitramar@andinet,com, French and English spoken, for travel arrangements throughout Colombia. *Bienvenidos*, Cra 62, No 127-72, T2531754, T/F2714517, biencol@cable.net.co, organises cultural, trekking, beach and adventure tours, can also advise on diving.

    Tierra Mar Aire, Cra 10, No 27-91, T2882088, is Amex agent, has several offices around town eg Santa Bárbara: Av 15, No 118-34, T6290277 and does city tours from *Hotel Tequendama* (T2861111). Similar tours of the City (4 hrs) can be arranged from *Hotel Nueva Granada* and other hotels. *Viajes Chapinero*, Av 7, 124-15, T 6127716, F 2159099, with branches at C 63, No 13-37, Chapinero, and Cra 40C, No 57-08, bloque A1, T2221311, helpful with information in English. *Vela*, Calle 100, No 19-61, T6353463, F6353827, viajes-vela@usa.net, student travel agency, for changing flights, cheap tickets etc, recommended. *Aviatur*, Av 19, No 4-62, T2827111, good, efficient.

Transport

Buses Buses stop (in theory) by 'Paradero' boards but there are very few left and normally passengers flag buses down near street corners. Bus fares are from US$0.30 up, depending on length of route and time of day. Most buses have day/night tariff advertised in the window. **Busetas** (small and green) charge a little more but can be dirty. There are some **'ejecutivo'** (red and white) routes with more comfortable seats, at US$0.50. **Colectivos** are small vans, cramped but faster, US$0.60. To go north, pick one up at C 19/Cra 3, or any bus marked Unicentro; they follow Cra 7. Fares are a bit higher at night and on holidays. The network is complicated and confusing. However, you will find people waiting for the buses more than happy to help you to find the correct bus. New red articulated buses are being used on the TransMilenio system (see Ins and outs) and green feeder buses link with the main routes. Through tickets can be

Fare way to heaven

You are newly arrived in Bogotá and have just embarked on your first taxi-ride. Within the first minute, you are aware that it is not quite like home. The skill of the driver at avoiding holes in the road, other vehicles, pedestrians and whatever else appears, whilst travelling at speeds the speedometer cannot register, is, you will soon realise, legendary. Taxi drivers seem to have divine protection. Well, they do.

President Kennedy's Guardian Angel slipped up one day in Dallas. Hauled before the Almighty to account for this, the Angel confessed his sin so contritely and with such humility that he earned himself just one more chance. This is it.

So, relax and enjoy your ride. However, do make sure that the driver knows exactly where you want to go. That aspect of your journey is not protected.

bought. 2 services are available: *corriente* (all stations) and *expreso* (limited stop. Service runs daily 0530-0030).

Car rentals Dollar Rent-a-Car, C 90, No 11A-09, T6914700/6113464.**Hertz** at airport, and at Av 15, No 106-82, T5209950/5201363. **Arrencar**, Transversal 17, No 121-12, Of 511, T2141413, T/F6203304, www.arrencar.com.co, good value. **Budget**, Av 15, No 107-08, T2136020/2155736. Check around for prices which range from, say, US$30/day for a small car to US$100 for 4WD. All companies have deals for more than 4 days.

Taxis If you are short of time, have luggage or valuables, or at night, take a taxi. They are relatively cheap, there are many of them about and the service is generally good. If you take one on the street, try to pick one that looks in good condition. It should also be yellow and the driver's official ID card with photo should be visible; non official taxis are not recommended. At busy times, empty taxis flagged down on the street may refuse to take you to less popular destinations.

All official taxis are metered. The meter registers units starting at 25 then calculates the time and distance travelled. The driver converts the total into pesos using a green fare table. If the conversion card is not displayed, the driver should show it to you. Check before taking your first taxi if there are any additional charges above what the meter/conversion card states eg: night charge or other surcharge; a list of legal charges should be posted in the taxi.

Radio taxis are recommended for safety and reliability. When you call, the dispatcher gives you a cab number, write it down and confirm this when it arrives. There is a small charge (US$0,25) but it is safer. Companies include: **Taxatelite** T222-2222, **Taxis Libres** T311-1111, T288-8888, T411-1111 and **TaxiNet** T366-6666 (recommended). Tipping is not customary, but is appreciated. If you are going to an address out of the city centre, it is helpful to know the section you are going to as well as the street address, eg Chicó, Chapinero (ask at your hotel). If you have any difficulty with a taxi driver, you can complain to Secretaría de Tránsito y Transporte de Bogotá, T2779627 or emergency line 127.

Long distance **Air** Since international and domestic flights use both the main El Dorado airport and the Puente Aéreo, **you must check which terminal your flight will use**.

The **main terminal**, T4139500, has been recently modernized. The departure areas with the usual duty-free shops are of a high standard and comfortable. There is free Colombian coffee inside the customs area and many snack bars and restaurants on first floor. International calls can be made from Telecom on 1st floor, open until 2100, credit cards accepted; post office in main arrivals lounge. There are two tourist offices run by the city tourist authority, one on the right near the international arrivals exit and the other in a similar position near the domestic arrivals exit. They are open daily during normal hours. Hotel and general information is available. Exchange rates are marginally less favourable than in the city, but pesos cannot be changed back into dollars at the airport without receipts. The Banco Popular by the barrier changes Travellers' Cheques (may request copy of purchase receipt) and the is a *Casa de Cambios* alongside which changes cash only. They may not be open at holiday times. When closed, ask airport police where to change money. Car hire counters are opposite the *Casa de Cambios*. Allow at least 2 hrs for checking in and the comprehensive security. There is no baggage deposit. You must reconfirm all flights around 48 hrs before flight time. The **Puente Aéreo** has ATMs which accept international credit cards, and two bookshops - *Oma* with a coffee shop attached and *Librería Nacional*. There is a *Presto* fast-food restaurant, *Telecom* with international call facilities but no exchange service. There is a ticket pick-up counter by the entrance. Otherwise, services are similar.

Buses The long-distance bus terminal, Terminal de Transportes, is near Av Boyacá (Cra 72) between El Dorado (Av 26) and Av Centenario (C 13). There is also access from Cra 68. The exact address is C 33B, No 69-59, T2951100. The terminal is divided into modules serving the 4 points of the compass; each module has several bus companies serving similar destinations. If possible, buy tickets at the respective ticket office before travelling. To get to the terminal take a bus marked **'Terminal terrestre'** from the centre or a *buseta* on Cra 10. At night take a colectivo taxi from Av 13 y Av Caracas, US$0.45 (no buses). A taxi costs around US$3.50, from the centre, with a surcharge at night. Fares and journey times are given under destinations below. If you are travelling north, enquire if the bus company has a pick-up point on the Autopista del Norte around C 160. Velotax busetas are slightly quicker and more expensive than ordinary buses, as are colectivos, which go to several long-distance destinations. The terminal is well-organized and comfortable, but, as usual, watch out for thieves who are also well organized – we have an increasing number of reports of baggage thefts. Free self-service luggage trolleys are provided. There are shops and restaurants. There are showers at the terminal (between Nos 3 and 4), US$0.50, soap and towel provided.

    International buses If going to **Venezuela**, it is better not to buy a through ticket to Caracas with **Berlinas de Fonce** as this does not guarantee a seat and is only valid for two Venezuelan companies; moreover no refunds are given in Cúcuta. Ideally, if you have time, make the journey to Cúcuta in two stages to enjoy the scenery to the full. Bus connections from San Antonio de Táchira in Venezuela to Caracas are good. There are buses from Lima (**Peru**) to Caracas (**Venezuela**) that travel through **Ecuador** run by **Transportes Ormeño**. This weekly service is not recommended mainly because of the several days it takes and the unreliability of the timetable. The cost to Lima is about US$150 (or US$130 from Cali). Much better (and cheaper) is to do the trip in stages and enjoy the countries you are travelling through.

Train Long distance services were suspended in 1992. There are no passenger services at present from Bogotá (La Sabana) station at C 13 y Cra 19 except a tourist steam train which runs on Sun at 0800 calling at Usaquén, C 110, Transversal 10, in the north of the city (see map) at 0900, going north to Nemocón (1200), returning at 1430 and back in Bogotá Usaquén at 1800 and La Sabana at 1900. Cost: adult US$8.50, child 2 to 10, US$5. Information, Turistrén Ltda, Transversal 17 A, No 98-17, T2563751. Tickets should be bought in advance here, at La Sabana station, at **Aguila Tours**, C 13, No 7-09, 2nd floor, T2839580/2828204 or from travel agents eg Tierra, Mar y Aire. There are short stops at La Caro, Cajicá, and Zipaquirá (where you can visit the salt cathedral and return in the afternoon) at which you can buy snacks and drinks, better value than those on the train. See under Nemocón for services at the destination. It is a popular trip for Colombian families, with lots of local colour and music on the train.

Bogotá

Directory

Airline offices **Local airlines**: *Aces*, Cra 10, No 26-53, T2830264/40, airport T4135511, Head Office, Cra 10, No 27-51, p 2, T2830064. *AeroRepública*, Cra 10, No 27-51, T3427766, airport T4139732. *Aires*, Aeropuerto El Dorado, T4138500, terminal, T4139517. *Avianca/Sam*, Cra 10, No 26-19, T4101011, flight information T2954611/243-1613, airport T413-8295. *Satena*, Cra 10, No 27-51, T3375000, airport T4138064, military airline, not best for comfort and delays. **International airlines** *Air France*, T2548950. *Alitalia*, T2871375. *American*, Cra 7, No 26-20, T3432424/2851111, airport T5050505. *British Airways*, C 98, No 9-03, T2180200 and 9003312777, airport T4148346. *Continental*, Cra 7, No 21-52, T 3122565, airport T4135137. *Iberia*, C 85, No 20-10, T 6166111/6109272, airport T4138715. *KLM* C 73, No 9-42, T3172919. *Lufthansa*, T6180300. *Mexicana*, C 100, No 19-61, T6353759, airport T4148428. *TACA*, Cra 13A, No 89-38, T6351100, airport T4148560. *Varig*, Cra 7A, No 33-24, T2858300, airport T4139500. Most airlines, local and international, have offices in both Central and North Bogotá. Many international airline offices are closed on Sat and Sun. The main airport telephone number is 4139500.

Banks Banks are everywhere in Bogotá where there is commercial activity. Some head offices are grouped around the Avianca building at the corner of Plaza San Francisco, others have moved to North Bogotá on or near C 72. *Lloyds TSB Bank*, Cra 8, No 15-46/60, T3345088, F3428505 and 23 local agencies, will cash Thomas Cook and American Express Travellers' Cheques with passport, will give advances against Visa, and will accept sterling, good rates. *Citibank Colombia*, Av 15, No 119-52, T2140961.

Much the best way to obtain pesos in Bogotá is to use credit or debit cards in Automatic Teller Machines (ATMs), using your pin number. Any other method will require your passport and, more than likely, timewasting queues. Look for the symbol, and try. Since it will probably require at least two or three attempts, either go to the downtown section or in the North where there are many banks. Unfortunately, there are no rules; there are countless ATMs accepting Mastercard, Visa and other cards, just look for your card's symbol; but machines may be down or out of cash, or just don't accept the cards stated. *Banco Ganadero* is consistently happy with **Visa**, *Conavi* with **Mastercard**. The major banks, *Banco de Bogotá, Banco de Occidente, Banco Popular, Banco de Colombia* will help, but if you need counter assistance, go early in the day.

Money changers *American Express*, Tierra Mar Aire Ltda, Edif Bavaria Torre B, Local 126, Cra 10, No 27-91, T2832955, does not change Travellers' Cheques, but will direct you to those who do, eg *Bancolombia*. Also very helpful in replacing lost Amex TCs provided you have full details, have a police report (*denuncia*) of the loss and preferably proof of purchase. Other offices at C 92, No 15-63, T2185666 and Cra 8/C 15 are reported as helpful. *International Money Exchange*, Cra 7, No 32-29, open Mon to Fri till 1600, check all transactions carefully. *Cambios Country*, Western Union agents, Cra 11, No 71-40, Of 201, T3466788, several other city offices, good rates, speedy service. *Western Union* also have their own offices, Cra 7, No 27-52, Of 603, T2456109, and C 94, No 15-32, Local 2, T6215316. *Orotur*, Cra 10, No 26-05 (very small, below *Hotel Tequendama*) is quick and efficient, cash only; *Money Point*, Cra 10, No 27, in Centro Internacional, unit 161, good rates, take passport photocopy. *Titan*, C 19, No 6-19, 2nd floor, open afternoons, several other branches. Other *cambios* on Av Jiménez de Quesada, between Cras 6 and 11, and in the north of the city. On Sun exchange is virtually impossible except at the airport. Other Latin American currencies are very difficult to change in Bogotá, except possibly at very poor rates. Better always to change at the borders or try at airports. As everywhere else in Colombia, never change money on the street.

Communications **Internet** There are an increasing number of Internet Cafés in Bogotá, with more opening all the time. As an example, there are quite a number along Cra 7: Cra 7, No 66-38 (T6916042); No 64-38 (T2553378); No 46-20 (T2457857); No 44-29 (T2882886). Most of the Shopping Malls (see **Shopping** above) have Internet centres. See also *Hotel Platypus* above. Prices per hour range from US$2.50 to US$5.50. The **British Council** (see **Cultural Centres** below), has an internet facility but only on a six month/US$26 membership basis. Instituto Colombiano Andino, C 19, No 3-16, US$3.30/hr.

Post Office The main airmail office and foreign **poste restante** is in the basement of Edif Avianca, Cra 7, No 16-36, open 0730-1900 Mon to Fri, 0730-1800 Sat, closed Sun and holidays (*poste restante* 0730-1800, Mon-Sat, letters kept for only a month, bureaucratic, US$0.40 for each letter retrieved). Also Cra7/C 26-27 near the Planetarium, and C 140, between Cra 19 and Autopista. The

Embassies & consulates

Argentina, Av 40A, No 13-09, T5720082.
Austria, Cra 11, No 75-29, T2356628.
Belgium, C 26, No 4A-45, 7th floor, T2828881. **Bolivia**, Cra 9C, No 114-96, T6298252.
Brazil, C 93, No 14-20, T2180800.
Canada, Cra 7, No 115-33, T6579800.
Chile, C 100, No 11B-44, T2147990.
Costa Rica, Cra 8, No 95-48, T6362681.
Cuba, Cra 9, No 92-54, T6217054.
Denmark, Cra 10, No 96-29, T6100887.
Ecuador, C 89, No 13-07, T6350322.
El Salvador, Cra 9, No 80-15, T2125932.
Finland, Av El Dorado, No 69A-51, T4109349. **France**, Cra 11, No 93-12, T6180511. **Germany**, Cra 4, No 72-35, 5th floor, T3484040.
Guatemala, Transversal 29A, No 139A-41, T2580746.
Israel, Edif Caxdac, C 35, No 7-25, T2320764.
Italy, C 93B, No 9-92, T2186680.
Japan, Cra 7, No 71-21, Torre B, T3175001.
Mexico, C 82, No 9-25, T2566121.
Netherlands, Cra 13, No 93-40, T6115080.

Norway, Cra 13, No 50-78, Oficina 506, T2355419.
Panama, C 92, No 7-70, T2575067. **Peru**, Cra 10, No 93-48, T2180133. **Portugal**, Cra 12, No 93-37, T6221334. **Spain**, C 92, No 12-68, T6181288. **Sweden**, C 72, No 5-83, T2352165. **Switzerland**, Cra 9, No 74-08, T2553945.
United Kingdom, Cra 9, No 76-49, 9th floor, T3176690. **USA**, Cra 50/Av El Dorado, T3151566.
Venezuela, Av 13, No 103-16, T6364011; for those who require visas, apply 0830-1200 and collect the following day, 1200-1630.
Note that citizens of Commonwealth countries which are not represented in Colombia may seek advice and help from the United Kingdom embassy.

Hours of opening and visa rules are changing all the time but official business is normally done only in the mornings up to 1230. Consulates are usually located with the embassy. Enquire by telephone before you go.

Bogotá

cost of airmail letters and postcards has recently increased and is now around US$2 to the USA and Europe. For parcels by air, contact Avianca. **Adpostal**, Edif Murillo Toro, Cra 7, No 12.00, one block north of Plaza de Bolívar, latest prices about US$0.65 for USA and the Americas, US$1.60 for Europe, but check.

Telephone International calls can be made from several Telecom offices in centre of Bogotá (eg C 12 y Cra 8, C 23, No 13-49, in the *Tequendama Hotel* complex, Cra 13, No 26-45, Mon-Sat 0800-1900; all close within half an hour of 2000 and may be closed on holidays. Purchase of phone cards is recommended if you are using call boxes.

Cultural Centres *British Council*, C 87, No 12-79, T2363976 has a good library and British newspapers. *Centro Colombo Americano*, Av 19, No 3-05, T3347640, English and Spanish courses, recommended. *Alianza Colombo-Francesa*, Cra 3, No 18-45, T3411348 and Cra 7, No 84-72, T2368605, films in French, newspapers, library monthly bulletin etc. *Goethe Institut*, Cra 7, No 81-57, T2551843. *Biblioteca Luis Angel Arango*, C 11, No 4-14, see No **8** on the map of Candelaria. *Instituto Colombiano de Cultura Hispánico*, C 12, No 2-41, T3413857, important collection of colonial books and documents, not normally available to the public, but researchers or interested visitors can ask for permission to use the reading room. An authoritative headed letter from an academic institution could be very helpful. Occasional lectures on colonial history here are open to the public. Another institution of interest for history research is the *Archivo General de la Nación*, Cra 6, No 6-91, T3372050, open Mon-Fri. In an interesting Moorish style building is the repository of historical documentation available to researchers.

Medical Services *Cruz Roja Nacional* (Red Cross), Av 68, No 66-31, T2319027/2319008/4280111, open 0830-1800, consultations, US$12.50, inoculations and vaccinations including tetanus, typhoid and yellow fever, US$12.50. *Centro Médico La Salud*, Cra 10, No 21-36, 2nd floor, T2431381/2824021. Also for injections, *Centro de Atención al Viajero*, Cra 7, No 119-14, T2152029. New and recommended but more expensive, about US$25 for hepatitis B (Harvix 1440 and Twinrix replacing gamma globulin), open Mon-Fri 0830-1730, Sat 0900-1200. *Walter Röthlisberger y Cía Ltda*, C 26, No 13-37, T2836200, imports medicines, including Vivotif for typhoid and gamma globulin; trade prices. Embassies will advise on doctors, dentists, etc. *Clínica Marly*, C 50, No 9-67, T2871020 and *Clínica del Country*, Cra 15, No 84-13, T6228764, are well-equipped private hospitals. *Dr Arturo Corchuelo*, C 89, No 12-21, T2188710, recommended for orthopaedic problems. *Clínica Barraquer*, Av 100, No 18A-51, T2366033, internationally known eye clinic. **Dentist** Dr Kamel Joseph Huayek Assis, Cra 17, No 60-41, Int 101, T2127203/2490862, speaks English.

There are good *farmacias* everywhere but generally medicines are expensive. *Farmacia Santa Rita*, Cra 5, No 11-09, also has a wide range of natural products and gives good advice if you are travelling to remoter regions. English spoken. For ambulances, T125 (24 hrs). *Cruz Roja* T132.

Language courses
The best Spanish courses are in the **Universidad Nacional** (see map) US$180 for 2 months, 8 hrs/week, contact María del Rosario Benitez, T2697592 or **Universidad de los Andes**, US$300, 6 weeks and **Pontificia Universidad Javeriana**, Centro Latino Americano de Relaciones Humanas e Interculturales, Cra 10, No 65-48, T2123009. Accommodation with local families can be arranged. Most other schools in Yellow Pages offer one-to-one private tuition at US$10/hr.

If coming from abroad, make sure you have a student visa, preferably before you arrive, if not, from DAS in Bogotá, before starting the course. You may not study on a tourist visa.

Laundry
Ask in your hotel, or locally. **Burbujas**, Edif Procoil, Av 19, No 3A-37, open Mon-Sat 0730-1930, manager speaks English. **Lavoseco Servitex**, C 15A, No 2-19, 24-hr service, average load price US$1.50/kg.

Useful addresses
DAS (Departamento Administrativo de Seguridad) Immigration office, Cra 27, No 17-85, open 0730-1530. **Dirección de Extranjería** (for extending entry permits), C 100, No 11B-27, T6107314/7371, or T2776666 (emergency) open Mon-Thu 0730-1600, Fri 0730-1530. DAS will not authorize photocopies of passports; look in Yellow Pages for notaries who will.

Emergency numbers Fire T119, Ambulance T125, Red Cross T132, Red Cross ambulance T127. **CAI Police** T156 or 112.

Around Bogotá

Cundinamarca Department
All around the Distrito Capital of Bogotá is the Department of Cundinamarca (of which Bogotá is also the capital). Much of it is the rich agricultural land of *La Sabana de Bogotá*, but it also includes a section of the high *páramos* of the Cordillera Oriental and the valleys going down to the west and the Río Magdalena. Most of the Department is within easy reach of the capital.

East from Bogotá

To the east of Bogotá is **Choachí**, an attractive village set in a valley, where there are hot springs (good food at *El Colonial*, 1½ blocks from main square). A turnoff from the Choachí road leads to the Santuario de San Francisco, with better views of Bogotá than from Monserrate.

Transport Buses from Bogotá with Flota Macarena, several a day; Transoriente also go there from Av 6A, No 15-48, T2435599, every 15 mins, US$2, (take a taxi to the terminal in Bogotá, don't walk).

Parque Nacional Chingaza
Above Choachí is the **Parque Nacional Natural Chingaza**, an area of over 50,000 ha that rises to over 4,000 m. A good walk is from the north (La Calera) entry to Laguna Siecha, which is named after the Muisca goddess of fertility, Sie. This is one of a number of lakes in the Park which, like Laguna de Guatavita (see below), were used by the Muisca Indians for ritual ceremonies.

Near here is the **Carpanta Biological Reserve**, a remnant of high Andean cloud forest with dozens of species of mosses, trees and epiphites. South from here past Chusa and Monteredonda, (where there are plans for a visitor centre with accommodation) is the Laguna de Chingaza.

Ins and outs   Access from Bogotá is through Choachí and Fomeque or alternatively a dirt road which turns off the La Calera/Guasca road. Unfortunately, this park is closed from time to time for security reasons. Enquire in Bogotá if access is available. You will probably not be allowed to stay overnight, but should permission be given, there are cabins of various sizes for US$6 per person per night, and camping, US$15 for 5 persons. Entry to the Park is US$3 per person, vehicle US$3. See also page 96.

There are many *frailejones* in the upper *páramo* section of the Park, and it was here that the biologist José Celestino Mutis took specimens of the plant which he presented to Alexander von Humboldt about 1800. These were used to identify and catalogue the *Espeletia grandiflora*. There are some steeper areas with deep ravines and a wide range of interesting flora. Chingaza Park is the main source of water for Bogotá and Villavicencio.

South from Bogotá

Due south from Bogotá is Usmé, of little interest, but the road continues more or less along the spine of the Cordillera to Nazareth and San Juan de Sumapaz. Between these two small towns, by Laguna Chisica, is an access point to the **Parque Nacional Natural Sumapaz**, 154,000 ha of highland páramo where the Departments of Cundinamarca, Meta and Huila meet. Towards the south is Laguna Cajones and from here treks can be made in the Park to Pántano Andabobos, where there is some basic accommodation (about US$4 per person). Entrance (including guide) US$3.50 per person. Also see page 96.

Parque Nacional Sumapaz

Ins and outs   Getting there   From Bogotá, bus to Usmé, US$3, 2 hrs, and another bus to San Juan.
   Warning   Unfortunately this area has seen some guerilla activity recently, and it is rumoured that the FARC has a command centre within the Park boundaries. Take careful local advice before visiting.

The highest point of the Park, called **Cerro Nevado** is 4,560 m, though it is no longer above the permanent snow line. It is a beautiful, wild, treeless moorland with many areas of *frailejones* and a number of lakes. Several rivers rise here, notably the Sumapaz, which joins the Magdalena near Giradot, and the Ariari, which flows through Amazonas to the Orinoco. Walking round the Laguna Chisica takes about four hours and it is possible to camp on its shores. There is at present no Park Visitor Centre.

Southwest from Bogotá

The Simón Bolívar Highway runs from Bogotá to Girardot. This 132 km stretch is extremely picturesque, running down the mountains.

About 20 km along this road from the centre of Bogotá is Soacha, now the end of the built-up area of the city. A right fork here leads along a poor road to the Indumil plant, 3 km after which there is a large sign for the **Chicaque Parque Natural**. The entrance booth is 300 m down a track.

Chicaque Nature Park

Bogotá

José Celestino Mutis

Although he was trained as a medical doctor, **José Celestino Mutis**, born in Cádiz, Spain, found that botany was his main interest in life. After a time at the Spanish court, he was appointed as physician to the Spanish viceroy in Bogotá in 1761. In 1766, he set up residence in the university of Pamplona (Norte de Santander), which was then one of the most important places in Nueva Granada, teaching medicine, but spending his time researching plants for medicinal purposes. He is credited with discovering quinine, distilled from cinchona bark, a native tree of the Amazon region.

In 1782, the new viceroy put him in charge of official botanical research in Spanish America. Supported by researchers on expeditions in Central and South America, he amassed thousands of drawings of the new plant species being discovered, and built a library and a botanical garden in Mariquita, near Honda on the Río Magdalena. The library became one of the finest in the Americas but was later transferred to Spain. The botanical garden was relocated to Bogotá and now bears his name.

He and his associates recognised the richness of the local flora and he has inspired the academic investigation which has continued in the country ever since his death in 1808 in Bogotá. You will find that botanical gardens are always worth visiting in Colombia.

Ins and outs The Park is open daily 0800-1600, entrance US$2.50. Take a bus to Soacha and ask for continuing transport to the Park. On Sat, Sun and public holidays there is a minibus service from the National Stadium (*Campín*) in Bogotá at 0800 and 0900 returning at 1600, US$5 return, limited number of places, enquire at Montañas de Chicaque Ltda, Bogotá, T3683114/3118, F2868834. If driving from Bogotá, there is a better route through Fontibón to Mosquera on the Honda road, left towards La Mesa and, after 11 km, left again on the road to Soacha. The park sign is 6 km along this road. There is parking close to the entrance.

The Park is a privately owned 300 ha estate of principally cloud forest between 2,100 m and 2,700 m on the edge of *La Sabana de Bogotá*. The property, which has never been developed, now has some 10 km of trails down and around 500 m of cliffs, with a supplementary peak and a 80 m waterfall to be visited. It is a popular spot for walkers and riders at weekends with good facilities for day visitors and a new Swiss style *refugio* at the bottom level, about one hour down the trail from the entrance. This provides meals and accommodation for 70 or so costing US$20-25 a day including meals and other facilities for day visitors. There is an abundance of birds, butterflies and a great natural diversity of forest cover. The owner also reports frequent sightings of UFOs.

Tequendama Falls Take the exit from the Giradot Highway marked El Colegio to **Salto de Tequendama** (5 km), where the water of the Río Bogotá (also called the Funza) falls 132 m over the lip of the Sabana. The water is dirty with sewage but the falls are still a spectacular sight though the smell can be most unpleasant. The site is in an amphitheatre of forest-clad hill sloping to the edge of a rock-walled gorge. There is a good bus service from Bogotá (31 km).

About 8 km beyond the falls is the **Zoológico Santa Cruz**, a private collection of local animals, birds and reptiles. ■ *Open daily, 0900-1700 US$2.*

After the Tequendama Falls turning is **Fusagasugá** which lies in a rich wooded valley famous for its fruits, its good climate and Sunday market. Splendid orchids can be seen in the Jardín Luxemburgo (best flowering November-February but it is a long walk out of town) and in the Jardín Clarisa. There is another pleasant garden at the Casa de la Cultura.

Fusagasuga
Phone code: 91
Population : 70,000
Altitude 1,740 m

Sleeping E *Castillo,* recommended. **E** *Scala,* Cra 8, No 10-30, T8672511. Recommended. There are many luxury hotels on the road to Melgar. Near Fusagasugá is **C** *Miramonti.* Italian-run family place, very quiet.

Transport Buses: To **Bogotá**, Autos Fusa and Cootransfusa, US$1.20.

About 2 km down the main road from Fusagasugá is a side road left to **San Bernardo**, a pretty little town. The cemetery has a macabre attraction; looking through a window near the central 'altar' you see mummified figures, including a woman and child, assembled in the dimly lit cellar (entry US$0.25). A further 24 km down is **Boquerón**, below which is a spectacular rock overhang known as El Nariz del Diablo (Devil's Nose). From Boquerón is a turning right to **Pandi** (10km), where there is a park with ancient stones. Nearby, on the road to **Icononzo,** is a famous natural bridge in a spectacular and very deep gorge through which runs the Río Sumapaz. Pandi can also be reached from the road to San Bernardo (see above) by turning right 3 km short of the village. There's a bus from Fusagasugá to San Bernardo (1½ hours).

Around Bogotá

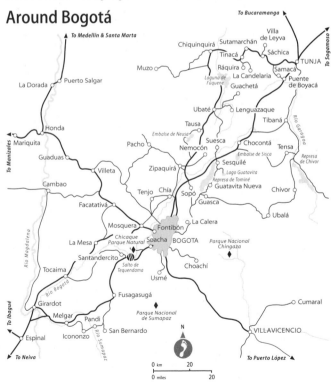

Melgar This is a popular weekending place, near Girardot, for Bogotanos who like a
Phone code 91 little warmth. There are three tolls between Bogotá and Melgar (not always
Population 20,000 staffed). For those driving south towards Neiva there is a new bypass avoid-
Altitude 324 m ing Girardot.

Sleeping Plenty of hotels in the area most of which have swimming pools; it is best to
try whichever you like the look of and move on to another if it is full. Camping sites are
available and the state-subsidized Cafam vacation centre, best visited in midweek.
Many good places to stop for snacks and meals, often with family facilities, eg *Parador
Las Villas*, near the Girardot bypass.

Northwest from Bogotá

La Sabana de Bogotá is dotted with white farms and groves of eucalyptus. The
road to Honda passes through two small towns, Fontibón and Madrid.
   Fontibón, 10 km from Bogotá, has a good colonial church, and about 3 km
outside the town are stones with Indian pictographs. Nearby, on the road from
the old Techo airport to Bogotá, there are replicas of San Agustín statues.
   Facatativá is 40 km from Bogotá. Some 3 km from Facatativá, on the road
to the west, is the park of Piedras de Tunja, a natural rock amphitheatre with
enormous stones, numerous Indian pictographs and an artificial lake. A road
goes southwest from Facatativá to Girardot through **Tocaima**, a small, attractive holiday town with several hotels, including **D** *Bella Vista*, clean, friendly,
good simple food, swimming pool, no hot water.
   There are several attractive roads that run from the Bogotá to Honda highway through Tocaima and down to Girardot as alternatives to the Simón
Bolívar highway.

Villeta Some 71 km from Facatativá on the road to Honda, **Villeta** is another popular
Phone code: 91 weekend resort for Bogotanos. It is a busy town at the centre of the *panela*
Population 13,000; (unrefined sugar cane) industry and is in a cattle raising area. Not far away are
Altitude 950 m the waterfalls of Quebrada Cune. There is a Tourist Office in the Alcaldía
building on the Plaza, T8444412. They are helpful and have a good map of the
town; open 0800-1200, 1400-1800. The annual National Panela Festival is for
three days in January and a Band Festival in mid-August.

Sleeping AL *Mediterraneo*, C 6, No 8-68, T8444134. Pool, nice rooms, restaurant,
parking. Recommended. **B** *Báltico*, C 7, No 10-35, T8444061. Pool, pleasant. Recommended. *Pacífico*, C 5, No 6-38, T8444533, one block from Plaza. Pool, good. **C** *Colonial Plaza*, Cra 4A, No 6-07, T8444969, on corner of main plaza. Good restaurant, with
pool, pleasant. **E** *Gran San Diego*, C 3, No 4-173, near old railway station. A line of very
tall palm trees outside the entrance, pleasant, friendly. Recommended. **E** *Tropical*, C
4, 2 blocks from Tourist Office. Basic, clean.

Eating *El Maná*, C 6, No 6-52. Vegetarian, good. *Llamarade*, near the centre. Good
value. *Pizzería*, C 4, near plaza. Good. Many places to eat and several bars, ice cream
parlours and cafes around the plaza.

Transport Buses The terminal is at the edge of town, a short walk downhill from the
centre. To **Bogotá** with Expreso Bolivariano, frequent, 2 ½ hrs, US$3.70. To **Honda**, 1
hr, US$2. Look out for *Piedra de Bolívar*, on which is marked all the occasions when
Bolívar passed through the town.

About 16 km east of Villeta, on the new road which goes up to Bogotá, is **La Vega**, a pleasant, quiet town surrounded by coffee farms and *fincas*. **C** *Cabañas Río Ila,* on main road, T8457067/8403. Pool, restaurant. About 15 km north of Villeta, near **Tobia**, a new area of rafting has opened up on the Río Negro. For information, call *Kumandai*, T2557518 (Bogotá).

Midway between Villeta and Honda is **Guaduas**. In the towns of the *tierra caliente* northwest of the capital, Guaduas preserves its colonial charm more than the others. Founded three times between 1572 and 1644, it was a stopover on the *camino real* between Bogotá and the river at Honda. **Policarpa Salavarrieta**, heroine of the independence movement, was born here on 26 January 1796. There is a statue of her in the plaza and the **Casa de La Pola** where she lived is one block from the plaza and now an interesting museum. ■ *Entry free.*

The **Catedral de San Miguel** also on the plaza is worth a visit. **Calle Real** is the best preserved colonial street. The **Casa de los Virreyes** on the corner of the plaza at Calle Real/Cra 4, houses a small museum: Joaquin Acosta, scientist, historian and another figure in the independence movement was born here on 29 December 1800. Opposite, at Calle 2, No 4-14, is the **Museo Virrey Espelta,** which has a good collection of antiques from the Viceroy era in a beautiful colonial house. ■ *Entry US$1.*

The museum has been recently restored. **Museo de Arte y Tradiciones Populares** is open Sat-Sun and holidays. ■ *Entry US$1, tickets from the shop next door.*

The oldest house in town is the **Alcaldía** on Avenida José Antonio Galán. Simón Bolívar slept in the room on the second floor before leaving by river for Santa Marta.

About 10 km outside the town is the **Salto de Versalles**, a lovely 45 m waterfall, now a National Monument. There is a public swimming pool in Guaduas and a Sunday market. Best local dish is *quesillos*.

Sleeping D *Hostería Colonial,* C 3, No 3-30, on plaza, T8466041. Beautifully restored mansion run by English/Colombian couple, big comfortable rooms around a central patio, good restaurant. Recommended. **B** *Tacuara,* T2559193 (Bogotá). Swimming pool, riding, *cabañas*. **E** *Central Plaza,* C 4, No 3-34, T8466016. Clean, restaurant. The plaza and neighbouring streets are dotted with cafes and restaurants.

Transport Bus to **Honda,** US$1.45, 1 hr.

Guaduas
Phone code 91
Population 23,000
Altitude 1000 m

Bogotá

North from Bogotá

Interesting day trips can be made to the attractive rolling antiplano, leaving Bogotá on the Autopista del Norte (extension of Avenida 13), or on the parallel Carretera del Norte (the old road, extension of Avenida 7). On the latter, once out of Bogotá, there are many old fincas and good typical restaurants, eg *El Pórtico*, a converted *hacienda*. The two roads join at Km 24 at La Caro where a road leaves left (west) to Chía and Zipaquirá. Overlooking this junction is a large sinister house once owned by Rodríguez Gacha one of the former drug barons. By contrast, opposite is the graceful colonial bridge over the Río Bogotá, now preserved and bypassed by the road to Chía.

Chía is a busy market town with a good, typical Sunday market (bus from Avenida Caracas in Bogotá, US$0.30). Near Chía is **Tenjo**, whose metalworks are famous. On the way there you pass through Fonqueta, where tapestries are made. Walk or take a bus to La Barbanera church on a hill overlooking Sabana de Bogotá. Good restaurant just outside Chía, *Andrés Carne de Res*, with good music, nice atmosphere, good food from 1600 and lunch at weekends.

From Chía it is 6 km to **Cajicá**, a pleasant little town with good shopping for ponchos and carpets. (*La Isla*, bar, good music, reasonable prices, *La Cabaña*, opposite Texaco, good traditional food, live music, open every day).

Zipaquirá
Phone code 91
Population 62,000
Altitude 2,600 m

A further 13 km beyond is **Zipaquirá**, (commonly called Zipa) centre of a rich cattle farming district, and famous for its rock salt mine, which has been exploited for centuries, and fabulous salt cathedral (see next page). The **church** in the attractive central Plaza is also worth a visit for its stonework (despite its external appearance, it has a modern interior). The market on Tuesday is good for fruit and vegetables.

■*Entry to the new cathedral is US$4, half price on Wed, including 1¼ hrs guided tour, car park US$1, Tue-Sun 0930-1630, Sun Mass at 1200, admission by ticket. The entrance to the cave is in hills about 20 mins walk west of the town. There is an information centre and a museum at the site.*

The **Museo Quevedo Zornozo**, Calle 3, No 7-69, has interesting displays musical instruments and paraphenalia including the piano of General Santander. ■ *Open Tue-Fri 0930-1200, 1400-1600, Sat-Sun 0900-1700, US$1.*

Sleeping C-D *Hostería del Libertador,* Vía Catedral de Sal, T8523060, F8526851. Restored colonial mansion, near the mine, good food. **E** *Colonial,* C 3, No 6-57, T8522690. Showers, clean and friendly. Restaurants on main square, *El Mesón del Zipa.* Good, cheap food, US$2.50-3.00. *Asadero Colonial,* C 5/Cra 7. Good food, *arepas, bandejas.*

Transport Buses From **Bogotá:** Many from Cra 30 (Av Ciudad de Quito) from C 22 northwards, marked 'Zipa', Flota Alianza, or others, US$0.75 each way, 1¼ hrs. There is no official stop but buses go by with the 'assistant' shouting the destination. Signal and they will stop. The Zipaquirá bus station is 15 mins walk from the mines and cathedral. Zipaquirá can also be reached from Tunja (see below) by taking a Bogotá-bound bus and getting off at La Caro for connection to Zipaquirá, US$2.40. Leave plenty of time for the return journey as it can be difficult to stop Bogotá-Tunja buses at La Caro. It can also be difficult to get on a bus from Zipaquirá going north towards Villa de Leiva. You can also take the Sun tourist train from Bogotá and return in the afternoon.

Around 15 km northeast of Zipaquirá, at **Nemocón**, there are salt mines and a church, but the mines are now not operating and closed to visitors. However, there is a small but interesting **Museo de Sal** on the plaza, which includes local history and the beginnings of the salt industry in the time of the Muisca Indians. ■ *Entrance US$1.*

The main salt mine is four blocks above the museum, with some bizarre lampposts on the approach road.

Eating *El Colonial,* 100 m from the station, on the left side of the main street. Good trout and try the *chísquay* (cheesecake!). Several others nearby with chicken, meat and fish dishes, plus drink about US$3. Busy on Sun. A side (dirt) road connects with the Bogotá-Cúcuta highway.

Transport A steam-hauled *tren turístico* runs on Sun from Bogotá to Zipaquirá and Nemocón. See page 99.

Suesca About 8 km beyond Nemocón, also with access from the Bogotá to Tunja road (5 km), is **Suesca**, population 12000, noted for some interesting rock outcrops just outside the small town.

Zipaquirá – a symphony in salt

The new salt cathedral at Zipaquirá should not be missed by visitors to Colombia. The sight of this remarkable architectural and artistic achievement is enough to leave even the most cynical atheist genuflecting in awed appreciation.

It is believed that the salt dome at Zipaquirá originated from deposits around 200 million years ago which were uplifted in the late Tertiary, say 30 million years ago, and concentrated in the present site. Under pressure and heat, salt moves rather like a glacier, so signs of stratification may be lost and a homogeneous mass of salt created.

Fortunately the deposit is conveniently in the hillside above Zipaquirá, and adit mining, ie tunnelling straight into the hillside, was possible. Salt has been mined here since the 15th century, long before the Spaniards came and established the town in 1606. Many kilometres of tunnels have been excavated since then.

There was a shrine in the cave carved by the miners into the salt many years before the original cathedral started to take shape in 1950. It was dedicated in 1954 to Nuestra Señora del Rosario (patron saint of miners). It consisted of three monumental naves with rough hewn columns dominated by a large

illuminated cross. There was a special circuit that you were allowed to drive through. Continuing deterioration made the cave unsafe and it was closed in 1990.

A new salt cathedral was begun in 1991 and opened on 16 December 1995 by President Samper. It is 500 m from, and 58 m below the old cathedral. From the formal courtyard at the entrance surrounded by wax palms, you enter the cave. There is a short section before the 14 stations of the cross. Each station has been sculptured by a different artist; at their centre is a cross 4 m high, subtly lit and imaginatively executed. This is followed by sections representing the choir, narthex, baptistry (with a natural water source) and sacristy. Finally, at the lowest point in the cave, 180 m below the surface, are the nave and the north and south aisles with huge pillars growing out of the salt and dominated by the central cross, 16 m high. All is discreetly illuminated and gives a modern and austere impression.

It is not quite unique in the world. There are, for example, three salt chapels in mines at Wieliczka, 15 km southeast of Cracow, in Poland. There is even room for an underground sanatorium for patients with asthma and allergies!

The main rock escarpment is 1 km from the road alongside the Río Bogotá, which the railway follows. There are routes of every grade of difficulty on fine Cretaceous sandstone (limonite). Across the river there is another area, Los Halcones, private access only. The railway station was renovated in 2000 with the help of the British Embassy, to become the local centre for environment projects in the upper Río Bogotá region. Nearby are several equipment shops which offer climbing courses at around US$30/day including full equipment hire. Ask for Fernando Gonzalo-Rubio at *Gravedad Escuela de Montaña*, T933-443729 (mobile) or T8563326. There is a good deal of activity here particularly at weekends. Enquire in Bogotá for the possibilities of transport. There is an excellent route guide: *Escaladores en Suesca y Valle de Los Halcones* by G A Montoya and A Bonilla, 1997, US$8.

Further upriver, the Río Bogotá goes through a gorge (Cañón de Suesca) which can be visited.

About 40 km northwest of Zipaquirá, on a road which eventually leads to the Río Magdalena, is **Pacho** in a pleasant hilly landscape at about 1,600 m, which is good for walking and riding. **A3** *San Nicolás*, Calle 7, No 28-277, on the outskirts of town, gardens, pool, restaurant, negotiate price during week. Colectivo from Zipa US$2.

Continuing north from Zipaquirá towards Chichinquirá, the road crosses a high ridge with some impressive mountain scenery, followed by a turning left to Tausa and **El Embalse de Neusa**, which is popular at weekends for watersports, and 48 km north of Zipaquirá is **Ubaté**, the cheese-making centre of the Sabana. There's a good restaurant, *La Rueda* in Plaza Catedral, with trout from the local lakes a speciality. A spur from the road to Lenguazaque branches left to Guachetá, 21 km from Ubaté, near which is the **Laguna de Fúquene** (Devil's Lake), now about 4,850 ha of water with four cultivated islands. In times past the lake was much more extensive as can readily be seen as the main road follows the old shore line. Not only is a good deal of the lake permanently silted up but thick sea-weed like reeds cover much of the remainder though progress is now being made to clear the reeds and open up the lake for fishing and leisure activities. For Chichinquirá, see the next chapter.

Bogotá

Bogotá to Cúcuta

4

Bogotá to Cúcuta

The main road route from Bogotá to Venezuela passes through some of the most interesting and attractive places and scenery in the country. In some places the route is spectacular; nowhere is it dull. Recently a new road to the Caribbean coast was built in the Magdalena valley which is longer but quicker than the old. This has marginally reduced the heavy traffic on this route making it all the more attractive for the visitor.

It starts in **Cundinamarca,** *north of Bogotá and makes for Tunja, the capital of* **Boyacá** *Department. Almost immediately the traveller is plunged into the fascinating history of the country, the homeland of the Muisca Indians, the Laguna de Guatavita (perhaps the nearest the Spanish conquistadores came to finding their El Dorado), and the site of the Battle of Boyacá, the most decisive point in Simón Bolívar's career, all before reaching the fine Spanish legacy of Tunja.*

Beyond are several almost untouched colonial towns, for example, Villa de Leiva and Barichara, cobblestone villages and ancient ways. The finest peaks of the Colombian Andes are here too, in the enticing shape of the Sierra Nevavda del Cocuy, a paradise for trekkers and a part of the country which few people visit. Further north, through **Santander** *Department, the road swoops down to the Río Fonce, then the Chicamocha canyon, where river sports compete with hang gliding, caving and climbing. Then the road climbs over the high pass into* **Norte de Santander** *Department for the ride down through more history around Pamplona to Cúcuta, on the border with Venezuela.*

Highlights of Bogotá to Cucutá

★ Reliving Simón Bolívar's victories at Puente de Boyacá and Pantano de Vargas.

★ Feeling the history and meeting the dinosaurs of Villa de Leiva.

★ Making a pilgrimage to Chiquinquirá or La Candelaria.

★ Trying homemade chicha in Guane and hormigas culonas in Bucamaranga.

★ Looking over the edge of the Chicamocha canyon.

★ Admiring the heliconias of San Gil's Parque El Gallineral after canoeing the Río Fonce.

★ The majesty of the snow peaks of El Cocuy.

★ Absorbing the precolumbian past in the Chibcha Bohío in Sogamoso.

Bogotá to Sesquilé The road out of Bogotá is the *autopista* to La Caro, from where the road goes through rich agricultural country, an area of market gardens, pastures and many crops including fruit and flowers.

At Km 32.5 is the Alpina Yogurt factory and the Parque Puerto de Sopó with artificial lake. 30 km east into the Sabana is **Sopó,** where an image of the Saviour has appeared in an eroded stone; the paintings of angels in the church are strange and worth seeing (ask at the Casa Cural for entry to the church - give a tip).

Continuing north from Puerto de Sopó is the large Jaime Duque amusement park created by one of Colombia's pioneer pilots. A replica of the first Avianca aircraft is the centrepiece. A few kilometres east of the main road is **Sesquilé**, with several restaurants but no accommodation. On your right beyond the town is the large lake and dam **Represa de Tominé**. There is a campsite on the lakeside.

Guatavita

Phone code: 91
Colour map 2, grid C5
Altitude: 2,650 m

About 17 km from Sesquilé (75 km from Bogotá), overlooking the lake is the small, modern town of **Guatavita Nueva**, which was built in colonial style when the old town of Guatavita was submerged by the reservoir. The original inhabitants were unwilling to stay in the new town, so it is now a weekend haunt for Bogotanos and tourists. There is a cathedral, artisan workshops and two small museums; one devoted to the Muisca Indians and the other to relics of the old Guatavita church, including a delightful Debain harmonium (Paris 1867). The Sunday market is best in the morning, before Bogotanos get there.

Balsa Muisca, Guatavita (Museo de Oro, Bogotá)

The Gilded Man

The basis of the El Dorado (Gilded Man) story is established fact. It was the custom of the Chibcha king to be coated annually with resin, on which gold dust was stuck, and then to be taken out on the lake on a ceremonial raft. He then plunged into the lake and emerged with the resin and gold dust washed off. The lake was also the repository of precious objects thrown in as offerings;. There have been several attempts to drain it (the first, by the Spaniards in colonial times, was the origin of the sharp cut in the crater rim) and many items have been recovered over the years. The factual basis of the El Dorado story was confirmed by the discovery of a miniature raft (balsa muisca) with ceremonial figures on it, made from gold wire, which is now one of the most prized treasures of the Museo de Oro in Bogotá. Part of the raft is missing; the story is that the gold from it ended up in one of the finder's teeth! (Read John Hemming's The Search for El Dorado on the subject).

Transport Bus from Bogotá (Flota Valle de Tenza, Cra 25, No 15-72, recommended; Flota Aguila, Cra 15 No 14-59), US$1.45, 2-3 hrs, departures 0730, 0800 and 0930; last return bus at 1730. There is no formal accommodation. However, the tourist information booth can find places to stay for visitors.

Laguna de Guatavita Also called Lago de Amor by locals, this is where the legend of El Dorado originated. The lake is a quiet, beautiful place. You can walk right round it close to the water level in 1½ hours, or climb to the rim of the crater in several places. Opinions differ on whether the crater is volcanic or a meteorite impact, but from the rim at 3,100 m there are extensive views over the varied countryside.

Getting there You can walk (2-3 hrs) or ride (US$7/horse) from Guatavita Nueva to the lake. An easier approach is from a point on the Sesquilé-Guatavita Nueva road (the bus driver will let you off at the right place) where there is a sign 'Vía Lago Guatavita'. Nearby, on the main road, are good places to eat at weekends, eg *Pinos*, 3 km south of the turning, trout, *carne asada* and *chorizos* are specialities. There is a good campsite nearby. From the main road to the lakeside the road is paved as far as a school, about half way. Follow the signs. This road and subsequent track can be driven in a good car to within 300 m of the lake where there is a car park and good restaurant, *Hostería Caminos a El Dorado*, open at weekends.

A short distance beyond Sesquilé, the main road north goes past the end of the **Sisca** reservoir, a fishing and windsurfing centre, popular at weekends. At the *Refugio de Sisca* restaurant, try the outrageously delicious *empanadas de trucha*, (cornmeal and trout snack), US$0.60. For information on windsurfing, contact Erhard Martín (see page 50).

Boyacá Department

Boyacá has a lot going for it. Among the Department's many attractions are some elegantly-wasted colonial towns, Indian sites, a major religious centre, budget-busting craft villages and plenty of achingly beautiful wild scenery, best of which is El Cocuy, with its jaw-dropping range of ice peaks, which have to be seen to be believed. The Department is mostly highland with a pleasant, invigorating climate, it has good road communications and is very accessible from Bogotá.

Southeast Boyacá

The main road from Bogotá crosses into Boyacá Department at Villapinzón. About 20 km into Boyacá, at Km 103, a turning right leads through delightful, rich open country to Nueva Colón and, 26 km from the main road, to **Tibaná.** Nearby, hidden in the lush countryside is the **A** *Hacienda Baza*, T98-7338033, once a small Dominican monastery, now a very attractive hotel, with modern comforts set in a 17th century building, very carefully restored by the Ospina family. Excellent home-produced food, horses available, fine walking in a very peaceful environment. Recommended.

Occasonal earthquakes do, however, disturb the area, as the church in Tibaná shows. This has a fine façade but the interior was badly damaged, and is yet to be repaired. There are fine flowering trees in the plaza. A paved road runs north through Jenesano to Tunja. South from Tibaná, the road follows the Río Jenesano to Chinavita and Tenza.

Tenza
Phone code: 98
Population :2500
Altitude: 1,600 m

There are three ways to approach the Tenza valley in the southern corner of Boyacá Department, one from the north described above, the more usual route from Bogotá turning off the main road just past the Sisga reservoir, or by the poor road which comes up from Villanueva (Casanare) in the Llanos. The famous bridge of the battle of Boyacá crosses the river (at Tenza called the Río Garagoa) which flows south to the **Represa de Chivor** and eventually joins the Río Meta and the Orinoco. Before reaching the Chivor dam, the valley opens out as the **Valle de Tenza**, a pleasant comfortable contrast to the highlands.

Tenza itself is a friendly town, popular at weekends, with many possibilities of country walks. There is a monument in the Plaza Principal to the heroes and martyrs of the independence movement, of which it was an important centre at the time. The area is also renowned for basketry, carved wooden bowls and decorative hand-woven textiles. Try *Artesanías Diana*, same building as *Hospedería Zue*, which offers good value.

Sleeping AL *Turística de Tenza,* Cra 5, No 5-36, on plaza, T7527019. Clean, comfortable, pool, good restaurant, try the *trucha al ajillo.* **E** *Hospedería Zue,* Cra 7, No 4-63, T7527051. With bath, good value. Also several restaurants on the main street.

About 10 km beyond Tenza is the Chivor reservoir, set dramatically in a deep valley. Above is the small town of **Chivor**, noted for its emerald mines, and 16 km short of Tunja on the main road from Bogotá, is the site of the **Battle of Boyacá,** one of the most significant events in the history of Colombia. Overlooking the bridge at Boyacá is a large monument to Bolívar. Bolívar took Tunja on 6 August 1819, and next day his troops, fortified by a British Legion, the only professional soldiers among them, fought the Spaniards on the banks of the swollen Río Boyacá. With the loss of only 13 killed and 53 wounded they captured 1,600 men and 39 officers. Only 50 men escaped back to Bogotá, and when these told their tale, the Viceroy Samao fled in such haste that he left behind him half a million pesos of the royal funds.

There are actually three bridges here; the new modern one taking the main road, the previous road bridge, and the reconstructed original bridge (illustrated), an important symbol of the famous battle. This 'original' bridge in fact replaced the first wooden crossing. The river here is not significant but the defile through which it flows was an important natural barrier. Apart from the fine bronze monument of the Liberator, there is a *ciclorama* (audiovisual and exhibition hall) and restaurant (not operating in early 2000), with a triumphal arch and obelisk on the north side. Also marked is the vantage point from which Bolívar directed the battle. ■ *Open 0800-1800 daily, entry (per car) US$1.50.*

Tunja

Tunja is capital of Boyacá Department. Like many South American towns and cities, it doesn't look anything special from around the bus terminal, but it's worth stopping for at least a few hours as Tunja has some of the finest colonial treasures of Colombia.

Phone code: 98
Colour map 2, grid B5
Population 120,000
Altitude 2,780 m

Bogotá to Cúcuta

Getting there There are 4 routes that converge on Tunja, all busy and in good condition. The main road from Bogotá through to Bucamaranga and the Caribbean bears left at the northern outskirts of the town. Straight on leads to Sogamoso, the Lago de Tota and Yopal and to the Sierras of Cucuy. West lies Villa de Leiva and Chiquinquirá. There are good bus services along all these roads; the bus station is near the main highway which skirts the east side of town. There is no air service to Tunja and the railway no longer takes passengers.

Ins & outs

Getting around From the bus station to the main square is a steep walk up, but the centre of the town and the main things to see are readily accessible from the Plaza de Bolívar.

Tunja is 137 km from Bogotá. It stands in a cool dry mountainous area, on a platform which slopes down to the north and east to the valley of the Río Chulo. There are good views from the centre and the Parque Centenario of the rolling hills to the east and the continental divide between the Magdalena and Orinoco river systems. The climate is cool, with a mean temperature of 12°C.

When the Spaniards arrived in what is now Boyacá, Tunja was aleady an Indian city, the seat of the Zipa, one of the two Muisca kings. He ruled over the northern part of the Muisca territories, the most populous and well developed Indian area of what is now Colombia. It was refounded as a Spanish city by Gonzalo Suárez Rendón in 1539. The city formed an independent Junta in 1811, and Bolívar fought under its aegis during the Magdalena campaign of 1812. Six years later he fought the decisive battle of Boyacá, nearby (see previous and next pages).

The **Cathedral**, on the Plaza de Bolívar, has a romanesque façade and right tower, with an unusual balustrade along the roof of the west front. It dates from the end of the 16th century. Inside, it is a mixture of styles, gothic and moorish, with ornamented pillars and colonial paintings. There are several fine side chapels and a mausoleum honouring Gonzalo Suárez Rendón, founder of the city. The **Casa de la Cultura**, opposite the cathedral, also 16th century, contains the **Museo de Museos** in which there are many reproductions of famous, principally European, masterpieces. This is where Simón Bolívar stayed before the

Sights

👉 *Bolívar – the liberation campaign*

In May 1819, a force of about 2000 men set out from Venezuela and met up with Santander's forces at Tame. It was the beginning of the rainy season and they (correctly) believed that the Spaniards would not expect an attack at this time of the year. On 22 June, after a very difficult march across the flooded plains, crossing the many rivers, they came to the foot of the Andes where they proposed to cross. Bolívar chose the rarely used route across the Páramo de Pisba, a barren windswept area of the Cordillera Oriental, the lowest pass over 3,200 m and consequently very cold, especially at night. Given that many of his troops were poorly clad and untrained llaneros from the hot plains, it's no wonder there were many deaths from exposure and few of the 800 horses they began with survived. They descended from the páramo and reached Socha on 6 July.

There were several skirmishes during the next few days, including at Bonza and Tópaga as they moved south. On 20th July, a British detachment under Colonel Rooke that had been guarding the rear, arrived. Asked if he had suffered any losses crossing the páramo, he replied, no. When it later transpired that a quarter of Rooke's men had perished, he replied: 'It is also true that they deserved their fate; for those were the most poorly behaved, and the corps has profited by their death'.

By the 25th July, the Spaniards had realised the situation and the patriots

met a strong force near Paipa at the Pantano de Vargas. The ensuing battle did not go well for Bolívar's men and they were on the brink of defeat when they were saved by two heroic actions: a desperate last-ditch counter-attack by the English Legion in which Colonel Rooke was killed, and a subsequent wild charge by a squadron of llanero lancers who had just arrived on the battlefield. Although the Battle of Boyacá 13 days later is remembered as the crowning glory of Bolívar's military career in Colombia, defeat at the Pantano de Vargas would certainly have changed the course of history.

On 6 August 1819, Bolívar reached Tunja and the following day came up against the royalist army, 16 km south of Tunja, intent on blocking his advance towards Bogotá. The Río Boyacá here is little more than a stream but the river valley is narrow and steep-sided and a good natural line of defence. The Spaniards held the bridge and the steep southern slopes of the valley. Yet despite the strength of their position, they disintegrated and fled almost at the first patriotic attack. 1600 prisoners were taken (about half the army) including the Spanish general and most of his officers for the loss of 13 killed and 53 wounded patriots. Three days later, on 10 August, Bolívar entered Bogotá to a hero's welcome.

battle of Boyacá. Cultural events are held here from time to time. Also on Plaza Bolívar is the **Casa del Fundador Suárez Rendón**, one of the few extant mansions of a Spanish conquistador in Colombia (1539-43). See the attractive peaceful courtyard with a fine view of the countryside through the gateway and the unique series of plateresque paintings on the ceilings. ■ *Open Wed-Sun. On the left at the entrance is the Tourist Information Office.*

Of the many colonial buildings, the most remarkable is the church of **Santo Domingo**, one block west of the plaza, a masterpiece begun in 1594, with its splendid interior covered with wood most richly carved. There are several chapels in the side aisles, but the Chapel of Our Lady of Rosario, the work of Fray Pedro Bedón, glistens with gold and glass ornamentation and is one of the finest examples of the period in Colombia.

Two blocks east of the plaza is another fine building, the **Santa Clara La Real chapel** (1580), with some fine wood carving in the Moorish style particularly in the ceiling of the single nave chapel. There is fine ornamentation everywhere, interesting oil paintings and wall decorations revealed after a recent restoration. This was the chapel to the Santa Clara convent, begun in 1574, which was probably the first to be established in Colombia. One of the nuns, Sister Josefa del Castillo y Guevara lived in a cell near the choir for over 50 years and was buried here. Some of her writings are exhibited in the museum into which part of the former convent has been converted.

Most of the churches, except the San Lázaro chapel, are open for visitors during the day, or at least at Mass times. All are indicated on the map

One block from the plaza, on Calle 20, is the house of the writer **Casa Don Juan de Vargas,** built 1590, has been restored as a museum of colonial Tunja, with many interesting exhibits relating to the city. Note the murals, gold candelsticks and particularly the fine ceiling of the upper floor. ■ *Entry US$0.50 includes guided tour in several languages, open 0800-1200, 1300-1800.*

One block south, on Calle 19, is the **Casa Juan de Castellanos**, a chronicler and friend of Suárez Rendón, is another notable colonial building, much of it carefully restored and again contains some fine ceiling paintings, both religious and of flora and fauna. **Casa de Capitán Antonio Ruíz Mancipe** is now a bank, on Calle 18, but much of the original has been preserved or restored.

Four blocks from the plaza, on Carrera 11, the church of **Santa Bárbara** dates from 1592 and also has much fine ornamentation and a *mudejar* ceiling. The treasury has many valuable items of gold and silver, part donated by the mother of Charles V of Spain. The chapel of La Epístola is the best of several. In the nearby parish house are some notable religious objects, including silk embroidery from the 18th century.

A short walk further south, in **Parque Bosque de la República**, is the adobe wall against which three martyrs of the Independence were shot in 1816. The wall, and bullet holes, are protected by a glass screen. Ask the tourist police guarding these buildings for information: they are helpful and knowledgeable.

The church and convent of **San Francisco** is another 16th century construction notable for its white colonial façade, sculptures of San Francisco and Mary Magdalen, striated pillars and the gilded arch over the central retable. Also note the Altar de los Pelícanos, believed to have been brought from Quito, which is in the chapel of the Virgin de las Angustias.

The church of **San Ignacio** has an interesting embossed façade constructed by the Jesuits in the 17th century. It is now used for cultural presentations.

The small **San Lázaro** chapel, dating from 1587, restored during the 18th century, has four semi-circular arches supporting an ornamental ceiling. It is at 2940m overlooking the town and is a fine viewpoint. (Take advice before walking up there).

Further from the centre, but also worth a visit, is the chapel of **El Topo** monastery, built in the 17th century with interesting silverwork and a statue to the Virgin de los Milagros, and **San Agustín,** the moorish church of the former Augustinian monastery, completed about 1600. This church is now a library and the monastery houses the Boyacá archives and the history department of the Universidad Pedagógico y Tecnológica de Colombia, whose main campus is just north of the city.

Excursions There are two precolumbian sites to visit outside the city. The **Cojines del Zaque** (literally the cushions of the Zaque, who was the principal chief of the Muisca government) is a ritual site around a large rock with pillow-like features carved into the rock. It is thought that sacrifices were made here.

Bogotá to Cúcuta

The **Pozo de Donato**, a short distance northeast out of town on the road to Paipa, was a well or pond also used for Muisca rituals. Legend had it that this included gold offerings. In the early days of the colonisation, a Spaniard by the name of Jeronimo Donato drained the pool looking for gold – which he did not find. The Pozo de Donato is in the grounds of the Universidad Pedagógico, which has done considerable archaeological work in the region. There is a small attractive park now around the pond.

Tunja

■ Sleeping	3 Casa Colonial	6 Hostería San Carlos	9 Lord/Dux/Saboy
1 Americano	4 Conquistador	7 Hunza	10 San Francisco
2 Boyacá Plaza	5 El Cid	8 Imperial	11 San Ignacio Plaza

AL *Hunza,* C 21A, No 10-66, T7424111,(Bogotá 3470099) F7424119. Modern, break- **Sleeping**
fast included, good restaurant, pool, sauna. **AL** *Boyacá Plaza,* C 18, No 11-22,
T7401116, F7427635. Modern, including breakfast, parking, good. **A** *San Ignacio
Plaza*, C 18 No 10-51, T7437583, F7423472. Modern, pleasant.

B *Hostería San Carlos*, Cra 11, No 20-12, T7423716. Colonial style, interestingly furnished, good restaurant, friendly. Highly recommended. **B** *Conquistador*, C 20, No
8-92, T7431465, F7423534, corner of Plaza de Bolívar. 22 traditional rooms round
courtyard, tartan blankets, nice restaurant, good. **C** *San Francisco*, Cra 9, No 18-90,
T7426645. 3rd floor, on Plaza de Bolívar near cathedral, clean, friendly. **C** *El Cid*, Cra 10,
No 20-78, T7423458. Comfortable, nothing special.

E *Lord*, C 19, No 10-64, T7423556. Small rooms, hot water, friendly but rundown.
E *Dux*, next to *Lord*. Nice creaky old hotel, good rooms, cold water, good value.
E *Saboy*, C 19, No 10-40, T7423492. Nice covered patio, clean, friendly, family run.
E *Americano*, Cra 11, No 18-70, T7422471. Friendly, hot water, attractive lobby.

F *Príncipe,* near bus station, 5 mins from Plaza de Bolívar. Limited hot water, small
rooms but clean. Recommended. **F** *Casa Colonial*, Cra 8, No 20-40. Clean, safe,
friendly. **F** *Imperial*, C 19, No 7-43. Clean, basic, cold water, friendly, use of kitchen.
F *Bolívar*, opposite bus station. Clean, basic. The area around the bus station is said
not to be safe at night.

San Ricardo, C 19, No 8-38. Good. *Surtipan*, C 20, No 12-58. Good cakes and coffee. **Eating**
Estar de Hunzahúa, C 20, No 11-30 (2nd floor). Good value. Recommended. *Pollo
Listo*, Cra 11, No 19-30. Good. *Santo Domingo*, Cra 11, No 19-66. Good. *Americano,*
Cra 11, 18-70. Light meals. *Café El Rinconcito*, C 20, No 9-14. Good coffee and *arepitas*
until late. *Doña Cecilia*, Cra 8, No 18-18. Good *comida corriente*. Also many fast food,
pizza etc outlets in the pedestrianised streets near Plaza de Bolívar.

The main local festival is in late May, culminating on the first Sunday in June with the **Festivals**
crowning of the queen amid popular and cultural festivities. There is a special ceremony at the chapel of El Topo at this time. During the week before Christmas, there is
a lively festival with local music, traditional dancing and fireworks.

The market is near the Plaza de Toros on outskirts of town, open every day (good for **Shopping**
ruanas and blankets). Fri is the main market day.

The bus station is a 400 m walk steeply down C 17 from the city centre. To **Bogotá**, **Transport**
2½-4½ hrs, US$5. To **Villa de Leiva,** colectivos, every 30 mins, 1 hr, US$1.60. To
Duitama, Cotrans, and others. To **Bucaramanga,** hourly, 7½ hrs, US$17.

Banks Several banks in the C 20/Cra 10 area. *Joyería Frances* next to the *Banco de Bogotá* **Directory**
changes TCs.
Communications Internet: *Coffenet*, Cra 9, No 19-98, upstairs, US$2/hr.
Tourist offices In *Casa del Fundador*, Plaza de Bolívar, helpful. Also try 'Fondo Mixto' Cámera
de Comercio building, C 21, No 10-52. For information on Boyacá: tourist office adjacent to the
Hotel Hunza.

Villa de Leiva

About 40 km west through the mountains is the colonial town of **Villa de Leiva**   *Phone code: 98*
(also spelt Leyva). This is one of Colombia's very special places. It is not on any   *Colour map 2, grid B5*
important through route and there are no significant natural resources nearby to   *Population 4,500*
be exploited, so it has been left alone and now is prized by Colombians and visi-   *Altitude 2,144 m*
tor alike. Although it can be quite busy at weekends and holidays, even then it is a
quiet, charming place where you can feel the past. There are many places to stay

Bogotá to Cúcuta

and you can judge the character of most of them by their names. The one modern full service hotel, like the bus station, is discretely well away from the **Plaza Mayor** where you have simply to stand for a few minutes and stare.

Ins & outs   **Getting there**   To reach it from Bogotá, turn left at the Puente de Boyacá monument, and go through the small attractive town of **Samacá** which has a pretty plaza ornamented with bougainvilla arcades. The church has a bright white/yellow interior and a fine gilt retable. Alternatively, go through Tunja and out by the northwest corner of the town. The two roads join and you must turn right at Sáchica for the final 6 km to Villa de Leiva. Most of the public transport goes through Tunja. There is an alternative from Tunja, staying on the main road towards Bucaramanga, and after 34 km, turn left at Arcabuco. This is an unsurfaced road and rough in places but you will see fine scenery as it goes alongside the Iguaque National Sanctuary.

Getting around   This is very much a place for walking around. Many of the streets are cobbled and such traffic as there is, travels at a snail's pace. If you want to visit the attractions outside Villa de Leiva, there are taxis who will take you. Roads locally are poor and dusty, and, with little tree cover it can get hot in the middle of the day.

Tourist offices *Oficina Municipal de Turismo*, Cra 9, No 13-04 just off the plaza, open daily 0800-1800, local maps, gives advice on cheaper accommodation. The staff are most helpful.

Villa de Leiva

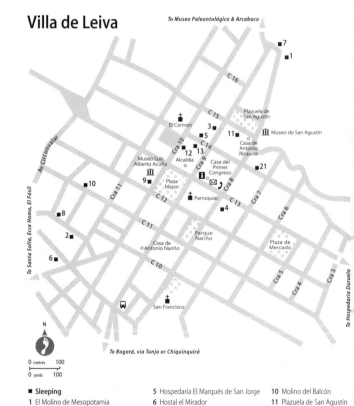

■ **Sleeping**
1 El Molino de Mesopotamia
2 Estancia El Olivo
3 Hospedaje El Mesón de los Virreyes
4 Hospedaje El Sol de la Villa
5 Hospedaría El Marqués de San Jorge
6 Hostal el Mirador
7 Hostal la Candelaria
8 Los Llanitos
9 Mesón de la Plaza Mayor
10 Molino del Balcón
11 Plazuela de San Agustín
12 Posada de los Angeles
13 Posada San Martín

The Bachué Legend

Shortly after the dawning of the first day, a woman called **Bachué** and a three year old boy arose from the icy waters of Iguaque lake, high in the sierra. They descended into the plains, where the boy grew up, married Bachué and they proceeded to populate the world. Having done so, they returned to the lake, changed into serpents and disappeared into the waters. This was the origin of the Chibcha/Muisca people, and small statues of gold and wood of Bachué and the boy have been venerated ever since.

The town dates back, like Tunja, to the early days of Spanish rule, but unlike Tunja, it has been declared a National Monument so will not be modernized. It was founded by Hernán Suárez de Villalobos in 1572 by order of the first president of Nueva Granada (see page 397), Andrés Díaz Venero de Leiva.

Sights

Two **colonial houses** are particularly worth a visit. One is the house in which **Antonio Nariño** lived, at Carrera 9, No 10-39. He translated the *Rights of Man* into Spanish. This is expected to reopen in 2000 after renovations. ■ *Open Tue-Sun 0900-1230, 1400-1800.*

The second is the building known as the **Casa del Primer Congreso** in which the first Convention of the United Provinces of New Granada was held, at Calle 13 and Carrera 9, on the corner of the plaza, part of which is used by the Tourist Office.

Also worth a visit is the restored birthplace of the independence hero **Antonio Ricaurte** at Carrera 8 and Calle 15. Ricaurte was born in Villa de Leiva and died in 1814 at San Mateo, Venezuela, in a famous act of courageous self-sacrifice while fighting in Bolívar's army. The house has an attractive courtyard and garden. ■ *Wed-Sun 0900-1200, 1400-1700. There is a statue of Ricaurte on Plazuela San Agustín.*

On the Plaza Mayor is the **Casa-Museo Luis Alberto Acuña**, housing fascinating examples of Acuña's work, is well worth a visit. ■ *Entry US$0.75, (extra to take photographs).*

The **Monasterio de las Carmelitas,** at Calle 14 and Carrera 10, has one of the best museums of religious art in Colombia. ■*Open Sat-Sun 1400-1700.* The monastery also includes the **Convento** and the **Iglesia del Carmen**, a simple, dignified church with a large fine Lady Chapel, all worth a visit. The **Iglesia de San Agustín** is now being converted into a museum.

An interesting and well displayed **palaeontological museum** has been opened 15 minutes walk north of the town on Carrera 9. ■ *Entrance US$0.75.*

Sleeping

Villa de Leiva is usually quiet on the early days of the week and some places may be closed

L3 *Hospedería Duruelo*, C 13, No 2-88, T7320222. Modern colonial style, beautiful views, nice gardens, also conference hotel, good food.

AL *El Molino la Mesopotamia*, C del Silencio (top of Cra 8), T7320235. A beautifully restored colonial mill originally dating from 1568, 10% rebate for booking 10 days ahead, imaginative use of water in garden landscaping including natural swimming pool, excellent home cooking, unique dining room around original millstone, beautiful gardens, a memorable hotel. Recommended. **AL** *Plazuela de San Agustín*, C 15, No 8-65, T7320842, F7320447. Well appointed hotel, attractive patio, nicely decorated.

A *Mesón de la Plaza Mayor*, Cra 10, No 12-31, T7320425, (T2187741 Bogotá). Beautifully restored *hospedaría*. **A** *Hospedaje El Mesón de Los Virreyes*, Cra 9, No 14-51, T7320252. With hot water, parking, good restaurant. **A** *Hostal La Candelaria*, C 18, No 8-12, next to *Molino de Mesopotamia*, T7230534, 7 rooms, family atmosphere, delightful, excellent breakfast. Recommended.

B *Hospedaría El Marquéz de San Jorge*, C 14, No 9-20, T7320240. With breakfast, colonial mansion, beautiful courtyard, very clean, parking. **B** *Los Llanitos*, C 9, No 12-31, T7320018. 5 mins' walk from main plaza, quiet, hot water, very friendly, good food. **B** *Posada de Los Angeles*, Cra 10, No 13-94, T7320562. With breakfast, attractive small hotel, balconies, restaurant.

C *Molino del Balcón*, Cra 12, No 11-51. Colonial building, garden, friendly.

D *Hospedaje El Sol de la Villa*, Cra 8, No 12-28, T7320224. Safe, clean, hot shower, very good breakfast, cooking facilities on request, good value. Recommended.

E *Posada San Martín*, C 14 between Cras 9/10. With bath, breakfast, good value. **E** *Estancia El Olivo*, Transversal 10, No 7-91. Bed and breakfast, simple. **E** *Hostal El Mirador*, Transversal 8, No 6-94. New, good value.

It is also possible to stay at the Monastery of Ecce Homo, see above. Booking advisable during holidays and at weekends or get there early. It is also worthwhile to try bargaining Mon-Thu.

Youth Hostel *Los Aceitunos*, Transversal 10, No 9-41, T7320282/0822. 150 beds, family rooms, attractive courtyard, restaurant, pool, *cabañas*, camping area.

Camping *Estadero San Luis*, Av Circunvalar, T7320617, capacity 70. *Iguaque Campestre Camping Club*, Km 1 Vía Hipódromo, T7320889, 15 mins walk north of plaza on road to Arcabuco. Ask for advice on other sites at the Tourist office.

Eating *Nueva Granada*, C 13, No 7-66. Good value, friendly, classical guitar music on demand. *El Rincón Bachué*, Cra 9, No 15-17, T7320884, along from china shop on corner. Interesting decor, nice food. *Casa Blanca*, C 13, No 7-16. Good juices (try *feijoa*), and *comida corriente*, open till 2100. Recommended. *Tienda de Teresa*, Cra 10, No 13-72. Good breakfasts. *Café y qué Café*, C 12, No 8-88. Excellent *tinto*. *Zarina Galería Café*, C 14, No 7-67. Antique décor, good. *Real Audiencia*, Cra 9, No 13-99. Local and international dishes, open till 2100. *El Candelero*, Cra 9, No 11-28. Full menu, good. *La Gran Mojarra*, Cra 9, No 11-16. Fish, light meals. *La Misión*, in Centro Verarte, Cra 9, No 13-09. Salads, light meals, good.

Restaurants tend to close early in the evening, especially during the week

There are *pizzerías* and chicken restaurants round the Plaza and along Cra 10 towards the bus station. There are many small bars near the centre, especially on Cra 9.

Festivals Villa de Leiva celebrates the *Virgen del Carmen* each year from **13-17 Jul.** In **Aug** (check dates) an international kite festival is held in the Plaza Mayor and a festival of light is held every year in **mid-Dec**.

Shopping The shops in the plaza and the adjoining streets have an excellent selection of Colombian handicrafts and offer many bargains. Market day is Sat, held in the Plaza del Mercado (not the Plaza Mayor).

Tour Operators *Guías & Travesías*, C 12, No 8A-31, T7320359, arranges trips throughout the region, guides for Iguaque National Park, Enrique Maldonado is the director amd is very helpful.

Transport **Buses** The bus station is in the 8th block of Cra 9. It is a good idea to book the return journey on arrival. To **Tunja,** 1 hr, US$2 with Flota Reina or Valle de Tenza, minibuses US$1.60, every 30 mins. To **Bogotá** via Tunja, takes 4 hrs, US$6, several companies, and via Zipaquirá and Chiquinquirá, US$6.70. To **Ráquira** busetas at 0730, 0800, 1740, 1930 US$1, taxi, US$2.50. To **Moniquirá**, 1000 connects with bus to **Bucamaranga,** thus avoiding Tunja.

Directory **Banks** *Banco Popular* and *Banco Agrario* in the Plaza will give pesos against Visa, limited hours. There is a Visa ATM in the Plaza.
Communications Post Office: in **Telecom** building, C 13, No 8-26.

Useful addresses Instituto von Humboldt main office at Claustro de San Agustín, T7320174. Excellent research and documentation centre for environmental studies. Publications sold. Call before visiting.

Around Villa de Leiva

The wide valley to the west of Villa de Leiva abounds in fossils; 5 km along the road to Santa Sofía you will see the road signs for **El Fósil**. The skeleton displayed is a Plesiosaur group reptile, possibly a small Kronosaurus, found here in 1977, and the museum was built around it. The second exhibit is a baby of the same group, complete with tail, found in 2000 and placed alongside. They were similar to dolphins with flippers but had a fine set of teeth. The museum contains a wide selection of other Mesozoic and Cretaceous exhibits. ■ *Open daily 0800-1800, US$1.*

About 2 km from El Fósil along this road is the turning for (1 km) the well-endowed archaeological site of **El Infiernito**, where there are several huge carved phalluses (which make popular photo opportunties!) and a solar calendar. ■ *0900-1200, 1400-1700, closed Mon, admission US$0.50.*

About 6 km beyond the Infiernito turning is a track on the left for the **Monastery of Ecce-Homo** (founded 1620); note the fossils in the floor at the entrance. The monastery has had a turbulent history. It was built by the Dominicans between 1650 and 1695, but a century later it was taken over by the military and the friars expelled. It was later abandoned until 1920 when it was reclaimed by the Dominicans, and some restoration was done. It has been repeatedly robbed since then, and some of the religious art is now in the Chiquinquirá museum for safe-keeping. What can be seen of the church, chapel and monastery is impressive, but the fabric and roof are in a poor state. *Entry US$1, open normal hours, just knock on the door.* Efforts are being made to modernise the living quarters which are used for religious conferences, or for the public to stay, if unoccupied. It costs US$7.50-$10 for accommodation, meals at US$2.50 available if preordered, T(098)7320277 or (mobile) 0332264588. Camping with permission of the monks.

Getting there There are buses from Villa de Leiva (check times) going to Santa Sofía, US$0.50; it is 30 mins to the crossing, then a 2 km walk to the monastery. A good day trip is to take the bus to Ecce Homo and walk back to Villa de Leiva via El Fósil and El Infernito.

Beyond Santa Sofía is La Cueva de Hayal, a cave set in beautiful scenery. A tour including most of these attractions leaves the plaza at 0930, Sat/Sun, US$5, recommended.

Some 20 km from Villa de Leiva on the road to Arcabuco, there is a right turn for the **Santuario de Fauna y Flora de Iguaque,** run by MA as a National Park.

Iguaque National Sanctuary

Ins and outs The entrance to the Park is 3 km from the junction; the road is in poor condition but saloon cars can make it if there has not been heavy rain.

Getting around About 40 mins walk up the valley from the entrance is a tourist centre with accommodation for 60 and a restaurant with good food at reasonable prices and a fine view of the surrounding countryside. There are guided paths and a marked trail to Lake Iguaque, a steep walk of 2½ hrs. The most likely day for a lift is Sat, market day, but there is a daily bus at 0700 from Villa de Leiva that passes the junction for the Park. It returns at 1300. Entrance US$3, vehicles US$3.

The 6750 hectare Park is mainly high cloud forest of oak, pine and other temperate trees, much covered with epiphytes, lichens and bromeliads. There is a series of high level lakes, formed in the last Ice Age, at over 3,400 m, and the mountains rise to 3,800 m. The height creates cloud and there is frequent rain, about 1700 mm a year, giving the Park a deep green quality. At the entrance there is a ranger station car parking and camping.

Sleeping A dormitory place is about US$8 pp, camping space US$3.

Ráquira and around

Ráquira, is one of the most important Colombian pottery centres. Locals make the mainly earthenware pottery in several workshops in and around the village which is sold in about 10 shops on the main street. Apart from kitchen and houseware items seen in many Colombian homes, there are many small ornaments and toys to enjoy. The craftsmen are happy for you to watch them at work. The village is undistinguished but the Plaza has some unusual ceramic statues including, perhaps for Belgian visitors, a local *Manneken-Pis*.

Ins & outs From Villa de Leiva, take Cra 9 south past the bus station out of town to Sáchica, turn right to Sutamarchán (famous for its pork *longanisa* sausage) on to Tinjacá and left after 1 km at Tres Esquinas for Ráquira, a further 5 km. The road from Tres Esquinas continues to Chiquinquirá.

Sleeping & eating There are two good hotels, **B** *Nequeteba,* T7320461. Converted and recently brightly renovated colonial house, pool, restaurant, craft shop, helpful owner, parking. **D** *Norteño.* Nice and clean (both on Plaza). At weekends it is possible to eat at the *Museo de Arte y Tradiciones Populares*. Market day is Sun.

La Candelaria About 7 km along a very rough road, which winds up above Ráquira affording spectacular views over the whole region, is a beautiful 16th-century monastery, the Convento de la Candelaria. The monastery is set down beside the Río Guachaneco surrounded by trees in an otherwise dry area known as **El Desierto de La Candelaria**. There is a fine church, the altar of which displays the painting of the *Virgen de La Candelaria,* dating from 1597, by Francisco del Pozo of Tunja. The painting was miraculously saved from burning and was brought here by the Augustinian monks, who founded the monastery in 1604 on the site of a pagan altar. The anniversary of the painting is celebrated on 1st February and is an annual event in addition to 28th August, the saint's day of San Agustín. Next to the church is the cloister with anonymous 17th-century paintings of the life of San Agustín, and there's a simple but interesting museum. In one of the attractive courtyards are a number of animals from their mission in Casanare Department and a dwarf orange tree over 100 years old. Among other things, they sell a delicious honey to help finance the monastery. ■ *Open daily 0900-1200, 1300-1700, entrance and guided tour of church, cloister and museum US$1.*

Sleeping and eating C *Parador La Candelaria,* adjoining monastery, picturesque, good food. Some other very basic accommodation nearby.

Transport Buses Ráquira is best reached from **Tunja**, 1 hr, US$1.70, although there are direct buses from **Bogotá** (Rápido El Carmen, 0545, 0715, US$6, 6 hrs, returning 1300). Last bus to Tunja 1330. If stuck after 1330, walk 5 km to Tres Esquinas on Villa de Leiva-Chiquinquirá road, where buses pass between 1530-1630, mostly going east. There are busetas from **Villa de Leiva**.

Chiquinquirá

Chiquinquirá is on the west side of the valley of the Río Suárez, 134 km by road from Bogotá, and 80 km from Tunja. It is a busy commercial centre and the focus of a large coffee and cattle region. In December thousands of pilgrims honour a painting of the Virgin, whose fading colours were restored by the prayers of a woman. In 1816, when the town had enjoyed six years of independence and was besieged by the Royalists, this painting was carried through the streets by Dominican priests from the famous monastery, to rally the people. The town fell, all the same.

Phone code 98
Colour map 2, grid B5
Population 38,000
Altitude 2,550 m

Sights The **Basílica** is an imposing building faced with a light sandy brown stone. The interior is bright with white/gold ornamented pillars. There is an impressive blue inlaid dome and the altar contains the original painting by Alonso de Narváez from Andalucia of the Virgin with three angels. The cloisters on the north side of the basilica are currently being restored after earthquake damage and will house part of a local university when completed. However, the scene of the miracle was in what is now the **Iglesia de la Renovación,** in the Parque Julio Flores. This church has an unusual altar with a blue surround dotted with silver motifs, and some colourful murals just below the ceiling. Near the altar, you can descend to the well by which María Ramos received her vision.

Bogotá to Cúcuta

Sleeping **B** *Gran*, C 16 No 6-97, T7263700. Comfortable, TV, secure, good restaurant, parking, good. **B** *Sarabita*, C 16, 8-12, T7262068. Business hotel, pool, TV, sauna, restaurant, building is a national monument. **C** *Real Muisca*, C 16, No 9-22. Clean, bar, restaurant, TV. **C** *La Viña*, Cra 9, No 16-51, T7264695. New building above shops/offices, TV, staff a bit off-hand. **D** *Moyba*, Cra 9, No 17-53. Facing square, with bath (cheaper without), dingy. **F** *Residencias San Martín*, Cra 9, No 19-84. Basic. **G** *Hospedaje Occidente*, Cra 11, No 17-32, opposite basilica. A last resort, very basic. Many others.

Eating *El Escorial*, Cra 9, No 16-25, on Parque Julio Flores, T7262516. Good but expensive. *Plaza 17*, C 17 No 11-45, near basilica, good. Plenty of reasonable places to eat around and near Parque Julio Flores.

Festivals There are special celebrations here at Easter and in particular on **26 Dec**, the anniversary of the miracle. Chiquinquirá is known as the 'religious capital of Colombia' though there could be some competition for this title from Las Lajas, near Ipiales, in the south of the country.

Shopping The shops display a huge variety of locally-made toys, also ceramics painted in bright colours and others white and porous as they come from the kiln. There are tops and teetotums and other little things carved from tagua nuts which come from the Chocó and Amazonas, orange-wood balls to catch on a stick, the most durable tambourines in the world, shining, brightly coloured gourds, and diminutive nine-stringed guitars on which children try the first measures of the *bambuca*. There are also little pottery horses from Ráquira, and, by the same Indian craftsmen, little birds that whistle, hens with their chicks, and enchanting little couples dancing to an orchestra of guitars and mandolins. Along the south side of the basilica are several shops specialising in musical instruments, perhaps the best is across the square, *Almacén El Bambuco*, Cra 11, No 17-96.

Transport **Buses** To **Villa de Leiva** 1¾ hr, US$2.70. To **Tunja**, 3 hrs, US$4. To **Zipaquirá**, US$4.30. To **Bogotá**, 2½ hrs, US$5 (last returns at 1730). All from bus station southwest along Cra 9.

Muzo
Phone code: 98
Colour map 2, grid B5
Altitude: 850 m

A poor road, dangerous in the rainy season, runs 105 km southwest to the little town of **Muzo**, on the banks of the Río Carare. There are several cheap places to sleep and eat. Some 16 km away is the famous open-cast emerald mine which has been worked since 1567, and long before that by the Muzo tribe of Indians. You may be able to visit the mine, check at your hotel. Below the mine, prospectors, known here as *guaqueros,* pan the streams for 2 km down the gorge hoping (mostly in vain) to find stones of commercial value. This is interesting to see but do not get involved unless you have someone with you who knows the business.

From Tunja there are two possible routes to Cúcuta: the main road, entirely paved, goes via Bucaramanga, and the other heading northeast via Duitama and Málaga, which rejoins the main road at Pamplona. Both are interesting, though you will find few filling stations if you go north from Duitama.

Northeast of Tunja

Paipa
Phone code: 98
Colour map 2, grid B6
Population 21,000
Altitude 2,513 m

Some 41 km along the road northeast of Tunja is **Paipa**, noted for the popular thermal baths 3 km to the southeast. Paipa was founded in 1568 when the Spaniards came across the hot springs which have been the basis of tourism since early colonial times. Bear right off the principal highway at the entrance to the town and right again in the centre for the good road across the railway to the baths. There are no significant tourist attractions in Paipa, but the baths and the neighbouring **Lago Sochagota** are very popular with Colombians and increasingly so with foreign tourists.

The **Aguas Termales de Paipa** complex covers about 5 ha and includes a number of mineral bathing pools both public and available for private hire, sports and holiday facilities, shops and cafeterias. The water comes from an underground lake which comes to the surface at this point, is also tapped by nearby establishments and piped to others. The springs were visited in 1801 by **Alexander von Humboldt,** who was impressed by the quality of the water. Extensive therapeutic claims are now made for the water and the precipitate can be bought in bottles or packets labelled *barro volcánico termal* at US$10 for 500g. If that is too much, a tub of cream costs US$4.50. ■*Open daily 0600-2200, basic entrance US$5, children US$3.*

Sleeping and eating There are innumerable hotels on the main street of Paipa (Cra 19) and on the approach road to the Aguas Termales. Two exceptional hotels are: **L** *Dann Sochagota*, Vía Aguas Termales Km 2, T7850012, F7850501, on exclusive site overlooking lake. Thermal pool, sauna, water skiing, many sports and conference facilities, top class international hotel; and **A** *Casona del Salitre*, Vía Toca, Km 3, T7850603, to the right of the Aguas Termales. Discounts during the week, an authentic colonial hacienda, immaculately preserved, Bolívar stayed here with his lancers 3-4 Aug 1819 just before the battle of Boyacá, all facilities, thermal pool, original chapel now frequently used for weddings.
In town, all budgets are catered for: **A** *Casa Blanca*, Vía Aguas Termales Km 1 Zona Hotelera, T7850215. Pool, mud therapy etc, restaurant, well appointed. **B** *Daza*, Cra 19 No 25-29, T7850071. Breakfast included, TV, friendly. **D** *Capri*, C 25, No 18-43, T7850568. With bath, family hotel, good. **Youth hostel** *Cabañas El Portón*, Av Piscinas Termales, T7850864/0168, F7851391. 95 beds, restaurant, family rooms.
Restaurants are as numerous as hotels and in the same areas. One strong recommendation is *Los Tizones*, Vía Aguas Termales (C 6), No 3-63, T7850358. Full menu, excellent soups, good fresh salads, open Mon-Thu 1200-1800. Fri-Sun 1200-2200.

Transport From Paipa there is a minibus service, US$0.50, a taxi costs US$1, or you can walk in 45 mins between the lines of hotels on both sides of the road and then across the flats of the *Río Chicamocha* where you can see natural chemical deposits beside the water channels. Lago Sochagota is to the right of the road but is hidden by a high bank.

About 7 km beyond the *Aguas Termales* on a winding hilly paved road, through delightful countryside, is the **Pantano de Vargas**, the site of the battle on 25th July 1819 between the forces of Bolívar and the Spaniards (*pantano* means swamp, but the battlefield is now pasture and cultivated land). A huge bronze sculpture by Rodrigo Arenas Betancur, the largest in the country, commemorates the event featuring the 14 lancers under Colonel Juan José Rondón who, together with a small force of English mercenaries, were decisive in the patriots' victory. The spectacular monument, which appears on the back of the 1,000 peso note, was inaugurated on the 150th anniversary in 1969. There is a small village at the foot of the monument with restaurants and *tiendas*. Regular minibuses run to Paipa and Duitama for about US$0.50, taxis US$3.

Duitama, the third largest town in Boyacá, is about 15 km beyond Paipa. Its name comes from the Muisca 'Tundama', still used for the local district. It is essentially a market town for the surrounding rich agricultural area, known for its fruit and legumes and, more recently, some grape and wine production. The town is noted for basket weaving. It is also a communications centre for roads north to Santander and east for Yopal and the Llanos, and was a stop on the railway when it was active.

Duitama
Phone code: 98
Colour map 2, grid B6
Population: 95,000
Altitude: 2,532 m

About 5 km from Duitama on the valley road to Sogamoso is the colonial *hacienda* of San Rafael which houses the **Museo de Arte Religioso**, with eight rooms of items from churches and monasteries including a fine collection of works of art, relics, gold and silver etc. ■ *Open daily except Tue, US$1.* For information, Instituto de Cultura, Diag 16, No 20-45, T7604628, Duitama.

Sleeping A *Hacienda El Carmen*, C 8, No 35-14, T7602307, F7605870. Colonial style, restaurant, pool, comfortable. **B** *Marantá*, Cra 16, No 17-36, T7603595, F7600145. Restaurant, bar, parking. **D** *Santa Isabel*, Cra 18, No 18-59, T7602623. Clean, quiet.
   About 7 km from Duitama, on the road east to Belencito, is the **A** *Hostería San Luis de Ucuenga*, T7603260, in an old *hacienda* that has been turned into a distinctive hotel. Opposite is the **B** *Complejo Turístico Puntalarga*, T7605841, in the same style, but catering more for families and weekend visitors. Nearby is a furniture factory that makes colonial reproductions which you can visit. They also make bronze bells for sale to tourists, and there is a vineyard up the hill. Also nearby **B** *Chalets El Trebol*, T7606751/7624724. Family cabins with 4-6 beds, horseriding, organised walks.

Transport Buses To **Bogotá**, hourly or so, 4 hrs, US$8. To **Bucaramanga**, at 0900, 9 hrs, US$11. To **Málaga**, at 0800, sit on right side for best views, 6 hrs.

From the main valley road to Sogamoso, bear right 4 km from Duitama at the Y junction (it is called La Y) for **Tibasosa**, a small attractive village, centre of a large fruit, especially feijoa, growing area. The **Casa Santillana** is a fine colonial building now housing the Casa de la Cultura. Nearby is the tourist hotel **B** *Hacienda Suescún*, T7706828, another converted colonial house complete with bell tower and set in well kept gardens. You can continue along the road to Sogamoso.

Bogotá to Cúcuta

Sogamoso
Phone code 98
Colour map 2, grid B6
Population :70,000
Altitude :2,569 m

Sogamoso is a large town with an industrial area to the north. It's not a particularly attractive place, though not unpleasant, and is centred on its main square, **Plaza de la Villa**, with the modern romanesque **Cathedral de San Martín** on its east side. This has a pleasing white and yellow façade, was completed in 1917 on the site of an original church dating from 1584. In the plaza there is the simple but dramatic **Monumento al Sol**, the most important symbol of the Muiscas. Three blocks north is the **Plaza 6 de Septiembre** with government buildings in the centre.

Sogamoso was an important Muisca settlement, and a **Parque Archaeológico** has been set up on the original site in which 'Bohio' buildings have been reconstructed. The principal Chibcha structure was the Temple of the Sun. One of the most dramatic acts of the Spanish conquest was the burning, in 1537, whether by accident or design, of the original. This was the holiest place of the Muisca religious capital known as Suamox. It is from this name that Sogamoso is derived. For many years there were plans to reconstruct the whole site as it was in precolonial times and this is now well advanced. The last structure to be completed was the thatched Temple of the Sun.

On the site, a comprehensive museum has exhibits describing Muisca arts of mummification, statuary, as well as the many crafts, including gold working, in which they excelled (see page 132).The Parque Archaeológico is to the southeast of the town, follow the signs from Cra 8A up the hill. You will see the conical thatched buildings and the large sign near the site. ■*Open Tue-Sun 0900-1300, 1400-1800, US$1.50 adults, US$0.80 children. There is a cafeteria near the entrance and camping is possible in the grass car park opposite, with permission.*

For general information on the area, check with the Casa de la Cultura in the Plaza de la Villa, T7705410, or the Instituto de Desarollo de Sogamoso in the government buildings in Plaza 6 de Septiembre, T7707555.

Sleeping and eating A *Sogamoso Real,* Cra 10, No 13-11, T/F7701870. 1 block behind central plaza, business hotel, all facilities, conference rooms. **B** *Litavira,* C 12, No 10-30, T7702585, F7705631. Discounts at week ends, with breakfast, cable TV, private parking, good value. **D** *Bochica,* C 11, No 14-33, T7704140. Comfortable rooms, hot water, TV, good value. There are many hotels near the bus station: eg **F** *Hostal Aranjuez.* Basic, safe, very helpful. **F** *Residencia Embajador.* Clean, friendly, secure, Recommended. **G** *Residencia El Terminal.* Basic, clean, safe.

There are several reasonable restaurants near the centre, one of the best is *Susacá*, Cra 16, No 11-35, T7702587. Open 1200-2100, specialties include trout, good *comida*, large portions, good value. Recommended.

Transport Buses The bus station is in the east of the town, Av Libertadores C 11/Cra 17. To **Bogotá**, 4½ hrs, US$8.50. To **Yopal**, US$5, 4½ hrs, several daily. To **Monguí**, from Plaza 6 de Septiembre, buseta every ½ hr, US$0.75, 45 mins.

Lago de Tota   The main road south climbs quite steeply, with great views back towards Sogamoso, as it winds up for 16 km to the continental divide at El Crucero at 3,100 m. At this point, the main road continues to Yopal: turn right for Lago de Tota and the lake immediately appears to the south. Most of its 15km length and 10 km width can be seen, and is a fine sight. Most of the mountains on either side are cultivated or are covered with trees and shrubs except the highest elevations over 3,500 m which are bare *páramo*. Virtually all round the lake, onions are grown near water level, and the whole area smells of pine, eucalyptus and onion. There are reeds and algae along the shore in many places and few beaches, the notable exception being Playa Blanca in the southwest corner, but remember the lake is at 3,015 m, and the water is cold.

Feijoa

Feijoa is a tree fruit, similar in size and colour to a lime, but sweet (not citrus), that can be eaten raw, or used as a juice for drinking, flavouring ice cream etc. It is delicious in all these forms and is popular in Colombia. Try it! Recently, Colombia has begun to export feijoa, and it has now reached Europe.

The road down reaches the lake in 4 km, where there is nothing more than a *tienda* or two. A dirt road to the right leads round eventually to Aquitania, but is not recommended.

Sleeping 4 km along this road is a steep descent down to the lake where **A** *Hotel Génesis* is located, a remarkable set of buildings with cabañas for 4 to 10 people, (**D** per person), geared for watersports and fishing. There are hotel rooms in the main building and to crown it all, the onion dome houses the nuptial suite! (**AL**). Contact T6158711 (Bogotá) for reservations.

The main road continues to the left and in 2 km comes to **AL** *Camino Real,* Km 20 Vía Sogamoso a Aquitania, T7700684. On the lake, pleasant public rooms, colourful gardens, boat slipway, boats for hire. 3 km further on is the **AL** *Pozo Azul,* down a poor road to the right, in a secluded bay on the lake, T2576586 (Bogotá), entrance by way of a steep set of steps through well kept gardens, also cabins up to 6, suitable for children, over furnished but comfortable, full range of water sport facilities including water skiing (but bring your own equipment), good food, fresh trout, friendly. 3 km before Aquitania is **A** *Santa Inéz,* Km 29, T7794199. Also cabins, good position on lake, boats for hire/fishing, good food, helpful.

Aquitania is the principal town on the lake and serves as the market town of the region. There are plenty of food shops and a bright, simple but elegant restored church with modern stained glass windows.

 Sleeping and eating F *Residencia Venecia,* C 8, No 144. Clean, basic, reasonable. Numerous restaurants including *Luchos, Tunjo de Oro* and *Pueblito Viejo* together on corner of plaza. At Playa Blanca, across the lake, is *Las Rocas Lindas* campground, with bath and hot water, 2 cabins for 7, one for 8, boats for hire, dining room, bar, fireplaces, friendly. Recommended,.

Transport Aquitania is reached by bus from Sogamoso, US$1.10, 1 hr. To **Bogotá** (Rápido Duitama), via Tunja and Sogamoso, goes round the lake to Aquitania, passing Cuitiva, Tota and the *Rocas Lindas* hotel. Above the town is a hill (El Cumbre) with beautiful views. The road continues round the lake, past Playa Blanca, then ascending to **Tota, Cuitiva** (thermal springs, *Hostería El Batán*), and the colonial town of **Iza** with several hotels and a good restaurant, *Comamos Trucha,* Km 14 on the road to Sogamoso, with rainbow trout a speciality. Locally made wool products including blankets and *ruanas* can be bought here.

Just before the descent to the Lago de Tota, the main road continues left, leading in four hours to **Yopal**, capital of the Department of Casanare in the Llanos. The road passes through *páramo* and virgin cloud forest. For details of Yopal, see the **Llanos and Amazonia** chapter.

Leaving Sogamoso northeast on Carrera 11, you go through several kilometres of unappealing suburbs and huge industrial plants. Then climbing east into the mountains, the road takes you by a left fork to **Tópaga,** 9 km from

Bogotá to Cúcuta

Bogotá to Cúcuta

Indian gold

One of the greatest tragedies of the Spanish conquest was that they were interested only in gold as a metal, and normally took what they found and melted it down into ingots for ease of transport back to Spain. For Colombia, this was particularly galling because the quality of the objects created by the Indians was so high.

In the 17th and 18th centuries, a little of the gold inheritance from the Indian groups destroyed or dispersed by the Spaniards found its way into the colonial houses and the churches, and can still be seen. At the beginning of the 19th century, von Humboldt wrote of the Chibcha culture and the use made by them of gold for ornaments and offerings.

By the middle of the 19th century, however, it had become clear that what Indian gold there still was in existence was to be found in the ground. So excavations began in earnest and the age of the guaquero (grave robber) was born. Although some official archaeological investigations have made a significant contribution to finding and conserving the local Indian heritage, the guaqueros have excavated many sites and dispersed their finds to the highest bidder.

However, in 1939, Julio Caro, manager of the Banco de la República in Bogotá, supported by the governing body of the Bank, began to buy gold artifacts from private collectors, and ended up with an unequalled collection of ancient Indian gold. The show at the Gold Museum in Bogotá and the smaller exhibitions in the provincial branches are stunning and for all to see. How sad that so much of this wonderful heritage has been destroyed.

Sogamoso. Tópaga was used by missionaries in the 17th and 18th centuries as a stopping place on the way to Los Llanos. Visit the colonial church with its large single nave construction, and fine altar. Note also the unusual topiary in the plaza and the bust of Bolívar to commemorate the battle of Peñon of 11 July 1819. The views south are splendid, and in the hills to the north are coal mines which fuel the brick kilns you see on the road to Sogamoso. Beyond Tópaga, a visit to the churches of **Mongua**, a pleasant colonial town, is well worthwhile.

Monguí A right fork in the road leads to Monguí, which has recently earned the title of 'most beautiful village of Boyacá province'. All houses are brightly painted in green and white with added red and gold in the immediate vicinity of the central plaza.

The upper side of the plaza is dominated by the **Basílica** and convent, constructed by the Franciscans in the 17th century. The architects of the church were influenced by the designs of Juan Herrera for the Escorial near Madrid, which has a simple façade with doric columns. There are many oil paintings in the complex including La Sacrada Familia by the 18th century artist, Mejía, and the famous Virgin de Monguí which is a 16th century work sent over from Spain by Philip II. Notice also the painted ceilings. This is a pleasant place to wander in with interesting arts and crafts shops in all directions. Don't miss the walk down Carrera 3 to the Calycanto Bridge, originally built by the Spaniards out of stone cemented with clay, lime and bull's blood, in order to bring the large stones across the river for the church. At the top of Calle 4, to the right of the church, is the Plaza de Toros. If you feel energetic, take any path beyond the bull ring to the rock on which stands a shrine to the Virgin and Child, illuminated at night. From here there is a tremendous view in all directions.

The **tourist office** is in the Municipality building on Plaza, Janeth Tellez, T7782050. It is very helpful and local craftwork – eg leather and woollen items – sold. They can arrange walking excursions and will advise about guides. Excursions are especially recommended to the *páramo* (high altitude moorland) east of Monguí with particularly fine *frailejones* and giant wild lupins in the *Páramo de Ocetá*. There is a good one day tour to the Virgin waterfall, or longer trips staying at the E *Rincón de Duzgua* refuge, 5 km into the mountains.

Sleeping and eating C *Hostal Calycanto*, pink house next to the bridge (see above), lovely setting, restaurant (but give advance notice), looks good. **E** *La Cabaña*, chalet on road beyond river, (cross brige, turn left), basic but comfortable, food if advised, information from Miriam Fernandez at Cafetería La Cabaña next to the Municipality. There are several restaurants round the plaza. *Taller de Arte Colonial*, Cra 3, serves coffee and snacks.

Transport Bus office on plaza. To **Bogotá**, Libertadores daily at 0730 and 1600, US$9, 4½ hrs. To **Sogamoso**, every ½ h by buseta, US$0.75, 45 mins. Monguí is also famous in Colombia for its footballs made in various houses around the town and sold in craft shops.

The Chicamocha valley road north from the steel works leads to Paz de Río itself with the unusual accompaniment of a busy railway which transports raw materials, coal and iron ore, from mines in the valley to the steel works. At Paz de Río, a dirt road leads up to **Socha** and then a right turn takes you up to the **Parque Nacional de Pisba,** a bleak but dramatic area of lakes and *páramo*. Bolívar and his army crossed here to reach Boyacá in 1819. There are fine walking tracks which cross the area which rises to 3,800 m, but best to ask for information in Socha where there are some modest places to stay. There are no facilities in the Park. Access is also possible from the Sogamoso-Yopal road through Paya to the small village of Pisba.

From Paz de Río, the road continues north to meet the principal direct road coming northeast from Duitama which passes through Viterbo and Belén, famous for its dairy products. They join at **Soatá** (*Residencias Colonial*, excellent, good restaurant. **D** *Hotel Turístico*, swimming pool) before descending again to the dry, spectacular valley of the Río Chicamocha. This area specialises in tobacco and dates. See also below under San Gil.

Sierra Nevada del Cocuy

This is one of the most beautiful mountain ranges in South America, and one of the least visited. You could be here for days and never see another gringo. While the tough 8-10 day trek may be beyond all but the most fit and experienced, there are plenty of shorter walks, or you can hire horses to take you right up to a glacier, from where the views must rank as some of the most astoundingly beautiful anywhere in the country.

Getting there Güican to/from Bogotá: 6 buses a day; Gacela, Paz del Rio and Los **Ins & outs** Libertadores (most comfortable), US$15, 10 hrs. El Cocuy to/from Bogotá: 6 buses a day, 2 with Tricolor, 2 with Paz de Río, 1 Libertadores and 1 Gacela, either early am or between 1000-1800, 11 hrs, US$15. **Güican to El Cocuy,** several buses a day US$1.50, 1 hr, some of which continue to Bogotá. To/from Málaga, Bucaramanga and points north, change at **Capitanejo** (several hotels, all **F-G**, and more on the *parque* 1 block below the bus stop, all are basic). **From Capitanejo:** 3 buses a day to Bucaramanga, 4 to Cúcuta. **By car** There are 2 main approaches to the **Sierra Nevada del Cocuy**. From the south, turn right at Soatá and follow the road through La Uvita and Guacamayas to Panqueba, or alternatively continue 32 km north and cross the bridge over the deep valley of the Río Chicamocha at **Capitanejo**. From here, go southeast to El Espino.

Climate The best weather for the Sierra Nevada del Cocuy is from Dec to Apr, and the optimum trekking months are Jan-Feb: however, be warned, the weather can be unsettled for most of this period.

Safety Unfortunately, there has been guerilla and paramilitary trouble here in the recent past with occasional harassment of tourists. Latest information is not good, particularly with the renewed tension over the oil concessions in or next to the U'wa lands. Before setting out, especially on the longer treks, make careful enquiries of those knowledgable about the area.

The sierra is located towards the northern end of the Cordillera Oriental and consists of two parallel chains running roughly north-south for about 30 km. The highest peaks are in the western range, Ritacuba Blanco, 5,330 m and Ritacuba Negro, 5,300 m. This is the most heavily glaciated zone in Colombia and the snowline today is at 4,800 m. The major peaks were first climbed in 1928 by a Swiss diplomat and his team and is now a popular venue for local and international climbers. It is one of the training areas for Colombian expeditions to the Himalaya and Everest. There are 18 peaks with permanent snow. In addition to rock, snow and ice climbing, the park is excellent for spectacular trekking with many lakes and waterfalls. The flora is particularly interesting. Everyone wears *ruanas*, rides horses and is very friendly.

Güican
Phone code: 98
Colour map 2, grid B6
Altitude: 2,970 m

The centre for climbing the main peaks is Güicán, a faintly charming old colonial town about 50 km east of Capitanejo. The name means 'where the eagle flies' in the local U'wa language. The church on the plaza has a painting of the *Virgin del Moranito* which, according to legend, was found in the nearby Cueva de la Cuchumba by the U'wa Indians in 1756, blackened by smoke from old rituals. It is difficult to see the painting behind the main altar but there is a reproduction in the side chapel. The shops around the plaza sell *artesanías* made by the U'wa. There are colourful Easter processions here.

About 1 km outside the town along Cra 5, the old road reaches the Río Nevado, where a large cliff, **El Peñol de los Muertos** can be seen from where U'wa Indians jumped to their deaths when the Spaniards arrived. More recently, in 1997 and again in 2000, Indians threatened to do the same thing to prevent Occidental Petroleum from continuing exploration for oil on their territory, which is set aside officially by the government as an Indian Reserve.

Sleeping There are a few hostal-type hotels: **F** *La Sierra,* T897074/897109. Good value, clean, cosy, comfortable, hot water, the owner, known to everyone as 'Profe', is very helpful, has good maps of the region, and an informative visitors' book for trekkers, good meals available, Profe can also arrange transport. **F** *Los Andes*, just off plaza, basic. **F** *Las Brisas,* basic, hot water, food available. There are a few basic restaurants around the plaza and the nearby streets. International calls can be made from Telecom, next to *Hotel Las Brisas,*

El Cocuy
Colour map 2, grid B6
Phone code: 98

The other main town is **El Cocuy,** an attractive village of green and white painted houses. There is a model of the Sierra Nevada in the plaza showing the names of all the peaks, valleys and lakes. For information, contact Pedro Moreno, Carrera 5, No 8-36, T 890017. He also has a contact in Bogotá, T4545301. He is most informative and has done much to promote tourism in the region. There is a branch of the *Banco Agrario* in the village and you can make international calls from Telecom. White gas is available at the petrol station.

Sleeping and eating **E** *Gutiérrez,* friendly, hot water, meals, laundry facilities. **E** *Colonial,* hot water, clean, meals available, owned by Orlando Correa, a good source of information if planning to hike or climb in the southern part of the Park. **F** *Residencia Cocuy*, cold water, meals, laundry. There are several basic restaurants in town.

From Güican A path leads steeply east from Güicán towards the mountains, joining the road after about 2 km. A further 7 km brings you to **E** per person *Cabañas Kanwara*, at 3,920 m, 4 cabins for 4/6 people, hot water, showers, meals US$3.50, managed by Teresa Cristancho who is very friendly and helpful, camping **F** per site with use of facilities and kitchen, day trips on horseback arranged, US$8/10 for a horse and US$8/10 for a guide. Alternatively there is transport to the *Cabañas* by the *lechero* (milk truck) from Güicán leaving the plaza daily between 0600 and 0700 which goes via El Cocuy and other fincas arriving at 1100 at La Cruz, one hour's walk below the *Cabañas*, US$2.50, then returns direct to Guicán at 1230. Private jeeps can be hired through 'Profe', Luis Blanco or José Riano for about US$20 one way (1 hour).

Hiking in the Sierra

From here it is a steep but not too demanding three-hour walk up, on a clear trail, to the snowline on Ritacuba Blanco. This is a good acclimatisation day trek if you are planning to climb higher. Beyond here, rope, ice axe and crampons are recommended for the final section above 4,800 m. In common with most high mountains in Colombia, cloud usually covers the peaks from 1000 onwards, so you must start early.

Cabañas Kanwara is also the best base for the 3-4 day trek round the north end of the Sierra and into Ratoncito valley, which is surrounded by

Sierra Nevada del Cocuy

The U'wa Indians

Very few of the precolumbian Indian tribes have managed to live apart from the 'invaders' from the outside world, and the Kogi of the Sierra Nevada de Santa Marta are the only people of Colombia who have almost managed to keep their lands and customs free from outside influences – at least for the time being.

Until recently, the U'wa were in the same category. They live on the Eastern side of the Cordillera Oriental, close to and within the borders of the Cocuy National Park in a territory once the size of Wales. Unfortunately (for them), the Maracaibo oilfields extend southwards from Venezuela into Colombia and one of the biggest deposits is the Caño Limón field which has been in production for many years. The oilmen have been looking for further reserves and successful drillings deeper into the U'wa reservations have proved positive,

accentuating the cruel dilemma of indigenous culture versus economic progress. For the U'wa, the land and all that is in it is sacred and if the blood of the earth is extracted, so the earth itself will die.

The tribal chiefs of the U'wa threw themselves off the Peñol de los Muertos when the Spaniards invaded their territory in the 16th century, and the present leaders have threatened to do the same.

Oil development is but one of their problems. The land on the eastern side of the Cordillera Oriental is being used for coca and other drug production, and the oil installations have had frequent visitations from the guerrilla groups seeking to disrupt the pipelines. Right wing vigilantes and the Army are also involved, making this one of the most unstable political zones of the country. The outlook for the U'wa is not good.

snow-capped mountains. However, this involves crossing several passes significantly over 4,000 m in very difficult terrain. There are no settlements and no easy ways out and the weather can be very dangerous at any time of the year.

From El Cocuy Above El Cocuy you can sleep at E *Hacienda La Esperanza*, newly renovated, hot water, meals US$3, owned by Marco Arturo Valderrama, T(91)8633599 (cellular), horses and guides arranged, camping possible. He also sells delicious cheese and *arequipe*, both cost US$2/a pound (libra). La Esperanza is 7-8 hours walk from Güicán, a little less from El Cocuy or take the *lechero* (see above). Fifteen minutes walk above La Esperanza is a *finca* owned by a friendly family. You can sleep and eat there, or ask permission to camp, but negotiate a fee first. They can also arrange horses to hire.

La Esperanza is the base for climbing to the **Laguna Grande de la Sierra** (7 hours round trip), a large sheet of glacier-fed water surrounded by five snow-capped peaks, and also for the two-day walk to the Laguna de la Plaza on the east side of the Sierra, reached through awesome, rugged scenery. Between El Cocuy and La Esperanza is **Alto de la Cueva** where you can stay at *El Himat* meterological station for US$5, basic, including two meals. There is a fine walk from here to Lagunillas, a string of lakes near the south end of the range (5 hours there and back). Permission to camp can easily be obtained from friendly locals.

It is possible to trek from Lagunillas, over the southern end of the main range and north up through the central rift and the valley of the Río Ratoncito returning west eventually to *Cabañas Kanwara*. This takes 8-10 days. Crampons, ice axe, rope etc are necessary if you wish to do any climbing en route. Be prepared for unstable slopes and rockfalls, few flat campsites and treacherous weather including high winds and snowfalls at any time. The perpendicular rock mountains overlooking the Llanos are for professionals only. The views east towards Los Llanos are stupendous.

Santander Department

Like Boyacá, Santander has a lot to recommend it. At present mostly Colombians go there, but surely international travellers will follow. Again, the colonial history is well represented. The Spaniards established many towns and trade routes through the area, the latter now offering interesting one day, or longer trips along old trade routes or caminos reales. Also adventure sports are being promoted, such as rafting on the rivers that flow down from the highlands to the Magdalena, and parapenting at the Mesón de los Santos, south of Bucamaranga. The western part of the Department is covered in the **Up the Río Magdalena** *chapter.*

The area around **Málaga** is very picturesque: pretty red-tiled villages, riders in *ruanas* and cowboy hats, and mountains (some covered in flowering trees). The roads are twisty but spectacular.

Málaga
Phone code: 97
Colour map 2, grid B6

Bogotá to Cúcuta

Sleeping and eating E *Santander,* Cra 8, No 13-40, T6608027. Friendly, good value. **E** *Arizona Plaza,* Cra 8, No 13-64. With bath, modern, clean, friendly. **F** *Príncipe,* Cra 8, No 10-82, T6607456, near main square. Shared bathroom, clean, friendly, good meals, recommended. Restaurants, eg *La Riviera,* Cra 8, No 13-61. Good food. Nearby, *La Esperanza.* Good Colombian food.

Transport Buses Good services to **Duitama** (6 hrs), **Bucaramanga** (6-7 hrs, US$6) and **Pamplona.**

From Málaga to Pamplona is a beautiful, but hard journey. To Bucaramanga is another spectacular trip through the mountains, but the road is not good and is very tortuous. The main road going to Bucamaranga and on to Cúcuta or the Caribbean coast is northwest from Tunja and into Santander Department.

The road from Tunja skirts round the east and north sides of the Iguaque Sanctuary across open moorland. You will be lucky to see the summits, as they are usually covered in cloud. Indeed it may well be raining! After Arcabuco (the turn off for Villa de Leiva), the road descends an attractive wooded valley – watch for waterfalls in the hills – to **Moniquirá,** 64 km from Tunja.
   Moniquirá, which is in Boyaca Department, is a pleasant place to stay. Hotels (all on central plaza): **D** *Mansión,* good; **E** *Clara Luz,* OK; **E** *Casablanca,* with swimming pool; **F** *Tairona,* clean, friendly.

North from Tunja

Some 10 km beyond is Barbosa, in the Department of Santander, a small provincial town servicing the local area and the traffic on the main road.

Sleeping and eating C *Campestre Moncada,* Cra 10, No 16-70, T97-7486001. On edge of town, pool, restaurant, children's park. **D** *Emperador,* Cra 10, No 8-39, T97-7485711, F7485049. With bath, TV, covered parking, clean. **E** *Príncipe,* Cra 9, No 6-75, T97-7486066. Quiet, friendly, restaurant, patio, clean rooms with private bath, parking, OK. **E** *Magnolia,* Cra 10, No 5C-137, T97-7485332, 1st floor, with bath, TV, parking. Several basic hotels near the bus station, Cra 10/C 6. A number of local and chicken restaurants near the hotels.

A road runs northwest from Barbosa to the Magdalena at Puerto Olaya, opposite Puerto Berrío. About 18 km from Barbosa is **Vélez,** a charming little town where horses and mules are raised. It is also known for its *bocadillos* of *guayaba* and *ariquipe,* (delicious sweets) and the processions and music at the local festival in August. Veléz was one of the earliest Spanish settlements in Colombia.

Socorro

Phone code: 97
Colour map 2, grid B6
Population: 26,000
Altitude: 1,230 m

Northeast of Barbosa, on the road to Bucaramanga, is the historic town of Socorro, with steep streets and single storey houses set among graceful palms. Here, in 1781, began the peasant *comuneros* revolt against poverty. It was led at first by a woman, **Manuela Beltrán**, and then, when other towns joined, by **Juan Francisco Berbeo** and **José Antonio Galán**. They marched as far as Zipaquirá; rebel terms were accepted by the Spaniards, and sworn to by the Bishop of Bogotá, but when they had returned home, troops were sent from Cartagena and there were savage reprisals. Galán was hanged the following year in Bogotá. There is a statue of him in the central plaza. Another woman from Socorro, **Antonia Santos**, led guerrillas fighting for independence and was captured and executed by the Spaniards in 1819; a statue of her is in the corner of the main square. Socorro was the capital of the independent State of Santander from 1862-1886. The founder of the huge Colombian beer industry, Bavaria, Leo S. Kopp, was born here in 1889.

It has a singularly large stone **Iglesia de NS de Socorro** (cathedral), started in 1873 and finished 70 years later. It is majestic inside with an impressively lit altar, fine chandeliers and curious angels with lamps to lighten the otherwise dark interior. There is a fine cupola.

The **Casa de Cultura,** Calle 14, No 12-31, is in a fine colonial building around an exquisite courtyard with a fountain and balconied upper floor. The building was declared a National Monument in 1972. Bolívar stayed here for several days in 1819, 1820, 1827 and 1828. There are rooms with period furnishings, exhibits of the Guane Indians who peopled this area before the Spaniards arrived) and a room dedicated to a recent notable musician, José A Morales, who died in 1978. Perhaps the most moving exhibit is the small room where Antonia Santos spent her last night before her execution. ■ *Open daily 0800-1200, 1400-1730, US$0.50.*

Sleeping and eating **B** *Tamacara*, C 14, No 14-45, T7273515/17, F7273519. Nice open design, patio, comfortable, restaurant, pool, parking. **E** *Colonial*, Cra 15, No 12-45, T7272842. With bath, TV, restaurant, parking. **E** *Nueva Venezia*, C 13, No 14-37, T7272350. Shower, dining room, nice old rooms, good value. **E** *Saravita*, Cra 15, No 12-64, T7272282. With bath, TV.

La Gran Parrilla, Cra 14, No 10-64, good steaks. *Panadería Imperial*, C 14/Cra 13, very good, simple.

Transport The bus station is at the north edge of town.

Directory **Banks** There are two banks on the main plaza with cash machines. **Festivals** Annual music festival, third week of Sep. **Communications Telecom** office is on the corner of the plaza. **Tourist Office** *Oficina Municipal de Turismo*, Pasaje Popular (half a block from the plaza on Cra 15), T7272227.

San Gil

Phone code: 97
Colour map 2, grid B6
Population: 28,000
Altitude: 1,140 m

About 21 km northeast of Socorro, is San Gil, a colonial town with a good climate in the deep valley of the Río Fonce. San Gil is an important centre for adventure sports. The river systems of the Ríos Fonce and Chicamocha run through deep valleys and gorges in this part of Santander, providing good **rafting** and **canoeing** (see below under Sports). Given the town is astride the main Bogotá-Bucaramanga road, and traffic has to descend and ascend steep hills to cross the river, it can be noisy.

Near the centre of the town by the river is **Parque El Gallineral.** The park, created in 1919, covers 4 ha where the Quebrada Curití runs through a delta to the Río Fonce. There are streams everywhere to create a delightful botanical garden full of butterflies and birds. Notable are the heliconias and the huge ceiba near the *playa* where the canoes end their trip down the Río Fonce. Outstanding are the many fine trees covered with moss-like tillandsia. You will need mosquito repellent! There is a restaurant and public swimming pool (entrance US$0.30). ■ *The park is open daily entrance US$1.75, T7240821.*

In the centre, the **Parque Principal** has a fountain surrounded by huge trees, very attractive when illuminated in the evening. Overlooking it is the **church,** which has interesting octagonal towers. There is a good view of the town from **La Gruta,** the shrine overlooking the town from the north (look for the cross).

A *Bella Isla*, north of town, Vía Javel San Pedro, T7242971. Large condominium, full **Sleeping** services, great views, beautiful gardens, TV, refrigerators, a/c, children's park. **B** *Mansión Perla del Fonce*, Cra 10, No 1-44, T7243298, F7240821. With full breakfast, family hotel. **C** *Cabañas Mesón de Cuchicute*, on road to Bogotá near Pinchote, T7245836/2041. Cabins, with bath, hot water, TV, fan, restaurant, swimming pool (non-residents US$1.80, children US$1.25). **E** *Alcantuz*, Cra 11, No 10-15, T7243160. Clean, free coffee, good location, pleasant. **E** *Abril*, C 8, No 9-63, T7243381. secure parking, relatively quiet, helpful. **E** *Residencias Señorial*, C 10, No 8-14, T7244442. Pleasant, quiet. **E** *Victoria*, Cra 11, No 10-40, T7242347. With bath, clean, fan, attractive, helpful, good value. **F** *San Gil*, C 11, No 11-25, T7242542. With bath, cheaper without, clean, friendly, upstairs rooms are preferable, basic.

There are plenty of restaurants in town, also an open-air restaurant in Parque **Eating** Gallineral, T7244372, good in evening, music at weekends. There are a number of good restaurants on the road leaving San Gil towards Bucaramanga.

Rafting A consortium of 3 companies, *Ríos y Canoas, Planeta Azul* and *Rafting Club,* **Sports** work together to provide activities on the Río Fonce. Daily guided trips can be arranged, minimum 3 people, 1½ hrs on the water, 2½ hrs round trip, US$15 per person. At weekends, regular trips at 0800, 1000, 1300 and 1500. Longer trips up to level IV can be made. On the Río Chicamocha, rafting from Cepitá to Pescadero (55km north of San Gil), also level IV, with transport US$38 per person.

Parapenting is offered at Páramo, 26 km south of San Gil, **abseiling** (called *raphell* or *rapel*) down cliffs and waterfalls at Pinchote off the San Gil to Socorro road, **caving** at Caverna de Yeso near Curití, a short distance north of San Gil and other sites eg Cueva del Indio (near Páramo), La Antigua and del Alumbre. For all these activities, full information is available at the booth next to the entrance to the Parque El Gallineral, normally open daily T7240000/7679.

Universal de Turismo Ltda, Cra 9, No 13-24, T7243133, F7247346. Arranges tours to **Tour operators** places of interest including adventure sports in the area.

Bus station 5 mins out of town by taxi on road to Tunja, or *busetas* from the centre. To **Transport** **Bogotá**, US$16. To **Bucaramanga**, US$5, 2½ hrs. To **Baricharа** from C 12, US$1, 45 mins, every hour, taxi US$5.

About 20 km south of San Gil on the road to Duitama, is **Páramo,** (with some accommodation eg *Páramo* in the Plaza Principal) one of the centres of activity sports (see above). For local information T7258944. About 30 km further on is **Charalá,** which has a plaza with a statue of **José Antonio Galán,** leader of the 1781 Comunero revolt. It also has an interesting church and Casa de la Cultura.

Sleeping E *El Refugio*, with private bath, clean, safe. **E** *Florián*, Calle 24, No 16-83, T7258110. **E** *Yarima*, Calle 24, No13-59, T7258021. **Bus** to San Gil, US$1.

Above Charalá and south towards Gámbita, a new Nature Sanctuary has been established, part of the National Parks system, called **Sanctuario Flora y Fauna Guanentá,** incorporating part of the *Páramo de la Rusia* and the head-waters of the *Río Fonce*. Access is through Encino. ■ *Entrance US$1.25.*

A road runs east from San Gil to Onzaga (bus), through Mogotes and San Joaquín, dropping from high mountain ridges to tropical valleys. From Onzaga it is 20 km to Soatá (see page 133), no regular public transport.

Barichara

Phone code: 97
Colour map 2, grid B6
Population: 10,000
Altitude: 1,300 m

Barichara is a beautiful colonial town founded in 1741 and designated as a National Monument in 1975. There are several interpretations of this Guane Indian name, the best is 'the place of rest with flowering trees'. It has a wonder-fully, peaceful, bohemian atmosphere, with white and green or blue paint everywhere and a lot of fine stonework. It is built of the brown stone found all over Santander, and the streets are paved with it throughout. This is very much a place to relax as an increasing number of Colombians find at weekends, mainly from Bucamaranga but also Bogotá. Artists congregate here, too, but in midweek it is very quiet.

Ins & outs From San Gil a direct paved road leads in 22 km to Barichara. Another road, mostly unpaved, turns left off the main road near Socorro, and 21 km along, there is a dirt

Barichara

track off to Barichara. Though a shorter journey from the south, this road is in poor condition and can be difficult even with 4WD vehicles.

Among Barichara's places of historical interest, is the house of the former president, **Casa de Aquileo Parra Gómez.** If you wish to visit, ask the lady at the house next door who has the key. The **Casa de Cultura,** on the Parque Principal, has a small exhibition of local historical interest and archeological finds, ■ *Entry US$0.25.*

Sights

The **Catedral de la Inmaculada Concepción** is a fine colonial building which sets the tone for the town. The façade and twin towers are strikingly illuminated at night. The interior is all in finished sandstone, with fluted columns, a carved wooden ceiling, gallery, cupola and a bright, gold leaf reredos. There are three other interesting churches, **San Antonio**, Carrera 4/Calle 5 with a house for the elderly alongside, **Santa Bárbara,** Calle 6/Carrera 11, at the top of the town, **Jesús Resucitado,** Calle 3/Carrera 7, with the cemetery next to it – all with simple, even stark, interiors. There is a superb wide-ranging view from the *mirador* at the top of Carrera 10 across the Río Suarez to the Cordillera de los Cobardes, the last section of the Cordillera Oriental before the valley of the Magdalena. At the corner of the Carrera 10 and Calle 4, there is a **Piedra de Bolívar**, which shows the number of times the Liberator passed through the village.

B *Hostal Misión Santa Bárbara*, C 5, No 9-12, T7267163 (or Bogotá 2884949), F7267060. Old colonial house, quiet, fan, hot clean showers in rooms, pool, all meals available. **B** *La Posada del Campanario*, C 5, No 7-75, T7267255. Well appointed, good international and Colombian restaurant, good view of the town. **C** *Bahía Chala*, C 7, No 7-61, T7267236. Pool, parking, comfortable, owners have restaurant on Cra 8, No 8-62. **D** *Coratá*, Cra 7, No 4-08, T7267110, F7267071. With private bath, charming courtyard, restaurant, lovely cathedral views. **D** *Diez Desitos,* Cra 6, No 4-37, T7267224. Simple hostal, some rooms with bath. Ask at the Casa de Cultura about staying in private homes. The *Tienda* on C 6, No 7-56 may also be able to help.

Sleeping

Camping Just outside Barichara on the road to San Gil is *La Chorrera*, a natural swimming pool, T7267422, US$0.30 to bathe, US$1.60 to camp, meals by arrangement, clean, attractive.

La Casona, C 6, No 5-68, cheap, good food, friendly. *Bahía Chala*, C 8, No 8-62. Full menu, pool, goat-meat a speciality. *Cafetería Bachué*, Cra 7/C 7, good value. *Central Panadería*, C 6, No 5-82. Light meals available around the plaza.

Eating

Local craft items, including dolls and figurines made from maize leaves, can be purchased at *Sua-ty Artesanías*, C 6, No 9-29. Also *Hoja de Maíz*, Calle 6, No 9-50. On the left as you enter the village from San Gil is a stone mason's workshop with interesting pieces on sale. There is a *micromercado* on the plaza.

Shopping

To San Gil, hourly bus from 0600, Cotransangil, 45 mins, US$1.50.

Transport

Around Barichara

An interesting excursion is to Guane, 9 km away by road, or two hours delightful walk along a *camino real*. Here are many colonial houses and an archaeological museum, in the **Casa Parroquial,** that has a collection of coins, locally woven Guane textiles and a mummified woman, ■ *Open daily, 0800-1200, 1300-1700, US$0.60. Ask next door to the left for the key if closed: a very knowledgable lady will take you round.*

Guane

Bogotá to Cúcuta

There is a restaurant/bar on the other side of the museum, a good place to try *chicha*. In the plaza there is a monument to the last Guane Chief, Guanenta and several brilliant orange acacia trees with an ancient one next to the church. The church, of simple design, is very attractive with an interesting beamed and ornamented roof, fine wooden doors, a balcony at the west end and an elegant chapel to Santa Lucía to the left of the altar. Well worth a visit.

The valley abounds with fossils and you will be approached by children and adults selling them. You should not buy: they are part of the *Patrimonio Nacional.* There is nowhere official to stay, but you can ask around. There are places to camp near the village, with permission. Simple food is available round the plaza.

Getting there   If walking from Barichara, go to the end of Cra 10 and continue down-hill along the stone trail, reconstructed in 1995. There are fine views but remember to take water and suncream. There are morning and afternoon buses from Barichara.

Another interesting trip is to the waterfall **Salto de Mico,** a 30-minute walk along a trail to the left of the road to Guane, following the line of cliffs near Barichara.

About 20 km north of Barichara is **Zapatoca,** a town which at one time controlled the traffic between highland Santander and the Magdalena. Local products include juicy sweets (*cocadas*) and *pauche*, a balsa type wood painted and carved into many forms. There is also a small museum. Local excursions to the Cuevas del Nitro and to a natural swimming pool with waterfall, Pozo del Ahogado. Buses to Bucaramanga, 2 hours, US$4.20.

North to Bucamaranga   North of San Gil on the main road to Bucaramanga is **Curití** noted for handicrafts in *fique* (agave sisal). Mixed with cotton, it is used to make fabrics, shoes, bags and even building materials. You can see weaving at *Ecofibras* in the village. Near Curití are limestone caves. To visit, see under San Gil. At the entrance to the village is **D** *Vegas de San Diego*, T7278001, and in Curití, **E** *Santa Monica,* Calle 9, No 8-14, T7278229.

About 28 km north of San Gil, a little off the road, is the picturesque village of **Aratoca,** with a colonial church. Near Aracota you will become aware of the deep valley to the east of the road, the canyon of the **Río Chicamocha.** At one point in the next section, look for the place where the road takes to a narrow ridge with spectacular views on both sides as the river loops round to the southwest. The descent from the heights along the side of a steep cliff into the dry Río Chicamocha canyon, with spectacular rock colours, is one of the most dramatic experiences of the trip to Cúcuta, but, if driving, this is a demanding and dangerous stretch. The deep valley of the river at this point is becoming an interesting place for canoeing and white water rafting, especially between Cepitá and Pescadero, which is where the main road crosses the river. There is a grandstand view of this section of the river from near Aracota. See under San Gil for sporting possibilities in this region. After crossing the river, the road ascends again to the plateau for the remaining few kilometers to Bucaramanga.

Bucaramanga

Phone code: 97
Colour map 2, grid A6
Population: 465,000
Altitude: 1,000 m

Bucaramanga, 420 km from Bogotá, is the capital of Santander Department. It stands on an uneven plateau sharply delimited by eroded slopes to the north and west, hills to the east and a ravine to the south. The city's great problem is space for expansion. Erosion in the lower, western side topples buildings over the edge after heavy rain. The fingers of erosion, deeply ravined between, are spectacular. The metropolitan area has grown rapidly because of the success of coffee, tobacco and staple crops.

Getting there by air The airport is at Palonegro, on 3 flattened hilltops on the other side of the ravine, south of the city. There are spectacular views on take-off and landing. Taxi from town US$4; colectivo, US$1. Buses are scarce despite the fact that some bus boards say 'Aeropuerto' (direction 'Girón/Lebrija' from Diagonal 15). For flight details see under Transport section below.

Ins & outs

    By road To the Magdalena at *Barrancabermeja*, 115 km; to *Cúcuta*, 198 km; to *Bogotá*, 420 km; to *Santa Marta*, 550 km, all paved. The **bus terminal** is on the Girón road, with cafés, shops, a bank and showers. Taxi to centre, US$1.50; bus US$0.35.

Getting around Most taxis have meters; beware of overcharging from bus terminals. Buses charge US$0.45.

Tourist office On main plaza C 35/Cra 19, friendly and knowledgeable, (closed 1200-1400). City maps free. *MA*, Av Quebrada Seca, between Cra 30 and 31 (south side), T634941. *DAS*, Cra 11, No 41-13.

The city was founded in 1622 by Paéz de Sotomayor but was little more than a village until the 19th century. Simón Bolívar established his campaign headquarters here in 1813, and lived here for some time in the **Casa de Bolívar** around 1828. Perú de la Croix, a French officer in Bolívar's army wrote his *Bucamaranga Diary* here, an interesting study of his leader. Gold was found in the hills and rivers nearby, hence the Río Oro to the southwest, which were worked until the end of the 19th century.

The **Parque Santander** is the heart of the modern city, while the **Parque García Rovira** is the centre of the colonial area. There are a number of other parks in the city, notably **Parque de Mejoras Públicas**, Calle 36/Carreras 29-32, with an open-air concert shell (*concha acústica*) for public performances, **Parque de los Niños**, Calle 30/Carrera 26, and **Parque Centenario** from which buses used to leave before the new terminal was built.

Sights

    There are several churches of interest. The **Catedral de la Sagrada Familia**, Calle 30/Carrera 19, overlooks the Parque Santander, a clean white romanesque style building with twin towers and statues of the Virgin and San José in between. The church of **San Pío**, Calle 45/Carrera 36, has several paintings by Oscar Rodríguez Naranjo, and the **Capilla de los Dolores** (Chapel of Sorrows), Calle 35/Carrera 10, was the first chapel to be built in the town and is where the poet Aurelio Martínez Mutis is buried.

The **Museo de Arte Moderno** is at Calle 37/Carrera 26, US$0.50. Just off Parque García Rovira, is **Casa de Bolívar**, at Calle 37, No 12-15, T6422542. This is an interesting ethnographic and historical museum and a centre of research on Bolívar and his period. ■ *Open Tue-Sat 0900-1200, 1400-1700.*

    Across the street is the **Casa de La Cultura,** Calle 37, No 12-46, T6302046, in a fine colonial building with exhibitions, film showings and a local *artesanía* display. The nearby **Casa Perú de la Croix**, Calle 37, No 11-18, is another colonial mansion (closed at present). Also worth a visit is the **Museo Arqueológico Regional Guane,** in the Casa de Cultura 'Piedra del Sol', Carrera 7, No 4-35, T6394537, good collection of Guane culture artifacts and textiles ■ *Open Mon-Sat 0900-1700, US$0.50.*

Away from the centre, the **Club Campestre** is one of the most beautifully set in Latin America. There is an amusement park, **Parque El Lago**, in the suburb of Lagos, southwest of the city on the way to Floridablanca. On the way out of the city northeast (towards Pamplona) is the **Parque Morrorico**, well-maintained with a fine view. There is a sculptured Saviour overlooking the park, a point of pilgrimage on Good Friday.

The suburb of **Floridablanca**, 8 km southwest, has the famous **Jardín Botánico** Eloy Valenzuela (also known as El Paragüitas gardens), belonging to the national tobacco agency. The Río Frío runs through the gardens, which have been recently reconstructed. ■*Open at weekends 0800-1100 and 1400-1700. Entrance US$0.25. To get there, take the Cotandra bus (US$0.40) from Cra 22, Bucaramanga, either Florida Villabel which goes by the botanical gardens, or Florida Autopista (continuation of Cra 33) which goes direct to the square in Florida and you have to walk about 1 km. Taxi from the centre, US$1.50.*

Sleeping

Since Bucaramanga has numerous national conventions, it is sometimes hard to find a room in more expensive hotels

AL *Chicamocha Meliá*, C 34, No 31-24, T6343000. Luxury, a/c, clean, swimming pool (non guests US$1.50). **AL** *Guane*, Calle 34, No 22-72, T6451287, F6347021. Breakfast included, clean, secure, parking. **AL** *Dann Carlton*, Cra 29/C 47, T6431919, F6431100. Modern, large, pool, gym, nice terrace.

A *Ruitoque*, Cra 19, No 37-26, T6334567, F6302997. With bath, telephone, a/c, TV, very friendly. **A** *Granada*, C 45, No 14-75, T6420050, F6333495. Restaurant, a/c, parking, laundry service.

B *Asturias*, Cra 22, No 35-01, T6351914. With bath, TV, good restaurant.

C *Balmoral*, Cra 21/C 35, T6303723. Friendly, clean, a/c, comfortable, pool. **C** *Colonial*, C 33, No 20-46, T645-4125. Newly renovated, good information at reception. **C**

Bucaramanga

■ **Sleeping**

1 Aquarela	5 Colonial	9 Guane	13 Residencias Esmeralda
2 Asturias	6 Dann Carlton	10 Hostal Doral	14 Residencias Solo Suite
3 Balmoral	7 El Pilar	11 Las Bahamas	15 Ruitoque
4 Chicamocha Meliá	8 Granada	12 Residencias Amparo	16 Tamaná

0 metres 200
0 yards 200

Aquarela, C 35, No 30-08, T/F6343570/71, aquarela@b-manga.cetcol.net.co Restaurant, pool, local excursions arranged.

D *El Pilar*, C 34, No 24-09, T6347207. Clean, hot water, quiet, good service and food. Recommended. **D** *D'León*, C 56, No 21-49, T6436998. Parking, TV, friendly.

E *Tamaná*, Cra 18, No 30-31, T6304726. With bath, cheaper without, clean, friendly. Recommended. **E** *Las Bahamas*, C 55, No 17A-120, T6449002. Opposite Copetran terminal, friendly, good value. **E** *Residencias San Diego*, Cra 18, No 54-71, T6434273. Quiet, good. **E** *La Isla*, Diagonal 15, No 54-37. Clean, good value. **E** *Hostal Doral*, C 32, No 21-65. With bath, **F** without, family business, clean, safe, several nice tiny rooms, but varying reports.

F *Residencias Solo Suite*, C 33, No 24-43. Clean, friendly. **F** *Residencias Tonchala*, C 56, No 21-23, with bath, good. **F** *Residencias Amparo*, C 31, No 20-29, T6304098. Clean, with bath, friendly, safe. **F** *Hormiga*, Cra 17C, No 55-56, opposite market, clean, safe, laundry. **F** *Residencias Esmeralda*, C 32, No 21-49, next to *Doral*, T6452693. Basic but acceptable.

Camping 30 mins drive south of Bucaramanga, on left of dual carriageway, with swimming pool and waterside restaurant.

Eating *D'Marco*, C 48, No 28-76. Excellent meat. *La Casa de Spaghetti*, Cra 27, No 51-18, cheap and good. *La Tranquera*, Cra 33/C 40. Good Baby Beef. *Piz Pan Pum*, Cra 33, No 31-107 (next to Cinema Rivera), pizzas. *Tropical*, C 33, No 17-81. *Los Notables*, Cra 18, between Calles 34/35. Pleasant, good breakfast. *Zirus*, C 56, No 30-88. Friendly, owner speaks a little English. *Super Pizza*, Centro Comercial Cabecera (pizza by the slice, hamburgers, etc). Good **snack bars** include: *Muchos Pinchos*, C 54, No 31-07.

Vegetarian *Maranatha*, Cra 24, No 36-20. Good lunches and dinners, reasonable prices. *El Toronjíl*, Cra 33, No 52-123. A bit dear. *Govinda*, Indian vegetarian, Cra 20, No 34-65. Excellent lunch. *Berna*, C 35, No 18-30. Best pastries in town. *Fonda*, C 33, No 34-42. Good, cheap.

Try the *hormigas culonas* (large bottomed black ants), a local delicacy mainly eaten during Holy Week (sold in shops, not restaurants and also sold on main highways in Santander at that time).

Bars & nightclubs Several on road to Girón and on Cra 33/35. Worth taking a look at: *Barbaroja*, Cra 27/C 28, a *salsa* and *son* bar set in a renovated red and white, gothic-style mansion, happy hour 1700-1800. *La Capilla*, Vía Aeropuerto, Km 14, good view of the city at night, good disco. *Mister Babilla*, Anillo Vial, huge, good music, also restaurant.

Festivals The annual international piano festival is held here in mid-Sep in the **Auditorio Luis A Calvo** at the Universidad Industrial de Santander, one of the finest concert halls in Colombia. The university is worth a visit for beautiful grounds and a lake full of exotic plants and alligators. *Fería de artesanías* (Handicraft Fair) in first 2 weeks of Sep, usually near the Puerta del Sol.

Shopping **Camping equipment** *Acampemos*, C 48, No 26-30, last place in Colombia to get camping gas cartridges before Venezuela. **Handicrafts** in Girón (see above) and typical clothing upstairs in the food market, C 34 y Cras 15-16. Similar articles (*ruanas*, hats) in San Andresito. Also, handicrafts fair, see **Festivals** above.

Sports **Canoeing and rafting** see under San Gil above. **Parapenting:** opportunities at the nearby Mesón de los Santos and over the Cañón de Chicamocha, to the south of the city. Enquire where you are staying, or a local contact is Stefano Cagnucci, T6314501.

Transport **Air** To **Bogotá**, 15 flights a day with Avianca, Aces and AeroRepublica. To **Cúcuta** 2 daily with Avianca. To **Cartagena**, 1 daily with Aces. To **Medellín** 2 daily with Avianca.

Bogotá to Cúcuta

Direct flights also to **Barranquilla, Ibagué, Neiva, Santa Marta** and flights by Aerotaca and Satena to towns in Los Llanos.

Bus To **Bogotá,** 8-11 hrs, US$22 (Pullman) with Berlinas del Fonce, Cra 18, No 31-06 (this journey is uncomfortable, there are no relief stops, and it starts off hot and ends cold in the mountains, be prepared); Expreso Brasilia, C 31, Cra 18-19, T6422152, and Copetrán, C 55, No 17B-57, T6448167 also run to Bogotá. To **Barranquilla,** 13 hrs, US$27 first class with Copetrán. To **Cartagena,** US$29, 14 hrs. To **Santa Marta,** 11 hrs, US$25 with Copetrán. To **Valledupar,** 8 hrs, US$20. To **El Banco** on the Río Magdalena, US$15, 7 hrs, several companies, direct or change at Aguachica, this journey should be made in daylight. To **Barrancabermeja,** 3 hrs, US$5, a scenic ride with one rest stop, this road is paved. Hourly buses to **San Gil,** US$5. To **Tunja,** 7½ hrs, US$17. To **Berlín,** US$3. To **Pamplona,** Copetrán, 3 a day, US$5 (Pullman), US$4.50 (*corriente*). To **Cúcuta,** 6 hrs, US$7 (Pullman), Berlinas and Copetrán, *colectivo* US$8. The trip to Cúcuta is spectacular in the region of Berlín (see below). Other companies with local services to nearby villages on back roads, eg the colourful folk-art buses of *Flota Cáchira* (C 32, Cra 33-34) which go north and east.

Directory **Airlines offices** Avianca, C 37, No 15-03, T6426117.
    Banks *Lloyds TSB Bank,* Cra 19 No 36-43, T6304321, and 2 agencies. *Bancafé,* C 35, No 16-20, Visa agents. *Bancolombia,* by Parque Santander, will cash Thomas Cook and Amex TCs, long queues (cheques and passports have to be photocopied). Many other banks, many with cash machines. Cash changed at *Distinguidos,* C 36, No 17-52 local 1A33.

Around Bucaramanga

Lebrija, 17 km to the west, is in an attractive plain, and **Rionegro,** is a coffee town 20 km to the north with, close by, the Laguna de Gálago and waterfalls. One fine waterfall is 30 minutes by bus from Rionegro to Los Llanos de Palma followed by a two-hour walk through citrus groves towards Bocas. Complete the walk along an old railway to the Bucamaranga-Rionegro road.

Girón Girón, a tobacco centre 9 km southwest of Bucaramanga on the Río de Oro, is a quiet and attractive colonial town, filled with Bumangueses at weekends, with a beautiful church. The buildings are well preserved and the town unspoilt by modernization. By the river are *tejo* courts and popular open air restaurants with *cumbia* and *salsa* bands. In the square at weekends, sweets and *raspados* (crushed ice delights) are sold.

Sleeping and eating **B** *San Juan de Girón,* outside town on road from Bucaramanga, T6466430. Swimming pool, restaurant uninspired. **F** *Río de Oro,* in centre, but make sure you get a lock for the door. *Mansión del Fraile* on the square, in a beautiful colonial house, good food. Bolívar slept here on one occasion, ask to see the bed. *La Casona,* C 28, No 27-47. Friendly, try their *fritanga gironesa*. Recommended.

Transport Take the bus from Cra 15 or 22 in Bucaramanga, US$1.25.

Piedecuesta, 18 km southeast of Bucaramanga, is where you can see cigars being hand-made, furniture carving and jute weaving. Cheap, hand-decorated *fique* rugs can be bought. There are frequent buses to all these dormitory towns from the city, or a taxi costs US$6. Corpus Christi processions in these towns in June are interesting. To get there, take bus from Carrera 22, US$0.45, 45 minutes. Sleeping: **F** *Piedecuesta,* good, safe, clean).

The road (paved but narrow) runs east to Berlín, and then northeast, a very scenic run over the Eastern Cordillera to Pamplona, about 130 km from Bucaramanga. **Berlín** is an ideal place to appreciate the grandeur of the Eastern Cordillera and the hardiness of the people who live on the *páramo*. The village lies in a valley at 3,100 m. The peaks surrounding it rise to 4,350 m and the temperature is constantly around 10°C, although on the infrequent sunny days it may seem much warmer. There is a tourist complex with cabins and there are several basic eating places. Camping (challenging but rewarding) is possible with permission. At the highest point on the road between Bucaramanga and Berlín, 3,400 m, is a café where you can camp on the covered porch.

Norte de Santander Department

The border between Santander and Norte de Santander Departments is at the high pass near Berlín. Thereafter, the Cordillera Oriental slowly reduces in height to become a ridge, now the border with Venezuela, and ending at the peninsular of La Guajira and the Caribbean Sea. A spur, however, turns northeast, crosses the border at the Tamá National Park to become the Sierra Nevada de Mérida, the highest mountains of Venezuela.

The northeast of the Department is well down into the Maracaibo basin, the hottest place in South America. This border country with Venezuela was intimately linked with the wars of independence, and with Bolívar and Santander.

Pamplona

Pamplona is a lovely old town, and few modern buildings have as yet broken its colonial harmony. It was founded in the mountains in 1549 by Pedro de Orsúa and Ortún Velasco as Pamplona del Espíritu Santo. During the colonial era it was as important as Bogotá. The independence movement was started here in 1810 by Agueda Gallardo. It became important as a mining town but is now better known for its university.

Phone code: 975
Colour map 2, grid A6
Populaton: 43,700
Altitude: 2,200 m

Sights The severe earthquake of 1875 played havoc with the monasteries and some of the churches. There is now a hotel on the site of the former San Agustín monastery, but it is still possible to visit the remains of the ex-monasteries of San Francisco and Santo Domingo. The **Cathedral** is in the spacious **Plaza Central** (Plaza Aguela Gallardo), a massive building with five naves. It dates from the 17th century but has been damaged by earthquakes and rebuilt over the years. The **Iglesia del Humilladero**, adjoining the cemetery also dates from the 17th century, is very picturesque and allows a fine view of the city. The sculpture *Cristo del Humilladero* came from Spain. In September, there is an annual festival celebrating the *Humilladero*.

Museo de Arte Religioso at Calle 4/Carrera 5 is a collection from the region and has paintings by many Colombians including Vázquez de Arce y Ceballos. The fine **Casa Colonial** is now an archaeological museum, at Calle 6, No 2-56. It's a little gem, with artifacts from the Motilones and other Indian communities still living in the north of the Department. ■ *Open Tue-Sat, 0900-1200, 1400-1800; Sun, 0900-1200.*

Casa Anzoátegui, Carrera 6, No 7-48, is where one of Bolívar's generals, José Antonio Anzoátegui, died in 1819, at the age of 30, after the battle of Boyacá. The state in northeast Venezuela is named after him. The restored colonial house is now a museum covering the Independence period. **Museo de Arte Moderno,** Calle 5 on the Parque Central, principally exhibits the paintings and sculptures of Eduardo Ramírez Villamizar of Pamplona. The colonial building is a notable local example and was declared a National Monument in 1975.

Excursions Some 47 km south of Pamplona, on the road to Málaga, is the small village of **Chitagá** with attractive surroundings and extensive views. Colectivo from Pamplona; US$2.60, 1½ hours. This road continues south to Capitanejo and Tunja, see page 137.

Sleeping
Hotel accommodation may be hard to find at weekends, when Venezuelans visit the town

C *Cariongo*, Cra 5/C 9, T682645. Very good, excellent restaurant, US satellite TV, locked parking available. **E** *Residencia Dorán*, Cra 6, No 7-21. With bath, cheaper without), large rooms, good meals. **E** *Imperial*, Cra 5, No 5-36, T682571. On plaza central, large rooms, hot water, safe, restaurant. **F** *Orsúa*, C 5, No 5-67, T682470, on plaza central, clean, friendly, cheap, good food also available (good, cheap restaurant also to left of hotel). **F** *Los Llanos*, C 9, No 7-35, T683441. Shared bath, cold water, motorcycle parking. Recommended.

Eating *El Maribél*, C 5, No 4-17. Cheap lunch. *La Casona*, C 6, No 6-57, limited but good menu. *Las Brazas*, next door. Good, cheap. *Portal Alemán*, C 7/Cra 6. Good meals, especially breakfasts. *El Trigal de Oro*, near *Hotel Cariongo*. Good breakfast. *Angelitas*, C 7/Cra 7. Good coffee. *Piero's Pizza*, Calle 9/Cra 5. Good. Many places to eat round the Plaza Central.

Festivals The town's Easter celebrations are famous throughout Colombia, with processions, and cultural presentations.

Shopping Pamplona is a good place to buy *ruanas*. Good indoor market.

Transport **Buses** To Bogotá, US$26, 13-16 hrs. To **Cúcuta**, US$3, 2½ hrs. To **Bucaramanga**, US$5, 4 hrs, great views. To **Málaga** from plaza central, 5 a day from 0800, 6 hrs, US$5. To **Berlín**, US$3. Buy tickets only at the official office upstairs. Do not accept help from 'intermediaries'.

Directory **Banks** *Banco de Bogotá*, on the plaza central, gives Visa cash advances. There are several cash machines nearby. Also try the store at C 6, No 4-37, where 'Don Dólar' will change cash and TCs. **Communications** Post Office: Cra 6/C 6, in pedestrian passage. **Telephone**: C 7 y Cra 5A.

The road north follows the Río Pamplonita down to Cúcuta. About half way, at La Donjuana, there is a turn off to **Chinácota**, with a hacienda style inn where you can stop for refreshments. From here a road leads 44 km to **Herrán** on the Río Táchira (the Venezuelan border).

Tamá National Park Tamá National Park covers the point at which the Cordilllera Oriental continues across into Venezuela, where there is also a National Park. It is high, rising to the Páramo de Santa Isabel with several sections above 3,400 m, and extending over 48,000 ha.

Getting there Access is from Herrán. From here take the minor road to El Tabor, cross the Río Táchira into Venezuela (with a MA permit you will be allowed across) and go south through Villa Paéz-Betanía to Palmazola, where you cross back into Colombia, with about 30 mins to Orocué and the administrative centre of the Park.

There is a comparatively heavy rainfall (over 3,000 mm per year on the lower slopes) which, combined with a wide range of altitude, produces a full set of forest types from jungle to high temperate woodland and páramo, with a vast variety of flora and fauna, including anteaters, deer and spectacled bears. It is reported that a waterfall has recently been discovered in the Park about 820 m high. If this proves to be true, this would place the falls as the third or forth highest in the world.

Sleeping At Oracué, 1 cabaña for 2, US$12.50 per person, cooking facilities, comfortable. *El Kiosko*, bunks for 8 US$6 per person, no cooking facilities but locals will cook food you bring, price negotiable. Camping is possible, US$1 per person. The situation is reported stable mid 2000. Entrance to the Park US$1.50.

Cúcuta

Cúcuta, capital of the Department of Norte de Santander, is only 16 km from the Venezuelan frontier. It was founded in 1733 by Juana Rangel, severely damaged by the earthquake in 1875, and then elegantly rebuilt, with the streets shaded by trees. Anyone spending more than five minutes here will appreciate this latter fact, for Cúcuta is one hot place: the mean temperature is 29°C.

Phone code: 975
Colour map 2, grid A6
Population: 526,000
Altitude: 215 m

The **airport** is 5 km north of the centre, 15 mins by taxi from the town and the border, US$3. Buses from Av 3 take rather longer. The notorious **bus station** is on Av 7 and Calle O (a really rough area). Taxi from bus station to town centre, US$2.40. The new Berlinas del Fonce terminal is much safer; it is 2 km beyond the main terminal along continuation of Diagonal Santander. For more details see page 150. **NB** Cúcuta and the surrounding area is a great centre for smuggling. Be careful.

Ins & outs

Tourist offices *Fondo Mixto de Promotion*, C 10, No 0-30, T718981, helpful, has maps, etc. At bus station (1st floor), and at airport. Other maps obtainable from Instituto Geográfico, Banco de la República building, in the main plaza.

The **Catedral de San José**, Avenida 5 between Calle 10/11, is worth a visit. Note the oil paintings by Salvador Moreno. The **Casa de la Cultura**, Calle 13, No 3-67, also incorporates the **Museo del la Ciudad** which covers the history of a city very much involved with the independence movement. The **international bridge** between Colombia and Venezuela is southeast of the city. Just beyond it is San Antonio del Táchira, the first Venezuelan town, and 55 km on is San Cristóbal.

Sights

Just short of the border is the small town of **Villa del Rosario**, where the Congress met which agreed the constitution of Gran Colombia in the autumn of 1821, one of the high points of the the career of Simón Bolívar. The actual spot where the documents were signed is now a park beside which is the **Templo del Congreso**, in which the preliminary meetings took place. Formerly a church, it was severely damaged in the 1875 earthquake and only the dome has been reconstructed.

Excursion

Also nearby is the **Casa de Santander**, where General Francisco de Paula Santander, to whom Bolívar entrusted the administration of the new Gran Colombia in 1821, was born in 1792 and spent his childhood. It became a National Monument in 1959 and a museum in 1971 dedicated to the period of the independence campaigns and the contribution made then and later by General Santander. The **Casa de Nariño** (also called the *Casa de la Bagatela)* nearby is where Antonio Nariño, as the first Vice President, conducted the affairs of the new republic. It is now an archaeological museum with interesting relics from northeast Colombia, including Tairona, Muisca and Guane artifacts, ■ *Open Tue-Sat 0800-1200, 1400-1800, Sun 0900-1330. Buses leave Cúcuta for Villa del Rosario from the Parque in front of the Venezuelan consulate.*

● ●

 Cúcuta and the road to independence

Cúcuta, because it is the gateway of entry from Venezuela, was a focal point in the history of Colombia during the wars for independence. Bolívar captured it after his lightning Magdalena campaign in 1813. The Bolívar Column stands where he addressed his troops on 28 February 1813. At Villa Rosario, a small town of 8,000 inhabitants 14½ km from Cúcuta on the

road to the frontier, the First Congress of Gran Colombia opened on 6 May 1821. It was at this Congress that the plan to unite Venezuela, Ecuador, and Colombia was ratified; Bolívar was made President, and Santander (who was against the plan) Vice-President. (Santander was born at the Casa de Santander which is now being developed as a tourist centre.)

● ●

Sleeping **A** *Tonchalá*, C 10/Av 0, T731891. Good restaurant, swimming pool, a/c, airline booking office in hall. **B** *Acora*, C 10, No 2-75, T712156, F731139. A/c, restaurant, safes, TV, good value. **C** *Casa Blanca*, Av 6, No 14-55, T721455, F722993. Good, reasonable meals. Recommended. **C** *Lord*, Av 7, No 10-58, T/F713609. A/c, nice rooms, good restaurant and service, safe, car parking.

D *Cacique*, Av 7, No 9-66, T712652, F719484. A/c, cold showers only, reasonable. **D** *Amaruc*, Av 5, No 9-73, T717625, F721805. With fan, private bath, no hot water. **D** *Tundaya*, C 10, No 6-21, T716161. Clean, safe, very good restaurant, breakfast US$10.

E *Flamingo*, Av 3, No 6-38, T712190. Bath, fan, clean, with bath, noisy. **F** *Imperial*, Av 7, No 6-28, T712866, F726376. With bath, clean, secure. Highly recommended. **F** *Residencia Leo*, Av 6A, No 0-24N, Barrio La Merced. With bath, clothes washing, free coffee all day. Recommended. **F** *Residencia Los Rosales*, near bus station, C 2, 8-39. Fan, with bath, good. **F** *Residencias Nohra*, C 7, No 7-52, T725889. Shared bath, quiet. **F** *Moderno*, C 7, No 3-48, T718571. Friendly, safe, motorcycle parking. **G** *Residencia Zambrano*, C 4, No 11E-87. Breakfast, laundry facilities, family-run by Cecilia Zambrano Mariño.

Eating *La Brasa*, Av 5/C 7. Good *churrascos*, modest prices. *Don Pancho*, Av 3, No 9-21, local menus, try *lengua criolla* (beef tongue). *La Palma*, C 7, opposite Hotel Moderno. Good, cheap meals. *Punto Zero*, Av 0, No 15-60, T730153. Local dishes, open late. *El Molinito*, Av Libertadores, No 18-30, T 715804. Seafood, popular. *Pinchos y Asados*, Av Libertadores, No 10-121, T751719. Steaks, *brochettes*, good.

Shopping A good range of leather goods: try C 10, Av 8 for leather boots and shoes. *Cuchitríl*, Av 3 No 9-89, has a selection of the better Colombian craft work.

Transport **Air** There are only domestic flights from Cúcuta airport. For flights to Venezuelan destinations you must cross the border and fly from San Antonio airport. **NB** Do not buy 'airline tickets' from Cúcuta to Venezuelan destinations. All flights go from San Antonio. Flights to **Bogotá**, 4 a day, Avianca/SAM. To **Barranquilla**, daily, Avianca. To **Bucamaranga**, 3 a day, Avianca and Aerotaca. To **Medellín**, 2 daily, Avianca. To **Ocaña**, 1 or 2 a day, Aces.

It is cheaper to buy tickets in Colombia than in advance in Venezuela. From San Antonio, Venezuela (30 mins by taxi) there are daily flights direct to the following Venezuelan cities: Caracas (6 a day), **Barcelona, Barquisimeto, Maracaibo, Porlamar** and **Valencia.** There are also flights from San Antonio direct to Medellín, 2 a day, Servivensa. At this airport, be sure all baggage is sealed after customs inspection and the paper seals signed and stamped.

Bus To **Bogotá**, hourly, 17-24 hrs, US$28, with Berlinas del Fonce who have their own terminal (see Ins & outs), making 2 stops, one of which is Bucamaranga (US$2.50

extra for *cochecama*), or Bolivariano, 20 hrs. There are frequent buses, even during the night (if the bus you take arrives in the dark, sit in the bus station café until it is light). To **Cartagena**, Brasilia 1800 and 1930, 18 hrs, US$35. To **Bucaramanga**, US$7, 6 hrs, with Copetrán and Berlinas del Fonce Pullman, several departures daily. There are good roads to **Caracas** (933 km direct or 1,046 km via Mérida), and to **Maracaibo** (571 km). Bus to Caracas, 15 hrs, Expreso Occidente, or taxi colectivo.

Warning Travellers have been reporting for years that the bus station is overrun with thieves and conmen, who have tried every trick in the book. This is still true. You must take great care, there is little or no police protection. On the 1st floor there is a tourist office for help and information and a café/snack bar where you can wait in comparative safety. Alternatively, go straight to a bus going in your direction, get on it, pay the driver and don't let your belongings out of your sight. Don't put your valuables in bus company 'safety boxes'. Make sure tickets are for buses that exist; tickets do not need to be 'stamped for validity'. For San Cristóbal, only pay the driver of the vehicle, not at the offices upstairs in the bus station. If you are told, even by officials, that it is dangerous to go to your chosen destination, double check. If the worst happens, report the theft to the DAS office, who may be able to help to recover what has been stolen.

Airline offices *Avianca*, C 13, No 5-09, T717758.   **Directory**

Banks A good rate of exchange for pesos is to be had in Cúcuta, at the airport, or on the border. *Banco Ganadero* and *Banco de Los Andes* near the plaza will give cash against Visa cards. *Bancolombia* changes TCs. *Banco de Bogotá*, on Parque Santander, advances on Visa. There are money changers on the street all round the main plaza and many shops advertise the purchase and sale of bolívares. Change pesos into bolívares in Cúcuta or San Antonio as it is difficult to change them further into Venezuela. Similarly, do not take bolívares further into Colombia, change them here.

Cúcuta

Sleeping

1 Acora	4 Flamingo	7 Moderno	10 Residencias Nohra
2 Amaruc	5 Imperial	8 Residencia Leo	11 Tonchalá
3 Cacique	6 Lord	9 Residencia Los Rosales	12 Tundaya

Border with Venezuela

Colombian immigration

There is a 1 hr time difference between Colombia and Venezuela

Exit and entry formalities are handled at DAS office in the white house before the international border bridge. DAS also has an office at the airport, which will deal with land travellers. **NB** If you do not obtain an exit stamp, you will be turned back by Venezuelan officials and the next time you enter Colombia, you will be fined.

DAS office in town, at Av Primera, No 28-55, open 0800-1200, 1400-2000 daily. Take bus from city centre to Barrio San Rafael, southwards towards the road to Pamplona. Shared taxi from border US$1, will wait for formalities, then US$0.80 to bus station.

Entering Colombia

By air All Colombian formalities can be undertaken at the airport. Visitors arriving by air may not need a visa: unfortunately, there are no local flights from Cúcuta to San Antonio or to Santo Domingo (San Cristóbal), the 2 nearby Venezuelan airports.

By Road You must obtain both a Venezuelan exit stamp and a Colombian entry stamp at the border. Without the former you will be sent back; without the latter you will have problems with police checks, banks and leaving the country. You can also be fined. **Colombian customs** Aduana office on the road to the airport (small sign); has a restaurant.

Leaving Colombia by private vehicle

Passports must be stamped at DAS in town and car papers must be stamped at Aduana on the road to the airport, about 10 km from the border. The same applies for those entering Colombia who must present passport and vehicle documents.

Entering Venezuela

Many overland visitors to Venezuela need a visa and tourist card, obtainable from here or the Venezuelan Embassy in Bogotá (which may send you to Cúcuta). Citizens of most European countries do not need visas to enter overland: check with a Venezuelan consulate in advance. Requirements for visas: 2 passport photographs; proof of transportation out of Venezuela, with date (not always asked for in Cúcuta). Proof of adequate funds sometimes requested. In Cúcuta, pay US$30 in pesos for the visa at a bank designated by the consulate, then take receipt to consulate. Apply for visa at 0800 to get it by 1400. If the consulate is busy, better join the queue earlier. You may need a numbered ticket to get served. If you know when you will be arriving at the frontier, get your visa in your home country. **Venezuelan consulate** Av 0, C 8, T713983/712107, open 0800-1300, Mon-Fri.

Transport

From Cúcuta: for a bus to **Caracas** go to **San Cristóbal,** US$1.20 (Bolivariano), colectivo US$2.40. To **San Antonio,** taxi US$7.20, bus and colectivo from C 7, Av 4, US$1. On any form of transport which is crossing the border, pay the driver not an intermediary and make sure that the driver knows that you need to stop to obtain exit/entry stamps etc. You may be asked to pay extra, or alight and flag down a later colectivo. Just to visit San Antonio de Táchira, no documents are needed.

North of Cúcuta Catatumbo

A paved road leads 60 km north to Puerto Santander on the frontier with Venezuela, but this is not an official crossing point. Beyond, a dirt road continues to the **Catatumbo** oil fields, the first to be developed in Colombia (around 1920), which extend 150 km north to **Río de Oro** close to the Río Catatumbo. This is part of the Lake Maracaibo basin, one of the largest oilfields in the world. The Colombian oil is piped across the mountains to the Caribbean port of Coveñas.

Above this area is the **Parque Nacional Catatumbo-Barí,** a 158,000 ha section of tropial rain forest, also home to a community of Barí Indians. There are no tourist facilities in the Park.

Up the river Catatumbo, near its source, is the historic town of **Ocaña,** connected by road to Cúcuta but more easily accessible from the Magdalena valley. See the **Up the Río Magdalena** chapter.

The Northcoast & the Islands

5

The Northcoast & the Islands

Caribbean Colombia is very different in spirit from the highlands. Attitude, it seems, changes with altitude and the costeños *(those who live on the coast)* have a more light-hearted approach than their more sober highland cousins. Fiestas are raucous and good-humoured, none more so than the Carnival of Barranquilla , second only to Rio for its Latin pizazz but much less commercialized.

But there's more to coastal Colombia than drinking and dancing. Cartagena is a colonial gem, full of wonderful old buildings in flower-filled streets and a history so rich it should carry a government health warning. Ironically, its magnificent fortifications, built to repel invading navies, now attract armies of tourists. East of Cartagena is a more traditional Caribbean treat, Tayrona National Park, with its beautiful unspoiled beaches, backed by the massive Sierra Nevada de Santa Marta coastal mountains which rise sheeer out of the turquoise waters. Inland, high up in the mountains, is Ciudad Perdida, the Lost City, ancient centre of the once-great Tayrona culture. The exhausting six-day trek through tropical rainforest is the ultimate Indiana Jones adventure. Further east is the remote, arid Guajira Peninsula, home to flamingoes and the Gaujiros, *another of Colombia's indigenous* tribes. Meanwhile, west of Cartagena are strange mud volcanos and a huge mud lake, where you can bathe in the brown, sticky stuff before waddling off for a more conventional dip in the Caribbean.

Highlights of Cartagena and the the North Coast

In Cartagena

★ *Drinking fresh fruit juice on Muelle de los Pegasos.*

★ *An evening cocktail in Plaza Santo Domingo.*

★ *Strolling among the small plazas of the San Diego quarter.*

★ *Exploring the tunnels of Castillo San Felipe.*

Along the North Coast

★ *Enjoying the Caribbean in Islas del Rosario or Tayrona.*

★ *Whooping it up at the Barranquilla Carnival.*

★ *Mudbathing in Galerazamba or Arboletes.*

★ *The trek through rainforest up to Ciudad Perdida.*

Cartagena

Phone code 95
Colour map 1, grid B2
Population: 746,000

Cartagena is one of the hottest, most vibrant and beautiful cities in South America. It combines superb weather, a sparkling stretch of the Caribbean, an abundance of tropical fruit, and, above all, the most fantastic collection of colonial buildings this side of the 16th century. You can almost smell the history here – as well as the flowers tumbling from a thousand balconies into the city's narrow streets and which decorate the many gorgeous internal patios. As if you hadn't worked it out by now, this is a place not to be missed.

Ins and Outs

Getting there

By air The Rafael Núñez international airport is at Crespo, is 1½ km north of the centre. The bus ride costs US$0.20; taxi to the centre US$2.50, to Bocagrande US$6. Buses and taxis for the return trip can be found on Av Blas de Lezo close to Puerta del Reloj. Buses can be very crowded and if you have much luggage, a taxi is recommended. See page 172 for Cartagena airport facilities and flight details.

By bus The bus terminal is 30 mins from town. To get there, take an air-conditioned city bus, with luggage space, marked 'Terminal de Transportes' US$0.60, or taxi US$4.50. Arriving, your taxi fare may be a little more, to Bocagrande for example; agree the fare before you get in.

By sea Undoubtedly, the best approach is by sea. Regular sea lines are at present non-existant, but what is possible is detailed on page 172. Cartagena is, however popular for cruise ships and those who have their own sea transport: around 200,000 passengers pass through the docks each year. Equally, many tourists take trips to the offshore islands. A description of the sea approach to the city is given below under **History.**

Getting around

Local buses are crowded, slow, ramshackled but colourful, cheap and a good way to find out about the locals. As usual in Latin America, do watch your belongings. **Taxis** are also quite cheap and more convenient. There are no meters, journeys are calculated by zones, each zone costing about US$0.75, thus Bocagrande to Centro, 2 zones = US$1.50. It is quite common to ask other people waiting if they would like to share, but, in any case, always agree the fare with the driver before getting in. By arrangement, taxis will wait for you if visiting more remote places. Fares go up at night.

Best time to visit

The climate varies little during the year. Temperatures rise marginally when there is more frequent rain, (Aug-Nov), and there can be flooding. Freak weather, (as in 1999

● ●

The Sacking of Cartagena

In spite of its daunting outer forts and encircling walls Cartagena was challenged again and again by enemies. Sir Francis Drake, with 1,300 men, broke in successfully in 1586, leading to a major reconstruction of the ramparts we see today. Nevertheless the Frenchmen Baron de Pointis and Ducasse, with 10,000 men, beat down the

defences and sacked the city in 1697. But the strongest attack of all, by Sir Edward Vernon with 27,000 men and 3,000 pieces of artillery, failed in 1741 after besieging the city for 56 days; it was defended by the one-eyed, one-armed and one-legged hero Blas de Lezo, whose statue is at the entrance to the San Felipe fortress.

● ●

on the fringes of the Venezuelan disaster) is very unusual. Fiestas are taken seriously in Cartagena, and if you want a quiet time, take account of the **Festival** section below. If you want to join in, be sure to plan in advance or be prepared to struggle for accommodation and expect higher prices.

Cartagena Convention & Visitors Bureau, Salon Pórtico, Cra 8, Getsemaní, T6602418, F6602415. In the Convention Center, maps and general information. *Empresa Promotora de Turismo y Cultura de Cartagena* (Proturismo), Muelle de Los Pegasos, T6651843, has some information but is primarily selling boat trips, T-shirts etc. **Tourist Offices**

Carry your passport, or a photocopy, at all times. Failure to present it on police request can result in imprisonment and fines. Generally, the central areas are safe and friendly (although Getsemaní is less secure), but should you require the police, there is a station in Barrio Manga. Beware of drug pushers on the beaches, pickpockets in crowded areas and bag/camera snatchers on quiet Sun mornings. At the bus station, do not be pressurised into a hotel recommendation different from your own choice. **Security**

History

The full name of Cartagena is *Cartagena de Indias*, a name that is quite frequently used and a reminder that the early Spanish navigators believed they had reached the Far East. It was founded by Pedro de Heredia on 13 January 1533. The core of the city was built by the Spaniards on an island separated from the mainland by marshes and lagoons close to a prominent hill, a perfect place for a harbour and, more important at the time, easy to defend against attack. Furthermore, it was close to the mouth of the Río Magdalena, the route to the interior of the continent. In 1650, the Spaniards built a connection to the river, 145 km long, known as the **Canal del Dique,** to allow free access for ships from the up-river ports. This waterway has been used off and on ever since, was updated in the early 19th century and it is still used, mainly by barges, today.

The great Bay of Cartagena, 15 km long and 5 km wide is protected by several low, sandy islands. There were then two approaches to it, Bocagrande, at the northern end of Tierrabomba island – this was the direct entry from the Caribbean – and Bocachica, a narrow channel to the south of the island. Bocagrande was blocked by an underwater protective wall after Admiral Vernon's attack in 1741 (see below), thus leaving only one, easily protected, entrance to the approach to the harbour. The old walled city lies at the north end of the Bahía de Cartagena.

Cartagena declared its independence from Spain in 1811. A year later Bolívar used the city as a jumping-off point for his Magdalena campaign. After a heroic resistance, Cartagena was retaken by the royalists under **General Pablo Morillo** in 1815. The patriots finally freed it in 1821.

Cartagena today   Although Cartagena is Colombia's fourth largest city, the short term visitor will not be aware of the size of the place. Beyond and behind the old walled city, Bocagrande and Manga, is a large sprawling conurbation that stretches 10 km to the southeast. People have been moving in to add to the pressure on the poorer neighbourhoods as everywhere else in this part of the world, but Cartagena is a long way from the more heavily populated parts of highland Colombia, to the city's advantage.

Sights

The city's fortifications   Cartagena was one of the storage points for merchandise sent out from Spain and for treasure collected from the Americas to be sent back to Spain. A series of forts protecting the approaches from the sea, and the formidable walls built around the city, made it almost impregnable.

Entering the **Bahía de Cartagena** by sea through Bocachica, the island of Tierrabomba is to the left. At the southern tip of Tierrabomba is the fortress of **San Fernando**. Opposite it, right on the end of Barú island, is the **Fuerte San José**. The two forts were once linked by heavy chains to prevent surprise attacks by pirates. Barú island is separated from the mainland only by the Canal del Dique. In recent years, the city has been expanding down the coast opposite Tierrabomba and settlements can be seen as you approach the entrance to the inner harbour of Cartagena, protected by another two forts, **San José de Manzanillo** on the mainland and the **Fuerte Castillo Grande** on the tip of **Bocagrande** now the main beach resort of the city.

In the centre of the harbour is the statue of the Virgin with the port installations to the right on Manga island. There is a very good view of the harbour, cruise boats and port activity from the end of Calle 6/Carrera 14, Bocagrande, though access to Castillo Grande itself is restricted. Manga Island is now an important suburb of the city. At its northern end a bridge, **Puente Román**, connects it with the old city. This approach to the fortified city was defended by three forts: **San Sebastián del Pastelillo** built between 1558 and 1567 (the *Club de Pesca* has it now) at the northwestern tip of Manga Island; the fortress of **San Lorenzo** near the city itself; and the very powerful **Castillo San Felipe de Barajas** inland on San Lázaro hill, 41 m above sea-level, to the east of the city.

The first fortifications on the site were built in 1536 though the main constructions began in 1639 and it was finished by 1657. It is the largest Spanish fort built in the Americas. Under the huge structure is a network of tunnels cut into the rock, lined with living rooms and offices. Some are open and lighted, a flashlight will be handy in the others; visitors pass through these and on to the top of the fortress. Good footwear is advisable in the damp sloping tunnels. Baron de Pointis, the French pirate, stormed and took it, but Admiral Vernon failed to reach it (see box). In the *Almacén de Pólvora* (Gunpowder store), there is an interesting 1996 reproduction of Vernon's map of the abortive attempt to take the city in 1741. On the statue of Don Blas de Lezo below the fortress, don't miss the plaque displaying the medal prematurely struck celebrating Vernon's 'victory'. ■ *Open daily 0800-1800. Entrance fee US$3. Guides are available.*

Yet another fort, **La Tenaza**, protected the northern point of the walled city from a direct attack from the open sea. The huge encircling walls were started early in the 17th century and finished by 1735. They were on average 12 m high and 17 m thick, with six gates. They contained, besides barracks, a water reservoir.

The old walled city was in two sections, **outer** and **inner.** Much of the wall between the two disappeared some years ago. Nearly all the houses are of one or two storeys. In the **outer** city, the artisan classes lived in the one-storey houses of **Getsemaní** where many colonial buildings survive. Today, there is a concentration of all categories of hotels and restaurants here. Immediately adjoining is the modern downtown sector, known as **La Matuna**, where vendors crowd the pavements and alleys between the modern commercial buildings. Several middle range hotels are in this district, between Avenidas Venezuela and Lemaitre.

In the **inner** city, the houses in **El Centro** were originally occupied by the high officials and nobility. **San Diego** (the northern end of the inner city) was where the middle classes lived: the clerks, merchants, priests and military. Today, the streets of the inner city are relatively uncrowded; up-market hotels and restaurants are sprinkled throughout the area.

Just under a kilometre from the old city, along a seafront boulevard, **Bocagrande** is a spit of land crowded with hotel and apartment towers. Thousands of visitors flock to the beach with its accompanying resort atmosphere, fast food outlets, shops – and dirty seawater.

The old city streets are narrow. Each block has a different name, a source of confusion, but don't worry: the thing to do is to wander aimlessly, savouring the street scenes, and allow the great sights to catch you by surprise. However, if you do want to know what you are looking at, the maps are marked with numerals for the places of outstanding interest. Most of the 'great houses' can be visited. Churches are generally open to the public at 1800, some for most of the day. Weekends and holidays are the best time for photography when traffic is minimal. What follows is a walking route for the sights of the old city which you can pick up and leave wherever you wish. Note that the numbers below refer to the circled numbers on the Historical Centre map.

1 The **Puente Román** is the bridge which leads from Isla Manga, with its shipping terminals, into Getsemaní, characterized by its *casas bajas* (low houses).

2 The chapel of **San Roque** (early 17th century) is near the end of Calle Media Luna, and the hospital of Espíritu Santo.

3 Just across the Playa Pedregal (Carrera 11) is the Laguna de San Lázaro and the **Puente Heredia,** on the other side of which is the Castillo San Felipe de Barajas, see above.

4 In an interesting plaza, is the church of **La Santísima Trinidad**, built 1643 but not consecrated till 1839. West of the church, at No 10 Calle Guerrero, lived Pedro Romero, who set the revolution of 1811 going by coming out into the street shouting 'Long Live Liberty'.

5 Along Calle Larga (Calle 25) is the monastery of **San Francisco**. The church was built in 1590 after the pirate Martin Côte had destroyed an earlier church built in 1559. The first Inquisitors lodged at the monastery. From its courtyard a crowd surged into the streets claiming independence from Spain on 11 November 1811. The main part of the monastery has now been turned into business premises – take a look at the cloister garden as you pass by. Handicrafts are sold in the grounds of the monastery, good value, fixed prices, and, at the back, is the Centro Comercial Getsemaní, a busy shopping centre. On the corner of Calle Larga, formerly part of the Franciscan complex, is the **Iglesia de la Tercera Orden**, a busy church with a fine wooden roof of unusual design and some brightly painted niche figures.

6 The church and monastery front on to the Avenida del Mercado on the other side of which is the **Centro Internacional de Convenciones.** It holds gatherings of up to 4,000 people and is frequently used now for local and

Around the old city

Outer city

The Northcoast & the Islands

Cartagena historical centre

The Northcoast & the Islands

Caribbean Sea

Paseo de la Muralla

SAN DIEGO

CENTRO

GETSEMANI

Plaza de la
Independencia

Parque del
Centenario

Playa de
Barahona

Bahía de las Ánimas

To Bocagrande

N

0 metres 100
0 yards 100

■ **Sleeping**
1 Casa Viena
2 Charleston Cartegena
3 Del Lago
4 Doral

5 El Refugio
6 Familiar
7 Holiday
8 Hostal Baluarte
9 Hostal San Diego

10 Hostal Santo
Domingo
11 Las Tres Banderas
12 Montecarlo
13 Monterrey

international conventions. It was built in 1972 on the site of the old colourful market, now banished to the interior part of the city. Although the severe fort-like structure is more or less in keeping with the surrounding historic walls and bastions, not everyone believes this is an improvement. When not in use, ask for a guide to show you around.

Immediately to the north is **Plaza de la Independencia**, with the landscaped **Parque del Centenario** alongside. At right angles to the Plaza runs the **Paseo de los Mártires**, flanked by the busts of nine patriots executed in the square on 24 February 1816 by the royalist Pablo Morillo after he had retaken the city.

Inner City

At the western end of the Paseo is a tall clock tower, often used as the symbol of Cartagena. To the left is the **Muelle de los Pegasos** from where the tourist boats leave. Under the clock tower is the **Puerta del Reloj** and the three arches are the principal entrance to the inner walled city.

7 Inside is the **Plaza de los Coches**. As with almost all the plazas of Cartagena, arcades here offer refuge from the tropical sun. At one time, this plaza was the slave market, and later, it was from here that carriages (*coches*) could be hired for local journeys. On the west side of this plaza is the **Portal de los Dulces**, a favourite meeting place and where you can still buy all manner of local sweets and delicacies.

8 Plaza de la Aduana, with a statue of Columbus in the centre and the **Casa de la Aduana** along the wall, originally the tax office and now part of the city administration as the **Palacio Municipal**. Opposite is the **Casa del Premio Real** which was the residence of the representative of the Spanish King. In the corner of the wall is the **Museo de Arte Moderno,** a collection of the work of modern Colombian artists. There is a museum shop. ■ *Open Mon-Fri 0900-1200, 1500-1800, Sat 1000-1200, US$0.50.*

9 Past the museum is the **Plaza de San Pedro Claver** and the church and monastery of the same name, built by Jesuits in 1603 and later dedicated to San Pedro Claver, a monk in the monastery, who died in 1654 and was canonized 235 years later. He was called *El Esclavo de los Esclavos,* or *El Apostol de los Negros*: he used to beg from door to door for money to give to the black slaves brought to the city. His body is in an illuminated glass coffin set in the high marble altar, and his cell and the balcony from which he kept watch for slave ships are shown to visitors. There are brightly coloured birds in the small monastery garden. Several upstairs rooms form a museum, with many interesting items linked and not linked to Pedro Claver. In the pottery room, for example, is the chair used by the Pope on his visit to Cartagena in 1986. In another room there are several old maps, one of which shows the Caribbean maritime boundaries of Colombia, topical in that disputes with Nicaragua persist in 2000. ■ *Open daily 0800-1700. Entry, US$1.50, reduction with ISIC. Bilingual guides available.*

10 Following the wall round, it is well worthwhile climbing up the **Baluarte San Francisco Javier** for a good view of the city and the Caribbean. There is a **Naval Museum** with maps, models and display of armaments, near the Baluarte, ■ *Open Tue-Sun 1000-1800, entry US$1.50, children US$0.50.*

11 On the corner of Calle Ricuarte is the convent of **Santa Teresa,** founded in 1609 by a rich benefactor as a convent for Carmelite nuns. It had various uses subsequently, as a prison, a military barracks, a school and in the 1970s, was occupied by the police. It was recently purchased by the Banco Central as a heritage investment and has now been converted into a hotel. It is possible to visit the public areas of the hotel and admire the tasteful work of restoration. There is a great view from the roof. See under **Sleeping** for details of the hotel, now called the *Charleston.*

12 El Bodegón de la Candelaria, Calle Las Damas No 64, was a fine colonial residence. It has been faithfully restored and there is some fine panelling and period furniture to see. It is now a restaurant specialising in good seafood. A small shrine in one of the rooms marks the place where the Virgin appeared to a priest who was living there at the time.

13 One block away is **Plaza de Bolívar** with an equestrian statue of the Liberator in the centre. Formerly it was the Plaza de la Inquisición, with the Palacio de la Inquisición (see below), on its west side. The gardens of the plaza were given a face-lift in 2000 and is now an attractive corner of Cartagena.

14 On the opposite side of the Plaza de Bolívar to the Palacio de la Inquisición is the **Museo del Oro y Arqueológico**. Gold and pottery are very well displayed. Specially featured is the Zenú area to the south of Cartagena in the marshlands of the Sinú, San Jorge and Magdalena rivers, which is flooded by the river waters 6-8 months of the year. Early drainage systems are featured as is the advanced level of weaving techniques using the *cañafleche* and other fresh water reeds. This area was densely populated between the second to tenth centuries AD during which time the gold working-skills of the people were developed to the high level that can still be seen today at Mompós, at the northern edge of the Zenú region. ■ *Open 0830-1200, 1400-1800, Mon-Fri. Entrance US$0.75,*

15 The **Palacio de La Inquisición** is on the other side of the Plaza Bolívar. The jurisdiction of this tribunal extended to Venezuela and Panama, and at least 800 were sentenced to death here. There is a small window overlooking the plaza where the public were informed of the sentences. The Palacio houses a modest historical museum at the Palacio, though some of the exhibits are in poor condition. Of special interest are the model of Cartagena in 1808, copies of Alexander Von Humboldt's maps showing the link he discovered between the Orinoco and Amazon rivers (*Canal de Casiquiere)* and of the Maypures

24 hours in Cartagena

*The essence of historic Cartagena is in the walled city. Start at **Puerta del Reloj** and sample the delicacies of the Portal de los Dulces. **San Pedro Claver church** is nearby and as rewarding a stop as any. Wander along the Ramparts and admire the view but be tempted down either towards **Plaza de Bolívar** (for the glitter of the Gold Museum or a shiver in the Palacio de la Inquisición) or further along to **Plaza de Santo Domingo**, a good place for refreshments.*

*Enjoy a stroll along any of the streets going north, and make for **Santa Clara** for a buffet lunch (or something lighter nearby). Round the corner is the **Plaza de las Bóvedas** for a fine selection for things to buy and an interesting corner of the Ramparts above.*

*Back through the busier parts of San Diego and Centro to **La Matuna** for the local market, or along the streets you missed earlier to the upmarket boutiques near Plaza de Bolívar. Watch the sunset from the **Baluarte San Francisco Javier,** and have an evening meal in one of the good restaurants in that corner of the old city.*

For a relaxing alternative, return at any time to Puerta del Reloj and take a horse-drawn carriage ride around the sights.

rapids on the Orinoco – note that the longitude lines on the maps are west of Paris not Greenwich. The main attraction is the grisly collection of torture instruments. Historical books are on sale at the entrance. ■ *Open Mon-Fri, 0800-1700, US$1.50.*

16 The **Cathedral**, in the northeast corner of Plaza de Bolívar, begun in 1575, was partially destroyed by Francis Drake. Reconstruction was finished by 1612. Great alterations were made between 1912 and 1923. A severe exterior, with a fine doorway, and a simply decorated interior. See the guilded 18th century altar, the Carrara marble pulpit, and the elegant arcades which sustain the central nave.

Although established in 1610, the present building dates from 1706 with modifications up to 1770. The stone entrance with its coats of arms is well preserved and the ornate wooden door is very notable. The whole building, with its balconies, cloisters and patios, is a fine example of colonial baroque.

Across the street is the **Palacio de la Proclamación** named for the declaration of independence of the State of Cartagena in November 1811. Before that it was the local Governor's residence, and later was where Simón Bolívar stayed in 1826. The building was restored in 1950.

17 The church and monastery of **Santo Domingo**, built 1570 to 1579 is now a seminary. The old monastery was replaced by the present one in the 17th century. Inside, a miracle-making image of Christ, carved towards the end of the 16th century, is set on a baroque 19th century altar. This is a most interesting neighbourhood, very little changed since the 16th century. In Calle Santo Domingo, No 33-29, is one of the great patrician houses of Cartagena, the **Casa de los Condes de Pestagua**, until recently the Colegio del Sagrado Corazón de Jesús, now an annex to the *Hotel Charleston* (see under **Sleeping**). It has a fine colonnaded courtyard, marble floors and magnificent palm trees in the centre garden. Beside the church is the **Plaza de Santo Domingo**, one of the favourite corners of Cartagena, with popular restaurants, outdoor bars and cafés a delight at night. A new sculpture by Fernando Botero *'La Gorda'* has recently arrived in the Plaza.

18 North of Santo Domingo at Calle de la Factoría 36-57 is the magnificent **Casa del Marqués de Valdehoyos**, originally owned by the Marqués, who had the lucrative licences to import slaves and flour. The fine woodcarving is

The Northcoast & the Islands

some of the best in Cartagena and the ceilings, chandeliers, wooden arches and balustrading are special. The views of the city from the fine upper floor balconies are also recommended. Unhappily the tourist office here has been closed and the building is unoccupied; already there are signs of neglect. Hopefully, it will again be brought into use soon. Though not officially open to the public, it is worth a try to have a look inside.

19 A short walk north is the Plaza, church and convent of **La Merced**, founded 1618. The convent, a prison during Morillo's reign of terror, is now occupied by a private university (Jorge Tadeo Lozano), and its church has become the **Teatro Heredia**, which was beautifully restored recently.

20 Two blocks east is Calle de la Universidad, at the end of which is the monastery of **San Agustín** (1580), now the Universidad de Cartagena. From its chapel, now occupied by a printing press, the pirate Baron de Pointis stole a 500-pound silver sepulchre. It was returned by the King of France but the citizens melted it down to pay their troops during the siege by Morillo in 1815.

21 One block along Calle de San Agustín is **La Casa Museo de Simón Bolívar,** a collection of memorabilia in the first Cartagena house he stayed in, now the *Biblioteca Bartolomé Calvo* owned by the Banco de la República.

22 One block along Badillo (Cra 7) is the church of **Santo Toribio de Mongrovejo**. Building began in 1729. In 1741, during Admiral Vernon's siege, a cannon ball fell into the church during Mass and lodged in one of the central columns; the ball is now in a recess in the west wall. The font of Carrara marble in the Sacristy is a masterpiece. There is a beautiful carved ceiling (*mudéjar* style) above the main altar with a rear lighted figure of Christ. Opens for Mass at 0600 and 1800, closed at other times.

23 The church and monastery of **Santa Clara de Assisi** is close by. It was built 1617-21, and has been spectacularly restored. It is now yet another hotel but is the one you must not fail to see (see also below).

24 Behind the hotel is the orange **Casa de Gabriel García Márquez,** the most famous living Colombian author, on the corner of Calle del Curato.

25 Beyond the Santa Clara is the **Plaza de las Bóvedas**. Outwards towards the sea before Las Bovedas you will see a bank (*espiga*) leading to a jetty used in colonial times when the sea came up to the walls, as shown on the 1808 map displayed in the *Palacio de la Inquisición*. All the land below the walls has since been reclaimed, now with sports fields and recreational areas and the Av Santander/Paseo de la Muralla, a busy bypass to the city. The walls of Las Bóvedas, built 1799, are some 12m high and from 15 to 18m thick. At the base of the wall are 23 dungeons, now containing tourist shops. Both a lighted underground passage and a drawbridge lead from Las Bóvedas to the fortress of La Tenaza that guarded the approach to the city from the coast to the northeast.

26 Casa de Núñez, just outside the walls of La Tenaza in El Cabrero district was the home of Rafael Núñez, four times the president of Colombia. He brought in the constitution of 1886 and wrote the national anthem. His grandiose marble tomb is in the delightful small **Ermita El Cabrero** church opposite. ■ *Mon-Fri 0800-1200, 1400-1800. There is also a monument to the 1886 constitution in the small park beside the lagoon.*

27 Back along the lagoon is the old **Plaza de Toros**,(bull ring). It is an interesting wooden building but now abandoned and in a dangerous state. It can not be visited.

28 Closer to the centre, where the main road comes across into the city, is a traffic circle, in the centre of which is the monument to **La India Catalina,** Pedro de Heredia's Indian interpreter in the early days of the Spanish conquest. A miniature of this statue is given to the winner of the annual Cartagena film festival – a Colombian 'Oscar'.

The Northcoast & the Islands

In addition to being a spectacular feature of Cartagena, the city walls make a **The Ramparts** great walk and are an excellent way to visit many of the attractions inside. A good place to start is the **Baluarte de San Francisco Javier** (No **10**) from where, with a few ups and downs, it is continuous to **La India Catalina** (No **28**). From this point, there are two further sections along the lagoons to the **Puente Román** (No **1**). The final section along the Calle del Arsenal can be completed through the **Playa de Barahona**, a bayside park, busy at weekends. The entire walk takes about 1½ hours, though if you take a camera, considerably longer! It is a spectacular walk in the morning around 0600 and equally at sunset. At many points you can drop down to see the sights detailed above in the tour of the old city.

Three of the sights of Cartagena are off our map. Two of them, the Fortress of San Fernando and the Castillo San Felipe de Barajas, across the **Puente Heredia** (No **3**) have been described above.

The third is **La Popa** hill, nearly 150 m high, from which there is a fine view of the harbour and the city. Here are the Augustinian church and monastery of Santa Cruz and restored ruins of the convent dating from 1608. In the church is the beautiful little image with a golden crown of the Virgin of La Candelaria, reputed a deliverer from plague and a protector against pirates. The statue was blessed by the Pope on his visit in 1986. Her day is 2 February. For nine days before the feast thousands of people go up the hill by car, on foot, or on horseback. On the day itself people carry lighted candles as they go up the hill. There is an attractive, bougainvillia covered cloister with a well in the centre, and a museum with illuminated manuscripts, old maps, music books, relics, and an image of the *Cabro de Oro,* (golden goat) found by the Augustinians on the site, presumed to be an object of veneration of the Indians who previously inhabited the area. The name was bestowed on the hill because of an imagined likeness to a ship's poop. ■ *Entry US$1.50, children US$0.75, open daily 0800-1730. Guides available. It is not recommended to walk up on your own; either take a guided tour, or take a public bus to Teatro Miramar at the foot of the hill (US$0.50), then bargain for a taxi up, about US$2. If driving, take Cra 21 off Avenida Pedro de Heredia, and follow the winding road to the top.*

Beaches

Take a bus south from the Puerta del Reloj, taxi US$1.50, or walk to **Bocagrande**, whose beaches can be dirty in parts, and often crowded. You will also be constantly hassled. However, the sea is gorgeous.

Marbella beach is an alternative, just north of Las Bóvedas. This is the locals' beach, and therefore quieter during the week than Bocagrande and is good for swimming, though subject at times to dangerous currents.

The **Bocachica** beach, on Tierrabomba island, is also none too clean and you may be hassled here too. Boats leave for Bocachica from Muelle Turístico. The departure point is the two-storey glass building half-way along, which also has some tourist information. The round trip can take up to two hours each way and costs about US$8. *Ferry Dancing*, about half the price of the faster, luxury boats, carries dancing passengers. Boats taking in Bocachica and the San Fernando fortress include *Alcatraz*, which runs a daily trip from the Muelle Turístico. Alternatively, you can cross from Bocagrande, *lanchas* leave from near the Hilton Hotel and go to Punta Arena beach on Tierrabomba.

Boats to the Islas del Rosario (see below) may stop at the San Fernando fortress on Tierrabomba island and **Playa Blanca** on the Isla de Barú for one hour. You can bargain with the boatman to leave you and collect you later. Take food and water since these are expensive on the island. Barú, a long thin island, is mostly fine white sand beaches which are slowly being exploited by up-market hotel complexes which hopefully will respect this fragile environment. The stopping place for tourist boats from Cartagena is Playa Blanca which is crowded in the mornings, but peaceful after the tour boats have left at around 1400. Another alternative is to catch a fishing boat from the Mercado Bazurto (a short distance beyond *La Popa*) to Playa Blanca, leaving around 0830, US$3.50 one way, and take another one back when you choose. There are several restaurants on the beach, the best *La Sirena*, is run by Carmen 'La Española' (there are other Carmens around!), good food, hammocks for hire US$3.50 or you can take your own or a tent. Remember to take water, there is little on the island. You can also reach Playa Blanca by taking the bus to Pasacaballo, crossing the Canal del Dique by canoe and continue by truck or jeep to the beach. If walking, aloow 2½ hours in all. If staying the night at Playa Blanca in *cabañas* or tents, beware of ferocious sandflies. A *cabaña* will typically cost about US$12 per night. **NB** Pay for boat trips on board if possible, and be certain that you and the operator understand what you are paying for. See also **La Boquilla**, northeast of Cartagena.

Bocagrande

```
N
0 metres    200
0 yards     200
```

■ Sleeping		
1 Bahía	6 Costa del Sol	12 Las Velas
2 Capilla del Mar	7 Flamingo	13 Leonela
3 Caribe	8 Ibatama	14 Playa
4 Cartagena Hilton	9 India Catalina	15 Residencias Internacional
5 Casa Grande	10 Intercontinental	16 Residencia Mary
	11 La Giralda	17 Residencia Punta Canoa

Essentials

Hotel prices rise for the high season, Nov-Mar, and Jun-Jul. From 15 Dec to 31 Jan they can rise by as much as 50% on Bocagrande beach; in town you will find not find much below **E**, but price increases are not so steep. Hotels tend to be heavily booked right through to Mar.

In Bocagrande (10 mins by bus from city): **LL** *Cartagena Hilton*, El Laguito, T6650666, F6652211 Apartado Aéreo 1774. Best equipped. **LL** *Caribe*, Cra 1, No 2-87, T6653855, F6653707. Caribbean style with newer annexes, comfortable, a/c, convention hotel, nice grounds, swimming pool in the (expensive) restaurant.

L *Capilla del Mar*, C 8, Cra 1, T6653866, F6655145. Resort hotel, good French restaurant, swimming pool on top floor, no connection with restaurant of same name in the old city. **L** *Las Velas*, Av Las Velas No 1-60, El Laguito, T6656866/0590. Holiday resort, rooms with balconies overlooking beach, a/c, good restaurant. **L** *Intercontinental*, Cra 2,/C 6A, T6658261, F6658269. Large new highrise hotel, convention facilities, usual intercontinental standard, internet services.

AL-A range: *Bahía*, Cra 3/C 4, T6650316. Pool, good. *Casa Grande*, Av del Malecón, No 9-126, T6653943. Pleasant small hotel on beach, hot water, tropical garden, restaurant, owner speaks English, a/c, cheaper with fan only. *Flamingo*, Av San Martín No 5-85, T6650623. With bath and a/c, good breakfast included, garden, clean, helpful, pleasant, eat on the terrace, beach facilities included, parking. Recommended.

C *India Catalina*, Cra 2, No 7-115, T6655523. With breakfast, a/c, safe, clean, convenient for groups, good cafeteria, good value. **C** *Playa*, Cra 2, No 4-87, T6650552. All rooms with bath, a/c, very clean, open air bar, restaurant, swimming pool, noisy disco next door. **C** *Ibatama*, Av San Martín 7-46, T6651127, With breakfast, a/c, less with fan, convenient.

D *Residencias Internacional*, Av San Martín 4-110, T6650675. Small rooms, small bath, a/c, cold water, TV, uncomfortable beds, convenient location, friendly. **D** *Leonela*, Cra 3, 7-142, T6654761. Quiet, comfortable. **D** *La Giralda*, Cra 3, No 7-166, T6654507. Clean, friendly, with bath, fan, some a/c. There are plenty of small, pleasant **D** *residencias*, On Cra 3, eg *Mary*, No 6-53, T6652833. Small, respectable, with bath, a/c less with fan, clean and friendly.

E *Costa del Sol*, Cra 1/C 9, T6650844, F6653755. Youth Hostel, 280 beds, cheaper for members, in tower block opposite beach. **E** *Residencia Punta Canoa*, C 7, No 2-50, T6654179. Reasonable though somewhat rundown.

In Old City – Centro and San Diego: LL *Santa Clara*, Cra 8, No 39-29, T6646070, F6648040. French Sofitel group, magnificently restored early 17th century convent, French, Italian and Colombian restaurants (good value buffet lunch for US$4), terrace a fine place to watch sunsets (cocktails around US$5), swimming pool open to public, all services. Recommended; if you can't afford to stay or eat there, take a look anyway. **LL** *Charleston Cartagena* (formerly *Santa Teresa*), Cra 3A, No 31-23, T6649494, F6649448. Thoughtfully converted convent, opened as a hotel 1996, elegant restaurant, swimming pool on roof with public bar, fine hotel.

A *Hostal San Diego*, C de las Bóvedas, No 39-120, T6600982/83. Modern rooms in a nice old house.

C *Las Tres Banderas*, C Cochera de Hobo, No 38-66, T6600160. Very pleasant, quiet, friendly, good beds. Recommended.

D *Hostal Santo Domingo*, C Santo Domingo, No 33-46, T6642268. Basic but clean and quiet, attractive inner court, well located. Recommended. **D** *Veracruz*, C San Agustín, No 6-15. Opposite San Agustín church, fan (more with a/c), clean, safe, helpful but noisy disco on ground floor.

In La Matuna and Getsemaní: **AL** *Monterrey*, Paseo de los Mártires, Cra 8B, No 25-103, T6648560, F6648574, htlmonterreyctg@ctgred.net.co French-owned, terrace bar, business centre, jacuzzi, a/c, good.

B *Del Lago*, C 34, No 11-15, T6640111. A/c, phone, no singles, reasonable restaurant, laundry, credit cards accepted, no parking.

D *Montecarlo*, C 34, No 10-16, T6640115. With a/c cheaper without, good value, good laundry next door, decent restaurant, expensive breakfast. **D** *Hostal Baluarte*, Media Luna, No 10-81, T6642208. With bath and fan, converted colonial house, family run, helpful, will arrange day trips, well-priced restaurant. **D** *Villa Colonial*, C de las Maravillas, No 30-60, T6642409, T/F6645919. With bath, a/c, TV, friendly owner Marta, convenient, clean, good.

E *Doral*, Media Luna, No 10-46, T6641706. Nice, fan, large rooms but avoid ground floor, safe courtyard where you can park cycles/motorbikes, noisy at night and water problems. **E** *Holiday*, Media Luna, No 10-47, T6640948. Clean, fan, friendly, quiet, pleasant courtyard; free luggage store, safe. Recommended. **E** *Familiar*, C del Guerrero, No 29-66, near Media Luna, T6648374. Clean, cheaper in dormitory, friendly, safe, fan, space for bike or motorcycle, use of kitchen, laundry facilities, good value. **E** *Punta Arena*, C del Guerrero, No 29-87, T6601595, family run, friendly, clean but noisy. **E** *Casa Viena*, San Andrés, No 30-53, T6646242. Run by Hans, rooms with bath and TV, cheaper rooms available down to **G** per person for dormitory bed, a/c, clean, safe, cooking facilities, washing machine, book exchange, good information on tours etc, sometimes noisy, internet service US$2.60/hr. Recommended as an excellent travellers' guest house.

F *Residencias Venecia*, C del Guerrero No 29-108, friendly, some rooms with fan, garden, washing facilities, clean and secure. **F** *Tropicana*, Plaza de la Independencia (C 30), No 8B-58, T6642929. Rundown but friendly, helpful and clean. **F** *El Refugio*, C Media Luna, No 10-35, T6643507. Clean, friendly. Many cheap hotels on C Media Luna are brothels; area not advisable for women on their own.

Outside the centre On the road to the airport are several hotels and *pensiones*, particularly at Marbella beach, eg **D** *Bellavista*, Av Santander No 46-50, T6646411. A Republican style building with a nice patio, clean, fan, English-speaking owner, secure, nice atmosphere, recommended for longer stays. Right behind is **F** *Mirador del Lago*. Clean, large rooms, fan, friendly owner. Further on is **F** *Turístico Margie*, Av 2A, No 63-175, very close to beach in Crespo district. Convenient for airport (walking distance), 3 km to old city, family-run, clean, modern. Southeast of the city is **E** *Santa Maria de Los Angeles*, Pie de La Popa, Camino Arriba No 22-109, T6692149. Next to Anglican Church and run by them, simple, comfortable rooms, clean, safe, cafetría, parking.

Camping On the beach is not secure. Vehicle parking overnight is possible at the Costa Norte Beach Club, 2 km northeast on coast beyond the airport, US$4 per night.

Eating **In Bocagrande:** *Italia*, Av San Martín 7-55. Good Italian, excellent ice creams and sorbets. *Palacio de las Frutas*, Av San Martín, No 5-130. Good *comida corriente*. *La Fonda Antioqueña*, Cra 2, No 6-164. Traditional Colombian, nice atmosphere. *Pietros*, Cra 3, No 4-101. Italian and local dishes. *Farah Express*, Cra 2/C 9, T6656479. Arab food, good, also vegetarian dishes, open late, good value. *Coffee Bean Shop*, Cra 2/Cra 6. Coffee, drinks, snacks, French Canadian owner, internet US$ 3/hr. Good reasonably priced food in the chain restaurants eg *Crêpes y Waffles*, *Ricco Ricco*.

In Old City - Centro and San Diego: *Capilla del Mar*, Callejón de los Estribos, No 2-74, T6601129. 50 years of excellent seafood, Colombian specialities. Recommended. *La Vitrola*, C Baloco, No 2-01, T6648243. High quality, some Caribbean dishes, in-place, expensive but very good. *Bodegón de La Candelaria*, C de las Damas, No 3-64, T6647251, Good fish menu, a/c, good value, open for lunch daily, dinner

Mon-Sat. *Nautilus*, C San Pedro, No 10-76, San Diego. Facing statue of *La India Catalina*, very good seafood. *La Escollera de la Marina*, C San Juan de Dios/C Ricaurte, T6642040. Spanish food, bar and disco.

There are several good establishments on Plaza Santo Domingo: *Pacos*, good bar/fish restaurant, open evenings till late. *Café de La Plaza*, great atmosphere, open all day. *Dalmacia*, just off square, charming, run by a Croatian, closes 2000. *La Sartén por el Mango*, 2nd floor overlooking Plaza, good in the evening but poor service and expensive. *Carbon de Palo*, close to Plaza, steak house, good quality. *San Bernabe*, reasonable food, open 1100 till late. *El Burlador de Sevilla*, C Santo Domingo, No 33-88, T6600866. Spanish, open 1200-2400, busy at weekends.

La Fogacha, C de la Mantilla/C de la Factoría, No 3-37, T6649099. Italian, cheap but good, open daily 1000-2400. *San Pedro*, Plaza de San Pedro Claver. Tables outside, a/c inside, Asian and fish specialities, good value. Recommended. *Enoteca*, C San Juan de Dios, No 3-39, T6643806. Italian, pricey, pizzas served downstairs. *Café San Nicolas*, C Ricaurte, No 31-46, T6643058. Inexpensive snacks, relaxed atmosphere.

La Tablada, C de la Tablada, No 7-46. Arty, usually good music, basic, gay bar at night. *Le Bistrot de L'Alianza*, Parque Fernandez de Madrid, No 37-34, French, good food, excellent *crêpes*. *Café de la Casa Santisima*, C Santisima No 8-19, T6643316. Quiet, attractive, lovely leafy courtyard, good salads and sandwiches. *La Crepería*, Plaza de Bolívar 3-110. Excellent salads, fruit drinks, crêpes, gets busy around 1230. *La Dolce Vita*, Parque San Diego. Pasta and pizza, bar upstairs.

Several Chinese restaurants in Centro, eg *Dragón de Oro*, Av Venezuela, No 10-24. Good, inexpensive. *El Diamante*, C de la Soledad, T6644121. Large helpings, good. *Jumbo*, C Tabaco, good Chinese and local food, *churrascos*, large portions, reasonable prices.

In Getsemaní and La Matuna: *Nuevo Mundo*, Media Luna near plaza. Chinese, big portions, good typical menu, cheap, good value. *Café-Galería Abaloa*, C Espíritu Santo, No 29-200. Quiet, cultural ambience, books, music etc, drinks, breakfasts, also has 3 cheap rooms. *El Koral*, next to *Hotel Doral*, Media Luna. Good, cheap. *El Niño*, Medio Luna, No 10-32. Good breakfasts, large fruit juices, good value. Many restaurants around Plaza Independencia have good value meals, eg *Fonda El Socorro*.

Vegetarian *Tienda Naturista*, C Quero 9-09. Good, cheap. *Govinda*, Plaza de los Coches 7-15. Good set meal US$2.50. *Girasoles*, C de Quero/Calle de los Puntales, good. *Panadería La Mejor*, Av Arbeláez, No 8A-37, good for breakfast, fine wholemeal bread, coffee, yoghurt, expensive.

Outside the centre: *Club de Pesca*, San Sebastián de Pastelillo fort, Manga Island, T6605863/6607065. Wonderful setting, excellent fish and seafood, expensive. Warmly recommended. *La Fragata*, C Real del Cabrera, No 41-15, T6648734. Next to Casa de Rafael Nuñez (Map No **26**), very good seafood. *Bucarest*, Marbella, next to *Hotel Bellavista*. For seafood and juices.

At cafés try *patacón*, a biscuit made of green banana, mashed and baked; also from street stalls in Parque del Centenario in the early morning. At restaurants ask for *sancocho* the local soup of the day of vegetables and fish or meat. Also try *obleas* for a snack, biscuits with jam, cream cheese, or caramel fudge (*arequipe*), and *buñuelos*, deep-fried cheese dough balls. Fruit juices are fresh, tasty and cheap in Cartagena: a good place is on the Paseo de los Pegasos (Av Blas de Lezo) from the many stalls alongside the boats: it is hard to choose between them but Jimmy (long fair hair ponytail), next to Proturismo has been recommended for several years and uses bottled water.

Cartagena boasts a lively dance scene and atmosphere in the city after dark is addictive. A great place for a drink are any one of the cafés next to the Santo Domingo

Bars & Nightclubs

The Northcoast & the Islands

church. In **Bocagrande**, many of the hotels have evening entertainment and can arrange *chiva* tours, usually with free drinks and live music on the bus. There are good local nightclubs eg *La Escollera*, Cra 1, next to El Pueblito shopping centre, with other places nearby including spontaneous musical groups on or near the beach almost every evening.

In **Centro**, several of the most popular places are also restaurants and mentioned in the eating section. The place to go in the evening is from the Plaza de los Coches up to the Baluarte de San Francisco where you can pick your place or just enjoy the activities in the plazas and on the street. Try *Tu Candela*, a second floor bar in the Plaza de la Aduana, popular for salsa dancing. A recommended club is *La Escollera de la Marina* (see above under **Eating**).

Elsewhere in the old town is the bar *La Muralla* on the city wall west of Plaza Bolívar, live music at weekends, romantic, but drinks expensive. *El Zorba*, Parque Fernández de Madrid, small, cosy, good music. There are several clubs nearby eg *Hipnótica*, C Cachera de Hobo, No 38-27. The best for salsa is in Getsemaní, *Quiebra Canto*, C Media Luna at Parque Centenario, next to Hotel Monterrey, nice atmosphere, free admission, US$15 average for a bottle of rum. Round the corner by the Convention Centre, along C del Arsenal are several lively bars and clubs. *Quatro Vientos*, Media Luna 10-35, pleasant bar.

Gay Bars include: *Bar Disco Zona G*, C del Porvenir No 35-73, T6642330. *Vía Libre*, C de la Soledad, No 5-52.

Entertainment There are many **cinemas** in Cartagena, two of the most popular (*Cine Cartagena* and *Cine Colón*) are in the Plaza de la Independencia facing the Torre del Reloj. In Mar of each year, there is an International Film Festival – the 40th was held in 2000, the longest running festival of its kind in Latin America. Although mainly Spanish American films are featured, the US, Canada and European countries are represented in the week long showings (see Box). Of the several **theatres** in the city, the most notable is the *Teatro Heredia*, (Map No **19**) which has recently been lavishly restored.

Festivals La Candelaria (Candelmas) 2 Feb, see under **La Popa** above. *Independencía*, in the 2nd week of Nov to celebrate the independence of Cartagena. Men and women in masks and fancy dress roam the streets, dancing to the sound of *maracas* and drums. There are beauty contests and battles of flowers, and general uncontrolled mayhem. *Caribbean Music Festival* for several days in Mar (most years), groups from all over the Caribbean region and beyond perform salsa, reggae, etc. There is an *International Film Festival* for a week in Mar (see above). Average ticket prices US$2. The festival has an office at Beluarte San Francisco, C San Juan de Dios, T6601701/2, F6600970, www.festicinecartagena.com Avianca offices everywhere have details of festival dates.

Shopping There is a good selection of *artesanías* at *Compendium* on Plaza Bolívar. *Galeria Cano*, next to the Gold Museum has excellent reproductions of precolumbian designs. Pricey antiques in C Santo Domingo. Handicraft shops in the Plaza de las Bóvedas (No **25**) have the best selection in town but tend to be expensive – cruise ship passengers are brought here. Woollen *blusas* are good value; try the *Tropicano* in Pierino Gallo building in Bocagrande. Also in this building are reputable jewellery shops. *H Stern* has a jewellery shop in the Pierino Gallo shopping centre and at the *Hilton Hotel*. A number of jewellery shops near Plaza de Bolívar in Centro specialise in emeralds. Beware of 'Cuban cigars' sold on the street. For the genuine article, *Habanos*, C San Juan de Dios has a wide selection. In general you will pay less in Bogotá.

Comercial Centro Getsemaní, C Larga between San Juan and Plaza de la Independencia, a large new shopping centre has many establishments. Good *artesanías* next to it in the grounds of San Francisco convent. *Magali París*, Av Venezuela y C del Boquete, is an a/c supermarket, with cafeteria.

Colombia on screen

Cartagena has long been associated with film-making. An early film made here was Green Fire (1954) about the Colombian emerald business, starring Grace Kelly, Paul Douglas and Stuart Granger. Since then, the backdrop of colonial buildings and the blue waters of the Caribbean have been seen the world over. Several scenes of The Mission with Robert de Niro and Jeremy Irons were shot in Cartagena, notably in the Palacio de la Inquisición, and young(er), single Michael Douglas danced with Kathleen Turner in one of the main squares in the 1980s blockbuster Romancing the Stone. Quemado, starring Marlon Brando also featured Cartagena. The most recent production to be made here was Nostromo, a BBC/RAI co-production based on the novel by Joseph Conrad, which was shown to wide acclaim in Europe and the USA.

In 2000, Cartagena held its 40th International Film Festival which featured films from 12 Latin American and three European countries.

Bookshops *Librería Bitacura*, Av San Martín 7-187, Bocagrande, T6657281, (also in Plaza San Pedro Claver in the old city, T6601957), English and Spanish books, run by friendly lady. *Libreria Nacional*, Cra 7 (Badillo), No 36-27, T6641448. For **maps**, *Instituto Geográfico Agustín Codazzi*, Cra 10B, No 34-24, La Matuna T6644171 (see map).

Markets The main market is now to the south east of the old city near La Popa off Av Pedro de Heredia (*Mercado Bazurto*). Good bargains can be found in the market of *La Matuna*, open daily including Sun.

Bullfights These take place mainly in Jan and Feb in the new Plaza de Toros at the Villa Olímpica on Av Pedro de Heredia away from the centre, T6698225. The old, wooden Plaza de Toros **(No 27** on the map) is a fine structure, but is no longer in use. **Sports**
Cockfights are held throughout the year at weekends and holidays. On Sat and Mon at 1500 cockfighting takes place at the Gallerita Popular de la Quinta and on Sun at 1600 at Club Gallístico Pedro Rhenals in El Bosque.

Football *Estadio de Futbol, Pedro de Heredia* is in the Villa Olímpica in the south of the city. Seats for matches cost US$2 Sol (sun), US$5 Sombra (shade) and US$6 for the best seats.

Watersports Yachting *Club Nautico*, Av Miramar on Isla Manga across the Puente Román, T6605582, good for opportunities to charter, crew or for finding a lift to other parts of the Caribbean. Windsurf rental, Bocagrande, US$6.50/hr. **Diving** *Eco Buzos*, Edif Alonso de Ojeda, Local 102, Av Almirante Brion, El Laguito, Bocagrande, T6652707, T/F6551129, 2 dives including all equipment US$75, snorkelling US$35, also snacks and drinks, a 5-day course plus dives is about US$140. *La Tortuga Dive Shop*, Edif Marina del Rey, 2-23 Av del Retorno, Bocagrande, T/F6656995, 2 dives US$70. A faster boat, which allows trips to Isla Barú as well as Los Rosarios, is the same price at Hotel Caribe Dive shop, though discounts are sometimes available if you book via the hotels, enquire. Recompression chamber at the naval hospital, Bocagrande.

Gema Tours, Cra 2, No 6-15, T6551212. Also at airport, city and local tours, also *Rumba en Chiva* night tour of the city. *Aviatur*, Centro Comercial Pierino Gallo, El Laguito, Bocagrande, T6650081. *Contactos*, Centro Comercial Bocagrande, Av San Martín, No 8-142 T6651300. Boat trips, guided tours of the city, bus tours to Galerazamba etc. **Tour operators**
Tierra Mar Aire, Cra 4, No 7-196, Bocagrande, full travel service.

Local Car rental *National*, T6653336 and *Hertz* T6652852 at airport. International T6651164. *Budget* T6655520. *Autocosta* T6652427. Several of the bigger hotels have car rental company offices in their foyers. **Transport**

The Northcoast & the Islands

A horse-drawn carriage can be hired for about US$12.50 for up to 4 people for a trip around the walled city from Puerta del Reloj or from opposite *Hotel El Dorado*, Av San Martín, in Bocagrande, to ride into town at night (romantic but rather short ride). Motorbikes, cycles, scooters and rollerblades rented by **S&S Alquiler de Vehículos de Sport**, Av San Martín, No 9-184, T6650554, T/F6655342. Clients showing this *Handbook* get a 30% discount.

Long distance Air Direct flights daily to major Colombian cities and to smaller places in the north of the country. International flights direct daily to Miami and Panama. From Dec to Mar flights can be overbooked – even reconfirming and turning up 2 hrs early doesn't guarantee a seat; best not to book a seat on the last plane of the day if you can avoid it. **Airport facilities** include a good self-service restaurant and a *Casa de Cambio*, open 0830-2400 cashes TCs but not Bank of America. Better, often much better, rates in town. For information, ask at the Travel Agents' offices on the upper level.

Buses The new bus terminal is on the edge of town on Carretera La Cordialidad (the road to Barranquilla), 30 mins from town. To **Medellín** 665 km, US$31 (Brasilia Pullman, or Rápidos Ochoa, slightly cheaper, recommended), several buses a day, but book early (2 days in advance at holiday times), takes 13-16 hrs. The road is now paved throughout, but in poor condition. To **Santa Marta**, US$9 (with Brasilia, C 32, No 20D-55), 4 hrs, also cheaper lines, US$8. To **Barranquilla**, US$5 with Transportes Cartagena, 3 hrs, or US$6 with Expreso Brasilia Pullman or La Costeña, 2 hrs. To **Bogotá** via Barranquilla and Bucaramanga with Expreso Brasilia pullman or Copetran, 8 a day, US$46, may take 21-28 hrs, depending on number of check-points. To **Magangué** on the **Magdalena** US$12, 4 hrs with Brasilia. To **Mompós**, Unitransco, 0530, 12 hrs including ferry crossing from Magangué, US$17. To **Valledupar** with Expreso Brasilia Pullman US$13 (with a 30 min stop in Barranquilla), for Sierra Nevada and Pueblo Bello. To **Riohacha**, US$12. Bus to **Maicao** on Venezuelan frontier US$18 (with Expreso Auto Pullman, Expreso Brasilia at 2000, or Unitrasco), 12 hrs.

Shipping Intermittent boats go from Cartagena to Porvenir in the San Blas Islands (Panama); the journey takes about two days and the one way fare is US$185 per person, without food. The skippers will help with immigration paperwork. Two possible boats are **Shatzi** (recommended) and **Dragón** (not so good). For information contact Hotel Casa Viena or Dirk Seiffert at *CaribeNet* (see under **Communications** below). You can also ask at the Yacht Club (*Club Nautico*). In Panama, the only reliable information is in Porvenir.

Boats leave most days for points south along the coast, (for example to Turbo cargo boats take 24 hrs, all-in cost about US$25 per person), and up the Río Sinú to Montería, and the Atrato as far as Quibdó. Get full independent advice before making any direct arrangements with boat owners or captains. It is possible to ship a car from Cartagena to Panama. Three companies which can arrange shipment of vehicles to Panama: *Hermann Schwyn*, Edif Concasa, 10th floor, T6647450, *Mundinaves*, C 35, No 8B-05, Of 13, La Matuna, T6644188, and *Agencia Internacional Ltda*, Cra 2, No 9-145, Edif Nautilus, Bocagrande, T6657539, agents for King Ocean Services, 7570 NW 14th Street, Miami, T(305)5917595 serving Cartagena, Panama and Miami. **NB** On the street, do not be tempted by offers of jobs or passages aboard ship: jobs should have full documentation from the Seamen's Union office; passages should only be bought at a recognised shipping agency.

Directory **Airline Offices SAM** and **Avianca**, Cra 4, No 34-15, opposite the west end of the cathedral. Also in Bocagrande, Cra 3, No 8-129, T6655504. **Aces**, C 35, No 10-30, La Matuna, T6646858. **AeroRepública**, Av Malecón (Cra 1), No 6-130, Edif Hipocampo, Bocagrande, T6658495. **Copa**, C Gastelbondo, No 2-95, T6648289.

Banks *Banco Unión Colombiana*, Avenida Venezuela (C 35), No 10-26, La Matuna, has Cirrus ATM, changes American Express and Thomas Cook TCs. *Bancolombia*, cash advances on Mastercard, changes TCs and *Bancafé*, gives money on Visa cards, both on Av Venezuela. *Banco Sudameris*, Cra 8B, No 24-36, opposite conference centre in Getsemaní, for Visa cash advances. *Lloyds TSB Bank*, C Baloco, No 2-76, T6647003 and office in Bocagrande, Cra 2, No 6-33. *Citibank*, Centro Plazoleta, Av Venezuela, for Mastercard ATM. There are many ATMs, the most convenient are in the Plaza de la Aduana, eg *CONAVI*, C 32, No 30-13, Mastercard, *Banco Ganadero*, C 32 No 4-65, Visa, and the Av Venezuela areas. If you are changing TCs make sure you have your passport with you or you will probably be charged the 3% tax applicable to residents. There are *cambios* in the arcade at Torre Reloj and adjoining streets which change Amex TCs; also *Caja de Cambio Caldas*, Av San Martín, No 4-118, Bocagrande, and on the corner of Plaza de los Coches, in Centro. Be sure to count the pesos yourself before handing over your dollars. *American Express* (Tierra Mar Aire), Bocagrande, Cra 4, No 7-196, is a travel agency downstairs, and gives cash against credit cards upstairs. TCs can be changed on Sat mornings (arrive early) at *Joyería Mora*, Román 5-39, and at El Portal nearby, in the old city. If you have time, shop around for the best cash or TC rates, Some rates change on a daily basis. **Never change money on the street in any circumstances**.

Communications Internet *Microclub*, Centro Comercial, Bocagrande, next to cinema. *Cyber Café*, at C de las Palmas, 3-102. *CaribeNet*, C Santo Domingo, No 3-54, T6642326, good service. *Chalet Suizo*, Media Luna No 10-36, T6647861. *The Verge*, next to *Club Nautico* (see under **Sports**), Mon-Fri 0900-1230, 1400-1700 and Sat mornings, also sailing information. *Hotel Viena* (see under **Sleeping**). Many others in Centro and Bocagrande, cost around US$3/hr. **Post Office** in Centro, for airmail is at the Avianca office near the cathedral, open Mon-Fri 0800-1830, Sat 0800-1500, and Av Lemaitre, La Matuna. Adpostal, C 33, La Matuna (see map). **Telephone** next to Adpostal; long distance phones behind this building.

Embassies and Consulates *Austria*, Cra 9, No 32A-50, Edif Concasa, La Matuna, T6648490. *Belgium*, C 8, No 4-41, Bocagrande, T6652741. *Canada*, Cra 3, No 33-08, Apto 201, C Santo Domingo, El Centro, T6647393. *Chile*, C 32, No 5-09, Edif Andean, Of 705, Plaza de la Aduana, Centro, T6645811. *France*, Cra 7, No 37-34, Plaza Fernández de Madrid, San Diego, T6646714. *Germany*, C Real, No 42-02, Ap 102, Cabrero, T6600309. *Guatemala*, Edif Comercios, Of 312, La Matuna, T6643528/6640120. *Mexico*, Edif Arauco, La Matuna, T6643660. *Norway*, C 32, No 8A-65, Edif Banco Central Hipotecario, La Matuna, T6645557. *Panama*, C 69, No 4-97, Crespo, T6662079. *Peru*, Transversal 53, No 20-53, C de la Giralda, Bosque, T6694178. *Spain*, C de la Universidad, No 36-44, Centro, T6642658. *Sweden*, Cra 4, No 5A-19, Bocagrande, T6655832. *USA*, Cra 3, No 36-37, C de la Factoría, Centro, T6600415. *Venezuela*, Cra 3, No 8-129, Edif Centro Ejecutivo, Of 802, T6650382, Bocagrande. Open to 1500, possible to get a visa the same day (US$30): you need onward ticket, two photos, but ensure you get a full visa not a 72 hrs' transit unless that is all you need.

Hospitals *Hospital Bocagrande*, C 5/Cra 6, Bocagrande, T6655270.

Laundry *Chalet Suizo*, Media Luna, No 10-36, also email, information and tours arranged.

Useful Addresses DAS Just beyond Castillo San Felipe, Cra 20B, No 29-18, Plaza de la Ermita (Pie de la Popa), T6563007, helpful. DAS passport office is in Calle Gastelbondo, near the Ramparts. Get visa extensions here, they are free. **Police** For loss of documents etc ask for a *'denuncia'* from the *Policía-Inspección Urbana*, Centro Comercial La Plazoleta, Matuna. The office is in the *Pasaje* leading to Av Carlos Lopez.

Around Cartagena

The little fishing village of **La Boquilla**, northeast of Cartagena, is near the end of a sandy promontory between the Ciénaga de Tesca and the Caribbean, about 20 minutes past the airport. There is a camping area with an attractive pool surrounded by palm trees and parrots, entrance US$2. There is a good beach, El Paraíso, nearby, busy at weekends but quiet during the week, good fish dishes. On Saturday and Sunday nights people dance the local dances. Visit the mangrove swamps nearby to see the birds. Golf courses are under

The Northcoast & the Islands

development here. You can stay at E *Los Morros*, clean, good food; and campsite, good, clean, showers, restaurant and small market, tents rented with mattresses. Good fish dishes in La Boquilla. Go there by taxi, US$3; there is also a reasonable bus service, including one from Bocagrande that leaves from beside Hotel India Catalina.

On the coast, 50 km northeast is **Galerazamba**, no accommodation but good local food. Nearby are the clay baths of **Volcán del Totumo**, in beautiful surroundings. Climb up steep steps to the lip of the 20 m high crater and slip into the grey cauldron of mud, about 10 m across, at a comfortable temperature, and reputed to be over 500 m deep. ■ *Entry to the cone US$1.*

The unusual experience of a bathe will cost you US$2 and you wash off in the nearby *Ciénaga*. Masseurs are available for a small extra fee. Bus from Cartagena to Galerazamba, US$1.50, two hours, ask to be dropped off at Lomo Arena where the bus turns off to Galerazamba. Walk along the main road for 2 km to a right turn signposted to Volcán del Totumo which is 1½ km along a poor road. Hitching is possible. Taking a tour from Cartagena will cost more but will save a lot of time.

Islas del Rosario

The National Park of **Corales del Rosario** embraces the archipelago of Rosario (a group of 30 coral islets 45 km southwest of the Bay of Cartagena) and the mangrove coast of the long island of Barú to its furthest tip. Isla Grande and some of the smaller islets are easily accessible by day trippers and those who wish to stay in one of the hotels. Permits are needed for the rest, entrance fee US$2. The islands represent part of a coral reef, low-lying, densely vegetated and with narrow strips of fine sand beaches. Rosario (the largest and best conserved) and Tesoro both have small lakes, some of which connect to the sea. There is an incredible profusion of aquatic and bird life. An **Aquarium** (Oceanario – look for the huge catfish) in the sea is worth visiting, US$3, not included in boat fares. Many of the smaller islets are privately owned.

Apart from fish and coconuts, everything is imported from the mainland, fresh water included. *Hotel del Caribe* in Bocagrande has scuba lessons in its pool followed by diving at its own resort on Isla Grande, US$230 and up. A diving permit from MA costs US$31.

Sleeping L *San Pedro de Majagua,* mainland office at Cra 5, No 8-59, Bocagrande, T/F665-2745, inside Restaurant Capilla del Mar, under the same ownership. Complex occupies part of Isla Grande, in the Rosario archipelago. Price per person, including meals. *Casa Blanca*, white with arched windows, former family home, converted to luxury hotel. Ask about other places to stay. **AL** *Club Isla del Pirata,* mainland booking office at C 8, No 4-66, Bocagrande, T665-2873, F665-2862, complex occupies a tiny islet in the archipelago. Room price per person including meals.

Transport Travel agencies and the hotels offer launch excursions from the Muelle Turístico, leaving 0700-0900 and returning 1600-1700, costing from US$10 to US$25, lunch included; free if staying at one of the hotels. Overnight trips can be arranged through agencies, but they are overpriced. Note that there is an additional 'port tax' of US$2 payable at the entrance to the Muelle or on the boat. Book in advance. Recommended are *Excursiones Roberto Lemaitre*, C 8, No 4-66, Bocagrande, Tÿ665-2872 (owner of *Club Isla del Pirata*). They have the best boats and are near the top end of the price range. *Yates Alcatraz* are more economical; enquire at the quay. For 5 or more, try hiring your own boat for the day and bargain for around US$10 per person. This way you get to see what you want in the time available. The tour boats leave you with plenty of time with the beach vendors. For the cheapest rates, buy tickets from the boat owners (make sure they are!) at the dockside, but they may already be full with reservations.

South of Cartagena

The highway south towards Medellín goes through **Turbaco**, where there's a Botanical Garden, 1½ km before village on the left. ■ *Open 0900-1600, Tue-Sun and holidays.* It then reaches **San Jacinto**, recognized as a major craft centre of Colombia, specializing in hand woven hammocks, wood carvings, drums and Indian flutes (gaitas) which feature in typical and contemporary Colombian music: try Artesanías Clauli, 60 m beyond petrol station. **Sleeping F** *Hospedaje Bolívar*, no sign, at the turn off by a petrol station, clean, simple, showers, parking, good food at El Llanero next door. **Buses** From Cartagena US$5.

About 10 km before San Jacinto is **Los Colorados National Park**, a small 1000 ha, steep hilly area rising to 420 m, heavily forested. A pleasant, if neglected park, with good forest walking, the main attraction is the colorado monkeys – but you need to walk two hours into the hills to reach their habitat.

The Northcoast & the Islands

Around Cartagena

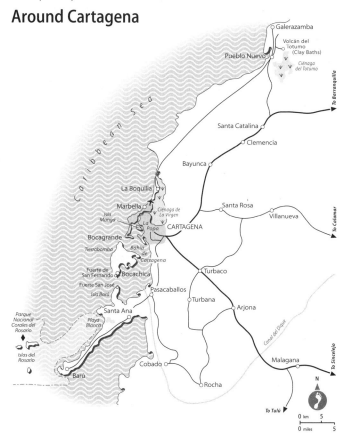

Mud volcanoes

At several points near the Caribbean coast between the Gulf of Urabá and Santa Marta there are strange 'mud volcanoes' where warm flows of black, grey or brown mud rise to the surface forming small lakes or pools. Sometimes a ridge builds up around the feature to form a cone that can be 20 m or more above the surroundings. The two best examples are near Arboletes and the Volcán del Totumo at Galerazamba between Barranquilla and Cartagena. Elsewhere there may only be fissures in the ground with occasional activity and emissions of sulphurous gases. Worth a visit if you are in the area are the pool near Necoclí on the Gulf of Urabá, several near Turbo (Rodosalín, El Alto de Mulatos, and Cacaual) and at San Pedro de Urabá on the borders of Antioquia and Córdoba Departments.

The cause of these phenomena is controversial. Most mud volcanoes are associated with underground petroleum oil and gas deposits, where volatile gases combine with water shales and mudstones and ooze to the surface. Many are found under the sea and have been an important help in the search for marine oilfields, in the Gulf of Mexico, for example. Some have recently been explored in the Caribbean near the coast of Panama, northwest of Colombia.

However, this coast of Colombia represents the border between the South American and the Caribbean tectonic plates which are slowly moving against each other at about 1-2 cm/year. Some kilometres inland there is an active line of instability, parallel to the coastline, known as the Sinú-San Jacinto fold belt, which also provides the low hills from Urabá northeast to Barranquilla. Geologists believe that this is the probable origin of the mud volcanoes. The heat generated by the movement between the plates and the gases released move up through the soft, porous sedimentary layers many km thick and bubble to the surface. These sediments have been built up by the major rivers that have been flowing northward for millions of years and may be additionally penetrated by sea water from the ocean. This process could also explain the happy absence of large interplate thrust earthquakes in this region.

Sincelejo
Phone code: 95
Colour map 1, grid B2

The capital of Sucre Department is a cattle centre 193 km south of Cartagena. The town is hot, dusty and power cuts are common.

Sleeping and eating **B** *Marsella*, Cra 24, No 20-38, T2820729, pool, comfortable. **C** *Ancor*, Cra 25, No 20A-45, T2824301, F2823561, a/c, garden, restaurant. **E** *Panorama*, Cra 25, 23-108, T2824301, F2822223, restaurant, secure parking. **E** *Santander*, corner of Plaza Santander, with bath, balconies, good restaurant, La Olla, opposite.

Festivals The dangerous bull-ring game in Jan is similar to the San Fermín festivities in Pamplona, Spain, in which bulls and men chase each other. At Eastertime there is the 'Fiesta del Burro' where they dress up donkeys and prizes go to the best and the funniest. A big party for three days.

Transport **Air** Flights are from **Corozal**, 13 km from Sincelejo. To **Bogotá**, 4 flights a week, 1 hour, **Satena** and **Aerotaca**. To **Medellín**, 3 flights a week, 45 mins, **Satena**. To **Cartagena**, Aires. To **Magangué** and **Montería**, Aires.

Bus To **Cartagena** frequent service, US$9. To **Medellín** hourly service, US$20. To **Megangué** (for Mompós), frequent service US$3.

Tolú
Phone code: 95
Colour map 1, grid B2

Tolú, 35 km northwest of Sincelejo, on the coast, is a fast developing holiday town popular with Colombians and, increasingly, foreign visitors attracted by visits to the offshore islands and diving. Tolú can also be reached more directly from Cartagena, though **San Onofre**, then, after 46 km from San Onofre, turn right for Tolú. Continue straight on from Toluviejo for 20 km to Sincelejo.

A good boat trip from Tolú is three hours to the beautiful beaches of Múcura island or Titipán (**D** *cabañas*) in the **Islas de San Bernardo**, about US$15. If camping, take your own supplies. Trips to the mangrove lagoons are also recommended. A good agency is *Mar Adentro*, Avenida La Playa 11-30, T2885481, another is *Club Náutico Los Delfines*, Avenida 1A, No 11-08, T2885202. They run daily tours to San Bernardo Islands at 0800, returning at 1600, which cost US$15, including the aquarium on Isla Palma.

Sleeping and eating **B** *Alcira*, Av La Playa 21-40, T2885334, F2885036, less off-season, a/c, restaurant, conference facilities, TV, pleasant. **C** *Ibatama*, Av La Playa 19-45, T/F2885150, T2885110, comfortable, air conditioning, patio, restaurant. **E** *Darimar*, C 17, No 1-60, T2885153, clean, with bath, fan. **F** *El Turista*, Av La Playa, No 11-68, T2885145, with bath, clean, basic, restaurant, comida US$2.50, best value. **E** *Residencias Familiar*, C 17, No 3-69, T2885066, with bath, parking, comfortable. **F** (no name), Cra 4, No 19-22, T2885412, comfortable, clean, run by Marjolene from Holland. Many other places to stay. *El Zaguán Paisa*, on Plaza, good *comidas*, open late. Other places to eat nearby eg Cafetería on the corner of the Plaza, good cakes.

Transport Tolú can be reached by colectivo from Sincelejo, or direct from Cartagena, several morning buses, 4 hrs, US$7; also service to Medellín with **Rapido Ochoa** and **Brasilia** 1100 and 1800, 10 hrs, US$24.

There are better beaches at **Coveñas**, 20 km further southwest, the terminal of the oil pipeline from the oilfields in the Venezuelan border area. **C** *Hostería Coveñas*, on seafront, T2880284, a/c, restaurant. Other hotels and several *cabañas* on the beach. Buses and colectivos from Tolú.

Further along the coast, turning right 18 km southwest of Coveñas at Lorica is **San Bernardo del Viento** from where launches can be arranged to **Isla Fuerte**, an unspoilt coral island with fine beaches and simple places to stay. A good place to dive, but there are very limited facilities on the island. Enquire at travel agencies in Medellín and elsewhere for inclusive trips or negtiate in San Bernardo.

The main road south from Sincelejo crosses into Córdoba Department and passes **Planeta Rica** (127 km), where it joins the road coming southeast from Montería (**E** *Río Negro*, several ground floor *cabaña*-style rooms, popular with cyclists).

South of Sincelejo

About 40 km further south is the *Zoocriadero Los Caimanes*, an aquatic zoo featuring crocodiles, iguanas and other reptiles. The restaurant has caiman on the menu. The gift shop sells shoes, bags, belts etc made of reptile skins 'farmed' in the zoo. ■*Entry US$2, children US$1, information, T8760165.* The main road continues south to Medellín and crosses the Río San Jorge near villa Fátima.

Next comes **Caucasia** (194 km), on the Río Cauca and just in Antioquia, a convenient stopping place between Cartagena and Medellín. Visit the Jardín Botánico (entry US$0.25).

Caucasia
Phone code: 94
Colour map 1, grid C2

Sleeping 11 km before Caucasia is *Parador Chambacú*, T8226946, with campsite. 5 km from town is the **C** *Mesón del Gitano*, T328-1882, F424-1886, family hotel, pool, restaurant, good; and **F** *Residencia Bonaire*, good, quiet, clean, TV in lounge. **In Caucasia** *Auto Hotel*, Cra 2, No 22-43, T822-6355, best, quiet, heavily booked. **D** *Colonial*, Cra 2, No 20-68, T/F822-7471, clean, pleasant, air conditioning, cheaper

How about a mud bath?

Of the various opportunities to enjoy mineral bathing in Colombia, mud is on the menu in several places eg Paipa (Boyacá), Santa Rosa de Cabal (Riseralda) and the mud volcanoes of the North Coast. Best of all, however, is Arboletes, where nothing has changed since prehistoric times; no special oils, no masseurs and no charge.

This is a circular mud lake about 30 m across with the mud level a slippery 2 m below the edge. Here you can bathe, or rather wallow, in the grey-black mud, the consistency of condensed milk, with no control over your buoyancy, but most entertaining. The bubbles are of sulphurous gases, but innocuous. When you have had enough (you will find that getting out is tricky – but most people make it), join the other surrealist figures for the short walk to the Caribbean, and a more conventional swim.

What is more, the stuff is an excellent conditioner for skin and hair.

with fan, good view of river, recommended for value. **D** *Yen*, near market, with bath, air conditioning cheaper with fan, friendly, clean. **E** *Del Río*, Cra 5/C 23, T822-6666, with bath, a/c, TV, clean, close to bus station, free morning coffee but avoid front rooms on street. **F** *Residencia El Viajero*, Cra 2, No 23-39, near centre, quiet, clean, ceiling fan.

Eating *La Posada del Gordo*, Carretera Troncal, steaks, bar. *El Rancho de Rey*, Carretera Troncal, facilities for children, accepts credit cards. *Sabor y Ricura*, Cra 4/C 21, pizzas, sandwiches, fast food. *Mundipollo*, Cra 5, No 23-41, chicken, burgers.

Transport **Air** To Medellín 5 flights a day, Aces, US$56. **Buses** To **Medellín** US$8, 7 hrs. To **Cartagena** US$21, with Brasilia, 6 hrs; US$19 with Rápido Ochoa.

Montería
Phone code 94
Colour map 1, grid C1

This small town, capital of Córdoba Department, stands on the east bank of the Río Sinú. It can be reached from Cartagena by air, by river boat, or from the main highway to Medellín. It is the centre of a cattle and agricultural area producing tobacco, cacao, cotton and sugar. It has one fine church, picturesque street life and extremely friendly people. Average temperature: 28°C.

Sleeping **D** *Alcázar*, Cra 2, No 32-17, T7824900, comfortable, friendly, restaurant. **F** *Brasilia*, clean, friendly, good value. **F** *Imperial*, Cra 2, No 35-20, T7825497. Also many cheap dives around.

Transport **Air** To Bogotá, 3 flights daily, SAM, AeroRepública. To Medellín, 2 flights a day, Aces, US$76. **Buses** To **Cartagena**, US$12, 5 hrs, with Brasilia, which has its own terminal in Montería, or colectivo, US$11, also 5 hrs.

Arboletes
Phone code: 94
Colour map 1, grid C1
Population 20,300

Some 67 km west of Montería, on the coast, is **Arboletes** a small quiet town, famous for its 'mud volcano'. You can drive up to the mud lake, no charge. (See the boxes on mud bathing, and the origins of mud volcanoes on previous pages).

Sleeping **E** *Ganadero*, T823-4086, fan, bath, good beds. **E** *Aristi*, T823-4125, very clean but small windows. **E** *La Floresta*, C Principal, T823-4056, reasonable. **F** *Julia*, on the main plaza, no private bathrooms. Other accommodation along the beach.

Eating *Guido's* restaurant is probably the best.

Transport Buses To **Turbo**, 4 a day, 5-6 hrs, US$6. To **Montería**, 10 a day, 3 hrs, US$3. To **Medellín**, Rápido Ochoa, US$25.50, 12 hrs.

From Arboletes, a mostly unmade road continues to Turbo (see below) and then up into the interior. Through extensive banana plantations, Apartadó is reached in 31 km.

Apartadó is a prosperous *paisa* town with clean tidy streets and modern build-ings but is very hot and it rains heavily at night much of the year. It depends on the local banana production which was troubled with labour problems in the mid to late 1990s. Recently things have improved though violence erupts from time to time between guerrillas and the paramilitaries in the region.

Apartadó
Phone code: 94
Colour map 1, grid C1

A local speciality is dried banana in strips, often covered with chocolate (cacao is also grown here). Ask for *chocoban*.

Sleeping B *Emberá*, C 100, No 103-49, T8281588, clean, comfortable rooms, a/c, minibar, cable TV, free coffee. **D** *Las Molas*, C 98, No 101-05, T8285214, a/c, cheaper with fan, free coffee, cable TV, good. There are plenty of *residencias* and basic hotels.

Eating *Barbacoa*, C 100F, No 117-109, T8282153, excellent fish, great prawn dishes. *Las Delicias*, C 99, No 103-18, good fish, superb *sancocho de pescado* and *arroz concoco*, good value. *Panadería la Inglesa*, 2 blocks from Hotel Embera, good sand-wiches and juices – *jugo de remolacha* (beetroot) recommended. Cheap food avail-able around the centre.

Transport Taxi Flat fare in town US$1. **Bus** To **Turbo**, collectivo US$1.50, taxi US$7. **Air** Daily flights to **Medellín**, Aces and Satena.

Some 31 km beyond Apatadó is **Chigorodó**: **E** *Eureka*, Calle 7, No 102-14, T8253262; **F** *Residencia Bonaire*, Calle 95, No 100-16, T8253015; **F** *Residencia Tobi*, a fan. A further 113 km to **Dabeiba**: **E** *Uraba*, Calle Uribe Uribe, No 9-73, T820016; **F** *Residencia Diana*, Calle Uribe Uribe, no 9-36, T8260027, simple, clean, helpful.

At Dabeiba the road begins to climb into the Cordillera Occidental up to **Canasgordas**, a centre for river fishing and bathing, cattle and coffee country. **G** *Doña Concha*, Cra Bolívar, No 19-34, T8264071, with bath, modern, good value. There is a branch of *Bancafé* in the Plaza Principal. This road continues to Santa Fe de Antioquia and Medellín, but is mostly unsurfaced, and four-wheel drive vehicles are recommended. There are road works in a num-ber of places and you can be stopped by Police, Military and other groups. At present it is regarded as dangerous and is not recommended in either private or public transport. If going south from Turbo, fly to Medellín and continue from there.

On the Gulf of Urabá is the port of **Turbo**, a rough frontier community and booming centre of banana cultivation.

Turbo
Phone code: 94
Colour map 2, grid A2
Population 127,000

Sleeping D *Castillo de Oro*, C 80, No 78-78, T8272185, best, reliable water and electricity, good restaurant. **D** *Playa Mar*, T8272205, good, but somewhat run-down. **D** *Sausa*, running water in the early morning only, helpful owners, pleasant dining room. **F** *Residencia Turbo*, Cra 78, No 20-76, T8272693, friendly, good. **F** *Residencia Marcela*, friendly, quiet, secure, best value. **G** *Residencia El Golfo*, friendly, good. Note that *residencias* also rent by the hour.

The Northcoast & the Islands

Transport Air To Medellín, Aces, 3 daily. To Necoclí, Aces, several a week. Local services to Caribbean and Pacific resorts. **Bus** To **Medellín** 6 buses a day, a gruelling 14 hrs, US$17; to **Montería**, 8 hrs, US$10, bad road, several army checkpoints. **Boat** Available to **Cartagena** (eg on timber boats) and up the Río Atrato to **Quibdó**, but you need plenty of time; services are intermittent and unreliable. Do not pay agents, or in advance.

Directory Banks Several banks including *Banco Ganadéro* but none are open for exchange of travellers' cheques on Mon or Tue; try exchanging money in stores. Rates are poor in Turbo
Useful addresses DAS, Postadero Naval, north of the town just before the airport, take transport along Cra 13, open 0800-1630. **MA** for information on Parque Nacional Los Katíos, office 1 km along road to Medellín.

The Northeast Coast

The main road from Cartegena to Barranquilla (124 km) goes inland, through agriculture and cattle country through Sabanalarga and Baranoa. A deviation, bypassing Sabanalarga, goes through **Usiacurí**, an attractive place with a cheerful blue and white church set on a rock in the centre of the village. It is well known for all kinds of basket weaving, especially using *palma iraca*, a local product. There is an interesting cooperative with a good selection of things to buy at the Barranquilla entrance to the village. Ask also for other places to see the work in the village. You will see the products on sale elsewhere in north Colombia at higher prices. The approach road from Cartegena to Usiacurí is poor with a ford to cross. The road out towards Barranquilla is paved. Bus service and tours arranged from Barranquilla.

There is also a quicker coast road through Galerazamba (see above) to Barranquilla, fully paved, passing near Puerto Colombia.

Barranquilla

Phone code: 95
Colour map 1, grid A2
Population: 1,064,000

Barranquilla, Colombia's fourth city, lies on the western bank of the Río Magdalena, about 18 km from its mouth. It's a seaport (though less busy than Cartagena or Santa Marta), as well as a river port, and a modern industrial city with a polluted but colourful central area near the river. First and foremost, however, Barranquilla is famed for its Carnival, reputed to be second only to Rio de Janeiro in terms of size and far less commericalized.

Ins & outs **Getting there Air** Ernesto Cortissoz airport is 10 km south of the city. City bus from airport to town, US$0.35 (US$0.40 on Sun). Taxi to town, US$5 (taxis do not have meters, fix the fare in advance). To town, take only buses marked 'centro' from 200 m to the right when leaving the airport; the bus to the airport (marked Malambo) leaves from Cra 44 up C 32 to Cra 38, then up C 30 to the airport. Taxi to Cartagena, US$40.

Bus The main bus terminal is south of the city near the Circunvalación. Take a bus marked 'Terminal' along C 45. Taxi from the centre or El Prado, US$5.

Tourist offices Tourist information at main hotels and at C 72, No 57-43, of 401, T333-6658. Tourist office at Cra 54, No 75-45, T345-4458. Maps and hotel information also at airport.

The city is surrounded by a continuous ring road called the *Vía Cuarenta* from **Sights**
the north along the river to the centre, *Avenida Boyacá* to the bridge (Puente
Pumarejo) which crosses the Río Magdalena for Santa Marta, and
Circunvalación round the south and west of the city. The long bridge over the
Río Magdalena gives a fine view of Barranquilla and the river.

In the centre the principal boulevard is **Paseo Bolívar** leading to **Parque
Simón Bolívar**. Two blocks south is a handsome church, **San Nicolás**, formerly
the Cathedral, in Plaza San Nicolás, the central square, and before it stands a
small statue of Columbus. The new **Catedral Metropolitana** is at Carrera 45,
No 53-120, opposite Parque la Paz. There is an impressive statue of Christ inside
by the Colombian sculptor, Arenas Betancourt. The small **Museo
Antropológico** is on Calle 68, No 53-45, with a big physical relief map on the
front lawn. ■ *Mon-Fri 0900-1200, 1400-1700.* **The Museo Romántico**, Carrera
54, No 59-199, covers the history of Barranquilla, including the establishment of
air services and radio in Colombia, with an interesting section on the local Carnival and a replica of 'Camellón Abello', an old street of Barranquilla.

The commercial and shopping districts are round the Paseo Bolívar, a few
blocks north of the old Cathedral, and in Avenida Murillo. The colourful and
vivid **market** is between Paseo Bolívar and the river, the so-called Zona Negra
on a side channel of the Magdalena.

One of the biggest and best maintained zoos in the country has some animals
not often seen in zoos. However, many are in small cages. All the trees are
labelled. It is at Calle 77/Carrera 68 (bus 'Boston/Boston' or 'Caldes/Recreo').
■ *Entrance US$1, 0830-1200, 1400-1800.*

Good parks to the northwest of the centre include **Parque Tomás Suri
Salcedo** on Calle 72. Stretching back into the northwestern heights overlooking the city are the modern suburbs of El Prado, Altos del Prado, Golf and
Ciudad Jardín, with *El Prado Hotel*. There is a full range of services including
commercial and shopping centres and banks between Bulevar Norte and

The Northcoast & the Islands

Barranquilla centre

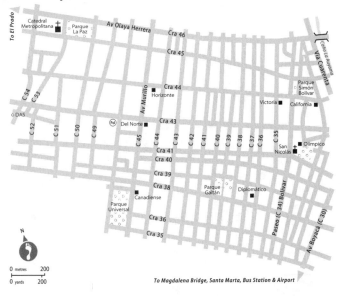

Avenida Olaya Herrera towards the Country Club. There are five stadia in the city, a big covered coliseum for sports, two for football and the others cater for basketball and baseball. The metropolitan stadium is on Avenida Murillo, outside the city where it meets the south stretch of the Circunvalación.

Excursions Regular buses from Paseo Bolívar and the church at Calle 33/Carrera 41 go to the attractive bathing resort of **Puerto Colombia**, 19 km (by bus US$0.60, 30 minutes), with its pier built around 1900. This was formerly the ocean port of Barranquilla, connected by railway. The beach is clean and sandy though the water a bit muddy. Nearby are the beaches of Salgar, where good fish dishes are served. Another place for good seafood is Las Flores, north of Barranquilla, 2 km from the mouth of the Río Magdalena at Bocas de Ceniza.

South along the west bank of the Magdalena, 5 km from the city, is the old colonial town of **Soledad.** The cathedral and the old narrow streets round it are worth seeing. A further 25 km south is Santo Tomás, known for its 'Good Friday flagellants' who symbolically whip themselves as an Easter penance. There are also street theatre presentations at this time. The small town of Palmar de Varela is a little further along the same road which continues to Calamar (see Up the Río Magdalena chapter).

Sleeping **LL** *El Prado*, Cra 54, No 70-10, T368-0111, F345-0019, some distance from the centre, best, the social centre, swimming pool and tennis courts, good restaurant, sauna, original 1920s building is national monument, new annex behind.

Barranquilla - El Prado

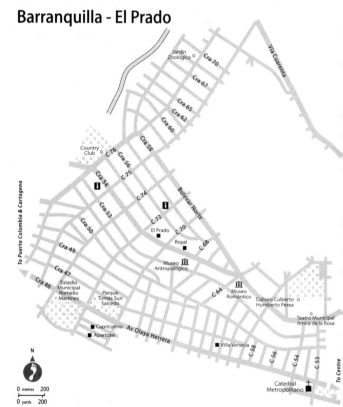

Catedral Metropolitano

The Northcoast & the Islands

A *Royal*, Cra 54, No 68-124, T3565533, F3562777, good service, with swimming pool, modern.

B *Apartotel*, Cra 44, No 70-242, T3561213, a/c, parking, large rooms. **B** *Olímpico*, Cra 42, no 33-20, T3518310/3517482, F3404750, 40 rooms with bath, fan, TV, restaurant, recommended;

C *Capricornio*, Cra 44B, No 70-201, T3565045, very clean, good service, with bath, a/c.

D *Canadiense*, C 45, No 36-142, fan, shower, noisy, but convenient for bus station 2 blocks away. **D** *Villa Venecia*, C 61, No 46-41, T3414107, clean, TV, a little noisy but recommended.

E *Victoria*, C 35, No 43-140, downtown, large, scruffy rooms with fan. **E** *Diplomático*, C 36, No 38-51, T3517954, with private bath, fan, TV room, washing facilities, cafetería. **E** *Del Norte*, Cra 43, No 44-43, T3409508, noisy.

F *Horizonte*, Cra 44, No 44-35, T3417925, with bath, clean, quiet, fan, friendly, safe. **F** *California*, C 32 y Cra 44, pleasant but about to fall down, enjoy the chickens. **NB** Hotel prices may be much higher during Carnival. Watch for thieves in downtown hotels.

Eating *La Puerta de Oro*, C 35, No 41-100, central, air conditioning good for meals (including breakfast); *El Huerto*, Cra 52, No 70-139, good vegetarian. *Jardines de Confucio*, Cra 54, No 75-44, good Chinese food, nice atmosphere. *La Ollita*, Cra 53, No 55-10, good local dishes. There are various Lebanese restaurants with belly-dancers, and several Chinese and *pizzerías*, including *Loca*, Cra 53, No 70-97, also at C 84, No 50-36. Many places, for all tastes and budgets, on C 70 from Hotel El Prado towards Cra 42. At C 70 y 44B are several estaderos, bars with snacks and verandas.

Entertainment **Theatre** *Teatro Amira de la Rosa*, one of the most modern of Colombia, has a full range of stage presentations, concerts, ballet, art exhibitions etc throughout the year.

Festivals Carnival is a long-standing tradition in Barranquilla, lasting for the four days before Ash Wed, comparable, some say, with those of Rio de Janeiro and Trinidad, and less commercialized. There are the usual parades, floats, street dancing, beauty contests and general mayhem. As normal on such occasions, take special care of your valuables.

Shopping **Bookshop** *Librería Nacional*, Cra 53, No 75-129, English, French and German books. Maps from Instituto Agustín Codazzi, C 36, No 45-101.

Market San Andrecito, or 'Tourist Market', Vía 40, is where smuggled goods are sold at very competitive prices; a good place to buy film. Picturesque and reasonably safe. Any taxi driver will take you there.

Sports **Bikeshop** *Bike House*, C 79, No 51-36, T3488989.

Tour Operators *Tierra Mar Aire*, C 74, No 52-34, very helpful for flights to Central America. *Aviatur*, Cra 54, No 72-96, T1565644.

Transport **Local Taxis** Within the town cost US$1.25 (eg downtown to northern suburbs).

Long distance Air Direct flights to **Bogotá**, 12 daily, Avianca, Aces and AeroRepública. At least 1 a day, Avianca, to **Bucamaranga, Cali, Cúcuta,** and Medellín. Aires to **Cartagena, Santa Marta** and **Ríohacha. International flights**: to **Maracaibo** (3 per week), to **Miami,** Avianca and American, each one daily; to **Panama City,** daily Copa-Avianca/SAM.

Bus Brasilia links all north coast towns and south as far as Bogotá, recommended air conditioned buses. To **Santa Marta,** US$3.25, Pullman (less in non-air conditioned, Coolibertador), about 2 hrs, also direct to Santa Marta's Rodadero beach; to **Valledupar,** 6 hrs, US$10; to **Montería,** US$11, 8 hrs; to **Medellín** by Pullman, 16 hrs, US$31; to Bucaramanga, US$27 with Copetran, air conditioning, first class, departures at 1130 most days, 9 hrs; to **Bogotá,** 20-24 hrs, US$45 direct; to **Caucasia,** US$17, 11 hrs. To **Maicao,** US$14.50, 5 hrs (with Brasilia, every 30 mins from 0100-1200); to **Cartagena,** 3 hrs, US$5 with Transportes Cartagena, US$6 with Expreso Brasilia, 2 hrs by colectivo, also from their downtown offices, US$7.

Ship See Warning under Cartagena Ins and outs regarding jobs and passages aboard ship. If shipping a car into Barranquilla allow 2 days to complete all paperwork to retrieve your car from the port.

Directory **Airline Offices** C 72, No 57-79, T3456207.

Banks *Lloyds TSB Bank*, Cra 52, No 72-131, T3686876, and 1 agencies; *Bancolombia*, *Banco de Bogotá* and other banks, many cash machines. *Western Union*, Cra 52, No 72-75 local 108, T3687996. *Casa de cambio El Cacique*, C 34, No 43-108, T3326392, reliable.

Communications Post Office in Parque Simón Bolívar.

Embassies & consulates *Germany*, C 80, No 78B-251, T3532078. *Finland*, Vía 40 de las Flores, Cementos del Caribe, T335-0080. *Netherlands*, Cra 42H, No 85-33, T3341282. *Norway*, C 72, No 57-33, T3581043. *Spain*, Cra 54, No 93-43, T3570664. *UK*, Cra 44, No 45-57, T3406936. *USA*, Centro Comercial Mayorista, C 77, No 68-15, opposite zoo (Apartado A, reo 51565), T3457088, 3457242 or 3457181 (visas obtainable only in Bogotá). *Venezuela*, Cra 49, No68-24, T3580048/3582832, 0800-1500 (take 'Caldas/Recreo' or 'Boston/Boston' bus), visa issued same day, but you must be there by 0915 with photo and US$30 cash; an onward ticket may not be requested.

Useful addresses DAS C 54, Cra 43, No 41-133. **Police** (for declarations of theft, etc), Policia F2, C 47 y Cra 43.

Magdalena Department

Magdalena Department includes a large area of low-lying marshland and lagoons, 60 km wide and 200 km long, associated with the delta region of the Río Magdalena. The river at present runs along the western edge of this area which is flooded for much of the year. There are few roads and most of the locals must use water transport. By contrast, the Department also includes the town of Santa Marta and a long stretch of rocky coastline behind which is the Sierra Nevada de Santa Marta massif, most of which is in the Department, and includes the main ice/snow covered ranges and the highest point in Colombia.

Ciénaga de Santa Marta

A *'ciénaga'* is literally 'a marshy place' and the *Ciénaga de Santa Marta* is officially the vast area of over 4,000 sq km of wetlands to the east of the last 50 km of the Río Magdalena. In fact the river, which brings down vast quantities of mud and silt, is slowly filling in the area which was formerly part of the Caribbean Sea.

The **Ciénaga Grande de Santa Marta** is the largest of about 20 recognizable lagoons and is 500 sq km in size. (The word *ciénaga* is more commonly used here to mean 'lagoon'). All types of water-birds, especially duck and heron may be seen in and near the *Ciénaga Grande*, with caimanes, iguanas and turtles plentiful in the rivers and *caños* (channels) which flow into the lake. Above all, however, it is the fish and shellfish that stock the *ciénagas* that are vital to the local economy, including *mojarra, lisa* and *chivo,* all local fish, and crab, oyster and shrimp. Between 4,000 and 5,000 tonnes of seafood are fished annually. Such is the value of the natural resources that the whole region has been denominated a Biosphere Reserve, and two sections of it are now under National Park control.

The **Santuario de Fauna y Flora Ciénaga Grande** is 300 sq km of remote marshland at the southern end of the principal lake with large sections of fresh water mangroves, very rich in wildlife. To get there is a long trip by motorised canoe from Tasajera on the coast road from Ciénaga to Barranquilla, or from Fundación, 56 km on an unpaved road to Pivijay and then by canoe. There is a ranger station near the lake but no accommodation or facilities and camping is difficult due to the terrain. Sleeping in hammocks is possible but you will need plenty of insect protection. Day trips are recommended, ask for information at MA or the Tourist offices in Santa Marta.

Several villages (not in the Park), among them Nueva Venecia and Buenavista, are built on stilts in the lake which can be visited, as can Trojas de Aracataca, a fishing village on the south east corner of the Ciénaga Grande. Ask about boats in Ciénaga, Pueblo Viejo or Tasajera.

At the coastal end of the Ciénaga de Santa Marta is the second protected area: **Parque Nacional Natural Isla de Salamanca,** another, more recent, product of the Río Magdalena. Silt from the mouth of the river with untold millions of seashells drifting along the coast have formed narrow sandbanks all the way to the town of Ciénaga, sealing off the end of the great Ciénaga lagoon. The western end, near the river, has become a significant series of sand dunes tapering off eastwards to a narrow strip at Tasajera, 60 km from Barranquilla and just short of the town of Ciénaga. This is now the National Park. Some 10 km from the Magdalena bridge at Barranquilla is **Los Cocos,** the headquarters of the 21,000 ha park, created in 1969 to protect the abundant birdlife and coastal mangroves. Near here is a raised walkway giving access to an excellent view of the saltwater mangroves which cover much of the Park. There are lots of possibilities for swimming from the beach which runs for many kilometers to the east eg at **Cangarú,** where prehistoric sites have been found. Beware of biting insects. It is possible to stay in basic conditions with some locals who live near Los Cocos, for a small charge, or camping at Cangarú, US$7.50 for 5 persons. Touring the Park by boat is recommended, Ask at Los Cocos. Further information at the MA office in Santa Marta.

The Barranquilla-Santa Marta highway runs through the Park but it became apparent shortly after its construction that the new road had seriously disrupted the ecology of the area by severing the connection between the waters of the lagoons and the sea. Many of the species of mangrove needed a precise combination of salt and fresh water and by disturbing the 'mix', the mangroves

100 Years of Solitude

1997 was the 30th anniversary of Gabriel García Marquéz' most famous book. It was also the year he decided once again to live outside Colombia. He first left for Mexico in 1981 in protest at the regime of Julio César Turbay. This time, after living in Cartagena for a number of years, he has left again for Mexico where he hopes he will feel more secure and find somewhere conducive to writing.

were destroyed. The result can be seen today – vast sectors of dead trees covering the landscape. The destruction stretches many kilometers inland and the knock-on effect has adversely affected the wildlife and the fish of the region.

A major effort has been started to redress the mistakes made. Channels have been restored between the Ciénaga Grande and the sea and more fresh water from the river has been diverted into the lake area. Young mangroves have begun to reappear near Nueva Venecia but it will be many years before regeneration will be complete. Much support has been received from overseas including the Interamerican Development Bank (BID) and the German government.

On the east shore of the lagoon is the town of **Ciénaga,** which is renowned for its Cumbias (see **Music and Dance** in **Essentials**). Cotton, bananas, tobacco and cacao are grown in the area. The hotels in Ciénaga are not recommended except in emergencies.

Aracataca & Fundación Aracataca, 60 km south of Ciénaga and 7 km before Fundación, is the birthplace of **Gabriel García Márquez**, fictionalized as Macondo in some of his stories (notably *Cien años de soledad*). His home, called a museum, may be seen in the backyard of La Familia Iriarte Ahumada; it is 1½ blocks from the plaza, ask for directions. There is not a great deal to see, but the huge tree associated with 'Coronel Buendía' can be seen in the back garden. The curator may give you a copy of the author's birth certificate as you leave! There are *residencias* (**G**), but it is better to stay in **Fundación**. There is a restaurant, *El Fogonazo*, Cra 4, No 6-40. Good food, local menu.

Banana growing in the area has now been partly replaced by African palm plantations.

Sleeping in Fundación **E** *Caroli*, Cra 8, No 5-30. Best. **E** *Fundación*. With a/c, cheaper without. **E** *Centro del Viajero*. With a/c, good value. Others in this price range.

Transport **Buses** Fundación/Aracataca to Ciénaga, US$1. To **Santa Marta,** US$2.50. To **Barranquilla,** US$2.50. Aracataca to Fundación, US$0.20. An all weather but unsurfaced road west from Fundación goes through Pivijay to Salamina on the Río Magdalena, ferry to Puerto Giraldo 0500-1800, then road to Sabanalarga and Barranquilla. By bus this route, Fundación-Barranquilla, US$3.20. South of Fundación the road continues into César Department, see under **Valledupar** below, and on to Bucaramanga and Bogotá.

Santa Marta

Phone code: 95
Colour map 1, grid A3
Population: 309,000

Santa Marta, the capital of Magdalena Department, is the third Caribbean port, 96 km east of Barranquilla. Santa Marta, unlike Cartagena, is no colonial beauty, and there's little to detain anyone, but there are some good beaches nearby and you can organize a trek to Ciudad Perdida from here. It also makes a convenient stopping point en route to Tayrona.

Getting there Simón Bolívar **airport** is 20 km south of the city. Bus to the centre costs US$0.25; taxi US$6, 30 mins. Taxi from Rodadero US$3. During the tourist season book well ahead and get to the airport early.

The **bus** terminal is southeast of the city, towards Rodadero, on the Troncal del Caribe. Minibus US$0.30, taxi US$1 to centre, US$3 to Rodadero.

Tourist Offices *Oficina Turística del Departamento de Magdalena*, is in the former Convent of Santo Domingo, now Casa de Cultura, Cra 2, No 16-44, T4235773/3597, F4211167. General information on the Department and Santa Marta. Open office hours Mon-Fri. *ETURSA Empresa Turística de Santa Marta*, C 19, No 2-09, T4211295/4357. There is also an office at Rodadero (see below).

Climate The climate ranges from normally hot and trying to hot but pleasant in Feb and Mar. It is relatively humid but the on-shore winds moderate the temperature much of the time. Occasionally the snow-clad peaks of the Sierra Nevada are visible to the east, less than 50 km away and 5,800 m high.

Security The north end of town near the port area beyond the old railway station, and areas south of Rodadero beach are dangerous and travellers are advised not to go there alone. If you arrive by bus, beware taxi drivers who take you to a hotel of their choice, not yours. Also beware of 'jungle tours', or 'boat trips to the islands' sold by street touts.

Santa Marta lies at the mouth of the Río Manzanares, one of the many rivers that drain the Sierra Nevada de Santa Marta, on a deep bay with high shelving cliffs at each end. The city's fine promenade offers good views of the bay and is lined with restaurants, accommodation and nightlife, though not of a very high quality. At the southern end, where the main traffic turns inland on Calle 22, is a striking sculpture dedicated to the Indian heritage of the region, *La Herencía Tairona*. The main commercial area and banks are on Carrera 5 and Calle 15.

History

This part of the South American coastline was visited in the early years of the 16th century from the new Spanish settlements in Venezuela. At the time many Indian groups were living on and near the coast and trading with each other and with communities further inland. The dominant group here were the Tayrona.

Santa Marta was the first town created (1525) by the *conquistadores* in Colombia. The founder, **Rodrigo de Bastidas**, chose it for its sheltered harbour and its proximity to the Río Magdalena and therefore its access to the hinterland. Also, the Indians represented a potential labour force for later developments and he had not failed to notice the presence of gold in their ornaments.

Within a few years, the Spanish settlement was consolidated, and permanent buildings appeared, (see below: the Casa de la Aduana). Things did not go well, however. The Indians did not 'collaborate' and there was continual friction amongst the Spaniards, all of whom were expecting instant riches. Bastidas' successor, Rodrigo Alvarez Palomino attempted to subdue the Indians by force, with great loss of life and little success. The Indians that survived took to the hills and their successors, the Kogi, are still there today, fearful and resentful, but with the good fortune of the remote wildness of the Sierra Nevada on their side, able so far to preserve their way of life.

By the middle of the 16th century, a new threat had appeared. Encouraged and often financed by Spain's enemies (England, France and Holland), pirates realised that rich pickings were to be had, not only from shipping, but also by attacking coastal settlements. The first raid was about 1544 by the French pirate Robert Waal with three ships and 1,000 men. He was followed by many of the famous sea-dogs – the brothers Côte, Drake and Hawkins – all sacked the city in spite of the forts built on a small island at the entrance to the bay and on the mainland. Before the end of the century more than 20 attacks were recorded, and the pillage continued until as late as 1779. The townsfolk lived in constant fear. Cartagena, meanwhile became the main base for the *conquistadores* and much was invested in its defences. Santa Marta was never fortified in the same way and declined in importance as a result and this accounts for the poverty of the colonial heritage here. Over the years caches of treasure have continued to turn up in old walls and floors – grim testimonies to the men and women of those troubled times who did not survive to claim them.

Two important names connecting Santa Marta with the history of Colombia must be mentioned. First, **Gonzalo Jiménez de Quesada** began his expedition here that led him up the Río Magdalena and into the highlands to found Santa Fe de Bogotá in 1538, and it was here that **Simón Bolívar**, his dream of Gran Colombia shattered, came to die. Almost penniless, he was given hospitality at the *hacienda* of San Pedro Alejandrino, see below. He died there on 17 December 1830, at the age of 47.

Sights

The centre of Santa Marta is the pleasant, leafy Plaza Bolívar, two blocks wide and four blocks deep leading back from the beach. It is complete with a statues of Bolívar and Santander and a bandstand. On the north side is the **Casa de la Aduana**, Calle 14/Carrera 2, which became the Custom House when Santa Marta was declared a free port in 1776. Previously it belonged to the Church and was used as the residence of the Chief Justice of the Inquisition. The house dates from 1531 and was probably the first house of brick and stone to be built in Colombia. An upstairs garret, added in 1730, offers an excellent view of the city and the bay. Simón Bolívar stayed here briefly in December 1830 before going to San Pedro Alejandrino (see below) where he died the same month. He lay in state here on the second floor from December 17th to the 20th before being moved to the cathedral. The Custom House now displays an excellent archaeological collection, with four rooms of exhibits mainly dedicated to the Tayrona Indian group. Especially interesting is the model of Ciudad Perdida, the most important of the Tayrona cities. A visit here is strongly recommended before going to Ciudad Perdida. Also housed here is one of the Banco de la Republica's **Museos de Oro** (Gold Museums), with a large number of precolombian gold artefacts held in the vault. ■ *Open Tue-Sat, 0800-1200, 1400-1800, Sun and holidays, 0800-1200, during the tourist season. Mon-Fri (only), 0800-1200, 1400-1800, during the rest of the year; entry US$1.*

Quinta de San Pedro Alejandrino, an early 17th century villa, is 5 km southeast of the city and dedicated to sugar cane production. This is where Simón Bolívar lived out his last days and the simple room in which he died on 17 December 1830, with a few of his belongings, can be seen. Other paintings and memorabilia of the period are on display in the villa and a contemporary art gallery featuring works by artists from Venezuela to Bolivia, ie the countries associated with Bolívar's life, and an exhibition hall have been built on the property. The estate and gardens, with some ancient cedars and *samanes,* and dignified formal statues and monuments can be visited. It is an impressive memorial to the man most revered by Colombians. ■*Open daily 0930-1630; entrance US$2.50, take a bus or colectivo from the waterfront, Cra 1C, to Mamatoca and ask to be dropped off at the Quinta, US$0.25.*

The **Cathedral** is at Carrera 4, Calle 16/17. The original building on this site was completed a few years after the founding of the city and was probably the first church of Colombia as proclaimed by the inscription on the west front. The present building is mainly 17th century with many additions and modifications, hence the mixture of styles. There are interesting shrines along the aisles, a fine barrel roof and chandeliers, a grey Italian marble altar decorated with red and brown, the whole giving a light, airy and dignified impression. Notable is the monument to Rodrigo de Bastidas, founder of the city, to the left of the main entrance and the inscription by the altar steps commemorating the period when Bolívar's remains rested here from his death in 1830 to 1842 when they were transfered to the Pantheon in Caracas. ■ *The cathedral is open for Mass daily at 0600 and 1800 (more frequently on Sun), and you may find it open at 1000.*

Convento de Santo Domingo Carrera 2, No 16-44, now serves as a cultural centre and houses a library and the tourist office.

Beaches There are rocky headlands and beaches in the bays and coves all along this coast, surrounded by hills, green meadows and shady trees. The largest sandy bay is that of Santa Marta, with Punta Betín, a rocky promontory, protecting the harbour to the north and a headland to the south on top of which are the ruins of an early defensive fort, Castillo San Fernando. The rugged Isla El Morro lies 3 km off Santa Marta topped by a lighthouse. Because of the proximity of the port and the city, the beach is not recommended for bathing. There is marine eco-system research science centre, run by Colombian and German universities near the end of Punta Betín.

Santa Marta

Related map
A Santa Marta centre, page 191

Playa **El Rodadero** (see below) is the most fashionable and tourist-oriented beach of the area, 4 km south of the city.

To the north of Santa Marta is the attractive resort of **Taganga** (see below) and there are further beaches in the bays near the Cabo (cape) and Isla de la Aguja. Villa Concha has a good beach, popular with locals at weekends, but a good day trip during the week. The bay is surrounded by tree covered hills and there are a number of restaurants. See also details of the beaches in Tayrona National Park.

Essentials

Sleeping Av Rodrigo de Bastidas (Cra 1) has several seaside holiday hotels while Cra 2 and connecting Calles have many budget *residencias*. For groups of 4 or more, ask about short rent apartments.

A *Yuldama*, Cra 1, No 12-19, T4210063, F4214932. Beachfront, clean, a/c, reasonable food. **B** *Panamerican*, Cra 1, No 18-23, T4211238, F4214751. A/c, less with fan, clean, tidy, safe, good restaurant, laundry, minibars, holiday hotel. **C** *Hostal Bahía*, C 12, No 2-70, T4230057. A/c, cheaper without, modern, plain, safe deposit, clean, recommended.

D *Andrea Doria No 1*, C 18, No 1C-90, T4214329. Clean, friendly with bath and fan, own parking. **D** *Andrea Doria No 2*, Cra 2, No 19-61, T4211458, T/F4312226. TV, pleasant, quiet. **D** *Bermuz*, C 13, No 5-16, T4210004, F4213625. Good, clean, also good vegetarian restaurant. **D** *Caribe*, C 18, No 2-28, T4234316. Clean, simple, fan, some dark rooms. **D** *Costa Azul*, C 17, No 2-09, T4212236. With bath and shower, some rooms with a/c, clean, fan, windows into courtyard, very friendly. **D** *Park*, Cra 1, No 18-67, T4211215, F4211574. On seafront, with shower, fan, reasonable, friendly, phone, popular with Colombians. **D** *Saratoga*, C 11, No 2-29, T4214858. A/c, less with fan, average, plain. **D** *Sompallón*, Cra 1, No 10B-57, T4214195. Modern, with *pizzería*.

E *Hospedería Casa Familiar*, C 10C No 2-14, T4211697/4622. With bath, cheaper in dormitory, very friendly, clean, family-run, will store luggage for US$1 if you don't stay there, good food opposite see **Eating**, excellent travellers' guest house. Highly recommended. **E** *Nueva Granada*, C 12, No 3-19, clean, old building with rooms round pleasant courtyard, quiet. **E** *Residencias Bahía Blanca*, Cra 1, No 11-13, T4214439. Private shower, friendly, clean, fan, safe deposit, will store luggage. Recommended. **E** *Tayrona*, Cra 1, No 11-41, T4212408. With fan, bath, friendly, no frills, not too secure. **E** *Yarimar*, Cra 1, No 26-61, T4212713. Outside the centre, clean, fan, noisy.

F *Miramar*, C 10C, No 1C-59, T4214756. 2 blocks from beach, the main gringo hotel, tends to be crowded, pretty basic but some nicer more expensive rooms, robberies have been reported, it is popular mainly because it is cheap, motorbike parking, restaurant, luggage stored, arranges trips. **F** *Residencias El Titanic*, C 10C, No 1C-68, T4211947. Friendly, large rooms with bath, fan, basic, safe, good value.

Eating *Yarimar*, Cra 1, No 26-37, next to hotel of same name. Good seafood. *El Gran Wah Yuen*, C 14, No 3-74. Good Chinese *à la carte* and *comida corriente*, plenty of fresh vegetables. *Terraza Marina*, Cra 1, No 26-38, T4231992. Very good fish, try the *bandeja*. *Manuel*, Cra 1, No 26A-167, T4231449. Fish and meat dishes, high quality. *La Casona*, C 16, No 2-06, T4212838. Family cooking. *La Gran Muralla*, Cra 5, No 23-77, T4214700. A/c, good oriental and international. *Café del Parque*, Parque de Bolívar, C 14 next to Casa de la Aduana. Great place for coffee and snacks and to linger outside in garden, try *café frappé* (with ice). *Reno*, C 10/Cra 3. Good local set meals, vegetarian dishes, open Sun evenings. *El Escorial*, Calle 11, No 1-60, T4213654. Popular, good food. *Asadero La Baranda*, C 22, No 2A-15, T4232940. Good grills. *Merkabar*, C 10C, No 2-11. Pastas, great pancakes, good juices, family run, good value, tourist advice. *Cafetería de la Calle*, Cra 3A, No 16-26, Good *empanadas*. *Juancho's House*, Cra 5/C 12, good fruit juices and snacks

. *Pizzeria*, Cra 1/C 20, good pizzas, soups, expensive fruit juices. Restaurant opposite Telecom (C 13/Cra 5), good menu and vegetarian dishes.

Festivals

Festival Patronal de Santa Marta in Jul celebrates the founding of the city with parades and musical performances. *Fiesta del Mar* in Aug has aquatic events and a beauty contest. *International Caribbean Theatre Festival* with contributions from many of the Caribbean countries.

Shopping

Look around for small artefacts and figurines in the Indian tradition, sometimes sold on the beaches. Best if you can find the artists who live in and around Santa Marta, eg José Pertuz, C 38, up the hill beyond Cra 17. Shopping malls: *El Barco*, C 13, No 5-22; *El Emporio*, Cra 9, C 11/12. The Market is at C 11/Cra 11, just off Av del Ferrocarril.

Tour Operators

For guided trips to Quinta San Pedro Alejandrino and other local points of interest, ask in your hotel, travel agencies or the tourist office. Similarly, if you wish to visit the Marine Centre at Punta Betín you will need a boat or a permit to pass through the port

The Northcoast & the Islands

Santa Marta centre

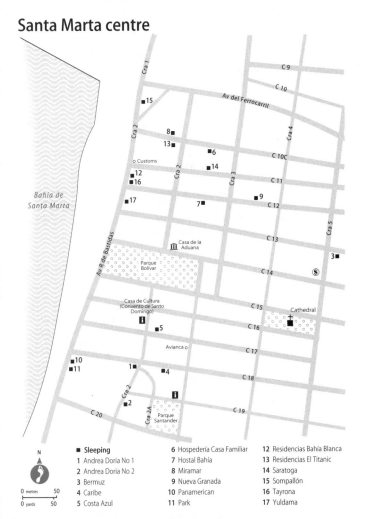

■ Sleeping	6 Hospedería Casa Familiar	12 Residencias Bahía Blanca
1 Andrea Doria No 1	7 Hostal Bahía	13 Residencias El Titanic
2 Andrea Doria No 2	8 Miramar	14 Saratoga
3 Bermuz	9 Nueva Granada	15 Sompallón
4 Caribe	10 Panamerican	16 Tayrona
5 Costa Azul	11 Park	17 Yuldama

area, so ask for guidance. For trips to Tayrona National Park, Ciudad Perdida and the Sierra Nevada, see under the relevant destination. Coach tours also go to Aracataca and Ciénaga de Santa Marta from Santa Marta. Ricardo Olarté, C 22, No 16-61, T/F4203413, has been recommended as a good guide for the remoter areas of Parque Tayrona, Guajira and the Sierra Nevada de Santa Marta. *Tierra Mar Aire*, C 15, No 2-60, T4215161. Amex agent and full tourist travel agent. *Aviatur*, Calle 23, No 4-17, T4213848. Good service. *MA* office, C 12, No 16D-05, T4203116, T/F4204506/04, Urb Riascos (Las Delicias). *Turcol*, Cra 1C, No 20-15, T/F4212256. Arranges trips and provides guide service (details in text), also covers Rodadero.

Transport **Air** See Ins and outs.

Bus To **Bogotá**, 22 hrs, US$45, 4 a day. If going direct, ask for 'Vía Dorada' buses, which go by the new road, US$43, 15 hrs, Brasilia at 1630 and 1830 good. Copetran to **Bucaramanga** about 9 hrs, US$25. Journey time will be affected by the number of police checks. There is a good meal stop at Los Límites. To **Barranquilla**, 2 hrs, US$3.25. To **Cartagena**, 4-5 hrs, US$8 (or US$10, Brasilia). To **Aracataca**, 1½ hrs, US$2.50. To **Riohacha** US$6, 3 hrs. To **Maicao**, with Rápido Ochoa US$12 a/c at 0500, also cheaper non a/c, 4-5 hrs. There are 3 buses a day (Brasilia) direct to **Rodadero** from Barranquilla, taking 2 hrs and costing US$2. They return to Barranquilla at 1300, 1530 and 1730. For **Venezuela,** Brasilia runs buses direct to Maracaibo around midday, enquire about times.

Sea Although cruise ships from various places eg USA, Puerto Rico, Panama and even Europe visit Santa Marta from time to time, it is difficult to find a passage here from overseas. For shipping vehicles to Santa Marta see **Shipping a vehicle** in the **Darien** section of this chapter. Without a *carnet de passages*, it can take up to 4 working days to get a car out of the port, but it is usually well guarded and it is unlikely that anything will be stolen. (See also under **Motorcycles** in **Essentials**.)

Train The railway has not been in use for some time and although new plans for revitalizing the line abound, there is little prospect of them coming to fruition in the near future. However, a stretch of line to the south of Rodadero has been rebuilt and freight trains run through Ciénaga to the loading port at La Loma.

Directory **Airline Offices** Avianca/SAM, C 17, No 2-76, T4210276. **Aires**, Cra 3, No 17-27, T4317024. AeroRepública, C 22/Cra 2, T4210120.

Banks Change money at *Banco de Occidente*, good rates for Mastercard. *Bancolombia*, Calle 13 y Cra 5 for Amex TC exchange, but in mornings only. *Banco de Bogotá* has Cirrus ATM. ATMs for other major cards available eg *Banco Ganadero*, for Visa. *Banco Santander*, Calle 14/Cra 3A, advances on credit cards, closed Mon, slow. Quicker is *Banco Caja Social*, opposite. *Amex*, see Tierra Mar Aire below. *Casas de cambio* in 3rd block of Calle 14, many others on this street. In Rodadero, Apto 201, Cra 1, No 9-23. Santa Marta is a good place to change pesos with Venezuelan bolívares.

Communications Internet *Cafenet Tayrona*, C 12, No 1-59, US$3 per hr, open Mon to Sat 0800-2030, Sun 0800-1300, queues in evening, free coffee. *Cybercafé*, C 23, No 6-18, Local 39, T4318804. Also, C 18, No 2-72. **Telephone** *Telecom*, C 13, No 5-17.

Laundry *Lavandería Paraíso*, C 14, No 8C-47.

Useful Addresses DAS Office, Cra 8, No 26A-15, T4231691/4215205. **Police** 112, *Cruz Roja* T4214509.

Around Santa Marta

Rodadero beach, 4 km south of Santa Marta, is one of the best along this coast. It is part of the municipality of **Gaira**, a small town, 2 km away, alongside the main road, on the Río Gaira which flows into the Caribbean at the southern end of Rodadero beach. Near here there are many apartment blocks owned by Colombians as holiday flats, and other holiday centres operated by public and social entities. The main part of the beach is high rise hotels of all standards. The attractive beach is tree lined and relatively clean and pleasant for bathing. Behind the promenade are the restaurants, cheaper accommodation and services. It is a popular place for family holidays.

Ins and outs To Santa Marta, local bus service US$0.35, taxi US$1.80. Many of the buses coming from Barranquilla and Cartagena stop at Rodadero on the way to Santa Marta.

Launches leave Rodadero beach for the 10 minute trip to the **Aquarium** north along the coast at Inca Inca Bay. Exhibits include sharks, seals and many colourful fish of the Caribbean. It is linked to a small museum with relics from Spanish galleons sunk by pirates and a collection of coral and seashells. Boats leave from Carrera 2, Calles 10/11 every hour from 0800, US$2.50 including admission, last boat back at 1600. From the Aquarium, one can walk (10 minutes) to the Playa Blanca and swim in less crowded conditions than elsewhere - food available at the beach. Sleeping and eating details for Rodadero are below. For services not listed see under Santa Marta.

Sleeping AL *Irotama*, Km 14, between airport and Rodadero Bay, T4320600, F4320077, www.irotama.com Own beach, full service, several restaurants, convention facilities, suites, rooms and nice bungalows. **AL** *Sol Arhuaco*, Cra 2, No 6-49, T4227166, F4227235. 200 m from beach, quiet, pool, bar. **AL** *Tamacá*, Cra 2, No 11A-98, T4227015, F4227028. Direct access to beach, fair rooms, good service, casino, fine pool. **A** *Betoma*, C 8, No 1-58, T4227340, F4228012 one block from beach. Clean, friendly.

C *El Rodadero*, C 11, No 1-29, T4227262, F4227371. Swimming pool, English-speaking manageress, very helpful. **C** *La Riviera*, Cra 2, No 5-42, Apdo Aéreo 50-69. Small, clean, safe, a/c. **C** *Edmar*, Cra 3, No 5-188, T4227858, F4228559. A/c, clean, cafeteria, welcoming.

D *Tucuraca*, Cra 2, No 12-53, T4227493. With bath, group discounts, fan, friendly, will store luggage. For groups of 4 or more, ask about apartments for short rent.

Youth hostels *Hostería Tima Uraka*, C 18, No 2-59, T/F4228433. Also known as *Casa de Luna*, new hostel, 110 beds, nice garden, friendly, owner speaks English. *Medellín*, C 19, No 1C-30, T/F4220220. Also 110 beds, both with full hostel services.

Eating *Pincho*, Cra 2, No 6-30. Good food, international menu, moderate prices, bar. *El Pibe*, C 6, No 1-26. Steaks, Argentine run. *El Banano*, Cra 2, No 8-25, also Cra 2, No 7-38. Good meat dishes and light meals, try their *carne asada con maduro* (banana) *y queso crema*, delicious. Recommended. There are also fast food restaurants and very good juice kiosks along the seafront.

Bars and nightclubs There are many bars and nightclub in Rodadero, one of the best is *La Escollera*, C 5, No 4-107, Lagunita, T4227859. Open till late.

Sports Diving Diving shops at Rodadero: *Centro de Buceo*, C 6, No 1-16, T/F4220178. *Tienda de Buceo y Salvamento*, C 8, No 2-21, 2nd floor, T4228179, 2 dives US$30 including equipment, 4 day course, US$180.

Tourist office *Fondo de Promoción Turístico*, C 10, No 3-10, T/F4227548, hotel and general information on Rodadero.

Taganga   Over the hills north of Santa Marta is the fishing village and beach of **Taganga**. The swimming is good, especially on Playa Grande, 25 minutes walk round the coast, but do not leave your belongings unattended. Taganga is quiet during week, but it is popular at weekends.

Ins and outs   From Santa Marta, minibus US$0.30, taxi US$2.50, 15-20 mins.

Trips by boat along the coast for fishing and to the many bays and beaches are run by Hotel Ballena Azul and by a syndicate of boatmen along the beach. Half an hour north of Taganga is Isla de la Aguja, a good fishing zone. Nearer to Taganga is Playa Granate, with excellent places to snorkle and dive around the coral reefs. Typical prices for round trips, maximum 10 people sharing the price are: Villa Concha, US$35; Arrecifes US$75.

Sleeping and eating **A** *La Ballena Azul*, T4219009/9005, F4219047, Apdo Aéreo 799, Santa Marta, info@ballena-azul.com French-owned, most attractive, own beach, friendly, comfortable, clean, good restaurant, also run boat tours to secluded beaches, ask about tours and diving, horses for hire. **B** *Bahía Taganga*, C 2, No 1-35, T4217620. With breakfast, overlooking bay, some rooms have balcony, clean, friendly owner. **D** *Playa Brava*, T4217309. Fan or a/c, quiet, clean, friendly owner, basic beds. **E** *Casa de Felipe*, 3 blocks from beach behind football field, T4219101, F4219022. With bath, cheaper without, kitchen facilities, owners Jean Phillipe and Sandra Gibelin. **E** *Guest House DIVA*, C 10, No 4, T4219092. Dormitory cheaper, good view of bay, clean, friendly, terrace, also own the dive shop (see below). **F** *Villa Altamar*, C 4, No 1B-12, T4129070, Aptdo Aereo 104, Santa Marta, 5 mins from beach. Excellent views over bay, shared bath, also new cabins with bath same price, all meals on request, Swiss

Around Santa Marta

owners Chris and Miriam von Allmen. Other cheap places to stay, shop around. Ask Joselito Guerra or Wilberto on the beach for **G** hammock space, may charge for use of kitchen, but make sure your luggage is secure.

Food is expensive but there is good fresh fish along the beach. Good pancakes at the *crêperie* at the *Ballena Azul*.

Sports Dive shops in Taganga include: *Centro de Buceo DIVA*, C 11, No 3-05, T4219001, PADI and NAUI courses at all levels, 4 day beginners US$140, 2 dives US$30, also single dives, French owner, English spoken. *Ser Buzo*, C 2, No 1-101, T4219007. Similar prices. *Oceano Scuba Club*, opposite the beach, T4219004. Bargain for courses with accommodation.

Southeast of Santa Marta beyond San Pedro Alejandrino is Mamatoca where the main road leads off to Riohacha. A short distance beyond, a dirt road leads south to a television relay centre on the high foothills of the Sierra Nevada, and on to Vistanieves. About 20 km along this road is **Minca**, at a height of about 600 m, surrounded by forests and coffee fincas.

Minca

Sleeping and transport E Hospedaje Las Piedras, C de las Piedras on the banks of the Río Gaira, some rooms with bath, hot water, German run, friendly, meals available, cooking facilities, local excursions, mountain bikes and horses for hire. Regular jeeps leave the market in Santa Marta for Minca, 40 mins.

The road continues to Vistanieves and La Tagua from where there is a hiking route to La Ciudad Perdida (see below). A further 5 km on the main road up the valley towards Riohacha is **Bonda**, a small village, once an important Indian settlement, off the road. Just before Bonda is a dirt road going south into the mountains. About 4 km along this road past Masinga at Paso del Mango is *Carpe Diem*, an ecological farm at an altitude of 400 m, which takes guests with rooms, dormitory and hammock space, meals available, free coffee, Dutch, French and English spoken. They provide transport from Santa Marta on Tuesday and Friday afternoons. Ask at *Hospedería Casa Familiar* in Santa Marta.

Tayrona National Park

Colombia without Tayrona is a bit like New York without the Empire State building. You just cannot contemplate missing it. So beautiful – and mostly unspoiled – is this stretch of wild coastal woodland that it attracts more than its fair share of new-age hippies. But don't let that put you off. This is a Caribbean paradise right up there with the rest of them, and the occasional mind-numbingly inane conversation will not detract from the experience.

Colour map 1, grid A3

The park is named for the Tayrona (also spelt Tairona) Indian culture, one of the most important of pre-colonial Colombia. It extends from north of Taganga for some 85 km of rugged coastline much of it fringed with coral reefs. You will see monkeys, iguanas and maybe snakes.

Getting there To get to the park entrance, take a minibus from the market in Santa Marta, Cra 11/C 11, about US$1, 45 mins, frequent service from 0700, last service back about 1630 or go to the Riohacha road police checkpoint (taxi US$1 or bus to Mamatoca) and catch any bus there going towards Riohacha. A tourist bus *(chiva)* goes from *Hotel Miramar* in Santa Marta, daily at 1030, to Cañaveral US$7 including park entrance but not food. This transport returns at 1200; visitors normally stay overnight. Hotels help in arranging tours, but there is no need to take guides (who charge

Ins & outs

US$20 or more per person for a day trip). A boat can be hired in Taganga to go to Arrecifes, about 2 hrs along the scenic coast, about US$75 for 10.

Park information Entry to the park is US$2.50 per person (US$3 in high season), US$1 for a motorcycle, US$3.50 for a car. It opens at 0800. If you arrive earlier, you may be able to pay at the car park at Cañaveral.

Check with MA in Santa Marta before visiting and obtain a permit if necessary. Normally, you are advised to book accommodation before going especially at holiday times. However, in the past few years, the park has been closed for safety, water shortages, local staffing and other reasons only to be reopened after a short break. Unfortunately, this has given rise to confusion and contradiction. The best place for information is Santa Marta, and hopefully you will find that the park is open when you wish to visit.

It is advisable to inform park guards when walking in the park. Wear hiking boots and beware of bloodsucking insects. Take your own food and water, but no valuables as robbery has been a problem. You may be able to hire donkeys for the Arrecifes-Pueblito stretch, US$5 each way, but watch them as these animals eat everything. Generally, there is litter everywhere along the main trails and around the campsites. In the wet, the paths are very slippery.

Around the park There are various places where there is access to the bays and beaches by road, including an unsurfaced road from the eastern edge of Santa Marta at Bastidas north 5 km to the beach at Villa Concha (see below). On towards Riohacha beyond Bonda (see above)there is a road in poor condition to Gayraca and Neguange (where the Indians had an important settlement to exploit marine salt resources), to a point near Ancón Cinto. You can reach Negangue beach by colectivo from Santa Marta at 0700, return 1600, US$6. Enquire also for transport to Villa Concha. Alternatively, take a boat from Taganga.

The normal entry to the park today is further on, turning off the main road at El Zaino, 35 km from Santa Marta and at the eastern end of the park. From there, a road leads within the park 4 km to the administrative and visitor centre with car park at **Cañaveral**, about 1 hr walk into the park from the gate. About 40 minutes west of Cañaveral on foot is **Arrecifes**, from where it is 45 minutes walk to El Cabo, then up inland along a stream (La Boquita) 1½ hours on a clear path to the archaeological site of **Pueblito**. A guided tour around the site is free, but check at the entry if it is available. There are many other smaller Tayrona settlements in the Park area and relics abound. At Pueblito there are Indians; do not photograph them. From Pueblito you can either return to Cañaveral, or continue for a pleasant two hour walk to Calabazo on the Santa Marta-Riohacha road. A circuit Santa Marta, Cañaveral, Arrecifes, Pueblito, Calabazo, Santa Marta in one day is arduous, needing an early start.

Beaches Bathing is not recommended near Cañaveral as there is often heavy pounding surf and the currents are treacherous, but the beach is less crowded and cleaner than Rodadero. About 5 km east of Cañaveral are splendid, deserted sandy beaches. You have to walk there, but take care as the park borders marijuana-growing areas. The beach at **Villa Concha** (see above) is one of the most beautiful beaches of the area, with camping space and several places to eat. Pirates used the bay on their way to sack Santa Marta. Beyond Arrecifes (the sea can be dangerous on this beach) near **Cabo** is La Piscina, a beautiful, safe natural swimming pool, excellent for snorkelling. Other safe bathing beaches can be found further along the shore but the going is difficult.

At Cañaveral Thatched 'ecohabs' (circular cabins built in the style of Indian *bohíos* **Sleeping** which hold 2-6 people). Charges for 2-4 persons, US$35-45/night high season, US$30-40 low, MA price. Great views over sea and jungle, good restaurant. Campsite US$15 for a 5 person tent, hammocks, US$4 each. There are facilities, but only a tiny store, take all supplies or eat in the restaurant. An attractive site but plenty of mosquitoes. Beware of falling coconuts and omnivorous donkeys. **At Arrecifes** there are 2 good campsites *El Paraíso* and *Rancho Bonito* charging around US$3 for a tent, US$1 for hammock space, US$1.50 to hire a hammock, US$20 for a hut. Fresh water showers and toilets (none too clean). There are 2 other basic sites and several places to eat (food poor quality but try the homemade coconut bread) and also a basic shop, a guardroom for gear, soft drinks and cooking facilities available. Bringing your own food is recommended.

On the path to Pueblito there is a campsite at **Cabo** where the path turns inland, with good bathing, showers and toilets. There is also a small restaurant and hammocks for hire; there are other camping and hammock places en route. You must obtain permission from MA to camp in the park if you are not staying at Cañaveral; this is normally forthcoming if you specify where you intend to stay. There is nowhere to stay at Pueblito.

Ciudad Perdida

Ciudad Perdida, (Lost City) is the third of the triumvirate of 'must-sees' on *Colour map 1, grid A3* Colombia's Caribbean coast (the other two being Cartagena and Tayrona, of course). The six-day trek is right up there with the Inca Trail in Peru and Roraima in Venezuela as one of the classic South American adventures and is a truly memorable experience.

Discovered only as recently as 1975, Cuidad Perdida was founded near the Río **The site** Buritaca between 500 and 700 AD and was surely the most important centre of the Tayrona culture. It stands at 1,100 m on the steep slopes of Cerro Corea, which lies in the northern part of the Sierra Nevada de Santa Marta. The site, known as Teyuna to the local Indians, covers 400 ha and consists of a complex system of buildings, paved footpaths, flights of steps and perimetrical walls, which link a series of terraces and platforms, on which were built cult centres, residences and warehouses. Juan Mayr's book, *The Sierra Nevada of Santa Marta* (Mayr y Cabal, Bogotá), deals beautifully with Ciudad Perdida.

Archaeologists and army guards will ask you for your permit (obtainable in Santa Marta, MA, Turcol or ask at tourist office). Don't forget that Ciudad Perdida is in a National Park: it is strictly forbidden to damage trees and collect flowers or insects. Note also that there are over 1,200 steps to climb when you get there.

Six day trips can be organized by the tourist office and Turcol in Santa Marta **Tours to** (addresses above) and cost US$150 per person. Price includes transport, **Ciudad Perdida** mules or porters, guide and food. It is three days there, one day (two nights) at the site, and two days back. The route goes beyond Parque Tayrona on the road to Riohacha, then past Guachaca turns inland to the roadhead at El Mamey. The climb broadly follows the Río Buritaca, and apart from crossing a number of streams, is up all the way. Ciudad Perdida is on a steep slope overlooking Río Buritaca.

Ask at hotels in Santa Marta (eg *Hotel Miramar*) or Taganga, or at Santa Marta market (Carrera 11/Calle 11) for alternative tours. If you are prepared to shop around and cook and carry your supplies and belongings, a tour could cost you less but you must take an authorised guide. Recommended guides:

Frankie Rey, known to German tourists as 'die graue Eminenz', very knowledgeable, or Edwin Rey, Wilson and Edilberto Montero, Donaldo and Rodrigo. Try to get views of the quality of guides from travellers who have done the trip. Under no cirumstances should you deal with unauthorised guides, check with a Tourist Office if in doubt.

An alternative route to the site can be arranged through *Hotel La Ballena Azul* (above). It costs about US$175-250 per person for the six-day round trip, all inclusive. Its advantage is that it avoids settlements, especially in the drug-growing lower valleys and Kogi villages which may not welcome foreigners. For this route take a jeep up to La Tagua (about three hours), where it is possible to rent mules and pay local guides (but see above). Unfortunately this route was closed in 2000, ask if it has been reopened.

For both routes you need to take a tent or a hammock and mosquito net (in organized tours these may be supplied by the guide), a good repellent, sleeping bag, warm clothing for the night, torch, plastic bags to keep everything dry, and strong, quick-drying footwear. Be prepared for heavy rain on the trip – the northern slopes of the Sierra Nevada have an average rainfall of over 4000 mm per year, a seriously wet climate. Small gifts for the Indian children are appreciated. Check conditions, especially information on river crossings, and ensure you have adequate food, water bottle and water purifying tablets before you start. Try to leave no rubbish behind and encourage the guides to ensure no one else does. Going on your own is discouraged and dangerous. Route finding is very difficult and unwelcoming Indians, paramilitaries and drug traders increase the hazards. Properly organised groups appear to be safe.

Those with little time, or more money than sense of adventure, can reach Ciudad Perdida by helicopter from Santa Marta in about 20 minutes. Ask at the airport, at Tourist Offices, or travel agencies in Santa Marta. *Sportur,* the travel company in the *Irotama* hotel near Rodadero T4320600, has good information; 15 days' advance booking may be required. Flights need a minimum of 5 people at about US$550 each, one hour each way and up to a three hour stay, but note that fog can be a problem. This service was available in 2000.

East from Tayrona Beyond Cañaveral and Guachaca along the coast, is **Palomino** with an attractive beach, camping possible at *La Casa de Rosa* with hammocks, food and cooking facilities. Tours can be arranged from there to Indian villages taking up to six days, cost around US$32/day. Enquire at Turcol in Santa Marta. The paved coastal road continues from Tayrona and crosses into Guajira Department at Palomino, 80 km from Santa Marta; 72 km from Palomino is Los Camarones and the entry to Santuario Los Flamencos, 25 km short of Riohacha.

Santuario Los Flamencos The Santuario de Fauna y Flora Los Flamencos is 7000 ha of saline vegetation including some mangroves and lagoons. There are several small and two large saline lagoons (Laguna Grande and Laguna de Navío Quebrado), separated from the Caribbean by sand bars. The latter is near Camarones (colectivo from Riohacha, new market) which is just off the main road. 3 km beyond Camarones is 'La Playa', a popular beach to which some colectivos continue at weekends. The two large lagoons are fed by several intermittent streams which form deltas at the south point of the lakes and are noted for the many colonies of flamingoes, some of whom are there all year, others congregate between November and May, ie during the wet season when some fresh water enters the lagoons. To see them take off against the deep blue of the sky is unforgettable. A zoom lens is recommended for photographs. The birds are believed to migrate to and from the Dutch Antilles, Venezuela and Florida. Across Laguna de Navío Quebrado is a warden's hut on the sand bar, ask to be ferried across by local fishermen or the Park guards who are very helpful. There is a visitor centre and some accommodation. Camping is permitted near the centre. Entry to the Park is US$2.50. Take plenty of water if walking. The locals survive, after the failure of the crustaceans in the lagoons, on tourism and ocean fishing. There are several bars/restaurants and two stores on the beach.

Riohacha

Riohacha capital of Guajira Department, 160 km east of Santa Marta, is a port at the mouth of the Río César. It is famed for its excellent white beaches lined with coconut palms. At weekends it fills up, and bars and music spring up all over the place. The sea is clean, despite the red silt stirred up by the waves.

Phone code: 95
Colour map 1, grid A5
Population: 142,000

Getting there The **airport,** José Prudencio Padilla, is south of the town towards Tomarrazón. The main **bus terminal** is on C 15 (Av El Progreso)/Cra 11. Some colectivos for Uribia and the Northeast leave from the new market 2 km southeast on the Valledupar road.

Ins & outs

Tourist offices There is a Tourist Office, *Cortguajira* at Cra 7/C 1, Av La Marina, T272482, F7274728, well organized.

The city was founded in 1545 by Nicolás Federmann, who, along with Gonzalo Jiménez de Quesada and Sebastián de Belalcázar founded most of the major Spanish settlements of Colombia. One of Riohacha's resources of those days were oyster beds, and the pearls were valuable enough to tempt Drake to sack it (see also under Cartagena). Pearling almost ceased during the 18th century and the town was all but abandoned. José Prudencia Padilla, who was born here, was in command of the republican fleet which defeated the Spaniards in the Battle of Lago Maracaibo in 1823. He is buried in the **cathedral**, and there is a statue in the central park which bears his name. *Riohacha y Los Indios Guajiros*, by Henri Candelier, a Frenchman's account of a journey to the area 100 years ago, is very interesting on the life and festivals of the Wayuú Indians.

A *Arimaca*, C 1, No 8-75, T7273481, restaurant, comfortable rooms, overlooking sea, clean and friendly. **B** *El Castillo del Mar Suites*, C 9A, No 15-352, T7275043, with breakfast, on beach, German owner. **B** *Gimaura* (state-owned), Av La Playa, T272266, including breakfast, helpful, recommended, they allow camping in their grounds, with outside shower.

Sleeping

D *Tunebo*, Cra 10, No 12A-02, T7273131, near market, some air conditioning. **E** *Almirante Pedilla*, Cra 6/C 2, patio, restaurant with cheap *almuerzo*, laundry, clean, friendly. **E** *Internacional*, Cra 7, No 12A-31, T7273483, opposite market, friendly, patio, free iced water, recommended. **E** *Yalconia*, Cra 7, No 11-26, T7273487, private bath, clean, safe, helpful, half way between beach and bus station.

Asadero La Brasa, C 11, No 10-37, steaks, local dishes. *La Santandereana*, Cra 8/C 1, Colombian menu. *La Tinaja*, C 11, No 9-48, seafood. *Glenppi*, Av La Marina, south end, T7273356, good, especially for fish. Many small restaurants along seafront.

Eating

Good hammocks sold in the market. The best places for buying *mantas* and other local items are *La Casa de la Manta Guajira*, Cra 6/C 12, be prepared to bargain; *Rincón Artesanal Dicaime*, C 2, No 5-61, T7273071; *Ojo de Agua*, C 2/Cra 9.

Shopping

Awarraija Tours, Av La Marina No 3-55, T7275806, tours anywhere in La Guajira about US$150 per day per jeep, negotiable for longer trips. *Guajira Tours*, C 3, No 6-47,

Tour Operators

The Northcoast & the Islands

T7273385. *Administradores Costeños*, C 2, No 5-06, T7273393. *Guajira Viva*, agency in Hotel Arimaca, T7270607. All do tours to El Pájaro, Musichi, Manaure, Uribia and Cabo de Vela, leaving about 0600, 12-hr trip, US$40 per person, minimum 4 people.

Transport **Air** Flights to **Bogotá**, daily with SAM, 1½ hrs. To **Cartagena**, daily, **SAM**, about US$120 return. To **Barranquilla, Maicao** and **Valledupar**, Aires.
Bus To **Manaure**, daily at 1300, 3 hrs. To **Maicao**, US$3, to **Santa Marta**, US$6.

Directory **Banks** *Banco de la República*, C 1, No 7-11; *BanColombia*, Cra 8, No 3-09; *Banco de Bogotá*, Cra 7, between C 2/3, for Visa.
Communications Post Office: C 2, Cra 6/7. *Avianca* for airmail, C 7, No 7-104, T7273624, also airline ticket agency. **Telephone** Telecom: C 15/Cra 10, T7272528.
Embassies and consulates *Venezuelan* Cra 7, No 3-08 (hrs 0900-1300, and closed from 1500 Fri to 0900 Mon). With 2 passport photographs, photocopy of passport and an exit ticket with date most can get a visa on the same day, if you get there early, but be prepared for an interview with the consul himself; visas cost US$30 and should not be a transit visa, valid for 72 hrs only. Travellers report it is easier to get a Venezuelan visa in Barranquilla.

Useful addresses DAS Office (immigration) C 5, No 4-48, T7272407, open 0800-1200, 1400-1800.

Riohacha

Going south from Riohacha on an alternative road to Maicao and the Venezuelan frontier, you come to **Cuestecita**, where you can turn southwest to **Barrancas**. Here a large coal mine (one of the largest in the world – El Cerrejón) came into operation in 1986. A good dirt road and an industrial railway (no passengers) have been built between the mine and the new Puerto Bolívar in the Bahía Portete; many millions of tons of coal are being exported annually. Visitors are apparently welcome, but it would probably be best to make arrangements first at the El Cerrejón main office in Barranquilla.

Guajira Peninsula

Beyond Riohacha to the east is the arid and sparsely inhabited Guajira Peninsula, with its magnificent sunsets. The Indians here collect *dividivi* (pods from a strangely wind-bent tree, the *caesalpina coriaria*, which are mainly used for tanning), tend goats, and fish. They are Guajiros, and of special interest are the coloured robes worn by the women.

Ins & outs To visit a small part of the Peninsula take a bus from Riohacha (twice a day from the Indian market) to Manaure, US$2.40, 3 uncomfortable hours through fields of cactus but offering fine views of flamingoes and other brightly coloured birds.

Manaure is known for its salt flats southwest of the town. Hundreds of workers dig the salt and collect it in wheelbarrows, a bizarre sight against the glaring white background. If you walk along the beach past the salt works, there are several lagoons where flamingoes congregate. Around 14 km from Manaure in this direction is **Musichi**, an important haunt of the flamingoes, sometimes out of the wet season, but they may be on the other side of the lagoon and difficult to see. From Manaure there are early morning busetas to **Uribia** (45 minutes, US$1), and from there to Maicao, 1 hour longer. In Uribia, known as the indigenous capital of Colombia, you can buy authentic local handicrafts by asking around. There is a Wayuú Indian festival here annually in May, very colourful, 'alijunas' (white people) are welcome, but ask permission before taking photographs. You can get *busetas* from Uribia to Puerto Bolívar (from where the coal is exported) and from there transport to **Cabo de la Vela**, where the lagoons seasonally shelter vast flocks of flamingoes, herons and sandpipers. Cabo de la Vela is where the Wayuú Indians believe their souls go after death, and is known as 'Jepirra'. It costs about US$3 from Uribia to Cabo de la Vela, 1½ hours. There are fine beaches.

Sleeping **In Manaure E** *Unuipa*, main street, T278113, popular with groups visiting the Los Flamencos. **E** *Manaure*, on beachfront, basic but clean and friendly. **In Uribia G** *Flamingo*; **G** *Uribia*, and one basic *residencia*, no running water. **In Cabo de la Vela** a basic but friendly, Indian-run hotel, *El Mesón* rooms and hammock veranda, showers, good meals – excellent fried fish, or sling a hammock at El Caracol where there is an expensive restaurant; better value next door at *La Tropicana* if you order food in advance. Also Conchita will hire out a large hut, hammocks for up to 5 and cook food with prior request. Along the coast, ask anyone, and you will probably be able to get fried fish and coconut rice and a place to hang a hammock for about US$3.

Macuira National Park Towards the northeast tip of the Guajira peninsula is the Serranía de Macuira, named after the Makui people, ancestors of the Wayuú. Makuira means tobacco, formerly grown here. The Park, of 25,000 ha, is entirely within the limits of the Wayuú reservation. It consists of a range of hills over 500 m which have a microclimate of their own creating an oasis of tropical forest in the

Sir Francis Drake

On his various voyages to the Caribbean, Drake visited the north coast of Colombia several times, not only sacking the main Spanish settlement at Cartagena in 1586, but also making unwelcome appearances in Guajira. Rather than looking for gold or other precious metals, he found the rich pearl grounds in the waters near Riohacha. He sacked the town in 1596 on his last voyage, shortly before he died of fever in Portobelo, Panama, where he is buried.

He presented the largest pearl he acquired here to Queen Elizabeth I of England, and it was set in one of her state crowns.

semi-desert. The highest point is **Cerro Palúa**, 865 m, and two other peaks are over 750 m. Moisture comes mainly from the northeast which forms clouds in the evening, dispersing in the early morning. The average temperature is 29°C and there is 450mm of mist/rain providing sufficient water for several more or less permanent streams that disappear into the sand once they reach the plains. Its remoteness gives it interesting flora and fauna and Wayuú Indian settlements little affected by outsiders. They cultivate cashew nuts, coconuts and plantains as well as collecting dividivi pods.

To reach the **Parque Natural Nacional Macuira** you must travel northeast from Uribia first along the mineral railway, then either round the coast past Bahía Portete, or direct across the semi-desert, to Nazareth on the east side of the park. There are no tourist facilities anywhere nearby and no public transport though trucks may take you from the Bahía Portete area to **Nazareth**, 6-8 hours (if you can find one). Nazareth is a Wayuú village where you can stay the night, food available. There are local guides in Nazareth. Entrance to the Park US$2.50. Rangers, all locals, are friendly. Notable wildlife includes the Cardinal bird and 15 species of snakes including coral snakes. Walks include a visit to the 40 m-high El Chorro waterfall, in a delightful area of lush, green vegetation. The best way to visit is to contract your own jeep and guide, recommended is Belisario Lugo Salas, T7276323 (Riohacha), who charges around US$150 per day or US$200 per two days, prices negotiable. See also Riohacha **Tour companies**. *Eco-Guías* in Bogotá arrange trips here from time to time.

NB The Guajira peninsular is not a place to travel alone, parties of three or more are recommended. If going in your own transport, check on safety before setting out. Also remember it is hot, it is easy to get lost, there is little cover and very little water. Locals, including police, are very helpful in giving lifts.

Maicao

Phone code: 95
Colour map 1, grid A5

The paved Caribbean coastal highway, continues from Riohacha inland to Maicao, 78 km, close to the Venezuelan border. Now that there are no flights from Barranquilla to Maracaibo, taxi or bus to Maicao, and colectivo to Maracaibo is the most practical route.

Maicao is full of Venezuelan contraband, and is still at the centre of the narcotics trade. It has a real Wild West feel to it, with unmade streets. Most commercial premises close before 1600 and after 1700 the streets are unsafe.

Sleeping **C** *El Dorado*, Cra 10, No 12-45, T7267242, a/c, TV, good water supply; **E** *Don Blas*, C 14, No 9-36, T7267262; **E** *Médanos*, Cra 10, No 11-25, T7268822.

Buses There is a new terminal to the east of town. To **Riohacha**, US$3; **Santa Marta** (Expreso Occidente), US$9; **Barranquilla,** last one at 1600, US$14.50. Cartagena, US$18. Colectivos, known as *por puestos* in Venezuela, Maicao-Maracaibo, US$5 per person, or infrequent microbus, US$3.50, very few buses to Venezuela after midday. Brasilia bus company has its own security compound: non-passengers are not allowed in (you can change money, buy bus tickets and food before your journey). *Por puestos* wait here for passengers to Maracaibo; it is a very easy transfer.

Entering Colombia If travelling by *por puesto* make sure the driver stops at the Colombian entry post. If not you will have to return later to complete formalities. With all the right papers, border crossing is easy.

Leaving Colombia There is now no Venezuelan Consul in Maicao. If you need a visa you must get it in Bogotá, Barranquilla, Cartagena or Riohacha. A transit visa which you may be able to get at the border but will probably cost more than a full consular visa will only suffice if you have a confirmed ticket to a third country within 3 days. There are frequent checks between the border and Maracaibo.

(margin:) **Border with Venezuela**

South from Santa Marta

Some 125 km south of Santa Marta the main road to Bucaramanga and Bogotá crosses from Magdalena into César Department. Several roads lead east to Valledupar, the best of which goes from Bosconia, 157 km from Santa Marta. At Km 303, El Burro, is the unpaved road to Talameque and El Banco on the Río Magdalena, and 31 km beyond is La Mata where the oil pipeline from the border area with Venezuela crosses on its way to Coveñas on the Caribbean coast. At San Alberto, 437 km from Santa Marta, the new highway goes right to follow the Río Magdalena to Honda and is now the quickest way to the centre of the country and Bogotá. The old road continues to Bucaramanga, 530 km from Santa Marta.

(margin:) The Northcoast & the Islands

Valledupar

A paved road also comes from the northeastern towns of Maicao and Riohacha to Valledupar, capital of César Department. The town is on the Río Guatapurí which rises in the heart of the Sierra Nevada de Santa Marta.

(margin:) Phone code: 95
Colour map 1, grid B4
Population 260,000

The Alfonso López **airport** is on the southern outskirts of the city, 3 km from the centre, a short walk from the bus terminal. Taxi US$3. The **bus terminal** is 3 km down Avenida Salguero (Cra 7A), the road to Robles and Maicao.

(margin:) **Ins & outs**

One of the few old buildings in the town, which was founded in the middle of the 16th century, is the **Iglesia La Concepción** which overlooks the central plaza named after a past president, Alfonso López Pumarejo. Nearby is a fine balconied colonial façade of the **Casa del Maestre Pavejeau**. There is an interesting display of Indian cultures in the **Casa de la Cultura**, Carrera 6, No 16A-24, T5723271. You can change money at *casas de cambio* on Calle 16.

Valledupar claims to be the home of the *vallenato* music. The annual festival is in the last few days of April (see **Music and dance** section in Background chapter).

A *Vajamar*, Cra 7, No 16A-30, T5743939, with breakfast, pool, expensive food. **F** *Residencia El Triunfo*, C 19, No 9-31, with bath, small rooms, fan, clean, good; next door is *Hotel/Restaurant Nutibara*, excellent cheap meals and breakfast, excellent fruit juices; several other hotels in this street.

(margin:) **Sleeping**

Transport **Air** To Bogotá, daily, Avianca. Other airlines fly to Cartagena, Barranquilla and Poucamacanga. Aires to **Santa Marta** and **Riohacha**.

　　Bus To Santa Marta, 6 hrs. To **Cartagena**, US$13 (with Expreso Brasilia); to **Barranquilla,** 6 hrs, US$10; to **Bucaramanga**, 8 hrs US$20: a paved road runs south through Codazzi to the Santa Marta-Bucaramanga highway at Curumaní (*Hotel Himalaya*).

The Sierra Nevada de Santa Marta

The spectacular Sierra Nevada, covering a triangular area of 16,000 sq km, rises abruptly from the sea, or from lowlands which nowhere reach over 300 m above sea-level. Indeed, the north slope is one of the most striking anywhere, lifting from the Caribbean to 5,800 m snow peaks in about 45 km, a gradient comparable with the south face of the Himalaya, and unequalled along the world's coasts.

Ins & outs **Getting there** From Valledupar one route is along the Guatapurí valley. Another route is by jeep from Valledupar, Cra 7A, C 18, Nos 37-55, to Pueblo Bello, 2 hrs US$2 (less, 1 hr, from the turning off the main road to Pueblo Bello).

　　Before leaving for the Sierra Nevada, check with MA, and ICAN in Bogotá (see **National Parks** section in Background chapter), and the **Fundación Pro-Sierra Nevada**, Edificio Los Bancos 502, Santa Marta, T4214697, F4214737, for information and guidance on what permits are required. Apart from the trip to Ciudad Perdida (see under Santa Marta), there are two 'normal' entry points into the Park. The first from Santa Marta is via the road to Minca, from which a side road leads to San Lorenzo (just outside the Park) where there are MA cabins at about US$4 per person per night. The second is from Valledupar, see below. Unfortunately, permission to enter the Park itself was difficult to obtain in 2000.

　　Climate The rainy season in these mountains ends Nov; Jan is best month for a visit.

　　Advice and information The Indians of the Sierra do not take kindly to being photographed without permission. (Do not leave litter or disrespect the Indians' sacred grounds; stay on paths and do not stray on to private land.) They like to be given sea-shells which can be ground into powder and mixed with coca leaves. Learning a few words of their language can work wonders.

The interior is made up of some eight east-west ranges with their intervening valleys. The lower parts of these interior valleys are flanked by forests – the homes of Indians as well as of pumas, jaguars, and a variety of snakes and birds – but for the most part the Sierra is almost lunar in its sterile grandeur, bleak *páramos* leading to naked crag and scree and glacier, where only an occasional hungry condor moves. In the rocky heart of the area are a large number of small, beautiful lakes, many in cirques. Hikes in the Sierra go through villages, valleys alive with butterflies, flowers and waterfalls, and to the lakes and the snowfields and summit of Pico Colón at 5,800 m, the highest point in Colombia. The Park goes down to the Caribbean between Ríos Don Diego and Palomino.

Trekking Trekking is very limited as the Arhuacos will not allow access deep into the Sierra. Climbing is not permitted (2000). Ñoco (see below) can arrange mules for trips (US$8.50 per mule including guide, per day). Ñoco himself occasionally acts as guide if he is free (he runs a grocery store); he is very knowledgeable. Also recommended is Ricardo Olarté, Padilla and Hans Kolland, Calle 22, No 16-61 Santa Marta, T/F4203413, who will arrange transport, food, accommodation for treks in the Sierra Nevada region and has a very good relationship with the local Indians.

Before hiking in the Sierra, visitors must get permission from the Arhuaco chief in San Sebastián (at the police HQ); a charge may be made for whatever walk you are allowed to do, this ranges from US$7 to US$15. **NB** Information in mid-2000 indicates that no permissions are being granted at present to go into the high sierra, but day trips with guides or on your own are permitted provided you report back the same day: for this, no charge is made. Walking upstream along the Río San Sebastián from the village is recommended.

There is plenty of drinking water, but Pueblo Bello is the only place to stock up with food. A tent is necessary for trekking (though not applicable in present circumstances). The best place for maps is Bogotá. It is also possible to hike on the coastal side of the Sierra, but it is absolutely essential to take a guide through the marijuana-growing areas. Trekking tours into the fringes of the Nevada de Santa Marta can also be arranged in the Santa Marta area, check with the Tourist Office.

In Pueblo Bello (F *Hotel El Encanto*, good meals US$1, friendly, but poor beds, hot, small, dark; F *Los Ensueños*, friendly, clean) enquire for jeeps to **San Sebastián de Rábago** (also called **Nabusimake**), the central village of one of the 4 tribes of Indians living in the Sierra, the Arhuacos (jeeps leave 0700-0800, 2-2½ hrs, US$3 to $6 depending on conditions, dreadful road). It is set in beautiful surroundings and is the epitome of an Indian village with stone, thatched roof houses and local costumes. Ask for El Salto, a 2-hr walk, guide US$4.50 (not really needed). Jeep drivers may be able to arrange for you to stay on a farm; Doña Inés recommended, **F** (arrange price on arrival), clean, friendly, good food. Also recommended is Ñoco, a mestizo who has lived in the valley for over 30 years; he has floor space, free camping (cold). Camping is also permitted in the valley.

Sleeping

San Andrés and Providencia

Colombia's Caribbean islands of the San Andrés and Providencia archipelago are small and attractive, but very expensive by South American standards. Nevertheless, with their surrounding islets and cays, they are a popular holiday and shopping resort. San Andrés is very crowded with Colombian shoppers looking for foreign-made bargains. Although alcoholic drinks are cheap, essential goods are extremely costly, and electronic goods are more expensive than in many other countries.

San Andrés and Providencia are famous in Colombia for their music, whose styles include the local form of calypso, soca, reggae and church music. A number of good local groups perform on the islands and in Colombia. Concerts are held at the Old Coliseum (every Saturday at 2100 in the high season); the Green Moon Festival is held in May. There is a cultural centre at Punta Hansa in San Andrés town (T25518). On **20 July** independence celebrations are held on San Andrés with various events, and in **November** is the *Reinado del Coco* (Coconut Queen) festival. Providencia holds its carnival in **June**.

After their discovery by Colombus on his fourth trip to the Caribbean, their early colonial history was dominated by the conflicts between Spain and England, though the Dutch occupied Providencia for some years. English Puritans arrived in 1627 on Providencia and later moved on to San Andrés. The English left in 1641, but English remained the dominant language until recent times and is still widely spoken. The original inhabitants, mostly black, speak some English, but the population has swollen with unrestricted immigration from

The Northcoast & the Islands

Colombia. There are also Chinese and Middle Eastern communities. The islands are 480 km north of the South American coast, 400 km southwest of Jamaica, and 180 km east of Nicaragua. This proximity has led Nicaragua to claim them from Colombia in the past.

San Andrés

Phone code: 9851
Colour map 1, inset
Population: 70,000

San Andrés, a coral island, is 11 km long, rising at its highest to 104 m. The town, commercial centre, major hotel sector and airport are at the northern end. A good view of the town can be seen from **El Cliff** (see map of the town).

Ins & outs

Getting there The airport is 15 mins' walk to town. For flight details see under Transport.

Getting around Buses cover the eastern side of the island all day (15 mins intervals), US$0.30 (more at night and on holidays). **Taxis** round the island, US$8; to the airport, US$3.50; in town, US$1.25, US$2.50 elsewhere, fares double after 2200; *colectivo* to the airport, US$0.50.

Train a 'tourist train' (suitably converted tractor and carriages) tours the island in 3 hrs for US$4.50.

Bicycles are a popular way of getting around on the island and are easy to hire, eg opposite Los *Delfines Hotel* on Av Colombia – usually in poor condition, choose your own bike and check all parts thoroughly (US$1.10 per hour, US$6 per day). **Motorbikes** are also easy to hire, US$8 for minimum 2 hrs. **Cars** can be hired for US$15 for 2 hrs, with US$6 for every extra hour.

A picturesque road circles the island. Places to see, besides the beautiful cays and beaches on the eastern side, are the **Hoyo Soplador** (South End), a geyser-like hole through which the sea spouts into the air most surprisingly when the wind is in the right direction. The west coast is less spoilt, but there are no beaches on this side. Instead there is **El Cove** (The Cove), the island's deepest anchorage, and **Cueva de Morgan** (Morgan's Cave), reputed hiding place for the pirate's treasure, which is penetrated by the sea through an underwater passage. Near Cueva de Morgan is the **Seaquarium** with a good selection of Caribbean sea life. Ask at *El Isleño* hotel about free transport. At El Cove, you can continue round the coast, or cross the centre of the island back to town over **La Loma**. This is the highest point on the island and nearby is **La Laguna** (Big Pond), a fresh water lake 30m deep, home to many birds and surrounded by palm and mango

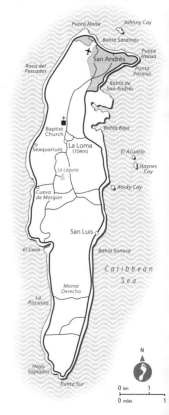

San Andrés Island

trees. On the town side of La Loma is the first **Baptist Church** to be built on the island(1847), acting as a beacon to shipping.

Boats go in the morning from San Andrés to Johnny Cay (frequently spelt Jhonny) with a white beach and parties all day Sunday (US$3 return, you can go in one boat and return in another). Apart from those already mentioned, other cays and islets in the archipelago are Bolívar, Albuquerque, Algodón (included in the Sunrise Park development in San Andrés), Rocky, the Grunt, Serrana, Serranilla and Quitasueño. **Beaches & cays**

On San Andrés the beaches are in town and on the eastern coast. Perhaps the best is at San Luis and Bahía Sonora/Sound Bay.

Diving off San Andrés is very good; the depth varies from 3-30 m, visibility from 10-30 m. There are three types of site: walls of seaweed and minor coral reefs, large groups of different types of coral, and underwater plateaux with much marine life. It is possible to dive in 70% of the insular platform. The Blue Wall (Pared Azul) is excellent for deepwater diving. Black Coral Net and Morgam's Sponge are other good sites. See also below under **Watersports**. **Diving**

AL *Aquarium (Decamerón)*, Av Colombia 1-19, T26926, F26174, rooms and suites, TV, a/c, large pool, marina. **AL** *Casablanca*, Av Colombia y Costa Rica, T24115, central, rooms and cabins, a/c, pool, restaurant, cafetería. **AL** *Casa Dorada*, Av Las Américas No 2A-69, T24056, salt water washing, reasonable food. **AL** *San Luis Decamerón*, road to San Luis Km 15, T23657, all-inclusive resort, pool, a/c, TV, good restaurant, recommended. **AL** *Cacique Toné*, Av Colombia, No 5-02, T24251, deluxe, a/c, pool, 2 restaurants, own generator. **AL** *El Isleño (Decamerón)*, Av de la Playa 3-59, T23990, F23126, 2 blocks from airport, in palm grove, a/c, good sea views. **AL** *Green Moon*, Av 20 de Julio, No 2A-51, T23491, good facilities, special rates for weekends and holidays. **Sleeping**
Some hotels raise their prices by 20-30% on 15 Dec

A *Bahía Sardina*, Av Colombia No 4-24, T23793, F24363 across the street from the beach, a/c, TV, fridge, good service, comfortable, clean, pool. **A3** *Verde Mar*, Av 20 de Julio, No 2A-13, T23498, F25494, quiet and friendly, a/c, cafetería, recommended. **A** *Viña del Mar*, Av de la Playa, 3-1145, T28298, T/F24791, spacious rooms, shower and bath, close to beach and centre, bargain for a good price.

B *Capri*, Av Costa Rica, No 1A-100, T24316, with bath and a/c, pool, restaurant, good value.

C *Mediterráneo*, Av Los Libertadores, T26722, clean, friendly, poor water supply. **C** *Nueva Aurora*, Av de las Américas, No 3-46, T26077, fan and private bath, pool, restaurant.

D *Coliseo*, Cra 5/Av Aeropuerto, T23330, friendly, noisy, good restaurant. **D** *Residencias Hernando Henry*, Av de las Américas 4-84, T24009, restaurant, fan, clean, good value, often full, on road from airport. Also near the airport is **D** *Olga and Federico Archibold*, C de la Bodega Marlboro, No 91-18, T25781, 3 self-contained apartments, modern, clean, friendly. **E** *Residencia Restrepo*, Av 8 near airport, very noisy, 'like sharing a room with a Boeing 727' main gringo hotel, much cheaper than others, less for a hammock in the porch, but you get what you pay for, the accommodation is in a poor state and the grounds are a junkyard, not recommended. Opposite Restrepo is a tobacco/paper shop whose owner rents air conditioned apartments with kitchen, **D**.

Out of town is **C** *Channel View*, Vía San Luis, on the east side of the island opposite Rocky Cay, T27057, F(932) 818965, with breakfast, 30 rooms, a/c, restaurant, bar, gardens, private beach, quiet, hospitable, good value.

Oasis (good), Av Colombia No 4-09; *El Pimentón*, Av de las Américas, good menú, cheap. *El Zaguán de los Arrieros*, Av 20 de Julio (50m after the cinema), good food and value. *Fonda Antioqueña Nos 1 and 2*, on Av Colombia near the main beach, and **Eating**

The Northcoast & the Islands

Av Colombia at Av Nicaragua, best value for fish. *Sea Food House*, Av 20 de Julio, at Parque Bolívar, good cooking, not expensive, second floor terrace; excellent fruit juices at *Nueva China*, next to Restrepo, reasonable Chinese; *Fisherman's Place*, in the fishing cooperative at the north end of the main beach, very good, simple. Cheap fish meals can be bought at San Luis beach.

Watersports **Diving** *Buzos del Caribe*, Centro Comercial Dann, T2893011, offer diving courses and equipment hire; *Sharky Dive Shop*, T33977, on the coast 10 minutes from town, PADI advanced certificate course, US$250. Also, try *Diver's Dream*, T27701, or *San André Divers*, T25158.

For the less adventurous, take a morning boat (20 minutes, none in the afternoon) to the so-called El Acuario (Aquarium) Cay (US$3 return), off Haynes Cay, where, using a mask and wearing sandals as protection against sea-urchins, you can see colourful fish, or to *Nautilus II*, a glass hull 'wreck,' a good way for non-divers to see marine life, entrance fee US$10.

Snorkelling equipment can be hired on San Andrés for US$4-5, but it is better and cheaper on the shore than on the island.

Pedalos can be rented for US$6 per hour. **Windsurfing, parasailing** (US$30 for a session, ask at hotels and Dive shops), and **sunfish sailing** rental and lessons are

San Andrés town

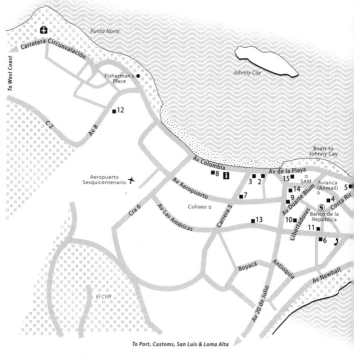

To Port, Customs, San Luis & Loma Alta

N

Not to scale

■ **Sleeping**	6 Casa Dorada	12 Residencia Restrepo
1 Aquarium	7 Coliseo	13 Residencias Hernando
2 Bahía Sardina	8 El Isleño	Henry
3 Cacique Toné	9 Green Moon	14 Verde Mar
4 Capri	10 Mediterráneo	15 Viña del Mar
5 Casablanca	11 Nueva Aurora	

available from *Bar Boat* on the road to San Luis (opposite the naval base), 1000-1800 daily (also has floating bar, English and German spoken), and *Windsurf Spot*, *Hotel Isleño*, T23990. **Water-skiing** at *Water Spot*, *Hotel Aquarium*, T26926, and *Jet Sky*.

From Tominos Marina there are boat trips around the island. Bay trips for 2 hrs cost US$8.75, for 4 hrs US$17.50, including 3 free rum-and-cokes. For all these sports, ask at your hotel and check around for the best prices. *Cooperativa de Lancheros*, opposite *Hotel Abacoa* for fishing and pleasure trips.

Air Terminal, T26110. To **Bogotá**, 3 flights daily, Avianca, US$160, cheapest if booked 14 days before flying. To **Cali,** daily, Intercontinental, US$150. To **Cartagena,** 3 a week, AeroRepública, US$90. To **San José** (Costa Rica), daily, Lacsa/SAM, US$260 return. To **Providencia,** 6 daily, West Caribbean Airways, US$45, 25 mins. **Transport**

A cheap way to visit San Andrés is by taking a charter flight from Bogotá or another major city for a weekend or a week, with accomodation and food. See the regional newspapers who usually have supplements on Wed or Thu. San Andrés is a popular, safe, local holiday destination for Colombians. However, booking a hotel and meal plan outside San Andrés is not always satisfactory. You may wish to go for a cheap airfare and choose where to stay on arrival.

Sea Cruise ships and tours go to San Andrés; there are no other, official passenger services by sea. Cargo ships are not supposed to carry passengers to the mainland, but many do. If you want to leave by sea, speak only to the ship's captain. (Any other offer of tickets on ships to/from San Andrés, or of a job on a ship, may be a con trick.) The sea crossing takes 3-4 days, depending on the weather. In Cartagena, ships leave from the Embarcadero San Andrés, opposite the Plaza de la Aduana.

Airline Offices All offices are in town accept Aces at the airport. West Caribbean Airways, T23184, F21222. **Directory**

Banks *BanColombia*, Av Costa Rica; *Banco de Bogotá* will advance pesos on a Visa card. *Banco Occidente* for Mastercard. Aerodisco shop at the airport will change dollars cash anytime at rates slightly worse than banks, or try the Photo Shop on Av Costa Rica. Many shops will change US$ cash; it is impossible to change travellers' cheques at weekends.

Communications **Internet** Café Internet, *Hotel Tiuna*, US$2 per hr, www.dol.net.co **Post Office** on Av Duarte Blum (Avianca);

Embassies & consulates *Costa Rican*, *Guatemalan* (Av Las Américas, No 3-136, T26357) and *Panamanian* consulates in San Andrés Town but they may not be able to issue visas which should be arranged, as necessary, on the mainland.

Tourist offices Av Colombia No 5-117, English spoken, maps.

Punta Hansa

Av Providencia

Punta Paraíso

Providencia

Phone code: 9851
Colour map 1, inset
Population 5,500

Providencia, also called Old Providence, 80 km to the north-northeast of San Andrés, is 7 km long and 3½ km wide. The Island is more mountainous than San Andrés, rising to 610 m, due to its volcanic origen and is much older than San Andrés which is uplifted coralline rocks. There are waterfalls, and the land drops steeply into the sea in places.

Ins & outs

Getting there Air West Caribbean Airways flies from San Andrés, 6 times a day, bookable only in San Andrés. (Return flight has to be confirmed at the airport, where there is a tourist office.) **Sea** Boat trips from San Andrés take 8 hrs, but are not regular.

Getting around *Chivas* circle the island at more or less regular intervals at US$0.50 standard fare.

Like San Andrés, it is an expensive island. There is a bank in Santa Isabel that will exchange cash, but it is best to take sufficient pesos with you. Exchange rates from shops and hotels are poor. Alternatively, use credit cards. The seafood is very good, water and fresh milk are generally a problem. English is widely spoken. Day tours are arranged through hotels round the island stopping typically

Providencia

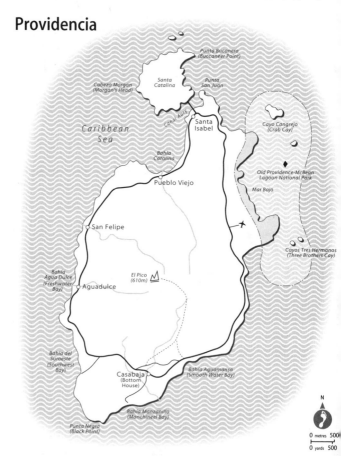

The Northcoast & the Islands

at Cayo Cangrejo to swim and snorkel, about US$10. Snorkelling equipment can be hired and diving trips arranged: the best place is Aguadulce.

In 1996 part of the east coast and offshore reefs and coral islands were declared a National Park (**Parque Nacional Natural Old Providence – McBean Lagoon**). The land position includes Iron Wood Hill (150 m), mainly small trees but including cockspur (*acacia colinsii*) which has large conical shaped needles, home to a species of ant (pseudomyrmex ferruginea) with a very painful sting. ■ *Entrance US$1.50, MA rent diving gear, T48885. An information centre is under construction.*

Around the island

Superb views can be had by climbing from Casabaja/Bottom House or Aguamansa/ Smooth Water to the peak, about one hour, mostly forested. There are relics of the fortifications built on the island during its disputed ownership. Horse riding is available, and boat trips can be made to neighbouring islands such as **Santa Catalina** (an old pirate lair separated from Providencia by a channel cut for their better defence), and to the northeast, Cayo Cangrejo/Crab Cay (beautiful swimming and snorkelling) and Cayos Tres Hermanos/Three Brothers Cay. Trips from 1000-1500 cost about US$7 per person. Santa Catalina is joined to the main island by a wooden bridge. On the west side of Santa Catalina is a rock formation called Morgan's Head; seen from the side it looks like a man's profile.

On Providencia the three main beaches are Bahía Manzanillo/Manchineel Bay, the largest, most attractive and least developed, Bahía del Suroeste/South West Bay and Bahía Agua Dulce/Freshwater Bay, all in the southwest.

Most of the accommodation is at Freshwater (Aguadulce): **A** *Cabañas El Encanto*, T48131, with meals. **B** *Cabañas Aguadulce Miss Elma's*, T48160, recommended for cheap food; also *Morgan's Bar* for fish meals and a good breakfast. On Santa Catalina is the German-owned **D** *Cabañas Santa Catalina*, T 48037, friendly, use of small kitchen.

Sleeping & eating

Many houses on both islands take in guests. Truck drivers who provide transport on the island may also be able to advise on accommodation. Camping is possible at Freshwater Bay, and elsewhere with permission.

The Darién Gap

The Isthmus of Darién, which links Central to South Amercia, has no road connection south of Yaviza, 60 km from the border with Colombia. It is a similar distance to the nearest road in Colombia. Various attempts have been made to bridge the gap, but none have succeeded. The terrain is very difficult, thick jungle on the Panamanian side, high ridges to cross near and at the border and treacherous marshes of the Río Atrato to negotiate before reaching the 'habitable' part of Colombia. The weather is terrible being in the Chocó climate belt with one of the highest levels of rainfall in the world. There are no roads of any kind, the only inland routes are by boat or on foot.

As a trek, it is rightly held in high regard. It requires considerable planning skill and a lot of effort. Parties have successfully completed it in the past. Indeed pioneers have tried everything and the occasional bicycle, motorbike, horse, canoe, even a jeep has made it. As more people have generally approached from the north, it is mainly written from that direction but the information is all there for doing it in reverse.

The Northcoast & the Islands

Colombia canal

In 1540, Philip II of Spain commissioned Hernán Cortés to study the possibility of a link across the Panama isthmus to join the Caribbean to the Pacific Ocean. In the rivalry of the day between Spain and England, he believed that control and efficient use of this link would benefit the Spanish Empire. Hernán Cortés looked seriously at the route from the Gulf of Urabá to the Pacific south of Darién.

In 1846, the US government concluded a treaty with New Granada (now Colombia, of which Panama was then part) whereby, in return for help in constructing a canal, its neutrality would be guaranteed. Ferdinand de Lesseps who built the Suez Canal, began to build a sea level canal in 1882, but the attempt failed as did a second effort started in 1894. This led to a US move to take over the construction for its own account in 1902, a major factor in Panama's declaration of independence from Colombia the following year.

Ever since then, Colombia has periodically considered whether a second canal should be built in the alternative site. The latest proposals, up for discussion in 1997, suggest a route up from Tanela on the Gulf of Urabá near Unguía to Cupica north of Bahía Solano on the Pacific. Arguments rage on whether it should be a sea level canal, or stepped, or a railway (canal seco), or simply a road or just a pipeline. Meanwhile, ecologists insist that the National Park (Los Katíos) should be extended and no development of any kind permitted. In any case, they say, the lower Atrato valley is to a large extent swamp, and even those proposing a completion of the Pan-American highway to close the Darién Gap have no solution to this problem other than staying near the Pacific coast and cross the Río Atrato at Quibdó.

Don't hold your breath.

At the end of 1992, Panama and Colombia revealed a plan to build a road through the Darién Gap which includes environmental protection. Construction had been halted in the 1970s by a lawsuit filed by US environmental groups who feared deforestation, soil erosion, endangerment of indigenous groups and the threat of foot-and-mouth disease reaching the USA. Of course, the more people who walk the Darién Gap, the greater the pressure for building a road link. Consider, therefore, the environmental implications of crossing between Panama and Colombia just for the sake of it. The Darién Gap road linking Panama with Colombia will not be open for many years, so the usual way of getting to Colombia is by sea or air. It is possible to go overland, but the journey is in fact more expensive than going by air.

Unfortunately, in the past several years, other serious problems have arisen. Those trafficking drugs from South to North America have found the density of the jungle a useful protection for running consignments. Bona fide travellers are not welcome. Indian communities still living in Darién have never truly accepted trekkers passing through. More difficult still is that both FARC and ELN guerilla groups have infiltrated the region and paramilitaries regard this as a threat to their land. As a result this has become a violent war zone, virtually deserted now by police and the military, a hostile environment for any tourist. For the moment only the foolhardy will attempt the land crossing.

By Land

The Pan-American Highway runs east 60 km from Panama City to the sizeable town of Chepo. There are no hotels or *pensiones* in Chepo, but if you are stuck there, ask at the fire station, they will be able to find a place for you. There is a document check in Chepo and at one or two other places. From Chepo the

Highway has been completed as far as Yaviza (225 km); it is gravel from Chepo until the last 30 km which are of earth (often impassable in the rainy season).

From **El Llano**, 18 km east of Chepo, a road goes north to the Caribbean coast. After 27 km it passes the *Nusagandi Nature Lodge* in the Pemansky Nature Park. The Lodge is in Cuna (often spelt Kuna) territory, in an area of mostly primary forest. Visits can be arranged through Centro de Aventuras, Parque Urracá, Panama City, T225-8946, F227-6477. The coast is reached at Cartí, 20 km from Nusagandi. From here there is access to the San Blas Archipelago, the long string of islands off the coast of Panama.

Some 35 km east of Chepo it crosses the new Lago Bayano dam by bridge (the land to the north of the Highway as far as Cañazas is the **Reserva Indígena del Bayano**). Lago Bayano dam supplies a significant amount of Panama's electricity, and has been a source of friction with the Cuna Indians who occupy the land around the lake and especially above in the catchment area. However, it was hoped that a new Indigenous *Comarca*, created in 1996, will confirm the Indian title to the land and set up conservation measures.

Buses From Piquera bus terminal in Panama City, buses leave every 2 hrs 0630-1430 **Transport** for Pacora, US$0.80, Chepo, US$1.60, Cañitas, 4 hrs, US$3.10, Arretí, 6 hrs, US$9, Metetí and Canglón, 8 hrs, US$11.20. Beyond, to Yaviza, in the dry season only, Jan-Apr, US$15, 10 hrs minimum. Plenty of pick-ups run on the last stretch to Yaviza, eg about 3 hrs from Metetí to Yaviza.

Darién

East of Chepo is known as Darién, which is over a third of the area of Panama and very little developed. Most villages are accessible only by air or river and on foot.

The main villages (Yaviza, Púcuro, Paya and Cristales) have electricity, radios and cassette decks, canned food is available in Yaviza, Pinogana, Unión de Chocó, Púcuro and Paya (but no gasoline). Only the Emberá-Wunan (Chocó) and Cuna women retain traditional dress. Organized jungle tours to Cuna Indians, Emberá-Wunan Indians and the Río Bayano costing from US$65 to over US$300 can be purchased through *Mar Go Tours*, Apartado 473, Balboa (Panama).

The bus service from Panama City (see above) has its problems, the road is bad and may be washed out after rains. Find out before you leave how far you can get. Alternatively there is an irregular boat to Yaviza, about once a week, US$12 including meals, leaving from the harbour by the market in the old city (Panama City), information from Muelle Fiscal, Calle 13 next to the Mercado Público. The only sleeping accommodation is the deck (take a hammock) and there is one primitive toilet for about 120 people. The advertised travel time is 16 hours, but it can take as much as two days.

Another possibility is to fly to La Palma (see page 221) and take the much **Yaviza/El Real** shorter boat trip to Yaviza, or direct to El Real (three a week, US$68 return), which is about 10 km from Yaviza. There is only one hotel at Yaviza: **E** *Tres Américas*, pay in *Casa Indira* shop next door, take mosquito coils – nowhere to hang a net, basic, noisy, meals available but not very sanitary. There is a TB clinic and a hospital. Crossing the river in Yaviza costs US$0.25. From Yaviza it is an easy 1-2 hours' walk to **Pinogana** (small and primitive), where you have to cross the Río Tuira by dugout, US$1 per person. From Pinogana you can walk on, keeping the river to your left to Vista Alegre (three hours), recross the river and walk a further 30 minutes to **Unión de Chocó** (some provisions and you can hammock overnight; you can sleep in the village hall but use a net to protect against *vinchucas* – Chagas disease).

About 1 km upriver is Yape, on the tributary of the same name, then 3-4 hours walking to Boca de Cupe. Alternatively you can go by motor dugout from Pinogana to Boca de Cupe (about US$65 per boat). Or you can take a boat from Yaviza to **El Real** (US$10), where there is a very basic place to stay, *El Nazareno*, for US$10 a night. Directly opposite there is a lady who will pre-pare meals if given notice. From there take a motor dugout to Boca de Cupe, about US$15-20 per person (if possible, take a banana dugout, otherwise bar-gain hard on boats). Boats from El Real are not very frequent and may only go as far as Unión de Chocó or Pinogana. A jeep track runs from El Real to Pinogana. There are various other combinations of going on foot or by boat, prices for boat trips vary widely, so negotiate. Parties of four or more will be in a stronger bargaining position. They tend to be lower going downstream than up. It is wise to make payment always on arrival.

Boca de Cupe   Stay the night at **Boca de Cupe** with a family. Food and cold beer are on sale here (last possibility if you are going through to Colombia) at *Restaurant Nena* (a blue building near the landing dock); meals US$2, good information. You can go with Emberá-Wunan Indians to Unión de Chocó, stay one or two days with them and share some food (they won't charge for lodging). The Emberá-Wunan are very friendly and shy, better not to take pictures. In Boca

Darién

de Cupe get your exit stamp (though you may be told to get it at Púcuro) and keep your eye on your luggage. Lodging in Boca de Cupe for US$12.50 with Antonio (son of María who helped many hikers crossing Darién, but who died in 1989). Don Ramón will prepare meals for US$2 and let you sleep on his floor. From Boca de Cupe to Púcuro, dugout, US$20-50, to Paya (if the river level is high enough) US$80. The section Boca de Cupe-Púcuro is possible on foot, first through a cultivated area then less easy terrain where careful route finding is necessary. About two days is needed with several rivers to cross.

Púcuro

Púcuro is a Cuna Indian village and it is customary to ask the chief's permission to stay (he will ask to see your passport – immigration here, if arriving from Colombia, can be very officious). The women wear colourful ornamented *molas* and gold rings through their noses. There is a small shop selling tinned meats, salted biscuits etc. Visitors usually stay in the assembly house. People show little interest in travellers. From Púcuro you can walk through lush jungle to Paya, which was the capital of the Cuna Empire: six hours (a guide costs US$20, not really necessary, do not pay in advance). From Púcuro to Paya there are four river crossings. The path is clear after the first kilometre.

Paya

In Paya you may be able to stay in the assembly house at the village, but it is mandatory to go 2 km away eastwards to the barracks. You can stay there, US$2.50 per person, recommended, and for US$2-2.50 you will get meals (passport check, baggage search and, on entry into Panama at least, all gear is treated with a chemical which eats plastic and ruins leather – wash it off as soon as possible). The Cuna Indians in Paya are more friendly than in Púcuro.

From Paya there are two routes:

Route 1

From Paya, the next step is a 4-6 hour walk to **Palo de las Letras**, the frontier stone, where you enter **Parque Nacional Los Katíos**, one of Colombia's National Parks (see below). The path is in theory not difficult, but it is frequently blocked up to the frontier. From there you go down until you reach the left bank of the Río Tulé, (in three hours, no water between these points), you follow it downstream, which involves seven crossings (at the third crossing the trail almost disappears, so walk along the river bed – if possible – to the next crossing). If any of these watercourses are dry, watch out for snakes. About 30 minutes after leaving this river you cross a small creek; 45 minutes further on is the abandoned camp of the Montadero, near where the Tulé, and Pailón rivers meet to form the Río Cacarica.

The Northcoast & the Islands

Cautions and general notes on crossing the Darién gap

In planning your trip by land or along the coast to Colombia, remember there are strict rules on entry into Colombia and you must aim for either Turbo or Buenaventura to obtain your entry stamp. Failure to do this will almost certainly involve you in significant fines, accusations of illegal entry, or worse in Colombia. Also, do not enter Darién without first obtaining full details of which areas to avoid because of the activities of drug traffickers, bandits and guerrilla groups, mostly from Colombia, but operating on both sides of the border.

Latest information from Colombia (mid 2000) is that armed groups, hostile to travellers including tourists, are particularly active in the northwest corner of Colombia which includes the area on the Colombian side of the border. If information has not improved before you set out to cross Darién by land either way, you are advised not to go.

The New Tribes Mission, after the kidnap of 3 missionaries, has withdrawn its staff from the area and therefore one of a traveller's main sources of assistance has disappeared.

The best time to go is in the dry months (January-mid-April); in the wet season (from May) it is only recommended for the hardy. Travel with a reliable companion or two.

Talk to knowledgeable locals for the best advice. Hire at least one Indian guide, but do it through the village corregidor, whose involvement may add to the reliability of the guides he selects. (Budget up to US$12/day for the guide and his food. Negotiate with the chief, but do not begrudge the cost.)

Travel light and move fast. The journey as described below takes about 7 days to Turbo.

Maps of the Darién area can be purchased from the Ministro de Obras Públicas, Instituto Geográfico Nacional Tommy Guardia, in Panama City (US$4, reported to contain serious mistakes). Information is also available from Asociación de Conservación de la Naturaleza, Calle Alberto Navarro, El Cangrejo, Apontado 1387, Panama city, T2648100, F2642836.

We must emphasize that the land route description below is past experience, and is retained hoping for better times to come. We have heard of no tourists in recent months who has completed the trip. There are several cases of parties that have made an attempt and apparently not survived.

Cross the Cacarica and follow the trail to the MA(Colombian National Parks) hut at **Cristales** (seven hours from Palo de las Letras). Guides (they always go in pairs) cost US$50-200. If you insist on walking beyond Montadero, a machete, compass and fishing gear (or extra food) are essential; the path is so overgrown that it is easier, when the river is low, to walk and swim down it (Cristales is on the left bank, so perhaps it would be better to stick to this side). The friendly rangers at Cristales may sell you food, will let you sleep at the hut, cook, and will take you, or arrange a dugout to **Bijao** (or Viajado); two hours, for around US$120 per boat. The rangers are often not there and there is no village nearby, so arrive prepared. It is possible to walk to Bijao down the right (west) bank of the Río Cacarica (heavy going). From the bend to the east of the river the path improves and it is one hour to Bijao. At Bijao ask for the MA station, where you can eat and sleep (floor space, or camp). **NB** At the end of 1998, guerillas siezed Bijao, killing several people and driving out others. It is still unclear what the situation is now.

From Bijao a motor dugout runs to the confluence of the Ríos Cacarica and Atrato at **Travesía** (also called Puerto América) for US$40 per person (2-3 hours), from where motorboats go to Turbo for US$10 (in scheduled boat – if it stops; if not it'll cost you about US$250 to hire a boat). Travesía has some accommodation and provisions but have been reported as expensive and anti-gringo. Once again, there is a walking route south to Limón (two hours) and east to La Tapa (30 minutes). A cargo boat may be caught from here to Turbo (price unknown). One *residencial* and a shop in Travesía. The last section from Travesía down the Atrato goes through an area full of birdlife, humming birds, kingfishers, herons, etc, and 'screamers', about the size of turkeys and believed to be unique to the Atrato valley.

On arrival in Turbo, you must go to the DAS office at Postadero Naval, north along Carrera 13 near the airport (open 0800-1630), to get your entrance stamp. If you fail to do this, you will have to wait until Cartagena, or elsewhere, and then explain yourself in great detail to DAS and quite likely be fined. If you arrive at the weekend and the DAS is closed, make sure you obtain a letter or document from the police in Turbo that states when you arrived in Colombia. The problems with this route are mostly on the Colombian side, where route finding is difficult, the undergrowth very difficult to get through, and the terrain steep. Any rain adds greatly to the difficulties, though equally, when the water is low, boats need more pole assistance, and the cost increases.

If you are coming into Panama from Colombia by these routes, and you have difficulty in obtaining entry stamps at Púcuro or Boca de Cupe, obtain a document from an official en route stating when you arrived in Panama. This may be equally hard to get. Then go to the Oficina Nacional de Migración in Panama City (who may send you to the port immigration) and explain the problem. One traveller reports hearing of several arrests of travellers caught without their entry stamp. Many of these 'illegals' stay arrested for weeks. It may help to be able to prove that you have sufficient money to cover your stay in Panama.

Route 2 The second route is a strenuous hike up the Río Paya valley through dense jungle (machete country) for about 16 hours to the last point on the Paya (fill up with water), then a further three hours to the continental divide where you cross into Colombia. Down through easier country (3-4 hours) brings you to **Unguía** (**F** *Residencias Viajero*, with bath; **G** *Doña Julia*, also with bath; several basic restaurants) where motor boats are available to take you down the Río Tarena, out into the Gulf of Urabá, across to Turbo. This trip should not be taken without a guide, though you may be lucky and find an Indian, or a group of Indians making the journey and willing to take you along. They will appreciate a gift when you arrive in Unguía. Hazards include blood-sucking ticks, the inevitable mosquitoes and, above all, thirst.

Overland from Puerto Obaldía This involves a four-hour walk to the foot of the Darién range (guide essential, US$10), crossing the hills to the Río Tuquesa (three hours) and following the river downstream with a great many crossings and one night camping out, to Maranganti (immigration post). From here a dugout can be taken to **Vigía**; walk to the next village, Villa Calleta (take care with directions on this stretch). From Villa Calleta you walk along the Río Chucucanaque to join the Yaviza-Panama City road near La Pinita. Note that locals on this route are very wary of foreigners (much illegal immigration).

There are many other possible routes from Panama crossing the land frontier used by locals. Most involve river systems and are affected by water levels. There are few tracks and no reliable maps. We have heard of successful crossings using the Ríos Salaqui and Balsas, and a land route Jaqué-Juradó-Riosucio. Good guides and serious planning are essential.

Health and general advice

Heat Acclimatization to a hot climate usually takes around three weeks. It is more difficult in humid climates than in dry ones, since sweat cannot evaporate easily, and when high humidity persists through the night as well, the body has no respite. (In desert conditions, where the temperature falls at night, adaptation is much easier.) Requirements for salt and water increase dramatically under such conditions. You will need to drink 12 litres per day to keep pace with fluid loss on some parts of the trip. It is important to remember that the human thirst sensation is not an accurate guide to true fluid requirements. In hot countries it is always essential to drink beyond the point of thirst quenching, and to drink sufficient water to ensure that the urine is consistently pale in colour.

Salt losses also need to be replaced. Deficiency of salt, water, or both, is referred to as heat exhaustion; lethargy, fatigue, and headache are typical features, eventually leading to coma and death. Prevention is the best approach. Recommended is the pre-salted water regime pioneered by Colonel Jim Adam and followed by the British Army; salt is added to all fluids, one quarter of a level teaspoon (approximately 1g) per pint – to produce a solution that is just below the taste threshold. Salt tablets, however, are poorly absorbed, irritate the stomach and may cause vomiting; plenty of pre-salted fluid should be the rule for anyone spending much time outdoors in the tropics. (Salted biscuits are recommended by Darién travellers.)

Food & water Diarrhoea can be annoying enough in a luxurious holiday resort with comfortable sanitary facilities. The inconvenience under jungle conditions would have been more than trivial, however, with the added problem of coping with further fluid loss and dehydration.

Much caution is therefore needed with food hygiene. Carry your own supplies, and prepare carefully yourselves. In the villages, oranges, bananas and coconuts are available, also freshly baked bread and rice.

Purify water with 2% tincture of iodine carried in a small plastic dropping bottle, 4 drops to each litre – more when the water is very turbid – wait 20 minutes before drinking. This method is safe and effective, and is the only suitable technique for such conditions. Another suggestion from is a water purifying pump based on a ceramic filter. There are several on the market. It takes about a minute to purify a litre of water. When the water is cloudy, eg after rain, water pumps are less effective and harder work. Take purification tablets as back-up. It is also worth travelling with a suitable antidiarrhoeal medication such as Arret.

Malaria Chloroquine resistant malaria is present in the Darién area, so appropriate antimalarial medication is essential. Free advice on antimalarial medication for all destinations is available from the Malaria Reference Laboratory, T0891 600 350 in the UK. An insect repellent is also essential, and so are precautions to avoid insect bites.

Insects Beside malaria and yellow fever, other insect-borne diseases such as dengue fever and leishmaniasis may pose a risk. The old fashioned mosquito net is ideal if you have to sleep outdoors, or in a room that is not mosquito-proof. Mosquito nets for hammocks are widely available. An insecticide spray is valuable for clearing your room of flying insects before you go to sleep, and mosquito coils that burn through the night giving off an insecticidal vapour, are also valuable.

It is said that ticks should be removed by holding a lighted cigarette close to them. New advice from Dr Hollins of Stockbridge, England is that cigarettes are definitely a no-no since it roasts the tick but leaves the mouthpiece in the skin. In the jungle, this could lead to a dangerous tropical ulcer. Ticks breathe through small openings in the skin. Smoothing with oil or vaseline will kill the tick and release the mouthparts. So too will alcohols. When removing, don't pull straight – the best way to break off the head – but gently and firmly twist to left or right while pulling to dislodge the barbs. Use tweezers, as close to the tiny head as possible.

Ticks

A yellow fever vaccination certificate is required from all travellers arriving from infected areas, and vaccination is advised for personal protection. Immunization against hepatitis A and typhoid are strongly advised.

Vaccinations
*See Health section
on page 52*

Attacks by dogs are relatively common: the new rabies vaccine is safe and effective, and carrying a machete for the extra purpose of discouraging animals is advised. In addition, all travellers should be protected against tetanus, diptheria and polio.

You can get some food along the way, but take enough for at least five days. Do take, though, a torch/flashlight, and a bottle of rum (or similar!) for the ranger at Cristales and useful items for others who give help and information. Newspapers are of interest to missionaries etc. A compass can save your life in the remoter sections if you are without a guide – getting lost is the greatest danger according to the rangers. It is highly recommended to travel in the dry season only, when there is no mud and fewer mosquitoes. A hammock can be very useful. If you have time, bargains can be found, but as pointed out above, costs of guides and water transport are steadily increasing. Buying pesos in Panama is recommended as changing dollars when you enter Colombia will be at poor rates. You will need small denomination dollar notes on the trip.

**General advice
& information**

Taking a motorcycle through Darién is not an endeavour to be undertaken lightly, and cannot be recommended. The late Ed Culberson (who, in 1986 after two unsuccessful attempts, was the first to accomplish the feat) wrote: 'Dry season passage is comparatively easy on foot and even with a bicycle. But it simply cannot be done with a standard sized motorcycle unless helped by Indians at a heavy cost in dollars... It is a very strenuous, dangerous adventure, often underestimated by motorcyclists, some of whom have come to untimely ends in the jungle.' Culberson's account of his journey (in the October 1986 issue of *Rider* and in a book, *Obsessions Die Hard*, published 1991 by Teakwood Press, 160 Fiesta Drive, Kissimmee, Fla, USA, 34743, Tÿ(407) 348-7330), makes harrowing reading.

By Sea

There are usually two or three boats a week from Coco Solo (Colón) to Colombia, making for various ports along the Colombian coast. Going only to San Andrés leaves you with an expensive gap to the mainland. Most of these boats are not licenced to take passengers and may be carrying contraband so you are entirely at your own risk; captains of these boats are reluctant to carry travellers (and you may have to wait days for a sailing – the customs officials will let you sleep in the wind-shadow of their office, will watch your luggage and let you use the sanitary facilities). A passenger travelling in a contraband boat had some problems in the DAS office about getting an entrance stamp: they wanted official papers from the boat's captain showing that he brought him in. You have to bargain for your fare on these boats. Accommodation can be very primitive. See also under **Cartagena Transport**.

Puerto Obaldía – Panama Boats also leave, irregularly, from the Coco Solo wharf in Colón (minibus from Calle 12, 15 minutes, US$0.80, taxi US$4) for **Puerto Obaldía**, via the San Blas Islands. These are small boats and give a rough ride in bad weather, cost around US$30 per person, take your own food, water and shade. With stops it takes 2-4 days. There are flights with Ansa (T226-7891/6881) and Transpasa (T226-0932/0843) at 0600-0630 from Paitilla, Panama City to Puerto Obaldía daily except Sunday for US$44 single (book well in advance). There are also flights with Aerotaxi and Saansa. Puerto Obaldía is a few kilometres from the Colombian border. There are expresos (speedboats) from Puerto Obaldía (after clearing Customs) to Capurganá, and Acandí (see below). You can walk from Puerto Obaldía to Zapzurro (also spelt Sapzurro), just beyond the frontier, for a dugout to Turbo, US$15, where you must get your Colombia entry stamp. It seems that most of the boats leaving Puerto Obaldía for Colombian ports are contraband boats. One traveller obtained an unnecessary visa (free) from the Colombian consul in Puerto Obaldía which proved to be useful in Colombia where soldiers and police took it to be an entry stamp. **NB** Arriving in Puerto Obaldía you have to pass through the military control for baggage search, immigration – proof of funds and onward ticket asked for, and malaria control.

Sleeping There is a good pensión in Puerto Obaldía: **E** *Residencia Cande*, nice and clean, which also serves very good meals for US$1.50, book in advance for meals.

Also in Puerto Obaldía are shops, the Colombian consulate and Panamanian immigration, but nowhere to change travellers' cheques until well into Colombia (not Turbo). Changing cash is possible, though.

Capurganá (Colombia) A short distance down the coast from Zapzurro is Capurganá, now a small tourist resort. There is a Panamanian consul in Capurganá (Roberto) who issues Panamanian visas. To walk to Capurganá takes four hours. A guide is recommended; they charge US$10. First to go to La Miel (two hours), then to Zapzurro (20 minutes), where there are shops and cabins for rent, then 1-1½ hours to Capurganá. Most of the time the path follows the coast, but there are some hills to cross (which are hot – take drinking water). Take pesos, if possible, to these Colombian places, the rate of exchange for dollars is poor. There are Twin Otter flights to Medellín.

Sleeping AL *Almar*, T421479 (Medellín), on beach. Nice rooms, a/c, pool. **AL** *Alcazar*, T4216850 (Medellín), comfortable rooms, Arab style, pool, excursions. **B** *Calypso*, also with a Medellín number for reservations, T2503921. **E** *Uvita*, clean, safe. There are cheaper pensiones and you can camp near the beach (where there is good snorkelling).

Acandí
Phone code: 9816
Colour map 2, grid A1
Alternatively you can get from Puerto Obaldía to Acandí on the Colombian side of the border, either by walking nine hours or by hiring a dugout or a launch to Capurganá (US$8). Then take another launch at 0715, one hour, US$3 to Acandí, with several *residencias* eg **F** *Hotel Central*, clean, safe; **F** *Acandí*, acceptable; **G** *Hotel Pilar*, safe.

Transport From Acandí you can go on to Turbo, on the Gulf of Urabá, a daily boat is scheduled to go at 0800 to Turbo (US$15, 3 hrs); take shade and drinks and be prepared for seasickness. Boats normally leave Turbo at 0900 daily, for Capurganá and/or Acandí. Enquire for the best passage. There are also cargo boats from Cartagena to Capurganá which take passengers, 30-50 rough hours, US$25-30, take hammock. Try to ensure that the boat you take is fully seaworthy and in good hands. We have had reports of unsafe boats, inexperienced operators and bad weather ending in tragedy.

On the Pacific side

There is another possible route to Colombia along the Pacific coast. Although not quick, it is relatively straightforward (spoken Spanish is essential). Take a bus from Panama (Plaza 5 de Mayo) to **Metetí**, 50 km from Yaviza (**E** *Hospedaje Feliz*, basic 'box' rooms), the junction for transport to **Puerto Quimba**, where boats can be taken to La Palma. Alternatively, take a bus to **Santa Fe**, which is 100 km short of Yaviza and off to the south, a rough but scenic 6-8 hours (US$8, three a day, check times). In Santa Fe it is possible to camp near the national guard post (no *pensiones*). Then hitch a ride on a truck (scarce), or walk two hours to the Río Sabanas at Puerto Lardo (11 km) where you must take a dugout or launch to La Palma, or hire one (US$5, two hours). La Palma is also reached by boat from Yaviza, US$3, eight hours.

La Palma is the capital of Darién; it has one pensión (friendly, English-speaking owners, **F**, pricey, with cooking and laundry facilities, or see if you can stay with the guardia). There are daily Aeroperlas flights from Panama City to La Palma and to Jaqué three days a week; also to Yaviza three days a week, but check with the airline Parsa, T226-3883/3803. They have an office at the Paitilla airport in Panama City. There is no public transport from La Palma to Jaqué, but you may be able to find a boat. The bank changes travellers' cheques in La Palma.

Jaqué is on the Pacific coast, near Puerto Piña, 50 km north of the Colombian border. There are direct flights from Panama City to Jaqué. At **Bahía Piña** is the Tropic Star Lodge, T2645549, where a luxury fishing holiday may be enjoyed on the sea and in the jungle for over US$1,000 a week. Bahía Piña has a runway, used mainly by the expensive fishing resort.

Alternatively, at the Muelle Fiscal in Panama City (next to the main waterfront market, near Calle 13), ask for a passenger boat going to Jaqué. The journey takes 18 hours, is cramped and passengers cook food themselves, costs only US$12 but you may be charged US$20 departure tax. Jaqué is only reached by sea or air (the airstrip is used mostly by the wealthy who come for sport fishing). There are small stores with few fruit and vegetables, a good *comedor*, one *hospedaje*, **F** *Hospedaje Chavela*, clean, basic, friendly (but it is easy to find accommodation with local families), and camping is possible anywhere on the beautiful 4 km beach. The guard post is open every day and gives exit stamps. Canoes from Jaqué go to Juradó (US$25, 4½ hours, very uncomfortable, make sure you have something to sit on) or Bahía Solano (US$45, 160 km, with two overnight stops) in Chocó. The first night is spent in **Juradó** (where the boat's captain may put you up and the local military commander may search you out of curiosity). There are flights from Juradó to Turbo, but it is possible to get 'stuck' in Juradó for several days. Take care to get good advice about Juradó and the other small fidhing ports near the Colombia/Panama frontier. Remember this close to the 'war zone.' Other occasional cargo boats go south to Bahía Solano and Buenaventura, eg M/V Fronteras. Bahía Solano is a deep-sea fishing resort with an airport and places to stay (see **Chocó** section, page 286). On this journey, you sail past the lush, mountainous Pacific coast of Darién and Chocó, with its beautiful coves and beaches, and you will see a great variety of marine life.

NB It is not easy to get a passage to any of the larger Colombian ports as the main shipping lines rarely take passengers. Those that do are booked up well in advance. The Agencias Panamá company, Muelle 18, Balboa, represents Delta Line and accepts passengers to Buenaventura. Anyone interested in using the Delta Line ships should book a passage before arriving in Panama. The only easy way of getting to Colombia is to fly (see **Getting there** in **Essentials**).

Shipping agencies do not have the authority to charge passages. Many travellers think they can travel as crew on cargo lines, but this is not possible because Panamanian law requires all crew taken on in Panama to be Panamanian nationals.

Colombia officially demands an exit ticket from the country. If you travel by air the tickets should be bought outside Panama and Colombia, which have taxes on all international air tickets. If you buy air tickets from IATA companies, they can be refunded. Copa tickets can be refunded in Cartagena (Calle Santos de Piedra 3466), but this takes four days, Barranquilla, Cali or Medellín. Refunds in pesos only. Copa office in Panama City, Avenida Justo Arosemena y Calle 39, T227-5000.

Shipping a vehicle

The best advice is to shop around the agencies in Panama City or Colón to see what is available when you want to go. Both local and international lines take vehicles, and sometimes passengers, but schedules and prices are very variable. To **Colombia**, agents include: *Sudamericana de Vapores*, T229-3844, Cristóbal-Buenaventura; *Boyd Steamship Corporation*, T263- 6311, Balboa-Buenaventura or Guayaquil. To Barranquilla: *Vicente Simones*, T Colón 195-1262, beeper 270-0000, code 700283, will arrange all paperwork for US$25: car passage US$800, motorcycle US$50, plus US$50 per passenger, no accommodation on ship other than hammock space, take food and drink for a week (even though the voyage should be three days). To Cartagena, Captain Newball, Edificio Los Cristales, 3rd floor, Calle 38 y Avenida Cuba, Panama City. On the same route Central American Lines sail once a week, agent in Panama, T Colón 441-2880, Panama City 236-1036. Also, *Geminis Shipping Co SA*, Apartado Postal No 3016, Zona Libre de Colón, Rep de Panamá, T441-6269/6959, F441-6571. Mr Ricardo Gil was helpful and reliable. Another agent Barwil, next door to Citíbank in Colón, T441-5533 (Colón), 263-7755 (Panama City), will arrange shipment to Colombia (Cartagena) and elsewhere in Latin America. If sending luggage separately, make enquiries at Tocumen airport, eg Tampa, T238-4439.

One alternative is to try to ship on one of the small freighters that occasionally depart from Coco Solo Wharf in Colón for Turbo in Colombia, which allow you to travel with your car. Obviously there is a considerable element of risk involved (suspect cargo, crews and seaworthiness), though the financial cost is lower than on a regular line. Once you have found a skipper, correct documentation is essential.

Warning The contents of your vehicle are shipped at your own risk – generally considered to be a high one! Anything loose, tools, seat belts, etc, is liable to disappear, or to be swapped for an inferior replacement (eg spare tyre).

Air-freighting a vehicle

Most people ship their vehicles from Panama to South America by sea but some find air-freighting much more convenient. Generally it is faster and avoids many of the unpleasant customs hassles, but is more expensive. Prices vary considerably. The major carriers, if they permit it on a regular commercial flight, tend to charge more than the cargo lines and independents. Prices and availability change from month to month depending on the demand by regular commercial shippers. You are generally not allowed to accompany the vehicle. For Copa Cargo, T238-4414, Tocumen airport, talk to Otto Littman.

Taking a motorcycle from Panama to Colombia can normally only be done on a cargo flight. Drain oil and gasoline, and remove battery before loading. You may be able to save space (and cost) by knocking down the vehicle. If possible, insist on loading the bike yourself. Documentation and customs fees may exceed US$50. Having bought your passenger ticket, and checked your bike in at the carrier's office, go to customs in Paitilla airport with your entry permit and freight papers, and pay US$4.20 to have the stamp cancelled in your passport. You may have to take your airwaybill to the Colombian Consulate for stamping 3 hours before flight time. Allow two days in Panama. Try Challenge Air Cargo (CAC) in Pamama, US$150 for a 200 kg bike, pallet system, good service. Remove anything breakable and tape cardboard over fragile bits. Retrieving the bike in Colombia, although costing very little (US$10 approximately), will take from 0900 to 1630 for paperwork (or up to two days if there are any peculiarities in your documents). You must normally go to customs in the arrival port for the bike to be released. If you bring the bike by air, try to stay as close as possible to it while it is cleared through the freight fowarders and customs to save time and damage. A *carnet de passages* is strongly advised (see under Shipping a Vehicle, above). At Bogotá airport, you can have your documents stamped and be through in two hours. Otherwise you must go to the Aduana Nacional, Calle 65 bis, no 904-35, Bodega España, T4309670, to complete formalities.

Shipping motorcycles

Border with Panama

DAS Office at the Postadero Naval, Turbo, near the airport, transport available on Cra 13 between C 101 and 102, open 0800-1630. If going from Colombia to Panama via Turbo you should get an exit stamp from the DAS office. There is also a DAS office in Capurganá, opposite *Hotel Uvita*, and a Panamanian consultate, but it's best not to leave it that late. If leaving Colombia, check the facts at any DAS office.
   NB Colombian pesos are impossible to change at fair rates in Panama.

Colombian immigration

Arriving from Panama, go to the DAS in Turbo for your entry stamp.

Entering Colombia

Panamanian immigration at Puerto Obaldía is sometimes obstructive (all baggage will be checked for drugs, adequate funds for your stay may have to be shown – US$400, travellers' cheques or credit card; a ticket out of Panama is required, although a ticket from another Central American country may do).
   NB If travelling from Panama to Colombia by coastal boat or land, we strongly advise you to aim for Turbo (or Buenaventura) and obtain your entry stamp from the DAS office there. If you arrive by boat at Cartagena or other Caribbean ports, you may require evidence to show how you got there. Travellers who have requested entry stamps at other DAS offices have been fined or accused of illegal entry. A police stamp, eg in Capurgana, is no legal substitute, though it can help.

Entering Panama

The Northcoast & the Islands

Los Katíos National Park

Colour map 2, grid A1 The Katíos National Park, extending in Colombia to the Panamanian border, contains several waterfalls, including the 125 m-high Tilupo, where the water cascades down a series of rock staircases, surrounded by orchids and fantastic plants. This is six hours return trip. A five-hour trip passing through splendid jungle is required for two other fine waterfalls, the Salto de La Tigra and Salto de La Tendal. A full day's hike is recommended to Alto de Limón for a fine view of primary forest. You can stay overnight in a hut. Also in the park are the Alto de la Guillermina, a mountain behind which is a strange forest of palms called 'mil pesos', and the Ciénagas de Tumaradó, with red monkeys, waterfowl and alligators.

Ins & outs **Getting there** The National Park can be reached by boat from Turbo most days, charging US$8. The boats, normally going up the Atrato to Riosucio, or beyond, will leave you at the MA headquarters of the Park in Sautatá. Ask in Turbo harbour when they are leaving. You should have a permit from MA in Turbo for the Park, or you can pay in the park. Arrange your return trip Sautatá – Turbo with the park guide at Sautatá beforehand. Boats do not normally stop. The Park can be visited with mules from the MA headquarters in Sautatá (cabins US$5.50 per person, or rangers may offer free space for your hammock, very friendly). Food can be ordered half a day in advance. All motorized vehicles are prohibited in the Park.

To visit the park, go first to the MA office in Turbo, where all necessary information is available. The office is 1 km along the road to Medellín. Because of violence and guerrilla activity in the region, MA discourages entry; if you insist you must sign a disclaimer. **NB** In mid 2000 the Park was closed to visitors and the MA ranger stations were unmanned. Best information on the Park is in Turbo. See the the warning at the beginning of this section.

Crossing Darién: Pacific Side

On the Pacific side, crossing into Panama involves travel by both boat and on foot, the quantity of each depending on the route chosen.

One sea route is from Bahía Solano or Juradó in Chocó Department, see details above.

Juradó can be reached by plane from Turbo, or overland from Riosucio by the Trans-Isthmus route, using both boat and walking (30-36 hours in all). Serious advance planning is essential, although the Trans-Isthmus route is well-trodden by local traders (legal or otherwise). The Embera and Wounan Indians encountered en route are wary, but hospitable. Besides the boat Juradó-Jaqu,, there is an overland route involving at least one night camping between Santa Teresita (Wounan village, Colombia) and Mamey (Embera, Panama), detailed local instructions are essential. Transport out of Jaqué is frustrating; you must obtain a DAS stamp in either Turbo or Buenaventura, without it you will have problems in Jaqué or Panama City.

We have heard of a number of routes successfully attempted across the land frontier. Well-equipped groups using local paths and information, armed with compass and machete, can more or less make their own way. However, accident or illness could be very serious, much of the area is sparsely inhabited, and getting lost is usually fatal.

Up the Río Magdalena

6

Up the Río Magdalena

The Río Magdalena, one of the great rivers of South America, has played an essential part in the history and the economy of the region since precolumbian times.

The Magdalena has also its assured its place in literature. It features in one of the classic Latin American novels, Love in the Time of Cholera, by Gabriel García Márquez. The Nobel-prize winning author had to make the trip twice a year as a child, up to Bogotá and back, and has stated that the only thing that would make him want to be a child again would be travel the river by boat. He describes the journey as slow and full of surprises, accompanied by the screeching of monkeys, the constant chatter of parakeets and the haunting cries of manatees.

Nowadays, the Magdalena bears little resemblance to the river of Márquez's childhood – it is badly polluted and most of the animals have been hunted to extinction. The great waterway, has also been replaced over the years by roads and railways as the main link from the Caribbean to the interior. But this isolation has brought its own benefits for curious travellers. Along its course, from Barranquilla to its upper reaches in the south of the country, is a string of sleepy old places, boasting the best of Spanish colonial legacy in the towns, churches and caminos reales in the area drained by the river.

Highlights along the Río Magdalena

★ Seeing the filigree gold work in Mompós.

★ Marvelling at the strange rock towers of Los Estoraques.

★ Having a meal at the historic Hotel Magdalena in Puerto Berrío.

★ Splashing through the limestone caves of El Nus or Río Claro.

★ Spending a sombre moment in the buried town of Armero.

★ Listening to every kind of music in Ibagué.

The Lower Magdalena

Ins & outs The Magdalena near its mouth is wide but shallow and difficult to navigate because of surface eddies, and there are little whirlpools over submerged rocks. Away to the north-east, in the morning, you can occasionally see the high snow-capped peaks of the Sierra Nevada de Santa Marta. Passenger travel by the lofty paddle boats on the river has come to an end, though the adventurous traveller may still find an occasional passage by cargo paddle boat. In general the only way of getting from one place to the other along the river is by motor launch (*chalupa*). The river trip from the north coast (best to take a bus from Cartagena to Magangué, see details under that town below) to Puerto Berrío or Puerto Boyacá and thence by bus to Bogotá can in theory be completed in about 4 days. Insect repellents should be taken, for mosquitoes are a nuisance.

The last 200 km of the Río Magdalena is sluggish and dull as a boat trip, but there are interesting places on its banks. **Calamar** is the terminus of the Canal del Dique which links the river with Cartagena and 50 km upstream, is Tenerife, where Bolívar had his first victory in the Magdalena campaign.

A short distance above Tenerife is **Zambrano** (**E** *La Española*, C 5, No 14B-07, T(95)2853068, with bath, friendly, good). It is in an important archeological area which has been continually occupied for over 4000 years. The large shell mounds found here have demonstrated that it was in contact with cultures throughout the northern Colombia of today. There is little to be seen here now but pots anf figurines discovered here are in many museums (eg Museo del Oro, Cartagena). Today Zambrano is a quiet port on the river in a cattle and tabacco producing area.

From here there is a road west to the north-south Cartagena-Medellín road at El Carmen de Bolívar, jeep from Zambrano, US$0.30. On the opposite (east) shore is Plato from where another road goes 108 km through to the Santa Marta-Bucaramanga road across the flat flood plain of the Magdalena valley.

Near Pinto, 40 km above Zambrano, the river divides: the eastern branch known as the Brazo Mompós, silted and difficult, leads to Mompós (full name Santa Cruz de Mompós or Mompóx) through cattle farming and tobacco country. *Chalupa* from Zambrano to Mompós, US$5, 2½ hrs.

NB At present this route is not considered safe. The section from El Banco to Puerto Berrío borders on lands dominated by ELN guerilla groups, and Barranca bermeja, as an oil refining and shipping town, is a target from time to time. This area, known as Magdalena Medio, should be avoided at present (2000).

Mompós

Phone code: 952
Colour map 1, grid B3
Population 33,000

Thanks to its comparative isolation, Mompós has retained its colonial character. This sleepy town, founded in 1537, was the scene of another victory for Bolívar: 'At Mompós', he said, 'my glory was born.'

At that time, this was the main channel of the river and Mompós became a major staging port for travellers and merchandise going to the interior. Prosperity followed, but by the beginning of the 20th century, the silting up of this branch of the river diverted traffic to the Brazo de Loba, and the Mompós section became a backwater.

Holy Week is an important and solemn celebration in Mompós with many of the churches' images paraded through the streets.

Sights The churches demonstrate the colonial origins of the town; five of the six are close to the centre. The church of **San Francisco** is probably the oldest dating from the end of the 16th century with an interesting interior. **Santo Bárbara**, on Calle 14 by the river, has a unique octagonal moorish tower and balcony. **San Juan de Dios, La Concepción, Santo Domingo** and **San Agustín** are all worth visiting. You may have to ask around for the key to see inside, they are not normally open except during Mass. Among the old buildings are the Casa de Gobierno, once a home of the Jesuits and now the **Alcaldía**, and the **Colegio Pinillos**. The cemetery has considerable historical interest. The town is well known in Colombia for handworked gold jewellery, especially filigree.

Simón Bolívar stayed in what is now called the **Casa Bolívariana** which houses memorabilia of his times and also has some religious art exhibits. The

Mompós (Santa Cruz de Mompox)

Up the Río Magdalena

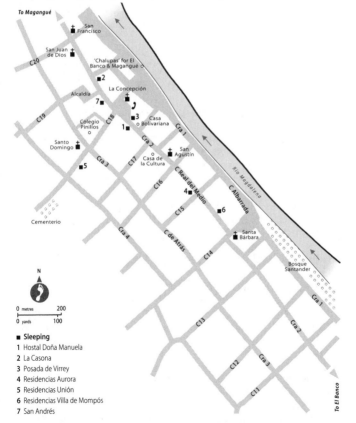

■ Sleeping
1 Hostal Doña Manuela
2 La Casona
3 Posada de Virrey
4 Residencias Aurora
5 Residencias Unión
6 Residencias Villa de Mompós
7 San Andrés

Air travel – Colombia

Travel from the north coast of Colombia to the major cities of the interior has always been difficult because of the terrain of swamplands, forests and mountains. The rivers were well used, but travel was very slow, particularly upstream. The main route was the Río Magdalena from Barranquilla, with access from Cartagena and Santa Marta by sea, canal and railway.

When air travel 'took off', Colombia was the first country in South America to benefit, and Barranquilla, with its varied experience of freight and passenger shipping, the obvious choice. The river figured prominently at the start because flying boats were employed. Around 1920, German entrepreneurs established the Sociedad Colombo-Alemana de Transportes Aéreos (SCADTA), and the first service from Barranquilla to Girardot was inaugurated using Junkers Frit Hammer aircraft powered by BMW engines. This cut the passenger time from eight days to eight hours. It still took another eight hours by train to Bogotá or three hours to Ibagué (followed by a mule trip over the Cordillera to Armenia, Pereira and Manizales). The idea caught on and the service was extended south to Neiva and eventually, with new aeroplanes, air travel reached Bogotá itself.

This service led to the establishment of AVIANCA, the first airline in South America. It attracted mail from the start and AVIANCA still runs the airmail service for the country. An early set of SCADTA airmail stamps has become a collectors item. The first AVIANCA aircraft is preserved and can be seen from the main road north from Bogotá.

Casa de la Cultura is a particularly interesting colonial building and home of the local Academy of History.

Sleeping

Malaria is endemic in the surrounding countryside. If staying overnight, mosquito nets and/or coils are a must

C *Hostal Doña Manuela*, C Real del Medio (Cra 2), 17-41, T855620, F855621, a converted 18th century colonial house, quiet and peaceful, restaurant is the best in town. **D** *Residencias Aurora*, Cra 2, no15-65, T855723, shower, fan, good meals, nice and friendly, bargaining possible. **D** *Residencias Unión*, C 18, No 3-43, T855723, with bath and fan. **D** *La Casona*, Cra 2, No 18-58, T855307, very friendly, recommended. **E** *San Andrés*, Cra 2, No 18-23, T855886, modern, with bath, fan, TV, central, clean, restaurant. **E** *Residencias Villa de Mompós*, 500 m east of Plaza Tamarindo, T855208, with bath, free mosquito spray, family run, friendly, free coffee. **E** *Posada de Virrey*, T855630, opposite *Doña Manuela*, shared bath, modern, clean, above medical practice.

Eating

El Galileo, next to the Plaza, good *comida corriente*. *Otra Parte*, Callejón de Santa Bárbara, No 1-42, food, and bar owned by Ruben Darío Vires. *La Pizzería*, opposite San Agústin Church, OK. Good bakeries on C 18 and Cra 3 for coffee, cakes and snacks.

Transport

Air To Cartagena, **SAM**, 3 a week, US$80 return. Taxi to town US$1.50.

Buses From **Cartagena** with Unitransco (0530, returns 0700), daily, 12 hrs, US$12. Otherwise take jeep and ferry to Magangué (see below). To **Valledupar** and **Santa Marta,** either go from El Banco (see below), or cross the river at **Talaigua** (between Mompós and Magangué, *carritos* leave Mompós early morning) to **Santa Ana**. Buses leave Santa Ana 0700 for Santa Marta and Valledupar, first 2½ hrs unpaved, then paved; US$10 to Valledupar.

River From Magangué you have to take a *chalupa* (launch) either direct to Mompós, 2 hrs, US$3.30, or to La Bodega, 45 mins, and from there by jeep or taxi 1 hr, US$2. You can also reach Mompós in 2 hrs, US$5 by *chalupa* from El Banco to the southeast. It is also possible to reach Mompós from Barranquilla by *chalupa* changing at Plato.

NB Most *chalupas* and buses run in the morning. There is little public transport after 1400.

Most vessels go now via the western arm of the loop (Brazo de Loba) which passes **Magangué**, the port for the *savannas* of Bolívar. A road runs west to join the north-south Cartagena-Medellín highway.

Magangué
Phone code: 952
Colour map 1, grid B3

Sleeping and eating There are 5 hotels including: **D** *Hans Burchardt*, C 17, no 4-36, T878332, a/c, private bath, fridge, friendly. **E** *Valle*, Cra 6/C 15, T875806, with bath, a/c, TV. **E** *Julia*, Cra 2A, no 12-37, T878933. Also 10 *residenciales*, the cheapest of which are *Londres*, *Brasil* or *Hotel Medellín*, all **F** per person. There are few places to eat, though *Terraza*, to the left of the plaza, is reasonable.

Transport Air To Cartagena, Montería and Corozal, Aires. **Buses** To and from *Cartagena*, Velox and Brasilia, several daily, 3-4 hrs, US$12. To Sincelejo, frequent service US$3.

Upstream from Magangué, the Río San Jorge, 379 km long, 240 km of it navigable, comes in from the Western Cordillera. Further up, the Río Cauca, 1,020 km long, comes in from the far south. Its Caribbean end is navigable for 370 km, and it is navigable again for a distance of 245 km in the Cauca Valley above the gorge. It is possible to get small boats from Magangué up the Cauca, via Guaranda and Nechí to Caucasia on the main road between Montería and Medellín. This trip costs about US$20 and takes two days allowing for unforseen breakdowns etc. A very attractive trip if you have time but check for security.

El Banco is an old, dirty but beautiful town (see under **Music and Dance** for its festival), 420 km from Barranquilla, where the river loops join. Along the river front are massive stone stairways. The Cordilleras are in the distance, a blue range on either side of the valley. Egrets, various species of heron and ringed kingfishers are much in evidence.

El Banco
Phone code: 95
Color map 1, grid C3

Sleeping D *Central*, near church, modern, fan. **E** *Continental*, near jeep terminal, friendly. **E** *Casa del Viajero*, C 8, T7292181, colour TV, fan, bath, clean, fridge with drikns, safe. **F** *Colonial*, one block from harbour, with bath and fan. **G** per person *Residencia Ocaña*, basic, clean, noisy. **G** *Residencia Edén*, C 9, friendly, free coffee. Also about a dozen others.

Transport Air 1 flight each weekday.
Buses Daily buses from El Banco to **Bucaramanga,** US$15, **Cúcuta** and **Valledupar**. To **Cartagena, Santa Marta** and **Barranquilla** take a jeep to El Burro on the main north/south highway and take a through bus from there. Don't get conned into taking an expensive boat across the river instead of the bus ferry. **River** *Chalupa* service El Banco-Barrancabermeja with Cootransfluviales, 0800, 7 hrs, US$16, but check for security.
River Continuing upriver are the small towns of **Puerto Boca, Tamalameque** (basic *residencia* and restaurant), La Gloria, **Gamarra** , San Pablo and **Puerto Wilches**, a centre of African palm plantations. All are connected by launch. To the east of the river is the main road from the coast to Bucaramanga and, eventually, Bogotá. To the east of Gamarra is Aguachica on the main road. From there, a minor road climbs into the Cordillera Oriental to Ocaña and continues a further 212 km on to Cúcuta.

Up the Río Magdalena

Ocaña
Phone code: 974
Colour map 1, grid C4
Population: 75,000
Altitude: 1,200m

Although nowadays in a little visited part of the country, Ocaña was founded by the Spaniards in the 16th century as a staging post between Pamplona and Cartagena, with the benefit of being in the mountains above the unhealthy plains of the Río Magdalena. Later in post-independence times it was here that the Convention was held that led to the split up of Gran Colombia in 1830.

The colonial Cathedral de Santa Ana overlooks the central Plaza 29 de Mayo. In the centre of the plaza is a monument commemorating the abolition of slavery in Colombia. Ocaña is near the headwaters of Río Catatumbo which flows down through picturesque forests to the Catatumbo – Bari National Park and the Venezuelan border.

Sleeping and eating B *Hacaritama*, C 10, No 12-57, T 625352, on the central plaza, pool, TV, restaurant. **C** *Real*, C 12, No 12-39, T610444, 1 block from the centre, restaurant. **E** *El Viajero*, Cra 11, No 9-17, with bath, cheaper without, pleasant, quiet. There are a number of other reasonable hotels and restaurants near the centre.

Transport Air Daily flights to Barrancabermeja, Cúcuta and Medellín, with **Aces**. **Buses** Buses leave from the central plaza for Aguachica, 1½ hrs, Cúcuta 7 hrs and Bucaramanga 5½ hrs, several a day to each destination.

Area Natural Unica Los Estoraques

About 15 km from Ocaña along a side road at **La Playa** is the Area Natural Unica Los Estoraques run by the National Parks service. Towering pinnacles of rock, of varying colours between red and white look down on interlocking river valleys in most of the 640 ha of the park. The geology is made up of horizontal strata of hard and soft volcanics probably dating from the pre-Jurassic era. They are now exposed and being eroded by the elements, including wind and the infrequent but often violent rainfall, reminiscent of a small scale 'badlands' of South Dakota, USA. There are many good walking trails around the park but few facilities, better to take food and water with you. It's a very pleasant and picturesque place but beware of snakes.

Ins and outs Entry to the Park US$0.75, children US$0.50, cars US$0.50. There is some basic accommodation at US$2.50, camping US$1.50 per person, tent hire (for 4) US$15, sleeping bags and lanterns available for hire. There are no official places to stay in La Playa but ask around if you are caught after the last buseta has left for Ocaña. There are busetas from Ocaña to La Playa from C 8 by the market, in the morning only, 1 hr, US$2.

Some 100 km north of Bucaramanga at San Alberto, a new road has been completed which runs comparatively close to the Magdalena, 400 km to Honda. This is now by far the fastest road from the capital to the Caribbean.

Barrancabermeja
Phone code: 97
Colour map 2, grid A5
Population: 181,000

Some 30 km above Puerto Wilches and 30 km from this new road is Barrancabermeja (or more commonly Barranca), so called because of the reddish-brown oil-stained cliffs on which it stands. It is an important oil refining centre. It is also a warm, humid place with an interesting indoor market.

Sleeping and eating C *Bachué*, Cra 17, No 49-12, T622599, a/c, private bath, restaurant, friendly, safe. **F** *Hostal Real*, opposite station, T6222239, clean, hot water, pleasant owner, safe (locked day and night), restaurant, good value. **F** *Iris*, Cra 3, No 48-46, T6222871, clean, friendly. **F** *Residencias Ferroviario*, C 12, No 35-21, T6224524, with bath, opposite the railway station, friendly. **F** *Santa Fé*, in town, clean and friendly; many more around the train station and in town. A shop at C 19, Avs 18 and 19 sells good bread and muesli.

● ●

Bolívar - the Magdalena campaign

New Granada accepted Simón Bolívar when he came to Santa Marta in 1812, and entrusted with a small contingent, he quickly embarked on a campaign to clear the royalists from the lower Magdalena valley. After a successful confrontation at Tenerife, he took Mompós in December 1812, attracting more volunteers as he proceeded. He took El Banco unopposed, defeated the royalists at Chiriguaná, siezed Tamalameque and then went east into the mountains to capture the important town of Ocaña. This effectively cut off Bogotá and the hinterland from the Caribbean ports. Hearing that the royalists had taken Cúcuta, Bolívar pushed on through the Cordillera to San Cayetano on the Río Zulia, then retook Cúcuta on 28 February 1813. A few months later, in command of a larger force, he went on into Venezuela and, after another lightning campaign, he retook Caracas, where he was given a hero's welcome. He was given the title of El Libertador, a name that he cherished more than any other.

● ●

Transport Air 10 mins by taxi from centre, 2 daily flights to Bogotá, **Aces**. Also daily flights to Medellín and 3 days a week to Ocaña. **Buses** Bucaramanga, 3 hrs, US$5; Medellín, 1045, US$17. **River Boat**: *Chalupa* to Puerto Boyacá, 0845, 6 hrs, US$12. Several daily to El Banco, 7 hrs, US$15. Fast launch to Gamarra,US$20, 4 hrs. **Train** To Medellín, daily 0500, US$10-12, 15 hrs, unreliable.

Directory *Banco de Bogotá* will change travellers' cheques.

Puerto Berrío is on the west bank 100 km above Barrancabermeja and 756 km   **Puerto Berrío**
from Barranquilla. It is the river port for Medellín and Antioquia Department.   *Phone code: 94*
A railway from Medellín runs down the slopes of the Cordillera Central and   *Colour map 2, grid B4*
over a low pass to Puerto Berrío, where it connects with the Bogotá-Santa   *Population: 26,000*
Marta line.

Sleeping E *Hotel Magdalena*, Cra 1, No 9-11, T823-2408, classic hotel, used for many years as the place to stay for travellers changing from river to railway for Medellín, good restaurant, pleasant, on a hilltop near river. **E** *Ayacucho*, Cra 1, No 8-20, T823-2312. **F** *Residencias El Ganadero*, C 7, No 1-34, T823-2192, on second floor, with bath, clean, modern, with ceiling fans. Many others.

Eating *La Buena Mesa*, good big meals. *Chava*, C 9, No 3-47. *El Turista*, Cra 4, No 7-10. *Las Palmas*, Cra 2, No 10-17. *Heladeria Joi*, good ice cream and sundaes.

Transport Air To Medellín, 3 flights a day, 2 **SAM**, 3 **Aces**. **Train** To Barrancabermeja and Medellín, check if trains are running at **Grecia** station, 4 km from the town (taxi service only).

The railway south to Bogotá runs along the west bank from Grecia (no passenger trains at present), and meets the road coming down from Medellín via San Carlos at **Puerto Nare** (several *residencias* and restaurants). This is the best place from which to visit the marble and limestone **Cavernas del Nus** some 20 km to the northwest along the Río Nare. Ask about directions to the caves and guides in Puerto Nare. See under Rio Claro below for a description of similar caves.

About 75 km upriver from Puerto Berrío, on the east bank, is **Puerto Boyacá** (several *residencias*). Rápido Tolima has regular buses to Honda (3 hours, US$4) on the Medellín-Bogotá highway. Boats to Puerto Berrío, US$4.10.

Up the Río Magdalena

About 10 km upstream from Puerto Boyacá on the other side (west) of the river is **Puerto Triunfo** (several *residencias* and places to eat) where the new main road from Medellín crosses the 1200 m long Puente de la Paz over the Magdalena and joins the new road from the Caribbean to Bogotá.

Río Claro   Some 12 km from Puerto Triunfo towards Medellín the small town of **Doradal** (**B** *La Colina*, pool, restaurant, smart). There are other facilities and restaurants in town. About 20 km further on, the road crosses the **Río Claro** where a privately owned nature reserve has been established. Near the bridge is **C** *Los Colores*, a modern hotel, restaurant.

The Reserve has many nature trails in the forest and along the river which here runs through deep gorges with several interesting caves. This is limestone country similar to that of the Río Nus further north. The **Gruta de la Cascada**, in a section known as **Parque Ecológico El Refugio**, is a waterfall emerging from a cave inhabited by *guácharos* (oilbirds). You can walk or wade through the cave in about 40 minutes. There is excellent swimming in the river, most refreshing after a trek through the humid jungle. There are several caves in the region, of various types of limestone. The biggest cave is **Cueva del Cóndor**, which is mostly of fine grain marble with some impressive stalagtites. Transport from the Reserve is needed, a good torch required and you will have to wade through waist-deep pools. A guide is recommended. There are many multicoloured hummingbirds, toucans and irridescent blue morpho butterflies to see in the area. ■ *Entrance to the Reserve is US$2 per day.*

Sleeping A *El Refugio*, within the park overlooking the river and surrounded by forest, includes meals, the terrace is a great place to watch the wildlife. There is also dormitory accommodation at US$6 per person, lunch/dinner US$4, breakfast US$2. Camping by the river, US$6 per tent.

Transport From Bogotá US$15, from Medellín US$10.

La Dorada   It is 151 km up river from Puerto Berrío to La Dorada on the west bank. The
Phone code: 96   old Medellín-Bogotá highway crosses the Magdalena by a bridge from **Puerto**
Colour map 2, grid B4   **Salgar**, on the east bank.

Sleeping La Dorada F *Rosita*, C 17, No 3-28, T8572301, with bath, friendly, pleasant, recommended; on the highway to Honda, *Magdalena Motel*. Others near the railway station. **Puerto Salgar**: **G** *Residencia Antioquia*, with fan.

Transport Buses To Bogotá via Honda (see next section), 5 hrs, US$11; to Medellín US$14.

The Lower Río Magdalena navigation stops at La Dorada as there are rapids above, as far as Honda. Currently there are no passenger services south of Puerto Boyacá. The Upper Magdalena is navigable as far as Girardot.

The Upper Magdalena

Standing on the west bank of the river, 32 km upstream from La Dorada in Tolima Department, is Honda, a pleasant old town surrounded by hills and with a picturesque colonial section of narrow cobbled streets and brightly coloured houses.

Honda
Phone code: 98
Colour map 2, grid B4
Population: 27,000

To reach the colonial part of town, go past the interesting indoor market. El Salto de Honda (the rapids which separate the Lower from the Upper Magdalena) are just below the town. Several bridges span the Ríos Magdalena and the Guali, at whose junction the town lies. In February the Magdalena rises and fishing is unusually good. People come from all over the region for the fishing and the festival of the Subienda, as the season is called.

Since Honda is a popular weekend spot for Bogotáños, hotels tend to be a little expensive for budget travellers but it is possible to bargain during the week. There are many resort style hotels on the road to Guaduas, most are in our **B/C** range with pools and leisure facilities. There is a tourist kiosk over the bridge near the market place, maps available. The former President of Colombia, Alfonso López, was born here. There's also a **Casa Cultural**, at Calle 13/Carrera 11, though restoration work is in progress.

Sleeping C *Campestre El Molino*, 5 km from Honda on Mariquita road, T2513604, swimming pools, fans in rooms, friendly. **C** *Ondana*, Cra 13A, No 17A-17, T2513127, swimming pool. **D** *Club Piscina*, Cra 12, No 19-139, T2513273, fan, swimming pool, clean, friendly, arranges safe parking at reasonable rates with neighbours, recommended. **D** *Royal Plaza*, near where buses/colectivos stop, T2513326, spacious rooms, a/c. **D-E** *Dorantes*, C 14, No 12-57, T2513423, clean, TV. **F** *Del Carmen*, on small street up from bus stop on main road, private bath, small rooms, clean.

Eating *La Cascada*, overlooking the river, good. There is a row of good cheap restaurants across the Río Magdalena bridge in Puerto Bogotá.

Buses From **Bogotá** (149 km) with Velotax and Rápido Tolima, US$8, 4 hrs. **Manizales,** US$6. Rápido Tolima run half-hourly buses to **La Dorada** (1 hr), and beyond, to **Puerto Boyacá** (3 hrs), US$4. The new Bogotá-Medellín highway passes round the town.

West from Honda a main road goes to **Mariquita** (21 km), the centre of a fruit-growing country, and **Fresno** (a further 30 km), the heart of a coffee growing area. The road continues up the slopes of the Central Cordillera to Manizales (83 km). A cableway from Manizales to Mariquita, carrying mainly coffee from the Zona Cafetera for export, operated from 1922 to the 1960s (see under Manizales).

Mariquita (founded 1551) has several old houses and buildings, the mint, the viceroy's house and the parish church. Here Gonzalo Jiménez de Quesada, founder of Santa Fe de Bogotá died of leprosy in 1579 and here also **José Celestino Mutis** lived for eight years during his famous Botanic Expedition towards the end of the 18th century (when he and his helpers accumulated a herbarium of 20,000 plants, a vast library, and a rich collection of botanical plates and paintings of native fauna). His colonial house leads off from the corner of the plaza. The collection was sent to Madrid, where it remains.

Mariquita
Phone code: 98
Colour map 2, grid C4
Population: 25,000

Between Mariquita and Fresno are the clean and pleasant bathing pools of El Diamante; the Club Deportivo is private, but visitors are welcome to its swimming pool. There is another, El Virrey, in Mariquita. Follow Carrera 7 out of town over the bridge and continue along a good road for 3 km to the Cataratas de Medina, with good rock pools for swimming against a backdrop of rolling green hills.

Up the Río Magdalena

Help from the skies

They say 'Tis an ill wind that blows nobody any good', and it was certainly an 'ill' landslide that swept down Nevado del Ruiz after the volcano's eruption in 1985, killing over 25,000 people.

One of the problems at the time was the difficulty of getting rescue services to the scene fast enough to save lives and hospitalize the injured. Now, specifically using the Nevado del Ruiz tragedy as a relevant example, Bell Helicopter Textron and Boeing Company have combined to

produce the V 22 Osprey, which will be the first 'tilt-rotor' passenger/cargo aircraft that can land and take off vertically, yet has a much greater range and twice the speed of a helicopter. It is expected that 500 of these aircraft will be delivered to the US Marines, starting in 1999.

Had they been available in 1985, it is calculated that a well co-ordinated rescue could have saved thousands of lives around Armero.

Sleeping A *Las Acacias*, on the Armero road, T2522016, F2522612, 3 pools, sports facilities. **B-C** *La Rosa*, C 5, No 4-21, T2522282, small rooms, TV, minibar, secure. **D** *San Felipe*, 8 km from Mariquita on the Armero road, T2522447, good, pool, restaurant with slow service. **D** *Josi*, C 7, No 3-18, T2522392, a/c, parking. **E** *Janeth*, Cra 5, No 7-69, T2522495, 5 mins from Expreso Bolivariano terminal, clean, fan, pool, friendly. **F** *Monaco*, Cra 4, No 5-12, T2522169, clean, basic. The main road from Honda is lined with **B-D** hotels with good facilities and parking. 1 km outside Marquita there is a well maintained **camping** site with swimming pool and restaurant, **F** per tent.

Eating Many restaurants to eat cheaply, excellent fruit selection in the market, very good juices.

Buses To **Bogotá**, Expreso Bolivariano, hourly, US$9, 4 hrs. To **Medellín** US$18. To **Ibagué**, Velotax, several a day, US$6; to **Cali** US$19. To **Honda**, Rápido Tolima, every 30 mins, US$1, 30 mins, colectivos US$1.80, 25 mins.

From Mariquita there is a good road south for 32 km to **Armero**, which used to be a cotton growing centre until it and surrounding villages were devastated by the eruption of the Nevado del Ruiz volcano, in November 1985. Over 25,000 people were killed as approximately 10% of the ice core melted, causing landslides and mudflows. The town has been abandoned and the mud and dust covered buildings left as a memorial to those who died. The upper stories of just a few buildings can be seen from the main road. Much is now overgrown. There is a moving annual ceremony on 13th November when helicopters drop rose petals over the site to commemorate the disaster. A large white cross marks the place where the Pope said Mass for the victims and decreed all of Armero a cemetery.

There may be roadside stalls at the crossroads in Armero for drinks and snacks (there are also lots of mosquitoes). Armero is now omitted from some maps.

A branch road runs 23 km east to Cambao on the Río Magdalena, the road continues to the highway for Bogotá. The nearest settlement and lodging to Armero is in **Lérida**, 12 km south. Beyond it, to the east on the Río Magdalena is Ambalema; **B** *San Gabriel*, Carrera 2, No 8-50, T2856031, pool,restaurant.

Ibagué

Phone code: 98
Colour map 2, grid C3
Population: 347,000
Altitude: 1,248m

The main road from Armero goes direct for 88 km to Ibagué, capital of Tolima Department. It is a large city with some interesting old parts. The town was originally founded in 1550 as Villa de San Bonifacio higher up the mountains near Cajamarca, where the Indians had a settlement ruled by the *Cacique* Ibagué. The following year, the town was moved to the present site. There is a strong musical tradition here. In the 1880s a French traveller noted that in every house people played *tiples*, guitars and other instruments and all sang with great gusto.

Getting there Perales **airport** is 9 km east of the centre. The **bus terminal** is between Cras 1-2 and Calle 19-20. The tourist police at the terminal are helpful.

Tourist offices Cra 3, between C 10 and 11; helpful; closed Sat and Sun. The *Instituto Geográfico Agustín Codazzi* has an office at C 14A, No 3-14, 3rd Floor, for maps and premises at C 13, No 3-60.

The city lies at the foot of the Quindío mountains on a sloping tongue of land between the Chipalo and Combeima rivers. It is cooler here (22°C) than in the valley.

The **Colegio de San Simón**, Carrera 5/Calle 33, is worth seeing, and so is the market. The **Parque Centenario** is pleasant where outdoor concerts are held in the *concha acústica*. Also worth a visit is the **Universidad del Tolima**, Carrera 1/Calle 41, near the east entrance to the city in which is the **Museo Antropológico** and a comprehensive **Jardín Botánico**. The **Museo de Arte**

Ibagué

Cerro Pan de Azúcar

Up the Río Magdalena

■ Sleeping
1 Ambala	5 Combeima Plaza	9 Lusitania
2 Bolivariano	6 Cordillera	10 Montserrat
3 Bram	7 Farallones	11 Nelson's Inn
4 Bremen	8 La Paz	12 Suiza

Moderno is in the Gobernación building opposite **Parque Murillo Toro**. There is an excellent Conservatory of Music which is officially recognized as a University. International choral festivals are staged here. The city specializes in hand-made leather goods (there are many good, cheap shoe shops) and a local drink called *mistela*.

Sleeping **A** *Ambala*, C 11, No 2-60, T2610982, F2633490, TV, pool, restaurant, bar, parking. **A** *Combeima Plaza*, Cra 2, No 12-21, T2618888, also suites, restaurant, bar, parking. **B** *Nelson's Inn*, C 13, No 2-94, T2611810, F2635897, cable TV, laundry facilities. **B** *Lusitania*, Cra 2, No 15-55, T2619166, F2619260, restaurant, attractive inner court-yard with pool, parking, laundry facilities. **C** *Bremen*, C 14, No 3-19, T2631519, friendly. **D** *Farallones*, C 16, No 2-88, T2613339, good, fan, clean, hot water. Opposite is **D** *Cordillera*, C 16, No 2-89, T2611084, also good. **E** *Bolivariano*, C 17, No 3-119, T2633487, good, clean, TV. **E** *Bram*, C 17 y Cra 4, T2632562, convenient, secure, insect-free, cold water. **E** *Suiza*, C 17, No 3-19, T2611271, good, hot water. **E** *Residencia Puracé*, opposite Tolima bus station. Nearby is **F** *La Paz*, C 18, No 3-119, friendly, free *tinto* in the morning. **F** per person *Montserrat*, C 18, Cra 1 y 2, clean, quiet, recommended. **F** *Boston*, near bus station clean, basic.

Eating *El Espacio*, Cra 4, No 18-14, large helpings, good value. *La Vieja Enramada*, Cra 8, No 15-03, local and international dishes, live music, pleasant atmosphere. *El Balcón de Ayer*, C 13, No 3A-58, local food with local music, good value. *Toy Wan*, Cra 4, No 11-14, Chinese, good value also at C 42, No 4C-39, in the east of the city along with other Chinese restaurants on C 42. *Govinda*, Cra 2 y C 13. Vegetarian. *Punto Rojo*, in the shopping precinct on Cra 3, open 24 hrs, good lunch.

Festivals The National Folklore Festival is held during the third week of Jun. The Departments of Tolima and Huila commemorate San Juan (24 Jun) and SS Pedro y Pablo (29 Jun) with bullfights (the Plaza de Toros is near the river at C 27/Cra 2 Sur), fireworks, and music. The choral festivals are held biannually in Dec.

Transport **Air** To Bogotá, 6 daily; to Bucamaranga, 3 per week; to Cartagena, 1 per week; to Florencia, 5 per week; to Medellín, 2 daily; to Cali, 2 daily; to Neiva, 2 or 3 daily; to Pereira, 1 or 2 daily; to Santa Marta, 3 per week. All **Aires**.

Bus To **Bogotá**, Expreso Bolivariano, Expreso Palmira US$11, 4 hrs; also buses to Pereira, Cali and Popayán. To **Medellín**, Expreso Bolivariano, US$20, 8 hrs. To **Neiva**, US$9.

Nevado del Tolima

From Ibagué, a dirt road northwest of the city up the Río Combeima valley, leads to the slopes of the **Nevado del Tolima**, southernmost 'nevado' in the **Parque Nacional Los Nevados**. For climbing the Nevado del Tolima (5,221 m) follow this road to Juntas and El Silencio (see Los Nevados map, page 296). There are good views of the mountain from the road. At **El Silencio** (2,400 m) you must register in the visitor's book (departure date, expected return date) and there is a shop with basic provisions and refreshments. However, it is better to buy supplies in Ibagué. From El Silencio, it is an easy hike along a clear path (45 minutes) to **El Rancho** 2,650 m, where there is basic accommodation – ie floor space – for US$2 per night, meals available on request. The natural thermal baths are administered by the University of Tolima, entry US$2. The water is hot and most welcome, particularly after the descent from the mountain, and is popular with visitors from the valley at weekends, though there has been some damage recently to the pools from rockfalls.

The climb starts from El Rancho. Follow the path behind the *termales* and **The route** climb steeply. You will shortly enter the National Park. It takes about five hours to **Campo La Cueva**, 3,750 m, where there is a flat spot to pitch a tent just before the cave on the left of the path. It is possible to sleep in the cave, there is a basic wooden shelter. Please do not add to the unsightly pile of rubbish at this point. There is water nearby, fill up here. An hour or so further up is another campsite, **Campo Los Cuatro Mil**, just above 4,000 m. From here it is a hard 3-4 hour trek through *páramo* to the rocky **Campo Latas**, 4,650 m. If you decide to camp here, it will be a longer trek next morning to the top; the final climb has to be done at sunrise because clouds and mist almost invariably rise around 0800. Better to continue and look for flat ground just below the snowline at 4,800 m. This is a bleak and windswept place and bitterly cold after about 1500. You should look for small rocks to help stabilise the tent.

Start early for the summit, the climb will take 3-4 hours from the snowline, depending on fitness and acclimatization. Most parties leave between 0300 and 0400, head torches and hopefully moonlight desirable. Part of the climb is quite steep ice climbing, and crampons and an ice-axe are necessary. A rope is helpful for the last difficult section near the top. From the top is a breathtaking view across the other snowcapped mountains of the Cordillera Central. The descent takes about two hours to the snowline and the rest can be completed in the day. The *termales* at El Rancho make it all worthwhile.

Continuing up the valley from El Rancho, it is 8 km to **El Boquerón** 4,100 m campsite, 5-6 hour trek, from which there are several high summits to visit and an alternative route up Nevado del Tolima. Also you can continue on to Laguna El Encanto or descend to Salento. For this area, see under **Salento**.

Information and guides Admission US$3, car (to El Rancho) US$2.50, camping US$12.50 per tent, space for 5. For information contact Cruz Roja Colombiana in Ibagué, Zona Industrial El Papayo, on the right hand side of the main road (Av Ferrocarril), near the east entrance to the city, T2646014, who can put you in touch with a climbing group, *Asociación Tolimense de Montañistas y Escaladores*. Helpful guides are: Claus Schlief, who speaks German and English; Manolo Barrios, who has some Himalayan experience and is well recommended, ask for information at the Cruz Roja; Fernando Reyes, C 28, No13-27, Fenalco, Ibagué, T2656372. He organizes 2/3 day hikes to Los Nevados and Nevado del Huila for US$50 per person including equipment, US$140 for a single climber, US$70 for each additional, maximum of 5, and rock climbing excursions to Chicoral, 45 mins from Ibagué on the Bogotá road, and to Juntas on the way to Nevado del Tolima. They can also arrange accommodation, supply equipment and make and repair backpacks. It is possible to buy 'benzina/gasolina blanca' for stoves at the Terpel service station in Ibagué.

Transport A milk truck (*lechero*) leaves the market in Ibagué for El Silencio daily between 0630 and 0730. Check the day before and reserve seats, US$2.50, 2½ hrs.

The Quindío Pass, 3,250 m (commonly called *La Línea*, which refers to the power lines that cross the mountains here) is on the road to Armenia, 105 km west of Ibagué across the Cordillera Central. At night, fog, reckless drivers and stray animals make the pass hazardous. On the east side of the Pass is **Cajamarca**, a friendly town in a beautiful setting (**G** *Residencia Central*, friendly; **F** *Nevados*, nearby, cold water, restaurant, friendly and clean). Bakers on corner of central plaza, good for breakfast and drinks. *Bar El Globo*, on another corner of the main plaza worth a visit, excellent coffee from an ancient *Aguila Roja* machine, and notice the instruction above the pool tables '*Por favor no limpia las manos sobre las mesas*'. There is an interesting market on Sunday.

Up the Río Magdalena

Train in vain

Colombia was not an obvious target for the railway in the late 19th century when they first arrived in Latin America. In countries such as Argentina and Brazil, the railway became the most important mode of transport, and even as late as 1971, Argentina had 33,000 km of paved highways but over 46,000 km of railways.

The reasons why Colombia lagged behind were simply that the main inhabited parts of the country, in the high Andes, made railway construction difficult and expensive, and fast, reliable services virtually impossible. At the same time, the two major navigable rivers encouraged the movement of passengers and freight from the north coast as far as Cali and Neiva in the south.

Eventually, railways were built, first to connect the rivers to the main towns (Girardot-Bogotá, Puerto Berrío-Medellín, Puerto Wilches-Bucaramanga) and the ports to the immediate hinterland (Buenaventura-Cali, Santa Marta-Fundación, Puerto Colombia-Barranquilla). By 1925, there was still no connection from the north coast to the south, and the railways of the Bogotá region, Medellín and Cali were all isolated, though ambitious plans abounded. A map published in 1927 showed projected lines from Florencia in the south to Bogotá, through Tunja, Bucaramanga and Cúcuta to Santa Marta, and a second line from Cartagena to Medellín and on through Cali and Pasto to Ecuador.

Some of the dream materialised, notably the 700 km line from Puerto Berrío to Santa Marta and the spur to Bogotá via La Dorada. Lines South as far as Neiva and Popayán were built. Armenia, Ibagué, Tunja and Sogamoso were connected to the system. All carried passengers, the autoferro (diesel railcar) was comfortable if unreliable, and the Tayrona Express between Santa Marta and Bogotá was an attractive experience in its day.

By the 1970s, however, there were serious problems. The roads improved, airlines expanded and the railways were mismanaged and underfunded. Serious storm damage in 1974 cut the line from Medellín to Cali which was never repaired. Eventually, in the early 1990s, all passenger services were suspended. Apart from weekend tourist trains out of Bogotá and Medellín, and some freight traffic here and there, that is all there is today.

Once again, however, there are ambitious plans to revive the system. The freight line from Cali to Buenaventura is being rebuilt and could again carry passengers. It is hoped that the fondo mixto (ie public and private capital) principal might work for the railways. There are published proposals to revamp the lines from Bogotá to Santa Marta and from Puerto Berrío to Medellín. 'Phase III' is planned to reconstruct the lines north from Bogotá to Chiquinquirá and to link up with the mineral line still operating near Sogamoso, serving the steel industry and mines at Paz de Río.

Meanwhile, the legacy of some fine station architecture, eg Medellín, Manizales and Chiquinquirá is happily being carefully preserved.

Another expression of local humour is the site of the huge cement works on this road between Ibagué and Girardot, officially named Buenos Aires.

Some 79 km east of Ibagué is **Girardot**, on the Upper Magdalena. The road from Ibagué runs through **Gualanday** (where there is accommodation and restaurants), joining the highway from Bogotá at **Espinal**, an important agro-industrial town (**B** *Hotel Yuma*; **F** *Hotel Bucaros*, central, clean, with bath, restaurant). From Ibagué it is one hour by bus to Espinal, whence buses run north and south. There are tolls between Ibagué and Espinal and between Espinal and Girardot.

Up the Río Magdalena

Girardot was the original railway terminal for Bogotá, the link, with Honda, between the upper and lower section of the Río Magdalena and the first inland scheduled point for an air service from the coast. There is a feeling of commercial history about the place. This is also the best place to find river fish dishes on the menu. Local fish include: *chacama*, *mojarra*, *bagre* and *viudo du capaz*.

Girardot
Phone code: 98
Colour map 2, grid C4
Population: 84,000
Altitude: 289m

The climate here is hot and there are heavy rains. Bogotanos come down here at weekends to warm up. Here significant navigation of the Upper Magdalena (ie from Honda) ends, although in dry weather some boats cannot get this far. Small commercial boats continue up to Neiva. Walk across the fine steel bridge to see merchandise being loaded and unloaded – coffee and hides are the main items. Large cattle fairs are held on 5-10 June and 5-10 December. Launch rides on the river start from underneath the bridge. A 1-hour trip to Isla del Sol is recommended (US$9). Also to Ambalema downstream and to La Chamba (see below) upstream.

Sleeping AL *Girardot Resort*, km 1 via Ricaurte, T8332875, large resort hotel, meals included, 2 restaurants, 3 pools, tennis, gym, disco. **AL** *El Peñón*, on the site of a former *hacienda* just outside the town, Cra 16, No 79-31, T34981, fashionable bungalow complex, casino, huge pool, lake, price per bungalow. **B** *Bachué*, Cra 8, No 18-04, T8334791, F8333830, modern, large cooled pool, excellent, rooms are a/c with bath and TV, restaurant. **D** *Río*, Cra 10, No 16-31, T8332858, TV, fan, restaurant, laundry, friendly, English and German spoken. **D** *Los Angeles*, on main plaza, clean, friendly, recommended. **E** *Miami*, Cra 7, No 13-57, large rooms, clean, fan, good, central location safe. Opposite the new bus terminal, **F** *El Cid*, Cra 13, No 28-06, T8311574, with fan. **F** *Rincón*, on main street, C 19, No 10-68, balcony, fan. **F** *Colonial*, Cra 11, no 16-32, T8333730, showers, bath.

Eating *El Castillo*, Cra 11, No 19-52, T8331742, a/c, seafood and meat dishes. *El Fogón*, C 19, No 19-01, T8323822. Fish, *viudo de capaz* is a speciality. Plenty of fast food and typical restaurants round and near Parque Bolívar.

Shopping There is a 2-storey market, at its best in the early morning but nevertheless good all day, and another good market on Sun mornings.

Transport Buses to **Bogotá**, 132 km, costs US$9, about 3½ hrs; bus to **Neiva**, US$6, 3½ hrs. To **Fusagasugá**, US$5.

South of Girardot, the highway and the Río Magdalena continue to Neiva. The river valley is highly productive with coffee and tobacco grown on the slopes, and cattle, mainly Brahman, raised in the valley. About 35 km south of Girardot is **Guamo**. Just before Guamo is a marked turn off to **La Chamba**, where internationally famous blackware pottery is made and sold, and 8 km beyond Guamo is **Saldaña**, where there are irrigation works that have made 15,000 ha available for rice, sorghum, sesame and cotton. There have been significant archaeological finds in this area where shaft graves contained pottery identified with the Quimbaya/Calima cultures of the Canca valley dated about 200 BC. Gold and ceramics were also found at Rioblanco in the upper part of the Saldaña river.

South of Girardot

A pretty spot is the Embalse del Río Prado reservoir located near **Prado**, Tolima, 25 km east of Saldaña; it is well signposted. There is a dirt road for the last 12 km past Purificación, where you cross the Magdalena. Buses can be caught in Bogotá, Ibagué and all intermediate towns. The pretty part of the lake is hidden from the end of the road and must be seen from a boat. Take an official boat trip from the mooring-point down the slope at the end of the road

Up the Río Magdalena

Deserts in Colombia?

In a country with one of the highest rainfall zones of the world, oceans on two sides and the Amazon Rain Forest on a third, deserts seem totally out of place.

Yet, if you are travelling with us through Colombia, you will already have noticed the arid zone of Guajira on the northeast coast and the Desierto de La Candelaria in a corner of Boyacá. The driest place of all, however is the Tatacoa desert here in Huila.

Approaching Neiva from the north, the lush agricultural land near the river quite quickly gives way to scrubland and then to stones and red sand with very sparce vegetation, with the Magdalena, already a substantial river, flowing strongly by.

About 50 km to the west is the massive

Nevado del Huila the second highest sierra in the country, with a substantial cap of ice and snow fed by constant moisture coming mainly from the Pacific. 40 km or so to the east is the Cordillera de los Picachos (see in the text), which form an arc, south to north-east, and collect an average of over 4,000 mm of annual rainfall from the Amazon weather systems. Interestingly, this precipitation is concentrated on the lower slopes and is much less on the summits at 3,500m.

So there is virtually no moisture left as the air flows into the deep Magdalena valley from either direction, a good example of another of Colombia's micro-climates, adding to the diversity of flora, fauna and wildlife.

(food is available here). Swimming is good and the water is warm, but wading is not advisable because of the fresh-water stingray.

Sleeping At **Guamo**: *Lemayá*, Cra 8 y C 9, T 270230, modern, swimming pool, best in the region. At **Saldaña**: *Hotel Saldaña*, not too good. At **Prado**: There are only cheap hotels and basic restaurants. **By the Lake**: government hotel, **B** in cabin, **D** in room, pleasant; free camping on shore.

The road the Neiva enters the Huila Department, and 37 km before Neiva you can turn left, cross a fence, and see the **Piedra Pintada de Aipe**, a stone not in fact painted but carved by precolumbian Indians with designs akin to the shapes of some of the pieces in the Museo del Oro at Bogotá.

About 50 km north of Neiva is a small area (300 sq km) of scrub and arid eroded red soil known as the **Tatacoa** desert, with large cacti, isolated mesas and unusual wildlife. Bus from Neiva to **Villavieja**, near the Río Magdalena, and the Neiva-Bogotá highway at Aipe daily 1030, 1½ hours, US$2. Contact Nelson Martínez Olaya, an official tourist guide at the *Restaurant La Tatacoa*, Villavieja, Carrera 4, No 7-32, for 4-5 hour walks through the desert. There is also a museum showing prehistoric finds in the area. You can cross the Magdalena by motorized canoe near Villavieja for US$0.75.

Neiva

Phone code: 98
Colour map 3, grid A5
Population: 248,000

The capital of Huila Department, Neiva, is a pleasant, modern city on the east bank of the Río Magdalena. **It** was first founded in 1539, when Belalcázar came across the Cordillera Central from Popayán in quest of El Dorado. It was soon after destroyed by the Indians and refounded in 1612.

Ins & outs   La Marguita **airport** is 1½ km from city. The new **bus station** is to the south of the town; bus from the centre leaves from the old terminal (Cra 2, Calles 5 and 6). **Warning** At the bus stations, both off and on buses, in Neiva, Garzón and especially Pitalito, theft is rife.

There is an interesting monument to the struggles for independence by Rodrigo Arenas Betancur by the riverside. There are rich coffee plantations around Neiva, for here the valley bottom is high enough to be in the coffee zone. The cathedral was destroyed by earthquake in 1967. The old, colonial railway station is worth a visit. There is a large and colourful market every day. Tourist information is given at the cultural centre, with museum and gallery, on the main plaza. A good local festival is held on 18 to 28 June, when the Bambuco Queen is elected. Much dancing and feasting to be had.

A 30-minutes drive south is **Rivera**, with thermal springs and swimming pools to cool off, entrance US$1.25. Also to the south is the Betania dam project with boat trips on the lake formed by the dam, from the village of Yaguará.

AL *Plaza*, C 7, No 4-62, T8710806, swimming pool, with a/c (cheaper with fan), pleasant, restaurant, disco. **B** *Sulicam*, Cra 3, No 5-51, T8713068, F8710159, restaurant. **B** *Tumburagua*, C 5A, No 5-40, T8712470, recommended. **C** *Hostería Matamundo*, in an old *hacienda* 3 km from the centre, on the road to Garzón and San Agustín, Cra 5, No 3S-51, T8730216, a/c, swimming pool, restaurant, disco.

Sleeping & eating

D *Americano*, Cra 5, No 8-67, T8713029, clean, swimming pool. **D** *Central*, Cra 3, No 7-82, T8712356, meals, near market, good value, recommended. **E** *Residencias Astoria*, C 6, No 1-41, with bath, cheaper with shared bath, clean, big rooms. **F** *La Cuerva*, right from the bus station, 50m on right, convenient, restaurant. **F** *Residencia Magdalena*, C 1A Sur, No 8A-57, T8733586, close to the new bus station, restaurant. *Maria's*, C 8, No 7-61, good *comida casera*. *Heladería La Pampa*, Pasaje Camacho 8, excellent juices.

Air Aires flies to *Bogotá*, 6 daily; to *Medellín*, daily except Sun; to *Cali*, daily; to *Florencia*, 3 daily; to *Ibagué*, 2 daily; to *Puerto Asís*, daily. Taxi to bus terminal about US$1.

Transport

Buses To **Bogotá** (331 km, paved road), Coomotor, 5½ hrs, US$10.50. Regular bus service with Autobuses Unidos del Sur, Cootranshuila (0600) and Coomotor to **San Agustín**, US$6, 5½ hrs (US$5.40 by colectivo). To **Garzón**, US$3.60; to **Pitalito**, Cootranshuila, US$6.50, 3½ hrs. To **La Plata,** for Tierradentro, US$6.50. To **Espinal,** 3 hrs, US$2.40, good road except for stretch between Aipe and Nataguima. To **Pasto,** US$10.75; to **Popayán**, US$9.25, ordinary bus at 0330, 1000, 1500, 1930, 11 hrs poor road; to **Florencia,** US$7.80. To Ibagué at 1200, US$9.

BanColombia, near Parque Santander, will change US$ cash and travellers' cheques.

Directory

Although over the continental divide, in the Department of Meta and Caquetá, access to the **Parque Nacional Natural Los Picachos** is from Neiva, east to Rovira from where it is a five hour hike to the park. It has the distinction of being the meeting place of the Amazon, Orinoco and Magdalena river basins. It is in a high Amazon rainfall area, over 5000 mm annually in parts with only January-February comparatively dry. The steep sided mountains are virgin forest with many reported waterfalls over 300 m. There are no facilities. Permission to visit is not easy to obtain, consult MA in Bogotá.

Los Picachos National Park

South of Neiva lie the plains of Huila Department, arid, but still capable of supporting cattle, dominated by the snow-capped Nevado del Huila to the northwest.

Up the Río Magdalena

Antioquia & Chocó

7

Antioquia & Chocó

Antioquia is the largest of the western Departments of Colombia. It stretches from the Río Magdalena in the east to the Río Atrato in the west, while the Río Cauca flows through its centre, these being the three most important rivers of the western half of the country. With its roots in two of the three Cordilleras and almost 100 km of Caribbean coastline, it is not surprising that it is one of the most diverse regions of Colombia.

Centred on Medellín, Antioquia is in many ways the dynamo of Colombia. The people are active and artistic and the city is full of interest for the visitor. The surroundings are delightful. Within one hour's travel in every direction from Medellín are historic towns and villages, parks and lakes, all in attractive countryside, enhanced by farms growing flowers and fruit, major exports of the region.

Chocó Department, on the other hand, while almost as large in extent, is all in the heavy northwest Pacific rain belt, thickly forested, sparsely inhabited and remote. To say that Chocó was not exactly chock-a-block with visitors would be a major understatement. This is one the least-visited parts of the country, which makes it potentially all the more rewarding to explore, particularly its beautiful coastline.

Highlights of Antioquia and Chocó

★ *Enjoying the riot of colour at the Desfile de Silleteros, in Medellín.*
★ *Seeing the city in minature at Cerro Nutibara.*
★ *Joining the revellers at Tangovía.*
★ *Climbing the Peñol stairway.*
★ *Visiting the stunning countryside around Rionegro.*

★ *Absorbing the charm of Santa Fé.*
★ *A weekend on the Pacific at Nuquí or Bahía Solano.*
★ *Making a date with the whales of Ensenada de Utria.*
★ *Visiting the orchids at the botanical museum in Urrao and the real thing in the National Park.*

Antioquia Department

Antioquia spreads into three distinct zones of Colombia. The eastern border is along the Río Magdalena, and is covered in the previous chapter. The north and west of the Department is dominated by the Atrato lowlands and the Caribbean coast, covered in the North Coast chapter. The core of Antioquia is, however, the central/south section, with the northern extremities of two of the *Cordilleras* of the Andes split by the deep valley of the Cauca river. The Andes here are do not reach the heights common further south; nevertheless the land rises to well over 3,000 m in both ranges within Antioquia, giving a wide range of climates.

History

The northern corner of Antioquia was probably the major route of migration of the prehistoric peoples of the continent. Important evidence of their settlements have been found here, especially of the Sinú tribes in the Urabá region and, further south, of the Katío/Embera groups near the Atrato. The 'core' section, however, was not an area of significant Indian cultures.

When the Spaniards arrived, they were looking for gold. Their first inland settlements in Antioquia were near the Cauca river at Peque, and then Frontino, where there were, and still are, some gold deposits. The town of Santa Fé de Antioquia was founded in 1546.

One of the early places to be explored by the Spaniards was the Valle de Aburrá, discovered in August 1541 by a unit under the command of Mariscal Jorge Robledo. There were several Indian groups in the valley, one of which was the Aburrá, hence the name given to the valley which is still in common use today, through the centre of which flows the Río Medellín. Later arrivals were farmers rather than *conquistadores* and intermarried very little with the indigenous people. Some of the 17th century settlers that came to Colombia from Spain were Jewish refugees who were deliberately seeking isolation, and found it in the highland valleys of Antioquia including the Aburrá. The city of Medellín was established here in 1616.

Generally the land was divided into small farms which the settlers worked themselves, living on the food they produced. Their only exports were a little gold and silver from the streams.

In the early 19th century the settlement began to expand, particularly to the south. The settlers occupied all the cultivable land on the western side of the Central Cordillera, which turned out to be ideal for coffee.

Spanish gold

Gold has played a very important role in the history of Colombia. The Indians discovered it in the Andean streams and rivers and used it to make ever more sophisticated ornaments. For them, it was never a store of wealth or a medium of exchange, only a beautiful, enduring material. By the time the Spaniards arrived, the Indians of this region had developed virtually all the techniques used today for refining and working the metal and were more advanced than any other group on the American continent.

To the Spaniards, finding gold was their primary objective. Later, it became an obsession. They took it from the living by torture and violence and from the dead by looting shrines and graves. The search for gold determined their sites for settlements and which territories they conquered. It was a measure of their success driven by the demands of the Spanish crown back home. The greatest possible achievement of the conquistadores would have been the discovery and capture of El Dorado, the city made of gold somewhere in the New World. Of course, they never found it, to the despair and disillusion of those who came, and perhaps this was the main reason why they were unable to hold off the independence movements, and hence lost an empire.

It was indeed coffee, introduced from Santander Department in the late 19th century, that brought stability and prosperity to this part of the country. Coffee was being exported from Antioquia by the end of the century, but it was the 1914-18 war which suddenly gave a fillip to the industry: within 20 years the Departments of Antioquia and Caldas to the south were producing half the coffee of Colombia. Together with Quindío and Risaralda, they are by far the most important producers today.

The agricultural development in Antioquia can be seen everywhere. The Andes are often cultivated up to 2500m and the significant height range gives a wide variety of 'climates', so that tropical, temperate and alpine crops can be grown. Cattle, fruits, and cereals are all important and Colombia's now well known flower industry has a significant centre here. Considerable forested areas remain, though under threat from today's settlers. At present, however, this also makes it scenically a very attractive and interesting place to visit.

Antioquia is considered by many to be the cultural heartland of Colombia. Its residents, referred to as 'Paisas', are renowned for their hospitality, distinctive accent and customs.

Antioquia & Chocó

Medellín

Medellín, capital of Antioquia Department, has long been synonymous with its infamous drug cartel. But this fresh, vibrant and prosperous city has made considerable progress in the past few years, exemplified by the new Metro system inaugurated in 1995. It is now one of the main industrial cities of Colombia, and here, you'll find the people very proud of their city. In the centre, the new has driven out much of the old and few colonial buildings remain. However, large new buildings must, by law, incorporate modern works of art which, together with plazas and parks that feature monuments and sculptures, makes for an interesting walking tour for the visitor. Music and arts festivals attract many visitors and the flower festival, Desfile de Silleteros, in August, is the most spectacular parade in Colombia.

Phone code: 94
Colour map 2, grid B3
Population: 1.7mn (city); 2.45 mn (metropolitan area)
Altitude: 1,487m

24 hours in Medellín

Start your tour in the **Parque de Bolívar** with a visit to the **Metropolitan cathedral.** Have a look around the square afterwards and end up in **Pasaje Junín**, a busy pedestrian street with balconied cafés, and savour the vitality of the city.

At Calle 46 is the **Parque San Antonio** with the characteristic sculptures of Botero. Go along Calle 46 and under the Metro to Cra 52 and the **Palacio Nacional,** one of many expressive modern building complexes in the city. Further along Cra 52 is the new **cultural centre,** with new artistic displays are being created next to it.

Returning to the other side of the Metro, it is a short walk to **Parque de Berrío** overlooked by the former cathedral, a fine building, well worth a look inside. On the south side of the square is the **Banco de la República,** with a library, music room and exhibition rooms, a refuge from the teeming city outside.

Don't miss the rare experience of a visit to the **Cementerio San Pedro** (Hospital station), then return to Pasaje Junín in the centre for a meal or something lighter, perhaps in the **Salón de Té Astor,** which has to be seen to be believed.

Ins and Outs

Getting there　**Air** The **José María Córdova international airport**, (sometimes called Rionegro airport) is 28 km from Medellín by the new highway, and 9 km from Rionegro. It is a modern airport completed in 1985. A taxi to town is US$12.50 (fixed), *buseta* to centre, US$1.70, frequent service, taking about 1 hr to the small road (Cra 50A/C 53) behind *Hotel Nutibara*. To Rionegro from airport, bus US$0.20, taxi US$8.

There is also the **Enrique Olaya Herrera metropolitan airport** in the city, where some internal flights arrive. Taxis between the airports, US$12.50.

Bus Long distance buses arrive either at Terminal del Norte or Terminal del Sur. A taxi from either costs US$2 to the centre, or there are local buses and the Metro.

Getting around　The best way to get around the city is by Metro which serves the three main sectors of Medellín, ie centre, south and west. It is efficient and safe. The town bus services are marginally cheaper but slower. There are plenty of taxis.

Orientation　Medellín is set in the comparatively narrow Aburrá valley surrounded by high mountain barriers of the Cordillera Central in nearly all directions. The built-up metropolitan area now extends from Copacabana in the north, to Sabaneta in the south, more than 25km.

The city is centred around the old and the new cathedrals, the former on Parque Berrío and the latter overlooking Parque de Bolívar. The main commercial area is three blocks away on Cra 46, with shopping and hotels throughout the area. Some streets have been pedestrianised.

In the south, El Poblado has become an up-market commercial and residential area and many companies have moved their headquarters there from the centre. The best hotels and restaurants are in or near El Poblado.

Also favoured is the area west of the centre between Cerro El Volador and the Universidad Pontificia Bolivariana. Around Cra 70 and C 44 are busy commercial and entertainment sectors with many new hotels, shopping centres and the huge Atanasio Girardot sports stadium nearby.

In our listings, we give the Calle (C) and Carrera (Cra) numbers for easy reference. Unlike most other Colombian cities, most central streets are named, and locally these are normally used. Refer to the maps which show both numbers and names.

Particularly important are: Cra 46, part of the inner ring road, which has several names but is known popularly as 'Av Oriental'; Cra 80/Cra 81/Diagonal 79, the outer ring road to the west, which is called 'La Ochenta' throughout; C 51/ 52, east of the centre is 'La Playa'; and C 33, which crosses the Río Medellín to become C 37, is still called 'La Treinta y Tres'.

For your first general view of the city, take the Metro. Most of the track in the centre is elevated, none of it is underground and you can ride the whole system on one ticket for US$ 0.28.

NB A new feature of Medellín is the pedestrianisation in the centre. Pasaje Junín (Cra 49) is now closed to traffic from Parque de Bolívar to Parque San Antonio (C 46). This gives walkers pleasant relief from traffic in the busy heart of the city. If driving out of Medellín, check routes carefully before leaving. There are few signs and information from officials and petrol stations is often less than clear.

Tourist Offices *Oficina de Turismo de Medellín*, C 57 No 45-129, T2540800, F2545233. For information on the city, staff helpful. TURISA office in the Centro Administrative La Alpujarra, Of 1034, T3859070. There are tourist booths at both airports but not at the bus stations – they have been closed because of lack of funds - but the information booths in the terminals will help. *MA:* Cra 76, No 49-92, T4220883.

Best time to visit Medellín's climate is generally warm and pleasant though it is often cloudy and rain can come at any time over the Cauca valley from the Chocó, which is only 100 km to the west. The city's festivals draw many visitors from the rest of Colombia and abroad and the *paisas* know how to have a good time. For details, see below under **Festivals**.

Safety Travellers should take the same safety precautions as they would in any large city, particularly at night. It is, nevertheless, a friendly place. For all police services T 112.

History

Though the Valle de Aburrá was discovered early on by the Spaniards (1541), there were few settlements here until early in the 17th century. The foundation of the town is considered to be in 1616 as San Lorenzo de Aburrá on the site of what is now El Poblado. It was given the official title of town (*villa*) in 1675 by Queen Mariana of Austria and named after Don Pedro Portocarrero y Luna, Count of Medellín, who achieved this recognition of the town by Spain. It was declared a city in 1813 and in 1826 it became the capital of Antioquia, by which time the city had become established around the *Basilica de La Candelaria* (now known as the Old Cathedral), which was built at the end of the 17th century.

The industrialisation of Medellín followed the coffee boom. The first looms arrived in 1902. Today the city produces more than 80% of the textile output of the country, and textiles account for only half its industrial activity. Other major local industries are brick making, leather goods and plastics. There has been limited immigration from overseas since the original settlement, but the natural growth in population has been extraordinary. Recently, the city has continued to expand at a great pace, a manifestation of which is the fine new Metro giving easy communication across the city.

Sights

Medellín is a well-laid-out city, comprising 10 municipalities, with the whole of 'greater Medellín' a metropolis of over 2,500,000 people.

Antioquia & Chocó

In the centre In the centre are two plazas. The **Parque de Berrío** is bounded on one side by the **Señora de La Candelaria** church. The original building on this site dated from the latter part of the 17th century. The present church was finished around 1767 and became the original cathedral of the city, consecrated in 1776, with the towers built five years later and the cupola in 1860. The clock was donated by Tyrell Moore (see below) in 1890. It remained the city's cathedral until 1931. It has a fine flat-roofed nave and interesting altar gilded by local artisans dedicated to the patron of Medellín. The most recent restoration of the façade was completed in 1997 and the interior in 1999. In the square is

Medellín

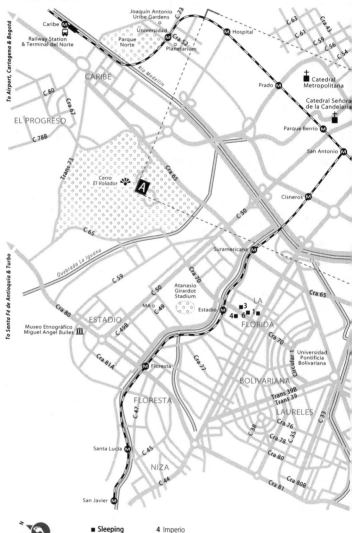

■ Sleeping
1 Arod
2 Dann Carlton
3 Florida

4 Imperio
5 Intercontinental
6 Lukas
7 Park 10

Fernando Botero's *Cuerpo Mujer* (generally known as *La Gorda* and not therefore immediately appreciated by half the local population).

Overlooking Parque Berrío is **Museo Filatélico**, on the 4th floor of Banco de la República building, Calle 50, No 50-21, T2515579, with an interesting stamp collection and special displays connected with postal services. Also music room with concerts on video in afternoons. ■ *Mon-Fri 0900-1800, free.*

The second square, **Parque de Bolívar**, four blocks away, is dominated by the new **Catedral Metropolitano**, one of the largest (sun dried) brick structures

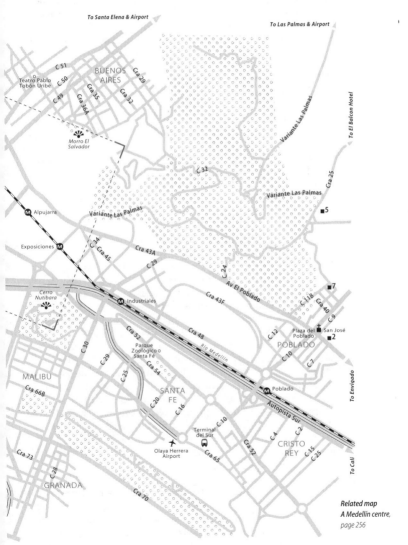

Related map
A Medellín centre,
page 256

Antioquia & Chocó

in the world, built between 1875 and 1931. It is also claimed to be the largest cathedral in South America. It is indeed impressive inside with marble used only for the pulpit, the altar canopy and some statuary around the nave. The Spanish stained glass windows are a good example of the period. There are several paintings of Gregorio Vázquez de Arce. There is a plaque in the square to Tyrell Moore, the Englishman who dedicated the land to the city for the park, in the centre of which is a statue of Bolívar. On the first Saturday of the month there is a craft market known as the *Mercado de San Alejo* in Parque de Bolívar.

The oldest church in the centre of Medellín is believed to be the **Iglesia de la Veracruz**, originally started in 1682 by early Spanish settlers. It was only finally completed around the end of the 18th century. Pablo Chávez was commissioned to decorate the interior and the main altar was brought directly from Spain. It has an attractive *calicanto* style façade. In the square outside, there is a statue of Atanasio Girardot, a hero of the war of Independence.

Nearby is the **Museo de Antioquia**, at Carrera 52A, No 51A-29, opposite the main post office, T2513636, F2510874. It shows contemporary pictures and sculptures, including the best collection of works by Fernando Botero, Colombia's leading contemporary artist, and a room of paintings of Francisco Antonio Cano. With auditorium, film shows etc. ■ *Tue-Fri 0930-1730, Sat 0900-1400, US$1.60, (guides free).*

They also have premises at Carrera 45, No 52-49, where there is an arts centre with classes, exhibitions and a good Colombian arts shop. Preparations are being made to move the displays to new premises in the old Palacio Municipal at Carrera 52, No 52-43 and to exhibit an additional collection of works by Fernando Botero in a plaza in front of the building.

Further south (see map), the **Iglesia de San Benito** was also founded about 1685 but its present baroque style dates from 1802. Another old foundation is the **Iglesia de San José** (see map) begun in the 17th century but modified several times up to 1903, the last work done by the Nicaraguan architect, Félix Pereira. It houses the oldest painting in Medellín – of San Lorenzo, the first patron saint of Medellín. The painting of San José is by Carlos Hefritter.

Three other churches are worth a visit, including **San Ignacio**, a Franciscan church in Plaza San Ignacio (see map), begun in 1793, has a colonial interior with a barrel vaulted central nave and a splendid red and gold altar. It was later taken over by the Jesuits forming part of the original group of buildings of the Universidad de Antioquia: this complex includes the auditorium (*paraninfo*) of the university, which was declared a National Monument in 1982 and over a period of 8 years was tastefully renovated and reopened in 1997 – there is a great view of the city from the top of the tower. The two others are **San Juan de Dios**, in colonial style, and **San Antonio,** designed by Benjamín Machiantonio and built between 1884 and 1902. It was inspired by San Antonio de Padua, a 13th century Venetian church, famous for its domes. This church has one of the biggest domes in the country.

The city's main business area, **Villanueva,** named after the nunnery which has now been converted into a commercial centre, is interesting for its blend of old and modern architecture, including many skyscrapers. To the north across Calle 58, is El Prado section, originally a finca named La Polka, where there were many fine old houses, most of which have been replaced or are in decay. Some however have been restored and the area attracts artists and musicians. There are many sculptures in the city (see below). One collection not to be missed is of the works of Fernando Botero in **Parque San Antonio** between

Calle 44/46 and Carrera 46 including the *Torso Masculino* (which complements the female version in Parque Berrío), *La Mujer Inclinada* and the *El Pájaro de Paz (Bird of Peace)* which was severely damaged by a guerrilla bomb in 1996. At the request of the sculptor, it has been left unrepaired as a symbol of the futility of violence. A new *Bird of Peace* has been placed alongside to make the point yet more dramatically. There is a garden beyond the plaza with the sculptures and a useful footbridge to cross the busy Calle 44 (San Juan).

On the other side of the Metro, at Carrera 52 and Calle 48, is the old **Palacio Nacional,** designed by Agustín Goovares in the Romantic style, built in 1925, now a commercial centre, recognisable by its brass coloured domes, stylishly renovated with sweeping marble staircases and spacious hallways. Another former official building, the old **Palacio Municipal,** Cra 52, No 52-43, was reopened in 1997 after extensive renovations as a cultural centre and renamed **Palacio Cultural**. Entrance is free and it is very pleasant to walk around. Most of the events are also free. These two *Palacios* have been functionally superseded by the **La Alpujarra** administrative centre, a nine block area from Calle 44/Carrera 52, from where the government of the city and the department is conducted. Within the complex is the fine old Medellín railway station building designed in 1914 by Enrique Olarte. This is currently being restored as a cultural centre.

Also in the centre is **Casa Museo Maestro Pedro Nel Gómez**, Carrera 51B, No 85-24, T2332633, house of the Colombian painter and sculptor (1899-1984) with many of his artworks, and a specialist library, ■ *US$1.60, students US$1.10. Mon-Fri 0900-1200, 1400-1700, Sat 0900-1200, but may be closed during school holidays.* **Archivo Histórico de Antioquia** is at Carrera 51, No 52-03, T2510823. It is a research library for the Department with over 30000 volumes.

Of the modern buildings, the **Edificio Coltejer** deserves a mention. It is the tallest building in Medellín (35 floors) and was built as the headquarters of the Compañía Colombiana de Tejidos, thus symbolising the importance of textiles to the city. It is uniquely in the form of a needle with the 'eye' clearly visible near the top. The building contains offices, a commercial centre, two cinemas and various other public facilities for cultural events.

An unusual attraction is the **Punto Zero** (Point Zero), an elegant steel double arch with a pendulum marking the 'centre of the city'. It was the initial idea of students at the neighbouring Universidad Nacional. It straddles the river where it is crossed by Calle 67.

The **Edificio Inteligente**, Calle 43, No 58-01, was completed in 1996. All the main public services in Medellín concentrate their administrative operations here in a highly energy-efficient building.

One of the city's more unusual sights , at Carrera 51, No 68-68, T2120951, near the Hospital Metro station, is the **Cementerio San Pedro**. It has the dubious honour of being the resting place of many notorious drug dealers, guerrillas, and the like, as well as of the best families of Medellín. Even for Latin America, some of the tombs (there are over 20,000 buried here) are spectacular, and the small chapel has some of the most colourful stained glass in Antioquia. It is also a place for some unique sculptures eg *Dolor de Madre*, depicting the anguish of a mother losing a young son, a replica of Michelangelo's *La Pietà*. ■ *Daily 0730-1730.*

South of the Río Medellín, in the Suramericano district, is the **Museo de Arte Moderno**, at Carrera 64B, No 51-64, T2302622. It has a small collection of paintings, collages, photographs etc. Particularly good of Débora Arango. Foreign films daily except Weds. Coffee shop. ■ *Mon-Fri 1030-1900, Sat 1030-1700.*

Antioquia & Chocó

Close by is the **Biblioteca Pública Piloto para América Latina**, at Carrera 64, No 50-32, T2302382/2302422. This is one of the best public libraries in the country, set up by UNESCO and the Colombian government in 1952. Also art and photo exhibitions, authors reading their own work, foreign films. There are several branches in Medellín and it has links to the *Biblioteca Luis Angel Arango* in Bogotá. ■ *Mon-Fri 0830-1900, Sat 0900-1800.*

Sculptures are hard to miss in Medellín. The best of Rodrigo Arenas Betancur are the *Monumento a la Vida*, in the forecourt of the Edificio Suramericana de Seguros on Calle 50/Carrera 64, where exhibitions of work by leading South American artists are held on the ground floor. More examples of his work, the *Energía Creadora* and *El Cristo Cayendo*, are on display at the new campus of Universidad de Antioquia, Calle 67, No 53-108. Here also is the **Museo**

Medellín centre

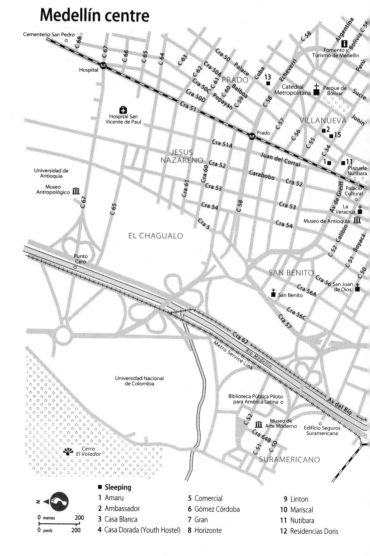

■ **Sleeping**

1 Amaru	
2 Ambassador	
3 Casa Blanca	
4 Casa Dorada (Youth Hostel)	
5 Comercial	9 Linton
6 Gómez Córdoba	10 Mariscal
7 Gran	11 Nutibara
8 Horizonte	12 Residencias Doris

0 metres 200
0 yards 200

Universitario, T2105180, which has a good collection of indigenous pottery. Also has exhibitions of modern art and incorporates a natural sciences section. ■ *Mon-Thu 0800-1200, 1400-1800, Fri 0800-1600, Sat 0900-1300, free.*

Fernando Botero, another major artist, is well represented in the city parks (see above) and in the Museo de Antioquia. There are many others, also murals, paintings, mosaics etc very much helped by the interesting decree approved in 1983 which requires all constructions in the city of over 2,000 sq m to incorporate a work of art. A notable colourful mosaic can be seen on the façade of the *Clínica Soma*, Carrera 46/Calle 51.

You will notice three prominent hills within the Aburrá valley. They are first, **The city's hills**
Cerro Nutibara, (across the river from Industriales station), where there is an outdoor stage for open air concerts, sculpture park (the idea of former

Antioquia & Chocó

President Belisario Betancur) with exhibits from other Latin American countries, a miniature Antioquian village (known as Pueblito Paisa), souvenir shops and restaurants. There is a statue of Chief Nutibara near the village. Every month, on the night of the full moon, there is a party here with music, dancing, food stalls, tango show etc, organised by the Department of Sports and Recreation. To get there, take a 301 bus from Carrera 43/Calle 54 which takes you to the bottom of the hill with 1½ km to walk, or a taxi from Industriales or Exposiciones Metro stations to the village, US$1. Second is **Cerro El Volador** (seen as the Metro turns between Universidad and Caribe stations), tree covered and the site of an important Indian burial ground; and third, **Morro El Salvador** (to the east of Alpujarra station), with a cross and statue designed by Arturo Longas in 1950 on top. This hill and its small public park have been more or less absorbed into building developments and is not recommended for visits on foot.

Outside the centre **Museo Etnográfico Miguel Angel Builes**, at Carrera 81, No 52B-120, T2642299/4216259, was originally founded in 1963 in Yarumal, Antioquia by missionaries and moved to Medellín in 1972. It has an extensive collection of artefacts from Indian cultures, two floors dedicated to Colombia, one to other Andean countries including Peru and Bolivia and another floor to Africa. There are models of Indian houses in a fine new building with a library and bookshop. ■ *Tue-Fri, 0800-1200, 1400-1700, free but voluntary contributions appreciated.*

Take the Metro to Floresta and walk along Carrera 81 (about 10 mins). The **Museo de la Madre Laura**, Carrera 92, No 34D-21, T2523017, has a good collection of indigenous costumes and crafts from Colombia, Ecuador and Guatemala collected by a community of missionary nuns. ■ *Tue-Fri 0900-1200, 1400-1700.*

Museo El Castillo, Calle 9 Sur, No 32-269, T2660900, formerly a landowner's home, constructed in 1930 in neo-gothic style, has interesting collection of painting, sculptures, porcelain and furniture. The house is set in beautiful grounds. There is also a 250 seat concert hall. Take a bus to Loma de los Balsos, El Poblado, then walk 1 km up the hill until you see the road lined with pine trees to the right. ■ *US$1.20, open Mon-Fri 0900-1130, 1400-1730, Sat 0900-1100.*

One other church should be mentioned: **Iglesia San José**, on the central park of Poblado in the south of the city where the Spanish first settled in the Aburrá valley in 1616. The present church is the third on the site, in which the architect Agustín Goovares was involved. There are commemorative plaques in the park.

Botanical & Zoological Gardens **Joaquín Antonio Uribe gardens**, Carrera 52, No 73-298, T2337025/2115607, was formerly the *Finca Eden* turned into a garden by the owner, the botanist, Joaquín Antonio Uribe. It was rescued from developers in 1972 and converted into a public garden with 600 species of plants and trees. There is a lake with various lilies on display – a cool and restful place. In March there is an international orchid show in the gardens in a covered exhibition area. There is a pleasant restaurant for lunches and snacks, facilities for children, a library and an open air auditorium. ■ *The gardens are open daily, 0900-1730, entrance US$1.60, children US$1. The library Mon-Fri 0900-1700, Sat 0900-1200. The public entrance is at Cra 52/Calle 78 about 300m away from Metro station: Universidad).*

Nearby, Carrera 55, No 76-115, is the **Parque Norte,** a recreational park with a lake and children's playground, ■ *Tue-Fri 1000-1700, Sat-Sun 1000-1900.*

Next to it is the old railway station *El Bosque*, now restored and converted into a recreation centre for the elderly. Also in this area is the **Planetario**, Carrera 52, No 71-117, T2332184, with a 300 seat projection room and an auditorium for 200, library and exhibition hall. ■ *Wed-Fri 1100-1600, Sat, Sun and holidays, 1100-1700.*

The **Parque Zoológico Santa Fe**, at Carrera 52, No 20-63, T2351326, mainly houses South American animals and birds and is concerned with the protection of threatened local species including the spectacled bear and the Andean condor. There are special exhibits of Caribbean fauna and a butterfly section. ■ *Daily 0900-1700, entry US$1. Take the Metro to Industriales, cross the river and walk along Cra 52 about 10 mins.* Within the complex is the **Museo Santa Fe** with exhibition halls including displays of furniture and pictures of Medellín's past, including the Antioquia railway and the construction of La Quiebra Tunnel, (additional charge US$0.50).

Also worth a visit is **El Ranchito**, an orchid farm between the towns of Itagüí and La Estrella, entry US$0.50, April to June is the best time to go.

Essentials

Sleeping

Central Medellín **AL** *Nutibara*, C 52A, No 50-46, T5115111, F2313713. Best in centre, casino (open Mon-Sat 2100-0400), swimming pool. *Residencias Nutibara*. An annex facing hotel of same name, slightly cheaper with all the same facilities. **AL** *Ambassador*, Cra 50, No 54-50, T5115311, F5132100, with breakfast, in connection with **AL** *Veracruz*, Cra 50, No 54-18, T2315757, F2310542. With bath, swimming pool, very good, restaurant on 11th floor gives fine view over city. **AL** *Gran*, C 54, No 45-92, T5134455, F3810068. With breakfast, some cheap offers, pool.

A *Amaru*, Cra 50A, No 53-45, T5112155, F2310321. Central, quiet, good, restaurant. Recommended.

B *Horizonte*, Cra 47, No 49A-24, T5116188. Good and popular restaurant. **B** *Mariscal*, Cra 45, No 46-49, T2515433. Hot shower, good service, clean. **B** *Villa de la Candelaria*, Cra 42, No 50-101, T2390345. With bath, modern rooms, TV.

C *Casa Blanca*, Cra 45, No 46-09, T2515211. Clean, small restaurant, safe but noisy. **C** *Samaritano*, Cra 45, No 45-25, T2517200, F2519588. 120 rooms, with bath, clean and friendly, pool.

D *Linton*, Cra 45, No 47-74, T2170847. With bath, very clean, TV, safe parking nearby US$0.50 per night, central. **D** *Comercial*, C 48, No 53-102. Friendly, clean, hot water available in some rooms, the best of which are on the top floor, doors barred to all but residents after 1800, good meals.

E *Residencias Doris*, Cra 45, No 46-23, T2515431. Family run, clean sheets every day, laundry facilities, locked night and day, good value. Recommended. **E** *Gómez Córdoba*, Cra 46, No 50-29, T5131676. With bath, good value, renovated, safe, clean, TV, central. **E** *Romania*, C 58, No 50-46, with bath, clean, a bit noisy.

Youth Hostel *Casa Dorada*, C 50, No 47-25, T5125300, F3815400. 155 beds, usual services.

South Medellín (in or near Poblado) **LL** *Intercontinental*, C 16, No 28-51, Variante Las Palmas, T2660680, F2661548, medellin@interconti.com The best, some distance from the city and isolated but excellent. **LL** *Poblado Plaza*, Cra 43A, No 4 Sur 75, T2685555, F2686949, 104551.341@compuserve.com Also very good. **LL** *Park 10*, Cra 36B No 11-12, T2668811, F2666155, park10@colomsat.net.co 55 suites, gourmet restaurant. **LL** *Dann Carlton*, Cra 43, No 7-50, Av El Poblado, T3124141, F2681316. All services.

L *Mercure*, Cra 43A, No 9 Sur-51, T3132020, F3131047, mercure@hotelsporton.com New in 2000, elegant, business services.

☞ *Flower power*

Santa Elena, up in the mountains on the way to Medellín airport, annually makes a unique contribution to the city – it is where most of the flowers are grown for the Desfile de Silleteros, the most important parade of the year in Medellín and a major tourist attraction. More than 400 local families compete to see who can grow the finest flowers and create the most fantastic designs. These are then mounted on wooden 'chairs' (sillas), a traditional way of carrying supplies – and people – in the remoter areas to the east of Medellín. The Silleteros carry the displays for three hours through the streets of the city on the final day of the August festivities, watched by vast numbers of locals and visitors. The parade now ends in the Atanasio Girardot Stadium where the selection of the best is made. The displays are distributed by the sponsors throughout the city and can be seen in hospitals, hotels, churches and other public places for days afterwards.

You can see the fields where the flowers grow, hardly any are grown under glass. The air is full of the scent of herbs and lavender and the fresh milk comes straight from the cow. Round Santa Elena is excellent walking through forests with rivers and waterfalls, popular at weekends for a day out in the country.

AL *El Balcón*, Cra 25, No 2-370, near *Intercontinental*, in Transversal Superior, T2682511. Beautiful view of the city, good meals.

West Medellín L *Lukas*, Cra 70, No 44A-28, T2601761, F2603765, lukas@epm.net,co. Best hotel in sector. **L** *Florida*, Cra 70, No 44B-38, T2604900, F2600644. New, smart, expensive but negotiable.
A *Arod*, C 44, No 69-80, T2601427, F2601441. Small, secure, clean, friendly, 1½ km from centre, basement parking. Recommended. **A** *Imperio*, Cra 70, No 45E-117, T2500311. 2 mins from Metro, price negotiable, opened 1997, friendly.

Near the airport Within a short distance of the airport are two luxury hotels: **LL** *Las Lomas Forum*, T5360440, F5360403. Elegant hotel with beautiful gardens, all services, conventions, nice walking countryside nearby. **L** *Hostería Llanogrande*, T5370511, F5370507. Weekend reductions, restaurants, pool, sauna, tennis, football field, also used for conventions.

Eating Central Medellín Palazzetto D'Italia, C 54, No 43-102. Excellent Italian, reasonable prices. Recommended. *El Viejo Vapor*, Cra 43, No 53-19, T2163646. Café, bar, artist clientèle, good meeting place, Polish chef, set lunch US$3. *Hacienda Real*, Cra 49, No 52-48, T5115330. Good steaks, soups, *paisa* décor, reasonable prices. *Hato Viejo*, Cra 49, No 52-170, upstairs, T2512196. Very good local dishes, reasonable prices, open till 2200. Recommended. Also at Pasaje Junín (Cra 49)/Plaza de Bolívar are several upstairs bar/cafés including *Bulevard de Junín* and *Café del Parque*, both good for food or refreshments while watching Medellín in action below.
Vegetarian *Trigo y Miel*, C 53, No 43-54. Very good vegetarian, set lunch US$3. *Govinda*, Calle 51 No 52-17. *Crepes y Waffles*, Cra 36, No 10-54. Good.
Cafés and snacks Excellent pastries at *Salón de Té Astor*, Cra 49, No 52-84, a delightful traditional tea house. *Versalles*, Cra 49, No 53-39. Good coffee and snacks, *menu económico* US$3. Recommended. *JC Delicias*, C 45, No 43A-08. Salads, *arepas*, light meals, hamburgers, good with other branches in the city.
There are many cheap and fast food restaurants in the centre of the city and else-where, eg *Taco Loco* and *Dogger* for cheap and filling meals.

South Medellín (in or near Poblado) *Frutos del Mar*, Cra 43B, No 11-51, T2665766. Good seafood. *Aguacatala*, Cra 43A, No 7 Sur-130. An old country house with patio and wandering musical trio, *comida típica*, quiet surroundings. Similar, *La Posada de la Montaña*, Cra 43-B, No 16-22, T2668540. Excellent Colombian food, very attractive setting. Recommended. Several good restaurants are on Variante a las Palmas: *Carbon*, Km 1, T2625425. Good grills, good view over city, live music at weekends; *Frutas de Mi Tierra*. Extraordinary fruit salads; *Hato Viejo*, opposite *Intercontinental Hotel*, T2685412. Good service, local dishes, large portions, good value. *La Grappa*, Cra 41, No 10-19, T2662326/2227. Good Italian. *Picante*, Calle 4S, No 43A-27. Varied menu, good. *Zócalo*, Cra 43B, No 11-84. Mexican, good value.

Restaurants in Poblado tend to be good quality & more expensive than elsewhere in the city

West Medellín *Manhattan*, Cra 70, No 42-39. Good international. *Asados La 80*, Cra 81, No 30-7, T2568194. Very good, large steaks. *El Palacio Chino*, Circular 4, No 74-69, T2506323. Good Chinese, reasonable prices. *La Llanera*, Cra 70, Circular 1-36. Local dishes, good quality. *La Casa del Majoral*, Cra 81, No 30A-37, T3417510. Steaks, bar. *La Crêperie*, Cra 77, No 35-67, T2503029. French. Plenty of cheap local restaurants and fast food outlets in the Cra 70 area and around the *Unicentro* shopping centre on C 34/Cra 66.

Bars All 3 areas have their bars of varied style and quality. In the **centre**, try *Don Eduardo*, Cra 45, No 48-57, for a pleasant atmosphere, modest prices.

In the **south**, the best are in the centre of Poblado near the Parque. *Blue Rock*, C 10, No 40-21 and *Belrin*, C 10, No 41-65 are both popular spots.

In **West** Medellín, you will find plenty of bars along Cra 70 and the adjacent streets. Try *Bar 242*, Cra 73/C 40, with punks and goths, a fun place. *Tacuba*, Cra 80 at Plaza Las Villas, good music, tasty Mexican food upstairs, open till 0130. There are several gay bars, eg *Ammabamba*, Calle 33/Cra 76, good music and videos.

Bars & nightclubs

Nightclubs In several hotels in the centre and in El Poblado. A popular place in the **centre** is *El Guanábano*, Cra 43, No 53-21 by the Plazuela de los Periodistas.

In the **south** there are many clubs along the Variante Las Palmas, try *Visagra* for salsa and rock. *Pub*, Cra 38, No 26-260, well established for rock. *Exilio*, C 18, No 35-81, and *Templo Antonia*, C 19, No 38-15, both very popular for trance music. South, beyond El Poblado, there is more nightlife in Envigado, near Plaza Envigado. *Taberna Viguerías* is a recommended place. Note that couples only are allowed in to many clubs.

In the **west**, 2 popular places along C 44 are *Rumbantanana* No 74-80, (salsa), and *Rumbantanita*, No 74-85, for son cubana. *Congo*, Cra 73, between C 43/44 (look for the blue light), good rock, cheap beer. Also there are many other clubs on C 50, between Cras 65 and 75, with *El Callejón del Gato* nearby at C 49B, No 67A-34 and Cra 70, between C 36 and 44.

See also under **Entertainment** for Tango shows which are popular in Medellín.

Cinema Free foreign/cultural films at *Universidad de Antioquia*, T2105140, *Museo de Arte Moderno*, T2302622 and *Centro Colombo Americano*, T5134444, check press for programme.

Entertainment

Music Monthly concerts by the Antioquia Symphony Orchestra in the *Teatro Metropolitano* (see below). *Palacio de Bellas Artes*, Cra 42, No 52-33, T2394820, has a *Salon Beethoven*, which has classical, contemporary and Colombian music concerts, plays and other events in a 300 seat auditorium. The octagonal building was designed in Republican style in 1925 by architect Nel Rodríguez. Band concerts and other entertainments in the Parque de Bolívar every Sun.

Antioquia & Chocó

Universidad de Medellín theatre has monthly tango shows. Tango also at *Vos Tango*, C 34, No 66A-13, opposite the Super Ley supermarket in Unicentro, T2659352, US$5.

Carlos Gardel, the legendary tango singer died in 1935 in an air crash in Medellín and was commemorated in a museum in Barrio Manrique in the northeast of the city. Unfortunately, it was closed when the Argentinean owner retired in 1997. The contents of the museum are at the University of Antioquia except for a small exhibition at the Enrique Olaya Herrera airport which is where Carlos Gardel died. '**Tangovia**' is a general term for occasions when streets, especially in Barrio Manrique, are closed to traffic for tango dancing. Cra 45 (Av Carlos Gardel), leads north east into the centre of Barrio Manrique and is normally the centre of activity. Enquire at the *Oficina de Turismo*, T2540800 when the next *fiesta* will be, usually once a month.

Theatre *Teatro Metropolitano* C 41, No 57-30, T2328584. A modern style brick building close to the river, inaugurated 1987, 1600 capacity, symphony concerts, opera, ballet, tango shows etc. Tickets usually between US$8 and US$20. *Teatro de la Universidad de Medellín*, Cra 87, No 30-65, T2569153. Home of the other Medellín symphony orchestra, the Philharmonic, also gives a wide range of cultural presentations. *Teatro Pablo Tobón Uribe*, Cra 40, No 51-24, T2392674. Traditional theatrical presentations, capacity 880. There are many other theatres of all types in the centre and *barrios* of the city. See local press for details.

Festivals **Feria de las Flores/Desfile de Silleteros** (Flower fair) is held annually in the first half of Aug, for several days ending on the Sat with parades and music. The parade goes from Cra 55 across the Puente Colombia to the Atanasio Girardot Stadium. The flowers are grown at Santa Elena in the Parque Ecológico de Piedras Blancas, 14 km from Medellín (bus from Plaza Las Flores). It has been growing in popularity since 1957 (see Box). A horse *Cabalgata* is a special feature – in 1999 over 6000 riders took part.

Exposición Equina de Medellín (Equestrian show), takes place annually in Apr in the Coliseo Aurelio Mejía, a short distance from Tricentenario Metro station.

Feria de Artesanias (Handicrafts fair), handicrafts of all kinds of craftsmen from all over the country, 17-26 Jul, held in the Atanasio Girardot stadium complex.

There is an annual **international poetry festival**, normally in Jun. For information, call T2911950, prometeo@epm.net.co, or Tourist offices.

20 Sep is celebrated as **Amor y Amistad** but in true Paisa style, this equivalent of St Valentine's day lasts for a whole week!

Semana Santa (Holy Week) has special Easter religious parades and **Christmas** is an important festival locally starting with a fantasy parade and dancing on Dec 7 to coincide with the switching on of spectacular illuminations.

Shopping **Handicrafts** Try the *artisanía* shops on the top of Cerro Nutibara, or the *Centro Libre de la Artesanía*, Pasaje La Bastilla/C 49, where you can buy, and watch articles being made from wood, leather etc.

Markets There is a small handicrafts market at C 52 near Cra 46 with many hippy stalls. *Mercado San Alejo*, Parque Bolívar, open on the first Sat of every month except Jan. Before Christmas it is there Sat and Sun with handicrafts on sale at good prices. Good shopping generally around Parque Bolívar.

Textiles Many of the textile mills have discount clothing departments attached where good bargains can be had. For more information ask at your hotel or at the *Cámara de Comercio*, Cra 46, No 52-82, T5116111. *Aluzia Correas y Cinturones*, Oviedo Shopping Center, Poblado, Unicentro Medellín, (also in Bogotá), for an incredible selection of belts, US$10-30. *La Piel*, at C 53, No 49-131, has an excellent selection of leather goods at very reasonable prices. *Almacenes Exito*, Cra 66, No 49-01, C 10, No 43E-135 Poblado, and other locations is reasonable for cheap leather bags.

Shopping centres *(Centros Comerciales)* are in all the main areas of the city, of which the most notable are: **Centre** *San Diego*, C 34/Cra 43; *Camino Real*, Cra 47/C 53 and *Villanueva*, C 57/Cra 49. **South** *Oviedo*, Cra 43A/C 6 Sur; *Monterrey*, Cra 48/C 10 and *La Candelaria*, Cra 43A/C 11. **West** *Unicentro*, Cra 66B/C 34A; *El Diamante*, C 51/Cra 73; *Obelisco*, Cra 74/C 48 and there is a new *Makro* (1996) at C 44/Cra 65.

Bookshops *Librería Continental*, Cra 50/C 52. *Librería Científica*, C 51, No 49-52, T2314974. Large selection, some foreign books. *La Anticuaria*, C 49, No 47-46, T5114969. Antique and secondhand books, including in English, helpful. *Centro Colombo Americano*, Cra 45, No 53-24, T5134444. Good selection of books in English for sale, (including *Footprint Handbooks*). **Maps** Virtually nothing in the bookshops. Good map of the city centre from the *Oficina de Turismo* (see Tourist Offices). Local and national maps from *Instituto Geográfico Agustín Codazzi* in Fundación Ferrocarril building, Cra 52, No 14-43, office in the basement.

Photography for developing, *Almacenes Duperly* (several branches, eg C 52, No 46-28), good quality. Camera repairs: *Clínica de Cámaras*, Centro Coltejer, Local 120. *Cámeras y Accesorios*, C 52, No 46-22, Local 140, T5132596.

Estadio Atanasio Girardot, is a sports complex at Cra 74, C 50. It was enlarged in 1978 for the Pan American games and has facilities for over 50 sports including football, baseball, olympic swimming pool, velodrome etc. It is next to the *Estadio* Metro station. **Sports**

Bullfighting at the bull-ring of La Macarena, C 44/Cra 63, T2607193, in Jan and Feb; cheapest US$12, usually fully booked.

Horse riding *Al Galope*, riding school in Rionegro, will pick up in Medellín Mon-Fri, many horses including Pasofino, US$16 per day. Stables in property formerly owned by the drug baron Pablo Escobar in fine riding country. For information, call Marta Niquía, T2358330/2713652.

Marco Polo, C 48, No 65-94, T2305944 some English spoken. *Tierra Mar Aire*, C 52, No 43-124, T5120922, helpful. *Realturs*, Cra 46, No 50-28, T5116000. Good. *Destino Colombia*, Cra 65, No 49B-21, local B209, T2606868. Day and evening trips in the city, tours to nearby attractions in Antioquia. *Turismo Maya Londoño*, C 54, No 45-29, T231-6204. City tours and trips to places around Medellín. **Tour Operators**

Comfama, a state social security organisation, runs a number of recreational facilities in Antioquia. Enquire at the *Unidad de Servicio - San Ignacio - Sección Turismo*, C 48, No 43-87, T2516155/2156580, in Plaza San Ignacio, for places to stay and trips that they run locally, good value, eg day trip to Parque Tutucán, including visits to El Retiro, Tequendamita Falls, La Ceja etc with lunch at the club in the Park, US$17; 3 day/2 night trip to Jardín, transport, accommodation, meals, guide etc, US$90 per person.

Buses US$0.30. Slow because of the volume of traffic, but many are smart and comfortable - a reaction to the new Metro. *Colectivos*, operating on certain main routes, US$0.35. **Transport Local**

Car hire Avis, Cra 43A, No 23-40, T3814433. **Hertz**, C 1A Sur, No 43A-35, T3119262. Also offices and vehicles at International airport. If driving in Medellín, check if there are any restricted routes (eg car-sharing, bus lanes, rush hour restrictions) that apply to hired cars.

Metro The Metro has 2 lines: Línia A from Niquía to Itagüí, Línea B from San Javier to San Antonio, where they intersect. One journey (anywhere on the system) US$0.28, two US$0.50, ten US$2.25. The system operates from 0500-2300 on weekdays, 0700-2200 Sun and holidays (see Box).

Taxis Taxis have meters, make sure they are used, minimum charge US$0.75. Radio taxis include: **Aerotaxi** for service to International airport, T5622837/2357676. **Tax Individual**, (Poblado) T3311111. **Coodetaxi**, (West) T3117777. **Cotaxis**, T2119393.

Antioquia & Chocó

The Metro

Organized public transport has been running in Medellín since the 1880s when horse-drawn trams were inaugurated. They ran eventually from what is now the Jardín Botánico in the north of the city, to Plazuela Veracruz in the centre, then up Ayacucho to the Barrio of Buenos Aires in the east. Subsequently electric trams took over in 1921 (some of the lines can still be seen in the streets), followed by trolley buses in the 1930s, all to be superseded by petrol and diesel buses, as in so many of the world's cities.

The idea of a Metro in Medellín was alive in 1950 when the city began to reserve land along the Río Medellín for a mass transit system, but it was almost 20 years before definitive plans were drawn up. Construction began in 1985, and after many setbacks it began operating in November 1995, and the full present 32 km were completed the following year. The total cost is given officially at US$1.8 bn of which about half was borrowed from overseas, principally Germany and Spain. Special local taxes on tobacco and petrol are helping to pay for the construction, but the economic benefit of the service to the community is very significant.

Line A runs 23 km along the length of the city following the Río Medellín (also called the Valle de Aburrá). Much of the 1.6 mn population live along this axis so the city was particularly suitable for a modern city railway. By constructing the central section on a viaduct, there is little hindrance to road traffic, and the elevated sections are a great way to go for an overview of the city. **Line B** runs 6 km from San Javier in the west of the city to the centre at San Antonio where there is an interchange with Line A,

and a plaque commemorating the opening by President Samper on 30 November 1995. There is a 3-km link between the lines not at present used for passengers. There are no present plans for further lines but Line B stops tantalisingly over the street at the present San Antonio terminus and East Medellín awaits.

At present, over 130,000 journeys are made daily and approaching 40% of public passenger traffic has been taken off the roads. Local city bus services have been preserved however by making the Metro a little more expensive.

Considerable efforts have been made to improve the immediate environment of the Metro by establishing pedestrian areas alongside and under the railway with new open spaces, parks, cafés and sections designated for street traders. A major ongoing project is the planting of 11,000 trees, many of them in specific blocks, red flowering near Berrío station, pink around Prado, yellow between Alpujarra and Exposiciones. The opportunity has been taken to introduce many more murals and sculptures, already a major feature of the city.

The Metro is now five years old and is regarded by the Paisas with great pride – and not only because it shows their superiority over Bogotá! It is efficient, clean, safe and a comfortable ride. There is plenty of exhortation in notices, over loudspeakers and in give-away pamphlets and many regulations including, for example, 'Don't take flash photos which might distract the driver of the train'. However, all instructions are followed with good humour and this must be, at least for now, one of the best mannered transit systems in the world.

Long distance **Air** The **Aeropuerto José María Córdova**, 28 km from Medellín, is reached by the new toll road or by two other routes, one of which enters the city along Variante Las Palmas through the south of the city. This is normally used by *busetas* and you can be dropped at a convenient point for transport to hotels in El Poblado. The modern airport, T5622828, was completed in 1985, has a *Presto* restaurant, shops, Telecom with email and fax service, no left luggage, but Tourist Office may oblige.

Domestic flights from **Aeropuerto José María Cordova** (sometimes called Rionegro airport): To **Bogotá,** 45 mins with Avianca, Aces, or AeroRepública (cheapest), each has several daily. To **Cali,** 1hr, Avianca 3 daily and Aces 2 daily. To **Barranquilla,** 1

Antioquia & Chocó

daily, Avianca. To **Bucamaranga,** 2 daily, Avianca. To **Cartagena,** 1hr, 1 daily each Avianca and Aces. To **Cúcuta,** 2 daily, Avianca. To **Ibagué,** 2 daily, Aires. To **Santa Marta,** 1 daily, Avianca. There are 2-3 a week also to **Florencia** and **Neiva,** Aires. Indicative one way fares are: **Bogotá** US$60, **Cali** US$85, **Cartagena** US$90, **Cúcuta** US$85.

International flights: direct to **Miami,** 1 daily each, Avianca and Aces. To **New York,** Avianca direct on Mon. To **Panama,** 1 daily, COPA. To **Aruba and Curaçao,** 5 flights a week, SAM/Air Aruba. To **San Antonio, Barquisimeto** and **Caracas,** 2 daily, Servivensa.

There is also an airport in the city, **Aeropuerto Enrique Olaya Herrera,**(sometimes called Medellín airport), with flights to nearby destinations in western Colombia. To get there, see under **Bus Terminal del Sur** below. It has the usual services, a bank *(Banco Santander* - open office hours), cash machines, a tourist office and several travel agents offices and impressive security.

There are one or more flights daily by Aces to: Apartadó, Armenia, Barrancabermeja, Caucasia, Chigorodó, El Bagre, Manizales, Monterría, Ocaña, Otú, Pereira, Puerto Berrío, Quibdó (3 flights daily, US$45 and 1 a day SAM), and Turbo. Daily flights by SAM also to Bahía Solano (US$65), Capurganá and Nuquí.

In addition, there are non-scheduled charter flights to coastal resorts eg San Andrés, and elsewhere, check with travel agents. To get the best price, shop around. Special offers can mean substantial savings. With difficulties on the road network from time to time, air services have become more comprehensive. **When leaving by air, make sure you go to the correct airport**.

Bus The terminal for long-distance buses going north and east is **Terminal del Norte** at Cra 64 (Autopista del Norte) y Transversal 78, (full address Cra 64C, No 78-580) T2308514/2677075, about 3 km north of the centre, with shops, cafeterias, left luggage (US$0.50 per day), two Visa/Mastercard cash machines and other facilities. It is well ordered with no unauthorised vendors allowed, even shoe blacks have fixed prices (from US$0.50 for a simple shine to US$0.90 for a Griffin Gris – whatever that is!). It is well policed and quite safe, though best not to tempt fate.

Bus service to city centre, US$0.30, buses to terminal from C 50, marked: 'Terminal de Transporte'. Much the best, by Metro to Caribe. Taxi to or from the centre about US$2.

To **Bogotá,** 9-12 hrs, US$14-19, every 40 mins or so, with 5 companies. To **La**

Medellín Metro

Dorada, US$12. To **Caucasia,** US$11, 7 hrs. To **Cartagena,** Brasilia or Rápido Ochoa, 15 hrs, US$29 (take food with you, the stops tend to be at expensive restaurants), road paved throughout but poor. To **Barranquilla,** 16 hrs by Brasilia US$31. To **Sincelejo,** 9½ hrs, US$23. To **Arboletes,** Rápido Ochoa, US$24, 12 hrs. To **Turbo,** US$15 with Gómez (the best), 14 hrs.

A new bus terminal for buses going south was opened in Jun 1995, **Terminal del Sur,** Cra 65, No 8B-91, alongside the Enrique Olaya Herrera airport, for information, T3611499/2859157. There are similar services to those of **Terminal del Norte.** To get there, take a bus No 143 marked 'Terminal del Sur' from C 51 (in front of the Banco Popular) along Cra 46 or the Metro to Poblado on Línea A, from where you will probably need a taxi for the remaining 1½ km to the bus station.

Frequent buses to Manizales, 7 hrs US$8, by Empresa Arauca. To **Pereira,** 8 hrs, US$10 by Flota Occidental Pullman. To **Cartago,** 7 hrs, Flota Magdalena, US$12. Many buses to **Cali,** eg Flota Magdalena US$17, 10-12 hrs. To **Popayán,** US$22, 12 hrs, Flota Magadalena at 1400 and 1800. To **Ipiales,** US$33, 22 hrs, Expreso Bolivariano (takes Visa). To **San Agustín,** Rápido Tolima, 0600, US$34, or change at Popayán. To **Quibdó,** 11-13 hrs, US$14. Some of the bus companies have offices downtown for tickets and information eg Rápido Ochoa, basement of the Colseguros building, Cra 46, C 53/54.

A taxi between the terminals costs about US$5, but it is quicker and cheaper to use the Metro.

Train For long-distance travel to **Barrancabermeja,** a train leaves daily 0700, US$8 or US$10 one way, 12-15 hrs (running 2000) No trains running at present beyond Puerto Berrío to Bogotá or beyond Barranca to Santa Marta. A tourist train to and from **Cisneros** runs on Sun and holidays, leaving Medellín at 0700 and Cisneros at 1600, return trip US$6 or US$8. For information call Terminales de Transportes del Norte, T2671157, or go to the station itself, Metro to Caribe on line A, cross to the bus terminal and go to the ground floor where there is a booth by the tunnel entrance to the railway platforms.

Directory **Airline Offices Domestic**: *Aces*, C 49, No 50-21, T5112237, Reservations T5141300. *AeroRepública*, Cra 66A, No 34-32, T3511266. *Aires*, Cra 65A, No 13-157, T3611331. *Avianca/SAM*, Cra 52, No 45-94, T2517710. *Satena*, Olaya Herrera airport, T2551180.

International: *Air Aruba*, C 10 Sur, No 50F-92, T3615265. *American*, Cra 43A, No 34-95, Local 211, T3814546. *COPA*, Cra 43A, No 34-95, Local 217, T3817277. *Servivensa*, Transversal 39B, Av Nutibara, No 73A-33, T2503431/4138180.

For information, purchase of tickets and general problems go to any good travel agent and they will serve you or find out where you must go.

Banks There are banks everywhere in the 3 business zones. Most of the major banks have automated cash machines, many will accept international cards, but you must plug into the appropriate system. *Lloyds TSB bank*, C 52, No 49-35, T5115820 in the centre, Diagonal 47, No 15 Sur-31 in Poblado, and Cra 76, No 33-83 in the west will cash Amex TCs with passport and purchase voucher, and give cash at the counter against credit and debit cards. *Bancolombia*, with many branches in the city, cash against Mastercard, good rates for TCs and cash. Their branch at Cra 54, No 47-49 in Parque de Bolívar is in a colonial building with an attractive courtyard. *Citibank*, Calle 50/Cra 47. Banks are increasingly opening later and on Sat. Main hotels will cash TCs for residents when banks are closed, but at less favourable rates. *Western Union*, Cra 50, No 57-72, T5137416, Centro Comercial Villanueva, and Cra 43A, No 17-240, T3112233 (south). *Diners Club*, C 49, No 50-21, T2515119.

Communications Internet: *R Computadores*, Cra 48, No 25 Sur-181. *Comfenalco*, C 52/Cra 46, has 12 terminals in the library, US$1.60/hr. Email is widely available in commercial sectors, shopping centres and, though usually more expensive, in many hotels. There are plenty of 'internet cafés' in Poblado. **Media:** The local daily newspaper is *El Colombiano*. There is also a weekly *El Mundo*. Two TV stations are *Telemedellín* and *Teleantioquia*. **Post Office:** main airmail

Medellín Cartel

In its heyday, the Medellín drugs cartel was renowned for the ruthless way all opposition was treated. Born in the used car trade in Medellín, it grew into one of the most powerful criminal groups ever seen on the continent. Its leader, Pablo Escobar, was eventually captured and imprisoned in Envigado in what became known as La Catedral. You can see the buildings overlooking the southern part of Medellín. From here he escaped in 1992 but the authorities were able to track down his associates and eventually Escobar himself

was killed, in Poblado, in December 1993.

Interestingly, it was the help of the local people, in spite of the enormous risks to themselves, which was vital in the final elimination of Escobar and the downfall of the cartel. Although the drug trade continues to thrive in Colombia and all the neighbouring countries, the deep shadow over Medellín was lifted, and there is a noticeable resolution by the Paisas to keep their capital free from any repetition of the horrors of the narcotraficantes.

(Avianca) office in Vicente Uribe Rendón building, Cra 46 (Oriental)/C 51 (La Playa), Mon-Sat, 0800-1800. Also, Avianca Veracruz post office, Cra 52, No 51A-01, T5116311, near Veracruz church, and at Almacenes Exito, Puerta No 2, Cra 66, No 49-01, on the corner of C 50 (Av Colombia), in Barrio Suramericana, open Sun and holidays. *ADPOSTAL* office for mail and parcels, Edif Furatena, C 50/Cra 47 with Federal Express on the ground floor. **Telephone**: *Telecom* C 49, No 45-63, international telephones and fax; also at Cra 49 (Pasaje Junín)/ C 49, open 0800-2200 and at C 50/Cra 47, Edif Furatena. Telecom (prefix 09 may be more expensive than 05 and 07 for intercity calls, especially at off peak times. Check for international calls, cheapest are direct dialled.

Cultural Centres *Centro Colombo Americano*, Cra 45, No 53-24, T5134444. English classes, library, bookshop (including *Footprint* Handbooks), daily films (see press), gallery for monthly exhibitions, very helpful. *Alianza Francesa*, Cra 49, No 44-94, Local 258, T5136688, near San Antonio church. *Biblioteca Público Piloto*, library, see above under **Museums**. *British Council*, Cra 42, No 16A Sur-41, T3131867. English lessons and cultural centre.

Embassies & Consulates *Argentina*, C 55, No 45-82, T2315622. *Austria*, Cra 43A, No 14-119, Of 600, T2665757. Closed Mon. *Belgium*, Diagonal 75B, No 2A-120, T3416060. *Brazil*, C 29D, No 55-91, T2657565. *Chile*, Cra 48, No 12 Sur-70, Of 808, T3132209. *Costa Rica*, Cra 43A, No 14-109, T3817539. Closed Mon. *Denmark*, Cra 49, No 50-21, Of 1904, T5135161/2165161. *Ecuador*, C 50, No 52-22, Of 802, T5121193. *El Salvador*, C 10B, No 35-27, T2665433. *France*, Cra 52, No 14-200, Of 204, T2358037 F2657291. Open only Tue and Thur 1430-1730. *Germany*, Cra 43F, No 17-419, T2621756/4119228. *Guatemala*, Autopista Sur, Cra 42, No33-173, Itagüí, T3722000. *Italy*, C 31, No 43A-172, T2621823. Open only Tue and Thur 0830-1130. *Mexico*, C 50, No 42-54, T2390456. Open Mon-Fri 1400-1700. *Netherlands*, Cra 52, No 51A-23, Of 401, T2510324. *Panama*, C 10, No 42-45, Of 233, T2681157. *Peru*, C 4 Sur, No 43A-195, Of 201D, T2687285. *Spain*, Cra 42, No 10-11, T3120400. *Sweden*, Cra 43A, No 1 Sur-31, Of 401, T2660498. *Switzerland*, Cra 36, No 48D-48, T2304563. *UK*, Cra 49, No 46A Sur-103, Envigado, T2709242/3318625, F3310046. Very helpful, take a taxi and phone for directions as it is hard to find. *Venezuela*, C 32B, No 69-59, T2350359/3511614. Note the Venezuelan consul will not issue visas.

Except where shown, consulates are normally open Mon-Fri, at least 0900-1100.

Medical Services There is a clinic with free consultations and basic treatment in the International airport buildings. *Hospital San Vicente de Paul*, C 64/Cra 51D, T2635333, close to the *Hospital* Metro station, is one of the best hospitals in the country. There is a special section for children's emergencies, T2633737. *Hospital General*, Cra 48, No 32-102, T2321000 (day), 3856204 (night). *Clínica Soma*, C 51 (Av La Playa), No 45-93, T2510555. Good general medical and specialist services, consultations about US$40, English spoken. *Cruz Roja* (Red Cross), Cra 52, No 25-310, T265-2200/235-3001 (emergency), T125 (ambulance). In general, Medellín's specialist hospitals are of high quality, attracting patients from all over Colombia, Central America and the Caribbean. Notable for heart disease and surgery are *Hospital Pablo Tobón Uribe*, C 78B, No 69-240, T4415252 and *Clínica Medellín*, C 53, No 46-38, T5116044.

Antioquia & Chocó

Doctor: Dr Lázaro Velez, Clínica Soma (see above), T5129664, general practitioner and immunologist, speaks English.

Optician: *Optica Andina*, Cra 49, No 49-40, T5113765.

Dentist: Dr Mario Jimenez, C 52, No 45-56, room 102, T5115155, English spoken.

Useful Addresses DAS, C 19, No 80A-40 in Belén La Gloria section, T3415900 and at main airport. Tourist Police at airport, T2872053, city T2532083, Terminal del Norte T2603724, Terminal del Sur, T3611182, recognisable from their olive-green uniforms and white armbands. Local police T112.

Southeast from Medellín

The new Medellín-Bogotá highway is totally paved, but between Medellín and Puerto Triunfo, the road through the Cordillera is subject to landslides in wet weather and several stretches are being rebuilt and improved, mostly by private contractors, to be paid for via tolls. There are four tolls to pay between Medellín and Puerto Triunfo.

Leave Medellín north on the west side of the Río Medellín and cross to the east side just before Bello where the highway leaves the main road to Cartagena. You then climb up on the 'Autopista' (toll US$1.60) to the crest of the Sierra and Guarne. At **Guarne** (22 km), is the Hipódromo Los Comuneros, with horse races twice a month on Saturday and Sunday, US$1, great atmosphere. On the road between Guarne and Santa Elena (see below) is the **Parque Ecológico de Piedras Blancas**, an 18 ha natural forest reserve with nature trails and hiking paths. Nearby is the large artificial Piedras Blancas lake, a water storage facility for Medellín.

The best route to the José María Córdoba airport branches right, 2 km beyond Guarne, and goes 7 km to a roundabout at the entrance to the airport. Another route goes from the centre of the city (up Calle 45), over the west ridge of the Cordillera, through Santa Elena. **Santa Elena** is where the flowers for the *Silletero* parades in August are grown – well worth a visit (see page 260). A third route goes directly up from Poblado through Las Palmas. **NB** This road is one way into Medellín from 1700 on Sunday evenings.

Just off the main road, 46 km from Medellín is **Marinilla**, with its fine white church and busy main plaza. It is known throughout Colombia for its guitars. There are many attractive corners in the town, not least of which is the small plaza of J M Córdoba with the chapel of Jesús Nazareno. This dates from the mid-18th century and has three bells above an attractive façade. There is an especially interesting balconied house alongside. There is also a small museum on Carrera 29.

Sleeping in Marinilla D *La Capilla*, C 31, Plaza Principal, T94-5485149. D *El Turista*, Cra 30, No 29-26, T548-4037. There are also 2 upmarket hotels on the main road.

El Peñol

Phone code: 94
Colour map 2, grid B3
Population: 13,000
Altitude: 2,250 m

Go through Marinilla (you may need to ask if driving) for the road northeast to El Peñol. It is 21 km to the town, strictly El Peñol Nuevo, which replaces the old town drowned by the nearby reservoir. It is an undistinguished place with a weird modern concrete church, the tower a miniature of the extraordinary rock of the same name 14 km further along the paved road. The whole of this area is noted for its production of tomatoes.

The original town of El (Viejo) Peñol was founded in 1714 on an Indian site known as Sacatín, with a large plaza dominated by a fine church. Before it was submerged, a 28 m pedestal was built, topped with a 12 m aluminium cross which can be seen marking the site of the old presbytery. Services are held on the lake around the cross notably on *El Día de Los Magos* (6 January).

El Peñol (La Piedra), the tourist attraction, is a precipitous, bullet-shaped rock which towers above the surrounding hills and the Embalse de El Peñol reservoir. There is a short, steep unpaved access from the main road to the base of the exposed rock. It has been eroded smooth, but a spiral staircase has been built into a crack from the base to the summit. ■ *Entry US$1, parking US$1. At the summit is a snack bar with fine views (meals at holiday times only).*

About 3 km beyond the rock is the pretty town of **Guatapé**. Here there is a 300 m frontage on the lake with a full range of water activities available including a rickety 'paddle steamer' for the brave. Across the bridge at the far end is a yacht marina and nearby two 'condominiums' where you can spend the day and use the facilities for a fee. The town has a bright red and white church with a surprising interior and skilfully painted and varnished wood surfaces to give a very attractive finish. Notice too the many houses with delightful designs on the *socle* (below the windows), and a ship's propeller incongruously on a plinth in the square (apparently awaiting the rest of a pleasure boat for the lake which never arrived). This is a popular place at weekends.

Sleeping and eating C *Refugio Campestre Bahía del Peñon*, 5 km from town, near the rock, on lakeside, reservations T2503388 (Medellín). **E** *La Florida*, on main plaza, T825-3600, clean, friendly, good restaurant, and several other places to stay on the lakeside. Ask for places for shorter or longer stays, very reasonable prices during the week out of holiday periods. There are plenty of restaurants, round the plaza and especially fronting the lake; one of the best is *La Tienda de Toño* on the lakeside, T8353680, *asados*, trout, *bandeja*, good view, pleasant, recommended.

Buses There's a bus to the rock and to Guatapé, with Cía Fco López, from Terminal del Norte, Medellín, US$2.70. A bus back to Medellín may have to be caught in the town of El Peñol Nuevo (take a *colectivo* from Guatapé or the rock).

The road continues, unsurfaced, past the power station (visits possible) to **San Rafael**. Several rivers run near to the town including the Río Bizcocho and Río Arenas, with waterfalls and pools, good for bathing. It is a busy place at weekends but quiet in the week. There is a small museum in the town. Bus from Guatapé, 1½ hours.

El Peñol, Guatapé

Antioquia & Chocó

El Peñol

Most of the northern part of the Central Cordillera is over 2,000 m and some over 3,000 m. However, it is not towering mountain scenery, but undulating countryside, dotted with farms and otherwise covered with temperate and pine forests. The whole area has, however, been deeply eroded, the hills are steep and the valleys tortuous. Roads forever wind back and forth, up and down and the proverbial crow has a much easier time getting from A to B than you will.

As implied, there are virtually no cliffs, rock faces or boulders to be seen, which makes the appearance of El Peñol particularly remarkable. It is a precipitous, black, bullet shaped rock, 200 m high, which dominates the immediate area including the nearby huge lake, Embalse del Peñol, created when the Río Negro was dammed in 1978. The rock is often called La Piedra or El Peñón, the latter the correct Spanish word for an outstanding rock (eg Gibraltar). It is much the largest of several

volcanic 'plugs' in the region, the cores of long extinct volcanoes, probably dating from the early Cretaceous, or say 120 mn years ago. They are composed of granite, quartz and feldspar, amongst the most basic of the earth's rocks, and exposed from under thousands of metres of other deposits laid down since that time. There is a remarkable resemblance with Rio de Janeiro's Sugar Loaf in geology and shape, though El Peñol is only half as high.

For many years the rock was regarded with dread and suspicion by the locals, and it was not until 1954 that the first recorded climb was made. Although the rock is almost perfectly smooth on all sides, there is an obvious crack on the north side running up to the summit. An intrepid local team consisting of the owner of the property, Luis Eduardo Villegas López, and three neighbours used a series of ladders and ropes to reach the top of this vertical crack in five days. Since

Sleeping E *Familiar*, close to the plaza, clean, comfortable. **E** *Magdalena*, Cra 30, very clean. **F** *La Plácida*, one block from the plaza. Other hotels and restaurants near the plaza. You can camp in several places. On the main river upstream are the **Cabañas Trocadero Nova Mayo**, T831-8643, with big family rooms, US$40 for 2 nights at weekends, cheaper during the week.

From Marinilla, the new road towards Bogotá continues through attractive country to **El Santuario** (**E** *Aires del Oriente*, on main road, Km 45, and several restaurants nearby including *El Pasajero* and *El Recreo*) and 65 km beyond, passes by **San Luis**, a short distance up a side road to the north. Here there are three ecological parks, all with walking paths and places to bathe on the rivers. The best is the **Parque Ecológico El Dormilón**, on the Río Dormilón and the notable *Cascada La Cuba* waterfall which tumbles 110 m down through the forest. There is a restaurant in the park and places to stay in the village. *Comfama* (see page 263) run weekend trips to San Luis from Medellín. Public transport from the village links with the many buses for Medellín on the main road and to Puerto Triunfo and Bogotá.

For the continuation of the road, several stretches of which were being improved in 2000, see under Puerto Triunfo in the previous chapter. Take advice on using this road – it has been under some threat from the ELN in 2000.

Rionegro
Phone code: 94
Altitude: 2,115 m

Some 39 km southeast of Medellín and 5 km from the airport is the town of **Rionegro**, in a delightful valley of gardens and orchards. This is an old town founded in 1663. Here was born one of Bolívar's generals, José María Córdoba, the hero of the battle of Ayacucho, and after whom the nearby international airport is named. His monument in the plaza is by Rodrigo Arenas Betancur. The

then, wood and later concrete, spiral stairways have been constructed and you can now ascend the rock in 30 minutes, 649 steps and about 140m from the top of the dirt access road where there is parking, refreshments and the usual tourist stalls. On the top there is a well protected space of about 2,000m^2 with more refreshments and a less than appropriate unfinished building.

Sr Villegas, born in 1917, still owns the rock and, in spite of official encouragement to sell for national tourist development, has no intention of doing so. Doubtless the whole area could be improved for visitors but the modest price for parking and to climb up would surely increase. There is more controversy. The letters G I on the side of the rock were to be completed as GUATAPE, since the rock is in the jurisdiction of Guatapé, and the locals wished everyone to be aware of this fact. This is (naturally) not the view of the town of El Peñol, who consider the rock to be morally theirs. The painters were, however, stopped in their tracks by superior authorities for `defamation of a national heritage' though no-one has dared to try and remove what is already there.

The view from the summit is very impressive and well worth the effort. The Embalse del Peñol is not, as many maps show, a regular body of water with roads and villages along the shores. Because of the terrain, the dam has created a series of connected drowned valleys and, at ground level, the road gives occasional glimpses and crossings of fingers of the lake as you approach the town of Guatapé, which is the only significant place actually on the lake. From the top of the rock, much of the surface area can be seen, apparently interspersed with a bewildering series of islands and peninsulas, very attractively covered with forests with small developments here and there. For now, it is a beautiful place.

Antioquia & Chocó

Casa de la Convención (where the 1863 Convention took place to decide the national constitution) is now an archive museum. ■ *Entry US$0.50.*

The **cathedral** of San Nicolás, with its gold and silver altar and an unusual high balcony round the nave and dome, deserves a visit. In the right transept is the tomb of Juan del Corral (president of Antoquia 1813-26) impressively set in the open crypt. A museum of religious artefacts is behind the altar; it includes a virgin's robe with 300,000 pearls, not to be missed, and you can climb up behind the Virgin donated by Philip II to look down into the cathedral. ■ *Entry US$0.25.* There are colourful processions in Easter Week.

Sleeping B *Gutier*, Cra 49, No 50-32, T561-0106, central, restaurant, near the market. **C** *Liborio Mejía*, Cra 50, No 46-91, T561-0804, hot water, clean, good. **D** *Dinastía*, Cra 50, No 46-47, T561-6165, with bath, hot water, clean, good value. **E** *Casa Vieja*, Cra 51, No 48-68, T531-4645, small, good. **E** *Dorado*, Cra 50, No 46-124, T531-1106/2030, OK. **E** *Casaloma*, Cra 46, No 51-68, with bath, friendly, safe, hot water.

Eating *Las Abedules*, C 48, No 50-51, good *ajiaco* US$3, recommended. *Los Cheffs*, C 49, No 50-41, central plaza, good. *Doña Bertha*, Cra 51, No 48-66, comida US$1.70, OK. Many other places to eat in and near the plaza.

Transport Buses from Medellín from Terminal del Norte via the autopista US$1.40, 1½ hrs, every 30 mins or so; others from Terminal del Sur go via Santa Elena. Also colectivos from C 49/Cra 42, US$2.50, 45 mins. To El Peñol, take a colectivo to Marinilla from near market, US$0.60.

Around Rionegro

There are many interesting pottery and ceramics factories in the Rionegro area, hardly mechanised, as well as leather working. They welcome visitors and explain the processes.

About 10 km southeast from Rionegro is **Carmen de Viboral** (E *Familiar*, Carrera 31, No 30-53, T5432381), well-known for its fine pottery: there are several factories just north of the market place, the best known is *Fábrica Cerámicas Continental*. Try also *Cristal y Lozo*, good prices for craftwork. A visit to the **Casa de la Cultura**, Carrera 30 is worthwhile.

Transport Buses To Medellín (Terminal del Norte), **Flota El Carmen**, US$2.20. From Rionegro, 15 mins by colectivo, leave when full from plaza, US$0.75; buses every 2 hrs, US$0.60.

A few kilometres due south from Rionegro on the road to Llanogrande, is the COMFAMA recreational park of Tutucán, T5313333, with a replica *paisa* town emphasizing local folklore, on a bigger scale than Cerro Nutibara in Medellín. There are extensive grounds and lakes for boating, a popular place for day outings. There is a good, reasonably priced handicraft centre. Next to it is another COMFAMA family park, Los Osos, mainly for children. For further information and transport possibilities check with COMFAMA (see under Medellín Tour Operators). The parks open Monday-Friday, 0900-1700, weekends and holidays, 0900-2100. Nearby is the *Club Campestre Llanogrande*, an upmarket country club for the wealthy *Paisas*. There is good water-skiing on the lake there and indeed this was the venue for the World Championships in September 1997.

Near Rionegro on the road southwest to El Retiro is **La Fé** reservoir, with a fine public park, **Parque de los Salados**, popular at weekends for aquatic sports amid attractive pine forests.

Also nearby is **Fizebad**, an old estate house, constructed in 1825, restored with original furniture and artefacts, and a display of flowering orchids. ■ *Entry US$2.50*. Many roadside stalls sell typical Colombian snacks: clotted cream, strawberries, *arequipe* (a soft caramel now also sold in small sachets), fruits and juices.

Near El Retiro is the attractive **Tequendamita Falls** with the **B** *Parador Tequendamita*, T5420054, and a good restaurant nearby. In **El Retiro** itself there is a small colonial church and an even older chapel, Capilla de San José, where a document to free local slaves was signed in 1800. If it is not open, ask for the caretaker. (To Fizebad, catch a La Ceja or El Retiro bus.) The scenery is gorgeous and you'll see typical Antioquian life.

The old Bogotá road continues to **La Ceja**, 16 km from Rionegro, with the attractive church dedicated to Nuestra Señora de Chiquinquirá. This is another flower growing centre and a local flower festival is held in December. Any of the surrounding hills affords an excellent view of the area, one of the best is known as Cerro Capiro.

Sleeping and eating D *Turin*, C 19, No 21-55, T5531316, near plaza, small rooms, with bath, hot water, cheaper rooms available, nice courtyard, TV, clean, friendly, laundry facilities, good value. **D** *Primavera*, Cra 20, No 20-61, with bath and TV, cheaper without, uncomfortable beds, small rooms, clean. There are several restaurants.

Buses Bus to Medellín (Terminal Sur), 1½ hrs, US$1.50; to Rionegro, every 30 mins US$0.90.

At **Sonsón**, 121 km from Medellín, the central plaza has many attractive colonial houses, most with balconies. The Casa de los Abuelos is an old house, now a museum with many historical objects, including a printing press which produces a weekly newspaper. There ia a second museum, of religious art, on Carrera 8.

Sleeping D *Tahami*, C 6, No 6-67, T847-5151, very good value. **E** *Imperio*, C 7, Plaza Central, T847-5235, and several *hospedajes*.

North from Medellín

The main road north from Medellín leads to Cartagena, 665 km. About 10 km north of Medellín is the industrial town of **Bello**, where a hut in which Marcos Fidel Suárez, president 1918-1922, was born, is covered in glass for its preservation. The main road follows the Río Medellín for 25 km to El Hatillo where it turns left to climb through well watered dairy country and over the Alto de Matasano pass to **Don Matías** (**D** *Cinco Estrellas*, Carrera 30, No 28-49, T8663587, good restaurant, recommended; also **E** *El Viajero*, T8663099, cold water, basic, and several restaurants). Just off the main road a few kilometres

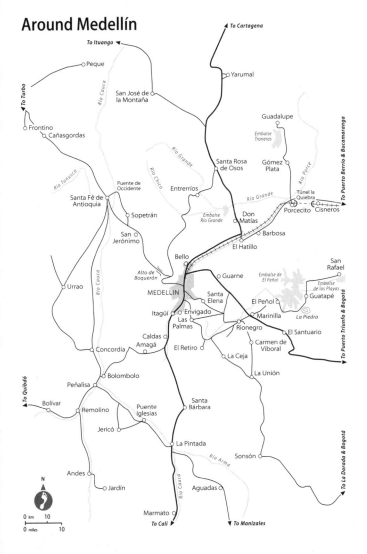

Around Medellín

from Don Matías is the Río Grande hydroelectric dam being developed for tourism. About 21 km north is **Santa Rosa de Osos**, 2,550 m, founded in 1636 and with several surviving colonial buildings including the Humildad chapel. There are sculptures of Rodrigo Arenas Betancur and Marco Tobón Mejía. (**D** *Cortejo Imperial*, T8609575; **E** *Nomar*, Plaza Principal, T860-8221): buses from Medellín to Yarumal stop here.

About 15 km southwest from Santa Rosa is **Entrerríos**, between the Río Grande and the Río Chico in attractive steep country, somewhat extravagantly called the 'Switzerland of Colombia', though the fishing is reported good. Nearby there is a 75 m *peñón*, El Monolito, which has proven to be of archaeological interest. **D** *Capilla del Río*, T8670109, there are several restaurants nearby.

Ituango   About 25 km north of Santa Rosa, a road to the west leads to San José de la Montaña, 2550 m, in the Páramo de Santa Inés, with cloud forest, caverns and waterfalls. 75 km beyond, over the gorge of Río Cauca, the rough road climbs again to **Ituango**, 1550 m, an active town with simple accommodation, banks, pharmacies and a supermarket. Bus Coonorte to Medellín.

From Ituango, rural transport is available to Badillo in the **Parque Nacional Natural Paramillo**, 460,000 ha of forest from the plains of the Río Sinú and the Río San Jorge to the headwaters of both rivers. There is páramo over 3000 m, the highest point, 3960 m, and a wide range of flora and fauna to see from caiman and turtles in the lower areas, monkeys, and many varieties of trees and birds at all levels. Unfortunately there are no facilities at present and there have been problems with guerrillas and paramilitaries recently. Enquire at MA for guidance.

Yarumal   The main road then climbs over to **Yarumal**, 122 km from Medellín, a friendly
Altitude: 2,300m   town in a cold mountain climate with fine views from Parroquia La Merced. There is a museum of religious art in the town hall and an interesting chapel, **Capilla de San Luis** nearby. There is a natural bridge 1 km from the town and several *peñoles* in the neighbourhood. There is also a bike shop at Centro de Servicios, Carrera 21, No 20-28, T8870772.

Sleeping E *Residencias Horizontes*, C Caliente, T94-8871281, hot shower, welcoming. **E** *Executive*, opposite *Horizontes*, good. **E** *Plaza Hostal*, C 19/Cra 20, T94-8871306. Also many *hosterías* on the main plaza and C Caliente.

A further high pass, Alto de Ventanas follows, then a drop to **Valdivia**, 159 km from Medellín. There are a number of good walking and riding trails here including to the gorges of Quebrada Valdivia and Quebrada El Oro and two waterfalls, Casacadas de Santa Inez and Chorros Blancos. There are **D-E** *Residencias* to stay on the main road and several typical restaurants.

It is a short distance north to Puerto Valdivia where the Río Cauca is crossed by the spectacular Simón Bolívar suspension bridge and the new concrete bridge.

Sleeping D *Hotel 2000*, Troncal Norte. **E** *Residencias Rondinella*, El Alto on the edge of town, with *Restaurant La Terraza* nearby.

Continuing north, in 60 km is **Tarazá**, 222 km from Medellín, noted for its many natural pools in the nearby rivers where you can camp and bathe.

Sleeping D *Fortuna*, T821-8739, by the bridge over the Río Tarazá, good but check doors and windows for safety. **F** *Residencia Magdalena*, friendly, fan, parking at the Mobil station, basic, noisy bar.

Crossing the Río Medellín and continuing down the valley from El Hatillo leads to Barbosa, near where a new theme park, **Parque de las Aguas** also known as Venturópolis, opened in 1997. It has a full complement of adventure rides, entertainments, restaurants and leisure facilities. ■ *Open Tue-Fri1000-1800, weekends and holidays 0900-2000. Entrance US$5, car parking US$2, with special arrangements if you go by Metro to Niquía and take the 20-minute bus ride – US$5 all inclusive. Information T407-1515.* Further expansion is planned, a lake for sailing, water skiing etc, and a small airport. The designer, José Villa, is a local Paisa but was involved in the planning of Disneyworld in Florida. Ask at the park for possibilities of staying overnight in the region.

East of El Hatillo

Beyond Barbosa is Porcecito. Here a road goes north to **Gómez Plata** near which is *Hosteria Lagos de Porce*, a comfortable hotel in an attractive setting. Beyond is another hydroelectric dam, Represa Troneras, and several power stations. About 24 km past Gómez Plata is **Guadalupe** (**E** *Central*, Plaza Principal, T8616140), with the Guadalupe waterfall between the two towns and a *teleférico* reputed to be the steepest in Latin America.

The road east from Porcecito climbs over the pass, under which the railway takes to the La Quiebra tunnel, to **Cisneros**, where there is a park and waterfalls, and where the tourist train from Medellín terminates at weekends. The first locomotive (Number 45) to cross the Magdalena and go through the La Quiebra tunnel is displayed here.

Sleeping and eating D *Del Turismo*, Plaza Principal, No 18-09, T863-1522, good restaurant. **E** *Residencia Colonial*, C Colón No 18-20, T863-1503. There are several other *residencias* in town. *Restaurant La Estación*, busy on Sun, good. Many others in centre.

Northwest from Medellín

To reach the road to Santa Fé de Antioquia (78 km) and Turbo (384 km) from Medellín, take Carrera 80 northwards and follow the signs. There is a steep short cut to the main road winding up the mountains between Calle 55 and Calle 65 – you should be on the latter when you meet the highway. The road climbs up to Alto de Boquerón, 22 km from the city. There are good views of Medellín on the way up (sit on the left of the bus) and even more stunning beyond the pass which, unfortunately, is often covered in mist. A newly paved road begins the long descent, again with views to the left. There are many places to eat along the road (called *estaderos, fondas* etc: one is called *El Derrumbe*, ie the landslide, aptly named). The road stones are measured from Santa Fé, therefore, the petrol station marked at 31 km is 47 km from Medellín.

Some 57 km from Medellín is **San Jerónimo**, through which runs the Río Aburrá which forms attractive swimming holes and waterfalls, with two holiday centres on the main road **L** *Lagoturs*, T94-8582204, almost a theme park, a bit over the top; **A** *Hostería Guaracu*, T94-8582104, F2505007 (Medellín), with breakfast (**AL** with all meals), pool, childrens playground, many facilities, often full at weekends, good value for families. There are other smaller places to stay in the town.

From here turn right for a 13 km paved road to **Sopetrán**, the centre of a tropical fruit growing area, and popular with weekenders from Medellín.

Antioquia & Chocó

Sleeping and eating D *Tamarindo*, T8541753. **E** *Paraíso*, good restaurant; enquire in the village if accommodation is available in the 'country clubs' nearby. There is a good restaurant *Mar de Occidente* on C 9.

Transport Bus, Sotraurabá, from San Jerónimo.

Beyond Sopetrán the road deteriorates but leads eventually to the Puente de Occidente (see below).

Santa Fé de Antioquia

Phone code: 94
Colour map 2, grid B3
Population: 12,000
Altitude: 530 m

A further 23 km along the main road is the crossing of the Río Cauca and Antioquia. Santa Fé de Antioquia (to give it its full name, but it is frequently called just Santa Fé), lies just west of the river. It was founded as a gold mining town by Mariscal Jorge Robledo in 1541, the first in the area, and still retains its colonial atmosphere, with interesting Christmas and New Year fiestas. For a time in the 19th century it was the capital of the Department, and retains much of its grandeur and character, little affected by the changing times since then. Its preservation is now assured since it was given National Monument status in 1960.

Ins & outs   The bus station is on the road to Turbo at the north end of Cras 9 and 10.

Sights   The **Catedral Metropolitano** is on the site of the first modest church in the town, built in the late 16th century. A second church was completed in 1673, with three naves, and other embellishments including chapels were added in the next 100 years. This in turn was replaced, in 1799, and the present building consecrated in 1837. It has an imposing white and coloured stone/brick façade (a sort of 'nougat' style, called *calicanto* seen in a number of local buildings) overlooking the main plaza. There is a fine 17th century Christ figure as the centrepiece of the high altar, and a notable Last Supper sculpture from the 18th century. The shrine with embossed silver ornamentation was the work of local artists, but unhappily, several fine gold pieces, also of local workmanship, were stolen from the Treasury in 1986. The tower was used as a prison in times past.

The **Plaza Mayor** is dominated by the fountain which has been supplying water to the town for 450 years and has a bronze statue of Juan del Corral, the President of Antioquia during its few years of independence between 1813 and 1826.

The **Iglesia de Santa Bárbara**, Carrera 8 y Calle 11, is also on the site of at least one previous building, which was passed to the Jesuits in 1728. They found it too small, and the present three nave church was finished by Juan Pablo Pérez de Rublas at the end of the 18th century. The broad west front, also of *calicanto* style as are the interior walls and arches, is crowned with turrets and bells. An interesting woodcarving of the Virgin is enshrined in the Altar of San Blas, which is the oldest altar in Santa Fé. The font, in rococo style, is also older than the building.

The church of **Jesús Nazareno** is another classical style building, this from the 19th century, and is notable for the wood sculptures of Jesus on the cross and the representation of the Crown of Thorns. The church of **Nuestra Señora de Chiquinquirá** is across the José María Martínez Pardo square from the *Hotel Mariscal Robledo*, whose statue stands in the centre. The present church was built in the late 19th century on the site of a 17th century Franciscan temple. An old painting of the Virgin of Chiquinquirá is built into the modern marble altar. This church too was used in the past as a prison. On the south side of the square is the **Palacio Arzobispal**, in republican style, well worth a look inside. Opposite is a music school, further evidence of the cultural life of the town.

Santa Fé de Antioquia

Mariscal Jorge Robledo came from Cali in 1541 to found the first settlement in this area of Antioquia. Up until this time the nearest Spanish settlements were on the coast – Alonso de Ojeda had founded San Sebastián de Urabá in 1509. The first location was to the north of the current site where Peque is today, then the settlement was moved in 1542 to Frontino, 93 km northwest of the present site. By 1546 this also had become unsatisfactory as a permanent location for the prime centre for the region, and Jorge Robledo founded Villa de Santa Fé beside the Río Cauca. It received parish status from the Bishop of Popayán in 1547 and, as Santa Fé de Antioquia, was declared the capital of Antioquia by Philip II of Spain in 1584. The reasons for these early moves are not clear though it probably had to do with the search for gold. Gold was found in Frontino and is indeed mined there to this day, but the narrow valley is not suitable for a city of consequence.

Pope Pious VII created the diocese of Antioquia in 1804, recognizing the cathedral which had been founded in 1799, and confirming the ecclesiastical and political supremacy of the city in the region. Meanwhile, the independence movements had been gathering pace in Nueva Granada and on 11 August 1813, Antioquia was one of the provinces that declared itself a sovereign state with Juan del Corral as its president and Santa Fé its capital.

From this point, however, things went less well for the town. By 1826, the independent state of Antioquia had collapsed and the capital of the Department (of what was to become Colombia) was transferred to Medellín. In 1868, the Catholic church also moved its diocesan centre to Medellín. Strenuous efforts of the faithful eventually restored its ecclesiastical status in 1873, and Antioquia was divided into two bishoprics.

The political decline has however continued. A number of other Antioquian towns are larger and Medellín has almost 100 times the population of Santa Fé. It is not on any vital trade routes: the Cauca is too swift and turbulent for significant river transport and the road to Turbo and the Caribbean unimportant compared to the routes that go through Medellín.

All this has preserved Santa Fé in a unique way. It is bounded on the south by the steep drop to the Río Tonusco, which joins the Cauca just below the town. On the northern side there is another ravine beyond which is the highway to Turbo. To the west and east the town quickly peters out. What is left is a unique, delightful colonial town, sleepy most of the time and not really 'busy' even on market days and holidays. Many of the streets are cobbled, there seem to be churches and little parks everywhere and those that live there have never been tempted to put up modern buildings. Now they cannot legally do so since the town was given National Monument status in 1960. The impression given is that no one would wish to make changes anyway.

The Museo Juan del Corral, has been incorporated into the **Museo de Arte Religioso** next to the Iglesia de Santa Bárbara on Calle 11, which is being reorganized. There is an interesting collection of historical items, paintings, gold objects etc from colonial and more recent times. It is open at weekends and holidays, 1000-1700. There are many fine colonial houses in the town, take a look inside where you can. Typical of the *calicanto* style are the *Casa de la Cultura*, and *La Casa Negra* (the birthplace of Fernando Gómez Martínez).

A trip to the **Puente de Occidente** is well worth while. It is about 3 km downstream from the main (new) bridge and about 6 km from the centre of Santa Fé. You can walk, drive or take a taxi. Hitching is difficult, there is very little traffic. Leave the town northeast on Carrera 9, cross the main Turbo road, and **Excursions**

Antioquia & Chocó

follow the signs to the 'Coliseo'. The paved road winds through the suburbs of the town, then drops down steeply through dry scrub country to the river. The fine slender suspension bridge across the Cauca was designed and constructed by José María Villa, who studied in the USA, between 1887 and 1895. It is single track with wooden cross slats, 300 m long. Small vehicles are allowed to cross the bridge but are not encouraged: have a look – you will see why very few do so! The bridge was declared a National Monument in 1978. On the far side there is the *Club Campestre La Florida* with a restaurant.

Sleeping **A** *Hostal de la Villa*, Cra 10, No 8-36, T853-1097/1065, with full board, pool, fan. **B** *Caserón Plaza*, Plaza Mayor, T8532040/2041, renovated charming colonial house built about 1570 and used as the Governor's mansion in the 1820s, restaurant, pool, parking, day rate of US$6 per person includes buffet lunch and use of pool, recommended.

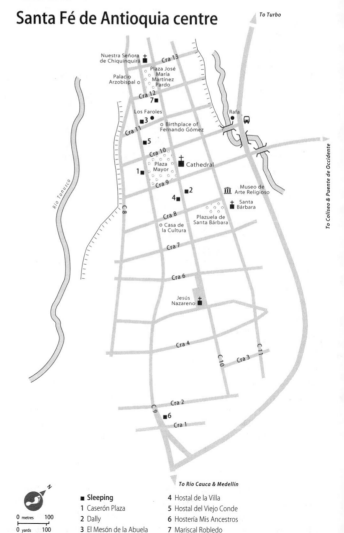

Santa Fé de Antioquia centre

■ **Sleeping**
1 Caserón Plaza
2 Dally
3 El Mesón de la Abuela
4 Hostal de la Villa
5 Hostal del Viejo Conde
6 Hostería Mis Ancestros
7 Mariscal Robledo

C *Mariscal Robledo*, Cra 12, No 9-70, T8531111, **B** with refrigerator and TV, always full holidays and most weekends, swimming pool, good restaurant with excellent buffet lunch US$5, recommended.

D *Hostal del Viejo Conde*, C 9, 10-56, T8531091, with bath, cheaper without, friendly, restaurant recommended. **D** *El Mesón de la Abuela*, Cra 11, No 9-31, T 8531053, with bath and breakfast, clean, friendly. **F** *Dally*, C 10, No 8-50, T8531376, clean, basic.

On the road between the centre and the bridge: **AL** *Hostería Real*, 2 km from town, T8531048, a/c cabins, full board, good food, pool. **AL** *Lago Antioquia*, 3 km from town, T8531154/1518, holiday hotel with many facilities, close to the river, plane at entrance crashed into the lake behind the hotel in 1992. **B** *Hostería Mis Ancestros*, C 9, No 1-192, T8531657, F8532499, pool, jacuzzi etc.

There is good food in the hotels and near the main plaza, eg *Porton del Parque*, local and international dishes, bar, good. *Los Faroles*, Cra 11, No 9-33. Cheaper meals are available near the bus station eg *Restaurant Rafa*, C 12, No 10-82, *menú* US$2.50. **Eating**

Holy Week is a major celebration here, and is followed by another week of festivities between the 2nd and 3rd Sun of Easter when there are many children's parades. This is known as *Semana Santica*. A music festival is held in the *Coliseo* annually in Aug-Sep. *Fiesta de los Diablitos*, 22-31 December: folk dancing, parades, bullfights etc. **Festivals**

Buses To Medellín US$3 (Socurabá or Transporte Sierra), 2½ hrs. To Turbo, US$14, 8 hrs, every 2 hrs or so. **Transport**

The road beyond Santa Fé continues over the Cordillera Occidental (Boquerón del Toyo) down the Río Sucio to Cañagordas, 53 km from Santa Fé. It is a further 250 km to Turbo through Dabeiba, and the banana cultivation area of Chigorodó and Apartadó.

Southwest from Medellín

The main route south from the city follows the Río Medellín as the *Autopista Sur*, marked to Cali. Across the river at **Envigado**, now a suburb 10 km south of Medellín, craftsmen in Jericó across the Río Cauca have for generations turned out the traditional *antioqueño* pouch called a *carriel*, carried by the men. Now used for money etc, one of its original uses was for coffee samples. They are sold here. Envigado is the site of the 'maximum security prison' which failed to hold Pablo Escobar.

Sleeping and eating D *Las Antillas*, C 44B Sur, No 36-04, Barrio La Paz, T3313969. Several Chinese restaurants, C 36S/Cra 43.

Envigado is followed by another industrial town, **Itagüí**, where visitors from all over Colombia come to buy textiles. This is the end of the Medellín Metro. There is a Rodrigo Arenas Betancur sculpture *El Flautista* in the Administrative Centre. There are some business hotels on Calle 85, eg **C** *Monterrey*, Calle 85, No 50A-41, T285-9497, and plenty of restaurants.

South of Itagüí is Caldas, famous for its ceramics and the interesting wood altar in its cathedral. Shortly after Caldas, a road to the right (west) descends through Amagá (two small hotels and restaurants) to cross the Cauca at Bolombolo. Turning right at Bolombolo, a road leads up, away from the Río

Cauca to **Concordia** near where there is attractive countryside with an 80 m waterfall, caves and a natural bridge nearby. **E** *Suroeste*, Carrera 20, no 20-37, T8446104. Some 70 km beyond is **Urrao**, a market town with several hotels (**E** *Colonial*, Plaza Principal, T8269263; **F** *El Turista*, also Plaza Principal, T8269478/9562; others nearby. Several places to eat around the plaza and in the adjacent Pasaje Peatonal).

Parque Nacional Las Orquídeas A poor road leads on to the settlement of Encarnación and the Parque Nacional Natural Las Orquídeas, 32,000 ha from 500 m to 3,400 m, mostly of rainforest. The great variety of flora in this Park is apparently partly due to this highland area remaining humid forest during the last Ice Age. Even the páramo boasts its unique variety of *frailejón* (Espeletia urraonensis).

Ins and outs Entrance to the Park is US$0.50 per person. Camping is possible in 2 sections of the Park at US$3 for 5 persons. Bus to Urrao from Medellín, Rápido Ochoa. There is an airstrip at Urrao, enquire in Medellín about flights. Check with MA before attempting to visit the Park.

There is extensive wildlife including lizards, snakes, squirrels and a few spectacled bears in the forest and very many species of birds. Especially fine is the variety of orchids, hence the name. A collection of 300 varieties of orchid found in the Park is on show in a small museum in Urrao which should be visited before going to the Park. Some of the varieties are found nowhere else.

Going left after crossing Río Cauca at Bolombolo, follow the river south to the next bridge, Puente Iglesias, where a dirt road climbs up 18 km to **Jericó**, an interesting Antioquian town, founded in 1851, with a large cathedral, several other churches, two museums (Arqueológico and Arte Religioso) and a good view from **Morro El Salvador** above the town. It is here that *carrieles* have been made for many generations. There is a Festival de la Cometa (kites) abd Fiesta de la Cultura in August. There are several daily buses to Medellín and transport to nearby Andes and Jardín.

Sleeping in Jericó D *Río Piedras*, main plaza, T843-7348. **E** *Casa Grande*, C 7, No 5-56, T8247554. **E** *La Casona*, T8437095.

Continuing along the Cauca upstream towards Riosucio and Cali, you pass near La Pintada (see below), join the principal road Medellín-Cali, cross from Antioquia into Risaralda Department and above, to the west is Marmato, known for its gold mines. Shortly a new road crosses the Cauca (east), passes through **La Felisa** (**F** *Remanso*, good) and rises in 55 km to Chinchiná on the main Pereira-Manizales road. The principal highway continues to Riosucio and Cali. The older route, all paved, goes through **Supía**, a pleasant town 140 km south of Medellín (**F** *Hotel Mis Ninietas*, near plaza, unsigned, with bath, clean). Further on is **Riosucio**, another delightful town with fine views and a large colonial church (many restaurants, bars and shops). At Anserma the road turns east to Manizales via Arauca.

Between Riosucio and Anserma (both in Caldas Department) is a small section of Riseralda Department. A few kilometres east of the road is Quinchía, near which is a large rock known as the **Cerro Batero**. There is a steep route to climb the rock with some 50 m of metal ladders to the top. Cars can be parked at the *Finca La Sierra*, about 3 km from the foot of the rock.

Antioquia & Chocó

If instead of following the Cauca upstream from Bolombolo you take the right fork at Peñalisa, you can keep to the valley of the Río San Juan for 19 km to Remolino where the road again divides, right for Quibdó and left for Andes and Jardín.

Andes is a busy town with several places to stay, eg *Los Cristales*, T8414263 and *Las Vegas*, T8414423, and a good number of restaurants all on Carrera 50/51. The **Iglesia San Pedro Claver** is worth a visit. There are also a number of attractive waterfalls, including Las Tinajas and Los Chorros, in the neighbourhood.

Jardín, 16 km from Andes and 135 km from Medellín, is a typical Antioquian village surrounded by coffee *fincas* and cultivated hills. It was founded in 1863 on the site of an Indian settlement (of the Embera-Katío group), who worked the naturally iodised salt in the river there. There is still an Indian reservation of the Cristianías community in the locality. It is a delightful place with an attractive fountain in the plaza which is full of flowering shrubs and trees, living up to its name. The neo-gothic church, **Templo Parroquial de la Inmaculada Concepción**, has a fine façade built of dark, dressed stone. It is a National Monument. It has an elegant, striking altar of Italian marble and an eight pointed star in the ceiling of the apse. There is a small museum in the *Casa Cultura* with paintings and artifacts of local artists, and a bank that accepts Visa cards. There is a rustic cable car (*garrucha*) that will take you to Filo de Oro hill, a fine viewpoint. Only 1 km towards Andes you can visit La Molienda to see the production of *panela* and *guarapo* (cane rum), open Saturday-Sunday 1100-2300. The Festival de las Rosas parade takes place in December.

Sleeping and eating in Jardín A *Hacienda Balandú*, 5 km from town, T8455561/8456848, comfortable rooms, pool, gardens, good restaurant, recommended. **E** *Jardín*, on plaza, T845-5651, with bath, hot water, friendly, clean, restaurant, balcony overlooking plaza, good value. **E** *Los Balcones*, Cra 2, no 9-09, T8455857/51. **E** *La Casona*, C 10, no 5-42, T845-5514, with bath, TV. Also several *residencias* on or near plaza. Also on plaza: restaurants, cafés and bars, eg *Restaurante Zodiaco*, good. 5 km out of town on the road to Riosucio is *La Truchería*, a trout farm and excellent restaurant, good value.
    Buses Bus to Medellín (Terminal Sur), 4 hrs. To Riosucio, 3 hrs, US$4.40.

The unpaved road continues south from Jardín to Riosucio (see above) through good walking country and friendly people who welcome your visit to local enterprises.

The right fork at Remolino continues for 17 km through coffee, tobacco and pineapple plantations to **Bolívar** (also called Ciudad Bolívar) in the centre of the coffee region where the evening's entertainment is to watch the local horsemen and women showing off their riding skills around the plaza.

Sleeping and eating D *Iberu*, C Principal, T8412626. **E** *Bahía*, T8411718, good. *Guillo's* restaurant nearby, good.

The road continues over the Cordillera Occidental divide at 3,000 m and down to the tropical forests of the Atrato valley, and Quibdó, 131 km from Bolívar.

South to Manizales

Apart from the route along the Cauca valley via Riosucio described above, there are two other ways to Manizales, either providing an alternative route to Bogotá. South of Medellín on the main road is **Santa Bárbara** (1,857 m), on a green hilltop, providing stunning views in every direction of coffee, banana and sugar plantations, orange-tiled roofs and folds of hills.

Sleeping E *Centenario*, C Santander, one block from plaza, T846-3085, restaurant, TV, recommended. **F** *Hotel Palomares*, on main plaza, clean, good; restaurants and cafés on main plaza, as is the large church. **Transport** Bus to Medellín, US$1.20.

La Pintada & Salamina It is a further 26 km to **La Pintada**, at the junction of the Río Arma and the Cauca (**B** *Mi Rey*, T8454697, cabins and rooms, a/c, restaurant, OK; **B** *Los Farallones*, T8454047; **E** *La Montaña*, with bath; **G** *Residencia Cosina*, basic, clean, fan, mosquitos, restaurant; camping also possible). The picturesque *ruta cafetera* goes back east across the Cauca and makes for Manizales through Aguadas, Pácora and **Salamina**, all perched on mountain ridges. At Salamina the **cathedral** was designed by English architects, large but with a single nave as if an extension of the main plaza on which it stands. The plaza has a fine Parisian fountain. The **Casa Cultura** museum on Cra 6 is in a traditional antioquian house dating from 1905 and has a fine collection of old photographs and other local items on display. ■Open Tue-Sat 0800-1200, 1400-1900, free.

Sleeping E *Hosteria Albares*, left of the church in the plaza, T595041, traditional house, patio, restaurant, clean, hot water. **F** *Residencia Puerto Nuevo*, opposite bus office, clean, good meals.

There are reasonable restaurants in all these towns. This *ruta cafetera* is strongly recommended by cyclists. At Aranzazu, a very picturesque place with lots of coffee shops, paving begins for the 51 remaining km to Manizales.

The third and fastest route from Medellín to Manizales follows a new road on the east side of the Río Cauca from near Supía, and joins the road from Arauca 15 km short of Manizales.

Chocó

Stretching like a ribbon for 400 km between the Cordillera Occidental and the Pacific Coast, from Panama to Valle del Cauca, Chocó is one of Colombia's least developed and most beautiful departments. It is also one of the rainiest regions on earth ('dry season': December to March). In the northern three quarters of the department, the mountain ranges of the Serranía de Los Saltos and Serranía del Baudó rise directly from the ocean to reach a height of about 500 m. The scenery of pristine rainforest descending the mountain slopes to the sea is spectacular.

Ins & outs The principal transport routes are along the Pacific coast from Buenaventura in the south and up the Río Atrato from the Gulf of Urabá and Cartagena to the north. The Ríos Baudó and San Juan flow to the Pacific in the south of the department. Road access is via 2 unpaved routes across the Cordillera Occidenta;, 1 from Medellín via Bolívar, the other from Pereira to the southeast via La Virginia and Pueblo Rico. Work is currently in progress to build a road to the mouth of the Río Tribugá, where a deep-sea port and industrial complex is planned as an alternative export terminal for the coffee and other products from neighbouring Caldas, Risaralda, and Quindío, thus complementing Buenaventura's lack of capacity.

However, it also represents a serious threat to Chocó's unique environment and to its inhabitants' way of life.

NB Malaria, yellow fever, and dengue remain endemic throughout Chocó, and the appropriate precautions (prophylaxis, vaccination, mosquito nets, etc) are recommended. Vampire bats are also common in the region, but fortunately, rabies is not.

Chocó is very sparsely populated. The coastline is dotted with fishing villages whose inhabitants, although also of African origin, are culturally distinct from the Caribbean Afro-Colombians. Inland along the rivers are Indian communities, whose lifestyle is based on hunting, fishing, and subsistence farming. Along the Río San Juan, in the south, there is much gold prospecting around the towns of Tadó and Istmina. For historical and geographic reasons, Chocó's ties are closer with Medellín than with Bogotá. A number of 'Paisas' (Antioqueños) have moved to the area, and virtually all outsiders are referred to as such.

Quibdó

Quibdó, is located on the eastern bank of the Río Atrato. Prices are higher here than in central Colombia, but they are higher still in the coastal villages, so it is a good place to get supplies. Despite its frontier town appearance, Quibdó is one of the safer cities in Colombia.

Phone code: 94
Colour map 2, grid B2
Population: 131,000
Altitude: 50m

There is an interesting mural in the cathedral. Hordes of birds fly in to roost at dusk and there are magnificent sunsets. A good place to view them is the permanently moored boat which houses the civil defence authority (bright orange roof, take insect repellent). The large Jorge Isaacs auditorium is used for cultural activities (see under **Music and dance** for festivals).

Sleeping & eating

E *Cristo Rey*, C 30, no 4-36, T6713352, bath, fan, clean, safe. **E** *Del Río*, good, with bath, safe, free coffee, its restaurant, *Club Náutico* on the 2nd floor has an excellent bar, good food and views. **F** *Dora Ley*, with bath, cheaper without, fan, rooms vary in quality, meals. **F** *Pacífico*, good rooms and beds. **F** *Residencia Darién*, Cra 4, No 26-68, T6712997, bath, fan, space to park motorcycle. **F** *Las Palmas*, with bath, cheaper without. **F** *Oriental*, no private showers, clean, quiet, charming elderly proprietor.

El Paisa, Cra 4, No 25-54, excellent. *Chopán* bakery, good pastries and coffee.

Transport

Air To **Medellín**, Aces and SAM fly daily, US$40. To **Bogotá,** Aces daily; to **Bahía Solano** and **Nuquí,** daily, Aces and SAM. Enquire about other non-scheduled flights at holiday times.

Buses Transportes Ochoa to **Medellín** via El Carmen and Bolívar, 5 daily, 10-12 hrs, US$14 luxury coach, cheaper by regular bus. Transportes Arauca to **Manizales** via Tadó, Pueblo Rico, La Virginia and Pereira, Tue, Thu, Sat, Sun at 0600, 14-17 hrs, US$16. Flota Occidental along same route to Pereira, daily at 0700, 8-10 hrs, US$15. Occasional buses to **Cali**, US$22 otherwise change at La Virginia. Bus to **Bogotá** US$27. Local service to Santa Cecilia and Tadó.

River From Buenaventura up the Río San Juan to Istmina and on by road; services infrequent. Irregular cargo service down the Río Atrato to Turbo and Cartagena takes passengers. Cost to Turbo US$26, food included; to/from Cartagena US$40-55, 4 days, take drinking water. Deal directly with boats. Also 20-seater power boats, 7 hrs to Turbo, about US$30. The lower Atrato was a very dangerous area in 2000 (guerrillas, kidnappings, drug running). Much caution and detailed advance inquiry are strongly recommended.

Directory

Banks *Banco de Bogotá,* cash against Visa, other banks do not change money. *Restaurant El Paisa, Farmacia Mercedes,* and a few shopkeepers sometimes change US$ cash, but rates are poor. Best to buy pesos in larger centres before arriving.

Useful addresses DAS Office: C 29, Cra 4. No entry or exit stamps (see also under **Los Katios National Park**, page 224).

Quibdó to The road to Pereira and Manizales begins in a very poor state, very slow, and
Pereira you can be stuck in mud for hours. Most is through pure jungle with luxuriant broad-leaf vegetation, flowers mostly red and yellow, colourful butterflies, waterfalls and few people. Las Animas is 60 km south, and if you continue south, 17 km further is **Istmina** where the road continues across the Río San Juan to **Condoto** (E *Condoto*, on the main street, friendly, washing facilities and two reasonable restaurants nearby). From Condoto you can visit the abandoned gold mines at Andagoya. At Las Animas there is a turning east to cross the San Juan, reaching **Tadó** (8 km from Las Animas), with a silver-fronted church. E *Hotel Macondo*, very basic but restaurant OK; **E** *Residencias Confort*, without bath, clean, friendly; good café/bar on corner of plaza. Further on is Playa de Oro, a very depressing area where people have been panning for gold. After crossing into Risaralda Department, the road improves before reaching the Cauca Valley.

Towns along the Pacific Coast

Nuquí On the Gulf of Tribugá, surrounded by estuaries and virgin beaches, Nuquí,
Phone code: 9816 is gaining popularity among Colombian sports fishermen and vacationers. A
Colour map 2, grid B1 number of luxury homes have been built nearby. To the south, 10 minutes away, lies the wide curve of the popular Playa Olímpica. Round the bay to the southwest is the fishing village of Panguí (cross first estuary by canoe, the second at low tide or swim), beyond which are various small settlements including Coquí, Guachalito and Arusí, near which are some *termales* (hot sulphur springs) testifying to the active vulcanism of the Serranía de Baudó. At the west end of this part of the coast is Cabo Corrientes. To the north is the small hamlet of Tribugá, a splendid beach and the proposed site of a deep-sea port (see below).

Sleeping There is a growing selection of places to stay along these beaches, often full at holiday times. Best to make arrangements in Medellín before going. The best deals are with travel agents, and watch the press. Along the beach at the north end of town, are **C** *Playa del Mar* and **E** *Ecotel Rocío del Mar*, T (Medellín) 5126854, T/F3815058, with breakfast, **C** with full board, cabins with bath, will organize trips to Ensenada de Utria, recommended. **D** *Cabañas del Pacifico*, T62098, T (Pereira) 270031, with breakfast, boat trips. **E** *Doña Jesusita*, at south end of town, basic. Felipe and Luz Largacha will sometimes rent rooms in their home (along the main street south of the town centre), **F**, basic, friendly. **On Playa Olímpica**: Guillermo and Doralina Moreno, run a small hotel, **E-F** range, shared bath, pleasant, very friendly. You can also pitch your tent in their coconut grove for a small fee, hammock not recommended because of heavy rains and vicious sandflies at night (mosquito net recommended, repellent a must). Meals available if arranged in advance. Near to Nuquí, *Hostal El Cantil*, 1 hr by launch from Nuquí, *cabañas* in lush jungle overlooking the sea, all inclusive package minimum 3 nights with excursions US$300, diving also available, T2520707 (Medellín) or 3348042 (Bogotá). *Cabinas Pijiba*, US$200 for 4 nights (more in high season), all meals, drinks, local transport, guided tips, contact T2608265 (Medellín). They received and award from Conservation International for high standards in ecotourism, www.pijiba.com

Eating Several small restaurants on the road to the airport serving mostly fish. Shops are well stocked with basic goods, prices somewhat higher than in Quibdó.

Transport Air To **Quibdó**, Aces, 20 mins; to Medellín, Aces and SAM, US$70, 50 mins. All flights on Mon, Wed, Fri, and Sun only, return the same day. Some extra flights are added around Christmas and Easter. **Overland** Construction is continuing on a road from Las Animas (see above) to Nuquí, which will eventually connect the port planned for Tribugá with the interior. At present, it is a strenuous 3-day trek along a jungle trail from the roadhead, through several Indian villages, to Nuquí. **Sea** There are launches south to Arusi (Mon, Wed, Fri), and, north to El Valle, there is a new twin engined boat, the *Magdalena* Mon, Wed and Fri calling at Jurubidá, US$4, La Esperanza, US$4, and El Valle, US$8, returning Tue, Thu and Sat, as well as occasional coastal vessels (small fuel barges) to Buenaventura, cost to Buenaventura about US$40. Sea taxis will take you to beaches and villages along the coast.

North of Nuquí at **Tribugá**, Mannuel Buitrago has cabins US$40 for 6, US$20 for 2, simple but very clean, friendly, knowledgeable owner who will arrange tours of jungle, swamps, waterfalls and beaches. Contact *Trinemar*, T4960037, Medellín. Tribugá is 1½ hours walk from Nuquí, transport can be arranged.

Some 50 km north of Nuquí along the coast, **El Valle** has the best bathing and surfing beaches in the area. With tourism development there has been a decline in friendliness. El Almejal, north of town, is the best beach. The entrance to El Valle's harbour is very tricky at ebb tide and many boats have been swept onto the rocks here. As yet there is no access for regular vehicles. If hiring boats privately, check carefully before accepting offers. Make sure there are life jackets for any sea journeys. Solomon and his son Absolom are recommended boatmen.

El Valle
Phone code: 9816
Colour map 2, grid B1

A local product is borojo marmalade, made from a local fruit tasting like tamarind. Guides are available for tours by canoe up the Río Baudó, and to other places of interest along the coast. El Nativo has been recommended. A beautiful isolated beach, El Tigre can be visited by boat, or a three hour walk. Near El Valle the Fundación Natura have a Tortugario where they protect turtle eggs from predators in season. Visits possible.

Sleeping Several large but simple tourist complexes at El Almejal, with rooms and cabins (**D-E** range), as well as bars and restaurants (deserted on weekdays off-season). **L** *Las Gaviotas Centro Vacacional*, T (Medellín) 341-3806, cabins, good facilities. **AL** *Cabañas El Almejal*, cabins with private bath, the best, clean, friendly, full board, reservations T (Medellín) 230-6060, price depends on the package arranged eg 3 nights/4 days, US$200. **D** *El Morro*, with breakfast, **C** full board.

Between El Valle and El Almejal is **F** *Cabinas Villa Maga*, friendly, safe, family run. There is other accommodation in **E** and **F** categories, for example *Carmen Lucia* or *El Nativo y Rosa*. Ask around.

Transport Road A rough road runs 18 km from El Valle to Bahía Solano (passes by the airport before town). Jeeps leave every morning, 1 hr ride, US$2.50, tickets can be purchased one day in advance. **Sea** There is a boat service to Nuquí (see above), and three times a week to Buenaventura.

Between Nuquí and El Valle is Parque Nacional Natural Ensenada de Utria. This 54,000 ha Park was created in 1987 to preserve several unique aquatic and terrestrial habitats. Steep, heavily forested mountains come down to the ocean to create dramatic scenery. Day trips may be arranged from El Valle, Nuquí, or Bahia Solano and special permits are sometimes granted for longer stays by MA in Bogotá. A (free) permit must be obtained from a MA office. The ranger welcomes volunteers to help in clearing rubbish from the beaches and other tasks (also best arranged in advance from Bogotá).

Ensenada de Utria National Park

Antioquia & Chocó

Getting there Entry is US$1.50 with a US$2 embarkation/disembarkation charge. Boats hired from El Valle take 1 hr and cost approximately US$16 return, from Nuquí 1½ hrs, US$24. Boats will not leave when the sea is too rough, which may be for several days. The launch which runs from Nuquí to El Valle can sometimes (depending on tides) leave you at Playa Blanca, a small, privately owned, island near the park boundary. Here Sr Salomon Caizamo has a simple restaurant, but the food is good and he rents space, US$2 for up to 5 hammocks (a nice spot). There is good snorkelling and fishing here. The park headquarters are 5 mins away by motorboat and you can generally hitch a ride with fishermen or park employees. There are also a road and trail leading through the jungle from El Valle to the head of the inlet (9 km, 4-5 hrs, can be very muddy), but you must arrange for a boat to pick you up as it is not possible to reach the park headquarters on foot.

The park is named after a large inlet (*ensenada*) at its centre, which is home to two varieties of whales, corals, needlefish, and many other aquatic species. This is one of the best places on the west coast of South America to see humpback whales migrating from late July to mid October. Motorboats are not allowed past the park headquarters, located halfway up the inlet, and the area is best appreciated if you paddle through in a canoe (try to rent or borrow). The surrounding hillsides are covered with pristine rainforest and there are several magnificent white sand beaches.

Sleeping At the park headquarters and visitors centre there are maps, good information and a display of whale bones and other exhibits, plus a small restaurant. There are several well marked trails. There is simple but comfortable accommodation for about 15 people in a guest house at US$6 per night and an outdoor kitchen with a wood stove, meals US$3, but camping is prohibited. Fresh fish can sometimes be purchased, but all other provisions should be brought from town. Mosquito nets are essential for protection against insects and vampire bats. Across the inlet from the headquarters is a private research station run by Fundación Natura as a base for biologists.

Bahía Solano
Phone code: 9816
Colour map 2, grid B1

Bahía Solano lies on a large bay set against jungle covered hills. As a resort, it gets busy during holiday periods when the deep-sea fishermen arrive and prices rise. The bay is rather muddy and there are no beaches by the town itself. Good bathing beaches may be reached by launch or by walking about 1½ hours at low tide (eg Playa Mecana. Be sure to return before the tide rises or you will be stranded).

Sleeping **B** *Mr Jerry's*, on Playa Huina, including all meals, hammocks cheaper, deep-sea fishing and diving, information T331-2406 (Cali). **B** *Balboa Palacio*, Cra 2, No 6-73, T27074, best in town, pool, boat service to bathing beaches. **D** *Estrellita*, Cra 1, with shower, family atmosphere. **E** *Bahía*, C 3, no 2-40, T27048, in same street as Satena office, with fan and private bath, good restaurant. **F** *Hostal del Mar*, across the street, T27001, run by Estelle and Rodrigo, good, excursions arranged. For information on cabins in Playa Potes near Bahía Solano, T265-6030, Medellín, cost about US$22 per day, boats for hire for fishing and diving, good whale-watching Aug/Sep. Several other places to stay. Good food at *Las Delicias* and at the restaurant run by Señora Ayde near the *Balboa* hotel.

Transport Air To Medellín, daily flights with **Aces**, 4 a week with **SAM**, US$65. To Quibdo, daily with **SAM**, US$35. Be sure to reconfirm return flights and arrive early when leaving. **Land** There is daily jeep service to El Valle (see above). **Sea** Occasional coastal cargo vessels north to Juradó and south to Buenaventura, eg M/V Fronteras, US$45, including food, 36 hrs, cramped bunks.

There are a number of small fishing villages along the coast northwards to Panama, including Juradó. For connections with Darién and Panama, see the Darién section, page 224.

La Zona Cafetera & the Cauca Valley

8

La Zona Cafetera & the Cauca Valley

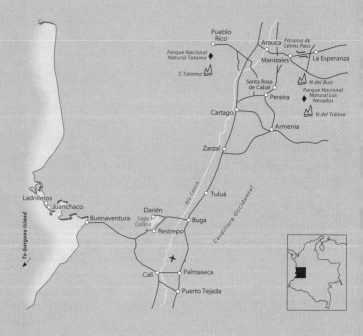

Colombia's best known legal export is coffee and La Zona Cafetera is the most important coffee growing area in the country. With the high mountains of the Cordillera Central a short distance away, the climate is ideal – and very comfortable for people, too. The three main cities, Manizales, Pereira and Armenia are all comparatively recent, each founded in the 19th century, and though badly damaged by recent earthquakes, are friendly, attractive places. Beyond the towns is stunning countryside, coffee fincas to visit and stay in, thermal pools, plenty of walking, trekking and climbing in the mountains.

Although linked by history and an economic interdependance, the hot and sultry Valle del Cauca is an altogether quite different place. The main city, Cali, is the most important place in Southern Colombia. This is the self-proclaimed world capital of salsa – la música tropical – and also boasts of having the most beautiful girls in Colombia. But what Cali lacks in modesty, it more than makes for in excitement. To the west is the southern part of Colombia's Pacific coast. Buenaventura is its largest Pacific port, an excellent place to enjoy the ocean, watch the whales and from which to visit Gorgona Island, Colombia's very own Alcatraz, which is now a place to escape to and not from.

Highlights of La Zona Cafetera & the Cauca Valley

★ Enjoying the views from Av 12 de Octubre, Manizales.

★ Getting a whiff of sulphur in the snows of Nevado del Ruiz.

★ Staying at Hotel Termales, Santa Rosa, relaxing in the hot pools and eating in the elegant restaurant.

★ Walking round the exotic Von Humboldt gardens in Marsella.

★ A visit to Salento and the huge wax palms of the Cocora valley.

★ An interesting day in the National Coffee Park's museum, gardens and adventure park.

★ Viewing the spectacular Pacific coastline in a launch from Buenaventura.

★ A few days on Gorgona, Colombia's virtually undisturbed Pacific island.

★ Enjoying the fine gold and pottery collections in the Calima Museum in Cali.

★ Dancing the night away to the world's best salsa in the grills of North Cali.

The three departmental capitals of La Zona Cafetera are in a north-south line, Manizales (Caldas) in the north, Pereira (Riseralda) 50 km away in the centre and Armenia (Quindío) a similar distance to the south, flanked to the east by the massif of Los Nevados. Because of the altitude, the climate is very agreeable and the road and transport facilities are good. There is much to see and enjoy and this is an excellent part of Colombia to visit with good services in the three cities. Much of the local transport in this region is by *chiva* (literally 'goat'), which are old, simple, brightly coloured buses, and jeeps, often called by the historic name 'Willys', also ancient but lovingly maintained. You will see that this area would be much the poorer without them.

All three can be reached from Bogotá by a road (309 km) passing through Facatativá and Honda and then over the Páramo de las Letras pass (3,700 m, the highest main road pass in Colombia), or through Girardot to Ibagué and over the high crest of the Quindío pass (3,250 m).

Manizales

Phone code: 96
Colour map 2, grid C3
Population: 335,000
Altitude: 2,153 m

Manizales is a comparatively new city, only founded in 1848 by a group of settlers from Antioquia looking for a peaceful place at a time of civil disturbances further north. As a result, Manizales has the feel of a late 19th century city with 'republic' period architecture and a fierce pride in Los Fundadores, the founders of the city. However, this area is unstable geologically and was struck by severe earthquakes in 1875 and 1879 only to be followed by fires which swept through the city in 1925 and especially 1926, severely damaging the centre. The city is now dominated by its enormous cathedral, not unreasonably of reinforced concrete, and still to be finished. Two previous cathedrals on the site were destroyed and even this one suffered during an earthquake in 1979. Yet another threat to the city is the Nevado del Ruiz volcano seen to the southeast, which erupted in November 1985, but most of the damage done was to communities on the side away from Manizales.

Ins and Outs

Getting there **Air** La Nubia airport is to the southeast overlooking the city. Buses to the centre US$0.30, taxi US$3. There are several daily flights from **Bogotá**, **Cali** and **Medellín** with Aces, though due to the altitude and humidity, services are often delayed by fog.

Road The bus terminal is 7 blocks from the centre of the city. There are good roads and comfortable bus services from the main cities of Colombia. From Bogotá and the east the Cordillera Central must be crossed, the most direct route via Honda crosses at 3,700 m. Alternatively, via Girardot and Pereira, the pass is lower at 3,250 m. Both are long winding climbs and descents.

The centre of Manizales is pleasant and convenient for walking, though narrow **Getting around** streets create traffic problems. An added attraction is the extensive views often seen over the local countryside. The key thoroughfare is Cra 23 whích runs the full length of the city, also called Av Santander in the east. It is the road to La Nubia airport, Honda and Bogotá.

Fomento y Turismo, C 29, no 20-25, T8846211, F8842266, guidebook and maps avail-   **Tourist Offices** able, open 0800-1200, 1400-1800, Mon-Fri.

The city was founded on a narrow saddle that falls away sharply to the north, west and south into adjacent valleys. Expansion has been to the east, along precipitous ridges between the Río Chinchiná and Quebrada Olivares using every available piece of flat land. Villages in the Valleys are gradualy being absorbed by the city, but though a spectacular site for the visitor, the terrain causes significant travel difficulties. The climate is extremely humid (average temperature is 17°C, and the annual rainfall is 3,560 mm), encouraging prodigious growth in the area around the city including the flowers that line the highways to the suburbs north and south. Frequently the city is covered in cloud but when it is clear, there are brilliant views in every direction. With luck, you may see the snows of the Nevados to the south east. The best months of the year are from mid-December through to early March. The city looks down on the small town of Villa María, 'the village of flowers', now almost a suburb.

Sights

Because of the earthquakes and fires much of the architecture is predominantly modern with high-rise office and apartment blocks. Traditional 19th century architectural styles are still seen in the suburbs and the older sections of the city.

The centre of the city is the **Plaza de Bolívar** with two ceramic murals by Guillermo Botero and a central plinth on which stands a bronze statue of Bolívar Condor (1991) by Rodrigo Arenas Betancur. On the north side of the plaza is the Departmental government building, **La Gobernación**, an imposing example of neo-colonial architecture, built in 1926 around a central garden patio. The building was declared a National Monument in 1984.

Opposite is the **Cathedral**, a new building constructed after the fires of 1925 and 1926 mainly of reinforced concrete, neo-gothic in style, with an elegant spire over 100 m high. It was designed and built by Italian architects between 1928 and 1939, although some work still continues, including strengthening the cupola. It now has four towers, one each dedicated to Saints Inés, Francis, Mark and Paul. Inside look for the fine decorated altar cover with a suspended cross above, the wooden choir stalls and colourful stained glass windows including a fine rose window at the west end. There is also a simple but elegant marble font to the left of the west door.

Nearby, at Carrera 23, No 23-06, the **Banco de la República** has a gold and anthropology museum, with classical music every afternoon, a good reference library, and records and videos. ■ *Open 0800-1130, 1400-1800, Mon-Fri, free.*

On Carrera 22 at Calle 30 the **Iglesia de la Inmaculada Concepción**overlooks **Parque Caldas**, again in neo-gothic style with cedarwood pillars and

La Zona Cafetera & the Cauca Valley

roof arching inside and the stained glass windows. It was built 1903-21. On Carrera 18, near the bus station is the **Iglesia de los Agustinos**, with its colonial style façade and the many spires around the building.

The **bull-ring** on the Avenida Centenario built around 1950 is an impressive copy of the traditional Moorish style, based on the one in Córdoba, Spain. It holds 20,000 people. The **University of Manizales** is housed in a fine building off Carrera 23 at Calle 40, originally the railway station, of considerable historic interest. **Universidad de Caldas**, Calle 65, No 26-10, has a natural history museum with a good selection of butterflies, moths and birds; open every day from 0800 to 1200 and 1400 to 1800. Take a 'Fátima' bus to the University, at the eastern end of the city. **The Teatro de los Fundadores**, Carrera 23/Calle 33, at the eastern entrance to the city centre is a good example of local architecture. This is well worth a visit with some fine murals and metal sculptures in the foyer and upper floors, including works by Guillermo Botero (see below).

La Galería del Arte, Avenida Santander (Carrera 23) at Calle 55, which has exhibitions of work by local artists. These can be bought. Further out on the road to Bogotá at Calle 65, you will see the tower of the Manizales terminal of the aerial cableway that went 75 km to Mariquita from 1922 till the 1960s carrying coffee, thus avoiding the difficult grind up to the Alto de Las Letras pass (3,700 m) and down the other side. From Mariquita the coffee was taken by road and rail to the Río Magdalena for shipment and export.

Chipre is a suburb in the northwest of the city and has, in its centre, the **Nuestra Señora del Rosario church** which is a replica of the previous city cathedral. Along Avenida 12 de Octubre, the west side is an open park with

Manizales

■ **Sleeping**
1 Amarú
2 Camino Real
3 Consol
4 Escorial
5 Europa
6 La Posada del Café

7 Las Colinas
8 Marana
9 Residencias Avenida
10 Residencias Caldas
11 Residencias Margarita
12 Rokasol
13 Tamá Internacional

La Zona Cafetera & the Cauca Valley

magnificent views over coffee country down towards the Río Cauca. Across to the east are views of the city. It is much frequented by locals at weekends. Stalls along promenade sell *obleas*, large wheat wafers, served with *arequipa*, coconut or *dulce de leche*, well worth a try. The large water tower, known as **El Tanque** is a local landmark. At the end of the avenue, a newm impressive sculpture, **Monumento a los Colonistas**, was being completed in 2000.

Visits to coffee farms in the area are warmly recommended. They are often included in local tours arranged by agencies or through hotels. You will also see the spectacular local countryside. For staying on coffee farms, see page 311. For visits to Los Nevados National Park, see page 295.

Excursions

Essentials

AL *Las Colinas*, Cra 22, No 20-20, T8842009, F8841590, central, 2 bars, good restaurant, very comfortable. **A** *El Carretero*, C 36, No 22-22, T8840225/0255, F8840281, good restaurant, business clientele, comfortable. **B** *Europa*, Av Centenario, No 25-98, T8971239, near bull ring, restaurant, comfortable, clean, very helpful. **B** *Camino Real*, Cra 21, No 20-45, T8845588, F8846131, central, good value. **B** *Escorial*, C 21, No 21-11, T8847646/7696, F8847722, with breakfast, good restaurant.

C *La Posada del Café*, Av Centenario, No 24-12, T8892385/2313, F8892528, restaurant, excellent breakfast, parking, safety box, satellite TV, good information, credit cards accepted, ask for room with view of Nevado del Ruiz. **C** *Tamá Internacional*, C 23, No 22-43, T8842124, F8847610, beside cathedral, 1st floor, old style, clean, restaurant, clean, good but noisy.

D *Amarú*, C 20, No 20-19, T8843560, F8844086, breakfast included, restaurant, well appointed, parking nearby. **D** *Rokasol*, C 21, No 19-16, T8843971. Good reports. **E** *Consol*, Cra 20, No 20-25, T8842084/8681, F8803847, with bath, hot water, clean.

F *Residencias Avenida*, C 21, No 20-07, T8835251, with bath, clean, safe, short stays. **F** *Marana*, C 18, No 17-34, T8843872, close to bus station, with bath, clean, friendly. **F** *Residencias Margarita*, C 17, No 22-14, quiet on second floor, safe, parking opposite, good. **F** *Residencias Caldas*, C 18, No 16-30, T8849361, quiet, not too clean.

Sleeping
In Jan, during the fiesta, hotel prices are considerably increased

Apart from the hotels, the best restaurants are on or near Cra 23 in the east part of the city. **Centre** *El Ruiz*, Cra 19, No 22-25, filling 3 course meal. *Chung Mi*, Cra 23, No 26-11, T8829281, Chinese, good value. *Punto Rojo*, Cra 23, No 21-41, T8833809, cafeteria, open 24 hrs, good value. *El Balcon del Arriero*, Cra 23, No 26-18, T8828375, Colombian food, good. *La Suiza*, Cra 23, No 26-57, good fruit juices and cakes. *Govindas*, Cra 23, no 22-26, vegetarian, open 1200-1400 only. *Café Tamanaco*, corner of Plaza de Bolívar, Cra 21/C 23, coffee and snacks, has information about local tours to Nevado del Ruiz etc, guided parties often meet here.

East *Las Redes*, Cra 23, No 75-97, mainly seafood, pricey but good. *Las Brasas*, Cra 23, No 75A-65, grills and *comida típica*. *Fonda Paisa*, Cra 23, No 72-130, T8865928, nice local dishes, coffee bar with Colombian music. *Las Cuatro Estaciones*, Cra 23, No 56-42, T8859358, Italian. *Caballo Loco*, Cra 61, No 23-07, good. *Casa Kena*, Cra 23, No 72-49, good Italian, Caruso recordings. *Las Geranios*, Cra 23, No 71-67, T8868738, good quality local dishes.

There are also a few restaurants in the west of the city on Av Centenario, eg no 33-50 *Los Sauces*, international menu and no 25-124, *Palacio Oriental*, Chinese. Behind Av 12 de Octobre, near El Tanque, is *La Teja*, T8830052, light meals, good *patacones*. There are many kiosks in the centre with cheap, fresh, delicious local snacks.

Eating

La Zona Cafetera & the Cauca Valley

Entertainment **Bars and clubs** Several on Cra 23 around C 63. Alternatively, try *Puerto Rico* or *Epsilon* on Av Centenario near the Hotel Posada del Café.

Cinema *Cinema Fundadores*, C 33/Cra 22 (next to Teatro de los Fundadores). *Multicíne Estrella*, Cra 23, no 59-70.
   Theatre *Teatro de los Fundadores* is a modern cinema-theatre auditorium. It has an interesting wood-carved mural by the famous local artist, Guillermo Botero. Events are held here and at the other locations during the Theatre Festival. Free films at the Universidad de Caldas on Wed at 1700. A good way to meet students.

Festivals Early in Jan for 8 days the *Feria de Manizales* is held, with bullfights, beauty parades and folk dancing. In the third week of Mar the *Exhibición Nacional Equina* horse show is held in the Coliseo, 3 km from the city on the road to Pereira. In Aug/Sep, there is an annual arts and theatre festival. The main events are in the *Teatro de los Fundadores*.

Shopping **Handicrafts** *Artesanías de Colombia*, Cra 21, no 26-10, T8847874, local arts and crafts; *Mil Cositas*, in the Centro Comercial Sancancio, Cra 27, no 66-30, T8871789. **Shopping Centres** In the east there are several along Cra 23. In the centre, try *San Andresito*, C 19/Cra 18, or *Cosmos*, C 19/Cra 20.

Tour Operators *Tierra Mar Aire*, Cra 23, no 55-100, T8863300 and office at airport, T8740506, helpful.

Transport **Air** Manizales has a small airport (Santaguida or La Nubia, 7 km east of the centre, T8745451). To **Bogotá**, Aces 7 flights daily. To **Medellín**, Aces 3 daily. To **Cali**, Aces 2 daily.
   Buses The terminal with good restaurant is at C 19 between Cras 15 and 17, T8849183. Buses to **Medellín**: via Neira and Aguadas, 6 hrs, US$8; via Anserma, 10 hrs, US$8; colectivo to Medellín, US$10. Bus to **Bogotá**, Expreso Bolivariano, US$12, 9 hrs; 7½ hrs by *buseta*, US$13.50. To **Honda**, US$5. **Cali** by bus, hourly, 6 hrs, US$9. To **Cartago**, 4 hrs, every 20 mins, US$3; **Pereira**, half-hourly, 1½ hrs, excellent road, beautiful scenery, US$2 ordinary. **Armenia**, 3 hrs, US$4. To **Quibdó**, Transportes Arauca, via Pereira, La Virginia, Pueblo Rico and Tadó, Mon, Wed, Fri, Satuday 0600, 14-17 hrs, US$16.
   Car To Medellín, see above. Manizales-Honda-Bogotá: all paved. The road climbs to 3,700 m, with most superb scenery. First accommodation is in Padua, then Fresno (cheap hotels), Mariquita and Honda.

Directory **Airline Offices** *Aces*, C 24, no 21-34, local 1B, T8832237, airport, T8745459; *Avianca/SAM*, C 23, no 21-19, T8847008.
   Banks *Lloyds TSB Bank*, Cra 22, No 17-04, T8844360, also agency Cra 23 no 56-42, in the east of the city; *Bancolombia*, Cra 22, no 20-60, T8841082, Titan, C 23, no 21-41, T8841789, and other banks. Exchange is not possible on Sat and Sun.
   Communications **Internet** Ask in your hotel for nearest service. **Post Office** (*Adpost*) C 21, no 23-39, T8821708; (*Avianca*) C 23, no 21-19, T8846861. **Telephone** *Telecom*, Cra 23, no 21-54, international call service 0800-1800.
   Embassies and Consulates *Germany*, via al Magdalena, no 74-71, 10th floor, T8872928. *Italy*, Edif 7 Banco de Bogotá, Of 501, T8831935. *Spain*, C 36, no 22-22, T8845960.
   Useful addresses *DAS*, C 53, no 25A-35, T8810600; *MA*, Cra 23, no 54-05, in front of Edif Triangulo, T8812210.

La Zona Cafetera & the Cauca Valley

Los Nevados National Park

The Parque Nacional Natural Los Nevados comprises 58,000 ha and straddles the departments of Caldas, Quindío, Risaralda, and Tolima. It is essentially a series of volcanoes that have coalesced into a highland area 30 km long, mostly over 4,000 m high, from Nevado del Ruiz (5,400 m) in the north to Nevado del Tolima (5,221 m) at the southern end. Ruiz is accessible from Manizales, Tolima from Salento or Ibagué. 'Nevado' implies permanent snow, but rising temperatures have lifted the snow line to about 4,850 m, though you can find intermittent snow much lower than that at any time.

You must check in advance if entry to the park is permitted. For information in **Ins & outs** Manizales contact MA, or the tourist office which organizes day trips to Nevado del Ruiz at weekends (US$16 one day, per person minimum 5, leave 0800, return via hot pools). For any climbing, a guide is required, US$50/day, maximum 6 people. A highly recommended guide is Javier Echavarría Carvajal, T8740116/8808300 (Manizales). See under Pereira, page 299, for access from Salento, and under Ibagué, page 236, for **Nevado del Tolima**.

For those planning an independent visit to Nevado del Ruiz with a vehicle, take the Bogotá road from Manizales to **La Esperanza,** (22 km) a little short of Las Letras pass. At La Esperanza is a good, simple restaurant. Take the right fork here for excursions towards the volcano. It is 17 km to the Park entrance, 25 km to the road head beneath the cone of **Nevado del Ruiz** or **Volcán Ruiz** (also known by its Indian name, *Cumanday)* and 62 km to Laguna del Otún.

An alternative route starts at La Enea just off the Carretera Panamericana (which links the road from Chinchiná to the road to Bogotá, bypassing the city and serving the airport). The road leads past the airport along the opposite side to the terminal, and in 5 km, comes to AL *Termales El Otoño*, T87402290, F 8746723, beautifully landscaped former *finca*, now a hotel with *cabañas* for 3-5 people (**LL-L**), complete with your own mineral hot baths and swimming pools. Water sourced from Volcán Ruiz also serves a public area, open 0700-2400 daily, US$4.50 adults, US$1.50 children. They have more accommodation (**A3**) a short distance away.

Continue along the now unsurfaced road, passing through outstanding primary forest, for 22 km upwards to **Termales del Ruiz** at 3,500 m, where there are thermal baths. About 2 km beyond is AL *Hotel Termales del Ruiz*, comfortable, with restaurant and its own good thermal pools on the premises, and camping in the grounds with permission. Further on (7 km), this road meets the road coming from La Esperanza. Turning right, and continuing 2 km brings you to **Las Brisas** below a prominent hill with several radio antennae on the summit. Unfortunately the *Restaurante Brisas del Cumanday* burnt down in 1995 but there is a small place to eat 2 km further on. You can camp there (there are some mattresses) but it is very cold and you will need a good sleeping bag. The surroundings are beautiful and this is the only place to overnight near the park entrance.

Past Las Brisas the road forks. To the left it continues over enormous landslides caused by the 1985 Nevado del Ruiz eruption (see below) to the village of Ventanas, a very scenic drive and on to Murillo in the department of Tolima. To the right it climbs steeply for 1 km to reach **the park entrance and visitors' centre** at 4,050 m. Entry is US$3 per person and US$2.50 per car; a camping permit for the Park is US$12.50 per tent, space for five. And 4 km from the entrance is the new *Chalet Arenales* at 4,150 m run by Carlos Alberto, **D** per person including sleeping bag and breakfast, hot showers, cooking facilities, good atmosphere, crowded at weekends. There is room for 20 people in the chalet, best to book through MA beforehand. At the nearest weekend to each full moon there is a special concert here.

The turnoff (left) to Nevado del Ruiz is 10 km beyond the park entrance and one can drive to 4,800 m, near the foundations of a large shelter (destroyed by fire before the eruption). Now there is a basic hut, with hot drinks and snacks during the day but no accommodation and very little water, ask at the entrance if it is open. This point is within a short distance of the permanent snow line. On foot from the entrance at 4,050 m to the summit takes 7-8 hours if you are acclimatised. From the end of the road, it is about three hours to the summit. An authorised guide is obligatory if you wish to climb beyond the snowline. The summit is the highest point of the snowfield, the Crater Arenales, the main vent of the volcano, is to the north. Another excellent climb nearby is La Olleta (4,850 m), the ash cone of an extinct volcano. You can descend into the crater, but note your route well as fog can obliterate landmarks very quickly.

Los Nevados National Park

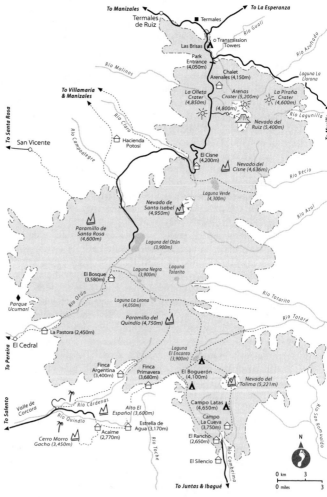

Nevado del Ruiz is 'dormant' at present though if you climb to the crater, beware of fumeroles of toxic gas. The principal road continues south below the Nevados del Cisne and de Santa Isabel between which you can visit the Laguna Verde, but you will need a special permit. A four-wheel drive vehicle is essential beyond Nevado del Ruiz. You can stay at the *Refugio El Cisne*, a small farm at 4,200 m, where a farmer lives with his family. He lets you sleep in his warehouse (very cold, but less so than outside) for US$3.50 and offers you milk and coffee.

From Refugio El Cisne you can climb Nevado San Isabel which has three snow capped summits around 4950 m. Go southeast towards Laguna Verde and turn right shortly before the lake aiming for the left side of the summit mound. The snow line is about 200 m below the summits. A round trip to the easiest summit is about seven hours. A guide is obligatory (and useful), crampons helpful, rope not necessary. Nevado del Cisne, 4,636 m (no permanent snow), can also be climbed from the Refugio. It is best to leave for these summits before dawn to arrive on the top about 0800 before the clouds roll in. A visitor centre is planned near El Cisne.

South of El Cisne there are two tracks leading down northwest eventually (about 35 km) to Villamaría and Manizales past various fincas with splendid views all the way. One can also walk from Las Brisas down to Manizales in a day, stopping along the way at the Termales del Ruiz.

Continuing south a further 13 km along the top road, and 39 km beyond the turnoff to Nevado del Ruiz is **Laguna del Otún**, trout fishing (between April and September) and camping with permission of MA, see also under **Ucumarí Park**.

If you do not have a car, it is still possible to reach Las Brisas and the park entrance with a milk truck that leaves the Celema dairy in Manizales, Carrera 22, No 71-97, T8864000, between 0500 and 0600 daily US$3, returning in the early afternoon, or the Rápido Tolima bus at 1430 from the Terminal in Manizales to Murillo passes near the entrance to the Park, US$3, 2 hrs.

Visitors to the park should come prepared for cold damp weather with snow possible at any time above 4,300 m, and remember to allow time to acclimatise to the altitude. Maps of the area are available at the Instituto Geográfico in Manizales, just behind the Club Manizales on Carrera 24.

Some 22 km southwest of Manizales is **Chinchiná** (F *Hotel Pielroja*, basic, but clean), noted for the attractive filigree steeple of the church, then over the Department line into Riseralda. It's then 15 km to **Santa Rosa de Cabal**, at 1,550 m, 12 km short of Pereira.

Santa Rosa de Cabal

Santa Rosa is a pleasant, small town increasingly involved in the tourist attractions nearby. There is some colonial architecture eg the **Cámara de Comercio** building on Carrera 15, and an attractive **Plaza de Bolívar** overlooked by the principal church of the town **Iglesia Las Victorias** with a fresh, light coloured façade with twin towers. The **Santuario La Milagrosa**, Carrera 14/Calle 6 on Parque Los Fundadores has a fine modern stained glass west window. Note also the old railway station on the road leading out to Manizales. There is a tourist office, *Oficina de Planeación y Desarrollo Turístico*, on Plaza de Bolívar, Carrera 14/Calle 12.

Sleeping and eating B *La Fragata*, above town off C 8, Barrio Cartaguito, T3641180. Cabins, pool, restaurant, family facilities. **B** *Finca*, C 12, No 7B-01, T3644338/40, F3644341. With breakfast, family hotel, bar, restaurant, cafetería, pool, attractive gardens. There are several hotels on or near Plaza de Bolívar. There are restaurants also in the centre and *El Champiñon* at Cra 10/C 10. **Camping** *Lagos de Venecia*, 2 km north of Santa Rosa off the road to Manizales. Food and fishing available.

La Zona Cafetera & the Cauca Valley

Nevado del Ruiz

This volcano has had a dramatic history of violent eruptions and irregular periods of quiescence for many centuries. Since at least 1595, pyroclastic explosions have been a characteristic form of activity, with vast quantities of rock and dust ejected from its craters. Noteworthy eruptions were recorded in 1805, 1845, 1928 and most recently, in 1985. An additional complication with this volcano is the considerable accumulation of snow on the summit because of the humid climate and the high altitude. When vast quantities of hot dust combine with the melting of the snow cap, gigantic mudflows are created which cascade down the mountainside.

The catastrophic eruption of 1985 took a chunk out of the north side of the volcano, and you can see the course of part of the landslide of rock and meltwater from the road as mentioned in the text. It is estimated that over 10% of the snowcap melted at that time and some of it rushed down to the west - round both sides of the La Olleta crater. The sand near Chalet Arenales and La Olleta was deposited at the time of this and previous eruptions.

Fortunately, the flow down the Río Molinos and Nereidos did little damage lower down though there was some material destruction near Chinchiná. The effect on the east side was another matter. The mud flows reached Armero, 50 km away, with widespread destruction and loss of life. A measure of the forces involved was demonstrated by the plume of steam and dust which rose 31 km above the volcano.

Of course, there will be further explosions – it is only a matter of time. However, geologists are closely monitoring Nevado del Ruiz, and hopefully there will be advance warning of the next event.

Termales de Santa Rosa is 8 km along an unpaved road east of town, and 1 km short of the main resort and hotel is *Balneario Termales* with hot and cold pools, food and camping. At the end of the road at 2,050 m is where waters from hot springs cascade down a mountain through lush tropical vegetation into a swimming pool, by which time the temperature is down to about 40°C. There are successive pools at cooler temperatures. It is claimed that the water contains 16 or more therapeutic chemicals. Entry US$4 (busy at weekends). Plenty of walking and riding in the neighbourhood, and fishing in the Marcelandia lakes nearby, which are famous for rainbow trout.

Sleeping AL *Hotel Termales* (also known as Hotel Arbeláez), T3645500, F3641490, termales@col2.telecom.com.co An elegant traditional building with a modern annex, with rooms for 1 to 6 people, also cabins, enquire about discounts, attractive balconied restaurant, bar and cafeteria, cold showers fed from a natural spring and mudbaths.

Another road, at present in a poor state, goes up to the northeast through Toboganes 18 km to **Ecotermales San Vicente** at 2,300 m in a spectacular setting of upland forest. Here there is an extensive choice of hot and cold pools and mud baths with varied chemical qualities fed by many hot springs. Accommodation is simple cabins but facilities good. Camping, riding and good trout fishing also available. Information and reservations at *Ecotermales*, Calle 16, No 14-08, T3335253, F3243258, Pereira, ecoterma@col2.telecom.com.co

Transport Bus Pereira-Santa Rosa, US$0.50; then bargain for a jeep ride, about US$1.50 per person, to the springs. Tours can be arranged from Pereira with overnight at the Termales at about US$35 per person. An afternoon or an evening excursion is a cheaper option. Enquire at the above address for buses at weekends/holidays at about US$10, including entrance. Similar arrangements can be made in Manizales. Bus Manizales-Santa Rosa, US$1.50.

Longer walks are possible from San Vicente and Hotel Termales through *La Cristalina* gorge up to the **Paramilla de Santa Rosa**, 4,600 m, one of the many extinct volcanoes of the region, about eight hours of ascent, much of it steep. It is possible to continue down to **Laguna del Otún**. There is much evidence of past volcanic activity and of more recent glaciation. Good information on hiking and trekking is available at the two *Termales* from where several trails to the mountains start.

Between Santa Rosa and Pereira look out for several restaurants noted for their local *chorizos* and craft shops selling cane furniture.

Pereira

Capital of Risaralda Department, 56 km southwest of Manizales, Pereira, stands within sight of the *Nevados* of the Cordillera Central. Pereira is situated on a small plateau, bounded to the south by the Río Consota and to the north, the Río Otún, about 140 m below. Beyond the Otún is Dosquebrados, an industrial town, now virtually part of the city, and dramatically linked by a new viaduct (see below). It is the largest city in this part of Colombia and acts as the centre of the Zona Cafetera with the appropriate range of official and commercial institutions and services. It has a very pleasant climate, though the green countryside around indicates a regular rainfall, usually short, sharp showers. Apart from coffee and cattle, there is a wide variety of local agricultural produce and you will notice the high quality of the food available here. Unfortunately this is an active seismic zone and earthquakes periodically damage Pereira. In 1995 significant damage was done to some buildings in the centre and again in January 1999 it was affected by the serious quake which devastated Armenia.

Phone code: 963
Colour map 2, grid C3
Population: 432,000
Altitude: 1,411 m

Air The airport is 5 km west of the city, taxi US$2, bus US$0.25. Daily flights from Bogotá, Cali, Ibagué and Medellín. Daily flights also from Miami and several a week from New York, calling at Bogotá.

Getting there

Road The bus terminal is 12 blocks south of the centre. Main roads are good in the Zona Cafetera. Frequent bus services from the main cities of Colombia. The direct road via Armenia to Ibagué, Giradot and Bogotá goes over La Linea pass (3,250 m).

The city is centred around Plaza de Bolívar and most points of interest are within walking distance. The centre is safe (subject to the usual common sense precautions) but the semi derelict area between Cra 10 and 12 is not a place to linger. Local taxi and bus services are of good quality.

Getting around

Tourist information at *Compañía Regional de Turismo de Risaralda* (CORTURIS), Edif de la Gobernación, Av 30 de Agosto, C 18/19, T3350786, F3353994. *Oficina de Fomento al Turismo*, Cra 7, No 18-55, p 2, T3357132/357172, F3267684, very helpful. *Corporación Autónoma Regional de Risaralda (Carder)*, C 24, No 7-29, pisos 4-5, T2354152, F3355501, for information and permission to visit local National Parks. For information on guides for Los Nevados contact ASOGUIAS through CORTURIS or Oficina de Fomento al Turismo.

Tourist offices

A settlement was established here around 1541 by Mariscal Jorge Robledo but about 1700 it was moved to the present site of Cartago on Río La Vieja after continuing difficulties with a tribe of Quimbaya Indians. Francisco Pereira from Cartago set out to re-establish a town here in the 19th century but died before achieving his objective. Remigio Antonio Cañarte, a priest and friend of Pereira, with a group of settlers, succeeded in 1863 and named the town after him.

History

La Zona Cafetera & the Cauca Valley

Sights The central square is the **Plaza de Bolívar**, noted for its *El Bolívar Desnudo*, a striking sculpture of the nude General on horseback by Rodrigo Arenas Betancur to commemorate the city's centenary in 1963. It caused a stir when unveiled, and brought a whole new meaning to the term 'liberator', but it is now accepted with pride by the local citizens. Enthusiasts of Arenas Betancur can find three of his other works in the city, *Monumento a los Fundadores* on Avenida Circunvalar/Calle 13, *El Prometeo*, in Universidad Tecnológico de Pereira (South on Calle 14), and *Cristo Sin Cruz* in the **Capilla de Fátima**, Avenida 30 de Agosto/Calle 49, towards the airport. There are many other examples of public art on display; look for works by Jaime Mejia Jaramillo and Leonidas Méndez. There is an interesting bronze of Benito Juarez, the Mexican patriot on Avenida 30 de Agosto. Also in Plaza de Bolívar is the **Cathedral**, drab and unimpressive from the outside but with an elegant interior, fine chandeliers down the central nave, two large mosaics depicting baptism and the eucharist and a fine dome with roof paintings. Also interesting are the two Lady Chapels and the stained glass windows.

There are three other parks with their churches. The **Parque del Lago Uribe Uribe** is the most picturesque with an artificial lake and a fountain illuminated at night. **Parque Gaitán** and **Parque La Libertad** (with its striking mozaic by Lucy Tejada) are also worth a visit (see map). Opposite the *Meliá Pereira* hotel is the **Templo Nuestra Señora del Carmen**, a gothic style church with a dull grey concrete finish outside but inside it has some good sculptures and stained glass.

Two early 20th century houses of architectural interest are **Casa de Luis Carlos Gonzalez**, Carrera 6, No 21-62, and **Casa Carrera,** Carrera 7, No 15-58. Both have been declared national monuments. Recently completed (1997) is the impressive new road bridge over the Río Otún connecting Pereira with Dosquebrados, known as **El Viadueto Gaviria Trujillo.** It was built by

Pereira

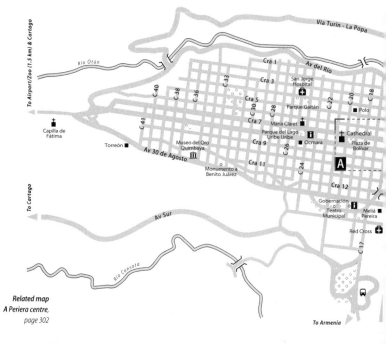

Related map
A Periera centre,
page 302

Colombian, German and US contractors to Italian designs. The Interamerican Development Bank (BID) contributed to the US$50 million cost. Traffic congestion in the city has noticeably improved.

An interesting old Spanish service is to be found in the centre of Pereira; *Los Escribanes*. These 'scribes' help locals with legal documents and filling in official forms, working on the street with their typewriters. They are to be found, in office hours, in front of the post office on Calle 19.

Some way from the city centre, but worth a visit, is the small **Museo del Oro Quimbaya**, of the Banco de la República, at Avenida 30 de Agosto, No 35-08. It features many Quimbaya pottery and gold items including 3 exquisite 2 cm high face masks. Alongside is a library and a music auditorium with a daily programme of classical music. Entry free. Also in the outskirts is the **Museo de Arte de Pereira**, Avenida Sur, No 19-88, T3255509, in a modern building near the bus terminal.

Sleeping

L *Meliá Pereira*, Cra 13, No 15-73 T3350770, F3350675, Aptdo Aéreo 4050, restaurant, bars, swimming pool, well appointed top hotel, tourist service in lobby.

AL *Soratama*, Cra 7, No 19-20, T3358650, on Plaza de Bolívar, restaurant, parking. **A** *Gran*, C 19, No 9-19, T3359500, including breakfast, early 20th century building, good restaurant, bar, travel agency, well managed, recommended. **B** *Marandúa*, Cra 8, No 14-73, T3357131/3356192, F3334081, clean, central, recommended. **B** *Torreón*, Av 30 de Agosto, no 41-37, T3360340, F3360304, with breakfast, business hotel, a/c, good services.

C *Cataluña*, C 19, No 8-61, T3336123/3354527, F3330791, 2 floors up, friendly, hot water, spacious, a bit gloomy. **C** *Royal*, C 16, No 7-56, T3358847, 2 floors up, with bath and hot water, clean, recommended.

D *Residencias Minerva*, C 18, No 7-32, T3334493, central, clean, safe, TV; **D** *Colón*, Cra 8, No 17-30, T3356400/3358339, F3356240, with bath, TV, meals to order. **D** *Ocmara*, Cra 8, no 24-55, T3350531, with bath/breakfast, cheaper without, fan, secure, hot water, clean, cable TV, friendly, recommended.

E *Polo*, C 20, No 4-21, T3250514, three blocks from plaza, TV. **E** *Residencia Edén No 1*, C 15, Cra 10, near market, clean, friendly, but not a safe area after dark. **E** *Fontana*, Cra 9, No 15-71, T3342061, with bath, cheaper without, near market, unsavoury area but otherwise OK.

Eating

El Vitral, Cra 15, no 11-55, T3250802, international food, very good. *Pastelería Lucerna*, C 19, No 6-49, large coffee shop, garden with fountain, good cakes, snacks, ice cream, Swiss owned, clean. *El Galeón*, C 20, No 8-29, *menú* US$2.50, good. *El Balcón de los Arrieros*, Cra 8, No 24-65, overlooking Parque del Lago, other branches elsewhere in the city, local and international, reasonable food. *Mezón Español*, C 14, no 25-57, T3215636, good Spanish food,

To Manizales

DOSQUEBRADAS

LA POPA

Parque La Libertad

Cra 8

Cra 10

Nuestra Señora del Carmen

Monumento a Los Fundadores

Av Circunvalar

Av Ricaurte

N

0 metres 500
0 yards 500

recommended. *A Mis Amigos*, Cra 15/C 5, T3314399, Argentine specialities, good. *Casa de Toño*, C 24, no 8-68, T3338560, good local dishes, friendly owner, good value. There are several Chinese restaurants in the city, eg *Nuevo Hong Kong*, C 21, No 8-66, and others nearby.

Vegetarian restaurants include *Naturista*, C 18, No 5-30, owner is doctor of natural medecines, good.

Cafeterías *Punto Rojo*, Cra 8, No 19-17, full meal service, open 24 hrs, good. *Grajales*, Cra 8, No 21-60, good food, also bakery. *Ricura*, Cra 8, No 21-03, quick meals. Many other fast food outlets in the centre.

There are good restaurants on the Av 30 de Agosto (the road west to the airport), including *Kisses Parilla*, No 46-05, good steaks. *La Posada Paisa*, no 48-60, T3363588, Colombian dishes, good. *El Dragón Chino*, no 48-175, Chinese. Also, past the Hotel *Meliá* on the Av Circunvalar going east, *Pizza Piccolo* at C 5, La Terraza, good Italian food, excellent pizzas, recommended.

Bars & nightclubs
There is a concentration of bars and discos along La Via Popa – Turín in Dosquebradas, cross the viaduct and then turn left through La Popa industrial zone or approach from Av del Río (see map). Try *La Cantina* or *Casa Pueblo*. There are 2 nightclubs *Remembras* and *Voces del Recuerdo* at km 5 on the road to Armenia, and several near Av Circunvalar/C 14 and C 10.

Entertainment
Cinema Several cinema complexes within 2 blocks of Plaza de Bolívar. **Theatre** *Teatro Municipal Santiago Londoño*, Centro Comercial Fiducentro, Av 30 de Agosto/C 19, T3357724, major stage productions. *Cámara de Comercio*, Cra 8/C 23, has an auditorium used for evening presentations, usually free. *Teatro Comfamiliar*, Cra 5/C 22, cultural activities.

Festivals
Feria del Libro (Book Fair), early Jul. *Fiestas de la Cosecha* (Harvest Festival), Aug. *Feria Gastronomica* (Food Fair), late Oct.

Shopping
Arts and crafts shops in the centre: *El Pitufo*, C 21, No 6-70; *El Turista*, C 23, No 7-20; *Sindamanoy*, C 23-No 7-78. **Shopping centres** (Centros Comerciales) *Alcides Arévalo*, C 19/Cra 6; *La 14*, C 17/Cra 21, opposite the bus terminal, with department stores etc.

Pereira centre

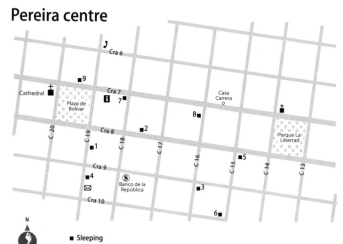

N
0 metres 100
0 yards 100

- **Sleeping**
- 1 Cataluña
- 2 Colón
- 3 Fontana
- 4 Gran
- 5 Marandúa
- 6 Residencia Eden No 1
- 7 Residencias Minerva
- 8 Royal
- 9 Soratama

Tierra Mar Aire, Av Circunvalar No 14-60, T3356565, general travel agency, good service; *Eco Sueños*, C 25, No 6-57, T3339955, F3245308, trips arranged to Ucumarí Park, Los Nevados etc, Manager: Soraya Quintana, very helpful and a fully qualified guide, recommended. Tour Operators also in the foyers of *Hotels Meliá* and *Gran*. **Tour Operators**

Local Car rental Hertz, T3360036; **National**, T3291185; **RentaCar**, T3252466. All offices at the airport. Motorcycle repairs **Bike House**, C 14, no 13-55, Local 5, T3343703. **Transport**

Long distance Air Matecaña airport is 5 km to the west of the city with good services including 2 banks with cash machines and a Telecom office with long distance facilities. Direct Avianca flights with a stop at Bogotá daily to Miami and 4 days a week to New York. To **Bogotá**, around 15 a day, Aces and Avianca. To **Medellín**, 4 most days, Aces. To **Cali**, 2 a day, Aires. To **Ibagué**, 2 a day, Aires, extended 3 days a week to Neiva and Florencia. Flights also Bucamaranga and the North Coast (Aires) local airlines to the Chocó.

Buses The new bus terminal, clean, with shops, is 1½ km south of the city centre on C 17. Bus to **Armenia**, 1 hr, US$2, a beautiful trip; to **Cali**, US$8, 4½-5 hrs, buses by night, take a colectivo by day, same price; to **Medellín**, 8 hrs, US$10; **Manizales**, US$2, 1½ hrs; to/from **Bogotá**, US$12, 7 hrs (route is via Girardot, Ibagué and Armenia).

Airline Offices *Aces*, Av Circunvalar, no 6-55, T3242237, airport T3360027; *Aires*, airport, local 28, T3261148; *Avianca/SAM*, C 19, no 6-28, T3355291, airport T3360029; *American*, C 14, no 13-55, T3344082; *COPA*, C 21, no 9-06, T3342050; *Iberia*, Cra 15, no 14-06, T3343761; *Varig*, Cra 8, no 18-37,Of 49, T3255489. **Directory**

Banks *Lloyds TSB Bank*, Cra 7, No 18-70, Suite 201, T3354389, changes Amex travellers' cheques with purchase receipt, cash against most credit cards, good rates, open 0800-1130, 1400-1600. Few other banks take travellers' cheques but many have cash machines, some of which take foreign cards, check. Many other banks in the centre. *Casas de cambio* change cash and some exchange travellers' cheques but check at what time of day: several around Cra 9/C 18, or try *Titan*, Centro Comercial Alcides Arévalo, Cra 6, C 19, good service; *Western Union*, Cra 7, No 16-50, local 111, T3351611.

Internet *Eccel*, Edificio Banco Ganadero, C 20/Cra 6A, 1st floor. *Café Internet Computar*, Cra 6, no 18-58, T/F3351474, open 0800-2100. *Netcenter*, CC Alcides Arévalo, local 108, open 0900-2100. Charges US$1.60 – US$2 per hr. **Post Office** For airmail, *Avianca*, C 19, No 6-28, T3355297. **Adpostal** C 19, No 9-75, T3341239. **Telephone** *Telecom*, Cra 6/C 18 and C 19, no 6-11. Also office in Centro Comercial Alcides Arévalo, local 108.

Laundry *Lava de Uno*, Cra 7, No 35-46, T3365447.

West of Pereira

A nice ride can be taken through the heart of coffee country along the road northwest to Tadó and Quibdó. The Río Cauca is crossed before **La Virginia**, 30 km from Pereira, which is at the point where the Río Risaralda, flowing down from the Antioquia border 60 km to the north, joins the Cauca, only to go back again to Antioquia. Sugar cane is an important product of this part of the Cauca valley. Boat trips are available on the river at La Virginia. (**E** *Nueva York*, Carrera 9, No 7-45, T3682277, F3682699; **E** *Riseralda*, Calle 8, no 6-62, T3682205, several others; also restaurant). The road then climbs the eastern slopes of the Cordillera Occidental to reach **Pueblo Rico** (basic hotels and restaurants). The many *veredas cafeteras* with their colourfully painted balconies decorated with flowers and the mountain scenery along the way are beautiful. A difficult road then continues to Quibdó (see under **Quibdó**). **Route to Chocó**

La Zona Cafetera & the Cauca Valley

An alternative route from Pereira to Pueblo Rico and the Chocó is northwest to 30 km **Marsella** noted for the **Alexander von Humboldt Gardens**, a well laid out and carefully maintained botanical display, with cobbled paths and bamboo bridges, fully worth a visit. There is an experimental *guadua* (bamboo) station here. Also nearby is the canyon of the Río Nona as it drops down from the plateau to the valley of the Río Cauca. From Marsella there is a path which leads up to a fine viewpoint, best in the early morning, when the Cauca valley and the Tatamá National Park can be seen to the West, and Pereira and the Nevado del Ruiz to the east. Just outside the town is **AL** *Ecohotel Los Lagos*, 1 km on the road to Pereira, T3685164, F3685430, mainly a convention hotel but enquire if you wish to stay or visit. This site was originally a gold mine which was then reclaimed to become a coffee *finca* only to have the business destroyed by the *broca* insect. The house has been restored as a hotel and the grounds are now a habitat for exotic plants and birds with several lakes for fishing. Buses run from Pereira to Marsella.

Continue west to cross the Cauca at Belalcázar and the Río Risaralda at Viterbo for Apia and Pueblo Rico.

Parque Nacional Tatamá

At Apia there is a road south to **Santuario** from where excursions can be made to the **Parque Nacional Tatamá**. This is an area of deep forested valleys and steep ridges rising to several peaks over 3,800 m. There is a recommended path up the Río San Rafael from Santuario to a series of waterfalls. Longer treks to the ridges and peaks are difficult because of the terrain, high rainfall and vegetation. Camping is possible at *fincas* lower down, and elsewhere in the Park there are religious establishments that may offer you hospitality. Permission to visit the Park is required: if you do not have a permit when you arrive, ask in Santuario.

East of Pereira

Otún Quimbaya National Sanctuary

About 14 km east of Pereira on an unpaved road is La Suiza at the entrance to the **Santuario de Fauna y Flora (SFF) Otún Quimbaya**; a 489 ha protected area administered by the MA as a National Park. The park protects one of the last remaining areas of Andean forest in Riseralda between 1,800 m and 2,400 m and includes Andean pine and wax palms.

It forms a biological corridor between Ucumarí Park (see below) and Los Nevados National Park. There are marked paths leading to waterfalls, including one of 130 m at El Topacio. There is a 40 bed *cabaña*, US$7.50 per night, camping US$12.50 per site for five people. Meals available. Fishing permit US$3 per day. Entrance to the park, US$1 per person, US$150 per vehicle. On foot, La Suiza is 5 hours from Salento and 8 hours from Laguna del Otún. From El Manzano on the main Pereira-Armenia road it is 4 hours walk to La Suiza. Bus from Pereira to La Suiza (Transportes La Florida) US$2.50. Permit and information from CARDER, Pereira.

Ucumarí Park

From Pereira, a 2-4 day excursion is recommended to the beautiful **Ucumarí Park** (Parque Ucumarí), about 25 km southeast of the city on the slopes of Los Nevados. The Park, over 4,000 ha in extent, stretches up from the Río Otún to the *páramo* of the Cordillera (see **Los Nevados** map, page 295). This is one of the few places where the Andean spectacled bear survives – the only native South American bear. Much of the Park is high Andean forest but above 4,000 m in Los Nevados National Park are spectacular *frailejón* plants. The Park also has many waterfalls and an abundance of butterflies. Permission to visit must be obtained from **Carder** (see above under **Tourist offices**). There is excellent camping, US$3 per person or US$30 for three good meals and room for the

night at *La Pastora* refuge (2,450 m), two hours walk from the roadhead at El
Cedral in the Park. Here Andean bears are kept in a compound in natural surroundings (you won't see them anywhere else in the Park). You can arrange
inclusive trips from Pereira, typically about US$45 per person for a two-day
visit. For public transport to El Cedral, see below.

From *La Pastora* a good path follows the Río Otún up toward its source in the **Laguna**
National Park. At 3,600 m there is the possibility to stay (prearranged) at *El* **Del Otún**
Bosque on the edge of the *páramo*, mules are also available. From there it is about
5 km through a zone dominated by *frailejones*, to **Laguna del Otún** at 3,900 m at
the foot of the Nevado de Santa Isabel. This 80 ha lake has many species of birds,
especially ducks, and rainbow trout thrive here. The lake's origin is a lava flow
which blocked the exit at the south end. Nearby there are several gas vents, some
bubbling into the lake, and bright yellow sulphur deposits can be seen. The walk
from *La Pastora* is about eight hours up. The higher areas are very exposed, frequently misty and storms can be violent and dangerous. A guide is strongly recommended. The lake can be reached by road from the North, and on foot from
Los Termales de Santa Rosa de Cabal. Fishing and camping permits required.

Long distance hikes can be made to the **Nevado del Ruiz** and elsewhere in
Los Nevados National Park (see also page 295). Take a *chiva* from Pereira at
0700/1100 daily, additional *chivas* at weekends, to **El Cedral** (1½ hours –
return at 1630), at the entrance to the Park. Reservations for the *refugio* must
be made in advance at **Carder**. Enquire there if a guide, eg Wilson Cardona or
Soraya Quintana, is available for tours to the volcano. Camping is possible in
the park, but check with the rangers.

Along the road from Pereira to Armenia are some nice places to eat, art galler- **Pereira to**
ies and craft centres. This is the heart of the *Zona Cafetera*. The coffee grows **Armenia:**
here up to about 2,000 m above which is forest providing some communities **Filandia**
with wood products as a livelihood. One such place is **Filandia**, a pleasant village 7 km off the main road. Unhappily, fire destroyed part of the town near the
central plaza in 1996, but the unusual church was not harmed. The town jail,
100 m down from the *Farmacia Bristol* on the plaza is worth a visit – from the
outside. The village was used for the popular local *telenovela* – TV soap – called
Café. Baskets for coffee picking and many other uses are made here. There is
no formal accommodation in Filandia, but ask around if you end up there at
the end of the day. Because it is higher than the intervening land to the east,
there are splendid views of the Nevados, especially dramatic if the weather is
unsettled, and if there has been a recent storm, you may well see snow on the
mountains well below the normal permanent snowline of about 4,800m.
There are frequent buses from Pereira and Armenia.

Well into the foothills of the Cordillera and on a promontory above the valleys **Salento**
which lead up to the Nevados of Quindío and Tolima, is the little town of *Phone code: 96*
Salento. This is a special place, clean and brightly painted with an attractive *Altitude: 1,985 m*
plaza with a curious old derelict building in the corner setting off the neatness
of the rest. Up Carrera 6 (continuation of the north side of the plaza) leads to a
250 step climb, 14 stations of the cross to measure your progress, to an outstanding viewpoint, overlooking the upper reaches of the Quindío and
Cardenas rivers known as the Corcora valley. To the west many kilometres of
the Cordillera Occidental can be seen. This is some of the finest countryside
and mountain views in Colombia. It is a popular weekend resort for Colombians for walking, riding and trekking but quiet during the week and relatively
few foreign tourists visit. The local *fiestas* are held in the first week of January.

La Zona Cafetera & the Cauca Valley

● ●

 Palma de cera – wax palm

Alexander von Humboldt called the stands of wax palms that he saw in this region 'the forest above the forest' to describe the strange sight of these trees which tower above the wooded areas in which they often grow.

There are many known varieties of palm tree (around 2,600), many of which are native to South America. From their leaves, nuts and bark come a multitude of products, from fibres, sugars, edible fruits to milk and oils. Several varieties produce oily waxes from their leaves or bark, the best known of the latter is the carnaube palm, a native of Central and South America: the resin is used for polishes, varnishes and tallow.

The wax palm was first identified by Alexander von Humboldt and Aime, Bonpland at the beginning of the 19th century who named the species Ceroxylon Alpinum. Around 1860, Hermann Karsten distinguished two varieties, naming the one seen in this part of Colombia Ceroxylon quindiunense, which is the official name today.

Formerly, these trees were to be seen in various parts of Colombia on the western flanks of the Cordilleras from Norte de Santander to Nariño and Antioquia to Valle de Cauca, where the land is between 2,000 m and 3,000 m, and the climate is cool and humid, typical of cloud forest. The trees take up to 15 years to establish themselves, ideally within a heavy forest environment unsuitable for animals interested in the young shoots as food. Once settled, however, they have a life span of 200 years or more and can grow to over 60m, the highest of all varieties of palm trees. Unfortunately, forest clearing for livestock and general cultivation has condemned the trees even where they were not specifically cut down, or their fronds collected for Palm Sunday festivals. Also, as the name implies, they were tapped or rather scraped for the wax, widely used in the past for candles. Eventually this also kills the tree.

In 1949, the palma de cera was proposed as the National Tree of Colombia, but it was not until 1985 that Congress passed the Decree, and prohibited the cutting or commercial use of the tree.

The Corcora valley is the best place to appreciate them. Some sections of cloud forest remain, and the trees can be seen towering over the canopy. Others are in magnificent isolation, particularly impressive when they show above the cloud filling the valleys, They do not reach the 90m of the highest Californian redwoods, but because of their slender cylindrical trunks, and their visual impact, you can forgive those who claim these are the tallest trees in the world.

● ●

Sleeping and eating A *Mis Bohíos*, on the road to the Corcora Valley (see below), **AL** with 3 meals, good facilities. **B** *La Posada del Café*, Cra 6, No 3-08, T7593012, F7593292, with bath and breakfast, clean, pleasant patio. **D** *El Caserón*, Cra 6, No 2-46, T7593090, with bath, pleasant patio, cooking facilities, good restaurant with trout specialities. *La Fogata de Salento*, Cra 3, esquina Las Colinas, T7593248, good foo.; *Café Patacón y Trucha*, on Plaza, good fish. There are other places to eat and to stay, ask around, but make arrangements early in the day. After a good day out, enjoy a hot drink of *agua panela con limón* in the cool of the evening.

Tourist offices For information about the area, contact *Fundación Herencia Verde*, C Real (Cra 6), No 2-15, Salento, T7593142 or the same organization in Cali, C 4 Oeste, No 3A-32, T880-8484, F881-3257. Trips can be arranged with guides and extended to the Parque Nacional de los Nevados and Nevado del Tolima.

Transport Microbuses (Cootranscir) to **Armenia** hourly, US$1.40, 40 mins, taxi US$7; to **Pereira** hourly, US$2.50, 1 hr; to **Medellín** colectivos 0400, 0930 and 1100 daily, US$14, 5 hrs.

Above Salento is the Cocora valley, part of the upper reaches of the Río   **Valle de Cocora**
Quindío. The centre of the valley (known as 'Cocora') is 12 km up from
Salento along a rough track, jeeps from the plaza take about 40 minutes, US$6.
Here there are three restaurants (*Las Orillas, Las Palmas,* T7593190, and
Bosques de Cocora, T7593212) all serving food at weekends, check in Salento if
they are open during the week. Camping is available at Bosques de Cocora.
There is also a trout farm.

About 5 km beyond Cocora is the **Acaime Natural Reserve**, at 2,770 m,
with a visitor centre, ponies for hire, accommodation for 20 and a small restaurant. This is the most important wax palm zone in Colombia (see previous
page), one of the reasons for the many varieties of humming birds, parrots,
toucans and other wild life that can be seen feeding on the fruit of the palm.

A little before Acaime is *Finca La Montaña*, the end of the vehicular track,
where there is a nursery for the wax palm. It is overlooked by Morro Gacho
(see below). Jeeps take 20 minutes from Cocora, and the remaining 2 km to
Acaime is a steep walk down across the infant Río Quindío and up the other
side; approximately one hour.

Above Acaime there are many trails into the high mountains. Day trips
include **Cerro Morro Gacho**, 3,450 m and **Alto El Español**, 3,600 m, both
steep walks through the forest of the Natural Reserve. The trip to **Paramillo
del Quindío**, 4,700 m, one of the principal mountains of Los Nevados, takes
3-4 days, via *Finca Argentina* (3,400 m, private *finca*, camping) and a total of
12 hours ascent from Cocora to the top. This is an exposed rocky summit but
not technically difficult. There are the remnants of a crater on the summit and
climbers occasionally pitch their tents here on the grey/yellow sand. There are
other *fincas*/camping sites that can be used on this trip.

The ascent of Nevado del Tolima 5,221 m, normally takes three days up, stay-   **Nevado del**
ing at *Estrella de Agua* (3,170 m) cabin, and *Finca Primavera* (3,680 m), and a   **Tolima**
two-day descent. Again there are variants, including camping at *Laguna El
Encanto* midway between Tolima and Quindío, from which both can be
climbed. You will need snow equipment for Tolima, ice axe and crampons recommended, but this too is not difficult. There is a shorter route from the south,
see under Ibagué.

The whole upland area is subject to wide temperature changes during the
day depending on cloud cover and very cold nights. Route finding in this fea-
tureless country can be especially difficult in mist and guides are strongly
recommended.

Details of what is available, prearranging places to stay, guides, transport etc
can be found in Salento. Guides cost around US$30 per day, mules US$20 per
day. An excellent map of the south part of Los Nevados, see under Armenia –
Tourist Offices below. See also under Ibagué (page 236).

Armenia

Armenia, capital of Quindío Department, has a tragic recent past. It has been   *Phone code: 967*
affected by some of the worst earthquakes in the area, with that of January 1999   *Colour map2, grid C3*
being particularly devastating. Most buildings in the centre of the city were   *Population: 220,000*
damaged, about 30% destroyed. Those who knew the city of high rise build-   *Altitude 1,838 m*
ings and rather dark, bustling streets will now find it unrecognizable. In early
2000 the centre was a major building site.

In spite of this, Armenia is a busy place, busier than either Pereira or
Manizales. The Rodrigo Arenas Betancur **Monumento al Esfuerzo** in the

Plaza de Bolívar poignantly portrays the present attitude of the local population. New construction is of high quality and hotels and restaurants are fresh and comfortable. There's no reason to leave Armenia out of your itinerary. Indeed, tourists and business visitors are especially welcome at this time, though some services remain in temporary buildings and will eventually move. Enquire locally in the meantime.

Ins & outs **Getting there** **Air** Direct Aces flights from Bogotá and Medellín connect with domestic and international flights. From Cali and the south, travellers use Pereira. The airport is at El Eden, 13 km south of the city. **Road** Comprehensive bus services run to Armenia from major Colombian cities. The bus station is at Cra 19/C 35, south of the city.

Getting around The interesting part of the city is within walking distance of the Plaza de Bolívar, and in 2000 this is the way to see the 'resurrection' after the earthquake. There are important attractions in Quindío outside the city for which buses, taxis, tours or your own transport will be required.

Tourist offices Tourist information at *Corporación de Fomento y Turismo,* C 20, No 15-31, T7410441. *Corporación Autónomo Regional de Quindío (CRQ),* Caja Agraria Building, Cra 17, No 18-20, 4, 5 y 6th floors, T7411633/7412810, for information on parks and natural reserves. For information on trips to Los Nevados, contact D Duque, T7476818. Excellent map of Paramillo del Quindío and Nevado de Tolima, scale 1:40,000, available. Also for maps and information, *Instituto Geográfico Agustín Codazzi*, Cra 17, No 19-29, open Mon-Fri 0730-1100, 1400-1600.

The surrounding Quindío countryside is a major coffee zone, and the slopes of the Cordillera here are home to the wax palm (see under **Salento** above). Armenia, founded in 1889, suffers when international coffee prices fall and they have been low since the mid 1990s, but this is an enterprising sector of Colombia and you will see many new and different agricultural crops and activities developing. One of particular interest is the opening of many fine *fincas* to visitors for holidays; see 'Staying on Coffee Farms', page 311.

Sights The central square, **Plaza de Bolívar**, has a fountain and two bronze sculptures, a conventional Bolívar by Roberto Henau Buritacá, and a fine example of

Palma de Cera

Rodrigo Arenas Betancur's work, the *Monumento al Esfuerzo*. The plaza has lost many of the surrounding buildings including part of the Quindío administration building (services relocated to the outskirts of the city). The striking modern **cathedral** was badly damaged but repairs are well advanced and we understand no changes will be incorporated, and, if so, the following description will stand: the facade is triangular in shape with a tall bell tower on the right. Inside, the nave continues the form and leaves a light airy feeling, accentuated by

Armenia

the fine modern stained glass. There is also an impressive bronze figure of Christ. Well worth a visit. Also of interest is the **San Francisco church** with some notable stained glass windows which overlooks the market covering four blocks in the centre of the city (this church is also closed as a result of the earthquake). There are many stalls of local *artesanía*, basket work is a local speciality, good prices. **Parque Sucre** is a colourful square with an ancient ceiba tree and a bust of Marshal Ayacucho. To the south in the oldest part of the city is Parque Uribe Uribe where concerts are held from time to time.

The **Museo Quimbaya**, Avenida Bolívar, Calle 40 Norte, T7493820, is on the edge of town on the road to Pereira, take a city bus or taxi. It was designed by Rogelio Salmona and opened in 1986 and has a fine collection of ceramics and gold pieces from the local Quimbaya culture, well displayed. There is a cafetería and an open-air theatre for cultural presentations. ■ *Open Tue-Sun 1000-1700.*

Sleeping Many hotels were lost to the 1999 earthquake. All those listed suffered damage but have been repaired or re-built and are therefore virtually new. Since hotel accommodation is reduced, prior reservation is recommended.

AL *Centenario*, C 21, no 18-20, T7443143, F7411321, central, fully refurbished 2000, restaurant, bar, sauna, parking, conference facilities. **B** *Zuldemayda*, C 20, no 15-38, T7410580, F7412343, enquire for discounts, restaurant, popular, business hotel. **B** *Maitamá*, C 21, no 16-45, T7410488, F7449308, friendly, central, moved and rebuilt 1999, recommended.

C *Mariscal Sucre*, Cra 17, no 18-33, T7410867, discounts possible, with bath, hot water, TV. **E** *Moderno Aristi*, C 18, no 19-67, T7441286, F7410873, with bath, hot water, TV. **F** *Los Viajeros*, Cra 18, no 17-22, T7442039, with bath, laundry services, cooking facilities, clean, OK.

Eating *La Fogata*, Av Bolívar, no 14N-39, T7495980, international menu, expensive but very good. *Casa Verde*, Cra 14, no 11A-25, T7466093, sea food, meat dishes, moderate-expensive. *Mateo Madero*, Cra 14, no 35N-96, T7493716, steaks, good value. *Rincón Costeño*, Cra 14, no 5-79, T7462443, seafood. *Pastelería Lucerna*, C 20, no 14-43, T7411946, light meals, good quality pasties, newly opened 2000, recommended. *Las Vegas*, Cra 14, no 11-46, T7459191, chicken and meat dishes, clean, open untill 0100, good quick meals. *Parador Los Geraníos*, Cra 14, no 53N-34 (on road to Pereira), T7493474, typical food, very popular, good value, speciality *frijol garra picada*, recommended.

Transport **Air** El Edén, 13 km from city. Scheduled direct flights only to: **Bogotá**, 4 daily Aces, and **Medellín**, 3 daily, Aces.

Buses Terminal 15 blocks from centre at Cra 19/C 35. To **Ibagué**, US$4. To/from **Bogotá**, hourly, 9 hrs, US$13. To **Neiva**, Flota Magdalena, 0100, 0400, 2230, US$16. **Cali**, Expreso Bolivariano, US$7, 3 hrs, frequent service. To Pereira, US$2.

Directory **Communications Post Office** Avianca (airmail, Cra 14, no 19-38; **Telecom** C 19/Cra 19.

Parque Nacional del Café Some 12 km northwest of Armenia is **Montenegro** (several basic *hosterías*, good restaurants and coffee shops) near which is the **Parque Nacional del Café**, 1 km from Pueblo Tapao, opened in 1994. You can tour this former coffee *finca* and see a fine view of the area from a tower in the park. There are restaurants, a botanical garden with a wide variety of exotic shrubs and orchids, ecological walks, a Quimbaya Indian cemetery and a children's section of Indian myths and legends illustrated with figures and storyboards. There is also an interesting museum which covers all aspects of the origins, cultivation, marketing and consumption of coffee.

La Zona Cafetera & the Cauca Valley

The full walk down past the 1946 Willys jeep, through the gardens, coffee plantations to the river (don't miss the fine stands of *guadua* bamboo) and back through the forest, the Indian section and the orchid garden takes a leisurely 1½ hours (good walking shoes advised). A cableway links to a children's theme park with many facilities (additional charges). ■ *The park is open Tue-Sun, 0900-1600, US$4, children US$2.50, parking US$1, T7524174, F7536095. Take a bus (US$0.35), or colectivo (US$0.45) from Armenia to Montenegro and then a jeep marked 'Parque' (US$0.25) or taxi (US$2) to the entrance. Taxi from Armenia, US$5.*

Quimbaya, an attractive small town 17 km north of Montenegro is known for its Festival of Light (*Fiesta de Velas y Faroles*) in December each year. Nearby is a new (2000) agricultural park known as PANACA (Parque Nacional de la Cultura Agropecuaria), centred on the country life of this region with sections on farm animals, milk the cows and ride buffaloes, but also demonstrates the prodigious variety and capacity of this part of Colombia. Well organised displays, good typical restaurant. ■ *US$4 adults, US$2.50 children, open daily, T7520464. Trips can be arranged from Armenia, Pereira and a day visit including transport and meals from Cali, US$17.50, T8837777 (Cali).*

Also in the region at Vereda Palermo is La Granja de Mamá Lulú, T7521260, a self sustaining family farm, which demonstrates the production of a wide range of local foodstuffs. Well presented, food and lodging available.

Southwest of Montenegro is Puerto Samaria on the Río La Vieja where guadua/balsa rafts are available. Trips can be arranged past fine stands of bamboo down river to Puerto Alejandría, return by jeep. Information in Quimbaya, at travel agents, or *Caminos del Mundo*, Calle 19, no 14-17, T7412123, Armenia.

The decline of coffee prices since 1992 has had a significant effect on the Colombian coffee *finca*. Coffee is still by far the most important agricultural product of the area, but there has been a good deal of diversification into other crops as varied as flowers, asparagus and bamboo amongst many others. Some *finqueros* have gone for cattle ranching but this appears to be something of a last resort in a land so basically productive. Some years ago the idea caught on to open the farms to tourism. Many of the traditional coffee *fincas* were large family homes or groups of homes on the family estate and letting these out to guests is a logical move. No two *fincas* are the same – they come in all shapes and sizes from beautiful historic country mansions to modest even primitive accommodation. All however bring you close to the people of the countryside and their way of life, and a chance to enjoy the hospitality and sample the fresh products of these friendly *finqueros*. Colombian families living in the cities are increasingly spending their holidays in such places and this is being broadened to include foreign visitors. For information on the possibilities, contact travel agents (*Eco-Guías* in Bogotá is specially recommended), or shop around in Manizales, Pereira and Armenia. *Turiscafé*, Calle 19, no 5-48, Oficina 901, T3254157, Pereira has good information. The tourist offices in these cities will also advise on visits to coffee farms and there is information at the Parque Nacional del Café (see above). Spanish is a help but not essential, ask about languages when booking. Also enquire about transport arrangements if you wish to tour around while staying on a *finca*.

Staying on Coffee Farms

La Zona Cafetera & the Cauca Valley

The Cauca Valley

From Pereira and Armenia roads run west to Cartago, at the northern end of the rich Cauca Valley, which stretches south for about 240 km but is little more than 30 km wide. The road, the Panamericana, goes south up this valley to Cali and Popayán, at the southern limit of the valley proper. There it mounts the high plateau between the Western and Central Cordilleras and goes through to Ecuador. From Cali a railway (no passengers) and a road run west to the Pacific port of Buenaventura. The Valley is one of the richest in Colombia. From Cartago south the Río Cauca is navigable by barges up to Cali.

Two roads go from Armenia to the Panamericana. A newer, direct road with heavy traffic, joins the highway 8 km south of Zarzal.

The slower old road emerges 9 km further south. Before it drops into the Cauca Valley is **Caicedonia**, near which is a coffee *finca* owned by Dolly and Umberto Samin de Botero, T(967)458530, who will show you around their plantations, make arrangements first. Further on is **Sevilla**; C *Hotel Sevilla*, good, Calle 49, No 49-70, T696434; others cheaper. In the main plaza of Sevilla is the *Cooperativa Café Cultores*, who have good information and arrange day trips to coffee *fincas*.

Cartago

Phone code: 965
Colour map 2, grid C3
Population: 130,000
Altitude: 920 m

Cartago, about 25 km southwest of Pereira, is on the Río La Vieja close to where it joins the Río Cauca which then takes to the gorge separating the two *cordilleras*. Coffee, tobacco and cattle are the main products. The town and the local area are noted for embroidered textiles, including clothing and table linen, some of the best in Colombia. There are believed to be more than 15,000 embroiderers in Cartago. A good place to see them is a *Fundación Pro-Bordados*, Carrera 4, no 15-09.

Founded in 1540 it was at one time the principal city of the region and was an important port on the Río Cauca (see also under Pereira, history). It still has some colonial buildings, particularly the very fine **Casa del Virrey**, Calle 13 no 4-29, T635979, mudejar style interior. It houses a small museum. Visit the neoclassical **Catedral de Nuestra Señora del Carmen** built about 1830, with the cross apart from the main building. There are three other churches in Cartago, **San Jorge** which overlooks the Plaza de Bolívar, **San Francisco** and **Guadalupe**, both on Carrera 4 and colonial in style. The oldest church is probably the **Capilla de San Jerónimo** on the outskirts of the town.

Sleeping D *Don Gregorio*, Cra 5, No 9-59, T 627491, swimming pool, a/c. **F** *Río Pul*, Cra 2, No 2-146, fan and bath, clean, recommended. **F** *Central*, Cra 6, No 11-51, safe, good parking. **F** *Casa Turista*, Cra 6 y Calle 11, clean, fan. Many others in the area around the bus terminals (Cra 9) and railway station (Cra 9 y C 6).

Eating *Mullipán*, Cra 6 y C 12, good cheap *meriendas*. *El Portal*, Cra 6 y C 11, good *churrascos*.

Transport Buses To **Cali**, US$6, 3½ hrs; to **Armenia**, US$1.75, 2-3 hrs; to **Pereira**, US$1.50, 45 mins; to **Medellín**, US$12, 7 hrs.

Directory Banks *Banco Popular*, and *Bancafé* in Plaza Bolívar will exchange cash, but not travellers' cheques. **Communications Internet**: *Compumax*, Plaza Bolívar, opposite Cathedral. **Post Office** on Plaza Bolívar.

La Victoria, 36 km south of Cartago, is a pleasant, small colonial town with a shady plaza (**A1** *Finca San Jose*, Cra 5, no 5-39, T2203608, luxury cabañas; **E** *Hotel Turista*, family atmosphere, clean, one block from the plaza; several restaurants.)

You can cross the Río Cauca by turning right off the road going to the south and 10 km (paved road) further on is **La Unión**, a small centre for grape production. **A** *Los Viñedos*, km 1, T2292020, rooms and suites; **B** *Bella Montaña*, Carretera Via Toro, T2293601, a/c, pool, restaurant, family hotel; **C** *Real*, Carrera 15, no 13-49, T2292601, with bath, a/c, including breakfast. The countryside around offers good walks.

About 18 km south of La Unión is **Roldanillo** (San Sebastián de Roldanillo), founded in the 16th century. It has several colonial buildings, eg the *Capilla La Ermita*. A special attraction is the modern museum of paintings by the Colombian artist Omar Rayo and other Latin Americans. There are several hotels. A road runs east to the Panamericana at Zarzal, 49 km south of Cartago along which are displayed more works of art. After the Armenia road junction is Andalucía (30 km – *Balneario Campestre*, car camping). **Tuluá**, 18 km south of Andalucía, is an important centre of sugar production, cattle ranching and banana plantations.There are several hotels, and many good places to eat along Calle Sarmiento in the centre of town.

Buga

Buga is an old colonial city which is a centre for cattle, rice, cotton, tobacco and sugar cane. Founded in 1650, its modern **Basílica del Señor de los Milagros** contains the image of the Miraculous Christ of Buga, who appeared to an Indian woman in the 16th century, and many miraculous cures have been claimed since then. It is a place to which pilgrimages are made especially in September. There are several other significant churches in the town including the original cathedral on the main plaza, **Catedral de San Pedro**, rebuilt after the 1766 earthquake with gold decorations on the altar, and a religious museum. On the road to Buenaventura, before the Río Cauca, is the **Laguna de Sonso Reserve**, which is good for birdwatching.

Phone code: 922
Colour map 2, grid C2
Ppulation: 99,000

Sleeping AL *Guadalajara*, C 1, no 13-33, T2272611, F2282468, comfortable hotel, some suites, pool, cabins for families, good restaurant, self service cafeteria. **A** *Condado Plaza*, C 7, no 13-48, T/F2284545, good restaurant. **F** *Residencial Palermo*, C 9, no 9-82, T2272552, with bath, clean. Other *residencias* near the *Basílica*, check room before taking.

Eating *La Barra*, Cra 14, no 4-02, near Basílica, local dishes, *Sancocho* speciality. *San José del Hato*, 2 km on road to Palmira, local dishes, family restaurant.

Transport Buses To Cali, US$2.50. Toll 22 km south of Buga.

Lago Calima

If you take the road from Buga across Río Cauca and over the Cordíllera towards Buenaventura you come to the man-made **Lago Calima**. Many treasures of the Calima culture are said to have been left, to be flooded by the lake, when the dam was built. The northern route round the lake goes through **Darién** with a new archaeological museum. ■ *Open Tue-Fri 0800-1700, Sat-Sun 1000-1800, with good displays of Calima and other Colombian cultures.* This is now an important centre for watersports and is good for sailing.

Sleeping There is a growing number of weekend houses and many leisure activities on the lake. **AL** *Los Veleros*, T(92) 661-3701 (Cali), swimming pool. **E** Darién, clean, cold showers, good, friendly. **E** *Sulevar*, clean, cold showers, restaurant, parking; also cabins available at a Centro Náutico on the lakeside. Camping possible near the village. Plenty of places to eat naer the lakeside.

Tourist office At C 10, No 6-21.

Buses There are direct buses from Buga, 2 hrs, and Cali, 4 hrs.

La Zona Cafetera & the Cauca Valley

🖙 House of bamboo

One of the increasingly important products of this region of Colombia is guadua, one of the largest varieties of bamboo. Bamboo is itself the tallest of the poaceae or grass family, and guadua is a genus of the bambusoideae sub family. Bambusa is the local name for guadua in Colombia.

It grows in clumps that virtually exclude other vegetation and to a height of 20 m or more, at altitudes of 1,500 m-2,000 m, best in well watered protected hollows. It is slow growing and takes years to reach maturity.

The Indians used guadua extensively for dwelling construction before the arrival of the Spaniards, but other building materials were favoured by the settlers: stone, brick and then cement and concrete. In recent years, however, the value of this resource has been rediscovered. Not only is guadua extremely strong and resilient, able to

support many times its own weight, but it also has a flexibility that is important in constructions subject to earthquake danger. Significantly, everywhere in Armenia, guadua is being used as scaffolding for the rebuilding after the 1999 earthquake. Apart from major building support, it is now being used for roofing, guttering, fencing, furniture, bridge construction and many other products.

The 'stigma' of it being synonymous with rural misery is fast disappearing and you will see many ways in which this natural renewable resource is being put to good use.

There is an interesting museum in Córdoba, 20 km south of Armenia, Centro de la Guadua, demonstrating the many uses now made of bamboo and selling typical items, including furniture.

Taking the southern route round the lake, 42 km from Buga is the **D** *Hotel del Lago Calima* set in very pleasant surroundings on the edge. There is no swimming pool, but some brave people swim in the lake, which is cold at about 16°C. Cabins and camping available.

Palmira
Phone code: 92
Colour map 3, grid A3
Population: 287,000
Altitude: 1,003 m

Palmira is 47 km south from Buga. Good tobacco, coffee, sugar, rice and grain are grown, and there is a College of Tropical Agriculture, specializing in vegetable research and agricultural diseases. The best road south is from Palmira through Candelaria and Puerto Tejada, avoiding Cali, to Popayán. It is paved, straight, with not much traffic. The town has a distinguished cathedral with an imposing 85m tower, and the *Bosque Municipal*, a small zoo.

Sleeping B *Las Victorias*, Cra 32 Vía a Candelaria, T2722666. **E** *Pacífico No 1*, C 30, No 32-55, T2725633, with bath, simple but nice. **F** *Residencias Belalcázar*, C 30, No 31-29, T2723782, with bath, **G** without, clean, friendly, good value. Many other cheap places.

Eating *Ricuras*, C 30, No 32-16, good local dishes. *Paradero los Parrales*, good breakfast, good service, clean.

Transport Taxi to Cali, 29 km southwest, US$8; bus US$0.75, Transportes Palmira, terminal on C 30, near Cra 33.

At La Manuelita, 5 km north of Palmira, is a famous sugar estate. Between El Cerrito and Palmira, any of three roads running east will reach, in 12 km, the fine restored colonial *hacienda* of **El Paraíso**, where the poet Jorge Isaacs (author of *María*, a Colombian classic) lived and wrote. Entry US$0.50; there is a café. About 9 km from El Paraíso is a **Museo de la Caña de Azúcar** (sugar cane museum) in the **Hacienda Piedechinche**, an 18th century finca, maintained with period furniture. On the second floor, the living quarters are surrounded by balconies with views over the estate. The museum covers the full story of sugar and the gardens have a wide variety of indigenous flora, with

Coffee talk

The wild coffee plant originally came from East Africa, possibly first discovered near Kaffa (Kefa) in Ethiopia. A favourite legend is that an Arab goatherd noticed his flock behaving oddly after eating the berries of the bush, so he tried it himself and was exhilarated by the experience and proclaimed his discovery to the world.

Coffee was first cultivated in South Arabia in the 15th century and in spite of a period when it was decreed intoxicating and therefore prohibited by the Koran, it gained increasing popularity first among the Arabs and their neighbours, then spread to Europe, Asia and the Americas. Coffee houses opened in London and Paris about 1650, and North America by about 1690, giving the drink a social dimension. By the end of the 17th century, production was being extended from Arabia (principally Yemen) to Ceylon, Indonesia and the West Indies (about 1715), Brazil (1727), and towards the end of the century, Colombia.

The two principal types of coffee are arabica and robusta, the latter cultivated mostly in Asia and the Indian sub-continent. Arabica varieties are milder, having about half the level of caffeine, but are less tolerant of warm humid climates and more susceptible to disease. They are however more popular with western coffee drinkers and have brought prosperity to many countries in Latin America including Colombia, which grows virtually no robusta coffee.

It is believed that coffee was brought into Colombia by Jesuit priests who first set up cultivation in Santander Department. Later it was tried in Cauca,

and only about 1850 was serious production taking place in what is now known as the Zona Cafetera. Since that time, coffee has grown in importance throughout the world and the industry claims that it is consumed by 30% of the planet's population in amounts larger than any other drink.

Colombia's coffee has been hit by several serious diseases, notably roya (rust: a leaf fungus) and broca (a bug that attacks the bean). The latter has been particularly destructive since 1988. Counter measures including the breeding of resistant plants have improved the situation. The other critical element is the world price which fluctuates wildly depending, mainly, on supply. Since 1960, efforts have been made to control the price by stockpiling and quota systems, but these have done little to help. Colombian coffee growers have suffered significantly since 1992 from low prices, exacerbated by unfavourable weather linked to El Niño reducing production while competition continues to increase. Bearing in mind that over 50% of the export earnings of the Zona Cafetera is from coffee, the need to widen the economic base is clear. Hence the move to diversify coffee farms to non-traditional agricultural products and to the new 'finca tourism' initiatives.

Anyone interested in coffee will find the full and well laid out exhibition in several rooms of the **Parque Nacional del Café**, and the connoisseur will enjoy the section of the gardens devoted to dozens of varieties of coffee trees. It is a worthy presentation of the most important money earning crop of the country.

some endangered species and examples of plants brought in by the colonists, now familiar 'residents' of Colombia. ■Open 0930-1630, closed Mon. US$0.50. Tours of Piedechinche and Hacienda El Paraíso are arranged by Comercializadora Turística Ltda, Cra 4, No 8-39, local 101, Cali (US$12, including transport, entrance fee, guided tour and lunch). Bus to El Paraíso from Palmira, Carrera 25 y Calle 26 (two before 1230), US$0.65, 30 minutes, return after 1500. There is no public transport connection between the two *haciendas*, so you must walk or arrange a taxi.

Palmira is the access point for the **Las Hermosas National Park** (Parque Nacional Natural Las Hermosas) which stretches 100 km along the spine of the

A sports crazy country

Colombians take sport very seriously. You only have to take a look at the sports facilities in the large (and even smaller) towns to see that. But you should go to a baseball or a football game while you are in the country. An international match will clear the streets and fill the bars and the atmosphere is unlike anything else you will ever experience – a cross between a riot and a giant party. Colombia's contribution to these two world games is significant. In 1997, for example, Edgar Rentería made the winning hit to clinch the World Series

baseball title for the Marlins and many Colombians, led by Faustino Asprilla have made an important impact on soccer in Europe in recent years.

Tuluá, in Valle de Cauca, was Asprilla's birthplace. Not far away in the same Department, María Isabel Urrutia was born to a humble family in the tiny village of Florencia. She startled Colombia by bringing home their first ever Olympic gold medal - and indeed the only gold medal for South America - from Sydney 2000, for the 75kg women's weightlifting.

Cordillera Central to the east of the Cauca Valley. It is a wild, remote area with virtually no facilities though MA have a cabin on the Río Nima at 3,800 m. There are canyons and waterfalls to see and the curious Toche 'stairways' near Santa Luisa, north east of Palmira. Check with MA in Cali for access.

Cali

Cali may be second to Bogotá in terms of size, but this vibrant, prosperous city is very much número uno when it comes to partying. Cali calls itself the Salsa capital of the world, and few could dispute that claim. The sensuous, tropical rythms are ubiquitous, seeming to seep from every pore of the city's being. Cali's other major claim, and rather more contentious, is that it boasts the most beautiful girls in the country. You can judge for yourself!

Phone code: 92
Colour map 3, grid A3
Population: 1.85 mn
Altitude: 1,030 m

Ins and Outs

Getting there Palmaseca **airport** (also called Alfonso Bonilla Aragón International Airport) is 20 km to the northeast of Cali. The best way to the city is by minibus, which you will find at the far end of the pick-up road outside arrivals. They will take you to the bus terminal (ground floor), on the edge of the centre, every 10 mins from 0500 up to 2100. It takes approximately 30 mins, US$1.50. From there *colectivos* to the city cost about US$1.20. Alternatively, take a taxi from the airport, US$11, 30 minutes. The minibuses to the airport, marked 'Aeropuerto', leave from the 2nd floor of the bus terminal. Note that there are direct flights to Cali from Mexico, Panama and several cities in the USA.

The **bus terminal,** at C 30N, No 2AN-29 is 25 mins walk from the centre following the river along Av 2N.

Getting around The centre of the city is comparatively small - most places of interest to the visitor are within comfortable walking distance. Transport by bus or taxi is tedious because of the density of the traffic. Cali's taxis have meters and can be flagged in the street, or ordered by telephone. Radio taxis include Taxi Libre T4444444, Taxis Valcali T4430000. Local buses cost US$0.25.

Best time to visit There is little climate variation during the year, average temperatures stay around 25°C. It is hot and humid at midday but a strong breeze which blows up in the afternoon makes the evenings cool and pleasant. Rain can come at more or less any time but Cali is shielded from the heavy rainfalls of the Pacific coast by the *Cordillera Occidental*.

Cali is bounded on the west by the *Cordillera* and to the east by the marshy plains of **Orientation**
the Río Cauca. Through the centre of the city runs the Río Cali, a tributary of the Cauca, **& safety**
with grass and exotic trees on its banks. North of the river, all streets have the suffix 'N',
and *Carreras* become *Avenidas*. The city extends southwards 15 km from the Río Cali.
Near the southern end a new area is building up around Cra 100 with the large
Unicentro shopping mall and the residential community of Ciudad Jardín.

Safety Although still associated with drug and anti-drug operations, the atmosphere in Cali is quite relaxed. However, carry your passport (or photocopy) at all times
and be prepared for police checks. At night, do not walk east or south of C 15 and Cra
10. Do not change money on the street in any circumstances and avoid all people
who approach, offering to sell. In 1999-2000, higher unemployment has increased
the incidence of robbery. Take advice on where, and where not to go.

Cortuvalle, Av 4N, No 4-10, T6615983/6605000, F6680862. *Fondo Mixto de* **Tourist Offices**
Promoción del Valle del Cauca, C 8, No 3-14, p 13, (*Cámara de Comercio* building),
T8861370, F8861399. General information on Cali and the Department of Valle de
Cauca. For national parks, **MA**, Av 3GN, No 37A-70, T6543719/20. For information on
Los Farallones de Cali and other parks, very helpful. Also *Fundación Farallones*, Cra
24B, No 2A-99 on the same subject. For information on the many privately owned
nature reserves in this part of Colombia, enquire at *Red de Reservas Naturales*, C 23N,
No 6AN-43, T6606133, F6612581. Ask for maps of Cali at these tourist offices. None are
very accurate. Try at *Instituto Geográfico Agustín Codazzi (IGAC)*, Cra 6, No 13-56,
T8811351. They have the best maps but probably out of date.

History

After the collapse of the Incas in 1533, Sebastián Belalcázar left Pizarro's army
in Peru and came north. He founded Quito in 1534 and established Popayán
and Cali in 1536. He intended to continue northwards and establish other new
settlements, but around Cali he encountered stiff resistance from the local
Indians which delayed him for several years so that others founded Antioquia
and Bogotá. The first site of the city was beside the Río Lili near the present
Ciudad Universitaria and Ciudad Jardín but it was moved north to the present
location in 1539. Cali remained a dependency of Popayán and was dominated
by Quito for 250 years, not surprising as north-south communications along
the line of the *cordillera* are so much easier than across the mountain ranges.
Indeed, until 1900 Cali was a leisurely colonial town. Then the railway came,
and Cali became a rapidly expanding industrial complex serving the whole of
southern Colombia. The railway has since been eclipsed by road and air links
but today Cali is economically closely tied in with the rest of Colombia.

The capital of Valle del Cauca Department is set in an exceptionally rich
agricultural area producing sugar, cotton, rice, coffee and cattle, and acts as the
southern capital of Colombia. It sits on the main route north from Ecuador
along the Río Cauca and controls the passage to the only important port of
Colombia's Pacific coast. Thanks to the port and the sugar industry, many
Caribbean blacks and other groups of people came to the rich valley and now
contribute to the wealth and entertainment of the city. It was originally named
Santiago de Cali, which name often officially used today. It has tropical climate, but with a freshness that makes for economic as well as cultural activity,
producing 20% of the country's GNP.

La Zona Cafetera & the Cauca Valley

Sights

Among the most interesting buildings in Cali are the church and monastery of **San Francisco,** Carrera 6, Calles 9/10. The brick church originates from 1757 and was structurally renovated inside in the 19th century and most recently in 1926. It has a fine ceiling and many 17th and 18th century images, carvings, and paintings. The altar came from Spain. A second church in the complex is the **Capilla de la Inmaculada**, with a long nave, well lit reredos and gold headed columns. The adjoining 18th century monastery has a splendidly proportioned domed belltower in the mudejar style known as the *Torre Mudejar*. On the opposite side of the square is the imposing 20 floor **Gobernación** building.

Cali's oldest church, **La Merced,** Carrera 4, No 6-117, T8804737, dates from 1545 and was constructed on the symbolic site of the founding of the city nine years earlier. It is in the classical style with a fine altar. It has been well restored by the Banco Popular. The adjoining convent houses two museums: **Museo de Arte Colonial** (which includes the church), a collection of 16th and 17th century paintings, and the **Museo Arqueológico,** Carrera 4, No 6-59, T8813229, which celebrated 20 years of operation in 2000. This houses a good precolumbian pottery collection highlighting Calima and other Southwest Colombia cultures. By the well in the courtyard is a replica of a Tierradentro tomb. ■ *Open Mon-Sat 0900-1300, 1400-1800, US$0.80.*

Opposite La Merced at Carrera 4, No 6-76, is the **Casa Arzobispal**. This is one of the earliest buildings of Cali and the only surviving two storied house of the period. Bolívar stayed here in 1822. Along Carrera 4, at No 7-17, more Indian pottery can be seen in the **Sociedad de Mejoras Públicas,** a colonial house being restored, with a very pleasant garden patio. The collection belongs to the Universidad del Valle. ■ *Open 0730-1130, 1400-1700.*

Nearby, in Banco de la República building, is the **Museo Calima (Museo de Oro),** at Calle 7, No 4-69. This is another of the national gold museums, of the usual high standard and well worth a visit. In addition to precolombian gold work, well presented, with some exquisite tiny items magnified, it has an excellent pottery collection. There is a music room and library in the basement and exhibition halls. ■ *Mon-Sat 0900-1700, entrance US$0.35.*

Another church the visitor cannot fail to notice is **La Ermita**, by the river at Carrera 1, Calles 12/13. The original church was built here in 1602, but was totally destroyed by the 1925 earthquake. It was rebuilt between 1926 and 1942 with funds from public subscription, with Cologne cathedral in mind. There is a fine marble altar and the painting 'El Señor de la Caña' reflecting the local importance of sugar cane, one of the few items that survived the earthquake. The neo-gothic blue and white exterior is striking. In the pleasant plaza in front of the church you can sit next to lifesize figures of notable *Caleños* of the past, including Joaquin de Caycedo and Jorge Isaacs. Across the street is an example of the older architecture of the city, the ornate *Colombia de Tabaco* building.

The city's centre is the **Plaza de Caicedo**, with a statue of one of the independence leaders, Joaquín de Caycedo y Cuero. Facing the square is the **Catedral Metropolitana**, a large three aisle church, with a clerestory, elaborate aisle niches and stained glass windows. The original church on the site dated from around 1539, the present building is mid 19th century. The **Palacio Nacional** is on the eastern side of the plaza, a French neo-classical style building (1933), now the city archive.

Cross the river by the delightful, pedestrianised **Puente Ortiz**, built in the 1840s, two blocks from the Plaza de Caicedo, to the **Paseo Bolívar**, alongside the Centro Administrativo Municipal (CAM) and the main post office. On the Paseo, are a bronze statue of *El Libertador* and a sculpture honouring Jorge Isaacs, the romantic 19th century novelist, depicting the characters of his novel *María*.

A special feature of the centre of Cali is the ribbon of green along the river, lined with exotic and ancient trees that always give a freshness to the heat of the day. Several sculptures were commissioned in the late 1990s, now in position along the river: look out for the *Maria Mulatta* a black bird seen everywhere along the coasts of Colombia and the splendid bronze *El Gato del Río* by Hernando Tejada, inaugurated in 1996. Also notable are the tall palms of Plaza Caicedo and the trees of the San Antonio park overlooking the west of the city. Cali prides itself on its trees. Several are marked out for conservation, for example, the huge *Ceiba* on Avenida 4N at Calle 10, by the viaduct.

Allong the river from the city centre is the **Museo de Arte Moderno La Tertulia**, Avenida Colombia, No 5-10 Oeste. It has exhibitions of South American including local art. ■ *Tue-Sat 0900-1300, 1500-1900, Sun and holidays, 1500-1900.* **Outside the centre**

To the west of the city, a popular morning 'run' is up the hill to the 18th century church of **San Antonio** on the Colina de San Antonio, built around 1747. It is a favourite place for weddings. There are some attractive colonial style houses on the way and pleasant parkland on the top with fine views of the city though partly obstructed by high-rise buildings.

For a full view of the city, you can take a taxi to the **Monumento Las Tres Cruces**, at 1,450 m, to the northwest of the city, a traditional pilgrimage site in Holy Week, or go to the huge statue of Christ **Monumento Cristo Rey**, at 1,470 m above San Antonio to the west of the city. This statue can be seen for 50 km across the Río Cauca. It is also worthwhile going up the skyscraper Torre de Cali for a view of the city, but you may have to buy an expensive meal as well.

Zoológico De Cali, Carrera 2A Oeste/Calle 14, entrance on the south bank of the Río Cali about 3 km upstream from the centre, T8927474. Interesting and well organised collection of all types of South American animals, birds and reptiles. It makes very good use of the river as it enters the city. There is a small aquarium and a new 'ant' auditorium showing interesting videos opened in 2000. ■ *Daily 0900-1700 US$2, children US$1.25.*

The orchid garden, **Orchideorama**, Avenida 2N, No 48-10, T6643256, is worth seeing: major international show annually in mid-November. ■ *Free, closed Sun.*

A popular family park is **Acuaparque de la Caña,** Carrera 8, No 39-01, El Troncal (about 4 km from the centre), T4384820, F4384817. Family entertainment including sports, swimming, riding and children's diversions.

Essentials

Central Cali L *Intercontinental*, Av Colombia, No 2-72, T8823225, F8939494. 4 restaurants including *La Taberna* with live music, casino, tennis and pool, pleasant garden, good barbecues and buffets, weekend discounts. **AL** *Dann Carlton*, Cra 2, No 1-60, T8933000, F8935000. Large rooms, art-deco comfortable restaurant, heated pool and spa, meeting rooms. **A** *Aristi*, Cra 9, No 10-04, T8822521, F8839697. Weekend discounts, art-deco style, large and old by Cali standards, unmodernized rooms cheaper, turkish baths, rooftop pool, restaurant. Recommended. **A** *Dann*, Av Colombia, No 1-40, in front of *Dann Carlton* with similar facilities, T8933000, F8934000. All spacious suites, good value. **A** *Obelisco*, Av Colombia, No 4 Oeste-29, T8933019, F8932995. Smart, some rooms have balconies, small but good. **Sleeping**

La Zona Cafetera & the Cauca Valley

B *Hostal Casa Republicana*, C 7, No 6-74, T8960949 F8960840. With breakfast, colonial house, central, attractively furnished, cable TV, restaurant, room service, parking, good value. **B** *La Merced*, C 7, No 1-65, T8824053, F8846330. Nice, comfortable, a/c, swimming pool, pleasant staff are very helpful, good restaurant, English spoken. Recommended. **B** *Royal Plaza*, Cra 4, No 11-69, T8839243, F8839955. On Plaza Caicedo, comfortable, restaurant with view, normal services.

C *San Antonio Plaza*, C 5, No 5-25, T8834219, F8811748. Friendly, central, good rooftop restaurant. **D** *Del Puente*, C 5, No 4-36, T8938290, F8938385. With bath, clean, will store luggage. Recommended. **D** *Los Angeles*, Cra 6, No 13-109, T6825616. Good. **D** *María Victoria*, C 10, No 3-38, T8823242. With bath, 24hr restaurant. **D** *Plaza*, Cra 6, No 10-29, T882-2560. Friendly, luggage stored, reasonably priced. **D** *Río Cali*, Av Colombia, No 9-80, T8803156, F8830354. With bath, good, reasonably priced meals available, old colonial building. **E** *Latino*, C 9, No 1-34, T8892435. Spacious rooms with bath, good view from roof. **F** *El Porvenir*, Cra 1, No 24-29. Shared bath, cold water, no keys, no windows but clean and quiet.

North Cali AL *Torre de Cali*, Av de las Américas, No 18N-26, T6674949 F6671817. Swimming pool, restaurant on top floor. **A** *Don Jaime*, Av 6N, No 15-25, T6672828, F6687098. With breakfast, good, restaurant. Recommended. **B** *Granada Real*, Av 8N, No 15A-31, T6614920, F6680166. Good location, a/c, restaurant, room service, parking, pleasant. **B** *Pensión Stein*, Av 4N, No 3-33, T6614927, F6675346. With breakfast, some cheaper rooms, friendly, quiet, excellent food, French, German and English spoken, Swiss-run, swimming pool, good value. Recommended.

E *Calidad House*, C 17N, No 9A-39, T/F6612338, big kitchen, laundry, will store luggage, cable TV with international channels, pleasant, good. Recommended. **E** *Iguana*, C 21N, No 9-22, T6613522. Some cheaper accommodation, converted villa, safe area, Swiss run, laundry, email service, luggage store, motorcycle parking, excursions and salsa lessons arranged, good value excellent travellers' guest house. **E** *JJ Hotel*, Av 8N, No 14-47, T6618979. With bath, cheaper without, friendly, safe area, good value. **E** *Sartor*, Av 8N, No 20-50, T6686482. Rooms with bath, central, TV available, restaurant with Italian dishes. **F** *Residencial Chalet*, Av 4N, No 15-43, T6612709. Friendly, clean, with shower, dark rooms, safe, quiet.

Out of town L *Pacífico Royal*, Cra 100B, No 11A-99, Urb Ciudad Jardín, T3307777, F3306477. In the south of the city, restaurant, good service, friendly. **C** *Turístico La Luna*, Autopista Sur, No 13-01, T5582611, F5586367. Friendly, safe, large pool, restaurant, good parking. At the airport is **B** *Aeropuerto Cali,* on the 3rd level. No restaurant service (but plenty in airport), a/c, good.

Camping on southern outskirts *Balneario Campestre*, Brisas Tropicales. Swimming pools, refreshments, car camping, armed guards and dogs.

Eating **Central Cali** *Cali Viejo*, Cra 1, Parque El Bosque, T8934927/4722. On south side of river near the zoo, colonial house, excellent local dishes, open daily except Sun. *Rancho Alegre*, Cra 1, No 1-155, T8930980. Good Colombian food. *Parilla de Esteban*, Cra 1, No 4-08. Good meat and fish. *Don Carlos*, Cra 1, No 7-53. Excellent seafood, elegant and expensive. *Hostería Madrid*, C 9, No 4-50. European specialities, good service, above-average price. *Restaurante Suizo*, Cra 30 y Diagonal 29. Swiss, excellent fondue bourguignonne, pleasant atmosphere, reasonably priced. *Chalet Suizo*, C 5, No 88-53. Good. *El Quijote*, Cra 4, No 1-64. Atmospheric, European dishes, expensive. *La Calima*, Cra 4, No 8-10. Good value, always open. There are at least 10 eating places in the bus station, *Doble Vía* is the best.

Vegetarian *Punto Verde*, Cra 6, No 7-40. Mon-Sat, lunch only. *Govindas*, C 14, No 4-49. Lunch at 1300, dinner 1900. *Casona Vegetariana*, Cra 6, No 6-56. Good food, ice-cream, juices and bread, open 0800-1800. *Sol de La India*, Cra 6, No 8-48, T8842333. A la carte or menu US$1.30, open 1200-1400.

North Cali *Las Dos Parrillas*, Av 6N/C 35, T6684646. Good steaks but expensive. *Los Girasoles*, Av 6N/C 35, T6684646. Excellent Colombian menu, fish, ask for the day's special. Recommended. *Da Massimo*, Av 5N, No 46-10. Good Italian. *Balocco*, Av 6N, No 14-04, T6612896. Italian and Colombian, good value. *Dominique*, Av 6N, No 15-25. Good Italian food and service. *Casa Ascoine*, Av 3N, No 7-32, T6673391. Very good Italian. *Le Bistro*, Av 8N, No 23-46, T6678393. French, good. *La Terraza*, C 16N, No 6-14. Elegant, music and dance, nice atmosphere. *Aragonesa*, Av 6N, No 13-68. Good breakfasts. *Fortissimo*, Av 6N, No 14-47. Good cheap Italian, nice atmosphere. *Primos,* Av 5BN, No 24-95. Good meat dishes and hamburgers. *Carbon y Leña*, in new Chipichape shopping centre, Av 6N. Excellent meat dishes, good prices, eg steaks US$3.50.

    Vegetarian *Centro Naturista Salud*, C 17N, No 6-39. Set lunch US$2. *Mi Tierra*, Av 8N, No 10-18. Regional food.

Outside town *La Fragata*, in Hotel Pacífico Royal (see above), T3307777. Branch of excellent seafood restaurants.

Cafés You can find lots of European style sidewalk places in the centre and along Av 6N in the north. Bread and pastry shops often have cafés or cafeterías eg *Punto Sabroso*, C 12, No 8-06, central, pastries, good selection of main dishes, good value, open 24 hrs; *Oasis*, Av 6N/C 17; *La Flora*, C 44, No 6-15; *Edad de Oro*, Av 5N, No 20-30, cheap, light meals, lunch only. Cafés and ice-cream parlours abound near the university, across the river from the main part of town.

    Cheaper still are the *fuentes de soda*, mostly with Colombian style cooking, a decent meal for US$2.50-3. There are also *Masserna* on Cra 7 between C 10 and 11 and *La Sultana*, C 10/Cra 9. Try their *buñuelos* (cheesy fritters) and the *pandebono* (cheesy buns) nearby at *Montecarlo*, C 10, No 8-69, also at Cra 5, No 14-22 and other branches.

Bars & nightclubs These are locally known as 'Grills'. The ones along Av 6N from C 16 upwards are the safest and best known. *Tropicali*, Av 6N, No15-66, T6671006, is one of the best with food and a range of entertainment. Nearby are *Las Brisas*, *Las Cataratas*, *Scarcha* and, across the road, *Douglas* and *Fandango*. Or try *Tin Tin Deo*, C 5/Cra 22, T5542830, good atmosphere, salsa at weekends. Typically they are open from 1500 to 0200. Many others elsewhere in the city including *Conga*, C 5, No 30-17; *Taberna Latina*, C 5/Cra 36, small and friendly; *Martins*, Av 4N/C 4, lively, popular, pop rock, crowded at weekends, moderate prices. *Caliwood*, C 16N/Av 4, salsa in a relaxed and alternative setting.

    There is a nightlife tour by *chiva* (open-sided bus) Fri-Sat, to various bar/discos US$14 per person including ½ bottle *aguardiente*, tickets from main hotels. There is a school, *Profesional Académia de Baile*, Cra 4B, No 44-24, T4462765, director Oscar Borrero, where you can perfect your Salsa, or ask at your hotel for recommended classes.

Entertainment **Theatre** *Teatro Municipal*, Cra 5, No 6-64, T8839107. Opened 1918, major cultural activities including opera, ballet and weekly classical concerts and home to the Cali Symphony orchestra. *Teatro Experimental,* C 7, No 8-63, T8843820. Theatre productions most weekends by resident company. *Teatro Aire Libre Los Cristales,* off Av Circunvalación in Parque Acueducto (San Antonio), all kinds of musical and artistic presentations. **Cinema** Films are shown on Wed nights at Centro Colombo-Americano (see below under **Cultural centres**). Also films on Fri nights at the *Alianza Colombo-Francesa*, Av 6N, No 21-34. Old, popular movies are shown at *Club Imbanaco*, C 5A, No 38A-14, T5589520. Good films also shown at the *Museo La Tertulia* (see above). Ask in your hotel for a free copy of the monthly magazine, *Cali Cultural*, for details of current events.

La Zona Cafetera & the Cauca Valley

Festivals *Feria Internacional de Cali* from 25 Dec to 3 Jan centred at Plaza Canaveralejo on C 5 but engulfs the whole city, with bullfights, horse parades, masquerade balls, sporting contests and salsa competitions everywhere with groups coming from all over the world. *Festival Internacional de Arte* in Jun (painting, sculpture, theatre, music, etc). Also in Jun Feria Artesanal at Parque Panamericano, C 5, handicrafts and excellent leather goods.

Shopping *Platería Ramírez*, Cra 11B, No 18-64, factory and shop good for gold, silver, brass, jewellery, table settings, etc: dubious area, best to take a taxi. *Artesanías de Colombia*, C 12, No 1-20 and for larger purchases Av 6N, No 23-45. For boots and shoes, *Botas Texana Chaparro*, Av 14N, No 6-27, T6653805, good, owner Edgar speaks a little English. *Paso Fino*, Av 8N, No 21-55, leather goods, prices negotiable. Best shopping districts are: Av 6N, from Río Cali to C 30 Norte culminating in the new shopping mall at Chipichape on the site of the old railway workshops, claimed to be the largest shopping mall in South America. It is spectacular but prices are high and in spite of the new high rise development around it, not yet an evident success. In the south of the city near Ciudad Jardín are two large shopping malls Unicentro and Holguines Trade Center facing each other across Cra 100, open also Sun 1000-1300.

Cali

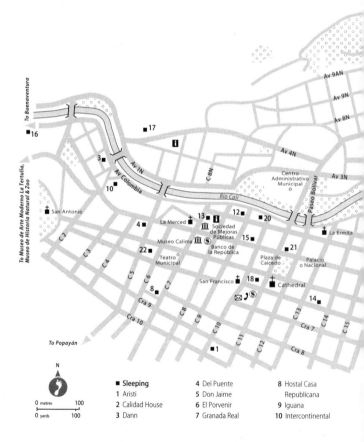

■ Sleeping	4 Del Puente	8 Hostal Casa
1 Aristi	5 Don Jaime	Republicana
2 Calidad House	6 El Porvenir	9 Iguana
3 Dann	7 Granada Real	10 Intercontinental

Bookshop *Librería Nacional*, Cra 5, No 11-50, almost next to the cathedral on Plaza de Caicedo, has a café, as do branches elsewhere in the city. Also at the airport. Bookstalls on the sidewalk on Cra 10 near C 10.

Within its Villa Olímpica along C 5 at Cra 34 in San Fernando, Cali has 3 stadia: the **Sports** Pascual Guerrero Stadium, holding 50,000 people, the Olympic Stadium, holding 7,000 people and the Piscinas Olímpicas, 3,000. Another stadium holding 18,000, the Monumental de Cali, is 10 mins from the city on the road to Meléndez.

Bullring The new, first-class bullring, the Plaza de Toros Cañaveralejo, is 5 km from the city centre along C 5. **Cycling** Cycleshops: *Bicicletas Todo Terreno*, C 5, No 57-54, T5521579, also at Av 8AN, No17-33, T6612456, bltcolombia@emcali.net.co *Bike House*, Av 20N, No 23AN-68, T6615572.

Viajes Sinisterra, C 11, No 4-42, T8893121. Good service especially for airline advice. **Tour Operators** *Viajes Camino Real*, Av 4N, No 21-84, T6613939. Trips locally and to Popayán, Puracé, Leticia etc. *Vela*, Cra 4, No 8-64, local 104, Edif Beneficiencia del Valle, T8890760, F8893683. Student travel agency for changing flights, cheap tickets. Recommended. *Viajar por Colombia*, C 10, No 29A-38, T5583140, F5585231, vpcol@emcali.net.co

La Zona Cafetera & the Cauca Valley

11 JJ	**15** María Victoria	**19** Residencial Chalet	**23** Sartor
12 Latino	**16** Obelisco	**20** Río Cali	**24** Torre de Cali
13 La Merced	**17** Pensión Stein	**21** Royal Plaza	
14 Los Angeles	**18** Plaza	**22** San Antonio Plaza	

English spoken, very helpful. Recommended. *Tierra Mar Aire SA*, C 22N, No 5BN-53, PO Box 44-64, T6676767. Clients' mail service, helpful.

Transport **Local Car Rental** Hertz, Av Colombia No 2-72, (Hotel Intercontinental), T8920437, also office at airport, T6663283. **Uno Auto Renta**, Av 5N, No 44-36, T6648635, and at airport, T6663317. **National**, C 5, No 39-36, T5524432, aiport, T6663016. **Taxi** ensure that meters are used. Prices, posted in the window, start at US$0.20. On holidays, Sun and at night, an extra charge is made.

Long distance Air Palmaseca, 20 km from city, T4422624, has banks, including Banco Popular, and cash machines near domestic departures/arrivals. The *Telecom* office with international telephone facilities, is near international departures, as is also the tax exemption office. Internet is available.

To Bogotá, 20 services daily. To **Medellín** 5 daily, Avianca and Aces. To **Buenaventura**, 2 daily, both SAM and Satena, US$75 return. One or two a day to **Barranquilla, Cartagena, Florencia, Guapí, Ibagué, Ipiales, Manizales, Neiva, Pasto, Pereira, Puerto Asís, Quibdó, Santa Marta**, and **Tumaco**. Direct international flights to **Miami**, Avianca, Aces and American daily. To **San Francisco, American daily. To Panama**, Copa daily. To **New York**, Avianca, 2/week. To **Mexico**, Avianca 4 a week. To **Los Angeles,** 4 a week.

Buses The bus terminal is at C 30N, No 2AN-29, 25 mins walk from the centre following the river along Av 2N. Bus information T6683655. Hotel information available, left luggage US$0.60 per item, good food at terminal. *Casa de cambio*, (cash only), banks and cash machines. Showers on second level (US$0.40). There are plenty of local buses between the bus station and the centre, which charge US$0.20. Taxi from centre to bus station, US$1.50.

Buses to **Popayán**, US$5, 2½ -3 hrs, also colectivos, US$6.50. To **Pasto**, US$11, 9 hrs. To *Ipiales* (direct), US$14, 12 hrs by Bolivariano Pullman or others, departures early morning. Coomotor and Sotracauca have direct services to **San Agustín** via Popayán, Coconuco and Isnos, 9 hrs, US$14; there are services to San Agustín via La Plata (much slower than the new road via Isnos) US$16.

To **Cartago**, 3½ hrs, US$4. To **Armenia**, US$7. To **Ibagué**, US$8, 7 hrs. To **Buenaventura**, US$5, 4 hrs. To **Manizales**, US$9, 7 hrs. To **Medellín**, US$17, 10-12 hrs. To **Bogotá**, 10-15 hrs, Magdalena (recommended) and Palmira, US$18 (sit on left hand side of the bus). **Busetas** (Velotax and others) and taxi-colectivos also available.

Directory **Airline Offices Local** *Aces*, Av 8N, No 24A-07, T6680909. *AeroRepública*, C 25N, No 6-42, T6604050. *Aires*, Av 6N, No 20-73, T6604777. *Avianca/SAM*, Av 4N, No 17-78, T6676919. *Intercontinental*, C 10, No 3-23, Of 109, T8807065. *Satena*, C 8, No 5-19, T8857709.

International *Aerolineas Argentinas*, Av 5CN, No 23D-37, T6602250. *Air France*, C 13, No 3-42, T8897733. *Alitalia*, Av 3AN, No 8-76, T8853200. *American*, C 11, No 4-47, T8842600. *COPA*, Centro Comercial Chipichape L 210, T6652399. *Iberia*, Av 5CN, No 23D-37, T6602250. *Lufthansa*, Calle 100, No 8A-49 T6180400. *KLM*, C 22N, No 8-65, T6607017. *Varig*, Av 6N, No 17-92, T6672610.

Banks *Lloyds TSB Bank*, Av 6N, No 25-11, T6640200 and several agencies. *Banco de Bogotá* on the Plaza de Caicedo quickest in giving Visa cash advances. *Bancolombia*, C 11, No 6-24, cashes Amex TCs, good rates. *Banco Union Colombiano*, C 2N, No 6-22, good rates for travellers cheques. *CONAVI*, Av 6N/C 18 for Mastercard and Cirrus. *Citibank*, C 11, No 3-50. Many other banks and cash machines in the main commercial areas. *Casas de Cambio* include *Titan Internacional*, C 11, No 4-48 and other offices. *Cambios Country* C 11, No 1-16. *Western Union*, Cra 4, No 10-12, T8857700, (Centro); Calle 8, No 31-04, T5565309,(Sur).

Communications Internet: *Cy@nco*, C 6N, No 13-27, US$3/hr, open Mon-Fri 0730-2000, Sun 0800-1800. *CosmoNet*, Av 6N, No 17-65, T6686522, open Mon-Sat 0800-2000. *Café-Web*, Calle 15N, No6-28, and many others in the north and centre. **Post Office** Adpostal for national service, C 10, No 6-25. Avianca for international service, C 12N, No 2A-37. **Telecom:** C 10, No 6-25. **Media:** Two local daily newspapers are *La Nación* and *El País*.

Cultural Centres *Alianza Colombo Francesa*, Av 6N, No 21-34, T6613431. *British Council*, C 22N, No 8-52, T6613612. *Centro Cultural Colombo-Americano*, C 13N, No 8-45, T6682836/6673539. *Fundación Cultural Colombo Alemana*, Diagonal 26A, No 27-31, T5564823. All give language classes, show films and have other events, enquire for programme.

Embassies and Consulates *Austria*, C 12, No 1-12, Of 408, T8821231. *Belgium*, Cra 113, No 11-49, T3320826. *Bolivia*, Cra 40, No 5C-102, T5584036. *Brazil*, C 11, No 1-07, Of 304, T8880282. *Chile*, C 47, No 1B-30, T4466704. *Denmark*, Av 4N, No 4-46, T6614368. *Ecuador*, C 4N, No 1-10, Of 703, T6604571. *El Salvador*, Av 4B Oeste, No 3-70, T8936250. *France*, Av 3N, No 8-24, Of 405, T8835904. *Germany*, Av de las Americas 19-08, T6611135. *Guatemala*, Cra 52, No 4B-06, T3474407. *Holland*, Av 2AN, No 9-09, T8817269. *Israel*, C 26, No 7-75, T4423737. *Italy*, C 20, No 8A-34, T8831445. *Japan*, Av 3N, No 21-62, T6606602. *Norway*, C 8, No 31-04, T5575780. *Mexico*, Zona Franca de Palmaseca, T6511120. *Panama*, C 11, No 4-42, T8809590. *Peru*, C 22N, No 3-21, T6602052. *Spain*, C 6, No 3-34, T8817085. *Sweden*, C 11, No 6-24, p 11, T8881561. *Switzerland*, Cra 100, No 11-90, Of 316, T3320491. *UK*, C 25, No 1N-65, T8881288. *USA*, for information, US citizens should contact *Centro Cultural Colombo-Americano* (see Cultural Centres below).

Laundry *Lavandería x kilo*, C 23 Norte, No 7N-08, T6612184. *Lavaprisa*, Av 8N, No 12-08. US$3.50 for a full load including drying. Recommended.

Medical Services Good health clinic for women, *Grupo Mujeres*, C 4, No 34-18, T6544294. *Centro de Ortopedia y Fracturas*, Av 2N, No 21-65, T6670400, for specialist treatments, doctors speak English and French. *Clínica de Occidente*, C 18N, No 5-34, T6603000, recommended clinic. *Cruz Roja*, Transversal 5, No 5-91 (Red Cross), T5140324. *Clínica de Oftalmología de Cali*, Av 4N, No 7-53, T6606809. Full service eye clinic. *Optica Cali*, Cra 5, No 13-105, good optician service.

Useful Addresses DAS office: Av 3AN, No 50-20, T 6643809/10.

From Cali it is 135 km south to Popayán. The road crosses the Río Cauca, then rejoins the main east bank route south at Villa Rica. About 17 km along the main road is **Santander**, an attractive town with a colonial chapel, Capilla de Dominguillo, worth a visit. Ceramics and *fique* handicrafts are sold here. Piendamó is at Km 101 from Cali – see next chapter under Silvia.

West of Cali

To the west of Cali is the northeast/southwest line of the Cordillera Occidental, which rises here to over 4,000 m. A large section of this area and down to 200 m on the Pacific side is the **Farallones de Cali National Park** (see below). North of this are the road and rail links to Buenaventura. Along the main road (toll) there is much heavy traffic to Colombia's main Pacific port. There are however places to stop, eg San Cipriano and Córdoba, both near the railway, where you can rent small *cabañas* in the forest, swim in the rivers and visit the rainforest. Busy at weekends and holidays but quiet otherwise. The railway is being refurbished for freight transport.

Both the toll and ordinary roads out of Cali and Buenaventura give beautiful views of mountains and jungle, and from the old road you can reach the **Parque Nacional Farallones**. Take the dirt road south from the plaza in El Queremal, at 1,460 m, about an hour from Cali, 3½ hours from Buenaventura. At El Queremal, a pleasant local mountain village, an Andean music festival is held each October (Encuentro Música Andina Colombiana). Alternatively, take the road southwest out of Cali, or *colectivo* (one hour), to Pance. From Pance there is a path, about 30 minutes, to the environmental centre at the entrance to the park at El Topacio. There is good walking and bathing in the park and peaks to climb, one of which is the Pico de Loro, a steep slippery

Farallones National Park
Note that in early 2000, the park was not open for safety reasons

La Zona Cafetera & the Cauca Valley

scramble for 2½ hours, but worth it for the views and the sound of the swoop-
ing birds. Busy at weekends, camping possible at US$6 for five people a night
at El Topacio or at Quebrada Honda, near the Río Pance. You will need a permit from MA in Cali (see under Cali-Tourist offices for address and where to
find more information). Entrance to the park, US$1.50 per person.

Buenaventura

Phone code: 92
Colour map 3, grid A2
Population: 202,000

Colombia's only important port on the Pacific is Buenaventura,145 km by
road from Cali over a pass in the Western Cordillera. The commercial centre is
now entirely paved and has some impressive buildings, but the rest of the town
is poor, with unpaved streets lined with wooden shacks. It is more expensive
than Cali and it is difficult to eat cheaply or well. On a hill near the centre is the
cathedral and a good view of the town can be seen from the nearby **El Mirador**
Edificio del Café. There is a festive atmosphere every night (see under **Music
and Dance** for festivals).

Around Cali

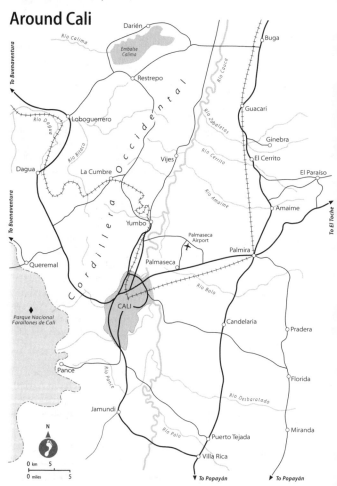

Getting there The **bus terminal** is at Cra 5/C 7. It is 560 km by sea from Panamá, 708 **Ins & outs** km by road from Bogotá. From Cali, the new road climbs 12 km to Saladito, a fresh 10°C cooler than the city. Many Caleños enjoy the roadside restaurants especially at weekends in this sector. The highest point is reached at Km 18 where the old road turns off left through El Queremal to Buenaventura. Dagua, 828m, 46 km from Cali, is in a semi-arid pineapple growing zone, a good place for refreshments. Here the railway comes alongside the road, both following the Río Dagua to the coast. Further down, tropical forests are continuous with several places to stop and bathe on the way.

Climate Mean temperature, 27°C. It rains nearly every day, particularly at night; the average annual rainfall is 7,400 mm (relative humidity 88%). There are some problems with malaria.

Buenaventura was founded in 1540, but not on its present site. It now stands on the island of Cascajal, 16 km at the end of the Bay of Buenaventura. The port handles 80% of Colombia's coffee exports, and 60% of the nation's total exports, including sugar and frozen shrimps. South of the town a swampy coast stretches as far as Tumaco (see page 362). To the north lies the deeply jungled Chocó Department.

A *Estación*, C 2, No 1A-08, T2434070, F2434118, French neo-classical style, good **Sleeping** restaurant. **C** *Majestic*, C 3, No 4-39, T2423010. With bath, a/c, TV. **D** *Felipe II*, Cra 3A, No 2-44, T2422775/2422820. A/c, with bath, restaurant, good. **D** *Balmoral*, C 3, No 4-19, T2423152. Cheaper for 4 bedded rooms. **D** *El Rey*, C 3, No 3-69, T2412128, F2423590. **D** *Cascajal*, Cra 2A, No 1-20, T2422962. With breakfast, a/c, TV, parking. **E** *Mi Balconcito*, C 3/Cra 4. Basic, clean. **E** *Continental*, Cra 5, No 4-05, with bath; opposite is **F** *Europa*, without bath. **F** *Las Gaviotas*, C 3, No 3-83, T2424652. Clean, friendly. **F** *Niza*, C 6, No 5-38. With bath and fan. Beware of the many brothels near the port area.

Los Balcones, C 2, No 3-94, T2423869. Very good, but expensive. *Mediterráneo*, C 3, **Eating** No 3-92. Local and international food. *El Arriero*, C 3, No 3-65, also at C 3, No 4-37. Good value. *La Sazón de Merceditas*, opposite Edif de Café. Good seafood, soups, friendly, reasonable prices. *Fat Choy*, C 7, No 3A-06. Chinese. *La Sombrita de Miguel*, near waterfront. Good seafood. Self-service restaurant on main plaza, clean, modern, open 24 hrs. Good seafood at Pueblo Nuevo market, but not very cheap. **Out of town** *El Palacio de Coco*, Km 15 via Cali, T2439700, traditional dishes, *sancocho de pescado*, also coconut delicacies.

Aviatur, Cra 3A, No 2-30, T2417250. *Viajes Balboa*, C 1, No 2-39, T2418067. **Tour Operators**

Air Local flights to **Cali**, SAM and Satena 2 a day each. To **Bogotá**, 3 a week, Satena. **Transport** **Buses** To **Cali:** there are plenty of buses, US$5, 4 hrs; colectivos also run at half-hourly intervals to Cali, US$5.75. To **Bogotá**: 1 a day, US$23, 10 hrs.

The toll road to Cali is fully paved; the toll is about US$1.30 for cars and US$0.30 for motorcycles. The ordinary road is not paved.

River From Buenaventura to Quibdó (see also page 246). Up the Río San Juan: boats are scarce out of Buenaventura (lumber boats from El Piñal only go about a day and a half upstream, and port authorities are strict about allowing passengers on cargo boats). One way is to take a bus from Pueblo Nuevo, Buenaventura to San Isidro on the Río Calima (28 km, 6 hrs, terrible road), then a motorized dugout (*panga*) to Palestina on the Río San Juan. From there take a dugout going upstream; they rarely go as far as Istmina, which is connected by road and bus to Quibdó. Try to get as far as Dipurdú (no hotels, but friendly locals who offer sleeping space, shops with tinned goods), from where daily boats go to Istmina.

La Zona Cafetera & the Cauca Valley

Sea Boats can be found going south to Tumaco. The *María Rita* goes north, 3 times a week, to **Bahía Solano,** 24 hrs, US$30. Also the *M/V Fronteras* takes cargo and passengers north along the coast towards Panama, food served but don't rely on it. Cramped bunks but OK.

Directory   **Banks** *Banco Popular*, Cra 2, No 2-37, changes US$ cash TCs. *Bancolombia*, C 1A, No 3-55, cash against Visa. *Banco del Occidente*, Cra 2, No 2-39, cash against Mastercard. *Western Union*, C 1, No 3-97, Of 205, T2422766.

Communications *Avianca Post Office*, C 8, No 26-05. *Telecom*, C 3/Cra 3.

Tourist Offices *Corporación Regional de Turismo del Valle*, C 1, No 1A-88, Mon-Fri, 0800-1200, 1400-1800, information on trips to beaches, boat excursions, hotel price lists etc. *Cámara de Comercio* nearby is also helpful; maps at CAM, 3rd floor of office block at the far end of the seafront.

Useful Addresses Shipping agent: *Navemar*, C 1, No 2A-25, T2422570, for Sudamericana de Vapores, for shipping vehicles to/from Panama. **DAS** near *Avianca* Post Office, T2419592.

Around Buenaventura

There are good black sand beaches on the northern shore of the Bahía de Buenaventura such as **La Bocana**, which can be reached by *lancha* in about 30 minutes. There are simple restaurants and some basic places to stay. Within walking distance further on round the coast is Piangüíta, an extensive, colourful beach.

About 45 minutes boat ride from Buenaventura to beyond the Bahía de Málaga is **Juanchaco** fishing village and beach with accommodation and restaurants. **Ladrilleros**, a better beach, is close by round the coast which has many sea caves and freshwater falls. From Juanchaco boats can be hired to visit places along the coast and in the Bahía de Málaga including La Sierpe, where a 65m waterfall cascades into the sea. Trips to beaches from Buenaventura cost between US$10-40 for 10-person launch (rate per launch, not per person). Check on safety before setting out, especially to the more isolated areas and bear in mind that the ocean can be very dangerous in bad weather.

Sleeping in Juanchaco: B *Asturias,* comfortable, restaurant. **C** *Malibu,* a/c, TV, restaurant. **C** *Villa de Mar,* a/c, food. In **Ladrilleros: E** *Oasis,* also has *cabañas* for 5 with showers. **E** *Estrella del Mar,* a/c, mosquito nets. Try bargaining outside peak times. Cheaper places are available, mostly on an ad-hoc basis, ask around. Good seafood everywhere but all other products have to be shipped from Buenaventura and hence are expensive.

Whale watching   About 25 km northwest of Buenaventura is the mouth of the Río San Juan, the largest river of South America to reach the Pacific. The Bahía de Malaga is a former mouth of the river and Juanchaco and Ladrilleros are on part of its delta. Partly because of the richness of the water in this region, this is the location of spectacular dolphin and humpback whale sightings with their calves which migrate south from August to early October each year. There are also all kinds of sea birds to see including pelicans, and frigate birds. A good place is near the Isla Palma, an island off Juanchaco owned by the Colombian Navy. You can visit this area by launch from Buenaventura US$22, one hour, and by boat US$16.50, three hours. Whale watching tours about US$12.50 for two hours.

Alternatvely tours to this part of the coast are arranged by the *Hotel Estación*, Buenaventura, mid/late Jul to end September, hopefully for whale sighting: three nights/four days from Bogotá, US$350 per person, including flight, accommodation and guides, T2434070 (Buenaventura), or T8838800

(Cali). *Hotel Asturias*, Juanchaco offers a similar package, T6676141 (Cali). Other travel agents include *Marvel Tours*, Calle 58N, No 3B Bis 42, T6651899, F6644839, and *Grupo Fiesta*, Avenida 4N, No 23C-22, T6612747, both in Cali.

Gorgona Island

The island of **Gorgona** is about 150 km down the coast from Buenaventura. It is 9 km long and 2½ km wide, with a small island (Gorgonilla) off its southwest tip. At one time, it was the country's high security prison – a sort of Colombian Alcatraz – and convicts were dissuaded from escaping by the poisonous snakes on the island and the sharks patrolling the 30 km to the mainland.

Getting there by boat If you wish to make your own arrangements, you will need to find a boat at Buenaventura. Boats normally leave daily except Sun at between 1500 and 1700 depending on the tides, from the El Piñal dock (Bodega Liscano) T2446106 or 2446091, in Buenaventura. The trip, US$40 return, takes up to 12 hrs depending on conditions and can be an experience in itself. **Ins & outs**

You may be able to make arrangements in **Guapí** on the mainland for the 1½ hr boat trip to Gorgona Island, but don't count on it. A launch costs US$250 to be shared by up to 10 passengers. Local basket-weaving is on sale in Guapí, as are musical instruments such as the guaza (a hollow tube filled with seeds) and the marimba (about US$10). The only passable place to stay in Guapí is the *Hotel El Río* run by Pedro Arroyo, who speaks a little English, and his brother Camilo. The only way out of Guapí is by boat or by plane one a day to Cali, US$36 or to Popayán, Satena, 3 days a week.

Information All visitors, research students and scientists must have a permit, obtainable from MA in Bogotá (other MA offices will give advice). Entrance US$4.50 per person plus US$2,60 embarkation/ disembarkation fee. At holiday times (Semana Santa, Jun-Jul, Dec-Jan and long weekends), application must be made at least 4 weeks in advance and you pay for 3 nights' accommodation at the time. Diving permit US$16 plus US$16 per instructor. If you want to volunteer your services as a Park guard, contact MA, Bogotá and speak to Dr Carlos Castaño Uribe, or Dr Luis Emiro Matallana. Facilities on the island are run by MA employees.

The island was made a National Nature Park in 1984. Many parts are unspoilt with deserted sandy beaches. Some sections have been closed to visitors owing to excessive traffic. There is a good hike across the island through the jungle via a series of lakes, now dry due to earthquake activity. From the paths you can see monkeys, iguanas, and a wealth of flora and fauna. Rubber boots are provided and recommended. There is an abundance of birds (pelicans, cormorants, geese, herons) that use the island as a migration stop-over. Snorkelling is rewarding, equipment can be hired (but take your own if possible), exotic fish and turtles to be seen. From July to September killer whales visit the area.

Organized tours: recommended are *Ecotur*, Cra 56, No 5-31, Cali, T5517248, with a 4 day, 3 nights (on the island) tour from Cali for US$275 including permission from MA, and an official guide. Another company is *Panturismo*, C 8, No 1-38, Cali, T8893135, who offer a 4-day visit via Guapi, or 6 days via Buenaventura. *Marvel Tours*, C 58N, No 3B Bis-42, T6651899, Cali offer a similar tour via Guapi with a night each end in Cali from US$410 a person or US$470 including diving (6 immersions) on the island. **Organized tours**

The total number of visitors at any one time is restricted to 72. You can stay in cabins on the island: for 4 US$50, for 8 US$90. Try to book bunk beds in advance; if you can't, prepare for a scramble. There is a restaurant with a mainly fish menu. You can take **Sleeping** your own food but all non-biodegradable items must be taken off the island. Collect your own coconuts, but there is no other fruit on the island. Don't take alcohol, it will probably be confiscated. Do take drinking water, it is in short supply and expensive on the island. Camping is not allowed.

Malpelo Island This remote island, 330 km west of Buenaventura, has recently been established as a natural sanctuary administered by the National Parks service as **Sanctuario de Flora y Fauna Isla Malpelo.** There are no facilities at present, and no permanent inhabitants. For information on the island and permission to land there, contact MA offices. Official charges are US$5 per person per day to visit and US$20 per day for a diving permit. For contracting a boat to visit the island, or for the good deep sea fishing near the island, enquire in Buenaventura. (See also under Land and Environment in the Background Section).

9

Popayán, Tierradentro & San Agustín

South of Cali, the Pan-American Highway follows the Cauca Valley, through rich pastures and sugar cane plantations, to the grand, old city of Popayán, one of the earliest Spanish settlements of the country and one of the best preserved, in spite of a history of damaging earthquakes. It has many churches and historical buildings, all in dazzling white, and is the most complete colonial city of Colombia. The landscape is dominated by the Cordillera Central and the Puracé volcano complex. In these mountains is Silvia, home of the disarmingly friendly Guambiano Indians and their colourful costumes.

From Popayán it's an unforgettably rough, but scenically stunning, bus ride across the páramo of Puracé to two of Colombia's major tourist attractions - the remarkable archaeological sites of Tierradentro and San Agustín. Here, you can explore the relics of ancient cultures on foot, horseback or by chiva and try to solve the mystery which has puzzled archaeologists for many years.

Highlights of Popayán, Tierradentro & San Agustín

★ A walk round the brilliant white colonial city of Popayán.

★ A trip to Silvia market to see the Gambiano Indians in their distinctive costumes.

★ A walking tour of the remarkable archaeological sites at Tierradentro.

★ The short walk to the white waterfalls behind Puracé village.

★ Enjoying the amazing colours of the mosses and lichens at Termales de San Juan in Puracé National Park.

★ Wondering who created the dramatic San Agustín statues.

Popayán

Phone code: 92
Colour map 3, grid B3
Population: 223,000
Altitude: 1,760 m

The city of Popayán has managed to retain its colonial character, which is remarkable given that it was partially destroyed by the March 1983 earthquake and extensively restored. Many of the streets are cobbled and the two-storey buildings are in rococo Andalucian style, with beautiful old monasteries and cloisters of pure Spanish classic architecture.

Ins & outs

Getting there The **airport** is 20 mins walk from the centre. Popayán's **bus terminal** is near the airport, 15 mins walk from the centre (Ruta 2-Centro bus, terminal to centre, US$0.30, or taxi, US$0.75). Luggage can be stored safely (receipt given); there is a charge to use the toilets, and a small departure tax. From the bus station, turn left to the statue of Bolívar, then take the second right to Parque Bolívar; here are the market and cheap hotels. Beware of thefts of luggage in the bus station.

Take care if you cross any of the bridges over the river going north, especially at night

Tourist offices Casa Caldas, C 3, No 4-70 (T8242251), has good maps of the city, prices of all hotels and pensions, and bus schedules and prices. All staff are helpful, giving information on places of interest, will tell you where horses may be hired for exploring, and will store your luggage. In addition to normal hours, they are open Sun until 1200. Ask at the Tourist Office about which areas of the city are unsafe. (For information on travel beyond Popayán ask elsewhere and check with other travellers.) They also sell local crafts at good prices; telephone and mail service. The Casa Caldas is a fine traditional Popayán house in its own right. Have a look around. The Tourist Office and the Colegio Mayor de Cauca have details on art exhibitions and concerts. Try also the *Casa de la Cultura*, C 5, No 4-33, for information on cultural events.

Warning Both Valle del Cauca and Cauca departments have had guerrilla problems in the recent past. Enquire locally before travelling on minor roads in the area and do not travel on any roads in the south at night

Popayán was founded by Sebastián de Belalcázar, Francisco Pizarro's lieutenant, in 1536, in the valley of the Pubenza, a peaceful landscape of palm, bamboo, and the sharp-leaved agave. The early settlers after setting up their sugar estates in the hot, damp Cauca valley, retreated to Popayán to live, for the city is high enough to give it a delightful climate. After the conquest of the Pijao Indians, Popayán became the regional seat of government, subject until 1717 to the Audiencia of Quito, and later to the Audiencia of Bogotá. Popayán has given no fewer than eleven presidents to the Republic. The scientist Francisco José de Caldas was born here in 1771. It was he who discovered how to determine altitude by variation in the boiling point of water, and it was to him that Mutis (of the famous *Expedición Botánica*) entrusted the directorship of the newly founded Observatory at Bogotá. He was a passionate partisan of independence, and was executed in 1815 during Morillo's 'Reign of Terror'.

Today, Popayán is the capital of the Department of Cauca. To north, south, and east the broken green plain is bounded by mountains. To the southeast rises the cone of the volcano Puracé (4,646 m). The Río Molino runs through the town, a tributary, of the Río Cauca, which rises near Puracé and flows past Popayán a few kilometres to the north.

The Cathedral, at Calle 5/Carrera 6, was built around 1900 and is the third on the site and has been beautifully restored after the 1983 earthquake. It has a fine marble madonna sculpture behind the altar by Buenaventura Malagón.

    San Agustín, at Calle 7/Carrera 6, is notable for the gilt altar piece and the unusual statue of Christ kneeling on the globe. **Santo Domingo**, Calle 4/Carrera 5, has some fine wood carvings, now used by the Universidad del Cauca whose building next door on Carrera 5, and is worth a visit. **La Ermita**, Calle 5/Carrera 2, on the site of the first chapel established by Sebastián de Belalcázar, dates from the 16th century. **La Encarnación**, Calle 5/Carrera 5, dates from 1764 and has a fine retable, is also used for religious music festivals. **San Francisco**, Calle 4/Carrera 9, dating from about 1775, has been frequently damaged by earthquakes and is now partly restored, note the fascinating figures on the pulpit stairs. **El Carmen**, Calle 4/Carrera 3, is a monastery church constructed about 1730 with *mudéjar* influences.

Sights

Museo de Historia Natural, Carrera 2, No 1A-25, has good displays of archaeological and geological items with sections on insects (particularly good on butterflies), reptiles, mammals and birds, US$1. Other museums are **Museo Negret**, Calle 5, No 10-23, with works, photographs and furniture of Negret (entry US$0.40), **Museo Guillermo Valencia**, Carrera 6, No 2-69, birthplace of the poet, and **Museo Casa Mosquera**, Calle 3, No 5-14, where General Tomás Cipriano de Mosquera lived, four times President of Colombia. A small collection of Indian artifacts is held in **Banco de la República**, Carrera 6, No 2-28.

Museums are not open on Mon

Walk to **Belén** chapel, Calle 4/Carrera 0, with a fine view of the city, seeing the statues en route, and then continue to **El Cerro de las Tres Cruces** if you have the energy, and on to the equestrian statue of Belalcázar on the **Morro de Tulcán** which overlooks the city. This hill is the site of a precolumbian pyramid. **NB** There are plenty of guides offering their services: check for safety before making these walks alone.

    A fine arched bridge built in 1868, **Puente del Humilladero** crosses the Río Molino at Carrera 6. Public presentations and concerts are given in the gardens below. It is said that Bolívar marched over the nearby **Puente Chiquito**, built in 1713.

NB Hotel prices include taxes, but are subject to a 30% increase in some cases for Holy Week and festivals, eg 5-6 Jan. Continental breakfast is included in most category **E** and above hotels.

Sleeping

In the centre AL *Monasterio*, C 4, No 10-50, in what was the monastery of San Francisco, T8242191, F243491, lovely grounds, swimming pool, very good.

    A *Camino Real*, C 5, No 5-59, T8241546, PO Box 248, good service, excellent restaurant, friendly, recommended. **A** *La Plazuela*, C 5, no 8-13, T8241071/2664, colonial style, courtyard, comfortable rooms, TV, restaurant. **A** *El Herrero*, Cra 5 No 2-08, T8244498, converted large colonial house, family owned, good restaurant, friendly, highly recommended.

Crown of the Andes

In the late 16th century, Popayán was threatened by an outbreak of the plague. The populace turned to the church and the Virgin Mary, and the plague passed them by. So grateful were they that they vowed to create the most beautiful crown in the world for her image in the cathedral.

After six years work, the goldsmiths and jewellers of the town produced a magnificent work of art, weighing over 2 kg, with over 450 fine emeralds, including one of the largest known named after Atahualpa, the Inca ruler killed by Pizarro in 1534. All were set in 18 and 22 carat

gold. The crown was duly placed in Popayán's cathedral.

Amazingly, in spite of the temptation it must have been to the conquistadores, theives and revolutionaries, it stayed there until the 20th century when, in 1909, the Vatican authorized the sale of the crown to provide funds for local hospitals and orphanages. It was bought by an American syndicate and disappeared, presumably into a bank vault. It reappeared, briefly, in 1995 when it change hands at auction, only to return once more to oblivion.

B *Hostal Santo Domingo*, C 4, No 5-14, T8241607, with bath, friendly, good value, in restored colonial building. **B** *Los Balcones*, C 3, No 6-80, T8242030, F241814, hot water, Spanish-style restaurant for breakfast and lunch, good, will change travellers' cheques, recommended.

C *La Casona del Virrey*, C 4, No 5-78, T8244237, hot water, big rooms with bath, friendly, nice colonial house, warmly recommended. **C** *La Posada del Rancho*, 5 km on the road to Cali, T8234710, hotel with excellent restaurant. **C** *Los Olivares*, Cra 7, No 2-48, T8242186, quiet, good local and international restaurant.

D *Pakandé*, Cra 6, No 7-75, T8240846, clean, good beds, hot shower, recommended. **D** *Casa Grande*, Cra 6, No 7-11, T8240604, family-run, attractive, friendly, hot water, convenient, will store luggage, highly recommended.

E *Casa Familiar Turística*, Cra 8, No 3-25, T8242100, clean, hot water, family-run, no sign, use of kitchen, German spoken, recommended. **E** *Don Blas*, Cra 6, No 7-87, T8240817, with bath, clean, modern, recommended. **E** *La Posada*, Cra 2, No 2-35, with bath, friendly, use of kitchen, TV room, cheaper for longer stays, Spanish lessons arranged. **E** *Casa Familiar El Descanso*, Cra 5 No 2-41, T8224-787, T/F8240019, clean, hot water, German spoken, use of fridge, nice courtyard, good breakfast, good information, highly recommended. **E** *Residencia Pubenza*, C 5, No 14-22, motorcycle parking. **E** *Bolívar*, Cra 5, No 7-11, T8244844, clean, hard beds, hot water, pleasant, good restaurant, spacious flowery courtyard, safe motorcycle parking, car parking across street.

F *Casa Suiza*, C 4, No 7-79, T8240751, friendly, hot water, clean, secure. **F** *Residencia Panamá*, Cra 5, No 7-33, hot shower, quiet, laundry service, good food, basic but recommended. Private accommodation at C 3, No 2-53, T8240602, with Karin and Luis Cabrera, **G**, food available, Spanish lessons arranged.

Outside the centre There are many hotels in the Mercado Bolívar area on Cra 6 to the north of the river, but this is not a safe area to walk alone at night. **F** *Plaza Bolívar*, Cra 6, No 2N-12, T8231533, with bath, good cheap restaurant, clean, safe, good value. **G** *Residencia Líder*, Cra 6, No 4N-70, T8230915, friendly, good. **G** *Residencias San Agustín*, Cra 6, No 1N-15, family run, clean, good beds, laundry facilities.

Also, on and south of C 8: **D** *Berioska*, C 8, No 5-47, T8223145, with bath, clean, well run. **E** *Residencias El Viajero*, C 8, No 4-45, T8243069, with bath, clean, otherwise basic, popular, watch your belongings, modern. **E** *Amalia*, Cra 6, No 8-58, hot water, same owners as *Berioska*, clean, cooking and laundry facilities, good base for young travellers, recommended. **F** *Residencias Cataluña*, Cra 5, No 8-27, clean, popular, friendly.

Just outside town are: **D** *Campobello Bed & Breakfast* (Myriam and André), C 33AN, No 14A-14, T8235545, just off Panamerican highway, 300 m down the road opposite the *Torremolino Restaurant*, no sign, run by the Galeanos, clean, friendly, safe, good view, meals available, take bus No 2 from centre to Torremolino or taxi US$1.40.

For longer stays, *finca* accommodation near Popayán suitable for families is available, enquire at the Tourist Office.

Eating

The best restaurants are attached to hotels. For good food at reasonable prices, take a short taxi ride to the road to Cali to *Rancho Grande*, Autopista Norte 32N-50, T8235788, 2 thatched restaurants, delicious *chuzos* (barbecued beef), credit cards accepted, recommended, or *Torremolino*, Autopista Norte 33N-100, T8234000, similar, also evening entertainment.

In the centre *La Viña*, C 4, No 7-85, open 24 hrs, good set lunch and dinner, also *panadería*. *Pizzería don Sebastián*, C 3, No 2-54, good food in a colonial mansion. *Cascada*, Cra 7, No 6-46, good for breakfast. *La Oficina*, C 4, No 8-01, huge servings, good value. *Los Quingos de Belén*, C 4, No 0-13, very good Colombian food, try *empanadas* and *tamales pipianes*. *La Brasa Roja*, Cra 8 No 5-90, set lunch and evening

Popayán

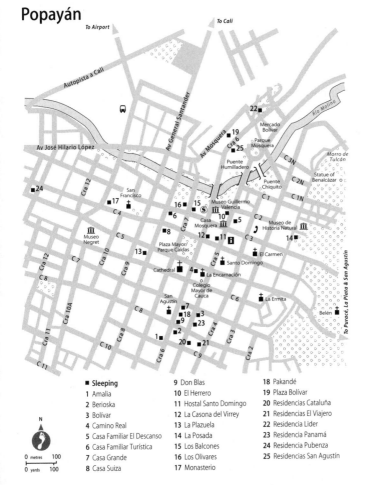

Popayán, Tierradentro & San Agustín

■ Sleeping	9 Don Blas	18 Pakandé
1 Amalia	10 El Herrero	19 Plaza Bolívar
2 Berioska	11 Hostal Santo Domingo	20 Residencias Cataluña
3 Bolívar	12 La Casona del Virrey	21 Residencias El Viajero
4 Camino Real	13 La Plazuela	22 Residencia Lider
5 Casa Familiar El Descanso	14 La Posada	23 Residencia Panamá
6 Casa Familiar Turística	15 Los Balcones	24 Residencia Pubenza
7 Casa Grande	16 Los Olivares	25 Residencias San Agustín
8 Casa Suiza	17 Monasterio	

meal, good food and value. *Jengibre*, Cra 8, No 7-19, T8242732, vegetarian. *Belalcázar*, Cra 6, No 7-55, T8241911, good value. *Caldas*, Cra 6 y C 8, filling 3-course set meals, their *sancocho* is recommended. *Mey Chow*, Cra 10A, No 10-81, good Chinese. *Chung Wah*, Cra 6, No 9-64, good Chinese, also vegetarian. *Pizzeria Italiano*, C 4, No 8-83, Swiss owned, good pizzas and pastas etc, vegetarian dishes, fondues, lunch US$2.40, friendly, good meeting place, recommended. *La Fontana*, C 6, No 7-72, excellent bakery with café serving meals, pizzas and sandwiches. *Peña Blanca*, Cra 7, No 6-73, best bread and cakes, recommended. *Comamos*, C 4, No 8-41, in front of cinema, friendly, cheap, try the *arepas de queso*. *Olafo*, C 6, No 7-42, good pizzas and *patacones con guacamol* and great vanilla ice cream. Near bus station: *Lo Máximo*, Cra 9A, sit outside, good, cheap.

Vegetarian *Delicias Naturales*, C 6, no 8-21, good, cheap.

Bars *Iguana Afro-Club*, C 4, No 9-67, good music, jazz, salsa, friendly owner; *La Topatolondra,* C 3, No 5-69, nice old bar with good salsa; *Pap-Ikar*, Cra 6, No 3-25, atmospheric bar, good drinks, snacks and music, open 1800 onwards. *Café Galería,* Cra 3/C 4; others on C 3.

Festivals Easter processions, every night of **Semana Santa** (Holy Week) until Good Friday, are spectacular; the city is very crowded. The childrens' processions in the following week are easier to see. The children assume all the rôles of the official processions to the delight of parents and onlookers. Also during Semana Santa there is an international sacred music festival, founded in 1964. Orchestras and groups from many countries have participated in the past. For information, T8232244. At the same time there are presentations at Santander de Quilichoa on the main road half way between Popayán and Cali. There are the **Día de los Negros** on 5 Jan and **Día de los Blancos** on 6 Jan, like those at Pasto, but a lot less wet!

Shopping During the week, the open markets are interesting – Bolívar market, C 1N, Cra 5 is best in the early morning – local foods such as *pipián*, *tamales* and *empanadas*.

Sports At weekends you will find people playing 'sapo', see under **Sports and special interest** in **Essentials**. A good place is along the La Plata road near Belén Church. At the Universidad del Cauca, Cra 3, there is a good, clean swimming pool, entry US$0.50.

Transport **Local Taxi** no meters; normal price within city is US$0.75, or US$0.90 at night.

Long distance **Air** To **Bogotá** with Avianca (Cra 7, No 5-77) daily, US$60.

Buses To/from **Bogotá**, Expreso Bolivariano, US$20, 16 hrs. To **Cali**, Cootranar, US$5, 2½-3 hrs, or Velotax microbus, US$6.50, colectivos leave from the main plaza; to **Pasto**,with various companies, about 5/6 hrs, US$7, spectacular scenery (sit on right); to **Medellín**, US$25, 12 hrs; to **Ipiales**, something runs every hour but many buses arrive full from Cali, book in advance; Supertaxis at 0645 and 1230, or bus, up to US$9, about 8 hrs. Alternatively, take a bus to Pasto and change. To **San Agustín** (confusing routes and schedules), La Gaitana, 11 hrs, at 0900 and 2000, Coomotor, 13 hrs, US$13 each once a day. Cootranshuila buses run over the new road via Isnos to San Agustín from bus terminal, twice a day (0600 and 1300), US$12, 6 hrs or more depending on the weather; also Sotracauca at 0900, 6 hrs, same price. Sit on the left side for the best views. To **Tierradentro** (Cruce de Pisimbalá, also known as Cruce de San Andrés), with Sotracauca, 5 a day between 0500 and 1500, US$6, 4-6 hrs, continues to La Plata. Flota Magdalena to **La Plata**, US$6, 5 hrs, also Unidos del Sur (not via Tierradentro) and Sotracauca at 0730. To **Puracé**, US$1.20, 2 hrs, Sotracauca at 0600, La Gaitana 0700, Coomotor later in morning.

Lucía Nates Turismo, C 4, no 8-79, T8242222 for tours in the region. **Tour Operators**

Banks *Banco Cooperativo*, Cra 6, will change Amex travellers' cheques 0900-1130, *Banco del* **Directory**
Estado also changes travellers' cheques. Some banks, eg *Banco Popular*, will give cash advances
against Visa cards or *Banco del Occidente* against Mastercard. Several automatic cash machines
are now operating eg *Bancafé*. *Almacen Salvador Duque*, C 5, No 6-25, on the main plaza, on the
left of the cathedral, T8241700, may change cash but rates are not good. Cash dollars can be
changed at the T-shirt shop in Central Comercial Martínez on Cra 7 between C 6 and 7, also open
on Sat. *Titam*, C 3, no 4-70, T8244659, reasonable rates, international money transfer service.
There are other *cambios*, but their rates are poor. Change dollars cash elsewhere; if coming from
the south, Pasto is a good place.
   Communications Post Office Cra 7, No 5-77. **Telephone Office** Telecom, Cra 4 y C 3; closes
2000. You can make international calls for less than 3 mins.
   Useful addresses MA: Cra 9, No 18N-143, T8239932, good library.

Across the Cauca Valley, west of Popayán is **El Tambo**, and beyond the small **Munchique**
village of Veinte de Julio, an entrance to **Parque Nacional Natural Munchique**, **National Park**
44,000 ha of steep, forested mountains. Another entrance to the north is through
Uribe. The highest point, accessible from Veinte de Julio is Cerro Munchique,
3,012 m. Heavy rain comes in from the Pacific, giving luxuriant growth and fine
waterfalls. The driest months are June-September. There are good viewpoints
from the trails. Entry US$2.50, cars US$3. Enquire about permits and
accomodation/camping at MA, Popayán. Buses run from Popayán.

Silvia lies in a high valley northeast of Popayán. The local Guambiano Indians **Silvia**
wear their typical blue and fuchsia costumes, and are very gregarious and *Phone code: 92*
friendly. You can watch them spinning and weaving their textiles. The Tues- *Colour map 3, grid A3*
day market seems to be full of Otavalo Indians from Ecuador and their goods – *Population: 5,000*
more expensive than in Otavalo, but sucres are accepted. The market is at its *Altitude: 2,520 m*
best between 0600 and 0830. There's not much to buy, but it's very colourful.
There are several Indian settlements in the hills around Silvia, a typical one to
visit is **La Campana**, 45 minutes on the bus, 2½ hours walk downhill back to
Silvia. It is not safe to park cars in the street at night in Silvia.
   There is a small **Museo de Artesanías**, Carrera 2, No 14-19 with exhibits of
local crafts, past and present. Tourist information is 1½ blocks up from the
plazuela on the righthand side. There are beautiful places to walk and ride
around Silvia. Horse hire from Señora Marco A Mosquiro, and others (take
advice) US$3 per hour.

Sleeping and eating C *Comfandi*, Cra 2, No 1-18, T8251253, F8251076, opposite the
church on the main plaza, clean, safe, restaurant. **D** *Casa Turística*, Cra 2, No 14-39,
T8251034, helpful, hot shower, good food, beautiful garden. **E** *Cali*, Cra 2, No 9-70,
T8251099, an old house, with good craft shop, including food, a little primitive, but very
pleasant. **E** *Ambeima* (3 beds per room), clean, friendly, efficient, good simple meals,
recommended. **F** *La Parrilla*, water supply erratic, basic, restaurant has reasonable,
cheap food. **G** *Residencias La Villa*, about 200 m up the main road, basic but friendly,
negotiate your price. *Taberna El Buho*, friendly, with live music Sat afternoons.

Transport Buses From **Popayán**, daily Coomotorista and Belalcázar, several *busetas*
in the morning (US$2), last transport back to Popayán, 1800; additional buses on Tue;
or take Expreso Palmira bus to **Piendamó**, every 30 mins, US$0.75; from there,
colectivo to Silvia, US$0.85. On market day (Tue) you can take a bus to **Totoró**, 1200,
US$1.50, 1 hr and then a bus to **Tierradentro**, 5 hrs, US$7.

Banks *Caja de Agraria* gives cash against Visa card.

Popayán, Tierradentro & San Agustín

Silvia is reached either through Totoró on the Popayán-Tierradentro road (partly paved), or through **Piendamó** (paved). Both are beautiful routes. **In Piendamó E** *Central*, behind old train station, clean, quiet, dubious electrics; **E** *Motel*, next to Mobil, with cold shower, clean, TV.

Tierradentro

Like San Agustín, Tierradentro is one of Colombia's great precolumbian attractions. Scattered throughout the area are man-made burial caves painted with red, black and white geometric patterns. Some are shallow, others up to 8 m deep. The surroundings have spectacular natural beauty, with small Indian villages in the mountains (get exact directions before setting out). Try to go to Tierradentro for a week and just walk in the hills. The people are very friendly, and you can stop and ask at almost any house to buy *guarapo*, a local slightly fermented drink. It's great to sit and talk and enjoy the hospitality and at night enjoy the spectacular night skies. If you don't have that much time, do try to stay at least two days.

The Páez Indians in the Tierradentro region can be seen on market days at Inzá (Saturday), and Belalcázar (Saturday); both start at 0600. An excellent guide to the Páez Indians and their culture is *Valores Culturales de Tierradentro* by Mauricio Puerta Restrepo, published by the Instituto Colombiano de Antropología, US$2.50.

Ins & outs **Getting there** The road from Popayán to **Tierradentro** is extremely rough, but this is compensated by the beautiful scenery; 67 km beyond Totoró is **Inzá** . There are several stone statues in the new plaza. About 9 km beyond Inzá is the Cruce de Pisimbalá, sometimes known as the Cruce de San Andrés or simply El Cruce, where a road turns off to **San Andrés de Pisimbalá** (4 km), the village at the far end of the Tierradentro Park.

Before reaching Pisimbalá, you pass the **Tierradentro Museum**. ■ *Open 0800-1700, but may close at lunchtime and the entry ticket is valid for the museum and all sites, US$1.50, students with ISIC card US$1, valid for 2 days.*

The well maintained museum is in two parts, an archaeological section including a model of the Tierradentro region with details of the sites and what has been found. The second floor is dedicated to an overview of the Páez Indians and their culture, past and present. This is all very well worth visiting before going to the sites and the staff are very helpful also with local information. Horses can be hired here at US$2.50 per hour.

At Pisimbalá, about 2 km beyond and up the hill from the museum, there is a unique and beautiful colonial missionary church with a thatched roof, dating back to the 17th century.

Tierradentro Archaeological Park At the archway directly opposite the museum, or at Pisimbalá village, you can hire horses (US$2 an hour, make sure they are in good condition) – or you can walk – to the burial caves. There are four cave sites – Segovia, El Duende, Alto de San Andrés and El

Tierradentro

Aguacate. The main caves are now lighted, but a torch (your own or one borrowed from the park administration) is advisable.

At Segovia (15 minutes' walk up behind the museum across the river), the guard is very informative (Spanish only) and turns lights on in the main tombs. Segovia has around 30 tombs, five of which are lit (but not opened until 0800-0900): nos 9, 10 and 12 are best decorated; Nos 8 and 28 are also impressive. Check if photography is permitted. Some 15 minutes up the hill beyond Segovia is El Duende (two of the four tombs are very good). From El Duende continue directly up to a rough road descending to Pisimbalá (40 minutes). El Tablón, with eight stone statues, is just off the road 20-30 minutes walk down. El Alto de San Andrés is 20 minutes from Pisimbalá (Nos 1 and 5 tombs the best – the guard is very helpful). From the back of El Alto it's 1½ hours up and down hill, with a final long climb to El Aguacate. Only one tomb is maintained although there may be 30 more. The views from El Aguacate are superb. You can continue to the museum.

Some say it's better to do this section starting from the museum. Either way, it is a splendid walk. The whole area is good for birdwatching. For a longer hike, ask about the Páez Indian Reserve at Tumbichutzwe, a strenuous 3-4 day walk, or less on horseback: for information ask Edgar at *Hotel Los Lagos*. **Note:** When walking between the sites, take a hat and plenty of water. It gets crowded at Easter. Single women are advised not to wander around this area at night unaccompanied.

Near the museum C *El Refugio*, restaurant and swimming pool (also available to non-residents). **E** *Residencias Pisimbalá*, near Telecom, T8252921, with bath, cheaper without, good, clean, set meal and good other meals, garden, laundry facilities (for non-residents at a small charge), mosquitos. **E** *Residencia La María*, next to Telecom, hot water. **F** *Hospedaje Luzerna*, next to museum, clean and friendly, hot showers with notice, quiet, excellent fresh orange juice, free coffee in morning, laundry facilities, very friendly, ask about walks and horseriding, highly recommended, will let you camp for US$0.50.

In the village F *Los Lagos*, T8252919, 100m past the church, family run, good restaurant, hot water, clean, pleasant, recommended. **F** *El Cauchito*, clean, pleasant, family atmosphere, meals available, will arrange horse rentals, recommended; camping US$1.50 per person. **F** *Residencia El Bosque*, cold showers, cheap meals, friendly dueña collects coins, recommended. **F** *Residencias El Viajero* (Marta Velázquez), meals US$1, clean, friendly, recommended. Ask about others who will rent rooms. **F** per person *Residencias Las Veraneras*, 2 houses run by friendly young couple, restaurant, attractive garden, murals painted by locals.

Pisimbalá, near museum, good food, cheap, recommended. *El Diamanto*, opposite the museum, big portions, good value, order in advance. *Restaurante 56*, next to *Luzerna*, small but very good meals, also vegetarian dishes (ordered in advance), good, friendly, also rents horses. Good fruit juices at the *Fuente de Soda y Artesanía* store. *Los Alpes* (try their juices, eg *mora con leche*), also good breakfasts. *La Portada*, at jeep/bus stop in village, built of bamboo, very good *comida corriente*, fresh soups, good value. *La Braza*, all meals, average US$2, also good juices, *gasolina blanca* for camping at US$1 per litre. The house of Nelli Parra de Jovar, opposite the museum with the long antenna, is recommended for huge portions, but you must book meals in advance. She can also give up to date information on accommodation.

Good Páez Indian artefacts at *Curiosidades Típicas*, rucksacks US$5-7. *Taller de Artesanías*, opposite *El Refugio*, ask for Fabien.

Sleeping

Eating

Shopping

Popayán, Tierradentro & San Agustín

Transport **Buses** There is in theory a daily bus to **Popayán**, at 0600, but services are very erratic and you may have to go from the Cruce. Sotracauca buses from Popayán, US$6, 4-6 hrs to **Cruce Pisimbalá**. Best to take the 0500 or 1000 bus, as the 1300 and 1500 will land you at the Cruce when it's dark, leaving you with a long unlit uphill walk. Walk (about 2 km) to the museum and on, 20 mins, to the village. Bus Cruce Pisimbalá-Popayán, 0600 (unreliable), 0800 and 1300, 4 hrs. If you want to go to **Silvia**, take this bus route and change to a colectivo (US$1.50) at Totoró. For Inzá market (Sat) buses leave Tierradentro from 0200, US$0.55; best to go into Pisimbalá and out again to be sure of a seat. Buses from the Cruce to **La Plata** leave at 1000 and 1600 (also unreliable), US$3, 4-5 hrs; if you cannot get a direct Cruce-La Plata bus, take one going to Páez (Belalcázar) (US$1.20), alight at Guadualejo from where there is a more frequent service to La Plata; or one can hitch. There are more frequent colectivo jeeps from El Cruce to La Plata, US$4. On Fri only, a bus leaves from Pisimbalá village for La Plata at 0400.

Directory **Communications** *Telecom*, a short distance up the hill from the museum.

On the road to Inzá is a turnoff at Alto de San Francisco for **La Pirámide** (2 km). There are two signposted tunnels beneath the mound. There is a good place to buy fresh bread and homemade cheese at the entrance. Also accommodation at **E** *Finca La Pirámide*, turn off at Alto de San Francisco and walk up the hill for 30 mins (2 km), nice rooms, food available, superb views over Tierradentro countryside.

Nevado About 17 km east of Inzá is Guadualejo, where one road heads southeast to La
del Huila Plata (see below), and another north to **Páez (Belalcázar)** (12 km, a dusty drive). A further 23 km north along this road to Santander de Quilichao is **Tóez** on the Río Páez from where there is an access track, following the upper reaches of the river, to the **Nevado del Huila** National Park. At 5,750 m, this is the second highest massif in Colombia and one of the least accessible.

The snow crest, elongated north-south to about 4 km, has four significant peaks, of which the central **Pico Mayor** is the highest, and which from time to time has fumeroles. The **Pico Sur** was unclimbed until 1978. Below are steep difficult ice masses and active glaciers. Climbing is normally attempted from the west side and there are three camp sites – Campamento Gringo, at 3,600 m, Polaco 4,300 m and Colombia 4,600 m. Below near the source of the Río Páez is an MA hut with some facilities. Entry to the Park is US$0.50 per person. There is some good trekking west of Río Páez to the Páramo de Santo Domingo and, cloud cover permitting, great views. There is heavy rain and snow in this area, especially April-June and October-December. There is also thermal activity which makes the area unstable. There have been a number of 'alerts' since 1995 when heavy precipitation led to dangerous slides and flooding below. Seek professional, general safety and MA advice before visiting or climbing in the area. One of the best sources of information is Manolo Barrios (see under Ibagué – Nevado del Tolima).

Popayán to San From Popayán a road crosses the Central Cordillera to Garzón on the paved
Agustín via La highway south of Neiva. At Km 18 from Popayán, the road turning up to the
Plata & Garzón right (south) leads to Coconuco and San Agustín (see below). The valley road climbs to the small town of **Puracé**, at Km 12 (30 km from Popayán), which has several old buildings. Behind the school a path leads for 500 m to Chorrera de las Monjas waterfalls on the Río Vinagre, notable for the milky white water due to concentrations of sulphur and other minerals. At Km 22, look for the spectacular San Francisco waterfall on the opposite side of the valley. At Km 23 is the turning right to Puracé sulphur mines (6 km) which can be visited by applying to

Industrias Puracé SA, Calle 4, No 7-32 Popayán, or, better still, through the Popayán tourist office. About 1 km along this road is a turning left leading in 1½ km to **Pilimbalá** in the **Puracé National Park** at 3,350 m (see below).

Sleeping and eating F *Residencias Cubina*, clean, safe, friendly, cold showers, secure parking. *Restaurant Casa Grande* just above the church, meals around US$2.50.

Buses There are several buses daily to Puracé from Popayán, the last returning about 1730.

Puracé National Park

The National Park contains Volcán Puracé (4,646 m), Pan de Azúcar (4,670 m) with its permanent snow summit, and the line of nine craters known as the **Volcanes los Coconucos**. A strenuous two-day hike can be made around the summits. The Park also encompasses the sources of four of Colombia's greatest rivers: the Magdalena, Cauca, Caquetá and Patía. Virtually all the park is over 3,000 m. The Andean Condor is being reintroduced to the wild here from Californian zoos, and there are many other birds to be seen. The Park's fauna include the spectacled bear and mountain tapir. Pilimbalá is a good base from which to explore the northern end of the park, where there are Páez Indian settlements. Although much of the park is *páramo*, there are also many species of orchids to be found.

Getting there All these places beyond Puracé village can be reached by any bus from Popayán to La Plata or Garzón. The last bus returning to Popayán in daylight leaves the visitor centre at about 1700. The bus service can be erratic so be prepared to spend a cold night at 3,000 m. The Park is open all week, but reduced service on Mon. Standard entrance fee to the park is US$0.60 (as shown above for the Termales at San Juan or climbing the volcanoes). **Ins & outs**

At Pilimbalá: saloon cars will struggle up the last stretch to the centre, but it is an easy 2½ km walk from Km 23. Here there are 7 sulphur baths at 28°C (not all in operation). Entrance US$0.60, children half price, bring your own towels. **Around the park**

The walk to the Cascada de San Nicolás is recommended, turn right when you see the abandoned cabin and continue steadily uphill through very muddy terrain, rubber boots advisable. The waterfall is spectacular, take care on the slippery overhanging rocks. **At Km 37**: The Visitor Centre has a good geology/ethnology museum (entrance US$0.60), and a cafetería which will also provide meals if arranged beforehand through the Popayán Tourist Office. Power for this centre is generated from a small artificial lake of crystalline water 1 km short of the Centre. The rangers are very helpful.

Sleeping and eating The rangers will allow you to stay in the visitor centre at the turning to Pilimbilá.The centre has picnic shelters, a good restaurant (rainbow trout a speciality) and 3 *cabañas* that hold 8, US$32.50 minimum for up to 5 and US$38 for 8 people. Firewood is provided. Camping costs US$3pp. Sleeping bags or warm clothing is recommended to supplement bedding provided. There's also a good scale model of the Park.

The hike to the summit is demanding; loose ash makes footholds difficult. Avoid getting down wind of the fumaroles, and do not be tempted to climb down into the crater. Although the best weather is reported to be **Climbing Volcán Puracé**

December-March and July-August, this massif makes its own climate, and high winds, rain and sub-zero temperatures can come in quickly at any time. A marked trail goes from behind the park office and eventually joins the road leading to a set of telecommunications antennae. These installations are no longer guarded by the military **but the area around them is mined, don't take shortcuts.** The summit is about one hour beyond the military buildings. Start early; the total time from Pilimbalá is at least four hours up and 2½ down, and you may need to take shelter if there is a sudden storm. Rangers will not allow you to start after 1200. An alternative route is from the sulphur mine (at 3,000 m), or driving, with permission, to the military base. It is also possible to walk round the crater (30 minutes). Rope and crampons are useful above the snowline if you want to continue to Pan de Azúcar and the Coconucos. For this trek, high altitude camping and mountaineering equipment are required and a guide is strongly recommended. A descent over the *páramo* to Paletará on the Popayán-San Agustín road is also possible.

Continuing on the main road to La Plata, at Km 31 there is a viewpoint for Laguna Rafael, at Km 35 the Cascada de Bedón (also chemically charged water) and at Km 37 the entrance to the most northerly part of the Puracé National Park where there is another park centre (see above). Here is the very interesting Termales de San Juan, 700 m from the road, entry US$0.60, where 112 hot sulphur springs combine with icy mountain creeks to produce spectacular arrays of multi-coloured mosses, algae and lichens – a must if you are in the area.

At the highest point on this road, still in the Puracé National Park, you leave Cauca and enter Huila Department, which includes the upper reaches of the Río Magdalena and San Agustín. At **Santa Leticia**, on the road to La Plata there is a cheap *hospedaje*, **F**, basic, to the right of the church.

A site of archaeological interest is **La Argentina**, 8 km off the Puracé-La Plata road beyond Santa Leticia. It is set in beautiful surroundings. The Museo Arqueológico de la Platavieja contains statues and ceramics as interesting as those found at San Agustín. Ask for Sr Carlos Hernández, who runs the museum and is extremely knowledgeable. (He also keeps bees and sells honey.)

La Plata
Phone code: 98
Colour map 3, grid B4
Population: 28,000
Altitude: 1,050m

La Plata, whose central plaza has an enormous ceiba tree planted in 1901, is 147 km from Popayán, 210 km from San Agustín. This is a historical town where it is claimed Bolívar stayed several times in local *haciendas*. About 3 km from the town at **La Quiebra Milagrosa** is a shrine much venerated locally. However, this is not a particularly interesting place for the tourist.

Sleeping D *Cambis*, C 4, No 4-28, T8370004, modern, clean, parking on the plaza, meals available, recommended. **E** *Berlin*, by the church on the square, three blocks from the bus office, with bath, **F** without, friendly, but unappealing toilets and bugs in the beds. **F** *Brisas de la Plata*, near the bus station, clean, door locked at 2300. **F** *Hospedaje Exclusivo*, near the bus station, clean, friendly. Next door to *Berlín* is **G** *Residencias Tunubalá*, OK, friendly. **G** *Viajero*, opposite Sotracauca office, basic but convenient. **G** *Residencia Orense*, near bus offices, clean, friendly, meals available. **G** *El Terminal*, clean, friendly, basic, near bus station.

Eating Most restaurants closed by 2000. *La Brasa Criolla*, just off the main plaza, chicken dishes, popular, very good. *Asadero Los Vikingos*, C 4, near *Cambis*, pizzas and all meals. *Noche y Luna*, just off main plaza, very good. *Café y Gelato*, C 4 No 4-32, good selection of coffees and snacks, closes 2030. Good set meals opposite Banco Cafetero. *Panadería Super Pan* excellent bakery on main plaza also serves meals.

Transport Buses To **Bogotá** Coomotor 2000, 2100, 9 hrs, and Cootranshuila 5 a day, 8 hrs US$18. To **Popayán** Sotracanca 0500 Coomotor 0800, 2000, 2200, 6 hrs, US$6 and on to **Cali** US$10; also La Gaitana. To **Tierradentro** Cootransplateña/Sotracauca/Cootranshuila, either to El Cruce or San Andrés, 5 a day, all US$4, 2-3 hrs. To **Garzon**, bus or jeep, 1½ hrs US$3. To **Neiva**, several companies, 2 hrs, US$6.50. To **San Agustín**, direct US$8 or take a colectivo to Garzón or Pitalito and change. Several *chivas* and jeeps daily. Private jeep hire La Plata-Tierradentro US$32, cheaper if you agree to pick up other passengers. Note that bus services in this area are changing all the time, ask around for best options.

Garzón, is a pleasant cathedral town set in mountains, 54 km southeast of La Plata, 92 km south of Neiva.

Garzón
Phone code: 988
Colour map 3, grid B4

Sleeping D *Damasco*, C 16, No 10-67, T2091, colonial building, recommended, good meals. **E** *Abeyma*, state hotel, recommended, Cra 10 y C 12; it is possible to camp in the grounds. **E** *Residencias Pigoanza*, on main plaza, with bath, recommended.

At Altamira, 29 km further southwest, a road heads southeast to Florencia, capital of the Department of Caquetá. Southwest leads to **Timaná** (basic accommodation in **G** range) and continues paved past Pitalito to San Agustín.

Pitalito has little to offer the tourist except that it is here that the brightly painted, imaginative ceramics are made that are often used in tourist advertisements for southern Colombia. Most notable are the extravagantly decorated *chivas*, the ubiquitous country buses of the region. Many other items are produced, a delightful art form expressing a popular culture.

Pitalito
Phone code: 988
Colour map 3, grid B4
Population: 63,000
Altitude: 1,231 m

Sleeping and eating At Pitalito there are 2 hotels with swimming pools: **C** *Calamó*, Cra 5, No 5-41, T8360600, hot water, and **D** *Timanco*, C 3 Sur, No 4-45, T8360666. **E** *Los Helechos*, C 7, No 6-48, T8360122, convenient for buses, clean, friendly, family run. **F** *Residencia Pitalito*, C 5 round corner from police station, without shower, reasonable. **F** *Residencial El Globo*, main street, clean, basic. *Crêperie*, 1 block south of main plaza, good value, excellent.

Transport Air Aires fly from Bogotá to Pitalito, via Neiva, variable service, 1¾ hrs, but the plane only goes if there are enough passengers (confirm tickets 24 hrs in advance). **Buses** go from C 3A. To **San Agustín** 0600, 0800, 1100, 1½ hrs, US$2, also colectivos on demand. To **La Plata** at 1800, 4 hrs, US$4. To **Garzón** colectivo, 1 hr, US$2.50. Taxis Verdes from the main plaza (US$18 to **Bogotá**). Bus to **Mocoa** (in the Putumayo), several daily, US$8.50, 7 hrs, also jeeps from market square, 2 in morning.

South of Pitalito is the Cueva de los Guácharos National Park. Between December and June swarms of oilbirds (*guácharos*) may be seen; they are nocturnal, with a unique radar-location system. The reserve also contains many of the unusual and spectacular cocks-of-the-rock. The rangers are particularly friendly, providing tours and basic accommodation; permission to visit the park must be obtained from the MA offices in Pitalito, Neiva or Bogotá.

Cueva de los Guácharos

Ins and outs Take a bus to Palestina, US$1.20, 1 hr, and then walk for 6 hrs along an eroded, muddy path.

The 9,000 ha park extends to the crest of the *Cordillera Oriental*, here rising to over 3,000 m. It is mostly rain and cloud forest with an abundance of wildlife,

Popayán, Tierradentro & San Agustín

Guácharos – oil birds

These unique nocturnal birds are native to the northern Andes of South America, living during the day in caves in colonies of up to 10,000, coming out at dusk to feed on insects and tree fruits, notably oil palms. This latter food source gives them a high natural oil content which the Indians traditionally used to render into an odourless oil for cooking and lighting, hence the name 'oil birds'.

The Spanish name guácharo probably comes from its shrill cry (perhaps when caught) which is another meaning of the word. Its Latin name is Steatornis caripensis and it is allied to the nightjar. An adult grows to about 40 cm long with a 80 cm wingspan, reddish brown with white and sometimes green markings. Its

unusual feature is its 'radar' method of finding its way in total darkness by sound echoes. The rapid clicking made by the birds can reach an astonishing 250 times a second, but is within the range of human hearing unlike the ultrasonic pulsations of bats. The clicking is not only the system of finding their way around, but also their normal method of communicating with each other.

In Colombia, they are found in caves in several places, particularly Antioquia and the Cordillera Oriental, but the Cueva de los Guácharos is believed to be the largest colony. It is probable that the guácharo, with its curved beak, is the inspiration for some of the San Agustín and Tierradentro stone carvings.

but inaccessible. The main interest centres on the valley of the Río Suárez, a tributary of the Magdalena, which here flows through limestone caves and gorges. There are three caves to visit, Cueva Chiquita near the entrance, Cueva del Indio, 740 m long with interesting calcium formations, and further upstream, the Cueva de los Guácharos with a natural bridge over the river. Entry to the park US$1.50. Accomodation (when available), US$5 per night per person.

Another unpaved road from Pitalito goes southwest to Mocoa through remote jungle, crossing the Río Caquetá 25 km before Mocoa. There are direct buses, some of which go on to Puerto Asís, 11 hours in all.

Popayan to San Agustín Direct Turn to the right off the Popayán-La Plata road at Km 18, then 7 km along is **Coconuco**. Coconuco is known for its baths, Aguas Hirviendas, 1½ km beyond the *Hotel de Turismo* on a paved road (mostly), which has one major and many individual pools with an initial temperature of at least 80°C. Entry US$0.60. There is one pool where you can boil an egg in five minutes. A track from town is quicker than the road. Coconuco and the baths are crowded at weekends, but during the week it is a fine area for walking and then relaxing in the waters. About 6 km beyond Coconuco are another set of hot springs, near the road, called Aguas Tibias, warm rather than hot water, with similar facilities for visitors.

Sleeping in Coconuco B *Hotel de Turismo*, 500 m out of town on the way to the baths, full service, colonial style hotel run by the Cali Tourist authority, restful atmosphere. **E** *Coconuco*, in town, basic. **F** *Casa Familiar*, basic. Several other modest hotels and restaurants in town. **At Aguas Hirviendas**: 3 cabins at US$20 per day that will hold up to 6.

Paletará is 24 km south of Coconuco, with the Puracé and Pan de Azúcar volcanoes in the background. Below the village (roadside restaurant and MA post) flows the infant Río Cauca. About 10 km south of Paletará, the road enters the Puracé National Park and there is a track northeast to Laguna del

Buey. The road then enters a long stretch of virgin cloud forest. This section links Paletará with Isnos and San Agustín. Heavy rains have weakened this stretch, 25 km of which is impassable to light vehicles and very tedious for buses and trucks. No efforts are being made currently to improve this road. Some 62 km from Paletará at the end of the cloud forest is Isnos followed by a steep drop to a dramatic bridge over the Río Magdalena and shortly to the main road between Pitalito and San Agustín.

Warning Avoid travelling by night between Popayán and San Agustín, the roads have been reported dangerous in the past. Cyclists should avoid the new direct route. Also we have received many reports of theft on the buses between these towns; do not trust 'helpfuls' and do not put bags on the luggage rack. Information in 2000 suggests you check carefully before taking this road even by day. Details of services are given under Popayán and San Agustín.

San Agustín

The little town of San Agustín seems an unremarkable place, but here, in the Valley of the Statues, are hundreds of large rough-hewn stone figures of men, animals and gods, dating from roughly 3300 BC to just before the Spanish conquest. Little is known of the culture which produced them, though traces of small circular bamboo straw-thatched houses have been found. Various sculptures found here are exhibited in the National Museum at Bogotá, and there are some life-sized copies of San Agustín originals along the highway from Bogotá to the superseded Techo airport, near Fontibón. There are about 20 sites, described below. The area offers excellent opportunities for hiking, although some trails to remote sites are not well marked.

Phone code: 98
Colour map 3, grid B3
Population: 7,000
Altitude: 1,700 m

Tourist offices Sr Joaquín Emilio García, who was well known as head of the office for many years, has now formed his own private company, *World Heritage Travel Office*, C 3, No 10-84, T/F8373940/8373567, open Mon-Sat 0800-2000, Sun 0800-1300, which we strongly recommend you visit on arrival. Sr Joaquía Emilio García is most helpful in all matters, he speaks English, French, Italian and a little German. Free maps to the area can only be obtained here. He has a list of all hotels, their prices and quality, cabins, and a price list for guides, taxi rides and horse hire. Tours can be arranged at the office.

Ins & outs

Climate The rainy season is Apr-Jun/Jul, but since the weather often comes up from the Amazon basin to the southeast, it rains somewhat during most of the year, hence the beautiful green landscape; the driest months are Nov-Mar. The days are warm but sweaters are needed in the evenings; average temperature 18°C.

Recommended reading The best books on the subject are *Exploraciones Arqueológicas en San Agustín*, by Luis Duque Gómez (Bogotá, 1966, 500 pages) or *San Agustín, Reseña Arqueológica*, by the same author (1963, 112 pages); a leaflet in English is obtainable from tourist offices. The Colombian Institute of Archaeology has published a booklet (English/Spanish), at US$1.80, on San Agustín and Tierradentro; it may be available at museums in San Agustín and San Andrés.

Warning Beware of 'guides' and touts who approach you in the street. Have nothing to do with anyone offering drugs, precolumbian objects, gold, emeralds or other precious minerals for sale. Enquire about safety before walking to the more distant monuments.

Popayán, Tierradentro & San Agustín

Parque
Arqueológico

The nearest archaeological sites are in the **Parque Arqueológico**, which includes the **Bosque de las Estatuas**. The Park, which was declared a World Heritage Site by UNESCO in 1995, is about 2½ km from San Agustín, less than 1 km from the *Hotel Osoguaico*. The statues in the Parque are *in situ*, though some have been set up on end and fenced in. Those in the Bosque de las Estatuas have been moved and rearranged, and linked by gravel footpaths.

Apart from the distinctive statues, the most notable features of the San Agustín site are the **Mesitas** (barrows) consisting of large vertical stone slabs, standing in circular enclosures about 25 m in diameter. These were probably originally roofed over with statues set inside and out. There is some doubt if they were primarily in places of ceremony or tombs. There are four Mesitas, Mesita D is beside the museum area near the entrance to the park, you will visit B,A and C following the trail. Beyond Mesita C are the carved rocks in and around the stream at the **Fuente de Lavapatas** in the Parque, where the water runs through carved channels. The park authorities have reduced the water flow to the Fuente as there was considerable damage being caused by too much water. It is however now easier to see the engravings on the rocks. The **Alto de Lavapatas**, above the Fuente, has an extensive view. It closes at 1600. There are refreshment stands at 'Fuente' and on the way up to Lavapatas.

Within the Park children sell various things including 'guama' fruit, which comes in a large pea-like pod: refreshing moist flavour but do not eat the black seeds!

There is a **museum** in the Parque which contains pottery and Indian artefacts and a good scale model of the local sites giving an excellent idea of the topography of the area (closes at 1700).

You can get a very good idea of the Parque, the Bosque and the museum in the course of three hours' walking, or add in El Tablón and La Chaquira (see below) for a full day. The whole site leaves an unforgettable impression, from the strength and strangeness of the statues, and the great beauty of the rolling green landscape. ■ *Open 0800-1600 daily, entrance to both costs US$2 (US$0.80 with a student card), valid 2 days, also permits entry to the museum and the Alto de los Idolos – see below). Guides: Spanish US$12.50/other languages US$20 per group up to 10, tour takes 2½ hours. Guidebook in Spanish/English US$3.75.*

In the town, at Carrera 11, No 3-61, is the **Museo Arqueológico Julio César Cubillos**. ■ *Open Mon-Sat until 2300, with cultural events in the evenings, a good library and videos in Spanish and English, light refreshments.*

Archaeological
sites

El Tablón is reached up Carrera 14, over the brow of the hill and 250 m to a marked track to the right. El Tablón (five sculptures brought together under a bamboo roof) is shortly down to the left. Continue down the path, muddy in wet weather, ford a stream and follow signs to the Río Magdalena canyon. **La Chaquira** (figures carved on rocks) is dramatically set half way down to the river. Walking time round trip from San Agustín is two hours. Plenty of houses offer refreshments as far as El Tablón. There are many pleasant paths to follow in this area, ask locally for ideas.

Continue along the road from San Agustín for the site of **La Pelota**, two painted statues were found in 1984. It's a three-hour return trip, six hours if you include El Tablón and La Chaquira, 15 km in all. The latest archaeological discoveries 1984/86 include some unique polychromed sculptures at **El Purutal** near La Pelota and a series of at least 30 stones carved with animals and other designs in high relief. These are known as **Los Petroglifos** and can be found on the right bank of the Río Magdalena, near the **Estrecho** (narrows) to which jeeps run.

Also part of the UNESCO site is **Alto de los Idolos**, about 10 km by horse or on foot (small charge, less if you have a student card). It's a lovely, if strenuous, walk, steep in places, via

Parque Arqueológico, San Agustín

Puente de la Chaquira. Here on a hill overlooking San Agustín are more and different statues known as *vigilantes*, each guarding a burial mound (one is an unusual rat totem). The few excavated have disclosed large stone sarcophagi, some covered by stone slabs bearing a sculpted likeness of the inmate (the site is open until 1600). About 500 m from the Alto is **D** *Parador de los Idolos* (3 rooms, bath, hot water).

Alto de los Idolos can also be reached from **San José de Isnos** (5 km northeast) 27 km by road from San Agustín. The road passes the **Salto del Mortiño**, a 300 m fall about 7 km before Isnos, 500 m off the road. Isnos' market day is Saturday. **Sleeping E** *Casa Grande*, central, with bath, cheaper without; **E** *El Balcón*. **Transport** Bus 0500, US$1.20, return 1100, 1300, otherwise bus from Cruce on the Pitalito road, or hitch.

About 6 km north of Isnos is **Alto de las Piedras**, which has a few interesting tombs and monoliths, including the famous 'Doble Yo'. Only less remarkable than the statues are the orchids growing nearby. Bordones is 8 km further on. Turn left at end of the village and there is (½ km) parking for the **Salto de Bordones** falls. Nearby is **D** *Parador Salto de Bordones*, hot water, restaurant.

Horse hire You are strongly advised to hire horses for trips around San Agustín through hotels or the World Heritage Travel Office. The centre for horses is along Calle 5 on the road to the Park (Asociación de Acompañantes y Alquiladores de Caballos) and costs about US$12 per day and US$3 per hour, per rider. If you require a guide, you must add the hire cost of his horse. There are fixed tariffs for 20 or so standard trips.

Tours around San Agustín

Vehicle tours Jeeps may be hired for between 4-5 people. Prices vary according to the number of sites to be visited, but the daily rate is about US$70. Try bargaining for a lower price. The Travel Office will often be able to fill the vehicle, make arrangements the day before. There is a popular tour in a brightly-painted *chiva*, daily at 0900, book the day before: US$16 per person to the narrows, Obando, El Palmar, Alto de los Idolos (entry not included), Isnos (lunch US$1.20), Alto de las Piedras, Saltos de Bordones and Mortiño. For those who like a good walk however, most sites can be reached on foot, see above.

Guides There are 25 guides available at any one time authorized by Turismo at US$15 for a half day, US$30 for a full day, up to 10 people for guide. You can make your own arrangements, and it may cost less (prospective horseriders and jeep passengers tend to congregate at the restaurants on Calle 5), but we have received many reports of unsatisfactory experiences of unregistered guides. Always ask to see a guide's identity badge; if you have any problems, ask at the World Heritage Travel Office.

Popayán, Tierradentro & San Agustín

Sleeping **Between San Agustín and the Parque Arqueológico AL** *Yalconia*, 1 km from town, T8373013, F8373001, full board, some rooms with hot water, very pleasant, swimming pool. **B** *Osoguaico*, T8373069, friendly, warm water, very clean, restaurant, laundry, swimming pool, camping site US$1 per person. **D** *Hostal Mulales*, T8373658, small cottage farm, discounts for longer stays, friendly, pleasant.

In town **D** *Cabañas Los Andes*, Cra 11, No 3-70, T8373461, cabins, hot water and rooms with excellent views, some cooking facilities. **D** *Central*, C 3, No 10-32, T8373027, near bus offices, with bath (cheaper without, or **G** for a room just to dump your luggage in during a day's visit), good meals, laundry facilities, clean and friendly, secure motorcycle parking, will hire horses, English and French spoken.

E *Colonial*, C 3, No 11-54, T8373159, hot shower, clean, pleasant, good restaurant, will provide good early breakfasts, parrots in the garden. **E** *Mi Terruño*, C 4, No 15-85, T8373516, 12 very nice rooms, some rooms with bath, hot water, friendly, attractive garden, motorbike parking, owner Carlos Arturo Muñoz also has 3 cabins, **E** *Los Andaqui*, C 5, No 23-71, T8373265, with restaurant *Pare y Come*. **E** *Residencias El Imperio*, Cra 13, No 3-42, without bath, free coffee, laundry facilities, good. **E** *Residencial Familiar*, C 3, No 11-47, T8373079, 20 rooms, hot water, laundry, friendly, book meals in advance or eat next door at the *Colonial*, horses for hire, but noisy disco nearby at weekends. **E** *Hospedaje D'Zuleg*, C 4, No 10-39, T8373111, with bath, hot water, safe, quiet. **E** *Residencias Menezu*, Cra 15, No 4-74, T8373693, shared bath, hot water, family atmosphere, clean, safe, central, quiet, recommended.

F *Residencias Eduardo Motta*, C 4, No 15-71, T8373031, has 5 rooms, friendly, clean, hot water, hard beds, but with morning coffee, quiet, recommended. **F** *Ullumbe*, Cra 13, No 3-36, T8373799, hot water, clean, helpful, TV, family atmosphere use of kitchen, motorcycle parking. **F** *Residencias El Jardín*, Cra 11, No 4-10, T8373455, hot water, clean, quiet, friendly,cooking and laundry facilities, free coffee. **F** *Ixchel*, C 5, no 15-39, T8373492, new, simple rooms, good restaurant, French/Guatemalan ruin, shows videos, internet services, sells organic coffee. **F** *Copacabana*, Cra 14/via Estrecha, T8373752, good restaurant.

G *Posada Campesina*, Cra 14, Camino al Estrecho (on the route to El Tablón), T8373956, owned by Doña Silviana Patiño, who makes good pizza and cheese bread, meals with family, simple working farm, nice garden, hot showers, clean, use of kitchen, camping possible, good walks nearby. **G** *Casa de Nelly*, Vía la Estrella, 1½ km west along 2 Av, T8373221, attractive peaceful *finca* run by Nelly Haymann (French), hot water, safe, good food nearby at *Tea Rooms* (see below), free coffee. **F** *Residencias Náñez*, C 5, No 15-78, T8373087, hot water, good value, friendly owner, kitchen facilities, horse hire, recommended. **G** *Apartamentos Diana*, C 5/Cra 13, with bath, hot water, good. There is accommodation in private houses for about US$2 per person.

Camping Next to *Yalconia* is *Camping San Agustín*, US$2 per person with own tent, US$3 to hire tent, clean, pleasant, safe (guards), showers, toilets, lights, laundry service, horse hire (see below).

Eating *La Brasa*, opposite *Yalconia Hotel*, good steaks, recommended. *Mulales*, next to Osoguaico, very good. *Brahama*, C 5, No 15-11, health food meals and *comida* including soup and drink (also meat dishes), good fruit salads, not expensive, recommended. *Surabhi*, C 5, No 15-10, friendly, vegetarian dishes or meat, pizzas, *menú*, good juices, desserts etc, recommended. *Bambú*, C 5, No 13-34, good food at fair prices, breakfasts, choice of vegetarian dishes, open all day. *Superpollo*, Diagonal a la Iglesia, chicken, good. *Acuario*, C 3, very good, breakfasts and juices, sandwiches etc, good music. *Bambu*, C 5, no 13-34, good food, fair prices. *Pueblito Viejo*, C 3, No 12-63, rustic decor, friendly, good food, big portions, popular with locals. *La Negra*, Cra 12, No 3-40, good tamales, weekends only. *La Cabaña*, opposite Telecom, oldest restaurant in town, standard fare, good. *Pizzería Arturo*, C 5, No 15-58, good pizzas,

Tap water in San Agustín is not safe to drink

juices, good prices, open to 2200. *Café Taza*, C 5, No 14-28, excellent coffees including organically produced, sit on gigantic Café de Colombia bean-bags, antique coffee machine, excellent pastries, owner Mary Wiede (Colombian) speaks English. *Tea Rooms*, 20m from *Casa de Nelly*, all day breakfasts, evening meals to order US$4, good food, roasts on Sun, good selection of magazines and games, run by an English couple, closed Jul-Aug, recommended.

The *fiesta* of **Santa María del Carmen** is held in mid-Jul (not on a fixed date) in San Agustín. Two festivals in Jun are **San Juan** (24th) with horse races and dances, and **San Pedro** (29th) with horse races, dances, fancy dress, competitions and other events. In the first week of Oct, the Casa de Cultura celebrates **La Semana Cultural Integrada**, with many folklore events from all parts of the country. There are cockfights in San Agustín on Sun 100m behind the church at 1900, US$1.

Festivals

Film is available in several shops. Leather goods are beautiful and priced reasonably. Machetes are good value here Many local shops make boots to your own design (double-check the price beforehand). *Intillay Artsanías de Eleazor Morad*, C 5, between Cra 14/16, good selection; also nearby *Almacenes de Artesanos*. Recommended handicraft shop is *Taller Orfebrería*, C 5, No 14-28, for masks using precolumbian designs, copper and gold items. C 5 leading out of town towards the Archaeological Park has many *artesanía* shops. Market day in San Agustín is Mon.

Shopping

Swimming at the *Piscina Municipal*, behind the *Hotel Yalconia*, clean, busy at weekends, US$1 per day.

Sports

Buses To **Bogotá** by colectivo (Taxis Verdes, C 3, No 11-57, T373068, 0700 and 1900 direct, US$15, 8-9 hrs or by bus Coomotor, C 3, No 10-71), 4 a day, day buses, US$14, night buses (often with long stops) US$16. Halcon has a 'luxury' service, US$20. From **Bogotá**, Taxis Verdes, T4297504/02, 0300 and 0800, 7 hrs. You can call their taxi service T3414000 to collect you, normal fare US$3.50 to Terminal. Alternatively there are frequent services from Bogotá to **Neiva** (approximately hourly, US$9.50, 6 hrs) as well as some to Pitalito (Taxi Verde costs US$14, leaving Bogotá at 0730 and 1030). To **Neiva**, 6 buses a day, including Coomotor and Cootranshuila, 6 hrs, US$6 and the 1000 Autobusco bus to Neiva arrives in time for a late Aires flight to Bogotá. To **Pitalito** 1½ hrs, US$2 by colectivo, or any bus to Neiva.

Transport

To **Popayán** and **Cali**, Coomotor daily via Pitalito, Garzón and La Plata, US$12 to Popayán, US$14-16 to Cali. The bus stops at La Plata, 5-6 hrs, US$5. To **Tierradentro**, check first if the Travel Service is running a jeep from San Agustín, price about US$120 for minimum 4 people or if there is any public transport in place at about US$17, 6 hrs. Otherwise, take early transport to Garzón (eg Taxis Verdes 0700, US$3.50), then a colectivo jeep to La Plata, US$2. With luck, you will get a *chiva* to Tierradentro the same day. Alternatively, make for **La Plata**, stay half a night at a hotel, then, next morning, take the 0500 Sotracauca bus to Cruce de Pisimbalá (more details and alternatives are given under La Plata). Buses to **Garzón** at 1230, 1430 and 1730, US$5, 3 hrs, from where more buses go to La Plata for Tierradentro. There are daily buses from San Agustín to **Popayán** via Paletará and Coconuco with Cootranshuila at 0700, 1000 and 1200 (office on C 3, No 10-81), slow, 6 hrs, US$12; also Sotracauca (C 3, No 10-53) at 0600, continuing to Cali (US$15) and Coomotor on this route to Cali at 1700, 13 hrs, US$18. It may be advisable to book seats the day before. (For information ask in the World Heritage Travel Office; the services are sometimes cut and prices vary.

Banks Travellers are advised to change travellers' cheques before arriving in San Agustín; enquire at the Travel Office and the small shop opposite the police station who may exchange cash. Caja Agraria, C 4/Cra 13, will give cash advances against Visa card.

Directory

Popayán, Tierradentro & San Agustín

Excursion to the source of the Río Magdalena

It is possible to walk from San Agustín to the Lago Magdalena, involving a bus ride or six hours' walk the first day, seven hours' walk the second, and 8-10 hours' walking on the third, either to the lake and back to the second *refugio*, or on to Valencia. From Valencia, there are buses to Popayán. It is also possible to ride from San Agustín via Lago Magdalena to Popayán, some 100 km, in five days or less. A recommended guide is Jorge Caitán, ask at the Travel Office, cost about US$70. Maps are also available here.

If walking in the opposite direction, take a bus from Popayán to Valencia, a dismal village with a very basic place to stay, but food available. A recommended guide for the way to San Agustín is Marnix Beching, Carrera 7, No 2-56, Aptdo 7, Popayán, T241850. He is a Dutchman working at the University of Popayán as a biologist. Seek advice on safety etc before committing yourself.

Sleeping Good bases for this excursion from San Agustín are **F** *Residencias El Paraíso*, at Puerto Quinchana, 30 km away on the road to the source of the Río Magdalena, 2 km from the Cementerio Indígena de Quinchana, owned by Sr Arsenio Guzmán, friendly, peaceful, restaurant. **F** *Residencias El Páramo* at Juntas, beautiful countryside, owner Alvaro Palechor, clean, safe, friendly, restaurant. San Antonio farm, owned by Sr Wilevaldo, riding, fishing.

Southern Colombia

10

Southern Colombia

From Popayán to Ecuador, the Panamerican highway travels through a wide range of scenery. First it drops down to the Patía valley, hot and humid agricultural land and pasture, before it climbs more or less straight into the highlands and Pasto. The old road, built by the Spaniards, takes time to go through small attractive towns to rejoin the new road in one of the highest sections of the country. From Pasto, it is highlands all the way to the border, except where there are spectacular gorges to cross. All of this is dominated by volcanoes: old ones overlook the routes to Pasto, active ones on the border with Ecuador, Azufral near a loop road to Ipiales and the dangerous Galeras above Pasto.

The páramo and the volcanic scenery of the highlands make for a trip full of interest in this pleasant cool climate. A short distance from Pasto is Laguna La Cocha with its exquisite Isla de la Corota National Park to visit. Close to Ipiales is the extraordinary Sanctuary of Las Lajas, an improbable Gothic-style church set in a deep gorge, a place of miracles and pilgrimage.

To the west is the long ride downhill to Tumaco on the Pacific and more of Colombia's Pacific coastline, with salt marshes and mangroves creating another distinct natural habitat for wildlife. On the way, a private nature reserve, La Planada, has a unique population of native birds and a conservation programme of special interest to ecologists.

Highlights of Southern Colombia

★ *Taking your chances in the wild Negros y Blancos fiestas in Pasto.*

★ *Watching them make you a Panama hat in Sandoná.*

★ *Walking up to Volcán Azufral where the crater lake is every shade of green.*

★ *Stopping at El Pedregal between Pasto and Ipiales for the best choclo (grilled corn-on-the-cob) in Colombia.*

★ *The extraordinary gothic-style Santuario de Las Lajas, a shrine at the bottom of a river gorge.*

★ *Visiting the fine private nature park of La Planada between Pasto and Tumaco, one of the finest of the country.*

★ *Crossing the lake to see the exquisite Isla de La Corota.*

Popayán to Pasto

The Pan-American Highway continues south from Popayán to Pasto (the entire road is now paved) and 19 km south of Popayán is Timbío with a clean *Residencial*. At 47 km south is Rosas, a small friendly town, **E** *Casa Familiar*, a small *hospedaje* and a good view to the valley of the Río Patía. **El Bordo** follows at 94 km (**E** *Hotel Patía*, fan, cold water, recommended; **G** *Residencias Central*, on Panamericana, basic, clean, fan). From El Bordo a road runs into the Cordillera Central to Valencia, from where there is a trail to the source of the Río Magdalena and San Agustín (see previous chapter). Some 101 km south of Popayán is a tourist complex, *El Patio*, with hotel, swimming pool and campsite with showers, toilets, barbecues, good, and at El Estrecho, Km 130, there are places to stay and eat.

At Mojarras, Km 140, the main road takes a new route and the full 285 km drive from Popayán to Pasto takes five hours. The road drops to 700 m in the valley of the Río Patía before climbing to Pasto with big temperature changes. About 38 km before Pasto is **Chachagüí**: **E** *Hotel Imperio de los Incas*, T218054, with bath, friendly, swimming pool, restaurant, 2 km from Pasto airport. **G** *Casa Champagnat*, with bath, cold water, swimming pool, friendly and helpful. There is also a tourist centre, **D** *Coba Negra*, with *cabañas*, swimming pools and a restaurant.

The old route via Mercaderes and La Unión can be done by bus; enquire at Popayán or Pasto bus terminals. Some 143 km south of Popayán is **Mercaderes**, a small town with a pleasant climate. Hotels (**F**) are good; *Restaurante Tropical*, recommended. There are three basic hotels at **La Unión** and, 68 km north of Pasto at **El Tablón**, three basic hotels; **G** *Residencial Ambalá*, the best, noisy from passing traffic but convenient for cyclists. To the east, above El Tablón, is the Volcán Doña Juana, with hot medicinal springs near the town of La Cruz. Also nearby is the leather working community of San José de Alban. And 37 km before Pasto on this road is **Buesaco**, a picturesque small town. There is a 19th century *cal y canto* bridge in the canyon below the modern one across the river. To the west of El Tablón is Berruecos where Antonio José de Sucre was assassinated in 1830.

Pasto

Phone code: 927
Colour map 3, grid B2
Population: 326,000
Altitude: 2,534 m

The capital of the Department of Nariño stands upon a high plateau in the southwest, 88 km from Ecuador. Pasto (full name San Juan de Pasto), is overlooked from the west by Galeras Volcano (when not in cloud) and to the east by green hills not yet suburbanized by the city, and enjoys a very attractive setting. It still retains some of its colonial character, but has not been helped by several serious earthquakes in the meantime. The people of Pasto have a reputation throughout the rest of Colombia as being very stupid and are the butt of many jokes. But it's probably best to keep quiet about that!

The **airport** is at Cano, 40 km north of Pasto; by colectivo (beautiful drive), 45 mins. US$2.40 or US$13.50 by taxi. There are no currency exchange facilities, but the shop will change US$ bills at a poor rate. All interurban **buses** leave from the new terminal, Cra 6, C 16, 4 km from the centre (just off the map where indicated). To get there by taxi, US$1 or take city bus No 4 from the centre.

Ins & outs

Tourist offices Just off the main plaza, C 18, No 25-25, T234962, friendly and helpful, open 0800-1200 and 1400-1800 Mon-Fri, closed Sat-Sun. It will advise on money changing.

The city was founded in 1539 by Lorenzo de Aldana, who came up from Quito, and is therefore one of the oldest cities of Colombia. During the wars of independence, it was a stronghold of the Royalists and the last town to fall into the hands of the patriots. Simón Bolívar directed the bloodiest battle of the independence war against the forces of Basilio García on 7th April 1822. His headquarters was nearby in Bomboná. Then the people of Nariño Department wanted to join Ecuador when that country split off from Gran Colombia in 1830, but were prevented by Colombian troops. Today Pasto is a centre for the agricultural and cattle industries of the region. Pasto varnish (*barniz*) is mixed locally, to embellish the strikingly colourful local wooden bowls.

A legacy of colonial times is the considerable number of churches. The **Cathedral** is a large but not distinguished building, sombre in its appearance and austere inside. **San Juan Bautista** church (St John the Baptist) is the oldest in Pasto, though the finely decorated building dates from 1669 which replaced the original of 1539 after damage by earthquakes. The church of **Cristo Rey** (Calle 20, No 24-64, near the centre), has a striking yellow stone west front with octagonal angelic turrets. **La Merced**, Calle 18 y Carrera 22, has rich decoration and gold ornamentation.

Sights

Nearby, at Calle 19, No 21-27, T215777, is the **Museo de Oro del Banco de la República**. It has a small well-displayed collection of precolumbian pieces from the cultures of South Colombia, a library and auditorium. ■ *0830-1150, 1400-1830, US$0.30*. Another museum in the city centre is the **Museo Alfonso Zambrano**, Calle 20, No 29-78, which houses a private collection of indigenous and colonial, especially *quiteño* (from Quito), and period arts. Alfonso Zambrano was a renowned local woodcarver. The **Museo Maridíaz**, Calle 18, No 32A-39, is mainly concerned with religious art and relics from the region.

From the church of **Santiago Apóstol** (Carrera 23 y Calle 13), there is a good view of the green mountains beyond the city. Four blocks to the north are the green tiled domes of the **San Felipe** church (Calle 12 y Carrera 27), opposite the monastery of the **Inmaculada Concepción**. The interior courtyard of the **municipal building** on the main plaza (corner of Calle 19 y Carrera 24) has two tiers of colonnaded balconies.

AL *Morasurco*, Av de los Estudiantes y C 20, T235017, F235639, recommended, reasonable restaurant. **AL** *Don Saul*, C 17, No 23-52, T230618, F230622, comfortable, good restaurant, recommended. **A** *Cuellar's*, Cra 23, No 15-50, roomy, T232879, well-furnished, bowling centre underneath, recommended. **A** *Galerías*, Cra 26, No 18-71, T233069, F 237069, above shopping mall, comfortable, good restaurant, recommended.

Sleeping

Southern Colombia

B *Eldorado*, Pasaje Dorado, No 23-42, T/F233260, good. **B** *Sindagua*, C 20, No 21B-16, T235404, recommended. **B** *Chambú*, Cra 20 y C 17, T213645, modern, with shower, hot water, TV, good but expensive.

C *San Diego*, C 16 A, No 23-27, T235050, good. **C** *El Duque*, Cra 20, No 17-17, T217390, including TV and shower, comfortable, recommended. **C** *El Paisa*, Cra 26, No 15-37, T234592, F239664, good restaurant, bar, laundry facilities.

D *Isa*, C 18, No 22-23, T236663, with bath, clean, helpful, safe. **D** *Río Mayo*, Cra 20, No 17-12, T212989, small rooms, with bath, noisy, restaurant downstairs. **D** *Metropol*, C 15, No 21-41, T214518, restaurant, laundry facilities.

E *Canchala*, C 17, No 20A-38, T213337, big, safe, clean, hot water, TV, central. **E** *Koala Inn*, C 18, No 22-37, T221101, cheaper without bath, laundry facilities, helpful English speaking, Oscar is the well-travelled owner, popular, hot water, cafetería including vegetarian dishes, book exchange, pleasant, excellent travellers guest house, highly recommended.

Pasto

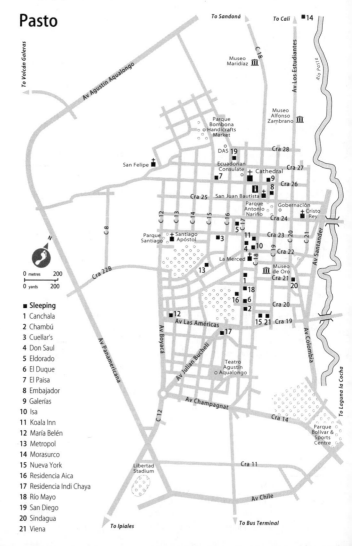

Sleeping
1 Canchala
2 Chambú
3 Cuellar's
4 Don Saul
5 Eldorado
6 El Duque
7 El Paisa
8 Embajador
9 Galerías
10 Isa
11 Koala Inn
12 María Belén
13 Metropol
14 Morasurco
15 Nueva York
16 Residencia Aica
17 Residencia Indi Chaya
18 Río Mayo
19 San Diego
20 Sindagua
21 Viena

Southern Colombia

F *Embajador*, C 19, No 25-57, quiet, private bath, motorcycle parking, cold water.
F *Nueva York*, Cra 19 bis, No 18-20, hot shower, friendly, motorcycle parking.
F *Residencia Indi Chaya*, C 16, No 18-23 (corner of Cra 19 y C 16, up the steps),
T 234476, good value, clean, good beds, carpets, safe. **F** *María Belén*, C 13, No 19-15,
F230277, clean, safe, quiet, friendly, hot water.

G *Residencia Aica*, C 17, No 20-75, T 235311, safe, shared bath, but dirty; **G** *Viena*,
clean, Cra 19B, No 18-36, cheap, restaurant downstairs, clean, noisy.

In the centre *La Merced*, Cra 22, No 17-37, pizzas and local dishes, good. *Punto Rojo*, **Eating**
Cra 24, Parque Nariño, self service, 24 hrs, good choice of dishes. *El Mundo de los
Pasteles*, Cra 22, No 18-34, cheap *comidas*. *Rancho Grande*, C 17, No 26-89, cheap and
open late. *El Vencedor*, C 18, No 20A-40, good value, open 0600-1900. *Las Dos
Parrillas*, Pasaje Dorado, No 23-22, steaks, chicken, reasonable prices. *La Cabaña*, C
16, No 25-20, varied menu. *Govinda*, Cra 24, No 13-91, vegetarian, set lunch US$2.
Riko Riko, various locations, good fast food.

Outside the centre *Sausalito*, Cra 35A, No 20-63, seafood, good. *La Casa Vasca*,
Calle 12A, No 29-10, Spanish, recommended. *Cokorín*, bus terminal, T 212084, meat,
chicken, local dishes. Try *arepas de choclo*, made with fresh ground sweet corn, at the
kiosks beside the main road going north.

Bars *Honey Bar*, C 16, No 25-40, T234895, pleasant atmosphere. **Theatre** *Teatro* **Entertainment**
Agustín Aqualongo, C 16/Cra 16.

During the new year's *fiesta* from Christmas to **6 Jan** there are parades and general **Festivals**
festivities. On **4 Jan,** parades commemorate the *Llegada de la Familia Castañeda.*
Apparently this peasant family, full of characters, came from El Encanio to Pasto in
1928. They are recreated in the parades. There is a *Día de los Negros* on **5 Jan** and a
Día de los Blancos next day. On 'black day' people dump their hands in black grease
and smear each other's faces (nice!). On 'white day' they throw talc or flour at each
other. Local people wear their oldest clothes. On **28 Dec** and **5 Feb**, there is also a
Fiesta de las Aguas when anything that moves gets drenched with water from balconies and even from fire engines' hoses. All towns in the region are involved in this
legalized water war! In Pasto and also in Ipiales (see below), on **31 Dec,** is the
Concurso de Años Viejos, when huge dolls are burnt. They represent the old year and
sometimes lampoon local people – which must be especially insulting here!

Casa del Barniz de Pasto, C 13, No 24-9. *Artesanías Nariño*, C 26, No 18-91. **Shopping**
Artesanía-Mercado Bombodá, C 14 y Cra 27. *Artesanías Mopa-Mopa*, Cra 25, No
13-14, for *barniz*. Leather goods shops are on C 17 and 18. Try the municipal market
for handicrafts. *Mercado Campesino*, southern end of C 16, esquina Cra 7.
Supermercado Confamiliar de Nariño, C 16B, No 30-53, recommended. *Ley* on C 18,
next to Avianca postal office. On the main plaza (C 19 y Cra 25) is a shopping centre
with many shops and restaurants.

You can buy maps of Colombia and cities from *Instituto Geográfico Agustín
Codazzi*, in the Banco de la República building, C 18, No 21-20, limited selection.

Every Sun a game of paddle ball is played across the border on the edge of the town **Sports**
(bus marked San Lorenzo) similar to that played across the border in Ibarra, Ecuador.

Girasur, C 20, no 33A-19, T/F292911, arranges day, weekend and longer tours of local **Tour Operators**
attractions, national and nature parks including Laguna La Cocha, La Planada, Cumbal
and Volcán Galeras.

Southern Colombia

Transport   **Air** To **Bogotá**, 2 flights daily, 1 hr 40 mins, Avianca. To **Cali**, 2 flights daily, 1 hr, Avianca.

Buses To **Bogotá**, 23 hrs, US$32 (Bolivariano Pullman). To **Ipiales**, Cooperativo Supertaxis del Sur US$3, 2 hrs, frequent; by bus, US$2.40, sit on left hand side for the views. To **Popayán**, ordinary buses take 10-12 hrs, US$7; expresses take 5-8 hrs, cost US$9. To **Cali**, US$11, expresses, 8½-10 hrs. To **Tumaco**, 9 hrs by bus, 7 hrs by minibus, US$9. To **Puerto Asís**, 11 hrs, US$10 with Trans Ipiales or Bolivariano (both on C 18), 0500 and 1100. To **Mocoa**, 8 hrs, US$7.25.

Directory   **Airline Offices** *Avianca*, C 18, No 25-86, T232044.

Banks For changing travellers' cheques, *BanColombia*, C 19, No 27. *Lloyds TSB Bank*, C 17, No 19-74, T213139, best rates, Visa advances. *Banco de Bogotá* will change travellers' cheques 0930-1130. If going to Tumaco, this is the last place where travellers' cheques can be cashed. *Casas de cambio*, at Cra 25, No 18-97, T 232294, and Calle 19, No 24-86, T 235616, by the main plaza, changes sucres into pesos and vice versa, and will change US dollars into either.

Embassies & consulates *Ecuadorean Consulate*, C 17, No 26-55, 2nd floor. Four photos needed if you require a visa.

Communications Post Office Cra 23, 18-42 y C 18, No 24-86. **Telecom** long distance calls, C 17 y Cra 23.

Useful addresses DAS C 16, No 28-11, T235901, will give exit stamps if you are going on to Ecuador. **Cruz Rosa** (Red Cross), Cra 25, no 13-26, T230409/232993.

Volcán Galeras   The volcano, Galeras (4,276 m), quiescent since 1934, began erupting again in 1989. A highway traversing all kinds of altitudes and climates has been built round it; the trip along it takes half a day. Check at the tourist office whether it is possible to climb on the mountain – it has been officially closed since 1995. There is a ranger station and police post at 3,700 m where you will be stopped. From there, a rough road goes to the summit near which there is a TV relay station. It is reported that this area is now mined to discourage unauthorised visitors, at least one of whom has died as a result. The volcano itself has claimed several victims including a British geologist, Geoffrey Brown, who died in 1993 when the volcano erupted just as he was setting up equipment to measure gravity changes which, it is hoped, will help eventually to predict volcanic activity. Information on Galeras, and the other volcanoes of Southern Colombia (Azufral, Cumbal and Chiles) can be found at in Pasto, at *El Observatorio*, Carrera 31, No 18-07. They also have a good selection of postcards.

On the north side of the volcano lies the village of **Sandoná** where Panama hats are made. They can be seen lying in the streets in the process of being finished. Sandoná market day is Saturday. There are four buses daily, US$1.50; the last back to Pasto is at 1700. There are good walks on the lower slopes through Catambuco and Jongovito (where bricks are made).

There is interesting country to the southwest of Galeras through Yacuanquer and **Consacá** (hotel/restaurant) to **Ancuya** which is on a tableland on the edge of the Guaitara gorge (restaurant at the right of the church; one *residencia*). Near Consacá is **Bombona** from where Simón Bolívar directed the battle of 1822 to take Pasto. The nearby Hacienda San Antonio was used as a hospital. A further 30 km through spectacular scenery is **Samaniego**, a big village with several hotels and restaurants, a service station and a hospital.

Pasto to   The 250 km road west from Pasto to Tumaco is paved, but is subject to land-
Tumaco   slides – check in Pasto. It leaves the Panamericana 40 km south of Pasto at El Pedregal, passing the brick factories of the high plains of the Cordillera Occidental. At **Túquerres** (3,050 m), the Thursday market is good for ponchos. **F** *Residencias Santa Rita*, Calle 4, No 17-29; several restaurants including

Cafetería La 14, Carrera 14, Calle 20 near Trans Ipiales bus office. Bus to Pasto US$2.25, 2 hours; jeep service to Ipiales from Carrera 14, Calle 20, US$2, 1½ hours). A short distance beyond Túquerres is a track to the right which leads in 2½ hours up to the Corponariño cabin where you can stay the night, US$2.50, and then a further 1½ hours to the spectacular **Laguna Verde** fed by sulphur springs. The lake is in the large crater of Volcán Azufral (4,070 m), still intermittantly active – beware of fumeroles. For information on walking and climbing in this area, enquire in Túquerres.

The road continues to El Espino (no hotels) where it divides, left 36 km to Ipiales, and right to Tumaco. About 90 km from Túquerres, before the town of Ricaurte, is the village of **Chucunez**.

A dirt road branches south here, and after crossing the river climbs for 7 km to Reserva Natural La Planada, a private 3,200 ha nature reserve created in 1982 by Fundación FES La Planada. This patch of dense cloud forest on a unique flat-topped mountain is home to a wide variety of flora and fauna and believed to have one of the highest concentrations of native bird species in South America.

Reserva Natural La Planada

Ins and outs To get there, take a bus to Chunes on the road to Tumaco, 3½ hrs and find a jeep to the Reserve, 20 mins. Alternatively, contact them direct, jeeps can be arranged from Pasto US$30 return.

The Foundation has initiated a programme reintroducing the spectacled bear to the reserve. There are also many orchids and bromeliads to be seen from the nature trails. Day visitors are welcome but camping is prohibited. Check at the tourist office on whether it is safe to climb on the mountain and whether you need a permit.The Visitor Centre has maps and details of nature trails.

Sleeping There is accommodation on site, comfortable cabins, hot water, with 3 meals US$12.50 per day. For further information contact Reserva Natural La Planada direct, Pedro Moreno, Director, T(927) 753396/97, Fundación FES has published a fine illustrated book on the Reserve, US$25, proceeds help conservation.

At Ricaurte is F *El Oasis*, central, the last reasonable place to stay before Tumaco. The road passes through beautiful cloud forest, excellent for bird-watchers (many species of tanager to be seen). About 10 km from Ricaurte is Altaquér where the *Reserva Natural Río Nambi* is located in a particularly rich and diverse ecological region. This reserve also has self guiding trails.

To the coast

At **Junín** (36 km from Ricaurte; restaurants), a road north, 57 km goes to the interesting town of **Barbacoas** on the Río Telembí, a former Spanish gold-producing centre which still retains the remains of an extensive water-front, a promenade and steps coming down through the town to the river. Gold is still panned from the rivers by part-time prospector-farmers. The town has *residencias* and restaurants. Bus to Pasto, US$7.20 (rough trip). The road to Barbacoas is limited to one-way traffic in places – ask the operator at the chain barring the road at Junín to see if the route is clear for you to pass.

This region is very different from highland Colombia, with two-storey Caribbean-style wooden houses and a predominantly black population. Small farms are mixed with cattle ranches, rice farms and oil-palm plantations. Cocoa is grown.

Southern Colombia

Tumaco

Phone code: 927
Colour map 3, grid B1
Population: 115,000

Tumaco isn't exactly the most appealing of places. It suffers from high unemployment, poor living conditions, poor roads and has problems with water and electricity supplies. To make matters worse, it is in one of the world's rainiest areas, and the yearly average temperature is about 30°C . The movement of the tides governs most of the activities in the area, especially transport. The northern part of the town is built on stilts out over the sea (safe to visit only in daylight). A natural arch on the main beach, north of the town and port, is reputed to be the hiding place of Henry Morgan's treasure. Swimming is not recommended from the town's beaches, which are polluted; stalls provide refreshment on the beach. Swimming is safe, however, at El Morro beach, north of the town, only on the incoming tide (the outgoing tide uncovers poisonous rays).

The area is noted for the archaeological finds associated with the Tumaco culture. Ask for Pacho Cantin at El Morro Beach who will guide you through the caves. The coastal area around Tumaco is mangrove swamp, with many rivers and inlets on which lie hundreds of villages and settlements; negotiate with boatmen for a visit to the swamps or the beautiful island tourist resort of **Boca Grande**. The trip takes 30 minutes, US$8 return; ask for Felipe Bustamante, Calle del Comercio, who rents canoes and cabins, has a good seafood restaurant on the island, where water and electricity supplies are irregular. There are several places to stay in the **F** category. There are water taxis north up the coast, across the bay to Salahonda and beyond.

Sleeping D *Villa del Mar*, C Sucre, modern, clean, with shower, toilet and fan, no hot water, good café below, also has well equipped cabins at El Morro Beach. **E** *El Dorado*, C del Comercio, near the water-front and *canoa* dock, friendly but basic. **E** *Barranquilla*, on El Morro Beach, clean, good but beware of ants. Children meet arriving buses to offer accommodation. Most cheap places are in C del Comercio, many houses and restaurants without signs take guests – nearly all have mosquito nets.

Be very careful of food & water because there are many parasites

Eating and entertainment The main culinary attraction of the town is the fish, in the market and restaurants, fresh from the Pacific. A number of good restaurants can be found on the main streets, C Mosquera and del Comercio, though the best is probably *Las Velas* on C Sucre. There are many discos specializing in Afro/South American rhythms; try *Candelejas*.

Transport Air There are daily flights to and from **Cali** with Avianca, 35 mins, and 3 a week with Satena, 1 hr. **Buses** Tumaco to **Pasto**, 9 hrs, US$9, with Supertaxis del Sur or Trans Ipiales (better), 4 a day, interesting ride; minibus 7 hrs. From Ipiales go to El Espino (US$0.75, colectivo, US$1.15) and there change buses for Tumaco (US$4.80).

Banks There are no money exchange facilities, except in some shops that will buy dollars and sucres at a poor rate; change money in Cali or Pasto.

Parque Nacional Sanquianga

The ranger headquarters are at La Vigía, north of Tumaco. The park was founded in 1977 and extends for some 30 km along the coast and a similar distance inland consisting of mangrove covered sandbanks formed by rivers flowing down from the Andes. There are fresh and salt water fish in abundance and a rich variety of bird life. It can also be reached from Guapí and Gorgona. The best time to visit is August-November, but it rains all year. The cost is about US$20 from Tumaco. Some primitive accommodation can usually be found at Playa de Mulatos nearby. Fundación Natura has produced a 'waterproof' guidebook to the mangrove swamps, US$4. Copies available at MA, Bogotá.

It is possible to travel to Ecuador by boat. Part of the trip is by river, which is very beautiful, and part on the open sea, which can be very rough; a plastic sheet to cover your belongings is essential. Take suncream. **Border with Ecuador**

Colombian immigration DAS Alcaldía Municipal, C 11 y Cra 9, Tumaco; obtain a stamp for leaving Colombia here; office open weekdays only.

Entering Colombia from Tumaco You will have to go to Ipiales to obtain the entry stamp. Apparently the 24/48 hrs 'unofficial' entry is not a problem, but do not obtain any Colombian stamps in your passport before presentation to DAS in Ipiales. DAS in Pasto is not authorized to give entry stamps for overland or sea crossings, and the DAS office in Tumaco seems to be only semi-official.

Ecuadorean consulate Visas for Ecuador (if required) should be obtained in Cali or Pasto. Entry stamps for Ecuador must be obtained in the coastal towns.

Transport Daily service at 0800 to San Lorenzo, 7 hrs (but can take 14) tickets from C del Comercio (protective plastic sheeting provided). Sr Pepello, who lives in the centre of Tumaco, owns two canoes: he leaves on Sat at 0700 for San Lorenzo and Limones in Ecuador – book in advance. Also ask around the water-front at 0600, or try at the fishing centre, El Coral del Pacífico, for a cheaper passage, but note that you should try to seek advice on safety before taking a boat (robberies en route reported). Fares: motorized canoe US$20; launch US$50.

About 25 km east of Pasto, on the road to Mocoa is **Laguna La Cocha**, 2,760 m, the largest lake in South Colombia (sometimes called Lago Guamuez). It is 14 km long and 4½ km wide. Near the north end of the lake is the Santuario de Fauna y Flora **Isla de La Corota** nature reserve (10 minutes by boat from the *Hotel Sindanamoy*). This is the smallest protected area administered by the Colombian National Parks service and can be visited in a day. The island was the ritual centre for Quillacinga and Mocoa Indian cultures for several centuries. There is now a small chapel near where you land on the island. There is a research unit and an interesting information centre and a marked path to see the many varieties of trees, small mammals and birds of the island. There are good viewing points of the lake which is also surrounded by forested mountains. A (free) pass to visit the island is needed. **Laguna La Cocha**

Around the lake are 15 or 20 private nature reserves run by a local association to protect prime forest areas and the páramo of the Guamuez river, part of the Putumayo river system. Several of these reserves have trails for visitors. Talk rubber boots (*botas pantomeras*) and wet weather clothing if you plan to hike. Average temperature at the lake is 12°C. For information on reserves around Laguna La Cocha, contact *Asociación para el Desarrollo Campesino*, Calle 10, No 36-28, Pasto, T/F231022/294044, cipar@cali.cetcol.net.co

Sleeping By the lake, 3 km from the main road, is the **C** *Chalet Guamuez*, T219306, recommended, particularly for the cuisine, cabins for 6 can be hired; free van-camping allowed. The chalet will arrange a US$22 jeep trip to Sibundoy, further along the road; boats may be hired for US$2.50 per hour. **B** *Sindamanoy*, T236433, chalet style, government-run, good views, inviting restaurant with good but expensive food, free van, and tent camping allowed with manager's permission. There are also cheap and friendly places to stay in and near **El Encano** (sometimes shown on maps as 'El Encanto') there are also many restaurants serving trout. You can also stay in various places around the lake, eg Tunguragúa and Encanto Andino, access by boat. Make arrangements in El Encano or at the hotels.

Transport La Cocha may be reached by taxi from Pasto, US$9, or colectivo from Calle 20 y Cra 20. Also you can take a bus to El Encano and walk the remaining 5 km round to the chalets area, or 20 mins from the bus stop direct to the lake shore and then take a *lancha* to the chalets for US$3.

South to Ecuador

Passing through deep valleys and a spectacular gorge, buses on the paved Pan-American Highway cover the 84 km from Pasto to Ipiales in 1½-2 hours. The road crosses the spectacular gorge of the Río Guáitara at 1,750m, near El Pedregal, where *choclo* (corn) is cooked in many forms by the roadside.

Ipiales

Phone code: 927
Colour map 3, grid C2
Population: 72,000
Altitude: 2,898 m

Ipiales, 'the city of the three volcanoes', stands close to Colombia's main border crossing with Ecuador and is famous for its colourful Friday morning Indian market. The Catedral Bodas de Plata is worth visiting.There is a small museum, set up by **Banco de la República**.

Ins & outs   San Luis **airport** is 6½ km out of town. **Buses** to most destinations leave from the main plaza. See under Transport on next page.

Excursions   The city's main attraction, 7 km east on a paved road, is the Sanctuary of the Virgin of **Las Lajas** which was declared a National Monument in 1987. Seen from the approach road, looking down into the canyon, the Sanctuary is a magnificent architectural conception, set on a bridge over the Río Guáitara. Close to, it is very heavily ornamented in the gothic style. The altar is set into the rock face of the canyon where the Virgin Mary appeared around 1750. This forms one end of the sanctuary with the façade facing a wide plaza that completes the bridge over the canyon. There are walks to nearby shrines in dramatic scenery. It is a 10-15 minutes walk down to the sanctuary from the village. There are great pilgrimages to it from Colombia and Ecuador (very crowded at Easter) and the Sanctuary must be second only to Lourdes in the number of miracles claimed for it. The Church recognizes one only.

There are several basic hotels and a small number of restaurants at Las Lajas. You may also stay at the convent, simple but cheerful. Try local guinea pig and boiled potatoes for lunch (or guinea pig betting in the central plaza may be more to your taste).

Getting there   Ipiales town buses going 'near the Sanctuary' leave you 2½ km short. Take a colectivo from Cra 6 y C 4, US$1 per person, taxi, US$6 return (it's about a 1½ hrs' walk, 7 km).

About 15 km northwest of Ipiales is **Cumbal** which sits beneath two 4,700 m volcanoes, Cumbal, immediately above the town (see next page), and Chiles, further south and on the Ecuador border. There is accommodation, **F**, at Carrera 8, No 20-47 (no name), basic, and very good food at *Rincón de Colombia*, Calle 18, No 8-48, good value. Jeep from Ipiales (Calle 15, No 7-23) US$1, 1 hour.

Sleeping   **B** *Angasmayo*, C 16, No 6-38, T252997, clean, comfortable, a little overpriced. **B** *Mayasquer*, 3 km on road to frontier, modern, nice restaurant, very good, T252643.

Volcán Cumbal

Volcán Cumbal, 4,764 m is the highest point in South Colombia. It can be climbed from Cumbal village using tracks made by miners who dig sulphur near the main crater which is used by industries in Ecuador and Colombia. The miners also bring down ice blocks for domestic use.

There is usually, but not always, snow on the highest summit for water, but you will find ice in the crevices. There are many fumeroles but there has been no serious activity for 70 years. Sleeping in the crater is popular with those wishing to see the

spectacular morning view, north to the Laguna La Bolsa (or Laguna Cumbal) and the other nearby volcanoes (Azufral and Galeras) and south to Volcán Chiles (4,748 m) on the border, but especially Cayambe, Antisana and a glimpse of Cotopaxi in Ecuador. You might even see a condor.

As a reward on your return, ask for a cholado, a mixture of fruit juices including lemon, sugar and aromatic aniline (from the indigo plant) – with crushed ice from the volcano.

D *Dinar*, Cra 4A, No 12A-18, T253659, cafetería, private parking. **D** *Korpawasy*, Cra 6, No 10-47, T252246, good food, plenty of blankets. **D** *Pasviveros*, Cra 6, No 16-90, T252622, bath, hot water, clean, interesting decoration.

E *ABC*, Cra 5, No 14-43, with bath, hot water, clean, good value. **E** *Bachué*, Cra 6, no 11-68, T252164, safe. **E** *Belmonte*, Cra 4, No 12-111 (near Transportes Ipiales), good beds, very clean, hot water, parking opposite, good value but crowded. **E** *Rumichaca Internacional*, C 14, No 7-114, T252692, clean, comfortable, good restaurant with reasonable prices.

F *Colombia*, C 13, No 7-50, hot water, clean except for toilets, helpful, parking for motorbikes. **F** *San Andrés*, Cra 5, No 14-75, clean, hot water.

G *India Catalina*, Cra 5a, No 14-88, T254392, hot shower, run down, 2 blocks from main plaza. **G** *Nueva York*, C 13, No 4-11, near main plaza, rundown, plenty of blankets, friendly. **G** *Oasis*, Cra 6, No 11-34, one block from main plaza, shower, ask for hot water, quiet after 2100, clean, helpful, also Oasis 2, nearby.

Camping Free behind last Esso station outside town on road north.

Eating *Don Lucho (Los Tejados)*, Cra 5, No 14-13 (*antioqueño*). *Don José*, Cra 5, No 14-53. *Panextra*, on Parque Central, good food, reasonable prices, popular. Plenty of cheap restaurants, better quality ones on Cra 7. *Panadería Galaxia*, C 15, No 7-89, for a good cheap breakfast. Outside town towards the frontier, *La Herradura*, good food, reasonable prices, try their excellent *trucha con salsa de camarones* (rainbow trout with shrimp sauce), recommended.

Transport **Air** To **Bogotá**, **Neiva** and **Puerto Asís**, 4 times a week, Aires. TAME (of Ecuador) has flights to Quito from Tulcán, Mon-Fri. Taxi to centre US$4.

Buses To **Popayán**, Expreso Bolivariano, US$9, 7½ hrs, hourly departures, 0430-2030; Transportes de Ipiales US$13 (neither on main plaza, best to take taxi from border), also transport from main plaza, Super Taxis and Cootranar *busetas*, sit on right side for views. Bus to **Cali**, US$14, 12 hrs, from main plaza. To **Pasto** from main plaza, colectivo US$3.25, 1½ hrs; Flota Bolivariano buses every hour, US$3, 3 hrs. Buses to **Bogotá** leave every hour from 0500, 24 hrs, US$35 (note, if coming from Bogotá, there is an hour's stop in Cali; bus leaves from a different level from which it arrived). To **Medellín**, Expreso Bolivariano, 22 hrs, US$33. To **Túquerres** and **Ricaurte** on the Tumaco road, *camperos* (4WD taxis) leave from in front of San Felipe Neri church; for **Tumaco** take a bus or *campero* to El Espino and wait for a bus from Pasto.

Southern Colombia

Directory **Banks** It is not possible to cash travellers' cheques, but cash is no problem; *Bancolombia*, cash against Visa. *Casa de Cambio* at Cra 6, No 14-09, other *cambios* on the plaza. There are money changers in the street, in the plaza and on the border, but they may take advantage of you if the banks are closed. Better rates if needing sucres are to be had in Quito. Coming from Ecuador, peso rates compare well in Ipiales with elsewhere in Colombia.

Communications International calls from Cra 6 between C 6/7, opposite Banco de Occidente. 3 min minimum for international calls.

Border with Ecuador

Ipiales is 2 km from the Rumichaca bridge across the Río Carchi into Ecuador. The frontier post stands beside a natural bridge, on a concrete bridge, where customs and passport examinations take place from 0600 to 2100.

Colombian immigration & customs All Colombian offices are in one complex: DAS (immigration, exit stamp given here), customs, INTRA (Dept of Transportation, car papers stamped here; if leaving Colombia you must show your vehicle entry permit) and ICA (Dept of Agriculture for plant and animal quarantine). There is also a restaurant, Telecom for long-distance phone calls, clean bathrooms (ask for key, US$0.10) and ample parking.

Ecuadorean immigration & customs The Ecuadorean side is older and more chaotic than the modern Colombian complex, but nonetheless adequate. There is a modern Andinatel office for phone calls. Ask for 90 days on entering Ecuador if you need it, otherwise you will be given 30 days. **NB** You are not allowed to cross to Ipiales for the day without having your passport stamped. Both Ecuadorean exit stamp and Colombian entry stamp are required. Although no one will stop you at the border, you risk serious consequences in Colombia if you are caught with your documents 'out of order'.

Crossing by private vehicle If entering Colombia by car, the vehicle is supposed to be fumigated against diseases that affect coffee trees, at the ICA office; the certificate must be presented in El Pedregal, 40 km beyond Ipiales on the road to Pasto. (This fumigation process is not always carried out.) You can buy insurance for your car in Colombia at Banco Agrario, in the plaza.

Ecuadorean consulate In the DAS complex described above; open weekdays 0830-1200, 1430-1800.

Exchange There are many moneychangers near the bridge on both sides. Travellers report better rates on the Colombian side, but check all calculations.

Transport From Ipiales to the border, colectivo from C 14/Cra 11, wait till all seats are full, US$0.40. From border to **Tulcán** (Parque Ayora near the cemetery six blocks from the centre) US$0.70, to Tulcán bus station, US$1. Taxi to or from border, US$3.50. From Ipiales airport to the border by taxi, about US$6.50. If arriving at Ipiales from the north by bus, ask the driver to drop you as close as possible to the point from which the colectivos leave for the frontier.

Los Llanos & Amazonia

11

Los Llanos & Amazonia

Eastern Colombia stretches for hundreds of kilometres from the Cordillera Oriental to the Río Orinoco and the borders with Venezuela, Brazil and Peru, and covers more than half of the country.

The northern part consists of vast plains known as Los Llanos, open scrub and grasslands, hot and dusty in the dry season but swampy and virtually impenetrable when it rains. Rivers provide transport all year round but, due to the flatness of the landscape, they meander and are slow-moving. This is Colombia's Wild West, where hardy cowboys tend huge herds of cattle. Most of the area is practically empty of people, save for a few settlers and occasional Indian tribes, but wildlife abounds, particularly birds, and it is a fisherman's paradise. Travellers to the region also frequently comment on the fantastic quality of the light in Los Llanos and the extravagant sunsets.

To the south is the transition to thick, humid Amazonian forest, where it rains all the year round. Many parts are continuously flooded, so the only way to get around is by boat or canoe. The forest is teeming with life. Colombia's Amazon basin is home to more species of birds, mammals and plants than almost any other country of the world. For the visitor, this means a wealth of things to see, helped by the creation of ten of the largest National Parks of the country. All, however, require considerable effort and time to reach, compounded by the unfortunate political situation at the present time.

Highlights of Los Llanos and Amazonas

★ Making your wishes come true at the
Obelisco near Puerto López.
★ Marvelling at the roaring waters of
the Orinoco at El Tuparro.
★ Learning about the way of life of the
indigenous groups protected by

Colombia's Amazonian National Parks.
★ Walking the rope bridge over the
jungle at Amacayacú.
★ Seeing the world's smallest monkeys
and largest water lilies in the wild near
Leticia.

Los Llanos

The vast region of Los Llanos comprises the Arauca, Casanare, Vichada, Guainia, Meta, Vaupes and Guaviare Departments. The economic value of Los Llanos is mainly as cattle country though large areas are unused. Roads go only so far into the plains, normally close to the main rivers, after which they are tracks which you can follow in dry weather but are impassable when it is wet. River transport is possible but tedious and requires considerable navigational skills because of currents and shallows. Distances are great and plenty of time is needed. Air travel is a good alternative but expensive. Apart from scheduled routes, there are many small airlines that run more or less regular services.

The people are warm and hospitable, great horsemen with a touch of the Wild West about them. Once you hear the music of the *llaneros*, however, you will never forget it.

Ins & outs   **Driving in Los Llanos** Plenty of reserve gasoline should be carried as there are few service stations. Take food and plenty of water with you. Fishing tackle could be useful. Everybody lets you hang up your hammock or pitch your tent, but mosquito nets are a must. Roads' are only tracks left by previous vehicles but easy from late Dec till early Apr and the very devil during the rest of the year. More information on the *llanos* can be obtained from the office of the Gobernación del Departamento de Meta, C 34/Cra 14, Bogotá.

Arauca and Casanare Departments

Access to Arauca Department is from Pamplona in Norte de Santander Department, then through the Cordillera Oriental, which crosses here into Venezuela. The road passes alongside the Tamá National Park (see under **Pamplona**) as it descends to the plains through Cubará to **Saravena,** a small town on the edge of Los Llanos with basic accommodation and an airport serving the nearby oilfields. From here the road follows the Río Arauca 150 km to **Arauca**, the capital of the Department, (accommodation and usual services), through some of the most important oilfields of Colombia, including the El Limón deposits. The pipelines following the road have often been the target of guerrilla groups (ELN), and, as a consequence, this is regarded as a dangerous area. Arauca itself in an uninteresting place but the bridge over the Río Arauca gives access to Venezuela (El Amparo) with routes to San Antonio, Barquisimeto and Caracas. This is not an official crossing point for vehicles and is mainly used by locals. On occasion there are border problems here between the two countries. The Río Arauca moves wholly into Venezuela (from being the border) a few km downstream from Arauca.

On a loop road from Saravena to Arauca is (or was, it appears to have been abandoned) a nature sanctuary known as the Parque Arauca, located between the Ríos Lipa and Ele. This as an area of little rain and high temperatures. The rivers, however, are fed by water from the Andes and there is plenty of wildlife, including capybara, a large hairy aquatic rodent, similar to a guinea pig. They are not an endangered species and you will find them on local menus.

From Saravena, a road runs south to **Tame**, another oil producing centre, within sight of the Sierra Nevada del Cocuy (see under **Boyacá**). From Tame, a poor road follows the foothills of the Cordillera for over 200 km to **Yopal**, capital of Casanare Department. This is another small but growing regional town, serving the cattle ranchers in the plains and the oil fields to the north. The main route to Yopal is through Boyacá via Sogamoso, and over the Cordillera above Lago de Tota with spectacular views. There is virtually no tourism here though there are future plans for visitors to stay on *fincas* in the region to see life on the llanos and experience their legendary hospitality at first hand.

South of Yopal, the road continues to Villanueva and Meta Department (see below), but it's a long and tedious journey. As it is running along the edge of the mountains, there are many rivers to cross, and often problems with the bridges. Settlements with tracks running down into the llanos are common, but there are no bridges over Río Meta.

Transport Air To **Bogotá** daily flights with Satena and Aerotaca; to **Bucamaranga** with Satena, 3 a week, and Aerotaca; to **Tame** 4 a week with Satena; to **Villavicencio** 3 a week with Satena, and to **Arauca**. Aerotaca, who also fly to **Cúcuta**. To **Sogamoso with Aerotaca. Bus** Frequent service to Sogamoso 4½ hrs US$5. To Bogotá several daily, 9 hrs, US$12.50. To Villavicencio, daily service.

Villavicencio

Locally shortened to Villabo (Vee-a-bo), Villavicencio is the capital of Meta Department. Founded in 1840 by Esteban Aguirre, it was originally a staging post and market for the ranching activities of the Llanos, conveniently on the way to Bogotá. Villavicencio is a good centre for visiting the *llanos* stretching 800 km east as far as Puerto Carreño and Puerto Inírida on the Orinoco. Cattle raising is the great industry on the plains, sparsely inhabited mostly by *mestizos*, rather than Indians.

Phone code: 98
Colour map 4, grid A1
Population: 310,000
Altitude: 498 m

A spectacular 110 km road runs south east from Bogotá to Villavicencio, at the foot of the eastern slopes of the Eastern Cordillera. A tunnel, completed in 2000, has reduced the journey by road from Bogotá to 1¼ hours. The **airport,** La Vanguardia, is 4 km northwest of the town. The **bus station** is outside town on the ring road to the east, on Av del Llano. A taxi costs US$1.

Ins & outs
For regional information:
www.villavo.com

Tourist offices *Instituto de Turismo del Meta,* Cra 32, No 38-70. Edif Promarco, T/F6716666, turimeta@villavicencio.cetcol.net.co Mon-Fri 0800-1230, 1400-1700 and information booth at Buenavista, 5 km from town on the road to Bogotá.

There is an attractive central plaza, **Parque de Los Libertadores** (also called Parque Santander), with many ancient *ceibas* and busts of Francisco Santander and Simón Bolívar. The cathedral of **Nuestra Señora del Carmen**, built in the middle of the 19th century, overlooks the plaza. A good place to see the city is from the **Monumento a Cristo Rey**, off Calle 40 to the southwest of the city. In the same direction, on the road to Acacias, is the **Monumento a Los Fundadores,** a sculpture by Rodrigo Arenas Betancur. There is a **botanical garden** 2 km from the centre. For local festivals See under **Music and Dance**.

Sleeping **AL** *Del Llano*, Cra 30, No 49-77, T6641716, F6641125. A/c, TV, bar, restaurant, gym, sauna, pools. **AL** *Villavicencio*, Cra 30, No 35A-22, T6626434, F6626438, hotvicio@andinet.com. Suites available, a/c, hot water, pool on terrace, very comfortable, good restaurant, they can arrange stays at **AL** *Colinas de San Genaro*, short distance outside town, horseriding, relaxed atmosphere. **B** *Imabú*, Cra 37A, No29-49, T6624402. A/c, cable TV, restaurant, parking, comfortable. **D** *Serranía*, C 37A, No 29-63, T6624190. Second floor, with bath, some a/c. **D** *Centauros*, C 38, No 31-05, T6625106, small rooms, reasonably clean and quiet, central. **D** *Don Lolo*, Cra 39/C 31, T6631824. Pool, restaurant. **E** *Central*, Cra 30A, No 37-06, T6625167. With bath, fan, quiet. **E** *Residencias Don Juan*, Cra 28, No 37-21 (Mercado de San Isidro). Attractive family house, with bath and fan, sauna, safe, recommended. **F** *Residencias Medina*, C 39D, No 28-27. OK, shared shower, washing facilities.

Youth Hostel: Granja Los Girasoles, Barrio Chapinerito, T6642712. 160 beds, 3 km from bus station.

Eating *Fonda Quindiana*, Cra 32, No 40-40. Central, local dishes. *Chop Suey*, Tra 25, No 41A-25, T6641461. Chinese, good. *Hato Grande*, C 35, No 17-07. Barbecued steaks, typical *llanera* grills, very good. *Ricardos*, C 37A, No 29-101. Central, local and international dishes, snacks, self service, good. *La Ragazza*, C 41A, No 35-15. Italian, good. Other Chinese restaurants in the centre and several fast food places eg *Kokorico* on or near the main square: other pleasant places to eat, some with swimming pools, on Cra 22, the road to Puerto López.

Shopping *Almacenes Ley*, C 37, No 29-83 is a good place to stock up with provisions if you are making for the *llanos*.

Transport **Air** To Bogotá: Aires 3 a day, Satena 1 a day. To **Puerto Carreño:** Satena 3 a week. To **Medellín:** Satena 2 a week. To **Puerto Inírida:** Satena 3 a week. Satena also flies to a number of other destinations in Los llanos. There are about 20 small companies flying air taxi services to local airfields, some depart from the Apiay Air Force Base to the south east of the town. Taxi from La Vanguardia to town, US$4, bus US$0.50.

Bus La Macarena and Bolivariano run from Bogotá about every ½ hr, US$4, 4 hrs; or colectivos Velotax, US$4.20, or Autollanos, who run every hour, US$6. Be prepared to queue for tickets back to Bogotá.

Directory **Banks** *Bancolombia* and other banks on or near the Plaza. Most have ATMs. **Communications Post Office** *Adpostal*, C 39/Cra 32. **Newspapers** *Llanos 7 Días*, a good weekly source of local information. **Useful addresses** Red Cross, Cra 30, No 39-30, T6623332/3. *Police*, T112 or T6625000. *Tourist Police*, T6625489.

North from Villavicencio A paved road goes north along the piedmont marking the transition between Los Llanos and the Cordillera. About 18 km from Villavicencio is **Restrepo,** with several interesting salt mines in the vicinity including **Salinas de Upía.** The paved road continues another 10 km to **Cumaral,** at 425m, where you can bathe in rock pools. Along this road are restaurants and places to stay. In another 10 km is Maya near the hot springs of **Guaicaramo**, in an area of exuberant vegitation. Beyond is Villanueva (in Casanare Department), with an impressive bridge over the river Upía (see Box page 115). This (now unpaved) road leads eventually to Yopal (see above), about 250 km from Villavicencio. Buses run along this road which, incidentally, was where many of the Spanish *conquistadores*, having laboriously crossed the llanos, usually in the wet season, then sought a route to climb up the mountains and find their elusive El Dorado.

A good asphalt road has been built east from Villavicencio which passes a large **Northeast from** rice mill, the La Libertad agricultural station, the Apiay oil field and two vaca- **Villavicencio** tion centres to reach **Puerto López** (87 km) on the Río Meta, more or less the limit of significant river transport from the Orinoco.

A few kilometers beyond Puerto López is the 21m high **El Obelisco** at Alto Menegua. This is a colourful hollow, four sided monument built in 1993. It has elements of local pre-history, cultural heritage, industrial achievement and a relief map of Colombia depicted on the sides. At the summer solstice, the mid-day sun illuminates the geographic centre of Colombia below the tower. If you stand at this place, your wishes will be granted. There is a wonderful view of the Llanos from the site.

Sleeping and eating E *Menegua*, Cra 8, No 4-35, T6450477. **E** *Tío Pepe*, Cra 5, No 7-39, T6450400. **F** *Morichal*. There are several other hotels and *residencias* and a number of basic restaurants.

You can, with some patience, arrange to go downstream by boat to Puerto Carreño, 3-6 days, about US$40 (negotiable). The road east (unpaved) con-tinues through horse and cattle country for another 150 km to **Puerto Gaitán**, a hot and dusty place. There are good views and great sunsets to be seen from the bridge across the Río Manacacías. Nearby it joins the Río Meta where there are good white sand beaches.

Sleeping and eating E *Manacías*, beside Texaco petrol station. **G** *La Playa*. **G** *Turista*. **G** *El Viajero*. All basic. Several simple restaurants, river fish, chicken and rice etc. The *Panadería* on the corner of the plaza provides meals and information.

Transport Several buses a day to **Puerto López**, Flota La Macarena, 3 hrs, US$3 and on to **Villavicencio**, 5 hrs, US$8.

The road continues more or less following the Río Meta for 40 km to **San Miguel,** passing through a Sikuané Indian reservation on the way. Near this rough village is a turning (8 km) to the Japanese-run agricultural project, *Fundación Yamato*, which has **D** cabins, price negotiable, clean and comfort-able. The Japanese director welcomes visitors. Ask at the *Fundación* office or the tourist office in Villavicencio or in Puerto Gaitán for possible transport to the *Fundación*. Otherwise take the bus (see below) but it will leave you with a 90 minute walk in the searing heat. Near the ranch are many isolated lagoons (*morichales*) where there is an incredible array of water bird life. Bus from Puerto Gaitán daily at 1400, 1½ hours.

It is another 20 kms to **San Pedro de Arimena**, after which the road to Puerto Carreño degenerates into a rough track impassable in the wet season.

Beyond San Pedro is a turn-off to **Oracué**, a port on the Río Meta from where gold (*oro*) and leather (*cuero*) used to be exported to Venezuela, Brazil and beyond. Times are less prosperous now but some fine old buildings have been preserved. There are amazing sunsets. The local Sikuané Indians have an arts and crafts cooperative, *Casa Indígena* T(987)565903. They will help you to find somewhere to stay and eat.

Transport: River boats, *Líneas Fluviales del Meta,* daily from Puerto Gaitán 0530 (or when the bus from Villavicencio arrives). There is an airstrip at Orocué and a poor road runs north to Yopal.

The road following the Río Meta crosses into Vichada Department for the remaining 500 km to Puerto Carreño. Vichada and Guainía Departments, the

Los Llanos & Amazonia

eastern bulge of Colombia, are remote, with few inhabitants, and more naturally lead to the Orinoco rather than to the populations of Colombia to the west. Indeed, many places are best visited from Venezuela than Colombia.

Puerto Carreño

Phone code: 9816
Colour map 4, grid A3
Population: 8000
Altitude: 51 m

Where the Río Meta joins the Orinoco, is **Puerto Carreño** . Overlooking the town is the **Pico de la Bandera,** a black rocky outcrop, which can be climbed. It offers an excellent view over the Llanos and the confluence of the rivers. There are good beaches and bathing during the dry season at Tiestero, 15 minutes from town by taxi, or a 1½ hour walk, popular with locals on weekends.

Sleeping & eating

E *Martha Helena*, 2 blocks from plaza near navy headquarters, T54086. Clean, friendly, family run, with private bath and fan. **E** *La Vorágine*, off Av Orinoco near the plaza, T54066. With bath, **F** without. Along Av Orinoco going from the plaza to the waterfront are the following: **E** *Apartotel Las Cabañas*, T54018. With private bath, fridge and TV. **E** *Safari*, T4302926 (Bogotá). With private bath, fan or a/c, clean, friendly, tame birds in courtyard, fridge facilities. **E** *Orinoco*. Clean, meals. **E** *Samanaré*, T54181. Rooms and 1 cabin for large group, disco-bar next door, a bit rundown but clean and friendly, set menu is good value, other food and drinks expensive. There are several restaurants along the same street, *Dona Margarita* is recommended; also *Donde Mery,* which serves breakfast. *Kitty,* near *Hotel Safari*, and *Oasis*, on main street, for refreshing juices.

Sports

For fishing excursions contact Victor Parra at *Taller Milton Guarín* near *Panadería Pompey* or Feliciano Morán, owner of *Almacén Safari*. Equipment can be bought in Puerto Carreño or Puerto Ayacucho.

Transport

Air To/from **Bogotá** Satena 3 times a week, US$160 round trip, tickets are sold at *Hotel Safari* and *Residencias Mami*, payable only in pesos, flights on Tue Thu and Sat. AeroRepública fly Sat. **Bus** There is a weekly bus to **Villavicencio** during the dry season, taking 2/3 days if you don't get stuck, US$30, take food and plenty of water. Check on safety before making the trip. **River** Launches upstream on Orinoco to Casuarito, 0800 and 1500, similar times return, US$6 one way. To La Primavera on Río Meta, 8-10 hrs, one or two a week, US$45. It is possible to carry on up the Río Meta on another launch, then bus to Villavicencio.

Directory

Banks Banks will not change cash or TCs. Shopkeepers will change cash, good rates for Venezuelan bolívares, extremely poor rates for US$. Try *Almacén Safari* or *Ferretería Pastuzo* on Av Orinoco. If arriving from Venezuela, best to bring enough bolívares to be able to pay for your onward transport into Colombia.
Useful addresses There is a **DAS** office on the plaza near the Casa de Cultura.

Border with Venezuela

Colombian immigration

DAS office is 2 blocks from the plaza, walking away from the river, near Casa de Cultura. Entry/exit stamps are given here.

The DAS agent meets all flights arriving from Bogotá or Villavicencio. Foreigners must show passport and register with him.

To Venezuela There are 2 routes. Launches run throughout the day to El Burro, US$2.50, via Pto Páez. From El Burro, *por puestos* leave when full for Pto Ayacucho, (DIEX office for documentation), US$3 total time from Pto Carreño is 2-3 hrs. Taxi US$8. Alternatively, take an 0700 boat to **Casuarito** (often full, buy ticket the day before at the foot of Av Orinoco) and then cross directly to Pto Ayacucho, US$0.30, reporting to the DIEX office there for your Venezuelan entry stamp (closes 1500). This takes 3-4 hrs, with an interesting ride along the river. There is no DAS in Casuarito, so that you must, in all cases, get your exit stamp in Pto Carreño.

NB It is very difficult to change US$ in any form into pesos or bolívares in Pto Ayacucho. There are some, but limited, possibilities in Casuarito.

On Av Orinoco, one block from the plaza, walking towards the river. Official requirements are onward ticket, 2 photos, and US$30, visa issued the same day, but procedures are extremely arbitrary. Only single entry visas are given here, maximum 30 days. Try to obtain visa, if required, in Bogotá.

Venezuelan consulate

El Tuparro National Park

The Park, created in 1980, is 548,000 ha in extent and bounded by the Río Tomo in the north and the Ríos Tuparro and Tuparrito, and Caño Maipures in the south. Birds, orchids, monkeys, snakes, bromeliads and dolphin can be seen, and there are excursions to river beaches, the burial site of the now extinct Maipure (or Maypure) Indians, and the **Raudales de Maipures** rapids on the Orinoco at the confluence with the Río Tuparro.

Here the Orinoco narrows and forms channels of raging water passing over a series of enormous flat rocks extending for about 5 km. The altitude at the Orinoco is 100 m, the highest point in the Park, 315 m. It is 85% savannah and 15% forest, much of which is *galería* forest, inundated in the wet season, in which there are many colonies of monkeys. It is a fine place to see birds.

Getting there The Park is in Colombia, but is normally reached via Venezuela. Follow the procedure as above for going to Pto Ayacucho, including having all documents stamped. From Pto Ayacucho take a taxi south along the road beside the Orinoco to Montaña Fría, US$10, where a launch can be hired for about US$80 (shared) to take you to the administative centre of the Park near the confluence of the Río Tomo with the Orinoco. There may be a tour boat from *Camturama Lodge,* a short distance upstream from Montaña Fría. It is about 1½ hrs by launch to the visitor centre. Bring your own food, which can be supplemented with local fish. Entrance to the Park US$2.50.

Ins & outs

For information on the Park and in general for the area and the border, try the *Casa Fiscal* in Puerto Carreño, which is where the rangers stay when in town.

The administrative centre (no accommodation) is on the Río Tomo near its junction with the Orinoco. There are camping facilities and a visitor centre at Maipures, up the Orinoco, near the rapids, 25 mins by boat from the administration centre. A 20 minute walk from the centre is the **Pozo Azul**, a swimming hole in attractive surroundings. Two hours walk away is **Piedra Canales** where there are caves with Indian pictograms and one hour by boat up the Río Tomo are several beaches and a short walk to **Cerro Peinillos**, one of the higher points of the park and more evidence of Indian occupation including burial sites.

At Maipures there are cabins, US$30 for 4 people/night, rooms have mosquito nets. Restaurant good, US$7 for all 3 meals. Otherwise, bring all your own supplies. Camping is US$12.50 for 5 people. In the dry season, visitors are asked to be especially careful not to cause fires.

Sleeping & eating

Los Llanos & Amazonia

Transport It is possible to reach the Park by road in the dry season (Dec/Mar and Jul/Aug) from Villavicencio, about 700 km, but there are only isolated settlements for the last 500 km beyond Puerto Gaitán. The route bears right after San Pedro de Arimena then left at Guacamayas to follow the Río Tomo to El Tapón, the western entrance to the Park, not nornally manned, no facilities. Navigation is crucial for this section and four-wheel drive essential. From El Tapón it is 190 km to the administration centre, about 6 hrs drive in good conditions. The whole trip from Villavicencio takes about three days.

There are 2 landing strips in the Park, one in El Tapón and one near the MA administration centre on the Río Tomo.

The dirt road from San Pedro de Arimena mentioned above continues beyond Guacamayas to **Santa Rita**, in Vichada Department, about 400 km through the llanos. Santa Rita is a port on the Río Vichada, 50 km or so from its confluence with the Orinoco. It has a few *residencias*, **G** per person, and it is possible to sling a hammock. It is expensive, like all the towns in the eastern llanos and it is useful to have US dollars or Venezuelan bolívares.

Transport There are 2 buses a week in the dry season from Villavicencio, US$50, journey time 2 days with an overnight stop at Gaviotas (basic *residencias*). There is frequent river transport from Santa Rita to ports on the Orinoco and to Puerto Inírida. The road ends at Santa Rita. This is a good area to experience the wonders of the changing light and colours of the Llanos as you travel.

Puerto Inírida Geographically due east of Villavicencio, near to the border with Venezuela, **Puerto Inírida** is the capital of Guainía Department. Except in the town, there are no roads, and indeed none in the Department. River and air the only alternatives.

To visit the local indigenous communities, you must go to the Oficina de Asuntos Indígenas and speak to one of the Community Leaders (Capitanes). The office is near the port. The local groups are Puinave, Guahibo and Curripaco.

About four hours upriver on the Río Inírida is the **Cerro de Mavecuré**, a collection of three mostly sheer sided black rocks with excellent views across the Llanos from the top, where you can camp. Other peaks are Cerro Mono and Cerro Pajarito (the biggest). A visit by boat from Puerto Inírida, US$30 per person is a well worth while excursion. The best way to see the region is to take a one week trip, about US$25 per person per day with a daily US$7 for fuel and US$4 for food, based on a party of four. The Indian groups along the river sell wood carvings and basketry using local materials like the bark of the *chiquichiqui* palm found by the Ríos Apaporis and Inírida. Take care not to offend them if you take photographs. One of the largest Puinave communities is close to the Cerro de Mavecuré at **El Remanso.** There is good river scenery and places to camp on white sand beaches. It is a good idea to take fishing tackle. Travel on the rivers in the dry season is more difficult due to shallows and rapids. Going up the Río Guaviare is not recommended at present on security grounds.

Sleeping and eating E *Safari,* beside the COMCEL antenna, meals, basic, good advice. **E** *Toninas,* owned by Carmen, cafeteria. There are a few basic *residencias* and places to eat.

There is an office of Telecom and basic facilities only.

Serranía de la Macarena

The oldest rock formations on the surface of South America are in Brazil and the Guiana Highlands of Venezuela and Brazil. The Andes chain is geologically recent, indeed is still being 'created' by movements of the earth. Yet right beside the Andes in Colombia is the Serranía de la Macarena, less than 100 km east of the Cordillera Oriental and the continental divide. Furthermore, the lower exposed formations have been identified as early Ordovician/late Cambrian which dates them as 350-400 million years old. Although several other areas of Los Llanos and Amazonas have examples of isolated inselbergs or tepuis, none is as massive as La Macarena, nor has such clear fossil identification as ancient as this.

It is located on the border between the comparatively dry area of the Llanos, and the tropical Amazonian forest region. The height of over 2,500 m creates its own microclimate, damp cool misty conditions with average temperatures varying from 12°C to 25°C within a small distance. Thus flora, fauna and people have a unique habitat, making this area a fascination for geologist, botanist and archaeologist alike.

Transport Air To **Bogotá**, 3 Satena flights a week and an AeroRepública flight via Puerto Carreño on Sat, US$125; taxi to the airport, US$1. **River** Travel is in launches called here *voladores,* and as the name implies, they are fast, necessary for the considerable distances involved. A weekly boat to **Santa Rita** (see above) 5 hrs, US$25. Launch to **Tuparro** (for Puerto Ayacucho) US$20 per person, about 5 hrs, more time coming back depending on water levels. For information on river transport, *Transporte Fluvial del Inírida,* T(9866)5656590, managed by Elmer Díaz. They also have a contact in Puerto Ayacucho (Venezuela) T048-212184. For organising trips, contact Orlando Isaza (known as Copetín), who can be reached through Hotel Safari. His wife, Luz Marina, is an excellent cook. Recommended.

In the south of Guainía Department is the large **Reserva Nacional Natural Puinawai** (also written Puinavi), a strange area of jungle and *tepuis*, encompassing some of the headwaters of the Río Negro. The Park borders on Brazil to the south. The only access is by the Río Guanía, one of its tributaries. The situation is similar to that of Nukak Maru (see below).

Puinawai National Reserve

South from Villavicencio

The road south from Villavicencio is paved through Acacias and San Martín, a cattle town, to **Granada** (bus 1½ hours, US$1.50), on the Río Ariari, which flows down to San José del Guaviare. It is an attractive trip, the latter portion marking the edge of the Serrenía de la Macarena National Park, but unfortunately out of bounds at present. From Granada, the road deteriorates rapidly. **Vista Hermosa** (Flota La Macarena bus from Bogotá, US$6, 9 hours), situated near the break-point between the Llanos and the jungle, lies further south along this road (G *Pampa Llanura*, opposite the Flota La Macarena office, clean and friendly).

Between Granada and Vista Hermosa is San Juan de Arama, near which is a road to the right (very muddy in the wet, March-November) leading in 6 km to the administration centre of the **Parque Nacional Natural Serranía de la Macarena**, a Tertiary outcrop 150 km long by 35 km broad (see Box). Its vegetation is so remarkable that the Sierra has been designated a National Park exclusively for scientific study, although the flora is under severe threat from colonization and drug cultivation.

Serranía de la Macarena

Los Llanos & Amazonia

Essentials If you wish to visit the Sierra, seek advice on conditions in advance, preferably from MA in Bogotá. There is also an office in the Park where you can hire guides (eg for hikes to waterfalls). Admission US$2.50, vehicle US$2.50 camping US$12.50 for five persons. The village of La Macarena, at the southern end of the Sierra, has flights from Villavicencio 3 times a week (Satena). It is close to some of the best river scenery in the Park with rapids and waterfalls, notably on the Río Guayabero. There are camping facilities at this end of the Park also.

Tinigua National Park Acting as a bridge between the Macarena and Los Picachos National Parks is the **Parque Nacional Natural Tinigua,** 202,000 ha of piedmont tropical forest, along the Ríos Duda, Lozada and Guayabero. It is approached via San Vicente del Caguán, but being partly within the FARC *zona de espeje*, it cannot be visited at present.

Guaviare Department A turn-off at Granada leads eventually (210 km) to San José del Guaviare, the most important settlement within the *zona de despeje* of the FARC. This road is closed to normal traffic. San José is on the Río Guaviare about 500 km by air up river from Puerto Inírida (at least double that distance by river). The eastward extension of the Macarena National Park borders Guaviare Department almost to San José.

At the opposite side of the Department bordering Vaupés is the **Reserva Nacional Natural Nukak Makú,** one of Colombia's largest National Parks and perhaps the remotest corner of the country. There are no facilities and the indigenous communities are among the most primitive of South America, little more than hunter-gatherers. Unhappily, increasing contact with the outside world is endangerinnng their habitat and introducing diseases (like influenza) fatal to them and their numbers are dwindling rapidly. So far, the goveernment has not managed to keep new settlers out of the territory and the future of these communities is bleak. It is very unlikely that permission will be granted for the time being.

Mitú To the southeast of Villavicencio, along the Río Vaupés, and near the border with Brazil, is **Mitú,** the only town of any size in Vaupes Department. Ask around for guides. In the wet season, traders will take you down river to Brazil (July-Aug). After several hundred kilometers, the Vaupés joins the Río Negro (see under **Up the Río Negro to Colombia** below). Good local buys are baskets and bark paintings. There is a small hospital near the airport.

Phone code: 9816
Colour map 4, grid B2
Population: 5000
Altitude: 170 m

Sleeping E *La Vorágine*. Shower, fan, clean, owned by Sr León, who will help you to arrange trips. **F** *JM*. Friendly, helpful, morning coffee, next to Satena office.

Eating Plenty of restaurants around. *De la Selva*, a meeting place of the pilots who fly into Mitú. Recommended

Transport Air Satena flies 2 times a week from Villavicencio and Bogotá.

Amazonia

Caquetá, Putumayo and Amazonas are the Amazon forest Departments of Colombia with the characteristic high rainfall fed by the airstream from the South Atlantic. Several major National Parks here are helping to conserve the many rare species of birds, flora and fauna of the region. The southern extremity of Colombia touches the Amazon itself at Leticia, and is a good place to visit Amazonia as a tourist with reasonable standards of services and good air communications.

At present, everything in the Leticia area and the Parque Amacayacú is open normally, and the zones around Villavicencio and Florencia have no problems. Elsewhere, you must seek local information, things are changing all the time. Those with special interests may find they can visit the Parks they wish but see the **National Parks** section for further advice.

Lying to the east of the Cordillera Oriental is the Department of Caquetá, reached by air, or by road from Altamira, 160 km south of Neiva on the road to San Agustín. The natural forest cover around Florencia, the capital of the Department, has been cleared, creating undulating pasturelands for livestock raising, dotted with tall palms, the fruits of which are a delicacy for grazing cattle. To the southeast, beyond the cleared lands, lie little-touched expanses of tropical forest inhabited by indigenous tribes and wide varieties of Amazonian flora and fauna.

The road Neiva-Florencia is 260 km and is possible in one day. It is recommended that the last 100 km from Altamira over the mountains into Florencia be driven by daylight. This is the only road into Caquetá. The climb up over the mountains goes through a region of small farms, through sugar-cane cultivation and up into cloud at the higher points of the route. Soon after the summit, and on a clear day, there are extensive views out over Caquetá and then the road winds down through substantial forests - ablaze with the colours of tropical flowers in the dry season (January-March) and into the lowlands. The lower section of the road into the lowlands is prone to frequent landslides. There is a thorough army check-point on this road.

The roads in Caquetá run from Florencia along the foothills of the Cordillera. Other routes are difficult and seasonal (although tracks, or *trochas*, are laid out as part of the settlement scheme) and the main lines of communication into the lowlands are the Ríos Caquetá and Caguán and their tributaries.

Florencia

Florencia, was originally established in 1908. It is the capital of Caquetá Department. The plaza contains sculptures, fountains, a large forest tree (*saba*) and flower beds. Overnight, cars are best left in the care of the fire-station (US$0.20 a night). The local Saint's day is 16 July, with a candlelight procession in the evening.

Phone code: 984
Colour map 3, grid B4
Population: 118,000
Altitude: 1300 m

Sleeping C *Kamani*, C 16, No 12-27, T354101/355760. Good value, safe. **D** *Metropol*, Cra 11, No 16-52, T354891. **D** *Royal Plaza*, Cra 11, No 14-64, T357504. **F** *Residencias Don Quijote*, Cra 11, No 13-28, T353190. and others in same price range.

Transport Air To *Puerto Asís* with Satena, on Thu and Sun. To *Neiva* several daily, Satena, Aires. To *Bogotá*, several planes a week, Satena and Aires. **Bus** There are regular services from Neiva (US$7.80, 7 hrs), Garzón and Altamira (bus Altamira to Florencia, US$3.75) and frequent services as far as Puerto Rico and Belén. Bus to Bogotá US$20.

Florencia to Puerto Rico

From Florencia the road runs northeast as far as San Vicente del Caguán. It is paved for 67 km to El Doncello, passing through **El Paujil** (*residencias* along the road into the town). **El Doncello** itself (*residencias*), is a pleasant town, overlooked by the church, which has a brightly painted steeple. There is a popular Sunday market. Next comes the small settlement of Esmeralda with a hotel, a ford for trucks and buses, wooden suspension bridge over the river for which there is a toll.

Los Llanos & Amazonia

Puerto Rico
Phone code: 988
Colour map 3, grid B5
Population: 32,000
Altitude: 250 m

Puerto Rico is a river port on the Río Guayas, which is crossed by ferry (US$0.10). Houses built down by the river are raised on stilts above possible flood levels. River boats are made and repaired by the riverside. Note that *residencias* are full on Saturday nights, so book a room early in the day. Buses then go as far as San Vicente where a mule-track goes over the Cordillera to Algeciras in Huila Department.

Warning San Vicente del Caguán is at the centre of the FARC *zona del despeje*. Near the boundary there is an army checkpoint beyond which tourists are not welcome. The area downstream of this road, along the Río Caguán and its tributaries is a cannabis growing region.

South from Florencia

The road southwest from Florencia is paved as far as Morelia, where a poor branch road goes west to **Belén de los Andaquíes**, passing through interesting scenery, and crossing fast-flowing rivers by metal bridges. There are places to stay here.

Beyond Belén further areas of settlement are reached by unsurfaced road. Another unsurfaced road goes south from Morelia to the Río Pescado, where a ferry will take you across the river to the town of **Valparaíso**, with several places to stay. From Valparaíso mule tracks go further into the lowlands.

Anyone wanting to see wildlife in Caquetá must travel beyond the settlement area. Toucans, monkeys, macaws etc are kept as pets, but there is little life in the wild. The main areas of interest are downstream from here. Boats and canoes are easily hired, but make enquiries about safety conditions and what services are available in the remoter regions. You must also have plenty of time.

The Río Pescado flows southeast from Valparaíso and soon joins the Río Caquetá, one of the major Colombian rivers which, renamed Río Japurá, joins the Amazon at Tefé in Brazil, after a journey nearly twice as long as the Río Magdalena.

Araracuara

Some 450 km downstream from Valparaíso is Araracuara which it is possible to reach by air from Bogotá, a spectacular flight over the Cordillera Oriental, Los Llanos and the northern part of the Amazonia forests. Araracuara is the starting point for trips to Cahuinarí and Chiribiquete National Parks, two of the biggest in Colombia. Both are 3-4 days away by boat. Araracuara features in a recommended book, *Perdido en el Amazonas* by German Castro Caicedo. It describes a fateful journey in the region during the years of the rubber boom when Araracura was an Alcatraz-style prison. It is set mainly in the Cahuinarí region.

Sleeping Accommodation is possible by prior arrangement with SINCHI research station US$10 per person, meals US$3. For information, ask at their office in Bogotá, C 20, No 5-44, T2836755, F3600365, open 0830-1130, 1400-1630. SINCHI are very helpful to visitors and will advise on guides for the forest. It is also possible to sling a hammock near the jetty. The town is 20 mins walk from the airport, look for the *flor de inírida* also called *estrella del sur*, a beautiful star-shaped flower around the runway.

Transport Air There is a military check at the airport and you must register with them when you arrive and leave. At the side of the runway you can see the burnt-out fuselage of a large aircraft on which is inscribed Trespassers will be shot. A nice welcome to Amazonia! To **Bogotá** via Villavicencio, Satena, once a week, USD$150 one way, buy your return passage on arrival. To **Leticia,** Satena, once a week.

Across the river at **Puerto Santander** (in Amazonas Department) there is a hotel **E** *El Turista*, clean, showers, pre-ordered meals US$3. From Puerto Santander, it is possible to walk through savannah and jungle to **La Chorrera** (see under **Amazonas** below).

This is true Amazon forest, high rainfall, high humidity and temperatures averaging 27°C with little variation though it can be cool at night. It is only 150 m above sea level. The wet season is from April to September and the river levels are higher at this time, but it rains most days all the year round. It was declared a National Park in 1987 and covers an area of 575,000 ha, 80% of which is an Indian Reserve. There are several ethnic groups, including the Andoque, Miraña and Bora, living in the Park which is home to the black and Amazon caiman and is one of only two known natural habitats of the Charapa turtle – the other is in Brazil. This species is the largest freshwater turtle in the world, can grow over 80 cm in length and up to 55 kg. The MA and Fundación Natura (Calle 61, No 4-26, Bogotá, T3456188, www.natura.org.co) are working to protect them from possible extinction. Problems include pressure from local trappers who trade in reptile skins.

Cahuinarí National Park *The Park is in Amazonas Department but is covered here because access is from Araracuara*

The Park is 2-3 days downriver from Araracuara, the guides usually stop for one night at the home of Luis Angel Lucho Trujillo, who operates an interesting agricultural project and is very informative on the local wildlife and the pink dolfin in particular. He has a good library. There are two fine waterfalls on side tributaries, the **Chorro del Sol** and the **Chorro de la Culebra.**

Information A permit is required to visit the Park, free from MA in Bogotá. It is best to arrange a group to visit Parks such as these to economise on costs of guides and transport, and also for safety. MA will give you advice. You will need to register with the Indian communities through whose territories you may be going and to know what the custom is with regard to taking photos of the local people and gifts. If you intend passing through the Miraña Indian lands ask in Araracura when you arrive for advice on local customs and arrange permits. You may be offered delicious smoked fish to eat and drinks made from local fruits (made with local river water). The cost of guides is about US$30 per day and a boat US$16 per day plus fuel at US$4 per US gallon. You will need to take your food and supplies with you, hammock, mosquito net, repellent, rubber boots and fishing equipment. All food and clothing etc should be in waterproof containers and bags. Protection against yellow fever, tetanus and especially hepatitis B are recommended. Cooking facilities are available at the ranger station in the Park and accommodation is in an indigenous *maloca* or palm-thatched wooden hut.

This is the largest National Park in Colombia, with an area of 1,280,000 ha. It is in a remote part of Caquetá and Guaviare Departments and there are very few settlements in the area. There are several *tepuis* – flat topped mountains – remnants of ancient geological formations, which have developed their own ecosystems with a remarkable variety of flora and fauna.

Chiribiquete National Park

Information The Park is officially closed to visitors for conservation reasons but those who wish to undertake research may obtain special permission. It is best to make arrangements well in advance. To get there is a 3-4 day trip from Araracaura first a short way down the Río Caquetá, then up the Ríos Yari and Mesay through very attractive scenery, with detours necessary in places where there are rapids. The best place for up-to-date information is in Araracaura but, before going, check with Fundación Puerto Rastrojo, Cra 10, No 24-76, Of 1201, T2849010, F2843028, (Bogotá), who maintain a cabin/research station in monkey territory at the entrance to the Park where you can stay, with permission. This is a scientific research institute and a very useful source of ecological and local information.

Los Llanos & Amazonia

Putumayo Department

The road from Pasto to the Putumayo deteriorates rapidly after El Encano. It is steep but spectacular. It is also dangerous between Sibundoy and El Pepino (the junction for Mocoa) and care should be taken (especially by cyclists), but there is a magnificent view out over the Putumayo by a large statue of the Virgin, just before the final descent.

Sibundoy
Phone code: 927
Colour map 3, grid B3
Population: 4,500
Altitude: 2,600 m

In Sibundoy there is a beautiful church on the main plaza, completed in 1968. About a quarter of the valley is now reserved for Sibundoy Indian occupation from the Inga and Kamza communities. They wear long purple, blue and white *ruanas*. During their rituals, they take *yajé*, a hallucinogenic drink from a local vine called *juipa* (banisteriopsis caapi). There is a local artist here, Carlos Jacanamijoy, whose colourful forest paintings can be found in Bogotá and are being sold in the USA. Market day is Sunday.

Sleeping and eating D *Turista*, clean, friendly; better meals at **F** *Sibundoy*, but hotel dirty, unhelpful, not recommended. **F** *Residencia Valle*, clean double rooms, hot water. *Restaurant Viajero*, just off main street. You can camp in the hills, where there are lovely walks and you can see all kinds of flora and fauna.

Transport Bus from **Pasto** (3 hrs, US$3), passing through Colón (*residencias*) and Santiago.

Mocoa
Phone code: 988
Colour map 3, grid B3

Mocoa, the administrative capital of the Department of Putumayo, has a very modern plaza, new offices and modern developments. Sugar-cane is grown in the area. The main **DAS** office for the region is in Mocoa.

Sleeping C *Continental*, C 8/Cra 6, T395428. With shower, cold water, new, TV, fan, clean. **D** *Central*, off main plaza. Very clean and friendly. **G** *Macaritama*. Safe, TV, cold water. **G** *Residencia Colonial*, Cra 6, No 8-10. Spartan but safe.

Transport Bus To **Pasto**, 8-12 hrs by bus and jeeps to US$5. To **Pitalito**, 7 hrs, US$6. To **Sibundoy**, US$3, 5 a day. To **Puerto Asís**, US$5, a few police checks.

Puerto Asís

Phone code: 98
Colour map 3, grid C3
Population: 55,000
Altitude: 250 m

The road continues from El Pepino, through cattle-ranching country, to Puerto Asís, the main town and port of the Putumayo. The water front is 3 km from the centre. River traffic is busy. For those interested in flora and fauna it is necessary to travel down river, beyond new areas of settlement or by canoe up the river for monkeys and many birds.

Warning Puerto Asís is a marketing centre for cocaine and has been the scene of much guerrilla and counter-insurgency activity.

**Sleeping
& eating**

C *Chilimaco*, C 10, No 20-06, T4227217/18, F4227191. A/c, cheaper without, cable and Ecuadorian TV, good restaurant. **D** *Tayrona I*. Cra 21, No 9-81, T4227029/8203. Good, clean, friendly. **D** *Tayrona II*, Cra 22, No 10-91, T4227490. Clean, quiet, friendly. **F** *Residencias Gigante*, C 10, 24-25, clean. **F** *Residencias Nevado*, Cra 20, close to the airport. Well kept and comfortable, a/c optional. **F** *Residencias Liz*, C 11. With bath, very friendly. *Rinconcito Paisa*, opposite Tayrona I. Good breakfasts and juices. Plenty of places to eat in town.

Transport Air To/from **Bogotá** 6 times a week by Satena direct or via Ipiales. Satena also fly to **Cali**, **Florencia**, **Pasto** and **Pto Leguízamo**. Aires fly to **Neiva**, and **Ipiales**. Flights also to **Lago Agrio** in Ecuador. Taxi to town from airport US$1.

Boat All boats that leave for **Leticia** (with connections to Manaus) are cargo boats, and only sail when they have cargo. They leave from the Hong Kong wharf (*muelle*), or the nearby Bavaria and Esmeraldas wharves. Local information in town is poor, you must check with the boat personnel yourself. We understand that at present, no boats are taking passengers. In any case, those carrying gasoline (and most do) are not supposed to take passengers. In the past, fares to Leticia were about US$100; at least 10-15 days travel. By boat to **Leguízamo** takes 2-3 days, or by speedboat (*volador* or *deslizador*), 7 hrs, US$25 one way. The trip is through dense jungle country, note the *chontadura* palms (bactris gasipaes), from which palm hearts are extracted. Planting of these trees is one of the projects to replace coca cultivation. Boats do not go unless the rivers are high because of shallows and sandbanks. Take supplementary food and water with you, meals on the boats are uninspired. Take comprehensive advice on safety before travelling downriver from Puerto Asís.

Bus To Bogotá US$24, 18 hrs. To Mocoa, 5 a day, US$5. To **Pasto** 4 a day, 10 hrs, US$8, be prepared for military checks. Jeep north to **Pitalito**, book in advance through bus company. Bus to **Sibundoy** US$4. For bus information: Transipiales, on corner of plaza, T4227279.

Communications *Telecom*, main plaza, open 0800-2100, also next to the mayor's office, C 10.

Five buses a day go from Puerto Asís to **San Miguel** (four hours, US$3.60), on the Río San Miguel, which is the Ecuadorean border here. The Sunday market provides a meeting place, and *canoas* may be hired to visit villages 2-4 hours away on the river.

To Ecuador from Puerto Asís
With drug and guerrilla problems, both on the Colombian side and in Lago Agrio, foreigners should stay away from this area for the time being.

There are several very basic hotels, eg **F** *Mirador*, safe and *Residencias Olga*.

Between Puerto Asís and San Miguel is La Hormiga, 30 minutes on the bus from San Miguel, but don't stay here. It is a dangerous place.

A few kilometres from San Miguel, canoes cross the river from El Puente (no road bridge) to La Punta in Ecuador. Get your exit stamp from the **DAS** office in Mocoa. The boat trip across the Río San Miguel to La Punta takes an hour and costs US$2.20. From La Punta there is a bus to Lago Agrio (US$0.60).

About 250 km downstream on the Río Putumayo is **Puerto Leguízamo** where there is a helpful MA office. **D** *La Frontera*, one block from plaza. Clean, friendly. Several basic hotels, all **G**, eg *Caucaya*, comfortable, nice owners. Places to eat nearby and good stalls on the plaza. *Banco Agrario* will give cash against Visa.

Transport Air To Bogotá, Satena 3 a week, US$180 return via Puerto Asís. **Boat** No boats on the Río Putumayo at present take passengers and the smaller local *voladores* are not considered safe for non-locals. Note that a large army anti-narcotics unit is stationed here and in the surrounds FARC guerrillas operate.

Just above Puerto Leguízamo, Parque Nacional Natural La Paya, has been established. It is 422,000 ha in extent bordering on both Ríos Putumayo and Caquetá, and has a hot, humid Amazonian climate. Most of it is undulating terrain between 180 m and 300 m and is, therefore, non-flooding forest so that a network of trails has been established. There is plenty of wildlife to be seen including manatí, anteaters and many species of monkey. Several Indian communities live in the forest, including Kamza, Inga and Uitoto. It is one of 17 of Colombia's National Parks in which there are Indian Reserves.

La Paya National Park

Advice and information For further information on El Paya, ask at the *Joyería El Ruby* in Pto Leguízamo, where Ramiro will give details and may offer to show you the

Park (where his family live). River transport from Pto Leguízamo to the Park costs about US$10, and takes about 40 mins depending on the river conditions. You should take water, food and a hammock. There are camping places on the banks of the Río Caquetá, and it is worth asking if you can stay at the Naval Base in Pto Leguízamo. There is a MA cabin on the Río Caucayá, a tributary of the Río Putumayo. There is coca and poppy cultivation in and around the Park with consequent safety problems. Take advice. If you wish to visit this Park and can obtain permission, we strongly advise you to fly in and out staying 2-3 days.

Amazonas Department

The Río Putumayo at Puerto Leguízamo is the border with Peru. A few kilometres below, on the Colombian side, it moves into Amazonas Department. A further 350 km downriver are El Encanto and the nearby village of **San Rafael,** stopping places on the river journey. About 40 km north of San Rafael on the Río Igara Paraná, which flows into the Putumayo, is **La Chorrera,** another small river village but with an airfield and weekly Satena services to Leticia, Araracaura and Bogotá. There is basic accommodation and an interesting cooperative run by local tribes, mostly of Uitoto Indians, who sell local craft items. The Río Cahuinarí, which flows down to the Parque Nacional Cahuinarí, is nearby.

The Putumayo continues as the international boundary, then flows for 50 km through Colombia before finally crossing into Brazil, becoming the Rio Iça to join the Amazon at Santo Antônio. The border town is **Tarapacá,** with an airport and basic *Residencial*. It can be quite cold at night. Tarapacá is joined by a dry season track to Leticia, 150 km further south.

Leticia is on the southern tip of a spur of territory which gives Colombia access to the Amazon, 3,200 km upstream from the Atlantic. There is a land frontier with Brazil a short distance to the east beyond which are Marco and Tabatinga. Directly south across the river is another important Brazilian port, Benjamin Constant, which is close to the border with Peru. On the north side of the Amazon, Colombia has a frontage on the river of 80 km to the land border with Peru. The growth of Leticia, Tabatinga, Marco and Benjamin Constant has imposed an artificiality on the immediately surrounding Amazon territory. Travellers interested in Amazonian wildlife should make for the Amacayacú National Park (see below). Alternatively the Putumayo, which forms the border with Peru towards the west, has much to offer both above Leticia (150 km to the north), or in its upper reaches, accessible from Pasto.

Leticia

Phone code: 9819
Colour map 4, grid C2
Population: 23,000

The city is clean and modern, thoughrun down near the river. It is rapidly merging into one town with neighbouring Marco in Brazil. There is a modern, well equipped hospital. The best time to visit the area is from June to August, the early months of the dry season. The river is at its highest level in May, lowest in September. At weekends, accommodation may be difficult to find. Leticia is a good place to buy typical products of Amazon Indians, and tourist services are better than in Tabatinga or Benjamin Constant.

Ins & outs The airport is 1½ km from town, taxi US$1.60; small terminal, few facilities. Expect to be searched before leaving Leticia airport, and on arrival in Bogotá from Leticia.

Note There is an obligatory US$5 environment tax payable on arrival in Leticia. You may also be asked for a yellow fever certificate. If you do not have one, you may have an inoculation administered on the spot (not recommended).

Tourist office at C 10, No 9-86. **MA** Cra 11, No 12-45, T/F27124, for general information on National Parks. *The World View of the Tukano Amazonian Indians,* Gerardo Reichel Dolmatoff, UK 1996. A good account of local ecology and cultures of the northwest Amazon.

There's precious little in the way of sights around town, but the **Banco de la República** has a museum which covers local ethnography and archaeology, housed in a beautiful building at Carrera 11 y Calle 9 with a library and a terrace overlooking the Amazon. There's also a small Amazonian **zoo** (with huge, scary anacondas) and **botanical garden** on road to airport, within walking distance of town (20 minutes). ■ *Entry US$1.*

On **Monkey Island** visits can be made to Yagua and Ticuna Indians. There are **Excursions** not many monkeys on the island now, those left are semi-tame. Agencies run overnight tours with full board. Other excursions are available to Benjamin Constant to see a rubber plantation. The trip lasts eight hours. Or there are longer trips to visit Indian communities with *Turamazonas*. The price depends on number of people in group. If you choose to go on an organized tour, do not accept the first price and check that the equipment and supplies are sufficient for the length of the tour.

Note On night excursions to look for cayman, the boat should have powerful halogen lamps. You can swim in the Amazon and its tributaries, but do not dive; this disturbs the fish. Do not swim at sunrise or sunset when the fish are more active, nor when the water is shallow in dry season, nor if you have a wound which may open up and bleed. Take water purification tablets since almost all the water here is taken from the river.

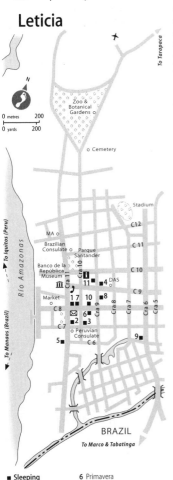

Leticia

AL *Anaconda*, Cra 11, No 7-34, T27119. **Sleeping** Large a/c rooms, hot water, restaurant, good terrace and swimming pool. **AL** *Parador Ticuna*, Av Libertador (Cra 11), No 6-11, T27241/3. Spacious apartments with bath, hot water, a/c, sleep up to 6, swimming pool, bar and restaurant. **A** *Amazonas*, C 8, No 10-32, T20824. Modern Central. Under the same ownership as *Parador Ticuna* is *Jungle Lodge*, on Monkey Island (see above) and, in town, **B** *Colonial*, Cra 10, No 7-08, T27164, with a/c or fans, cafeteria, noisy.

C *Residencias Fernando*, Cra 9, No 8-80, T27362. With a/c, less without, well

■ Sleeping
1 Amazonas
2 Anaconda
3 Colonial
4 Gringos House
5 Parador Ticuna
6 Primavera
7 Residencias Colombia
8 Residencias Fernando
9 Residencia Internacional
10 Residencias La Manigua
11 Residencias Marina

equipped, clean, recommended. **C** *Residencias Marina*, Cra 9 No 9-29 T27301/9). TV, some a/c, cold water, good breakfast and meals at attached restaurant, clean. **D** *Residencias La Manigua*, C 8, No 9-22, T27121. With bath, fan, clean, friendly.

E *Residencia Internacional*, Av Internacional. Basic, bath, between centre and Brazilian border, fan, friendly, hard beds, clean. **E** *Primavera*, C 8 between Cras 9 and 10, with bath and fan, noisy. **E** *Gringos House*, C 9/Cra 9. Small, run by French lady and Indian husband, basic but homely, ask about jungle tours.

F *Residencias Colombia*, Cra 10/C 8, good value, shared bath. **Youth Hostel** *Albergue Túristica Amazonas*, C 11, No 9-60, T27704, F27069. 50 beds, restaurant, usual services.

Eating   *Sancho Panza*, Cra 10, No 8-72. Good value, good meat dishes, big portions, Brazilian beer. *Señora Mercedes*, C 8 near Cra 11, serves good, cheap meals until 1930. Several small restaurants along Cra 10 with good value *plato del día*. Cheap food (fried banana and meat, also fish and pineapples) is sold at the market near the harbour. Also cheap fruit for sale. Many café/bars overlook the market on the river bank. Take your own drinking water and anything stronger that you desire.

Tour Operators   Companies include *Turamazonas*, T27241; *Amaturs*, in lobby of *Hotel Anaconda*; *Amazonian Adventures*, ask for Chiri Chiri; *Kapax*.

Independent guides Many guides can be found at the riverfront. They may be cheaper and better than organized groups, but you must seek advice about the guide's reputation and fix a firm price before setting out. Recommended are Luis Fernando Valera who can be found through the *Hotel Anaconda*, knowledgeable, speaks Spanish, Portuguese, English, runs a variety of tours; Daniel Martínez, also knowledgeable, speaks good English. Luis Daniel Gonzalez, often at the airport, has also been recommended. Tours can be arranged in Leticia for nearby areas in Brazil, for example, *Agencia Operadora de Turismo Río Javari,* Cra 10, No 11-27, T27457.

The cheaper the guide, usually the less experienced he will be. Check that adequate first aid is taken and whether rubber boots are provided (or buy your own in Leticia, US$5-6).

Transport   **Air** SAM and AeroRepública each fly to/from **Bogotá** (Tabatinga airport if Leticia's is closed) 2-4 days a week, US$80. Varig has 3 flights a week from Manaus to Tabatinga, and 2 of these flights call at Tefé (from where you can get direct to other places in Brazil. It is possible to fly to Iquitos (Peru), but the commercial service is very unreliable but it is worth a try to see what is available.

River The cheapest way to get to Leticia is by bus to Puerto Asís, and then by boat. There are boats connecting Leticia with Iquitos (Peru) daily, US$50, several companies, but check carefully. Passport formalities at Santa Rosa. If going upriver, the slower and dirtier the boat, the more mosquitoes you will meet.

Directory   **Banks** *Banco de Bogotá*, will cash TCs, has ATM on Cirrus network, good rates for Brazilian *reais*. There are street money changers, plenty of *cambios*, and banks for exchange. Shop around.

Communications Post Office *Avianca office*, Cra 11, No 7-58. **Telecom** Cra 11/C 9, near Parque Santander.

Amacayacú National Park

Some 60 km up the Amazon, at the mouth of the Matamatá Creek, is the entrance to the Parque Nacional Natural Amacayacú, which is 100km from north to south and a total of nearly 300,000 ha. It is bounded by several rivers flowing into the Putumayo and Amazon systems. At one point it touches the border with Peru. It is claimed that there are over 500 species of birds to be seen in the Park, and 150 or so species of mammals, including pink dolphin, danta and manatí. The smallest monkey in the world, *titi leoncito* (Cebuella pygmaea) may also be seen.

Getting there Boat from Leticia is US$10.50 one way, 1½ -2 hrs; two operators: **Ins & outs** Expreso Amazonas and Tres Fronteras (if you buy a return check that your operator runs the day you wish to return). Buy your ticket early to secure a seat. Boats leave about 1100 and go on to Puerto Nariño.

Park information Park entry US$3 with an additional dock charge of US$2.50 on arrival. For full information on the Park, go to their office at Cra 11, No 12-45, T/F 27124, Leticia. This is a very good place to see the Amazon jungle.

Only a small part is open to visitors, but this includes an area where a number **Around** of day and overnight treks are organised to villages and viewing platforms with **the park** abundant wildlife to see. A rope bridge has been constructed over the canopy with a wonderful view of the surrounding jungle. You will be accompanied by a ranger and fastened by a safety harness, US$7; an unforgettable experience. Guides come from the nearby San Martín village for US$8-10 per day, trips are mostly by dug-out canoe. Guides will point out plants, including those to avoid. Make sure you see the Victoria Regia water lilies (Victoria amazonica), the best are on the Isla de Mocagua (actually in the Amazon, not in the park). It is also possible to visit Tikuna Indian communities at Mocagua, San Martín and Palmeras, all within 2-4 hours from the Park Office.

The MA centre at Matamatá is well run, staff are helpful and friendly. There is a good introductory talk (in Spanish), and you decide what trips to take. Generally, travellers say that this is a better way to see the jungle than making standard arrangements in Leticia. As an alternative to MA tours, local fishermen will take you on canoe trips but take advice where possible. Wellington boots are useful especially in the high river season (normally January-March) though good walking shoes are sufficient for more limited trips. A good time to

Around Leticia

Los Llanos & Amazonia

Victoria Amazónica

There are two types of Victoria Regia water lilies, the V cruziana and the V amazonica. Both are native to South America, with the leaves and flowers growing separately from a submerged rhizome. The amazonica is the larger and therefore the most popular for cultivation elsewhere.

The flowers can grow to a diameter of over 40 cms and the round leaves, thickly veined with upturned edges looking like large, shallow pans, up to a massive 2 metres across.

Small wonder then that they were chosen as the focus of a prize winning garden exhibit at the Millenium Chelsea Flower show in London. Prince Charles came by and pointed an admiring 'green' finger at the vast, green lily saucers. To the consternation of all, a few minutes after his passing, the leaves reacted and turned brown.

All, that is, except the exhibitor who was Lady Walton, the widow of the British composer, Sir William Walton, in whose memory she had presented the garden with the flowers he greatly admired. She pointed out that amazonica has a short life span and is highly sensitive. Maybe the plant was very touched by the visit of the great-great-great-grandson and heir to the throne of the Queen after whom it was named.

visit is between May and October. Cover arms and legs, insect repellent is essential, waterproofs, torches advisable.

Sleeping and eating There is accommodation for 40-50 in three large, clean cabins with beds, US$9pp, and hammocks, US$7pp, mess-style meals, breakfast, US$2.50, lunch/dinner US$5, friendly, efficient; lights out 2130. There is a small handicraft shop run for the local Indian communities.

Puerto Nariño
Phone code: 9819
Colou map 4, grid C2

This small, quiet, attractive settlement lies up the Amazon, beyond the Parque Nacional Amacayacú. It is on the Río Loretoyacú, which reaches the Amazon at La Bocana nearby, a good place to see dolphins. Tours include fishing, visits to Indians and cayman watching, 4-5 days (eg with *Punto Amazónico*, Carrera 24, No 53-18, piso 2, Bogotá, T2493618).

Sleeping and eating C *Casa Selva*. With a/c. **E** *Brisas del Amazonas*. Charming location, friendly, simple rooms. **E** *El Alto del Aguila*, 20 mins walk from the village or 5 mins by boat, Hector, local school teacher/missionary has cabins, will arrange trips to Indian communities and to see dolphins at Lago Tarapoto. He has pet monkeys, parrots, *gavilanes* and a pair of young *caiman*.

Transport Daily boat from Leticia, Mon-Fri 1400, Sat-Sun 1200, 2 hrs, US$8.50.

Colombia to Brazil and Peru

Leticia is bordered on three sides by Brazil and Peru while the nearest Colombian town of consequence is hundreds of kilometers away. The Amazon river system provides the natural link.

Tefé Tefé is approximately halfway between Manaus and the Colombian border. The waterfront consists of a light sand beach, and there is a waterfront market on Monday morning. The nuns at the Franciscan convent sell handicrafts and embroidery.

Sleeping and eating D *Anilce*, Praça Santa Teresa 294. Clean, a/c, do not leave valuables in your room, very helpful. *Au Bec d'Or* by the port, French/Amazonian cuisine.

Transport Airport with connection to Manaus and Tabatinga for Leticia. If travelling on to Tabatinga, note that Manaus-Tabatinga boats do not usually stop at Tefé. You must hire a canoe to take you out to the main channel and try to flag down the approaching ship.

Benjamin Constant, is on the frontier with Peru, with Colombian territory on the opposite bank of the river. **Benjamin Constant**

Sleeping and eating B *Benjamin Constant*, beside ferry. All rooms a/c, some with hot water and TV, good restaurant, arranges tours, postal address Apdo Aéreo 219, Leticia, Colombia. D *Benjamin*. Very basic. D *Marcia María*. With bath, a/c, fridge, clean, friendly. Recommended. E *São Jorge*. Meals available. Recommended. E *Hotel Lanchonete Peruana*. Good food. Eat at *Pensão Cecília*, or *Bar-21 de Abril*, cheaper. The clothes shop on the road to port (left hand side) changes US$ cash.

Transport River Boat services from Manaus, 7 days, or more; to Manaus, 4 days, or more.

About 4 km from Leticia is Tabatinga. The Port Captain in Tabatinga is reported as very helpful and speaks good English. **NB** The port area of Tabatinga is called Marco. A good hammock will cost US$15 in Tabatinga (try *Esplanada Teocides*) or Benjamin Constant. A mosquito net is essential if sailing upstream from Tabatinga; much less so downstream. **Tabatinga**

Sleeping and eating *Hotel Martins*. Good but expensive. D *Residencial Aluguel Pajé*. With bath, fan, clean. D *Solimões*. Run by the military, close to the airport, with breakfast, other meals available if ordered in advance, excellent value, clean, some taxi drivers are unaware that this hotel accepts non-military guests, but there is a VW colectivo minibus from the barracks to town centre, harbour and Leticia. *Três Fronteiras*, excellent restaurant. *Canto do Peixado*, on main street. Highly recommended.

Transport Airport to Tabatinga by minibus, US$1. Regular minibus to Leticia, US$0,60.

Directory Banks It is difficult to change TCs in Tabatinga (try *Casa Branca*, *Casa Verde* or *Casa Amarela* on main road, or general manager of the main shopping centre), and far harder to purchase Peruvian soles than in Leticia. Good rates found at *Câmbio Cortez*, Av da Amizade 2205 (near *Banco do Brasil*).

Up the Río Negro to Colombia

It is possible to get a launch from Manaus up the Río Negro as far as **São Gabriel da Cachoeira**, berth US$240, hammock US$80. Boats leave from São Raimundo dock, north of the main port in Manaus. From there you can continue to Venezuela or go on by river to Colombia. In São Gabriel, Tom Hanly, an Irish Salesian brother, is helpful, friendly and informative. São Gabriel is near the **Pico de Neblina National Park** (Pico de Neblina is the highest mountain in Brazil, 3,014 m).

Sleeping E *Valpes;* another (better class) on the island, restaurant, recommended, shops, two banks but no exchange facilities, beautiful white beaches and, in the river, rapids for 112 km.

Los Llanos & Amazonia

Above São Gabriel, the Río Vaupés joins the Negro and boats go up the Vaupés to the Colombian border and Mitú. Cargo boats ply up the Río Negro on to **Cucuí** at the Brazil/Colombia/Venezuela border, also twice-weekly bus, US$5 (one hotel, ask for Elias, no restaurants). From Cucuí there are daily boats to Guadalupe (Colombia), infrequent boats to Santa Lucía (Venezuela). Beyond here, there is river transport to Bocas de Casiquiari and on up the Río Guainía into Colombia with various alternatives, depending on the seasons, to reach the interior of Colombia from its most easterly extremity.

Many of the **gold prospectors** (*garimpeiros*) expelled from the Yanomami reserves in Roraima have begun to move west to the middle and upper reaches of the Rio Negro, bringing conflict and destruction in their wake.

Border with Brazil and Peru

It is advisable to check all requirements and procedures before arriving at this multiple border. As no foreign boat is allowed to dock at the Brazilian, Colombian and Peruvian ports, travellers should enquire carefully about embarkation/disembarkation points and where to go through immigration formalities. If waiting for transport, the best place for accommodation, exchange and other facilities is Leticia, Colombia. **NB** When crossing these frontiers, check if there is a time difference (eg Brazilian summer time, usually mid-October to mid-February).

Brazilian immigration Entry and exit stamps are given at the Polícia Federal, 10 mins' walk from the Tabatinga docks, opposite *Café dos Navegantes* (walk through docks and follow road to its end, turn right at this T-junction for 1 block to white building). If coming from Leticia, it is one block from the hospital on the road to Leticia. The office is open Mon-Fri 0800-1200, 1400-1800; also at airport, open Wed and Sat only. Proof of US$500 or onward ticket may be asked for. There are no facilities in Benjamin Constant although it is possible to buy supplies for boat journeys. One-week transit in Tabatinga is permitted.

In this frontier area, carry your passport at all times. If coming from Peru, you must have a Peruvian exit stamp and a yellow fever certificate.

Colombian immigration **DAS**, C 9, No 8-32, T27189, Leticia, and at the airport. Exit stamps to leave Colombia by air or overland are given only at the airport. If flying into Leticia prior to leaving for Brazil or Peru, get an exit stamp while at the airport.

Entering Colombia To enter Colombia you must have a tourist card to obtain an entry stamp, even if you are passing through Leticia en route between Brazil and Peru (the Colombian consul in Manaus may tell you otherwise; try to get a tourist card elsewhere). The Colombian Consular Office in Tabatinga issues tourist cards. 24-hr transit stamps can be obtained at the DAS office. If visiting Leticia without intending to go anywhere else in Colombia, you may be allowed to enter without immigration or customs formalities (but TCs cannot be changed without an entry stamp). There are no customs formalities for everyday travel between Leticia and Tabatinga.

Peruvian immigration Entry/exit formalities take place at Santa Rosa. Every boat leaving Peru stops here. There is also an immigration office in Iquitos (Malecón Tarapacá 382) where procedures for leaving can be checked.

Consulates **In Leticia** *Brazil*, C 11, No 10-70, T27531. Open 1000-1600, Mon-Fri, efficient, helpful; onward ticket and 2 black-and-white photos needed for visa (photographer nearby); allow 36 hrs. *Colombia* Near the border on the road from Tabatinga to Leticia, opposite *Restaurant El Canto de las Peixadas* (0800-1400). Tourist cards are issued on presentation of 2 passport photos. *Peru*, Cra 11, No 6-80, T27204, F27825,

Leticia. Open 0830-1430; no entry or exit permits are given here. **In Iquitos** r *Brazil* (C Sargento Lores 363, T005194-232081) and *Colombia* (C Putumayo 247, T231461).

Travel between Colombia and Brazil and Peru is given below. Travel from/into Colom- **Transport**
bia is given under Leticia.

Tabatinga to Leticia Taxis between the two towns charge US$5 (more if you want to stop at immigration offices, exchange houses, etc. Beware of taxi drivers who want to rush you, expensively, over border before it closes'. Colectivo US$0.80 (more after 1800). If you ask for the port, you will be dropped where there is transport to Benjamin Constant (for Brazil and upstream boats to Peru). It is not advisable to walk the muddy path between Tabatinga and Leticia; robbery occurs here.

To/from Manaus by boat Boats from Manaus to Benjamin Constant normally go on to Tabatinga, and start from there when going to Manaus. Boats usually wait 1-2 days in both Tabatinga and Benjamin Constant before returning to Manaus; you can stay on board. Tabatinga and Leticia are 1½-2 hrs from Benjamin Constant by ferry/*recreio* US$2; much quicker by speedboat, US$4, about 25 mins.
    From Tabatinga and Benjamin Constant boats take 3 days to Manaus (depending on cargo and which river ports called at en route), and up to 8 days on the return trip up river, double berth US$250, hammock space US$75 pp (can be cheaper downriver). *Voyagers, Voyagers II and III* recommended; *Almirante Monteiro, Avelino Leal* and *Capitão Nunez VIII* all acceptable. *Dom Manoel*, cheaper, acceptable but over-crowded. Other smaller boats do the trip for US$50, low season.

To/from Iquitos Boats sail from Iquitos to a mud bank called Islandia, on the Peruvian side of a narrow creek a short distance from the Brazilian port of Benjamin Constant. The journey time is a minimum of 2 days upstream, 8-36 hrs downstream, depending on the speed of the boat. In ordinary boats, fares range from US$30-40 per person, depending on the standard of accommodation, food extra. Speedboats charge US$75 per person, 3 a week run by *Amazon Tours and Cruises*. Passengers leaving or entering Peru must visit immigration at Santa Rosa when the boat stops there. For entry into Brazil, formalities are done in Tabatinga; for Colombia, in Leticia. *Amazon Tours and Cruises* also operate a luxury service between Iquitos and Tabatinga leaving Sun from Iquitos, returning Wed from Tabatinga, US$695 per person in the *Río Amazonas*. Also *M/V Arca*, US$495 per person, leaves Iquitos Wed, returns Sat.

Los Llanos & Amazonia

Background

12

Background

History

Precolombian

Colombia was inhabited by various groups of Indians before the Spanish conquest. The most highly-developed were the **Tayronas**, who had settlements along the Atlantic coast and the slopes of the Sierra Nevada de Santa Marta. The Tayronas had a complex social organization, with an economy based on fishing, agriculture and commerce. They built paved roads, stone stairways, public plazas for ceremonies and aqueducts. Another major Indian group were the **Muisca**, a Chibcha speaking people who dominated the central highlands of Colombia at the time of the conquest. 'Muisca' and 'Chibcha' are us Indian group. Philologists identify the 'Chibchan' groued more or less interchangeably in Colombia to refer to thisp of languages as extending from Nicaragua in Central America to Ecuador, almost all of which have now disappeared. To confuse matters further, Muisca was one of those languages spoken by this group in Colombia. Carbon 14 dating places their earliest settlements at around 545 BC. Their village confederation was ruled by the **Zipa** at Bogotá, and the **Zaque** at Hunza (now Tunja). The Zipas believed they were descended from the Moon, and the Zaques from the Sun. Their livelihood came from trading at markets in corn, potatoes and beans. They were also accomplished goldsmiths, and traded emeralds, ceramics and textiles with other societies.

The **Sinú** Indians had their chiefdoms in the present-day Department of Córdoba and parts of Antioquia and Sucre. They farmed yucca and maize on artificial mounds in the local marshlands with complex drainage systems to make the best use of high and low water levels. They also cultivated reeds used for basket and textile weaving, as well as working with gold; much wealth was plundered from their tombs, known as 'guacas', by the Spaniards during the conquest. The **Quimbayas** were a people who inhabited parts of the Valle del Cauca. They had a class system, and a society similar to that of the Muisca and Tayronas, except that some evidence suggests they practised ritual cannibalism. Calima is a term used to classify the other groups of Indians living in the department of Valle del Cauca. They include the **Liles** (based near present-day Cali) and the **Gorrones** (based in the Cordillera Occidental). They were all organized into small chiefdoms with economies based on fishing, hunting, beans, yucca and corn. They traded in gold, salt, textiles and slaves. Two other significant groups prospered in the south of what is now Colombia, those of San Agustín and Tierradentro. Both left fascinating monuments but they had disappeared well before the conquest.

Indian cultures

Guajira..... Precolumbian
(Wayuú)..... Present day

N
Not to scale

● ●

🐟 Colonial town planning

Perhaps the most obvious influence of Spanish settlement for the visitor is the characteristic street plan of towns and cities.

A series of Royal Ordinances issued in Madrid in 1573 laid down the rules of town planning. The four corners of the main plaza were to face the four points of the compass 'because thus the streets diverging from the plaza will not be directly exposed to the four principal winds, which would cause much inconvenience'. The plaza and the main streets were to have arcades which were seen as 'a great convenience for those who resort thither for trade' Away from the plaza, the streets were to be traced out in the now familiar grid-pattern. Once this was done, building lots were to be distributed, those near the plaza being allocated by 'lottery to those of the settlers who are entitled to build around the main plaza'. Another Ordinance required that 'the church is not to be in the centre of the plaza but at a distance from it in a situation where it can stand by itself, separate from other buildings so that it can be seen from all sides. It can thus be made more beautiful

and it will inspire more respect. It should be built on high ground so that in order to reach its entrance, people will have to ascend a flight of steps'.

Cities and towns in Colombia conform quite well to these rules, some of the older colonial towns more so than those founded later. Surveyors had trouble in pointing the corners of the plaza to the cardinal points of the compass, (or perhaps they disputed the direction of 'the four principal winds'?), and few have their principal churches on a convenient isolated piece of high ground, but the steps up to the entrance are often present and the central plazas have elegant buildings and the required colonnades along a side or two.

Several of the finest colonial towns have now been designated National Monuments, to be preserved and maintained as they stand, one of the delights of a visit to Colombia. The grid pattern of calles and carreras is more or less standard everywhere and very easy for the visitor to follow. There is a full description at the beginning of the section on Bogotá.

● ●

Spanish Colonization

The first permanent settlement in Colombia was made in 1500-1507 by **Rodrigo de Bastidas** (1460-1526). He reached the country by sailing along the Caribbean coast as far as Panama. After his return to Spain to face trial for insubordination, he was given permission to establish a colony; he founded Santa Marta in 1525, and named the River Magdalena. Cartagena was founded in 1533 by **Pedro de Heredia**, and it was made into a centre for the growing Spanish collection of treasure. Massive fortifications were built to protect it from pirate attacks. Bogotá was founded by **Gonzalo Jiménez de Quesada** (1499-1579). He arrived in Santa Marta in 1535, then went up to the Sabana de Bogotá in 1536; 200 of his men made the trip by boat, 670 by land, and he founded Santa Fé de Bogotá in 1538. **Sebastian de Belalcázar** (1495-1551), the Lieutenant of Francisco Pizarro, was given instructions to explore Southern Colombia and the Cauca Valley in 1535. He founded Cali and Popayán in 1536, and was made governor of Popayán in 1540. **Nicolas Federmann** (1506-41), acting on behalf of the Welser financiers of Germany, led an expedition East to Coro and Cape Vela, then back to Barquisimeto and Meta. He arrived in the Sabana de Bogotá in 1538, where he met Belalcázar and Jiménez de Quesada.

Jiménez de Quesada named the territory he had conquered Nuevo Reino de Granada, because it reminded him of Granada in Spain. Santa Fé de Bogotá was named after the city of Santa Fé in Granada. The first secular government to be established after the conquest was the Audencia de Santa Fé de Bogotá, in 1550. After 1594, it shared ruling authority with the president of the New Kingdom of New

Granada, the name given to the whole conquered area, which included Panama. The Presidency was replaced in 1718 by a viceroyalty at Bogotá which also controlled the provinces now known as Venezuela; it was independent of the Viceroyalty of Peru, to which this vast area had previously been subject.

Independence from Spain

In 1793, a translation of the Rights of Man was published in Colombia by **Antonio Nariño** (1765-1823), an administrator and journalist, known as 'el Precursor' for his important role in the independence movement. He was imprisoned in Spain in 1794, but escaped and returned to Nueva Granada (as Colombia was then called) in 1797. He joined the patriot forces in 1810 and became president of Cundinamarca in 1812. He led a military campaign in the South in 1813, and was again imprisoned by the Spanish. Meanwhile **Simón Bolívar** (1783-1830) was leading a campaign for Venezuelan independence. Following the collapse of the first Venezuelan Republic in 1812, he joined the independence movement in Cartagena and had early successes in his 1812 Magdalena Campaign which ended in Caracas, where the Second Republic was proclaimed. Again, the patriots lost control and Bolívar returned to Colombia, but was forced to flee to the West Indies when **General Pablo Morillo** launched the Spanish reconquest.

Changes in Europe were also to affect the situation in Colombia. In 1808, Napoleon replaced Ferdinand VII of Spain with his own brother Joseph. The New World refused to recognize this, and several revolts erupted in Nueva Granada, culminating in a revolt at Bogotá and the establishment of a junta on 20 July 1810. Cartagena also bound itself to a junta set up at Tunja.

Simón Bolívar returned to the Llanos in 1816 and formed a new army. Their campaign for liberation involved a forced march over the Andes, in the face of incredible difficulties. After joining forces with **Francisco de Paulo Santander's** Nueva Granada army, he defeated the royalists at the Battle of the Pantano de Vargas in July, winning the decisive victory at the Battle of Boyacá on 7 August. From 1819-28 Bolívar was president of Gran Colombia, the new name for the union of Colombia, Venezuela, Panama and Ecuador, which lasted until the 1830s.

After the fall of Napoleon in 1815, the Spanish set about trying to reconquer the independent territories. The main Spanish general behind the task was Pablo Morillo (1778-1837), known as 'the Pacifier'. During his reign of terror (1816-19), more than 300 patriot supporters were executed. Morillo set up the 'Consejo de Guerra Permanente' and the 'Consejo de Purificación'. The latter's aim was to punish crimes of treason. There was also a board of confiscations known as the 'Junta de Secuestros'. Morillo was also linked to the re-establishment of the Inquisition, which saw many priests tried in military courts in South America.

The Spaniards left a considerable legacy behind in Colombia. Their main objective was to amass riches, notably gold, and ship them back to Spain. Protecting what they had collected from their English, French and Dutch rivals led to the massive fortifications of their main port, Cartagena. Most of what they built, remains and has to be seen to be appreciated. However, they also brought with them culture and life-style, and some of their best colonial public and domestic architecture can be found in Colombia. They left their language and their religion and many institutions, including universities, continue to thrive today. The towns they planned and built are now being preserved (see box). What they did not leave, however, were political institutions, and the search for a durable formula still continues, 200 years after the Spaniards left.

Simón Bolívar

There is no escaping the name of Simón Bolívar in Colombia. Statues of him are everywhere, streets and avenues bear his name and virtually every town and village calls its central square Plaza de Bolívar. His is the most revered name in the country – yet he was neither born nor is buried here. What is the explanation?

He was born in Caracas, now Venezuela, on 27 July 1783. His family originally came from Spain in the 16ᵗʰ century and they were well established in the New World by this time. Both his parents died when he was a child and he was cared for by an uncle, and a tutor, Simón Rodríguez, who was a liberal thinker and introduced him to Jean-Jacques Rousseau, Voltaire, Hobbes and Locke. At the age of 16, he went to France to further his education where he was strongly influenced by the post-revolution atmosphere in Paris and recognised its implication for South America. He also met Alexander von Humboldt on his return from expeditions to South America, one of the few independent travellers to that part of the world in those days. He watched the rise of Napoleon with admiration and dismay, when it was evident that the emperor was driven as much by personal ambition as idealism.

He returned to Caracas in 1807, having lost his wife to yellow fever 8 months after the marriage. He never married again, though his list of mistresses became legendary, culminating in Manuela Saenz, whom he met in Quito in 1822 and who stayed with him more or less for the rest of his life.

From the moment of his return, he became involved with the independence movement. Spain was in a weakened position attempting to retain its own independence from Napoleon, who removed the Spanish royal family from power in 1808. About this time, Bolívar visited England and asked for arms and support. This was not successful but he met the exiled Francisco de Miranda and persuaded him to return to Caracas to lead the fight for independence. In 1811, the Congress in Caracas declared independence from Spain and Miranda took over as leader with Bolívar as his deputy.

Things did not go well for the patriots and in 1812 the Spaniards regained control of Caracas, Miranda was jailed and Bolívar escaped to Cartagena in Colombia to 'follow the banner of freedom'.

Bolívar immediately set about the military campaign which secured his place as the leader of the liberation movement. See details of **The Magdalena Campaign** in the Box on page 203.

This ended in Caracas with the proclamation of the Second Republic but Caracas was soon again in turmoil. Powerful armed local groups supported the Spaniards, and in 1814 Bolívar again had to leave Caracas for Cartagena. Here he was again given troops, this time to clear Santa Marta, but conflicts within the republican movement led him to prudently leave for Jamaica in 1815. From there Bolívar renewed his contacts with England and the United States without much success but in nearby Haiti, recently freed from France, he obtained money and arms. In the meantime, however, Spain sent a strong contingent to the rebellious colonies, under the command of the

Gran Colombia

La República de Gran Colombia was established by the revolutionary Congress at present-day Ciudad Bolívar (Venezuela) on 17 December 1819. A general congress was held at Cúcuta on 1 January 1821, and it was here that the two opposing views which later sowed such dissent in Colombia first became apparent. Bolívar and Nariño were for centralization; Santander, a realist, wanted a federation of sovereign states. Bolívar succeeded in enforcing his view, and the 1821 constitution was drawn up, dividing Gran Colombia into 12 departments

'Pacifier' Pablo Murillo, with orders to regain the initiative for the Spaniards. There was much terror and bloodshed.

Bolívar returned to Venezuela in 1817 and built up a significant army including several thousand foreign mercenaries, mostly British and Irish. He set up his base in Angostura (now Ciudad Bolívar) on the Orinoco, well away from the Spanish garrisons on the coast. Francisco de Paula Santander commanded another group of patriots in the western llanos (Casanare and Arauca, Colombia) where it was evident there was a great deal of support for the patriots. Together they decided to attack the centre of New Granada, Bogotá.

There followed the most significant weeks of the colonial period as Bolívar led **The Liberation Campaign** to the heart of the Spanish control of this part of Latin America, culminating in the victory at the Battle of Boyacá and his arrival, in triumph, in Bogotá. See Box page 113.

Leaving Santander in charge in Bogotá, Bolívar travelled north through Colombia and eventually to Angostura where he was named President of Gran Colombia in December 1819. Negotiations with Murillo were hastened by changes in Spain, and the battle of Carabobo (Venezuela), won by the patriots, effectively led to the withdrawal of Spain from this part of South America. In June 1821, Caracas was free, and in the autumn of that year Bolívar convened the congress in Cúcuta which finally established Gran Colombia.

His vision was greater, however. In a frenzy of activity, he left the running of the new confederation, again to Santander,

and went south with Antonio José de Sucre, one of his finest generals. They captured Pasto in early 1822, completing the liberation of Ecuador in May of that year and Peru in 1824. The territory now called Bolivia was added in 1825.

This was the highest point of his career. Within two years, Gran Colombia was riven by disagreements and the break-up into the four countries of today began. An attempt on his life in Bogotá was unsuccessful only because of the vigilance of Manuela Saenz, and his precarious health began to fail. In 1830, disillusioned by the fractious behaviour of his generals and colleagues, he decided to leave for Europe. He left Bogotá on 8 May by the Río Magdalena, but on arrival on the Caribbean coast in June, he heard that Sucre, who he had hoped would be his successor, had been assassinated in Berruecos, near Pasto, while returning to his home in Ecuador. Bolívar was by now very ill and his journey to France was abandoned. He was invited by Joaquín de Meir, a Spanish admirer, to his sugar finca in San Pedro Alejandrino near Santa Marta, where he died of tuberculosis on 17 December 1830.

References to Símon Bolívar will be found throughout the travel section. Although a Venezuelan by birth, every Colombian regards him as an essential part of their history and admiration of him is unqualified. Some of the best paintings and sculptures of him are to be seen in Colombia and all places where he slept, or even passed by, are carefully documented. Following his travels through Colombia today is a rewarding journey.

Background

and 26 provinces. New laws were introduced to abolish the slave trade and allow free birth for the children of slaves born in Colombia, the distribution of Indian lands and the abolition of the Inquisition. This constitution lasted until 1830, when after the breakaway of Venezuela and Ecuador a new constitution was drawn up.

The next president after Bolívar was Francisco de Santander, from 1832-1837. After being Vice-President, he had led a campaign of dissent against the alleged dictatorship of Bolívar, culminating in an assassination attempt on Bolívar on 25 September 1828. Santander went into exile, but was later recalled for the presidency.

His was an important role in establishing the administrative structure of the new republic of Colombia. He went on to become leader of Congressional opposition from 1837-l840.

Colombia's Civil wars

The new country was the scene of much dissent between the centralizing pro-clerical Conservatives and the federalizing anti-clerical Liberals. The Liberals were dominant from 1849, throughout the next 30 years of insurrections and civil wars. In 1885 the Conservatives imposed a highly centralized constitution which was not modified for over 100 years. Civil war had disastrous effects on the economy, leading to the Paper Money Crisis of 1885, when Colombian currency suffered a dramatic fall in value and circulation had to be reduced to 12 million pesos in notes. Gold was not established as the standard for currency until 1903.

A Liberal revolt of 1899 against the rigidly partisan government of the Conservatives turned into the 'War of the Thousand Days', also known as 'La Rebelión'. It lasted from 17 October 1899 to 1 June 1903. The first Liberal victory was at Norte de Santander in December 1899, when government forces were defeated by rebel leader General Benjamín Herrera. The Battle of Palonegro, 11-26 May 1900, was won by the government forces, led by General Prospero Pinzón. This proved to be the decisive victory of the War of the Thousand Days. 100,000 people had died before the Liberals were finally defeated.

During the independence wars, Panama remained loyal to Spain. Although it had been a state in Nueva Granada since 1855, it was practically self-governing until 1886, when the new Colombian constitution reduced it to a mere department. A bid for independence in 1903 was supported by the US. The revolution lasted only 4 days, 3-6 November, and by 18 November, the US had signed a treaty allowing them to build the Panama Canal.

The authoritarian government of General **Rafael Reyes** (1850-1921), from 1904-1909, was known as the Quinquenio dictatorship. He created his own extra-legal national assembly in 1904. His territorial reorganization and his negotiations with the US over Panama increased his unpopularity, leading to an assassination attempt in 1906. The new president from 1910-14, **Carlos Eugenio Restrepo** (1867-1937), restored a legal form of government and began negotiations with the US for the Urrutia-Thomson Treaty of 1914. This resulted in a US$25 million indemnity payment to Colombia over US involvement in the Panamanian revolution.

Neighbouring Peru to the south was also engaged in a dispute with Colombia, over Leticia, capital of the Comissariat of Amazonas. Peru had repudiated the Lozano-Salomon Treaty of 1922 by occupying Leticia, a part of Colombia according to the treaty. The dispute was submitted to the League of Nations in 1933, who took over the Leticia area and handed it back to Colombia in 1934.

La Violencia

The late 1940s to the mid-1960s were dominated by a period known as 'La Violencia', incited by the assassination of the Socialist mayor of Bogotá, **Jorge Eliécer Gaitán**, on 9 April 1948. The riots that ensued were known as the 'Bogotazo'. La Violencia was characterized by terrorism, murder and destruction of property. Simultaneous, though un-coordinated, outbursts persisted throughout the 50s. Among the many victims were Protestants, who were persecuted 1948-1959. Some 115 Protestants were murdered and 42 of their buildings destroyed. Other contributing factors to La Violencia were anti-Communist sentiments, economic deprivation and the prevailing partisan political system. In 1957 a unique political truce was formed, putting an end to the violence. The Liberal and Conservative parties became the Frente Nacional, a coalition under which the two parties supported a single presidential candidate and divided all political offices equally between them. Political stability was maintained for 16 years. Ultimately the Conservatives gained more from this accord, and unforseen opposition was provoked in parties not involved in the agreement.

One of the biggest guerrilla organizations active after La Violencia was the Movimiento 19 de Abri1, known as M19. Their political wing was the Alianza Nacional Popular (ANAPO), founded by followers of the dictator General **Rojas Pinilla** (1900-75), whose Peronist tactics during his 1953-57 presidency had resulted in his trial by national tribunal when he was overthrown on 10 May 1957. ANAPO opposed both Liberals and Conservatives. They became a major protest force during the late 60s and 70s, believing that the 1970 presidential elections, in which Rojas Pinillo was a candidate, had been rigged, and that fraudulent results had placed **Misael Pastrana Borrero** in power. MI9 took their name from the date of the election, 19 April 1970.

M19's agenda was to achieve a democratic socialist society. Their first public act was the theft of Bolívar's sword from Quinta de Bolívar in Bogotá. They sought to identify themselves with the legacy of the leader of the 19th century independence movement. They also kidnapped José Rafael Mercado, President of the Confederation of Workers, in 1976, accusing him of fraud and misconduct in office, for which they tried and executed him. They then kidnapped Alvaro Gómez Hurtado, Communist Party leader and son of earlier president Gómez, to publicize demands for renewed talks with the government.

It was not until the late 80s that negotiations got under way. A peace accord was reached in late 1989. The following year M19 members surrendered their weapons, and formed themselves into a bona fide political party, named Alianza Democrática, or M19-AD, with which they achieved a significant portion of the vote in the 1990 elections.

The other main terrorist organization after La Violencia was Fuerzas Armadas Revolucionarias de Colombia (FARC). Formed in 1964 under leader **Pedro Antonio Marín**, known as 'Tirofijo', they were aligned with the Communist Party. After 20 years of guerrilla activity they signed a truce with the government on 24 May 1984. FARC joined forces with the legitimate Unión Patriótica and went on to win 10 seats in the 1986 election, while the Liberals took the majority.

In 1985 many of Colombia's guerrilla movements merged into the 'Coordinadora Guerrillera Simón Bolívar' (CGSB), joined by all organizations who had refused to sign the government amnesty offered by President **Belisario Betancur** in 1985. Their aim was to co-ordinate all their actions against the government and the armed forces. Most of their actions were based along the upper Río Cauca and the department of Antioquia. Peace talks with the government in the early 1990s collapsed, followed in 1992-93 by several indecisive but destructive offences on the part of both the guerrillas and the armed forces.

Background

Modern Colombia

Recent History

Ernesto Samper, another Liberal, won the 1994 presidential elections. The main thrust of his programme was that Colombia's current economic strength should provide resources to tackle the social deprivation which causes drug use and insurgency. He placed much emphasis on bringing the FARC and the Ejercito de Liberación Nacional (ELN) guerrillas to the negotiating table and on public spending on social welfare. Revelations during 1995-97 that Samper's election campaign had been financed partly by a US$6 million donation from the Cali Cartel set back the government's popularity. Charges in 1996 were brought against the president of further links with the drugs mafia, though he was acquitted. The charges led to political instability and the attempted killing of Samper's lawyer. When the opposition leader Alvaro Gómez was assassinated, Samper declared a state of emergency.

When it was revealed that other ministers had links with the drugs mafia, suspicion arose that Samper's acquittal had only been to protect their own positions. International confidence was lost: the USA decided, in March 1996, to remove (decertify) Colombia from its list of countries making progress against drug trafficking. This made Colombia ineligible for US aid. Ironically it increased Samper's ratings in the opinion polls, as support for him in the face of US sanctions came to represent a form of nationalism. However, Samper's reputation continued to decline in the international community. On 20 September 1996, the day before he was due to fly to New York to give an anti-drugs speech to the UN General assembly, 3.7 kg of heroin was found on his private aeroplane. The government claimed it had been planted to cause further embarrassment.

Colombia was decertified for the second time in March 1997 partly because the Cali leaders were continuing their business from prison having been given light sentences. Whatever progress was being made to eradicate drugs plantations and stocks, the denial of US aid permitted little scope for the establishment of alternative crops. Many rural communities were therefore left without a means of support. At the same time, the level of violence around the country remained high, with FARC and ELN still active. Colombia has received much criticism from international human rights organizations. In 1994, Amnesty International claimed that widespread political assassination by security forces was condoned by the government. They cited Colombia as one of the worst human rights violators in the world.

In May 1997 the government admitted for the first time to the escalating problem of paramilitary groups, and their links with members of the armed forces. The most infamous of these is 'Autodefensas Campesinas de Córdoba y Urabá' (ACCU), who receive financial support from drugs cartels. The state department admitted that 48% of violent episodes in 1997 were carried out by paramilitaries. This was confirmed by the annual report of the Inter-American Human Rights Commission in June 1997.

Background

Further violence was carried out during the October 1997 regional elections. A polling official was murdered by guerrillas in the Valle Department, and the ELN kidnapped two Organization of American States (OAS) observers, seeking to publicize the anti-democratic nature of the elections.

Nevertheless, the elections went ahead and a turnout of about 50% of voters overall was hailed as a 'vote for peace' by the government. In March 1998, congressional elections were relatively peaceful and a welcome boost to confidence was given when the US withdrew the decertification restrictions the same month. Two rounds of presidential elections in May and June 1998 also passed off without excessive guerrilla disruption. The new president, Andrés Pastrana, voted in on a promise to find a formula for peace, immediately devoted his efforts to bringing the guerilla groups to the negotiating table. After a long, tortuous process with FARC, a large *zona de despeje* (demilitarised zone), was conceded, centred on San Vicente del Caguán in Caquetá. Not everyone was in favour of Pastrana's initiative, not least because FARC violence and extortion did not cease. Nevertheless FARC and government teams have met regularly to discuss suggestions raised at FARC-led public hearings for the creation of employment in the countryside. ELN, meanwhile, angry at being excluded from talks, stepped up its campaign. In April 2000, the government proposed the ceding of a similar but smaller demilitarised zone to the ELN, situated on the west side of the Río Magdalena in the department of Bolívar and a small section of Antioquia, a *zona de encuentro*. Local communities of this agricultural area were dismayed and peacefully demonstrated by closing roads and causing disruption – another vitally interested group in the complicated political equation. More disruptive are the paramilitaries, armed groups of landowners and ex-militaries who wish to preserve their position in the country. They show no sign of ending their activities, which are often ruthless.

The position in mid 2000 remains tense, though all sides profess an interest in participating in the peace process. Yet another element, now confirmed is the Plan Colombia, designed to combat the drugs trade, which is as powerful and prosperous as even in Colombia. US Congress has approved (May 2000) a contribution of US$1.6 billion primarily to finance military and anti-narcotics equipment, but also directed to crop substitutions and other sustainable agricultural projects. Contributions from other countries and substantially by Colombia itself will hopefully bring the total to US$7.5 bn.

The narcotics trade

In Medellín and Cali, two cartels transformed Colombia's drugs trade into a major force in worldwide business and crime. Their methods were very different; Medellín's was ostentatious and violent, while Cali's was much more low-key. The Medellín Cartel processed and distributed 60-70% of cocaine exported to the US during the 1980s. It was headed by **Pablo Escobar Gaviria** and **Jorge Luis Ochoa Vásquez**. Many members of Ochoa's family were also working for the cartel. In the late 1980s he was listed as a billionaire by 'Forbes' Magazine.

In 1981, **Marta Nieves Ochoa Vásquez**, Jorge's sister, was kidnapped. MI9 were believed responsible. In response to the kidnapping, 'Muerte a Secuestradores' was formed by leaders of the drugs trade. Their strong anti-Communist beliefs led to alleged support from factions of the military. In 1984 Muerte a Secuestradores assassinated Carlos Toledo Plata, an ANAPO congressman who had later joined M19.

President César Gaviria Trujillo, the Liberal candidate who had won the 1990 presidential election, put into motion a pacification plan to end the drugs cartels' offensive and establish a peace agreement with the guerrillas. In a further display of reformist government, he appointed **Antonio Navarro Wolff**, former guerrilla leader now of the M19-AD, to the post of Health Minister.

As a result of the reform of the constitution in 1991, a further general election was held in October 1991 (although not due until 1994) and the Liberals retained a majority in the Senate and the House of Representatives. By 1991 the government had secured the surrender, under secret terms, of senior members of the Medellín cartel, namely Pablo Escobar and Jorge Luis Ochoa. One of the publicized conditions for their surrender was immunity from extradition and reduced sentences. Some of the senior traffickers and murderers got only 5-8 years. President Gaviria received international support, including the US, for his stance against the drugs problem, which contrasted with previous president Barco's tougher, and unsuccessful stand.

In the National Constituent Assembly elections of 1991 the M19-AD won 19 of the 70 contested seats; the Liberals won 24; combined Conservative factions 20. These results were followed by attempts to legitimize and modernize the political system, in an effort to deny remaining guerrilla groups cause for protest and therefore lead to peace. The judicial system was strengthened and extradition was banned. However, the early 1990s saw high abstention rates in elections: 60-70% of the electorate didn't vote. This was blamed on loss of confidence in the political system and disruption of voting by guerrillas in some rural areas.

During the Gaviria term, it was reported the Pablo Escobar was continuing to direct the Medellín Cartel from inside his purpose-built prison at Envigado. The Cali Cartel's trade was growing in the wake of reduced activity by the Medellín Cartel. In July 1992, Escobar escaped during a transfer to army barracks. Drug-related violence in Bogotá increased in 1993, thought to be Escobar's way of persuading the government to offer better surrender conditions for him. A paramilitary vigilante group was formed, called 'Perseguidos Por Pablo Escobar' (PEPE). This was allegedly made up of relatives of Escobar's murder victims and members of the Cali Cartel, and it targeted Escobar's family. Escobar was finally shot by the armed forces on 2 December 1993 in Medellín, giving a temporary boost to the government's popularity.

Economy

Structure of production

Colombia has varied natural resources and an economic structure which is no longer dependent on any one commodity. **Agriculture** is the major employer, providing about 15% of gdp and over half of total legal exports. The traditional crops are coffee, flowers, sugar cane, bananas, rice, maize and cotton. Colombia is the leading producer of mild Arabica **coffee** and second to Brazil in world production. Diversification since 1984, drought and disease have reduced output, but exports of coffee still amount to 15-20% of total exports, depending on world prices. About 900,000 ha are planted to coffee in the central Andes and production is around 10-11 mN bags a year. **Sugar** production at over 2 million metric tons is second only to Brzil in South America. **Flowers**, mostly grown near Bogotá because of ease of access to the airport, are exported mainly to the USA. Expansion has been so successful that Colombia is the second largest exporter of cut flowers in the world after the Netherlands. The USA accounts for 73% of total sales of over US$500 million a year. **Bananas** are grown on the tropical lowlands, about 56 mn boxes from around Urabá and 30 mn south of Santa Marta, while sugar cane is grown in the Cauca valley.

Manufacturing contributes 19% of gdp, with farming activities such as food processing, drink and tobacco accounting for about a third of the sector's value added. Textiles and clothing are also important and provide an outlet for home-grown cotton.

The most dynamic sector of the economy in the 1980s was **mining**, with average annual growth rates of 18%, although rates in the 1990s have declined. Mining (coal, nickel, emeralds, gold and platinum) now accounts for about a fifth of total exports. **Coal** reserves are the largest in Latin America, which partial surveys have put at 16.5 bn tonnes. The largest deposits are in the Cerrejón region, where a huge project mines and exports steam coal from a purpose built port at Bahía de Portete. Production was 30 mn tonnes in 1996 but was forecast to rise to 40 mn tonnes by 2000 and 55-70 mn tonnes by 2005. Coal is now the third largest export item by value. A mine at La Loma (César Department) and deposits in the Chocó are also being developed with railways and ports for export markets.

With the exception of a few major projects, mining of precious metals is concentrated in the hands of small scale producers with little technology or organization. Much of their output remains outside the formal economy. Colombia is a major producer of gold, platinum and emeralds, which have traditionally dominated the sector. Mining of precious metals, including silver, is primarily in the Department of Antioquia and El Chocó. Gold deposits have also been discovered on the borders of the Departments of Cauca and Valle, while others have been found in the Guainía, Vaupés and Guaviare regions near the Brazilian border.

Since the mid-1990s oil has held the position of top export earner contributing over a quarter of total exports. Traditionally, oil production came from the Magdalena basin, but these are older fields which are running down. The discovery of the Caño Limón field near Arauca raised output to around 450,000 b/d. The Cusiana and Cupiagua fields, in the Llanos, came into full production in 1995; average output in 1996 was about 580,000 b/d but has not been significantly expanded because of guerrilla attacks and operational problems. Cusiana also has substantial reserves of gas. Investment is taking place to raise oil output, build refineries, petrochemical plants and pipelines, although guerrilla attacks and high taxes make operating in Colombia costly for foreign oil companies and investment has dropped.

Despite abundant hydrocarbons, some 78% of installed generating capacity is hydroelectric. Three quarters of the nation's hydroelectric potential is in the central zone, where 80% of the population live, giving hydroelectricity a natural advantage over thermal power, but after a severe drought in 1992 the Government encouraged the construction of several thermal plants, due to come on stream in 1998-99. Further problems have been encountered by deforestation and the effects of El Niño, causing drought in 1997-98. Demand is forecast to grow annually by over 6% and there are plans to increase total capacity from 10,380MW to 13,000MW by 2000. Privatization of state electricity generating and distribution companies is in progress and it is forecast that up to two thirds of generating capacity could be privately owned by the end of the 2002.

Recent trends

Current account surpluses in the late 1970s during a coffee price boom were turned into large deficits in the first half of the 1980s because of lower export receipts and rapidly rising imports. However, Colombia was able to avoid having to reschedule its foreign debt and took steps to adjust its external accounts. The devaluation of the peso was speeded up, reinforced by import restrictions and export incentives. The fiscal accounts were also turned around and the public sector deficit was reduced while economic growth remained positive throughout and per capita income increased. The World Bank and the IMF endorsed the Colombian economic strategy and commercial banks continued to lend to the country to refinance loans falling due. The Gaviria Government accelerated the economic opening of the country and liberalized financial, investment, foreign exchange and tax legislation. High real interest rates encouraged capital inflows and economic stability encouraged foreign investors.

President Samper's 1995-98 development plan emphasized spending on the social sector and productive infrastructure (with private sector involvement) to help combat poverty. However, the transfer of responsibilities to the regions, as ordered by the 1991 Constitution, has been accompanied by mismanagement and the combination of uncertainty surrounding the government's links with drugs, guerrilla activity and strikes. In February 1997, Samper yielded to demands for 20% pay rises for public sector workers, putting further pressure on the inflation rate. The trade deficit was also cause for concern as the coffee and banana markets slumped and the peso became over-valued as interest rates were kept high to compensate for the fiscal deficit. However, in September 1997 the peso fell, helped by lower interest rates, and the Government turned to the domestic market for financing rather than raise capital abroad.

However, by the time Pastrama took office, unemployment had reached 15.8%, the fiscal deficit was rising, inflation was over 18% and gap growth falling. Pastrama

Departments & departmental capitals

1 ATLANTICO - Barranquilla   3 CALDAS - Manizales
2 RISARALDA - Pereira   4 QUINDIO - Armenia

instituted budget cuts but progress was hampered by the 1998 global financial crisis and the prolonged effects of El Niño which continued until 2000. High domestic interest rates fuelled the recession which persisted until early 2000 when unemployment reached almost 21%. The construction industry was particularly hard hit as was the banking sector in which some major changes have taken place, including takeovers by foreign banking groups.

The value of the peso has fallen, passing Col$2000 = US$1 in early 2000. Without a comparable rise in local prices, Colombia is now one of the cheapest countries to visit in South America. However, continuance of the recession has increased the hardship for many Colombians, and with joblessness at record levels, street crime has grown. In the second half of 2000, there is some optimism that the economy is turning the corner and a slow improvement has commenced.

Government

Senators and Representatives are elected by popular vote. The Senate has 102 members, and the Chamber of Representatives has 161. The President, who appoints his 13 ministers, is elected by direct vote for a term of four years, but cannot succeed himself in the next term. Every citizen over 18 can vote. Reform of the 1886 Constitution was undertaken by a Constituent Assembly in 1991 (see above, **History**).

Administratively the country is divided into 32 Departments and the Special Capital District of Bogotá.

Liberty of speech and the freedom of the press are in theory absolute but in practice more limited. The language of the country is Spanish. Its religion is Roman Catholicism. There is complete freedom for all other creeds not contravening Christian morals or the law.

Education

Education is free, and since 1927 theoretically compulsory, but many children, especially in rural areas, do not attend. There are high standards of secondary and university education, when it is available. The literacy rate is about 91% of those over 15 years of age.

Religion

The vast majority of Colombians (93%) are nominal Roman Catholics, and though observance is not particularly high, daily Masses in most town churches makes it possible for visitors to see the interior of many churches. As elsewhere in Latin America, Protestant Evangelical Churches have made some progress in Colombia in recent years.

Background

Culture

Arts and crafts

With the wide variety of climate, topography and geology, it is not surprising that Colombia has virtually all the materials, fibres, minerals and incentives to create useful and artistic products. Many of the techniques practised today have been inherited from the indigenous peoples who lived here before the conquest, some indeed have not changed in the intervening centuries and are as appropriate now as they were then.

Gold

Gold is very much associated with Colombia. It was gold that brought the Europeans to the New World, and where they found it first. The local Indians had been using it for many centuries though not as a simple 'store of value'. Only when it had been made into jewellery, body ornaments or items for sacrificial rites for their gods did gold have value for them. It must have been incomprehensible to them as well as a tragedy for posterity when the Spaniards melted down so much of the gold they obtained to ship it back to Europe.

Many of the *sierras* in the west of the country have traces of gold in the strata. Through erosion in the rainy climates of the region, panning for gold in the rivers was productive and probably has been practised here since around 800 BC. Even some deep shaft mines have been found in West Colombia.

The Quimbaya of the Cauca valley produced 24 carat gold containers, helmets and pendants in their ascendancy from 1000-1500 AD and also worked with *tumbaga*, a gold-copper alloy. The Tolima of the Magdalena valley made artefacts of pure gold and the Wayuú of the Guajira string beads, sometimes covered with gold, a tradition which continues today. When the Spaniards arrived, the Muisca of the Boyacá/Bogotá area were modelling figures in wax and covering them with clay. They then fired them, removed the melted wax and filled the mould with gold. By carefully prizing open the mould, they were able to make many replicas, thus inventing mass production.

Virtually all of today's techniques of the goldsmith were known to the early peoples of Colombia and there is a fine presentation on this subject at the museum in the Parque Archeológico in Sogamoso, Boyacá.

There are good bargains to be had in the cities of Colombia for gold items, notably Bogotá and Cartagena. Perhaps

Craft centres

Santa Marta
Barranquilla
Cartagena
San Jacinto
Mompós
PANAMA
Sampués
Turbo   Cúcuta
VENEZUELA
Bucaramanga
Medellín
Chiquinquirá
Carmen de   Ráquira   Tunja
Viboral   Tenza
Cali   Pereira   □ BOGOTA
La Chamba
Silvia   Neiva
Guapí   Popayán
Tumaco   Pitalito
Sandoná
Pasto
ECUADOR
BRAZIL

N
Not to scale   • Craft centre

PERU
Leticia

the most interesting place, however, is Mompós, Bolívar, where there is a tradition of fine gold filigree work.

No-one visiting Colombia should miss the Banco de la República's wonderful gold museums. The central collection of gold artefacts is in Bogotá but there are other smaller presentations in the main cities around the country, always worth a visit.

Textiles

Although Colombian textiles cannot rival those of Guatemala or Peru in terms of design and spectacular colour, some areas of the country have some fine traditions. For the Wayuú, *Ser mujer es saber tejer* (To be a woman is to know how to weave). Cotton was available in North Colombia and textiles were traded for wool from the Santa Marta *sierra* nearby, also used as a raw material. The Cuna Indians of Northwest Colombia still make the decorative panels for garments known as *molas*. A speciality is the *mola* made up of many layers of coloured cloth sewn together, then cut out using the different colours to create a pattern or a motif. Some are finished with embroidery.

One striking costume is found in the south near Silvia, Cauca, where the Guambiano Indians weave their own blue and fuschia costumes as well as many other wool garments and blankets.

Basketry

By its nature, articles made of vegetable fibres do not survive for very long, but we know that the Spaniards found many examples of Indian work in Colombia. The basket weaving techniques of the Muisca have continued in Tenza, Boyacá – still using *caña de castilla* (Arundo donax) which is easier to work with than bamboo. The whole local village works in this cottage industry.

Another similar community enterprise is in Sandoná, Nariño, where, in addition to basket weaving, Panama hats are a speciality. Panama hats are so named for where they were initially sold, rather than where made. The workers on the Canal in the early part of the 20th century were the first customers, followed by those passing through. They were made in Ecuador and in Sandoná where the local *iraca* palm fibre is used. Hats are also made in Sampués, Sucre, from 'arrowcane' which grows in the river lowlands nearby and good basket weaving using palma iraca can be found at Usiacurí, south of Barranquilla.

The finest quality basket weaving in the country is to be found along the northwest Pacific coast of Chocó where the Cholo Indians use *werregue* palm to weave a texture so fine that the finished product can look like clay and be used to carry water. They have a flourishing trade nowadays in coarser but more colourful palm weaving products.

Wood

The Cholo Indians also make interesting 'healing sticks' which have magical as well as healing powers. These are about 50 cm long with a pointed end and carved figures above. Held against the stomach of the patient, they drive away the evil spirits and cure the illness. Carved wooden masks are a feature of Indian crafts in the Sierra Nevada de Santa Marta in the north and the Sibundoy Indians of Putumayo in the extreme south of the country, used for festivities and rituals. Interesting wood carvings are made by the Puinave Indians near Puerto Inírida. Wooden masks appear in the Carnival in Barranquilla.

Perhaps the most important wood *artesanía* is found in Chiquinquirá (Boyacá). Carved musical instruments are a speciality and many other items including all sorts of items made of *tagua* nuts gathered in the forests of the Chocó and Amazonas. Guitars are also found in Marinilla near Medellín.

Leather

Leather and woodwork often go together, and the arrival of cattle brought the necessary raw material. Now, finely engraved leather covering carved wooden chairs and other furniture is made in Pasto (Nariño), one important centre.

Barniz

An added craft is that of the resin locally called *barniz*. This comes from seed pods of *Eleagia Utilis*, which grows over 2,000m in Putumayo. The resin is extracted now by passing through a mill or by hammering. Previously this was done by chewing the seeds, commonly known as *mopa-mopa*, supposedly because of the strange sound made by the chewers attempting to speak as well as chew at the same time. After extraction, the resin is dyed and expertly stretched to paper thin sheets from which are cut designs which decorate wooden objects including masks, each colour produced individually, finally covered with a protective lacquer. Pasto is the most important centre for *barniz*.

Pottery

The best known pottery centre in Colombia is Ráquira, Boyacá. A large selection of products is made for household and ornamental use including many small items and are sold here and in towns round about. The large earthenware pots made here today are identical to those made by the Chibcha centuries ago. A similar pottery centre across the country, Carmen de Viboral, Antioquia, also produces ceramics that are known throughout Colombia.

Imaginative and amusing ceramics are made in Pitalito, Huila. This form of popular art, pottery adorned with scenes of everyday life, is typified by representations of the *chiva*, the omnipresent brightly coloured bus seen in many parts of Colombia.

A more unusual line of production is the 'blackware' made at La Chamba, Tolima. This small village is beside the Río Magdalena near Guamo, not generally marked on maps. The process involves using closed kilns, thus cutting down the use of oxygen which thereby causes the iron in the clay to turn from red to black. La Chamba is now a household name in Colombia and is finding acceptance abroad.

Fine art and sculpture

The colonial art of Colombia is rich and diverse, perhaps reflecting its geographical position between the Caribbean and the Pacific, but also because of the early rivalry between the two first important colonial settlements of Bogotá and Tunja. Both cities boast numerous museums and religious foundations with good collections of painting, sculpture and decorative arts. Throughout the colonial period works of art were imported from Europe and elsewhere in the Spanish territories, particularly from Quito to the south. Artists too came from far afield to work in the wealthy Colombian centres. In contrast to colonial practice in Mexico and Ecuador there seems to have been little attempt to train native craftsmen in the dominant European artistic modes of painting and sculpture, perhaps because indigenous expertise lay in pottery and metalwork rather than carving or painting.

The conquerors brought the Christian religion and Christian art. The cathedral sacristy in Bogotá preserves what must be one of the first European imports: a fragile silk standard traditionally believed to have been carried by Jiménez de Quesada's troops at the foundation of Bogotá in 1538, and known as the **Cristo de la Conquista**. The emaciated, blood-spattered figure of Christ is in a mixture of paint and appliqué, with a swirling length of loin cloth around his hips. This seems to billow in the breeze, an impression that would have been all the stronger in its original context. It is hard to imagine anything more alien to native beliefs or native forms of art. Other early Christian images, especially pictures of the Virgin, must have tapped into local beliefs because they soon became the focus of popular cults: the **Virgen de Monguí**, for example, is a 16th century Spanish painting which tradition holds was sent over by Philip II, while the **Virgen de Chiquinquirá**, the patron of Colombia, was painted by the Andalucían **Alonso de Narváez** who settled in Tunja in the 1550s. Neither is outstanding as a work of art but both have been attributed with miraculous powers and versions can be found all over Colombia.

Although religious commissions dominated artistic production throughout the colonial period some remarkable secular wall paintings survive in Tunja which show another side to colonial society. In the late 16th and 17th centuries the houses of the city's founder, Gonzalo Suárez Rendón, of poet Juan de Castellanos and of city notary Juan de Vargas were decorated with colourful murals based on a wide range of printed sources. Those in the **Casa Vargas** are the most sophisticated, the combination of mythological figures, exotic animals, grotesques, heraldic cartouches and occasional Christian monogram resulting in a complex humanistic programme, probably devised by Castellanos. The diversity of style reflects the diversity of sources which can be traced to French, Flemish, German and Spanish originals. The rhinoceros, for example, is derived from Dürer's famous woodcut of 1515 but reached Tunja via a Spanish architectural treatise by Juan de Arfe, published in Seville in 1587. The murals in the **Casa Suárez Rendón** derive in part from those in the Casa Vargas, but are less philosophical, more straightforwardly decorative. Nevertheless, these paintings imply that a highly cultured society imported the most-up-to-date books and prints from Europe.

The new religious foundations in the Americas created a huge market for paintings and sculptures with which to adorn their altarpieces, and workshops in Andalucía flourished as a result. An outstanding example of imported polychrome sculpture is the dignified Crucifixion group of 1583 on the high altar of the chapel of the wealthy Mancipe family in the cathedral in Tunja, sent by **Juan Bautista Vázquez** (died 1589) from his workshop in Seville. Sculpture workshops were soon established in the Americas, however, and Colombian churches preserve a wealth of carved and polychromed wooden altarpieces, choirstalls, confessionals and pulpits, as well as decorative wooden ceilings, screens and wall panels. An early example is the ambitious high altar of the church of San Francisco in Bogotá. The central bays were redesigned in the late 18th century but the wings date from about 1620. The tightly ordered Renaissance structure frames panels of relief carving in two distinctive styles: in the upper storey each has a single, clearly-defined saint, while in the lower storey the panels contain crowded narrative scenes, overflowing with energy (the torso of the figure of St Jerome leans right out towards the high altar) and lush vegetation. The unknown artist was probably trained in Andalucía.

Such altarpieces usually involved several different craftsmen. The carvings for that in the Jesuit church of San Ignacio in Bogotá (1635-40), for example, were by an Italian, **Gian Battista Loessing**. Another important sculptor working in Colombia in the 17th century was **Pedro de Lugo Albarracín**, whose devotional images of the suffering Christ appealed to popular piety, and several, such as the powerful figure of the fallen Christ known as el **Señor de Monserrate** (1656) in the eponymous

Early art from Spain

Woodcarvings & sculpture

Background

shrine on the hill above Bogotá have become pilgrimage destinations. Records of other sculptors with the same surname working in Bogotá and Tunja in the 17th century suggest that Pedro de Lugo was the father of a dynasty of craftsmen. **Lorenzo de Lugo**, for example, executed the eight large reliefs for the high altar of the chapel of Rosary in Santo Domingo, Tunja (c 1686). The architectural frame of this oustanding altarpiece includes numerous anthropomorphic supporting figures, *atlantes*, a common feature of colonial church furnishings in Colombia, and a change for craftsmen to indulge in fanciful invention constrained by Christian orthodoxy. A famous example is the androgynous figure on the pulpit stairs in San Francisco, Popayán, a basket of exotic fruit on its head, and a pineapple in its hand, but grotesque figures, sometimes semi-angelic, sometimes semi-demonic, can be spotted amongst the fronds of tropial foliage on almost any baroque altarpiece. In 18th century figure sculpture **Pedro Laboria** from Andalucía introduced a new lightness of touch with his sinuous, almost dancing saints and angels (examples in Tunja cathedral and Santo Domingo, Bogotá).

Early paintings As with sculpture, the demand for painting was met from a variety of sources. Works were imported from Europe, particularly from Andalucía and from the Netherlands. In the 17th century enterprising sea captains would find room in their holds for a roll or two of canvases from the workshops of Zurbarán or Rubens to sell in the colonial ports. Itinerant artists worked their way round the viceregal centres in pursuit of lucrative commissions such as **Angelino Medoro** (c 1567-1631) from Rome who also worked in Quito and Lima before returning to Europe (see the two large canvases in the Mancipe chapel in Tunja cathedral, 1598). Quito was an important source both of artists and of works of art. Born in Quito, the Dominican **Pedro Bedón** (c 1556-1621) worked in Tunja in the late 16th century and his influence can be seen in the bogotano miniaturist **Francisco de Páramo** (active early 17th century), while **Miguel de Santiago** (c 1625-1706) sent numerous works to Colombia, including his esoteric 'Articles of the Faith' paintings now in Bogotá cathedral museum.

Santiago was an important influence on Colombia's best 17th century artist, **Gregorio Vázquez de Arce y Cevallos** (1638-1711) who trained in the workshop of the extensive Figueroa family of painters but who was working independently by the time he was 20. A prolific and eclectic artist, Vázquez drew on a variety of sources: sometimes his stiff, hieratic figures reveal his debt to popular prints, sometimes his soft landscapes and sweet-faced Virgins demonstrate his familiarity with the work of Zurbarán and Murillo (good examples in the Museo de Arte Colonial, Bogotá). 18th century painting in Colombia follows the well-trodden paths of earlier generations of artists, with none of the confident exuberance found in sculpture. You will find his work in many of Bogotá's churches.

After independence Independence from Spain did not bring independence from the traditions of colonial art. A survey of the galleries of ponderous churchmen and other civic dignitaries in the various museums suggests a more or less seamless production from the 17th to the 19th centuries: some appear sophisticated, some brutish, and the artist is not necessarily to blame. But if artistic style changes little the struggle for independence did provide some new subject matter. Bolívar is endlessly celebrated in painting. An inventive example is that of 1819 in the Quinta de Bolívar in Bogotá, by **Pedro José Figueroa** where he stands with a protective arm around the shoulders of a diminutive female figure personifying the new and newly-tamed republic, dressed in a silk gown, but still with bow, arrows and feather head-dress, and seated on a cayman. The events of the wars of independence are recorded by **José María Espinosa** (1796-1883) in a series of paintings of the 1813-1816 campaigns (examples in the Quinta de Bolívar and the Academia de Historia,

Bogotá). The painting of the death of General Santander of 1840 by **Luis García Hevia** in the Museo Nacional is sincere in its naiveté, whereas **Alberto Urdaneta** (1845-1887) who studied in Paris with Meissonier and is a much more versatile artist, sometimes makes his subjects from recent history seem artificial and melodramatic (*Caldas marchando al patíbulo*, Museo Nacional). But Urdaneta is also remembered as an uncompromising caricaturist, so much so that on one occasion he was expelled from the country. The Museo Nacional in Bogotá has two contrasting portraits of the heroine Policarpa Salvatierra, executed by the Spanish in 1817, one a popular anecdotal version shows her *en route* to the scaffold, the other attributed to **Epifanio Garay** (1849-1903) nicely contrasts the formal society portrait with the drama of the event: she sits poised and beautiful while the ominously shadowy figure of a soldier appears in a doorway behind.

Interest in Colombia's natural resources produced scientific missions which although organized by foreigners – the first by the Spanish botanist **Celestino Mutis** in the 18th century and the next by the Italian geographer **Agustín Codazzi** in the 19th – nevertheless helped to awaken an appreciation of the landscape, peoples and cultures of Colombia, past and present. The Venezuelan **Carmelo Fernández** (1811-1877) worked for Codazzi in 1851, producing carefully observed watercolours of the peoples and traditions of different provinces (examples in the Biblioteca Nacional). **Manuel María Paz** (1820-1902) held the same position in 1853 and his drawings of the precolumbian culture of San Agustín are the first of their kind. **Ramón Torres Méndez** (1809-1895) was not a member of the mission, but like them he travelled extensively in the countryside and his scenes from everyday life helped to make *costumbrista* subjects respectable.

During the first decades of the 20th century Colombian artists preferred to ignore the upheavals of the European art scene and hold on to the established traditions of academic figure and landscape painting. Almost the only interesting figure, **Andrés de Santamaría** (1860-1945), spent most of his life in Europe and developed a style that owed something to Cezanne and something to 17th century Spanish art, but with an over-riding concern for a thickly textured painted surface that is entirely personal (*Self-portrait*, 1923, Museo Nacional, Bogotá). During the 1930s the more liberal political climate in Colombia encouraged the younger generation of Colombian artists to look for a more socially and politically relevant form of art which, conveniently, they found in the Mexican muralists. Instead of having to embrace the violent rupture with the past represented by modern European movements such as Cubism and Futurism, the muralists offered a way of continuing in a figurative tradition but now with a social conscience expressed in images of workers and peasants struggling against the forces of oppression. **Pedro Nel Gómez** (1899-1984) was the first to paint murals in public buildings, particularly in his native Medellín, and was followed by others such as **Alipio Jaramillo** (born 1913) and **Carlos Correa** (1912-1985). The sculptor **Rómulo Rozo** (1899-1964) was also influenced by the rhetoric of the Mexican muralists but also by the forms of Aztec and Mayan sculpture, and strove to achieve a comparable combination of simplicity and monumentality.

Only in the 1950s did Abstraction have any impact in Colombia. **Guillermo Wiederman** (1905-1968) arrived from Germany in 1939 and after a spell painting tropical landscapes began to experiment with an expressionist form of abstraction, full of light and space and colour. **Eduardo Ramírez Villamizar** (born 1923) also began painting in a figurative mode but moved into abstraction in the 1950s and subsequently into sculpture, to create, alongside his contemporary **Edgar Negret** (born 1920), some of the most interesting constructivist work in Latin America. Both work in metal and have produced large, often brightly painted pieces for public spaces. Another important artist of this generation, **Alejandro Obregón**

20th century

Background

García Márquez's Yellow Caribbean

In an interview published in 1982, the year in which he was awarded the Nobel Prize for Literature, Gabriel García Márquez, was asked what were his favourite book, composer, painter, film director, etc. (If you are wondering, Oedipus Rex, Bartok, Goya, both Orson Welles and Kurosawa, respectively.) The day of the week he hated most was Sunday and the historical character he said he most detested was Christopher Colombus. This was a lighthearted interlude in an otherwise wide-ranging and serious conversation (El olor de la guayaba/The Smell of the Guava, by Plinio Apuleyo Mendoza), but it is worth noting that without Columbus, the seeds of the Latin America that García Márquez has consistently written about would never have been sown. If Columbus had not inspired Europeans to cross the Atlantic, the pioneers on José Arcadio Buendía's trek north, through a 'paradise of dampness and silence, going back to before original sin', would not have found an enormous Spanish galleon 4 days march from the sea, with orchids in the rigging and a thick forest flowers in the hull (in the first chapter of One Hundred Years of Solitude*). The ship is just there, occupying 'its own space, one of solitude and oblivion'. José Arcadio and his followers do not wonder about it (if anything, it is a trick), but we do. In the same way, we ask ourselves about the trajectory of Colombia after it broke away from Spain, about the legacy of those who won independence,*

Bolívar's broken dream of Gran Colombia, and why it has led to violence, oppression and injustice. García Márquez writes about these things, often using Colombia's Caribbean region as a backdrop, a world which is not merely Spanish, but also full of legends, of indigenous and African influences. Yet his style appears so matter-of-fact, so transparent, that our incredulity is not aimed at the magical things, but at the brutal realities.

García Márquez has made no secret of his desire to rid society of oppression and violence, nor of his support for socialism as a means of achieving this end. His long friendship with Fidel Castro has been well documented, as has the refusal of the US to grant him a visa because of his politics. But his writing is not protest fiction. Through a multitude of techniques, not just the famous magic realism, he has demonstrated his preoccupation with people's efforts to maintain personal integrity in the face of political and social degradation. At the same time, he does not ignore the solitude of the oppressed and the oppressor alike. As he sees it, the way to attack injustice and individualism is through the word and the imagination, to transform reality by suggesting that the extraordinary is part of the ordinary. He wants to replace the chaotic with a more harmonious existence, and the inauthentic with a shared commitment between people. The only way that he, a writer, can do this, in fact the writer's true

(1920-1992), avoided pure abstraction, preferring to include colourful figurative references with nationalistic overtones: carnations, guitars, condors. The slightly younger and internationally famous **Fernando Botero** (born 1932) has also tended to favour national themes. Working both as a painter and a sculptor he takes figures from Colombian society – dictators, drug barons, smug priests, autocratic matrons, prostitutes, spoilt children – and inflates them to ludicrous proportions. His gigantic bronze figures and the angular, two- dimensional sheets of metal of Negret and Ramírez Villamizar represent the two poles of 20th century artistic expression.

For the subsequent generation of artists Colombia's turbulent political history remains a recurrent preoccupation. **Luis Caballero** (1943-1995) was a masterful draughtsman who expressed his sympathy for the victims of officially-sanctioned violence by the tender attention he devotes to their tortured, naked bodies. **Beatriz González** (born 1938) uses a pop idiom to present military and political leaders as big and bold but essentially empty. **Juan Camillo Uribe** (born 1945) manipulates

revolutionary duty, is to write well.

Everyone knows, Plinio Apuleyo Mendoza said, that García Márquez' favourite colour is yellow, but exactly what shade of yellow? 'The yellow of the Caribbean Sea at three in the afternoon, as seen from Jamaica.' It was the Caribbean which taught him to see reality in a new way, to accept supernatural elements as things which form part of our everyday life. The history of the Caribbean is full of magic, a magic brought by the African slaves and by the pirates from Sweden, Holland and England, who were capable of staging an opera in New Orleans and filling their women's teeth with diamonds. The human synthesis and the contrasts which you find in the Caribbean you will not find anywhere else in the world. And what do you think García Márquez said was the Caribbean's first magical work of literature? – a book which tells of fabulous plants and mythological worlds, the Diary of Christopher Columbus.

Gabriel García Márquez was born in Aracataca in 1928. He studied in Barranquilla and Bogotá. In the 1950s and 1960s he worked as a journalist in Venezuela and Europe. His first novel, La hojarasca/Leaf Storm was published in 1955, then followed El coronel no tiene quien le escriba/No one writes to the Colonel (1958), the stories of Los funerales de la Mamá Grande/Big Mama's Funeral (1962) and La mala hora/In Evil Hour

(1966), before Cien años de soledad/One Hundred Years of Solitude (1967) took the literary world by storm. His first novels and stories either showed the early steps towards the magic realism that came to prominence in Cien años de soledad, or an almost journalistic, subtle handling of the horrors of La Violencia (the civil war of the 1940s and 1950s). After Cien años de soledad came various short stories before his 'dictator novel', El otoño del patriarca/The Autumn of the Patriarch (1975). Crónica de una muerte anunciada/Chronicle of a death foretold (1981) saw a return to the spare style of some of the earlier works, while El amor en los tiempos del cólera/Love in the Time of Cholera (1985) was a much more expansive novel. El general en su laberinto/The General in his Labyrinth (1989) and Noticias de un secuestro/News of a Kidnapping (1996) were both a mixture of documentary and fiction, but very different in their subject matter. The first deals with the last days of Simón Bolívar as he sailed down the Río Magdalena to die near Santa Marta; the second is an account of the kidnapping of a woman by Pablo Escobar. Previous to this book, García Márquez published the novel Del amor y otros demonios/Of Love and Other Demons in 1994. Throughout his career, he has continued to produce articles for the press and has been involved in the cinema, writing film scripts of his own and other people's stories.

the paraphernalia of popular religion – prayer cards, plastic angels, metalic trinkets – to construct wittily disturbing collages. Younger artists are exploring the tensions between the national and international demands of art, and are experimenting with a tremendous diversity of styles and media. There is certainly no shortage of talent. Many cities in Colombia now boast a lively art scene with regular public exhibitions of contemporary art and a good range of commercial galleries.

Rodrigo Arenas Betancur (born 1921) followed in Rozo's footsteps to become Colombia's best known sculptor of nationalistic public monuments. His gigantic and often rather melodramatic bronzes can be found in towns and cities throughout the country, as, for example his heroically naked Bolívar in Pereira, Monumento a la Vida in the Centro Suramericano in Medellín and the complex Lanceros del Pantano de Vargas near Paipa which must have been quite a challenge to the foundrymen. His sculptures are eminently worth seeking out.

Literature

The Colombian Indians' written language was discovered to be at its earliest stages at the time of the Spanish conquest in the 16th century. Consequently there are practically no records of pre-conquest literature. The Indian poetic tradition was oral; one of the few transcribed examples of their spoken poetry is 'El Yurupapy', an oral epic gathered from the Indians of the Vaupés region in the 16th century, though not published until 1890.

The literature produced during the colonial period (1500-1816) was mainly by an ecclesiastical elite, written for the benefit of an upper-class minority. The predominant themes were the conquest itself, Catholicism and observations of the New World. The two major writers of this period had themselves been major conquistadores. **Gonzalo Jiménez de Quesada** (1499-1579), the founder of Bogotá in 1538, wrote *Antijovio* in 1567. The main purpose of this book was to defend Spain's reputation against accusations made by the Italian Paulo Jovii in his *Historiarum sui temporis libri XLV* (1552). Quesada sought to put the record straight on matters concerning the behaviour of his nation during the conquest of the New World.

Juan de Castellanos (1522-1607) wrote a lengthy chronicle of the conquest called *Elegías de varones ilustres de Indias* (*Elegy of Illustrious Men of the Indies*, 1589). It was written in the Italian verse style popular at the time, and has been called one of the longest poems ever written. The most important piece of narrative prose written during this period was *El carnero* (*The Butcher*, 1638) by **Juan Rodríguez Freile** (1566-1642). This is a picaresque account of a year in the life of Santa Fé de Bogotá, using a blend of historical fact and scandalous invention to create a deliciously amoral book for its time. Mystic writing was also popular during the middle years of the conquest. **Sor Francisca Josefa de Castillo y Guevara** (1671-1742) was a nun who wrote Baroque poetry, but was best known for her intimate spiritual diary *Afectos espirituales* (date unknown). Another Baroque poet of renown was **Hernando Domínguez Camargo** (1606-1659), who chronicled the life of Saint Ignatius in his epic *Poema heróica de San Ignacio de Loyola* (*Heroic Poem of St Ignatius of Loyola*, 1666).

The first major Colombian writer after the declaration of independence in 1824 was **Juan José Nieto** (1804-66). His *Ingermina, o la hija de Calamar* (*Ingermina, or the Child of Calamar*, 1844) is a historical novel about the conquest of the Calamar Indians in the 16th century. The mid-19th century saw the publication in Bogotá of *El Mosaico*, a review centred around a literary group of the same name, founded by **José María Vergara y Vergara** (1831-72). The prevailing style in the capital was *costumbrismo*, the depiction of local life and customs in realistic detail. Major *costumbrista* novels were *Manuela* (1858) by **Eugenio Díaz** (1804-1865) and *María* (1867), by **Jorge Isaacs** (1837-1895). Romantic poetry also defined the early years of independence, reflecting the strong influence Europe still had over Colombia. One of the exceptions was a poet from Mompós, **Candelario Obeso** (1849-84), the first Colombian poet to use Afro-American colloquialisms in poetry. His *Cantos populares de mi tierrra* (*Popular Songs of my Land*, 1877) marked a progressive shift from the Romantic style, into a poetic language which reflected the true variety of Colombia's indigenous population.

Another important region in the development of Colombian literature was Antioquia, whose main city is Medellín. This region spawned the first crop of writers who were not of the upper-class elite which had dominated Colombian letters until the late 19th century. **Tomás Carrasquilla** (1858-1940) produced three major novels which reflected his humble middle-class background, and used a casual, spoken style to portray local customs and speech, and above all a love of the land.

Another Antioquian of renown was **Samuel Velásquez** (1865-1941), whose novel *Madre* (*Mother*, 1897) gives a strong sense of the simple life of the countryside coupled with the religious passion of its inhabitants.

The beginning of the avant-garde in Colombia is marked by the publication of *Tergiversaciones* (*Distortions*) in 1925 by **León de Greiff** (1895-1976), in which he experimented with new techniques to create a completely original poetic idiom. Another important Modernist poet was **Porfirio Barba Jacob** (the pseudonym of Miguel Angel Osorio, 1883-1942), who was influenced by the French Parnassian poets and published melancholic verse, typified by *Rosas negras* (*Black Roses*, 1935).

Other novelists of the same era were pursuing a much more social realist style than their avant-garde counterparts. *La voragine* (*The Vortex*, 1924) by **José Eustacio Rivera** (1888-1928) deals with the narrator's own struggle for literary expression against a backdrop of the Amazonian rubber workers' struggle for survival. **César Uribe Piedrahita** (1897-1951) also chronicled the plight of rubber workers, and in *Mancha de aceite* (*Oil Stain*, 1935) he looks at the effects of the oil industry on the land and people of his country. The problems facing indigenous people began to get more attention from these socially aware writers; **Bernardo Arias Trujillo** (1903-28) examined the lives of Afro-Americans in Colombia in *Risaralda*.

The late 1940s to the mid-1960s in Colombian society were dominated by La Violencia (see **History**). Literary output during this intensely violent period reflected the political concerns which had led to the violence; among the novels to stand out from the many personal tales of anger and disbelief was *El jardín de las Hartmann* (*The Garden of the Hartmanns*, 1978) by **Jorge Elicier Prado** (born 1945), which charts the history of La Violencia in Tolima, one of the most severely affected regions. What makes this book readable is the lack of historical facts and figures, typical of books set during La Violencia, and a more generalized view of the troubles.

Two important poetry movements to come out of La Violencia were the 'Mito' group and the 'nadaistas'. *Mito* was a poetry magazine founded in 1955 by **Jorge Gaitán Durán** (1924-62). It included **Eduardo Cote Lemus** (1928-64), **Carlos Obregón** (1929-65) and **Dora Castellanos** (born 1925). Their influences were contemporary French writers such as Genet and Sartre, and the Argentinean José Luis Borges. *Mito* came out during the dictatorship of Rojas Pinilla, and was one of the few outlets for free literary expression in the country. The *Nadaista* group were concerned with changing the elitist role of literature in the face of the violent conflict which affected everyone, and they felt should be addressed directly; they used avant-garde styles and extreme techniques to achieve this.

By far the biggest influence on Colombian fiction was the publication, in 1967, of *Cien años de soledad* (*A Hundred Years of Solitude*) by **Gabriel García Márquez** (born 1927). He had published many short stories and novels in the 1950s and early 1960s. Among the most significant were *La hojarasca* (*Leaf Storm* in 1955) and *El coronel no tiene quien le escriba* (*No-one Writes to the Colonel* – 1958), a portrayal of a Colonel and his wife struggling to cope with the tropical heat, political oppression and economic deprivation in their final years. But it was with *Cien años de soledad* that he became recognized as the major exponent of a new style generic to Latin American writers. Events were chronicled in a deadpan style; historical facts were blended with pure fantasy, the latter written matter-of-factly as if it were the truth; characters were vividly portrayed through their actions and brief dialogues rather than internal monologues. The style came to be known as Magic Realism in English, a translation of the Spanish 'Lo real maravilloso'. In 1975 Márquez published *El otoño del patriarca* (*The Autumn of the Patriarch*), which was a return to a favourite theme of his, the loneliness that power can bring.

Crónica de una muerte anunciada (*Chronicle of a Death Foretold*, 1981) was set in an unnamed coastal city, but no doubt not far from Márquez's birthplace of Aracataca. It captures the docility and traditional stubbornness of the people of

Colombia's Caribbean seaboard, an area in which Márquez had worked as a journalist in the 1950s. *El amor en los tiempos de cólera* (*Love in the Time of Cholera*, 1985) is set at the turn of the century, and concerns the affair between a couple of septuagenarians against the backdrop of another fictional city; Márquez skillfully blends Cartagena, Barranquilla and Santa Marta into one coastal town. Márquez has published nine novels in total, as well as much journalism and essays, and is currently writing his autobiography.

Other important writers in the 1970s and 1980s include **Fanny Buitrago** and **Manuel Zapata Olivella**. In novels such as *Los Panamanes* (1979) and *Los amores de Afrodita* (*The Loves of Aphrodite*, 1983), Buitrago contrasts the legends and culture of the Caribbean coast with the needs of young people to move on, at the risk of being swallowed up by modern North American culture. Zapata Olivella has published a monumental novel, *El fusilamiento del diablo* (*The Shooting of the Devil*, 1986) covering the six centuries of African and Afro-American history.

Colombian Postmodern literature has followed European theoretical trends, with many of Colombia's more avant-garde writers living and working in Europe. While retaining the Magic Realist tradition of dispensing with a subjective, authoritative narrator, the postmoderns have greatly distanced themselves from the Colombian tradition of orally-based, colloquial story-telling. But it is García Márquez who has done the most to capture the public imagination. By borrowing from Colombian traditions with a modernist approach, he has created a style which translates well and has made him an internationally renowned literary figure.

Music and dance

No South American country has a greater variety of music than Colombia, strategically placed where the Andes meet the Caribbean. The four major musical areas are (a) the mountain heartland (b) the Pacific coast (c) the Caribbean coast and (d) the Llanos or eastern plains.

The mountain heartland

The heartland covers the Andean highlands and intervening valleys of the Cauca and Magdalena and includes the country's three largest cities, Bogotá, Cali and Medellín. It is relatively gentle and sentimental music, accompanied largely by string instruments, with an occasional flute and a *chucho* or *carángano* shaker to lay down the rhythm. The preferred instrument of the highlands and by extension Colombia's national instrument, is the *tiple*, a small 12-stringed guitar, most of which are manufactured at Chiquinquirá in Boyacá. The national dance is the Bambuco, whose lilting sounds are said to have inspired Colombian troops at the Battle of Ayacucho in 1824. It is to be found throughout the country's heartland for dancing, singing and instrumentalizing and has long transcended its folk origins. The choreography is complex, including many figures, such as la Invitación, Los Ochos, Los Codos, Los Coqueteos, La Perseguida and La Arrodilla. Other related dances are the Torbellino, where the woman whirls like a top, the more stately Guabina, the Pasillo, Bunde, Sanjuanero and the picaresque Rajaleña. Particularly celebrated melodies are the 'Guabina Chiquinquireña' and the 'Bunde Tolimense'. The following fiestas, among others, provide a good opportunity of seeing the music and dance: La Fiesta del Campesino, ubiquitous on the first Sunday in June, the Fiesta del Bambuco in Neiva and Festival Folklórico Colombiano in Ibagué later in the month, the Fiesta Nacional de la Guabina y el Tiple, held in Velez in early August, the Desfile de Silleteros in Medellín in the same month and Las Fiestas de Pubenza in Popayán just after the New Year, where the Conjuntos de Chirimía process through the streets.

The Pacific coast

On Colombia's tropical Pacific coast (and extending down into Esmeraldas, Ecuador) is to be found some of the most African sounding black music in all South America. The Currulao and its variants, the Berejú and Patacoré, are extremely energetic recreational dances and the vocals are typically African-style call- and-response. This is the home of the *marimba* and the music is very percussion driven, including the upright *cununo* drum plus *bombos* and *redoblantes*. Wakes are important in this region and at these the Bundes, Arrullos and Alabaos are sung. Best known is the 'Bunde de San Antonio'. The Jota Chocoana is a fine example of a Spanish dance taken by black people and turned into a satirical weapon against their masters. The regional fiestas are the Festival Folklórico del Litoral at Buenaventura in July and San Francisco de Asís at Quibdó on 4 August. Quibdó also features a Fiesta de los Indios at Easter.

The Caribbean coast

The music of Colombia's Caribbean lowlands became popular for dancing throughout Latin America more than 30 years ago under the name of 'Música Tropical' and has much more recently become an integral part of the Salsa repertory. It can be very roughly divided into 'Cumbia' and 'Vallenato'. The Cumbia is a heavily black influenced dance form for several couples, the men forming an outer circle and the women an inner one. The men hold aloft a bottle of rum and the women a bundle of slim candles called 'espermas'. The dance probably originated in what is now Panama, moved east into Cartagena, where it is now centred and quite recently further east to Barranquilla and Santa Marta. The most celebrated Cumbias are those of Ciénaga, Mompós, Sampués, San Jacinto and Sincelejo. The instrumental accompaniment consists of *gaitas* or *flautas de caña de millo*, backed by drums. The *gaitas* ('male' and 'female') are vertical cactus flutes with beeswax heads, while the *cañas de millo* are smaller transverse flutes. The most famous conjuntos are the Gaiteros de San Jacinto, the Cumbia Soledeña and the Indios Selectos. Variants of the Cumbia are the Porro, Gaita, Puya, Bullerengue and Mapalé, these last two being much faster and more energetic. Lately Cumbia has also become very much part of the Vallenato repertoire and is therefore often played on the accordion. Vallenato music comes from Valledupar in the Department of César and is of relatively recent origin. It is built around one instrument, the accordion, albeit backed by *guacharaca* rasps and *caja* drums. The most popular rhythms are the Paseo and the Merengue, the latter having arrived from the Dominican Republic, where it is the national dance. Perhaps the first virtuoso accordionist was the legendary 'Francisco El Hombre', playing around the turn of the century. Today's best known names are those of Rafael Escalona, Alejandro Durán and Calixto Ochoa. In April the Festival de la Leyenda Vallenata is held in Valledupar and attended by thousands. Barranquilla is the scene of South America's second most celebrated Carnival, after that of Rio de Janeiro, with innumerable traditional masked groups, such as the Congos, Toros, Diablos and Caimanes. The Garabato is a dance in which death is defeated. Barranquilla's carnival is less commercialized and more traditional than that of Rio and should be a 'must' for anyone with the opportunity to attend. Other important festivals in the region are the Corralejas de Sincelejo with its bullfights in January, La Candelaria in Cartagena on 2 February, the Festival de la Cumbia in El Banco in June, Fiesta del Caiman in Ciénaga in January and Festival del Porro in San Pelayo (Córdoba). To complete the music of the Caribbean region, the Colombian islands of San Andrés and Providencia, off the coast of Nicaragua, have a fascinating mix of mainland Colombian and Jamaican island music, with the Calypso naturally a prominent feature.

Background

Alexander von Humboldt

Von Humboldt is known principally for the cold current that flows northwards off the coast of Chile and Peru, which he discovered, measured and bears his name. This is a minor achievement of a man who was one of the great explorers of the world and had a important impact on many branches of natural science.

He was born in Berlin (Prussia) in 1769, the same year as Napoleon. He trained as a mining engineer, and worked for a time in the gold and copper mines near Bayreuth, but his main passion was botany and he had his eye on South America, which had never been open to scientific investigation. After much frustration, he finally obtained permission from Charles IV to go with the French botanist, Aim, Bonpland, to Spanish America in 1799. During the next five years they travelled 10,000 km on foot, horseback and in canoes in South and Central America.

From 1804 to 1827 von Humboldt analysed and published his conclusions from the mass of data he had brought back from his travels. Apart from the basis he created for the area's botany, he made important contributions to world meteorology, to the study of vulcanism and the earth's crust and the connection between climate and flora. One of his spectacular achievements was to make the first ascent of several volcanoes including Chimborazo in Ecuador, where he and Bonpland reached the summit bergschrund (where the glacier meets the summit rocks) but not the top. Nevertheless, no one recorded a higher ascent anywhere for 30 years, and as a result of this climb, he correctly concluded that mountain sickness was caused by a lack of oxygen at high altitudes.

His first impact on Colombia was itself unusual. He came with Bonpland up the Orinoco, discovered the Maipures rapids and explored the Vichada, Guaviare and the rivers of Guainja until they heard about the 'lake from where the Orinoco and the Negro begin'. After a week of exploration they found the Casiquiare 'canal' which does indeed flow both ways after heavy rains. In 1801, he made the first map of the lower Magdalena, measured the width, flow and temperature and predicted important changes to the channels through the swamplands. There are many references to the two explorers as they made their way through the country, including identifying the wax palm, now Colombia's national tree and the nocturnal guácharos (oil birds). Von Humboldt went to Bogotá also in 1801 and was apparently fascinated by the colonial churches and continued on to Ecuador on horseback, roughly along the route of the Panamerican Highway that in those days was little more than a mountain trail.

He spent the last 25 years writing Kosmos, an account of his scientific findings. A measure of its importance and readability is that, within a few years, the book had been translated into nearly all European languages. Darwin, who followed von Humboldt to South America and was a great admirer, called him the greatest naturalist of his time. In spite of the illnesses and strains of his explorations, he lived to the ripe old age of 90, a good omen for ardent travellers.

The Llanos

The fourth musical region is that of the great eastern plains, the so-called Llanos Orientales between the Ríos Arauca and Guaviare, a region where there is really no musical frontier between the two republics of Colombia and Venezuela. Here the Joropo reigns supreme as a dance, with its close relatives the Galerón, the slower and more romantic Pasaje and the breathlessly fast Corrido and Zumba que Zumba. These are dances for couples, with a lot of heel tapping, the arms hanging down loosely to the sides. Arnulfo Briceño and Pentagrama Llanera are the big names and the harp is the only instrument that matters, although normally backed by *cuatro*, guitar, *tiple* and *maracas*. Where to see and hear it all is at the Festival Nacional del Joropo at Villavicencio in December.

People

The regions vary greatly in their racial make-up. Antioquia and Caldas are largely of European descent, Nariño has more Indian in the mixture, and the Cauca Valley more African who were originally brought to the area when sugar was introduced. Afro-Caribbeans are also prominent in the rural area near the Caribbean and the northwest Pacific coastline. No colour bar is legally recognized but is not entirely absent in certain centres. Population figures of cities and towns in the text are the best we can find but should not be relied upon. They will, however, give the traveller an idea of the size of the place and therefore the level of facilities that may be expected. The major cities are official 1995 estimates.

The birth and death rates vary greatly from one area of the country to another, but in general are similar to those of neighbouring countries. Likewise infant mortality rates, though these are only half those of Brazil. Hospitals and clinics are few in relation to the population. About 66% of the doctors are in the departmental capitals, which contain about half of the population, though all doctors have to spend a year in the country before they can get their final diploma. The best hospitals, notably in Bogotá and Medellín, are well equipped and have fine reputations attracting patients from other countries of Latin America.

An estimated 400,000 tribal peoples, from 60 ethnic groups, live in Colombia. Groups include the Wayuú (in the Guajira), the Kogi and Arhuaco (Sierra Nevada de Santa Marta), Amazonian Indians such as the Huitoto, the nomadic Nukak and the Ticuna, Andean Indians and groups of the Llanos and in the Pacific Coast rain forest. Although the national and official language of Colombia is overwhelmingly Spanish, many Indians use only their own languages. The largest ethnolinguistic group are the 150,000 Chibchas. On the Caribbean coast, especially the islands, English or Creole are widely spoken. The diversity and importance of indigenous peoples was recognized in the 1991 constitutional reforms when Indians were granted the right to two senate seats; the National Colombian Indian Organization (ONIC) won a third seat in the October 1991 ballot. State recognition and the right to bilingual education has not, however, solved major problems of land rights, training and education, and justice.

Land and environment

Geology and landscape

Colombia is the fourth largest in size of the 10 principal countries of South America, at 1,142,000 sq km slightly smaller than Peru and slightly larger than Bolivia. In terms of Europe, that is the size of France and Spain combined. The latest estimate of population (2000) is 42.2 million, marginally more than Argentina and second only to Brazil in the continent. The people are concentrated in the western third of the country: nevertheless the population density of 31.2 per sq km is only greater in Ecuador within South America. To the east, it is bounded by Venezuela and Brazil, to the south, by Peru and Ecuador and in the northwest by Panama. It is the only South American country with a coastline on the Pacific (1,306 km) and the Caribbean (1,600 km), with two small offshore islands in the Pacific. In the Caribbean, there are various coastal islands including the Rosario and San Bernardo groups and the more substantial San Andrés/Providencia archipelago off the coast of Nicaragua, plus several cays towards Jamaica.

Its greatest width east-west is 1,200 km and it stretches 1,800 km north-south, from 12°N to 4°S of the Equator, with virtually all of one of its Departments, Amazonas, south of the Equator. The borders of Colombia have been stable since 1903 when Panama seceded, though Nicaragua occasionally revives a claim for the San Andrés group of islands and there are three minute uninhabited reefs claimed by Colombia and by the USA: Quita Sueño Bank, Roncador Cay and Serrana Bank.

Structure   As with other countries on the west side of the continent, Colombia is on the line of collision between the west moving South American Plate, and the Nasca Plate, moving east and sinking beneath it thus creating the Andes. Almost 55% of the country to the east is alluvial plains on top of ancient rocks of the Guiana Shield dating from the Pre-Cambrian era over 500 million years ago. This was at one time part of the land mass called 'Pangea' which geologists believe broke up between 150 and 125 million years ago and the Americas floated away from what became Africa and Europe. It is presumed that prior to this, what is now the Caribbean Sea was an extension of the Mediterranean Sea and in the course of time this expanded to separate the two halves of the Americas. During the Cretaceous period, around 100 million years ago, the Atlantic was undoubtedly connected to the Pacific Ocean, at least from time to time, but by the end of the Cretaceous, the Tertiary mountain building had begun and the emergence of Central America and eventually the Isthmus of Panama, sealed off the connection.

All the rest of Colombia to the west, apart from the islands, is the product of the Andean mountain building activity which continues to the present day. This began earlier in the Jurassic and Cretaceous eras with intense volcanic activity, but the maximum was in the late Tertiary (around 25 million years ago). Large areas of molten material were formed beneath the surface and were uplifted to form the large high plateaux with peaks formed from later volcanic activity. Some areas were folded and contorted and the original rocks metamorphosed to lose their former identity. In general, it is the mountain ranges to the west that were most affected in this way. Continuous weathering, especially during the ice ages of which the most recent was in the Pleistocene up to 10,000 years ago, has been responsible for deep deposits in the valleys and the plains of North Colombia and in the inland slopes of the Andes towards the Orinoco and Amazon.

Other than the coral islands just off the north coast, the Colombian islands of the Caribbean are all on a submarine ridge which extends from Honduras and Nicaragua to Haiti, known as the Jamaica Ridge, which separates the Cayman Trench from the Colombia Basin, two of the deepest areas of the Caribbean Sea. Providencia is probably volcanic in origin but San Andrés has a less certain past, perhaps being an undersea mount which has been colonized by coral for millions of years, evidenced by the white sands and the limestone features. Little is known about the other reefs, banks and cays which belong to Colombia. The two Colombian island groups in the Pacific are quite different. Gorgona is one of the few islands off the South American Pacific coast which is on the continental shelf and no more than 30 km from the mainland. There is evidence of past volcanic activity on the island and it may represent a point on an otherwise submerged ridge parallel to the coast. By contrast, the Isla de Malpelo is on one of the structural lines of the East Pacific which runs due south from West Panama along the line of longitude 81°W which peters out off the coast of Ecuador. There is a deep trench between this line and the coast with depths down to 5,000m and clear signs of tectonic activity along the ridge including Malpelo which is the top of a volcanic structure. Further to the west there is another ridge running south from Central America, the Cocos Ridge, which leads to the Galápagos Islands.

The Andes

To the south of Colombia, the Andes of Ecuador are a single high range with volcanic peaks up to nearly 5,000 m, but north of the border they quickly split into three distinct *cordilleras* named Occidental, Central and Oriental. The first two are close together for 400 km but separated by a fault line occupied by the Río Patía in the south and the Cauca in the north. The Cordillera Oriental gradually pulls eastwards creating a valley basin for Colombia's most important river, the Magdalena. This range crosses the northeast border into Venezuela and continues as the Cordillera de Mérida. A subsidiary range, called the Sierra de Perijá, continues north within Colombia to reach the Caribbean at Punta Gallinas on the Península de Guajira, the northernmost point of the South American mainland. Near this point is the Santa Marta massif, one of the biggest volcanic structures in the world with the highest mountain peak in Colombia at 5,775 m.

All three of the *Cordilleras* have peaks, mostly volcanic, over 4,000 m, the Central and Oriental over 5,000 m, with permanent snow on the highest. Many are active and have caused great destruction in the past, both with gas and ash explosions and by creating ice and mud slides. The whole of the western half of the country is subject to earthquakes, demonstrating the unstable nature of the underlying geology, and the significant situation of the country at the point where the Andes make a dramatic turn to the east. Also, in the northwest, another range to the west of the Cordillera Occidental appears, the Serranía de Baudó, which becomes the spine of the Darién isthmus of Panama, eventually continuing westwards. Thus north Colombia is at the tectonic crossroads of the Americas.

Background

The Valleys

A glance at the map of Colombia will show the physical dominance of the *cordilleras* and the human dependence on the valleys between them. The fact that they run more or less north-south was a great advantage to the earlier explorers interested in finding gold and silver and the later settlers looking for good cultivable land. Even the earliest inhabitants were interested in the protection that the rugged land offered them but also in ways to migrate further south. As a consequence, the eastern half of the country has, until very recently, been ignored and still remains largely unexplored.

The valleys are structural basins between the *cordilleras* and not simply products of river erosion. In some places they are many kilometres broad, as for example between Cali and Popayán, yet the Patía and Cauca rivers flow in opposite directions. Elsewhere, the rivers go through narrow passages, eg near Honda on the Magdalena where rapids interrupt river navigation. However, the basins have been filled many metres thick with volcanic ash and dust which has produced very fertile terrain. This, together with the height above sea level has made for an agreeable environment, one of the most productive zones of the tropics world-wide.

By contrast, the *cordilleras* create formidable obstacles to lateral movements. The main routes from Bogotá to Cali and Manizales must cross the Cordillera Central by passes at 3,250 m and 3,700 m respectively, and virtually all the passes over the Cordillera Oriental exceed 3,000 m. Many of the volcanic peaks in these ranges are over 5,000 m and are snow capped, hence the name *nevados*. Such is the nature of the terrain, no railway was ever built to cross the *cordilleras* except from Cali to Buenaventura.

The rivers themselves do not provide the most attractive human corridors as can be seen by the frequent diversions from the rivers by the main trunk roads. Fortunately, the surrounding countryside is frequently dominated by plateaux. These make good level sites for towns and cities (Bogotá itself is the best example). They also give long stretches of easy surface travel but are interrupted by spectacular descents and climbs where there are natural rifts or subsidiary river gorges. This makes for dramatic scenic trips by road throughout this area of Colombia.

The Caribbean Lowlands From the Sierra de Perijá and the Sierra Nevada de Santa Marta westwards are the great plains of the lower Magdalena, which collects most of the water flowing north in Colombia to the Caribbean. The Cordilleras Central and Occidental finish at about 4°N, 350 km from the mouth of the river at Barranquilla. About 200 km from the sea, both the Magdalena and the Cauca flow into an area of swamps and lagoons which becomes a vast lake when water levels are high. This lowland is the result of the huge quantities of alluvium that has been brought down over the years from the mountains in the south of Colombia. Whilst not comparable in length with the major rivers of the world, the average discharge at the mouth of the Magdalena is 7,500m^3 per second similar to that of the Danube or about one third that of the Orinoco. To the north, the land slopes gently to the sandy beaches of the Caribbean and a string of inshore islands of considerable tourist attraction.

Beyond Barranquilla to the east, a sandbar encloses a salt lake that was formerly part of the Magdalena delta, now abandoned by the river which flows to the sea further west. On the far side of the lake, the Santa Marta massif comes down to the sea creating a interesting stretch of rocky bays and headlands. Further east again, the flatter land returns extending finally to the low hills of the Guajira peninsula at the north tip of the continent. This is a sandy, arid region, and is the modest northern end of the Cordillera Oriental.

At the west end of this section is the Gulf of Urabá and the border with Panama. The Río Atrato, which drains most of the area between the Cordillera Oriental and the Serranía de Baudó, reaches the sea here via another large swampy area where no land transport is possible. It is probable that this was formerly linked to the Gulf of Urabá which is itself now being filled up with material brought down by the Atrato and many other small streams. This was also probably an area where, in the much more distant past, the Atlantic was joined to the Pacific, a point not lost on the Colombians who periodically quote this as the site of a future rival to the Panama canal (see box, page 212).

There is little seismic activity in this region though there are occasional earthquakes and the mud lakes near Arboletes, Galerazamba and elsewhere near the coast are volcanic in origin.

The Serranía de Baudó runs from Panama south to 4°N just north of Buenaventura. The basin between it and the Cordillera Occidental is drained by the Río Atrato to the north and the San Juan to the south with another river, the Baudó assisting the centre. This is an area of very high rainfall and access by any means is difficult. This coastline is very different from the north coast. Most of it is heavily forested but with very attractive small beaches interspersed with rocky stretches and affected with a wide tidal range, absent from the Caribbean. It has only recently been 'discovered' by the tourist industry and remains quiet owing to the difficulties and cost of getting there. **The Pacific Coast**

South of Buenaventura, there is another 300 km of coastline to Ecuador, but reasonable access is only possible at Buenaventura, and Tumaco in the extreme south. Rainfall here is still copious with many short rivers coming down from the Cordillera Occidental and creating alluvial plains along the coast typically with mangrove swamps, which continue into Ecuador. This part of the Colombian coast is also remote and unspoilt with a few fishing communities though tourism is beginning to take hold at the end of the two access roads. Further inland there are a few mineral deposits and gold mines which have attracted interest. There is no range of Tertiary hills here between the Andes and the coastline as in Ecuador.

This section, representing more than half of Colombia, is in two parts. In the north are the grasslands known as *los llanos*, which stretch from the Cordillera Oriental across into Venezuela and on to the mouth of the Orinoco. 40% of *los llanos*, which means 'plains', are in Colombia. They are noted in both countries for the quality of the land for cattle raising which has been going on since the 16th century and are second only to the *Pampas* in Argentina for ranching in South America. Several important rivers, eg the Meta, flow from the mountains through this region to the Orinoco and act as transport routes. Slowly roads are being made into the interior but all-weather surfaces are virtually non-existent and land transport in the wet season is impossible. All important towns and villages and many *fincas* have their airstrips. In the extreme north of the area, near the border with Venezuela, oil was found some years ago and new finds are still being made. **The Eastern Plains**

The southern part of the section is tropical forest associated with the Amazon basin. As far as the vegetation is concerned, the transition is, of course, gradual. However, the Río Guaviare is the most southerly tributary of the Orinoco and, with headwaters (here called the Guayabero) rising near Neiva in the Cordillera Oriental, has its source some 350 km further from the sea than those of the official source of the Orinoco in the Sierra Parima on the Brazil/Venezuela border. Two important rivers join to form the Guaviare near the town of San José, the Guayabero and the Ariari. Between them is an extraordinary geological anomaly, the Serranía de Macarena. It is a huge dissected block of crystalline rocks partly covered with stratified later formations, 140 km long and 30 km wide, that stands isolated 2,000 m above the surrounding undulating forest and has been identified as a chunk of the Guiana Shield, the rest of which is hundreds of kilometres to the east, forming the border area between The Guianas, Venezuela and Brazil. Although there are some other low formations in this area of the country which are founded on the ancient basal rocks, as a remnant of 'Pangea', Macarena displays by far the oldest exposed rocks of Colombia.

South of the Guaviare basin, all the waters of the region flow into the Amazon system. However, in the extreme east of the country, the Río Guainía drains the south part of the Department of the same name which connects with another geographical curiosity, discovered by the great explorer Alexander von Humboldt. 250 km before joining the Guaviare, the Orinoco divides, with part of its flow going

Background

southwest as the 'Brazo Casiquiare' which eventually joins the Guianía to form the Negro and thence the Amazon. Other Colombian rivers feed the Negro, in particular the Vaupés, the longest tributary. Colombia therefore has the distinction of providing the true sources of the Orinoco and the Negro.

In the southern area, the climate becomes progressively wetter. Thick jungle covers much it though Colombia is no exception to the gradual destruction of the environment. The rivers Caquetá and Putumayo are important water routes to the Amazon proper but there is virtually no tourist traffic.

The extreme south of Colombia is Leticia, on the Amazon itself, a reminder of the original drawing of the maps which allowed all the western countries of South America except Chile to have access to the river and an exit to the South Atlantic.

Climate

Temperatures in Colombia are mainly affected by altitude and distance from the north and west coasts. The highest average temperatures in South America are in the Maracaibo lowlands of which Colombia has the southwest corner and the northwest extension into the Guajira peninsular. The Caribbean lowlands have typically mean annual temperatures in excess of 25°C, modified downwards on the coast, yet, within sight of the coast are the permanent snows of Sierra Nevada de Santa Marta due to its altitude of over 5,500 m. The temperature becomes oppressive where there is also high humidity.

Rainfall depends on the migrating northwest and southeast Trade Wind systems, the effect of the Andes acting as a weather barrier and some local situations along the coasts. There is high rainfall in the southeast where the southeast Trades bring moisture all year into the Amazon basin that is continually recycled to produce heavy daily precipitation all along the east edge of the Andes. This however tails off northwards into the *llanos* especially November-March when the wind systems move south and the southeast Trades are replaced by the northeast system. This is less effective in bringing moisture into the area because of the protection of the Venezuelan Andes. The rainfall in the lower reaches of the Magdalena basin is also high, aided by the large swampy area which keeps the air saturated. The highest rainfall in the country is in the northwest near the border with Panama, brought about by the convergence of the Trade Wind systems interacting with warm, saturated air coming in from the Pacific. Here it rains daily most of the year with some respite January-March but with a total on average of 8,000 mm per year. This is one of the highest in the world. This heavy rain belt extends down the coast tailing off as Ecuador is approached. Unlike further south, the ocean here is warm and air over it readily condenses when it moves on to the land. However, this is a generalized pattern only. Aberrations in the weather systems between November and March, when less rain normally falls, now labelled the *El Niño* phenomenon, also affect the western part of Colombia at least as far east as Bogotá. So far at least, the consequences have been much less dramatic than in Peru and Ecuador. Nevertheless, the tourist is warned that the words of the tour operator or travel book writer 'the best time to visit' will sometimes be totally misleading!

Inland local features often determine the level of precipitation. To the east of Nevado de Huila, 5,750 m, for example, there is a small area of near desert caused by the effect of rain shadow. Near desert conditions also can be found on the tip of the continent, between Riohacha and Punta Gallina which is probably caused by descending air collecting rather than expelling moisture. Although there are occasional storms here (Colombia was marginally affected by the heavy rains that brought disaster to the Venezuelan coast in 1999), the normal Caribbean hurricane track fortunately passes well to the north of the Colombian coast.

Wildlife and vegetation

This neotropical zone is a land of superlatives, it contains the most extensive tropical rainforest in the world; the Amazon has by far the largest volume of any of the world's rivers and the Andes are the longest uninterrupted mountain chain. The fauna and flora are to a large extent determined by the influence of those mountains and the great rivers, particularly the Amazon and the Orinoco. There are also huge expanses of open terrain, tree-covered savannahs and arid regions. It is this immense range of habitats which makes Colombia one of the world's regions of high biological diversity.

This diversity arises not only from the wide range of habitats available, but also from the history of the continent. South America has essentially been an island for much of its geological past, joined only by a narrow isthmus to Central and North America at various times between 50 million and 25 million years ago. The present connection has been stable only for a few million years. Land passage played a significant role in the gradual colonization of South America by both flora and fauna from the north. When the land-link was broken these colonists evolved to a wide variety of forms free from the competitive pressures that prevailed elsewhere. When the land-bridge was re-established a new invasion of species took place from North America, adding to the diversity but also leading to numerous extinctions. Comparative stability has now ensued and has guaranteed the survival of many primitive groups like the opossums.

There are three *cordilleras* of the Andes dominating the western part of Colombia. The rivers draining the area are referred to as white water (although more frequently coffee coloured because they contain a great deal of sediment). This is in contrast to the rivers that drain the Guiana shield in neighbouring Venezuela which are referred to as black or clear waters. The forests of the latter are of considerably lower productivity than those of the Andean countries.

The Llanos

Northeast of the Andes and extending almost to the Caribbean coast, the lowland habitat characterized by open grasslands and small islands of trees is called the *llanos*. Poor drainage leads to the alternation between standing water and extreme dessication, leading to large areas being devoid of trees except for some species of palm. Fire has also been responsible for maintaining this habitat type. Above 100m this gives way to predominantly dry forest with seasonal rainfall and a pronounced drought. Gallery forest persists only in the regions surrounding rivers and streams. In contrast, arid conditions are also found in the vicinity of the northern Caribbean coast.

The Pacific West

The wet forests of the Pacific slopes of the western Andes provide an interesting contrast with the Amazon region by virtue of their high degree of endemism – species unique to an area. The region is often referred to as the Chocó and extends from the Darién Gap in Panama to northern Ecuador. The natural vegetation is tropical wet forest. Clouds which hang over the forest provide condensation, and this almost constant drenching by mist, fog and rain leads to a profusion of plants with intense competition for space, such that the trees and shrubs are all covered with a great variety of epiphytes – orchids, mosses, lichens and bromeliads. The area has been referred to by birders as the 'tanager coast' owing to the large mixed flocks of these colourful birds. There are many other species of endemic birds here apart from the tanagers. At La Planada, between Pasto and Tumaco, there is one of the highest concentrations of native birds in the continent and the forest reserve contains an immense diversity of orchids.

Background

Overall, the fauna shows some interesting biogeographic patterns. Some species found here are those more common to Central and North America than to South America. The westernmost range defines a coastal strip with a fauna similar to Panama. Meanwhile, to the southeast, the fauna south of the river Guaviare is more typical of upper Amazon basin of Brazil and Peru.

The High Andes From about 3,600 m to 4,400 m, the high Andes are covered by *páramo* typified by the grass (*Stipa-ichu*) or *pajonal* which grows here. *Páramo* is a distinct type of high-altitude moorland vegetation comprised of tall grasses and *frailejones (Espeletia)* a member of the Compositae family, which are only found in the Colombian *cordilleras* and the Sierra Nevada de Mérida in Venezuela. These extraordinary plants that grow to as much as 12 m, also frequently attract hummingbirds such as the Black-tailed Trainbearer and the Great Sapphirewing. Lakes and marshes are also a common feature since the ground is generally level. Interspersed among the grasses are clumps of club-moss and chuquiraguas. In the zone of the high *páramo* there are many lakes. Birds frequently seen in this area include the Andean teal, Andean coot and a variety of hummingbird species. **Andean Condor** (*Vultur gryphus*) the largest land bird, weighing 12 kilos and with a wingspan of 3 m, may be seen effortlessly gliding on the updraught from the warmer valleys below.

Some protection from the severe climate and the icy winds that can blast this harsh environment may be provided in the deeply incised gorges. Here there may be a lush growth of shrubs, orchids, reeds and dwarf trees providing a marked visual contrast to the superficially drier *páramo*. In the favourable sheltered micro-climatic conditions provided in the gaps between the tall clumps of grass there nestle compact colonies of gentians, lupins and prostrate mosses. There is little evidence of mammal life here save for the occasional paw print of the Andean fox. **White-tailed deer**, once common here have been over-hunted.

Under 3,600 m, the condensation of the moisture-laden upwelling air from the warm humid jungles to the east creates cloud forest. With a similar wide variety of epíphytes as dound near the west coast. Both giant and dwarf tree ferns are characteristic. These are highly resistant to fire, the traditional manner of maintaining grazing lands. Pollination is effected by a variety of agents. Fragrant odours and bright colours are used by some orchids to attract nectivorous birds including some species of humming birds and insects. Others exude putrid smells to attract flies to carry out the same process. Tangled stands of bamboo intermingled with the *Polylepis* forest are the dominant vegetation feature.

At high altitude *Polylepis* forest clothes the deeply incised canyons and sides of the valleys. This is a tangled, lichen and fern be-decked world, dripping water from the moisture-laden air on to a mid-storey of tangled bamboo and lush tree ferns. A plentiful supply of bromeliads provide food for **spectacled bears**, now an endangered species. The steep slopes of the gullies are clothed in a dense blanket of giant cabbage-like paraguillas or umbrella plant. Tracks of mountain tapir are commonly found along river beaches, and the prints of the diminutive **pudu** – a small **Andean deer**, are also occasionally found. Mammals are rarely seen on the *páramo* during the day since most seek refuge in the fringing cloud forest, only venturing on to the open moors at night or under the protection of the swirling mists. But their presence is demonstrated by the tracks of **Andean fox** and marauding puma. Birds of the *páramo* include the mountain **caracara** and a variety of other raptors such as the **red-backed hawk**. Andean swifts, tapaculos, hummingbirds, fringillids and thrushes are common.

Masked **trogons** are also common in the Aliso (birch) forests, evidence of recent colonization of areas devastated by the frequent landslides. Colourful tanagers and tiny hummingbirds are frequently encountered flitting between the myriad of flowers. At night the hills reverberate with the incessant croak of frogs and toads.

The cloud forests of South America are found in a narrow strip that runs along the spine of the Andes from Colombia, through Ecuador and into Peru. On the western side of the Central Cordillera between 2,000 m and 3,000 m are the remaining stands of the **wax palm** (*Ceroxylon Alpinum*), the tallest variety of palm tree that grow dramatically above the surrounding forest and often appear above the cloud blanket. On the eastern side of the Cordillera Oriental the dense, often impenetrable, forests clothing the steep slopes protect the headwaters of the streams and rivers that cascade from the Andes to form the mighty Amazon as it begins its slow 8,000 km journey to the sea. A verdant kingdom of dripping epiphytic mosses, lichens, ferns and orchids grow in profusion despite the plummeting overnight temperatures. The high humidity resulting from the 2 m of rain that can fall in a year is responsible for the maintenance of the forest and it accumulates and leaks from the ground in a constant trickle that combines to form myriad icy, crystal-clear tumbling streams that cascade over precipitous waterfalls. In secluded areas flame-red Andean **Cock-of-the-Rock** give their spectacular display to females in the early morning mists. **Woolly monkeys** are also occasionally sighted as they descend the wooded slopes. Mixed flocks of colourful tanagers are commonly encountered, and the golden-headed **quetzal** and Amazon umbrella bird are occasionally seen.

Eastern Slopes of the Andes

At about 1,500 m there is a gradual transition to the vast lowland forests of the Amazon basin; surprisingly less jungle-like but warmer and more equable than the cloud-forests clothing the mountains above. The daily temperature varies little during the year with a high of 23-32°C falling slightly to 20-26°C overnight. This lowland region also receives some 2m of rainfall per year, most of it falling from November to April. The rest of the year is sufficiently dry, at least in the lowland areas, to inhibit the growth of epiphytes and orchids which were so characteristic of the highland areas. For a week or two in the rainy season the rivers flood the forest. The zone immediately surrounding this seasonally flooded forest is referred to as *terra firme* forest.

The lowland Amazon region can be seen at its best as the river passes the Amacayacu National Park. Flood waters from the Peruvian catchment area inundate the forest for a short period starting in January in its upper reaches to create a unique habitat called *várzea*. *Várzea* is a highly productive seasonally inundated forest found along the banks of the white-water rivers; it is very rich as a consequence of the huge amount of silt and nutrients washed out of the mountains and trapped by the massive buttress-rooted trees. One of the commonest trees of the *várzea*, the Pará rubber tree, is the source of latex. The Brazilian rubber industry foundered in the 19th century when seeds of this tree were illegally taken to Asia to form the basis of huge rubber plantations and flourished in the absence of pest species. In the still-flowing reaches of the *várzea* permanently flooded areas are frequently found where vast carpets of floating water lilies, water lettuce and water hyacinth are home to the Amazonian manatee, a large herbivorous aquatic mammal which is the fresh-water relative of the dugong of the Caribbean. Vast numbers of spectacled caiman populate the lakes feeding on the highly productive fish community.

Colombian Amazonas

Background

In the lowland forests, many of the trees are buttress rooted, with flanges extending 3-4 m up the trunk of the tree. Among the smaller trees stilt-like prop roots are also common. Frequently flowers are not well developed, and some emerge directly from the branches and even the trunk. This is possibly an adaptation for pollination by the profusion of bats, giving easier access than if they were obscured by leaves.

The vast river basin of the Amazon is home to an immense variety of species. The environment has largely dictated the lifestyle. Life in or around rivers, lakes, swamps and forest depend on the ability to swim and climb; amphibious and tree-dwelling animals are common. Once the entire Amazon basin was a great inland sea and the river still contains mammals more typical of the coast, eg manatees and dolphins.

National Parks

Colombia established its first National Park in 1969 (Tayrona on the Caribbean coast) and now has 46 reserves comprising 34 National Nature Parks (PNN), 9 Flora and Fauna Sanctuaries (SFF), two National Nature Reserves and one Unique Natural Area (ANU), spread throughout the country and in virtually every Department (see map). They vary in size from the tiny island of Corota in the Laguna de la Cocha near the border with Ecuador to large areas of forest in the eastern lowlands. All the significant mountain areas are National Parks including the Sierra Nevada de Santa Marta, El Cocuy, El Nevado de Huila, Los Nevados (Tolima and Ruiz) and Puracé. There are 14 on or near the Caribbean and Pacific coasts including the off-shore islands.

All except the smallest parks normally have one or more centres staffed with rangers (*guardaparques*) who offer information and guidance for visitors. Most, however, are remote with difficult access and few facilities. Unlike some Latin American countries, most National Parks in Colombia are virtually free of 'tourism' and are thus of particular interest to those looking for unspoilt natural surroundings. Permits from MA offices are required (usually free) and admission is charged at entrances, some based on high and low seasons. High season includes: weekends, June-July, December-January, public holidays and Semana Santa. You will find details of costs, accomodation, camping and facilities available in the text.

Until 1995, the National Parks were administered by Inderena in which various government ministries were involved. Inderena has now been disbanded and the service is the responsibility of the Unidad Administrativa Especial del Sistema de Parques Nacionales Naturales (UAESPNN) or (UAE) at the Ministerio del Medio Ambiente (Ministry of the Environment). In this guide we use **MA** to refer to the National Parks Offices.

The central office of the authority is in the Banco Agrario building at Carrera 10, No 20-30, Bogotá, T2433004, F2414174. Ask for the Oficina de Ecoturismo on the 4th floor where they have information about Parks, maps, and videos showing facilities and accomodation. They publish a National Parks Guide, attractive and informative, US$50, with scientific information and lavishly illustrated, though the previous edition (US$10) was more practical. There is a library and research unit (Centro de Documentación) with more detailed information. You can also visit their website: The office is open 0900-1200, 1330-1630. Permits to visit the parks are obtainable here and at the many MA offices near the parks themselves (see text). If you intend to visit the parks, this is a good place to start and ask for up-to-date details. Information is also available here on possibilities to work as volunteer rangers, minimum 30 days. There are 20 or so Parks participating in the scheme, and we have heard from several who have volunteered as rangers; *Corales del Rosario NP* is particularly recommended.

If you have a specific or professional scientific interest and would like to study in one of the Parks, contact Juan David Herrera on the 4th floor. It is helpful to bring a letter from an educational or research institution from your home country indicating your subject of interest. He is very helpful. Anyone interested in filming

National parks & reserves

8 Corales del Rosario PNN
9 Los Colorados SFF
10 Catatumbo Bari PNN
11 Los Estoraques ANU
12 Los Katíos PNN
13 Paramillo PNN
14 Tamá PNN
15 Las Orquídeas PNN
16 El Cocuy PNN
17 Guanenta SFF
18 Pisba PNN
19 Iguaque SFF
20 Ensenada de Utría PNN
21 Tatamá PNN
22 Los Nevados PNN

23 El Tuparro PNN
24 Chingaza PNN
25 Isla Malpelo SFF
26 Sumapaz PNN
27 Las Hermosas PNN
28 Farallones de Cali PNN
29 Nevada de Huila PNN
30 Isla Gorgona PNN
31 Cordillera de los Picachos PNN
32 Serranía de la Macarena PNN
33 Tinigua PNN
34 Munchique PNN
35 Sanquianga PNN
36 Puracé RNN
37 Nukak RNN

38 Puinawai RNN
39 Cueva de los Guácharos PNN
40 Chiribiquete PNN
41 Galeras SFF
42 Isla de la Corota SFF
43 La Paya PNN
44 Cahuinari PNN
45 Amacayacu PNN

PNN Parque Nacional Natural
SFF Santuario Flora y Fauna
RNN Reserva Nacional Natural
ANU Area Natural Unica

♦ National parks & reserves
1 Old Providence PNN
2 Macuira PNN
3 Los Flamencos SFF
4 Sierra Nevada de Santa Marta PNN
5 Tayrona PNN
6 Isla de Salamanca PNN
7 Ciénaga Grande de Santa Marta SFF

0 km 200
0 miles 200

of photography for publication purposes should contact Ivonne Mejía, Coordinator of the Ecoturismo office. Obtaining permission is a lengthy process, best apply well in advance.

For various reasons, unlike many countries where the main problem for national parks is visitor overcrowding, many of the parks in Colombia are difficult to visit. Unfortunately, because of their remoteness, some have been sanctuary to guerrilla groups or drug traffickers, some are sensitive Indian territories and many are of difficult access and have few or no facilities. Lovers of wilderness, however, will enjoy the richness of the natural attractions and the freedom from oppressive tourism.

Apart from the National Parks, there are a considerable number of private nature reserves, some exclusively for research, others open to the general public. Many of these are worth visiting: details are given in the text.

Other useful address: *Red de Reservas Naturales*, Calle 23N, No 6AN-43, piso 3, Cali, T 661-2581, F 660-6133, also for private reserves around the country. *Instituto Colombiano de Antropología* (ICAN), Calle 12, no 2-41, T2811051/5619600, Bogotá, colicam@col1.telecom.com.co Monday-Thursday 0830-1630, Friday 0830-1230, also very helpful. See also **Useful websites** in **Essentials**.

Footnotes

13

434

Footnotes

Useful words and phrases

No amount of dictionaries, phrase books or word lists will provide the same enjoyment as being able to communicate directly with the people of the country you are visiting. Learning Spanish is an important part of the preparation for any trip to Colombia and you are encouraged to make an effort to grasp the basics before you go. As you travel you will pick up more of the language and the more you know, the more you will benefit from your stay. The following section is designed to be a simple point of departure.

General pronunciation

The stress in a Spanish word conforms to one of three rules: 1) if the word ends in a vowel, or in **n** or **s**, the accent falls on the penultimate syllable (vent*a*na, vent*a*nas); 2) if the word ends in a consonant other than **n** or **s**, the accent falls on the last syllable (habl*a*r); 3) if the word is to be stressed on a syllable contrary to either of the above rules, the acute accent on the relevant vowel indicates where the stress is to be placed (pantal*ó*n, met*á*fora). Note that adverbs such as cuando, 'when', take an accent when used interrogatively: ¿cuándo?, 'when?'

Vowels

a	not quite as short as in English 'cat'
e	as in English 'pay', but shorter in a syllable ending in a consonant
i	as in English 'seek'
o	as in English 'shop', but more like 'pope' when the vowel ends a syllable
u	as in English 'food'; after 'q' and in 'gue', 'gui', **u** is unpronounced; in 'güe' and 'güi' it is pronounced
y	when a vowel, pronounced like **'i'**; when a semiconsonant or consonant, it is pronounced like English 'yes'
ai, ay	as in English 'ride'
ei, ey	as in English 'they'
oi, oy	as in English 'toy'

Unless listed below **consonants** can be pronounced in Spanish as they are in English.

b, v	their sound is interchangeable and is a cross between the English 'b' and 'v', except at the beginning of a word or after 'm' or 'n' when it is like English 'b'
c	like English 'k', except before 'e' or 'i' when it is as the 's' in English 'sip'
g	before 'e' and 'i' it is the same as **j**
h	when on its own, never pronounced
j	as the 'ch' in the Scottish 'loch'

Footnotes

ll   as the 'y' in English 'yacht'; sometimes as the 'lli' in 'million.' In Antioquia, normally as 'ge' in 'large,' eg Medellín.

ñ   as the 'ni' in English 'onion'

rr   trilled much more strongly than in English

x   depending on its location, pronounced as in English 'fox', or 'sip', or like 'gs'

z   as the 's' in English 'sip'

Greetings, courtesies

hello	*hola*
good morning	*buenos días*
good afternoon/evening/night	*buenas tardes/noches*
goodbye	*adiós/chao*
see you later	*hasta luego*
how are you?	*¿cómo está?/¿cómo estás?*
pleased to meet you	*mucho gusto/encantado/encantada*
please	*por favor*
thank you (very much)	*(muchas) gracias*
yes	*sí*
no	*no*
excuse me/I beg your pardon	*con permiso/ disculpe*
I do not understand	*no entiendo*
please speak slowly	*hable despacio por favor*
what is your name	*¿cómo se llama?*
Go away!	*¡Váyase!*

Basic questions

where is_?	*¿dónde está_?*
do you have_?	*¿hay_?*
how much is it?	*¿cuánto es?*
too much	*¡es mucho!, ¡demasiado!*
is there something cheaper	*¿hay algo más barato?*
when?	*¿cuándo?*
when does the bus leave?	*¿a qué hora sale el bus?*
– arrive?	*– llega –*
why?	*¿por qué?*
what for?	*¿para qué?*
what time is it?	*¿qué hora es?*
how do I get to_?	*¿cómo llego a_?*
is this the way to the church?	*¿la iglesia está por aquí?*

Basics

bathroom/toilet	*el baño*
is there toilet paper?	*¿hay papel higiénico?, - papel de baño?*
police (policeman)	*la policía (el policía)*
hotel	*el hotel (la pensión, el residencial, el alojamiento)*

restaurant	*el restaurante*
post office	*el correo*
telephone office	*la oficina de Telecom*
public telephone	*teléfono público*
phone call	*la llamada telefónico*
supermarket	*el supermercado*
bank	*el banco*
exchange house	*la casa de cambio*
exchange rate	*el tipo de cambio*
notes/coins	*los billetes/las monedas*
travellers' cheques	*los travelers/los cheques de viajero*
cash	*el efectivo*
breakfast	*el desayuno*
lunch	*el almuerzo*
dinner/supper	*la cena*
meal	*la comida*
drink	*la bebida*
mineral water	*el agua mineral*
soft fizzy drink	*la gaseosa/cola*
beer	*la cerveza*
without sugar	*sin azúcar*
without meat	*sin carne*

Getting around

on the left/right	*a la izquierda/derecha*
straight on	*derecho*
second street on the left	*la segunda calle a la izquierda*
to walk	*caminar*
bus station	*la terminal de buses*
train station	*la estación (de tren/ferrocarril)*
bus	*el bus/el autobus/el colectivo/ el micro etc*
train	*el tren*
airport	*el aeropuerto*
aeroplane/airplane	*el avión*
first/second class	*primera/segunda clase*
ticket	*el boleto, el pasaje*
ticket office	*la taquilla*
bus stop	*la parada, el paradero*

Accommodation

room	*el cuarto/la habitación*
single/double	*sencillo/doble*
with two beds	*con dos camas*
with private bathroom	*con baño*
hot/cold water	*agua caliente/fría*
noisy	*ruidoso*
to make up/clean	*limpiar*
sheets	*las sábanas*
blankets	*las mantas*
pillows	*las almohadas*
clean/dirty towels	*toallas limpias/sucias*
toilet paper	*el papel higiénico*

Health

Chemist, drug store	*la farmacia*
(for) pain	*(para) dolor*
stomach	*el estómago*
head	*la cabeza*
fever/sweat	*la fiebre/el sudor*
diarrhoea	*la diarrea*
blood	*la sangre*
altitude sickness	*el soroche*
doctor	*el médico*
condoms	*los preservativos*
contraceptive (pill)	*anticonceptivo (la píldora anticonceptiva)*
period/towels	*la regla/las toallas sanitarias*
contact lenses	*las lentes de contacto*
aspirin	*la aspirina*

Time

at one o'clock	*a la una*
at half past two/ two thirty	*a las dos y media*
at a quarter to three	*a un cuarto para las tres/ a las tres menos quince*
it's one o'clock	*es la una*
it's seven o'clock	*son las siete*
it's twenty past six/ six twenty	*son las seis y veinte*
it's five to nine	*son cinco para las nueve/ son las nueve menos cinco*
in ten minutes	*en diez minutos*
five hours	*cinco horas*
does it take long?	*¿tarda mucho?*
Monday	*lunes*
Tuesday	*martes*
Wednesday	*miercoles*
Thursday	*jueves*
Friday	*viernes*
Saturday	*sábado*
Sunday	*domingo*
January	*enero*
February	*febrero*
March	*marzo*
April	*abril*
May	*mayo*
June	*junio*
July	*julio*
August	*agosto*
September	*septiembre*
October	*octubre*
November	*noviembre*
December	*diciembre*

Numbers

one	*uno/una*
two	*dos*
three	*tres*
four	*cuatro*
five	*cinco*
six	*seis*
seven	*siete*
eight	*ocho*
nine	*nueve*
ten	*diez*
eleven	*once*
twelve	*doce*
thirteen	*trece*
fourteen	*catorce*
fifteen	*quince*
sixteen	*dieciseis*
seventeen	*diecisiete*
eighteen	*dieciocho*
nineteen	*diecinueve*
twenty	*veinte*
twenty one, two	*veintiuno, veintidos etc*
thirty	*treinta*
forty	*cuarenta*
fifty	*cincuenta*
sixty	*sesenta*
seventy	*setenta*
eighty	*ochenta*
ninety	*noventa*
hundred	*cien or ciento*
a hundred and one	*ciento uno*
two hundred	*doscientos*
thousand	*mil*
two thousand	*dos mil*

Key verbs

To Go   ir

I go '*voy*'; you go (familiar singular) '*vas*'; he, she, it goes, you (unfamiliar singular) go '*va*'; we go '*vamos*'; they, you (plural) go '*van*'.

To Have (possess)   tener

tengo; tienes; tiene; tenemos; tienen (also used as To Be, as in 'I am hungry' '*tengo hambre*')

(**NB** haber also means to have, but is used with other verbs, as in 'he has gone' '*ha ido*'. he; has; ha; hemos; han.

'*Hay*' means 'there is'; perhaps more common is '*No hay*' meaning 'there isn't any')

To Be (in a permanent state)   ser

soy (profesor – I am a teacher); eres; es; somos; son

To Be (positional or temporary state)   estar

estoy (en Londres – I am in London); estás; está (contenta – she is happy); estamos; están.

Index

Map index

Shorts

Footprint travel list

Footprint publish travel guides to over 120 countries worldwide. Each guide is packed with practical, concise and colourful information for everybody from first-time travellers to travel aficionados . The list is growing fast and current titles are noted below. For further information check out the website **www.footprintbooks.com**

Andalucía Handbook
Argentina Handbook
Bali & the Eastern Isles Hbk
Bangkok & the Beaches Hbk
Bolivia Handbook
Brazil Handbook
Cambodia Handbook
Caribbean Islands Handbook
Chile Handbook
Colombia Handbook
Cuba Handbook
Dominican Republic Handbook
East Africa Handbook
Ecuador & Galápagos Handbook
Egypt Handbook Handbook
Goa Handbook
India Handbook
Indian Himalaya Handbook
Indonesia Handbook
Ireland Handbook
Israel Handbook
Jordan Handbook
Jordan, Syria & Lebanon Hbk
Laos Handbook
Libya Handbook
Malaysia Handbook
Myanmar Handbook
Mexico Handbook
Mexico & Central America Hbk
Morocco Handbook
Namibia Handbook
Nepal Handbook
Pakistan Handbook

Peru Handbook
Rio de Janeiro Handbook
Scotland Handbook
Singapore Handbook
South Africa Handbook
South American Handbook
South India Handbook
Sri Lanka Handbook
Sumatra Handbook
Thailand Handbook
Tibet Handbook
Tunisia Handbook
Venezuela Handbook
Vietnam Handbook

In the pipeline – Turkey, London, Edinburgh, Rajasthan, Scotland Highlands & Islands, Syria & Lebanon

Also available from Footprint
Traveller's Handbook
Traveller's Healthbook

Available at all good bookshops

Sales & distribution

Footprint Handbooks
6 Riverside Court
Lower Bristol Road
Bath BA2 3DZ England
T 01225 469141
F 01225 469461
discover
@footprintbooks.com

Australia
Peribo Pty
58 Beaumont Road
Mt Kuring-Gai
NSW 2080
T 02 9457 0011
F 02 9457 0022

Austria
Freytag-Berndt Artaria
Kohlmarkt 9
A-1010 Wien
T 01533 2094
F 01533 8685

Freytag-Berndt
Sporgasse 29
A-8010 Graz
T 0316 818230
F 3016 818230-30

Belgium
Craenen BVBA
Mechelsesteenweg 633
B-3020 Herent
T 016 23 90 90
F 016 23 97 11

Waterstones
The English Bookshop
Blvd Adolphe Max 71-75
B-1000 Brussels
T 02 219 5034

Canada
Ulysses Travel Publications
4176 rue Saint-Denis
Montréal
Québec H2W 2M5
T 514 843 9882
F 514 843 9448

Europe
Bill Bailey
16 Devon Square
Newton Abbott
Devon TQ12 2HR. UK
T 01626 331079
F 01626 331080

Denmark
Nordisk Korthandel
Studiestraede 26-30 B
DK-1455 Copenhagen K
T 3338 2638
F 3338 2648

Scanvik Books
Esplanaden 8B
DK-1263 Copenhagen K
T 3312 7766
F 3391 2882

Finland
Akateeminen Kirjakauppa
Keskuskatu 1
FIN-00100 Helsinki
T 09 121 4151
F 09 121 4441

Suomalainen Kirjakauppa
Koivuvaarankuja 2
01640 Vantaa 64
F 09 852751

France
FNAC – major branches

L'Astrolabe
46 rue de Provence
F-75009 Paris 9e
T 01 42 85 42 95
F 01 45 75 92 51

VILO Diffusion
25 rue Ginoux
F-75015 Paris
T 01 45 77 08 05
F 01 45 79 97 15

Germany
GeoCenter ILH
Schockenriedstrasse 44
D-70565 Stuttgart
T 0711 781 94610
F 0711 781 94654

Brettschneider
Feldkirchnerstrasse 2
D-85551 Heimstetten
T 089 990 20330
F 089 990 20331

Geobuch
Rosental 6
D-80331 München
T 089 265030
F 089 263713

Gleumes
Hohenstaufenring 47-51
D-50674 Köln
T 0221 215650

Globetrotter Ausrustungen
Wiesendamm 1
D-22305 Hamburg
T040 679 66190
F 040 679 66183

Dr Götze
Bleichenbrücke 9
D-2000 Hamburg 1
T 040 3031 1009-0

Hugendubel Buchhandlung
Nymphenburgerstrasse 25
D-80335 München
T 089 238 9412
F 089 550 1853

Kiepert Buchhandlung
Hardenbergstrasse 4-5
D-10623 Berlin 12
T 030 311 880
F 030 311 88120

Greece
GC Eleftheroudakis
17 Panepistemiou
Athens 105 64
T 01 331 4180-83
F 01 323 9821

India
India Book Distributors
1007/1008 Arcadia
195 Nariman Point
Mumbai 400 021
T 91 22 282 5220
F 91 22 287 2531

Israel
Eco Trips
8 Tverya Street
Tel Aviv 63144
T 03 528 4113
F 03 528 8269

For a fuller list, see www.footprintbooks.com

Italy
Librimport
Via Biondelli 9
I-20141 Milano
T 02 8950 1422
F 02 8950 2811

Libreria del Viaggiatore
Via dell Pelegrino 78
I-00186 Roma
T/F 06 688 01048

Netherlands
Nilsson & Lamm bv
Postbus 195
Pampuslaan 212
N-1380 AD Weesp
T 0294 494949
F 0294 494455

Waterstones
Kalverstraat 152
1012 XE Amsterdam
T 020 638 3821

New Zealand
Auckland Map Centre
Dymocks

Norway
Schibsteds Forlag A/S
Akersgata 32 - 5th Floor
Postboks 1178 Sentrum
N-0107 Oslo
T 22 86 30 00
F 22 42 54 92

Tanum
Karl Johansgate 37-41
PO Box 1177 Sentrum
N-0107 Oslo 1
T 22 41 11 00
F 22 33 32 75

Olaf Norlis
Universitetsgt 24
N-1062 Oslo
T 22 00 43 00

Pakistan
Pak-American Commercial
Hamid Chambers
Zaib-un Nisa Street
Saddar, PO Box 7359
Karachi
T 21 566 0418
F 21 568 3611

South Africa
Faradawn CC
PO Box 1903
Saxonwold 2132
T 011 885 1787
F 011 885 1829

South America
Humphrys Roberts
Associates
Caixa Postal 801-0
Ag. Jardim da Gloria
06700-970 Cotia SP
Brazil
T 011 492 4496
F 011 492 6896

Southeast Asia
APA Publications
38 Joo Koon Road
Singapore 628990
T 865 1600
F 861 6438

In Hong Kong, Malaysia,
Singapore and Thailand:
MPH, Kinokuniya, Times

Spain
Altaïr
C/Balmes 69
08007 Barcelona
T 933 233062
F 934 512559

Altaïr
Gaztambide 31
28015 Madrid
T 0915 435300
F 0915 443498

Libros de Viaje
C/Serrano no 41
28001 Madrid
T 01 91 577 9899
F 01 91 577 5756

Il Corte Inglés – major
branches

Sweden
Hedengrens Bokhandel
PO Box 5509
S-11485 Stockholm
T 08 611 5132

Kart Centrum
Vasagatan 16
S-11120 Stockholm
T 08 411 1697

Kartforlaget
Skolgangen 10
S-80183 Gavle
T 026 633000
F 026 124204

Lantmateriet Kartbutiken
Kungsgatan 74
S-11122 Stockholm
T 08 202 303
F 08 202 711

Switzerland
Office du Livre OLF
ZI3, Corminboeuf
CH-1701 Fribourg
T 026 467 5111
F 026 467 5666

Schweizer Buchzentrum
Postfach
CH-4601 Olten
T 062 209 2525
F 062 209 2627

Travel Bookshop
Rindermarkt 20
Postfach 216
CH-8001 Zürich
T 01 252 3883
F 01 252 3832

Tanzania
A Novel Idea
The Slipway
PO Box 76513
Dar es Salaam
T/F 051 601088

USA
NTC/ Contemporary
4255 West Touhy Avenue
Lincolnwood
Illinois 60646-1975
T 847 679 5500
F 847 679 2494

Barnes & Noble, Borders,
specialist travel bookstores

Will you help us?

We try as hard as we can to make each Footprint Handbook as up-to-date and accurate as possible but, of course, things always change. Many people write to us - with corrections, new information, or simply comments.

If you want to let us know about an experience or adventure - hair-raising or mundane, good or bad, exciting or boring - we would be delighted to hear from you. Please give us as precise information as possible, quoting the edition number (you'll find it on the front cover) and page number of the Handbook you are using.

Your help will be greatly appreciated, especially by other travellers. In return we will send you details about our special guidebook offer.

email Footprint at:
col2_online@footprintbooks.com

or write to:
Elizabeth Taylor
Footprint Handbooks
6 Riverside Court
Lower Bristol Road
Bath BA2 3DZ
UK

What the papers say

"If 'the essence of real travel' is what you have been secretly yearning for all these years, then Footprint are the guides for you."
Under 26

"Footprint can be depended on for accurate travel information and for imparting a deep sense of respect for the lands and people they cover."
World News

"Footprint Handbooks, the best of the best."
Le Monde, Paris

"The guides for intelligent, independently-minded souls of any age or budget."
Indie Traveller

"Intelligently written, amazingly accurate and bang up-to-date. Footprint has combined nearly 80 years' experience with a stunning new format to bring us guidebooks that leave the competition standing."
John Pilkington, writer and broadcaster

Mail order
Available worldwide in bookshops and on-line. Footprint travel guides can also be ordered directly from us in Bath, via our website **www.footprintbooks.com** or from the address on the imprint page of this book.

Advertisers

Map 1

San Andrés & Providencia archipelago

Cayos de Roncador

Providencia

San Andrés
Cayos de ESE

Cayos de Alburquerque

Caribbean Sea

PANAMA

ECUADOR

Caribbean Sea

Cañaveral
PNN Pueblito & Tayrona
Taganga Calabazo
Santa Marta Bonda
Rodadero
Minca El Campano
Ciudad Perdida
Cienaga

PNN Isla de Salamanca

Barranquilla
Pto Colombia
Ciénaga de Sta Marta
Soledad

Galerazamba Baranoa Palmar de Varela
Pueblo Nuevo
Usiacuri SFF Ciénaga Grande
Luruaco
Santa Catalena Sabanalarga Aracataca
Bayunca Pto Giraldo Salamina Fundación
Santa Rosa Pivijay
La Boquilla Villanueva MAGDALENA
Cartagena
Tierrabomba Turbaco Calamar Caracolicito
Santa Ana Turbana
PNN Corales del Rosario Arjona
Islas del Rosario Malagana
Baru Cobado
Rocha San Cayetano
Los Colorados
SFF Nepomuceno Tenerife Dificil
San Jacinto
Islas de San Bernardo Zambrano Plato
San Onofre El Carmen Arjona
Tolú Ovejas Pinto
Coveñas Toluviejo Santa Ana Chimichagua
Corozal Mompós
Lorica Sincelejo Magangué El Banco
Chinú
SUCRE
Sahagún
Cereté
Montería
Map 2
Arboletes
Caribia BOLIVAR
Planeta Rica
Turbo San Pedro CORDOBA
de Urabá
Apartadó Caucasia
Montelíbano
Chigorodó Tarazá

ATLANTICO

ATLÁNTICO

Río Magdalena

Brazo Mompós

Brazo de Loba

Río San Jorge

Río Cauca

Río San Jorge

Río Sinú

Río Mulatos

N

0 km 100
0 miles 100

1 2 3

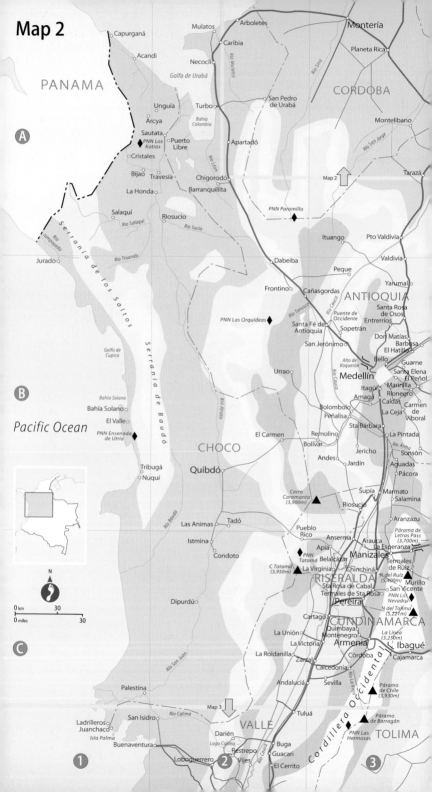

Map 2

PANAMA

Capurganá
Acandi
Unguía
Árcya
Sautata
PNN Los Katios
Cristales
Bijao
Travesía
La Honda
Salaquí
Riosucio
Jurado

Mulatos
Arboletes
Caribia
Necoclí
Golfo de Urabá
Turbo
San Pedro de Urabá
Bahía Colombia
Puerto Libre
Apartadó
Chigorodó
Barranquillita
Río Salaquí
Río Sucio
Río Truando

Montería
Planeta Rica
CORDOBA
Río Sinú
Montelíbano
Río San Jorge
Tarazá

PNN Paramillo
Río León

PANAMA — Río Jampavado
Serranía de los Saltos
Golfo de Cupica
Bahía Solano
Bahía Solano
El Valle
PNN Ensenada de Utría
Tribugá
Nuquí

Serranía de Baudó

Ituango
Pto Valdivia
Dabeiba
Valdivia
Peque
Yarumal
Frontino
Cañasgordas
ANTIOQUIA
Santa Rosa de Osos
Entrerríos
PNN Las Orquídeas
Río Tonusco
Santa Fé de Antioquia
Puente de Occidente
Sopetrán
Don Matías
Barbosa
El Hatillo
San Jerónimo
Bello
Guarne
Alto de Boquerón
Santa Elena El Peñol
Urrao
Río Cauca
Medellín
Itagüí
Marinilla
Rionegro
Amagá
Caldas
Carmen de Viboral
Bolombolo
Peñalisa
La Ceja
Río Amura
Sta Bárbara
La Pintada
El Carmen
Remolino
Jericó
Río Arma
Sonsón
Bolívar
Andes
Jardín
Aguadas
Pácora

Pacific Ocean

N

0 km   30
0 miles 30

CHOCO

Quibdó

Cerro Caramanta (3,900m)
Supía
Marmato
Salamina
Riosucio
Aranzazu
Las Animas
Tadó
Páramo de Letras Pass (3,700m)
Istmina
Pueblo Rico
Anserma
Arauca
La Esperanza
Condoto
Apía
Belalcázar
Manizales
Termales de Ruiz
C Tatamá (3,950m)
PNN Tatamá
La Virginia
Chinchiná
N del Ruiz (5,400m)
RISERALDA
Murillo
Sta Rosa de Cabal
San Vicente
Termales de Sta Rosa
PNN Los Nevados
Dipurdó
Pereira
N del Tolima (5,221m)
Río San Juan
Cartago
CUNDINAMARCA
La Línea (3,250m)
La Unión
Quimbaya
Montenegro
Armenia
Ibagué
Palestina
La Victoria
Córdoba
Cajamarca
La Roldanilla
Zarzal
Ladrilleros
Juanchaco
Isla Palma
San Isidro
Río Calima
Map 3
Andalucía
Sevilla
Calcedonia
Páramo de Chile (3,930m)
Buenaventura
Loboguerrero
Darién
Lago Calima
VALLE
Tuluá
Páramo de Barragán
PNN Las Hermosas
TOLIMA
Restrepo
Buga
Vijes
Guacarí
El Cerrito
Río Cauca
Cordillera Occidental

A

B

C

1   2   3

Map 2

Map 3

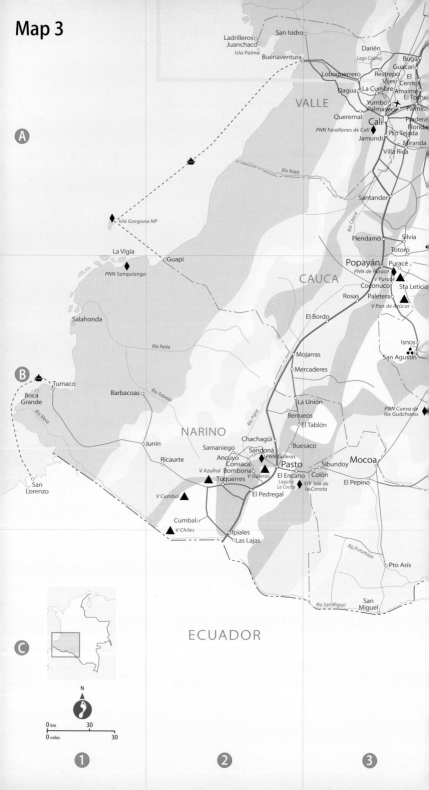

Ladrilleros
Juanchaco
Isla Palma
San Isidro
Buenaventura
Darién
Lago Calima
Buga
Guacarí
Restrepo
El
Cerrito
Loboguerrero
Vijes
Amaime
La Cumbre
El Toche
Dagua
Yumbo
Palmira
Palmaseca
Queremal
Cali
Pradera
Florida
PNN Farallones de Cali
Pto Tejada
Jamundi
Miranda
Villa Rica

VALLE

A

Santander

Río Naya

Río Cauca

Isla Gorgona NP

La Vigia
Guapi

Piendamó
Silvia
Totoró

Popayán
Puracé
PNN de Puracé
V Puracé
Sta Leticia
Coconuco
Rosas
Paletera
V Pan de Azúcar

CAUCA

PNN Sanquianga

Salahonda

El Bordo

Río Patía

Isnos
San Agustín

Mojarras
Mercaderes

B

Tumaco
Boca
Grande

Río Mira

Barbacoas

Río Telembí

Río Patía

La Unión
Bertueos
El Tablón

PNN Cueva de los Guácharos

NARINO

Junín

Chachagüí
Buesaco

San
Lorenzo

Ricaurte

Samaniego
Ancuyo
Consaca
Bombona
Sandoná
PNN Galeras
V Galeras
Mocoa
Sibundoy

V Azufral
Túquerres
El Encano
Colón
El Pepino
Laguna La Cocha
Pasto
SFF Isla de la Corota

V Cumbal
El Pedregal

Cumbal
V Chiles
Ipiales
Las Lajas

Río Putumayo

Pto Asís

Río San Miguel
San
Miguel

ECUADOR

C

N

0 km   30
0 miles   30

1   **2**   **3**

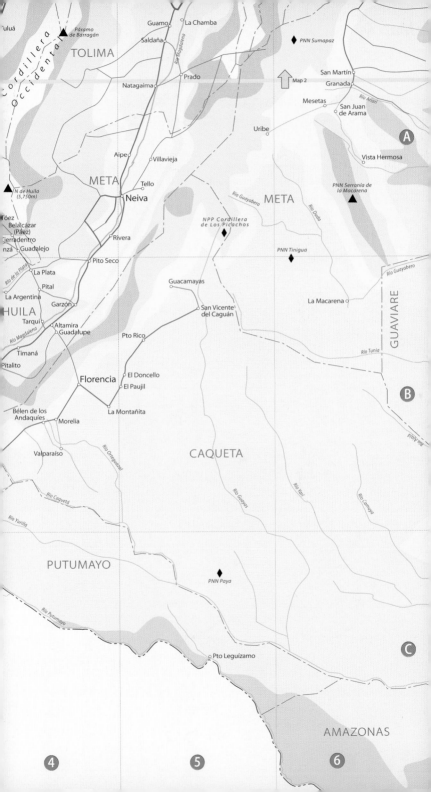

Map 4

Cúcuta
Pamplona
Chitaga
Bafrancabermeja
SANTANDER
Bucaramanga
San Gil
Barbosa
Duitama
Chiquinquirá
Tunja
Sogamoso
Yopal

Rio Arauca
Arauca
PNN Tamá
Sierra Nevada del Cocuy
Tame
PNN El Cocuy
ARAUCA

Rio Casanare
Pore
El Pretexto
Trinidad
La Primavera
CASANARE
Oracué
San Pedro de Arimena

Rio Meta
Rio Meta
Puerto Carreño
Casuarito
Rio Tomo
PNN El Tuparro
Rio Tuparro
Santa Rita
Rio Vichada
VICHADA
Rio Orinoco

BOYACA
A
BOGOTA
PNN Chingaza
Cumeral
Villavicencio
Puert López
San Miguel
Pto Gaitán

Rio Manacacías
META
Granada
Mesetas
San Juan de Arama
Vista Hermosa
PNN Serranía de la Macarena
La Macarena
San José del Guaviare
Calamar
B
GUAVIARE

Rio Guaviare
Pto Inírida
Rio Infreda
GUAINIA
Rio Guainia
Bocas de Casiquiare
RNN Puinawai

Nukak RNN
Rio Vaupés
Mitú
VAUPES
PNN Chiribiquete
Rio Mecay
Rio Apaporis
CAQUETA
Araracuara
Puerto Santander
Rio Caquetá
Rio Caquetá
PNN Predio Putumayo
AMAZONAS
La Chorrera
PNN Cahuinari
Bocas de Cahuinari
Rio Cahuinari
Rio Igara Paraná
San Rafael
El Encanto
Rio Putumayo
C

Tarapaca
PNN Amacayacu
Pto Nariño
Rio Amazonas
Leticia

N

0 km   100
0 miles   100

1   2   3

Acknowledgements

Thanks are due to a large number of people for their help in the preparation of this book, including the many travellers who wrote, faxed and emailed corrections and additions to the first edition of the *Colombia Handbook* and to its companion, the *South American Handbook*. In particular, Peter Pollard would like to recognize the great help given by Mark Duffy in Bogotá, whose wide experience of the country is reflected in many of the preceding pages. David Broom, from Caterham, England, travelled with Peter all over Colombia in 2000 and such was his enthusiasm for the country, he continued to give valuable assistance in the writing and proof-reading back in England.

Of the many in Colombia whose friendship, information and advice have been invaluable, special thanks are due to Nadia Diamond, Enrique Larotta, German Escobar and Adriana Rubio, all of Bogotá.

Others for particular mention are: Barbara Jahn and her students in Medellín; Soraya Quintana and her staff; Claudia Narváez of Pereira; Catherine Cushman; the staff of Lloyds TSB Bank; Patricia Acosta, Bogotá; Julian Restrepo; Dirk Enrique Seiffert, Cartagena; Javier Echavarria and friends, Manizales; María Eugenia Ledesma; Angela Maria Rojas, Cali.

Others have given continuing help since the first edition. Especially valuable have been contributions from: Joaquin Emilio García, San Agustín; Haydee de Varela, Popayán; Lynda Cheetham, formerly of Medellín; and the staff of the Colombian Embassy in London and the British Embassy in Bogotá.

Finally, thanks must go to Ben Box, editor of the *South American Handbook*, who has contributed much valuable advice and given his usual level of untiring support.

Thanks are also due to the following for specialist contributions: Dr Nigel Dunstone (University of Durham) for Flora and Fauna; Gavin Clark for History and Literature; Dr Valerie Fraser (University of Essex) for Fine Art and Sculpture; Mark Duffy for Adventure Tourism; Nigel Gallop for Music and Dance; Sarah Cameron for Economy; David Snashall for Health; and a major source for the relevant section was Arts and Crafts of South America by Lucy Davies and Mo Fini, 1994, published by Tumi.

The illustrations are the work of Colleen Bowler and Kevin Pollard.

Peter Pollard

Peter Pollard, a Cambridge Geography graduate and Fellow of the Royal Geographical Society, first arrived in Cartagena, Colombia, at the start of a career that kept him working in South and Central America for 12 years. In spite of working in other continents subsequently, he found he could not keep away from Latin America and jumped at the chance to work for Footprint Handbooks in 1990. This gives him the perfect excuse to go back frequently, notably to Colombia, the most diverse and welcoming country on the continent.

Peter has a Guatemalan wife and three children born in the Americas. His many interests include music, mountain climbing and local affairs in Surrey (which often makes him wish he was back in Latin America).